PHYSICAL EDUCATION for CHILDREN

Daily Lesson Plans for Elementary School

Second Edition

Katherine T. Thomas, PhD
Iowa State University

Amelia M. Lee, PhD
Louisiana State University

Jerry R. Thomas, EdD
Iowa State University

D1065586

Human Kinetics

Library of Congress Cataloging-in-Publication Data

Thomas, Katherine T., 1948-
      Physical education for children : daily lesson plans for elementary school / Jerry R.
Thomas, Amelia M. Lee, Katherine T. Thomas.--2nd ed.
      p. cm.
      Jerry R. Thomas' name appears first on the earlier edition.
      ISBN 0-87322-681-X
      1. Physical education for children--Study and teaching (Elementary)   2. Lesson
planning   I. Title.   II. Lee, Amelia M., 1938-   III. Thomas, Jerry R.

GV443 .T49 2000

99-045026

ISBN: 0-87322-681-X

Table F3.3 is reprinted with permission from the *Journal of Physical Education, Recreation & Dance*, volume 56, number 1, p. NCYFS-24. *JOPERD* is a publication of the American Alliance for Health, Physical Education, Recreation and Dance, 1900 Association Drive, Reston, VA 20191.

Table F3.4 is reprinted with permission from the *Journal of Physical Education, Recreation & Dance*, volume 56, number 1, p. NCYFS-23. *JOPERD* is a publication of the American Alliance for Health, Physical Education, Recreation and Dance, 1900 Association Drive, Reston, VA 20191.

Table H3.1 is reprinted, by permission, from M. Merki, 1983, *Choosing good health* (Austin, TX: Steck-Vaughn), 144.

Form H3.1 is reprinted, by permission, from K.T. Thomas, A.M. Lee, and J.R. Thomas, 1990, *YMCA youth fitness program for grades 1-6* (Champaign, IL: Human Kinetics), 485.

Figure on page 793 is reprinted by permission from the American Alliance for Health, Physical Education, Recreation and Dance, 1900 Association Drive, Reston, VA 20191.

Acquisitions Editor: Scott Wikgren; **Developmental Editor:** Kristine Enderle; **Managing Editor:** Amy Flaig; **Assistant Editor:** Derek Campbell; **Copyeditor:** Bonnie Pettifor; **Proofreader:** Jim Burns; **Permission Manager:** Heather Munson; **Graphic Designer:** Stuart Cartwright; **Graphic Artist:** Denise Lowry; **Cover Designer:** Keith Blomberg; **Photographer (cover):** Tom Roberts; **Art Manager:** Craig Newsom; **Illustrator:** Argosy; **Printer:** Versa Press

Printed in the United States of America   10   9   8   7   6   5   4   3   2   1

Human Kinetics
Web site: http://www.humankinetics.com/

United States: Human Kinetics, P.O. Box 5076, Champaign, IL 61825-5076
1-800-747-4457
e-mail: humank@hkusa.com

Canada: Human Kinetics, 475 Devonshire Road Unit 100, Windsor, ON N8Y 2L5
1-800-465-7301 (in Canada only)
e-mail: humank@hkcanada.com

Europe: Human Kinetics, P.O. Box IW14, Leeds LS16 6TR, United Kingdom
+44 (0)113-278 1708
e-mail: humank@hkeurope.com

Australia: Human Kinetics, 57A Price Avenue, Lower Mitcham, South Australia 5062
(08) 82771555
e-mail: liahka@senet.com.au

New Zealand: Human Kinetics, P.O. Box 105-231, Auckland Central
09-523-3462
e-mail: humank@hknewz.com

3201

CONTENTS

This book, *Physical Education for Children: Daily Lesson Plans for Elementary School*, and its companion, *Physical Education for Children: Daily Lesson Plans for Middle School*, form a complete developmental program for physical education specialists and classroom teachers alike. So complete and detailed is this program that it can serve as a curriculum guide or model for those developing a kindergarten through eighth grade scope and sequence.

Beyond providing such an overview, these books include the detailed lessons that are the building blocks of any sound program. Based on our knowledge of the developmental needs of children as they grow, mature, and change, this attention to detail both makes the lessons easy to use and ensures that students experience a developmentally appropriate, progressive program.

Specifically, we have designed this program to lay a firm foundation in basic motor skills then gradually build these skills through increasingly challenging activities. Thus, as students progress from kindergarten through eighth grade (see also the middle school book), they learn, then apply, skills in developmentally appropriate ways. This approach provides both the breadth and depth essential to producing physically educated individuals.

Although these two companion books provide a complete program, we encourage you to tailor these materials to your situation. Teacher interest and background; available equipment, materials, and facilities; program and school-wide goals; and initial student skill levels should all influence your choices. Next choose the units you feel comfortable teaching, then repeat the lessons as needed to ensure students master the skills. Then feel free to expand or extend the program and individual units as needed.

As you use and adapt this material, keep in mind that the lessons assume that all but kindergarten students have previous physical education experience. If this is not the case, use more basic units and lessons to bring such students up to grade level. For example, second graders with little exposure to gymnastics may benefit from experiencing certain units in the Grades K-1: Gymnastics section. In any case, use your judgment to tailor this material to your students' needs.

Be sure to study the basic concepts about motor development and effective teaching practices in the book introduction (pages xvi-xxvi) to get the most out of the lessons. This knowledge will help you plan your program, tailor the lesson plans to your situation, and teach more effectively, providing a quality physical education program to your students. Moreover, the organization of this book and its field-tested units, lessons, and activities will make delivering this material easy and enjoyable. Simply review the overall content at the beginning of the year, gather the equipment and materials (most of which should be readily available), and review the lesson plan before teaching each day.

As you use these lessons, you will see your students become more skilled and physically fit and more interested in physical activity. Indeed, both parents and children will love this enjoyable program. In short, these lessons make it easy for you to make a long-term contribution to health, physical fitness, and motor skill development in your students. Children who gain skill and fitness tend to develop lifelong habits of engaging in regular physical activity both because they feel competent and because they have positive memories of physical activity in school. Certainly, there is no better way to contribute to a lifetime of physical and mental health than by encouraging a healthy lifestyle through a developmentally appropriate, progressive, enjoyable physical education program.

To summarize, our hope is that this program will accomplish three objectives:

- Allow you to focus on the teaching-learning process, instead of wasting time and energy on details

- Encourage quality physical education by serving as a guide for developmentally appropriate physical education programs

- Help you understand the process of skill development and use that knowledge to be an effective teacher

Best wishes for a successful and enjoyable school year!

INTRODUCTION

This book is a collection of daily lesson plans for kindergarten through fifth grades. We have designed each unit to present a complete set of lessons, enabling you to efficiently organize and teach a daily program for elementary school students. The lessons have proven successful for many teachers and can help you get started as a new teacher or streamline your efforts as an experienced teacher. Then as you become more comfortable with the content and approach, you will be able to incorporate your own ideas into your own lessons or expand the ones presented here.

THE VALUE OF PHYSICAL ACTIVITY

Participation in physical activity during the childhood years can promote overall health and well-being. Physical activity is included as a national health promotion objective in *Healthy People 2000* (1991). This report was the result of a national effort to enhance the quality of life for all American children. It challenges both parents and teachers to involve children in physical activity programs beginning at an early age.

Indeed, childhood is a critical time for fostering the development of a healthy lifestyle. Some aspects of a child's basic orientation to life are well-organized by the time the child starts school; however, individuals can make lifestyle changes. Change, for example to an active lifestyle, could be a result of encouragement by significant others, including teachers who care. Certainly, teachers play a vital role in helping children develop attitudes and behaviors related to physical activity, diet, and health; these often persist into adulthood. Educators can also help youngsters feel positive about their own movement behavior, including their movement confidence, physical activity choices and motor skills, and confidence about reaching movement goals.

Regular physical activity enhances overall health and well-being. Children who are physically educated are more likely to become and remain active. Specifically, having basic information regarding exercise and the benefits of exercise as well as mastering sets of basic movement skills are essential to a child's initiating and continuing a regular exercise program. Individuals will not participate in activities they do not know about. Moreover, they are less likely to participate in activities they do not know how to do reasonably well. Researchers have identified a child's movement competence (i.e., skill) and enjoyment of physical activity as primary factors in how physically active an individual is during childhood and adolescence (Welk 1999). In addition, physical activity experiences during childhood need to be positive to encourage an active lifestyle during adulthood. Thus, we must provide children with the knowledge and skills they need to make healthful decisions regarding their exercise behavior and the positive memories to encourage them to pursue an active lifestyle after they leave our programs.

GOALS AND OBJECTIVES OF PHYSICAL EDUCATION

We have designed the activities and decision-making experiences in this book to guide children

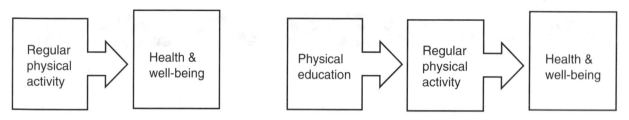

Figure I.1 Physical education relationships.

along the path toward becoming physically educated, the overall goal of physical education. As a result of participating in the curriculum outlined for kindergarten through fifth grades, we can expect students to demonstrate competence in combining the locomotor and manipulative skills into specific sport, rhythmic, and gymnastics skills. To this end, the lessons provide opportunities for students to refine and apply the specific skills, stunts, and dance steps they're learning in game-like drills and structured dance activities.

The first of two specific goals at the elementary level is to make the movement and sport patterns more efficient so that students can apply them in specialized sport activities and a variety of folk and square dances. In addition, students should become more proficient at the traditional tumbling and balance stunts as well as participate in advanced partner stunts. We also emphasize creative expression, encouraging students to invent new forms of games and develop new rhythmic sequences and tumbling routines.

The second goal for elementary students is to develop and/or maintain physical fitness. Thus, we have incorporated a variety of moderate to vigorous physical activities that promote health-related fitness into the daily lesson plans, no matter the content area. In addition, we have provided several options for implementing a fitness program, including fitness units, fitness contracts, and homework.

In addition to the goals of developing motor skills and physical fitness that are the primary and unique goals of elementary level physical education, outcomes in the cognitive and affective domains are also important. For example, children should learn and understand the principles involved in physical fitness development and begin to plan individual exercise programs. Students also need to understand the healthful benefits of regular exercise and participate in moderate to vigorous physical activities both in and outside of class.

Another goal is to teach students in ways that encourage them to think critically about their own learning. To this end, the lessons in this curriculum offer learners many opportunities to identify errors in their own and others' performances.

Finally, we know that students must feel good about themselves and be confident about their success before they can move forward toward a healthy lifestyle. Thus, our program uses specific strategies to build confidence and avoid anxiety. Moreover, we encourage social interaction and student appreciation of the successes and achievements of others.

ORGANIZATION OF THE LESSON PLANS

You can organize the lesson plans in many different ways as long as you present the lessons within a unit (e.g., tennis or rope jumping) in numerical order. The lower-numbered lessons cover basic skills, while higher-numbered lessons present skills that build on the lower-numbered lessons in the unit. There are four broad categories of activities, including games and sports lessons, gymnastics, rhythmical activities, and fitness and health. In addition, often you'll find you should repeat many lessons so students can master or review the skills or simply enjoy doing familiar activities again.

If you prefer to teach lessons in units, begin the school year with organization and fitness testing (weeks 1-4), then follow with gymnastics (weeks 5-10), fitness (weeks 11-14), games and sports (weeks 15-23), health (weeks 24-25), rhythmical activities (weeks 26-31), fitness testing (weeks 32-33) and repeating or free choice (weeks 34-36). This plan may work well in situations in which you must rotate equipment and share facilities or plan indoor units around weather patterns. We suggest another plan that alternates activities in table I.1. Tables I.2 and I.3 suggest plans for Grades 2-3 and 4-5, respectively. These plans are simply examples; we encourage you to teach the units in an order that works for your situation.

Beginning the School Year

During the first week of each school year we recommend that you spend a week or so teaching the organizational and management techniques presented in the organization sections. Then reinforce organizational and management techniques during the early weeks of the fall and as needed throughout the year.

To run classes efficiently, you should be especially sure to establish five aspects of management and organization: the signals you will use, how to get into and change formations, handling equipment, the social skills you expect, and other rules (and consequences) for good and poor behavior. In addition, consider how you will manage routines such as getting water, entering and leaving

Table I.1: Two Sample Weekly Formats for Grades K-1

Sample weekly format 1		
Month one	**Month two**	**Month three**
Week 1–Organization: rules, signals, and formations Week 2–Fitness: testing Week 3–Fitness: Hustles, circuit training Week 4–Fitness: Hustles, circuit training	Week 5–Fitness: vigorous games Week 6–Fitness: fitness challenges Week 7–Games and sports: identifying body parts, throwing, and catching Week 8–Games and sports: throwing, catching, and moving objects	Week 9–Games and sports: running, kicking, and striking Week 10–Games and sports: manipulative skills Week 11–Rhythmic activities: body shapes and locomotor skills Week 12–Rhythmic activities: moving to a beat and singing games
Month four	**Month five**	**Month six**
Week 13–Rhythmic activities: movements to lyrics and action words Week 14–Rhythmic activities: rhythm sticks Week 15–Gymnastics: locomotor skills Week 16–Gymnastics: warm-up routine and pre-tumbling	Week 17–Gymnastics: tumbling Week 18–Gymnastics: partner stunts Week 19–Fitness: testing Week 20–Sports and games: locomotor skills	Week 21–Sports and games: locomotor skills Week 22–Sports and games: locomotor skills Week 23–Sports and games: manipulative skills Week 24–Sports and games: fun and choice
Month seven	**Month eight**	**Month nine**
Week 25–Fitness: Hustles Week 26–Rhythmic activities: rope activities Week 27–Rhythmic activities: rope activities and marches Week 28–Health: health concepts	Week 29–Health: health concepts Week 30–Gymnastics: small equipment Week 31–Gymnastics: large equipment Week 32–Gymnastics: review	Week 33–Classroom lessons Week 34–Classroom lessons Week 35–Fun and choice activities Week 36–Fitness: testing

(continued)

Table I.1: *(continued)*

Sample weekly format 2

Month one	Month two	Month three
Week 1–Organization: rules, signals, and formations Week 2–Fitness: Hustles Week 3–Fitness: testing Week 4–Rhythmic activities: body shapes and locomotor skills	Week 5–Rhythmic activities: moving to a beat and singing games Week 6–Rhythmic activities: movements to lyrics and action words Week 7–Rhythmic activities: rhythm sticks Week 8–Fitness: circuit training	Week 9–Games and sports: identifying body parts, throwing, and catching Week 10–Games and sports: throwing, catching, and moving objects Week 11–Games and sports: running, kicking, and striking Week 12–Games and sports: manipulative skills

Month four	Month five	Month six
Week 13–Games and sports: locomotor skills Week 14–Fitness: Hustles review Week 15–Gymnastics: locomotor skills Week 16–Gymnastics: warm-up routine and pre-tumbling	Week 17–Gymnastics: tumbling Week 18–Gymnastics: partner stunts Week 19–Fitness: testing Week 20–Fitness: vigorous games	Week 21–Games and sports: locomotor skills Week 22–Games and sports: locomotor skills Week 23–Games and sports: manipulative skills Week 24–Health: health concepts

Month seven	Month eight	Month nine
Week 25–Health: health concepts Week 26–Fitness: Hustles review Week 27–Fitness: challenges Week 28–Gymnastics: small equipment	Week 29–Gymnastics: large equipment Week 30–Gymnastics: review Week 31–Rhythmic activities: rope activities Week 32–Rhythmic activities: rope activities and marches	Week 33–Classroom lessons Week 34–Classroom lessons Week 35–Fun and choice activities Week 36–Fitness: testing

the gym or playground, using the bathroom, and taking attendance (if necessary). For example, you might wish to make a small sign with "Stop" on one side and "Go" on the other to hang on the wall or place in a pocket taped on the wall as a pass for water or the bathroom. When a student leaves the gym, he or she turns the sign so "Stop" shows, meaning no one else may leave until that student returns; when all students are in class the sign says "Go." You can read the sign to know if someone is gone, the students don't misplace the pass, one student is gone at a time, and class is not interrupted each time someone needs to use the bathroom.

Although it may seem a week of instructional time is lost to the organizational lessons, ultimately, the purpose of organization and management is to prevent problems, creating more time for instruction. See also the section in this introduction entitled "Practical Knowledge About Teaching."

We also suggest you do three other activities during the second and third weeks in the fall: teaching and reviewing the Fitness Hustles, administering the health-related fitness test battery, and developing the semester fitness contract. The purpose of the growth and fitness assessment is to monitor growth and fitness by measuring

Table I.2: Sample Weekly Format for Grades 2-3

Month one	Month two	Month three
Week 1–Organization: review and teach rules Week 2–Fitness: testing Week 3–Fitness: warm-up and Hustles Week 4–Games and sports: throwing and catching	Week 5–Games and sports: tossing and kicking Week 6–Games and sports: kicking and striking Week 7–Fitness: Hustles Week 8–Gymnastics: warm-up pre-tumbling and review	Week 9–Gymnastics: stunts and tumbling Week 10–Gymnastics: stunts and tumbling Week 11–Fitness: circuit training Week 12–Games and sports: striking and dribbling

Month four	Month five	Month six
Week 13–Rhythmic activities: locomotor skills Week 14–Rhythmic activities: nonlocomotor skills Week 15–Rhythmic activities: singing games and folk dances Week 16–Fitness: vigorous games	Week 17–Health: health concepts Week 18–Gymnastics: partner activities Week 19–Gymnastics: small equipment Week 20–Gymnastics: large equipment	Week 21–Health: health concepts Week 22–Games and sports: locomotor skills Week 23–Games and sports: locomotor skills and parachute games Week 24–Games and sports: locomotor skills and parachute games

Month seven	Month eight	Month nine
Week 25–Rhythmic activities: rope jumping Week 26–Rhythmic activities: folk dancing and singing games Week 27–Rhythmic activities: rhythm sticks and skill testing Week 28–Fitness: challenges	Week 29–Games and sports: manipulative and locomotor skills Week 30–Fitness: Hustles Week 31–Fitness: testing Week 32–Games and sports: manipulative skills and review	Week 33–Classroom lessons Week 34–Classroom lessons Week 35–Fun and choice or testing Week 36–Fun and choice or testing

height, weight, body composition, aerobic endurance, muscular strength and endurance, and joint mobility (flexibility).

The items on the health-related fitness test battery are the one-mile run, sit-ups, backsaver sit-and-reach, and push-ups. During the second week, allow children to practice these items several times before you administer the actual tests. The objective of practicing the mile run is to learn about pace.

Then during the third week, administer the health-related fitness test battery and develop a fitness contract with each child. The contracts can focus on maintaining or increasing fitness in each

component of health-related physical fitness, depending upon individual needs and test results. The Fitness Hustles also supplement class activities during this week. By this point, students should know them well, and you can easily revisit them throughout the school year.

Health and Health-Related Fitness

The health lessons cover topics such as personal health and safety, relationships, feelings, communication, growth, nutrition, and substance use and abuse. You'll find the lessons to be both age-appropriate and helpful in sparking important

Table I.3: Sample Weekly Format for Grades 4-5

Month one	Month two	Month three
Week 1–Organization: review and teach rules Week 2–Fitness: warm-up for fitness Hustles and Hustles Week 3–Fitness: measurements and practice testing Week 4–Fitness: testing	Week 5–Games and sports: tossing, throwing, and catching Week 6–Games and sports: Frisbee tossing and games Week 7–Games and sports: juggling and soccer Week 8–Gymnastics: warm-up routine and gymnastics and tumbling skills	Week 9–Gymnastics: tumbling skills Week 10–Gymnastics: tumbling skills and tumbling checklist Week 11–Fitness: circuit training Week 12–Games and sports: soccer and basketball

Month four	Month five	Month six
Week 13–Rhythmic activities: locomotor and nonlocomotor sequences and streamers Week 14–Rhythmic activities: folk dances and rope jumping Week 15–Rhythmic activities: rope jumping and country dance Week 16–Fitness: rope jumping and individual skills	Week 17–Health: health concepts Week 18–Gymnastics: gymnastics skills and movement challenges Week 19–Gymnastics: small equipment and large equipment Week 20–Games and sports: basketball and softball	Week 21–Health: health concepts Week 22–Games and sports: softball and volleyball Week 23–Games and sports: volleyball and track and field Week 24–Games and sports: track and field and football

Month seven	Month eight	Month nine
Week 25–Rhythmic activities: folk dancing Week 26–Rhythmic activities: rhythm sticks Week 27–Fitness: wands and vigorous games Week 28–Fitness: vigorous games, Hustles; and Games and sports: raging river	Week 29–Rhythmic activities: review dances Week 30–Fitness: Hustles Week 31–Fitness: testing Week 32–Games and sports: review	Week 33–Classroom lessons Week 34–Classroom lessons Week 35–Fun and choice or testing Week 36–Fun and choice or testing

discussions. We designed the health lessons for classroom use, but you can adapt them for use on the playground or in the gym.

You can either teach these lessons straight through as a single unit or integrate the concepts with fitness or skill lessons where appropriate and logical throughout the school year. They are not meant to represent a comprehensive health education program, and you may want to supplement the plans by introducing other concepts. The ideas they present, however, will help you get started as they offer meaningful content for those students who get no other formal instruction in health. Furthermore, you may choose to use the health lessons to inspire and introduce larger units you develop on each of the topics covered.

The health-related fitness lessons include practicing fitness tests and testing, introducing the Fitness Hustles, circuit training, moderate to vigorous games, and fitness challenges. You can repeat or expand each of these lessons or units as well.

We believe that physical activity is an important goal, and physical fitness is one way of demonstrating a healthful level of physical activity. The lessons include moderate to vigorous activities and warm-ups that provide physical activity itself as well as promote the value of being physically active. In addition, we include units on physical fitness because physical fitness is like any other motor skill: it must be practiced to be learned so that students can enjoy participating in the activities.

As mentioned, we believe that children and adults are more likely to continue participating in activities in which they feel competent. The goal is to first teach the skills necessary to be physically fit, then, second, to make physical activity enjoyable and challenging. For some programs a third goal may be to influence actual physical fitness. This is a viable program goal when you have enough time devoted to physical education to meet the criteria of three days per week for physical fitness and additional days per week to teach other skills (Plan D later in this introduction is an example). Since very few schools designate this much time for physical education, we offer three alternative plans (A, B, and C), with the idea that teaching children to enjoy physical activity will enhance the chances of becoming physically fit and staying physically fit as an adult. If you must follow an alternative plan it is especially important to encourage physical activity outside of class through fitness contracts, journals, and homework (see additional information on this topic later in this introduction). You should also take opportunities to touch upon concepts more in other types of lessons, for example, mentioning that aerobic endurance enhances basketball performance and that playing basketball can enhance aerobic endurance, helping children see both one benefit of and one avenue to health-related fitness.

The advantage of plans A, B, and C are that these accommodate to situations with less than five days per week of physical education and programs that are skill- rather than fitness-oriented. Children are exposed to physical fitness in plans A, B, and C, but the focus is on skill development, fun, and lifetime physical activity. In plan D, physical fitness could be a major program goal; however this would be at the expense of presenting all the skill related lessons (e.g., nearly 50% of the gymnastics, rhythmic activities, and games and sports would not be presented in this plan).

Plan A

In this plan, the year begins with two weeks of fitness training and testing as previously described. You can then repeat the process of practicing and taking the fitness test at the end of the school year (weeks 31-33). Of the three fitness units presented in the fitness section (circuit training, moderate to vigorous games, and fitness challenges), you can use two of these units in the fall, one in the spring, and the Fitness Hustles to provide four, one-week units of fitness (for example at weeks 11 and 12 and weeks 24 and 25). You may also use the Fitness Hustles during the fun and choice weeks to include more fitness lessons.

Plan B

For this plan, fitness testing occurs at the beginning and end of each year. You teach a fitness lesson one or two days each week, rotating through the Fitness Hustles, challenges, circuits, and moderate to vigorous games. You use most of these lessons twice in a 36-week school year. You teach other activities the other three or four days per week from the gymnastics, rhythmic activities, and games and sports units. You give the children fitness homework or fitness contracts to round out their fitness training if a program goal is to develop physical fitness.

Plan C

For this plan, you conduct fitness testing at the beginning and end of the school year. Then you teach fitness as a unit, scheduled as a four-week unit, one week each for the Fitness Hustles, circuits, challenges, and moderate to vigorous games.

Plan D

This plan was designed for schools with five days of physical education for which physical fitness is a major goal of physical education. For this plan, fitness testing occurs at the beginning and end of the year. You schedule fitness lessons three days per week, and rhythmic activities, sports and games, and gymnastics on the other two days each week for the entire school year. Within this plan, you have many options for scheduling a rotation of the fitness lessons throughout the year. Table I.4 presents an example that uses the fitness lessons six or seven times each throughout the year. You can also introduce the Fitness Hustles in a rotation. To maximize training ben-

Table I.4: A Sample Fitness Training Program for the Year

Weeks	Day 1 of the week	Day 2 of the week	Day 3 of the week
4, 9, 14, 19, 24, 29, 34	Vigorous games 1	Vigorous games 2	Vigorous games 3
5, 10, 15, 20, 25, 30	Vigorous games 4	Vigorous games 5	Challenges 1
6, 11, 16, 21, 26, 31	Challenges 2	Challenges 3	Challenges 4
7, 12, 17, 22, 27, 32	Challenges 5	Circuit 1	Circuit 2
8, 13, 18, 23, 28, 33	Circuit 3	Circuit 4	Circuit 5

efits, schedule the three days of fitness training on alternate days (Monday, Wednesday, and Friday).

Fitness Testing

An important consideration is how you will use the fitness testing information you gather. You can expect students to maintain or improve their fitness levels through your program if you do

- fitness two days a week and fitness homework or fitness contracts throughout the school year,
- three days per week of fitness throughout the school year, or
- fitness units (three days per week for eight or more weeks).

However, if you are not including at least these minimum amounts of fitness training within your program, you should not expect improved fitness test scores when comparing the beginning to the end of the year except those caused by natural maturation (growth). In any scenario in which you work on fitness less than three days each week, the fitness test information must be for informational or monitoring purposes only, rather than to evaluate the program or assign grades.

Note, too, that we do not advocate grading on physical fitness; this is especially problematic if the program is not meeting the criteria to train physical fitness. We suggest reporting and interpreting physical fitness scores to children and parents and using the scores to monitor behavior and health and develop fitness contracts.

As you can see, it is important for you to know your goals for fitness testing and fitness activities *and* to explain this to your students and their parents. If you are monitoring fitness, that is fine; just say so. If you are doing fitness activities two days per week, then explain to the children that they must do at least one more additional workout per week in order to achieve or maintain physical fitness.

Fitness Contracts, Homework, and Journals

You can use fitness contracts to encourage students to adopt an active lifestyle. For such an approach, students, with your help, plan individualized fitness programs to complete on weekends and after school. This places responsibility on the students and therefore empowers them. Lifetime fitness is a result of self-discipline and the decision to be physically active; fitness contracts can be the beginning of students' learning this process.

Be sure to individualize such programs, as some children will need more challenging goals, while others will need more moderate goals. In addition, encourage the children to keep journals that describe their personal feelings about the activities.

It is important to carefully assess each child's fitness contract program, revising each as needed. This will help ensure goals are reasonable and help you reinforce each child's feelings of accomplishment in fitness endeavors.

Fitness homework is vital to supplementing your program, especially if you meet with each class less than every day. You can present it on a calendar or assign it at the end of each lesson. Fitness homework is also helpful for maintaining fitness levels over long vacations. Examples of fitness homework include the following:

- Take a 30-minute walk with a family member.
- Do 10 push-ups and 30 curl-ups.
- Play an active game for 20 minutes.

Require the children to write down what they did (e.g., where they walked, when, and with whom) and turn in their written reports. Students may also use journals to log their daily physical activity. Remind children that the fitness test battery will indicate whether they have been keeping their fitness contract by maintaining their fitness level and doing their homework.

Instructional Program

As mentioned earlier, you can and should repeat many of the games and sports, gymnastics, and rhythmic activities lessons. For example, you may want to continue a unit by repeating lessons for mastery. So revisit lessons or groups of lessons the children have difficulty with.

In addition, some teachers like to set aside Fridays for either (a) using the Fitness Hustles or (b) offering fun choices. Which might work for you? On the one hand, the Fitness Hustles are fun and vigorous, and the kids enjoy doing them regularly. On the other hand, teachers have successfully motivated students by offering Friday as a fun choice day as a reward for working hard the rest of the week. You can offer a choice of activities for fun choice days or allow the students to suggest choices.

Decide how to organize the lessons based on several factors. The schedule for physical education is one factor; for example, some schools do not have physical education every day. Moreover, children enter a physical education program with varying backgrounds. Older children accustomed to a developmental physical education program should be ready for the activities presented here. Kindergartners are yours to teach properly right from the start; seize the opportunity! However, individual children may vary, and groups of children with different experiences may need time to master more basic skills before doing the more advanced activities in these lessons and units. Certainly, the older the children, the more likely you will notice a wide range of skill levels, especially if they have not been in a well-planned and executed physical education program.

In addition, both facilities and equipment influence what you can teach. The lessons require basic equipment; however, you may not have all of the equipment for all the lessons. Also influencing your decisions may be a school or district that has curricular goals that emphasize a particular aspect of physical education. For example, one school may emphasize cooperative learning while another gives priority to physical fitness (although these two examples are certainly not mutually exclusive).

Finally, you must consider your own skills, strengths, and values when selecting what to teach. But don't be afraid to stretch your repertoire and try something new.

The lessons in this book represent a wide variety of physical activities that are developmentally appropriate for children from kindergarten through fifth grade from which you may choose. Simply keep in mind that we have arranged the lesson plans sequentially within each general activity category. Thus, the later lesson plans assume that you have taught the previous lessons.

Classroom Lesson Plans

We have included classroom lesson plans for those times when you need to teach physical education in the classroom or some other confined space. The reasons for teaching in the classroom vary from weather to activities in the gymnasium that interfere with your regular schedule. Even though the venue is more confining, simply being willing to carry on through classroom lessons reinforces the value of physical activity in students' minds. Certainly, when you choose to be creative and are dedicated to presenting opportunities for physical activity on a regular schedule, children understand the value you are assigning to physical activity.

USING THE LESSON PLANS

The lessons include hints on how to teach, specific to the particular activities. Here, we look more closely at lesson plan structure. We have divided the lesson plans into distinct sections, including objectives, equipment and materials, safety tips, warm-up activities, skill development activities, and concluding activities. You should read the entire lesson before you try to teach it. Some teachers make notes about the lesson to take to class; others take the entire lesson plan. Find what works for you.

Student Objectives

We have stated the lesson objectives in behavioral terms so you can see the exact purpose(s) of each lesson. Keep in mind that informing the students about the objective of the lesson (e.g., what they should expect to learn) facilitates learning. In most lessons, there are motor skill objectives (e.g., The student will be able to dribble a basketball using correct form), cognitive objectives (e.g., The student will state three characteristics of a correct basketball dribble), and affective objectives (e.g., The student will work with a partner practicing dribbling and passing the basketball). You may, however, want to make these objectives more specific when presenting it to the class; for example, "By the end of class today everyone should be able to dribble the ball, using correct form, five times in a row with each hand." Of course, you can include additional objectives as appropriate.

Equipment and Materials

We have listed all equipment and materials you will need in its own section at the beginning of each lesson to help you gather everything quickly before class. We recommend that, whenever possible, you have enough equipment so that each child or pair can have their own for maximal practice opportunities. If you do not have enough equipment, you may have to modify the lesson accordingly to keep time on task high. We recommend using cones to mark boundaries even when lines are available.

Warm-Up

At the beginning of each section (e.g., Grades 2-3: Games and Sports), we have explained the various warm-ups appropriate for that course of study. Then whenever the warm-up is used in a lesson, we offer a reference to the page explaining it. Most of the warm-up activities focus on physical fitness by requiring moderate to vigorous movement or stretching. Note, however, that the warm-ups do not provide enough exercise to train physical fitness and so must not replace a program of regular physical activity. However, the warm-ups do get the body ready for the activities to follow. Some warm-ups are general; others specifically prepare the muscle groups for the activities that follow. Children benefit from several bouts of moderate-to-vigorous activity each day lasting at least 10 minutes each, in addition to more extended periods of activity and skill instruction. So if you have time for a 10-minute warm-up, the warm-up activities are often activities you could use to help meet that need for brief periods of activity. Finally, during the warm-up, you should stress doing the activity correctly, that is, using correct form and following the rules.

Skill Development Activities

This is the body of the lesson in which you demonstrate skills, present instructions, and provide practice opportunities and feedback. Stress performing the movements correctly. The lessons include information about the correct movement (the process or qualitative aspects of the movements) to help you do so. In this section the following formatting is used: Italicized phrases and sentences = Statements by the teacher to the students and (Answers.) = Sample answers to questions.

Most skill development activities begin by introducing a new skill. However, some skill development activities begin with a review of skills from a previous lesson or a previous level. We suggest how to do the skill, and often give cues and instructions or statements you can make directly to the students. You will have to decide how long to practice, when to give feedback, and when to move on to the next activity. Within each lesson, we introduce skills from the least to most difficult. Practice should continue on the easier skills until most of the students have mastered the skill. Then you can show the students how to combine the skills with other skills or introduce new, more difficult skills as suggested in the lessons. Sometimes you may need to introduce a more difficult skill or task to challenge higher-skilled students while lower-skilled students continue to practice more basic skills and tasks. Just be sure to monitor all students at all times to ensure their safety.

Concluding Activities

Finally, most lessons have one or more concluding activities—often a game in which students apply the skills practiced during the lesson. Sometimes for the concluding activities, we suggest you ask students to reflect on or review what they have learned. Other times, the concluding activities serve as a cool-down after strenuous activity. You may also take this opportunity to informally evaluate students to assess progress. Finally, some lessons suggest homework or follow-up activities in this section.

MOTOR DEVELOPMENT

Children are not miniature adults. Assuming they are can lead to inappropriate expectations. Motor development provides information about how children grow, mature, become more efficient,

Student objects

GRADES 2-3

GAMES AND SPORTS

LESSON 5
TOSSING AND CATCHING WITH A SCOOP, ROLLING AT TARGETS

Student Objectives
- Toss and catch a self-tossed beanbag with a scoop.
- Hit a 2-ft-square target from 20 ft with a rolled ball.

Equipment and Materials
- Enough scoops and beanbags for half the class
- Enough targets (e.g., tires, bicycle tubes, pictures) and playground balls for half the class

Equipment and materials

Warm-Up Activities (7 minutes)

Warm-up activities

Nose Tag
See Grades 2-3: Games and Sports, Warm-Ups, page 467.

Reviewing an activity

Skill-Development Activities (18 minutes)

Skill-development activities

Divide the class into two groups. Have one group begin with the Underhand Toss With a Scoop activity and the other with Playground Balls activity. Switch groups after nine minutes.

Underhand Toss With a Scoop
Arrange half the class in scatter formation with the beanbags and scoops.

1. Tell the children: *Toss and catch the beanbags with the scoops as many times in a row as possible.*
2. *Point the scoop high (low; where you want the beanbag to go.)*

Setting up an activity

Playground Balls
Arrange the other half of the class in scatter formation with the playground balls and targets.

Introducing an activity

1. Have the children practice rolling (underhand), then tossing (underhand), then throwing (overhand) the ball at the targets. Tell the children: *Reach your hand to the target.*
2. Move among and between the two groups to correct and encourage.

After nine minutes, have groups trade equipment.

3. Have students do the activity they have not yet done.

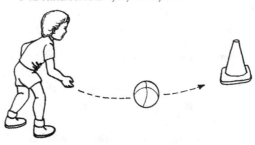

Concluding activities

Concluding Activities (5 minutes)

Encourage the children to practice whichever skill they had the most difficulty doing (rolling, tossing, or throwing at the targets, or tossing and catching with the scoops).

learn, respond to exercise, and feel about physical activity. In this section, we will discuss a few key factors that will help you to understand the lessons and how to maximize the physical education experience for each child. For further information, refer to the many books available that provide information about motor development.

Growth and Maturation

As you probably know, each person grows and matures on an individual schedule. The environment, specifically exercise, has little effect on height or maturation. But exercise can help children develop more skeletal mass, a little more muscle bulk, and have less fat. During the elementary school years, growth and maturation is steady. Children generally gain two to three inches in height each year from kindergarten to fourth or fifth grade (Roche & Falkner 1975).

Rapid changes in growth and maturation occur around puberty. Girls enter puberty between 9 and 11 years of age, and most girls are finished growing taller by 13 years old. Boys enter puberty between 11 and 13 years of age and are still growing at 15. These are only general ranges, however; some children mature earlier, others later. For boys, early maturation may present a short-term advantage in sport and physical education. Sometimes, these boys are shorter and more muscular compared to others as adults than boys who mature later. For girls, early maturation may be a disadvantage since early-maturing girls tend to be more pear-shaped and may have a greater percent body fat. Later-maturing children (both male and female), may have an advantage in sport and physical activity as adults since they are often taller (because they grow over a longer time period), and they are often more linear (leaner for their height). Rapid growth is usually a sign of maturation, which means a cadre of other changes will be forthcoming. In fourth and fifth grades, you will observe some girls and perhaps an early-maturing male entering puberty; however, many of the children this age will be four or more years from their growth spurt (Malina 1984).

Children have different body proportions than adults, sometimes affecting their movement performances. Understand that certain skills may be more difficult for young children than for adults because of these differences in body proportions, which influence balance and leverage. Specifically, young children have relatively larger heads, relatively shorter legs, and shoulders that match their hips so they look "straight up and down." As we grow and mature, our legs become longer, making our heads appear smaller on our bodies. In contrast, in young children, the head is heavy and sometimes difficult to control when doing balance activities. At puberty a male's shoulders grow broader, which is an advantage in many physical activities. So early-maturing males will have longer legs and broader shoulders to help them perform better than later-maturing children. For example, longer legs and arms help a person run faster and throw farther.

Bones, muscles, and organs also grow during childhood, and we can observe the bones getting longer as children increase in height. The bones should increase in breadth and density as well. Exercise has a positive influence on bone growth. For example, children who exercise have more robust skeletons, which means that the bones are wider, and they have greater bone mass and mineralization (Malina 1994).

During childhood many girls and some boys may have too much body fat. This may be a sign of a health problem or a result of environmental factors related to diet and exercise. All of us need some fat; however, children and adolescents should not gain large amounts of fat.

At puberty males experience rapid gains in muscle, and females tend to gain fat. The observed differences in fat between males and females at puberty is due in part to environmental factors, for example, levels of physical activity. So encourage young females to remain physically active. Indeed, it is important to recognize that few biological reasons exist to explain motor performance differences between boys and girls before puberty. Most observable differences in motor performance between boys and girls, even in the primary grades, are the result of different treatment and encouragement by parents, teachers, and others. Girls, just like boys, need to develop motor skills, participate in physical activity, and enjoy the benefits of regular exercise. To encourage optimal skill and physical development you should

- expect normal variation in physical growth and maturation among children,
- recognize the influence of body proportions on leverage and balance,
- consider physical size and maturation when grouping students for practice,
- encourage females to be and stay physically active,

- talk to children about the effects of growth and maturation on performance, and
- have similar expectations for males and females prior to puberty.

Cognitive and Psychological Factors

If we look closely we can see the differences in body proportions between children and adults. However, it is impossible to see the differences in the way children think and feel. Sometimes, we can infer these from observing the child's behavior. Before anyone can do a skill he or she must understand what to do—and then remember what to do. Teachers explain how to do skills and give instructions and demonstrations to help children learn. However, young children do not do anything special to help themselves remember. Most adults repeat to themselves (often aloud) the things they need to remember. Repeating helps young children, but unless you tell them to do so, they will not. Children begin to repeat to remember at about 7 years of age; by 11 years of age many are using a variety of methods to help themselves remember. The simplest solution for teachers is to tell children ages 7 and younger to repeat the things they need to remember. Also keep the pieces of information small, i.e., only ask them to remember one or two steps at a time. For students 7 to 11 you can tell them how you solve learning problems (e.g., share methods to aid memory), and your solution will probably work for them.

Most adults understand the relationship between practice and learning, but children may not see it. So, when a child is not able to perform a task, she may assume she "just can't." You can help by identifying parts of a skill or task with which you expect students to have trouble. For example, you might say, "I think the most difficult part of this to learn is the. . . ." You can also state the benefits of practice. For example, you might say, "It took me a long time and a lot of practice to learn this." Such statements help children see the relationship between practice and learning. Furthermore, they help children feel "normal" when they need to practice to learn a task.

Observe your students; when you give them time to practice, what are they doing? What are you doing? Most teachers provide feedback during practice, especially encouragement, which is good. However, specific feedback about the skills is also helpful. Children want to improve; improving their skills is important to them. Thus,

children appreciate specific information that will help them improve.

Young children, however, may not be able to apply the information. One reason is that children under 12 years of age will need more time than you do to answer questions and incorporate feedback into their movements. So, allowing more time and focusing on quality of practice—not just quantity—is often helpful. As a rule provide at least 10 seconds for young children to formulate solutions. In addition, be aware that children under seven interpret neutral and negative facial expressions as negative and smiles as positive. Facial expressions tend to "override" other sources of feedback. So if a teacher is saying "good job" but has a neutral expression, the child may interpret the expression to mean "The teacher is unhappy with me." Such misperceptions can be discouraging and defeating.

In addition to the differences in learning rates and methods, children have different feelings and motivations for physical activity than adults. Young children focus on the task; they are motivated to learn new skills to help them determine if they are normal and if they are improving. Some children shift from learning the task as a motivating factor to the status performance brings. Children who are task-motivated tend to persist in physical endeavors longer than children who are ego- or status-motivated. Therefore, you should encourage children to focus on task mastery and the positive feelings associated with improvement. Help children identify areas in which they have improved as well as the relationship between improvement and effort (practice and hard work).

Learning to cooperate with others is a vital life skill. Learning to understand another person's feelings or duties, however, is difficult. Certainly, children under 12 have difficulty taking another person's perspective and therefore may have trouble with teamwork. Moreover, competition is not important to young children; remember, improvement and fun are their goals. So they will demonstrate enthusiasm and be excited during game play in the absence of competition. This excitement will keep them interested in learning and trying hard.

Note, too, that competition can be stressful for children. In part, this is because the display of their motor skills is very public; everyone sees how they are doing. Competition can increase this stress. We are not suggesting that all competition is bad, but we believe that during physical education competition should be minimized. The lesson plans focus on cooperation and skill development.

As mentioned, children's perceptions about their abilities influence their motivation levels in physical education. Children who perceive themselves as poorly skilled may spend instructional time thinking "I am the worst student, everyone is looking at me, I am different because I am so bad." Meanwhile, children who perceive themselves as skilled may spend instructional time listening more closely to the teacher. This leads to a downward spiral: the lower-skilled child is not receiving the same instruction as the higher-skilled child. Then the higher-skilled child probably improves, making the lower-skilled child look even worse. Therefore, help children focus their attention on the task at hand. Specifically, you can teach children to redirect their attention from negative self-talk toward positive self-talk and then toward the instructional task. For example, teach all the children to say "listen, practice, and improve." Encourage them to say this silently to themselves whenever they are doubting their ability to learn and perform.

Children will "buy into" the idea and practice of positive self-talk, because they enter school with a persistent optimism about their chances for success. This leads to a keen level of eagerness in most learning situations. They believe that increased effort can improve their ability, and their beliefs about their performance exceed their actual performance—and this is OK. By fourth or fifth grade their beliefs and performance begin to match. Girls tend to have higher self-confidence about more "female" activities (e.g., dance) as compared to more "male" activities (e.g., football). Overall, girls tend to have slightly lower self-confidence about movement than boys. Ultimately, girls tend to decrease in self-confidence with age (Greendorfer et al. 1996). Parents, peers, and other significant persons (e.g., teachers) likely influence the feelings of children by encouraging boys in sport and physical activity. Girls may be discouraged, or the value of physical activity may be discounted for them.

Children make choices about activities: they decide to participate or not, to try or not, and how to approach learning. These decisions are influenced by their beliefs about their performances. So, if, for example, a girl's culture expects her to do poorly in a sport, she will have less self-confidence, which could lead to the decision not to try very hard, which results in less skill learning.

Less skill leads to lower self-confidence, and so forth. Thus you must actively seek to change the ability and value perceptions in children who view certain tasks as being inappropriate for them. Specifically, you should

- allow children more time to formulate decisions,
- provide children with the strategies (solutions) they can use to remember and learn,
- relate practice to improvement and learning,
- smile at everyone,
- provide general encouragement and specific feedback about skills,
- provide opportunities to cooperate,
- have similar expectations for boys and girls, and lower- and higher-skilled children,
- provide equal opportunity, feedback, and encouragement to all children regardless of skill level, and
- make it clear to students that you value each of them and believe each can succeed.

The Effects of Exercise

Physical fitness is one way to demonstrate a physically active lifestyle. Sedentary people are at greater risk for cardiovascular disease and other health problems. The good news is that sedentary individuals who become active reduce their health risks. There are many ways to be physically active: walking, gardening, housework, sports, or being physically fit. Moderate to vigorous physical activity has immediate benefits—a better-conditioned and more-trim body, a more healthful lifestyle, and better mental health. It also brings long-term benefits—reduced blood pressure, a more efficient and effective heart, weight control, and, potentially, a longer life span. Health-related physical fitness has five components: cardiovascular fitness, muscular strength, muscular endurance, flexibility, and body composition. To help children achieve health-related physical fitness, you must understand how the physiological systems develop and how exercise can influence development.

The body makes two major adjustments to prolonged rhythmic exercise, such as running, cycling, and swimming. First, muscles do their work during exercise by using fuel and oxygen. The more intense the work, the more oxygen and fuel the body uses. The body uses oxygen very rapidly, so the blood must deliver more oxygen (and fuel, too, but that is not a problem at most levels and durations of exercise) as work continues or increases. This means the lungs and heart must work harder. Generally, heart and respiration rates increase as the intensity of exercise increases. Fatigue sets in when the circulatory system can no longer keep up; then the person must slow down or stop.

The second effect of exercise is heat production. The body dissipates some heat through breathing, but most heat is lost through sweating. The circulatory system increases the blood flow to the skin, and heat is lost by radiation and evaporation of sweat. Children have less ability to handle heat than adults (Powers 1984). During exercise, especially during hot, dry weather, dehydration can occur. Thus, you must facilitate and always permit as much water as students want before, during, and after exercise. Note that water is as good for fluid replacement as commercial products.

Another fact you should know is that children (8 to 15 years of age) may not respond to training as adults do for several reasons. First, children tend to be very active, so they may be more fit than adults to start with. Second, children have higher resting and maximal heart rates. Boys' average heart rate at 6 years old is 86 beats per minute; this drops to 66 beats per minute by about 13 years old. Girls follow a similar pattern beginning at 88 beats per minute and dropping to about 70 (Powers 1984). One theory is that children have to train at a higher rate than adults to get the same benefits. Another issue is that a large part of cardiovascular capacity is inherited; therefore, the differences between individuals may be largely due to genetics. Individual adults respond differently to training, since this is an inherited characteristic, and it is likely that children do too. So the job of becoming fit may be more difficult for some children than for others (Bouchard and Pérusse 1994). (For a child who has already achieved a baseline of health-related fitness, simply maintaining fitness levels is a viable option.) Children who struggle with fitness or physical activity need encouragement. Physical activity for health may be a more realistic goal for some children than the goal of fitness.

There is a minimum amount of work necessary to train the cardiovascular system. An individual must train for at least 20 minutes (duration), three times per week (frequency), at a training heart rate for fitness. To train for health, three 10-minute bouts most days of the week are rec-ommended. Calculate intensity, the training heart rate, using the following formula: 220 minus age in years multiplied by percent of maximum heart rate desired, usually 60-90 percent for fitness and 40 percent for health. So for a 10-year-old child the maximum heart rate (MHR) is 210. If the intensity desired is 80 percent of maximum, calculate the training heart rate by multiplying .80 times 210: 168 beats per minute. By middle school students should be able to take their pulse at the carotid artery (the large artery in the neck) to get heart rate and calculate the training heart rate. An elementary school student can learn to take a carotid pulse by third grade. You may have to do the math for them. The youngest children can place a hand on the heart to feel it beat faster than before an active game. Cardiovascular fitness occurs after 8 to 12 weeks of regularly training at the appropriate intensity, frequency, and duration.

Muscular strength and endurance also develop as a result of training. *Muscular strength* refers to a person's ability to perform a movement one time against a maximal resistance. *Muscular endurance* refers to how well a person can perform several repetitions of a movement over time. An individual's muscular strength and endurance affect how fit she or he may be in the other components of health-related physical fitness. Muscular endurance influences our ability to train the cardiovascular system; for example, the heart rate may be low, but the legs are too tired to keep running because muscular endurance of the legs is poor. In addition to those muscles needed for cardiovascular training, fitness training in physical education should focus on two other muscle groups: the abdominal muscles, because weak abdominal muscles are associated with lower back pain in adults; and the arm muscles, because the arms are used in a variety of physical activities, for example, gymnastics.

For some individuals the fitness issue is first muscular strength, because he can't do one repetition of the task (e.g., one sit-up). After the individual gains the muscular strength necessary to do one repetition, the focus should shift to muscular endurance. To train muscular endurance, we think of many repetitions, for example, three sets of 10 repetitions, interspersed with rest intervals. Muscular endurance is also based on the idea of low intensity. For example, push-ups require us to lift part of our body weight; chin-ups, all of our body weight. So a child with low muscular endurance of the arms might begin by concentrating on push-ups, then proceed to chin-ups. In contrast, strength training uses fewer repetitions and greater intensity (weight or other resistance). Children can improve their strength levels but will not add muscle bulk before puberty.

Flexibility is the range of motion in a joint. Good flexibility is associated with injury prevention, and in some sports with superior performance. Flexibility varies greatly within individuals when comparing one joint to another. Fortunately, flexibility is relatively easy to improve. The most common test of flexibility is the backsaver sit-and-reach. The reason is that flexibility in the legs and lower back may prevent or reduce lower back pain.

To summarize regarding health-related physical fitness training, you should

- allow children to drink water before, during, and after moderate to vigorous exercise,
- be aware of individual differences in responses to training,
- teach children to count their heart rate by counting the carotid pulse, or feel increased heart rate by placing the hand on the chest, and
- teach children the short- and long-term value of regular exercise.

Changing Movement Patterns

We are all too familiar with the insult "You throw like a girl." It means the thrower did not take a step or stepped on the same foot as the throwing hand, exhibited very little body rotation, and may have moved the object more like a shot put or dart than a baseball. Ironically, it is normal for all children to throw using this pattern when they are young; with practice the pattern becomes more efficient and vigorous. Most motor patterns follow a similar trend. For example, think about how a baby walks: his steps are short with the feet spaced far apart. He often moves with his arms held rigid at shoulder height.

Researchers can usually describe a motor skill in two ways. First, they can detail the ideal pattern to produce the most efficient and effective outcomes. This is the way experts try to do the skill. Second, they can outline the common stages observed as individuals learn the skill. Unfortunately, many of us never reach the ideal technique in a motor pattern. However, the ideal is helpful for teachers and students to know as a model and goal. Furthermore, understanding the typical

changes will help you identify normal performance progression, so you know what to expect and encourage next as the child practices. Experienced teachers may have studied or learned through experience the normal progression of motor patterns. They use this information to help children by altering lessons or providing feedback. As you observe children, you will notice the orderly progression of skill development, and soon will be able to make predictions about what the child will do next. First, changes are more rapid in this (qualitative) area; second, children can obtain outcome (product) information for themselves. Thus, we recommend that you

- use motor pattern information to identify the qualitative goal of the movement,
- understand the progression of movements so they know what to expect, and
- focus on the qualitative aspects of movements for feedback and instruction.

PRACTICAL KNOWLEDGE ABOUT TEACHING

To be an effective teacher, you need to be aware of "whom," "how," and "what" you teach. The previous section covered "whom"—the developmental changes you will expect to see in your students. This section covers "how," and the lesson plans present "what" to teach. Here we discuss how you can arrange the teaching-learning environment to facilitate learning by developing a management system, starting lessons and activities smoothly, and making sure students stay on track. You should be able to apply these guidelines directly in most teaching settings, but feel free to modify them as needed.

Developing a Management System

Effective management techniques are a must to ensure each child has the opportunity to learn. As you might anticipate, every child will not behave perfectly during instructional time. Wise teachers develop a management plan before the first day of teaching, then they teach the behaviors associated with the plan during the first classes of the year, and follow the plan consistently throughout the school year. Children feel comfortable with routine and rules, and good management helps children know what to expect and to feel comfortable. A good management plan covers the following topics:

- A plan for entering and leaving the gymnasium or play area
- A signal for starting and stopping
- A plan for distributing and gathering equipment
- A set of rules for behavior
- A set of consequences for violations of the rules

Establish rules for behavior to facilitate a positive learning environment, then enforce the rules and procedures at all times. State rules in a positive way, describing the expected behaviors, for example, "Listen and do" instead of "Don't talk while the teacher is talking." Rules should cover following directions, stopping on a designated signal, and using equipment as intended. You must also clearly state that you expect students to show respect to others, listen, cooperate with a partner or in a group, encourage others to succeed, and generally behave in a socially responsible way. An example of a set of effective physical education rules follows:

1. Follow directions the first time they are given.
2. Stop and listen on the signal.
3. Use equipment only as it is intended.
4. Listen to and respect others.
5. Avoid using hostile gestures, fighting, or otherwise disrupting activity.

Post the list of the rules in a prominent place and spend time teaching each rule and desirable social skill at the beginning of the school year, offering concrete examples. Explain that the rules make sure everyone has an opportunity to learn, help students to know what to do, and keep class a safe place to be. Children appreciate having and knowing the rules, because this establishes boundaries and allows the child to fit in, to avoid embarrassing him- or herself by having negative attention directed at him or her. Then remind children as necessary about the rules throughout the year. For example, have the students practice them and think of more examples of acceptable and unacceptable behavior.

Inseparable from rules are consequences for rule violations; children must know and understand these consequences. The following consequences might be appropriate for fourth grade in schools where consequences are not established grade- or school-wide:

- First time a child breaks a rule—a warning
- Second time a child breaks a rule—4-minute time-out
- Third time a child breaks a rule—8-minute time-out
- Fourth time a child breaks a rule—talk to the parent

Giving a warning should be a private event; we recommend you move into the child's space and explain the warning. Some teachers prefer to warn children publicly, so the entire class can hear. This may embarrass a child and result in further misbehavior. General statements like "someone is breaking the rule" are ineffective since children do not know who is breaking the rule. However, teachers who make a regular habit of speaking to individual children can provide a warning which is indistinguishable to classmates from feedback, reinforcement, or conversation.

Time-out means that you remove the child from the activity to spend time in isolation. During time-out a child should not receive any positive reinforcement, including from peers. Set up time-out areas in the activity area where you can still see any children in time-out, but away from the other children and activity. Asking the child to sit on the edge of the play area with her or his back turned to the group is appropriate.

A key to managing children's behavior is to communicate clearly and specifically what you want the children to do. As mentioned, this starts with teaching the children your rules from the first day. Be firm and assertive when you present the discipline guidelines and make sure the children understand the system. Beyond these basic steps, you should establish organizational routines for the activities the children can automatically carry out without your direct input or supervision. The following guidelines can help you maintain control of the learning environment (see also the organization sections for each level):

- Have a designated place to gather for all instructions (e.g., under the tree, against the wall, standing on the circle).
- Provide instruction or directions only when all eyes are on you and there is absolute silence.
- Make sure that your directions are clear and complete (e.g., who goes where, how many in a group, what to do when you finish, how long you exercise).

- Have the practice area ready (e.g., clearly marked).
- Establish a plan for the distribution and collection of materials and equipment.
- Practice various formations so children can quickly get into a line, circle, square, and so forth.
- Use a signal to tell the children when you are finished with instructions and ready for them to move.

These guidelines help organize classes so that children get the maximum practice in both quality and quantity. *Quantity* is the number of turns or time doing the task, while *quality* is related to the process of improving, which is usually a result of student understanding, through teacher feedback and error correction. The following guidelines are also helpful in maximizing practice:

- Select some simple activities and some that are more difficult and challenging.
- Encourage children to master all tasks, but allow each child to progress at his or her own rate.
- Select activities that have wide appeal so that children will see that others are engaged and thus be motivated to participate themselves.
- Have enough equipment and practice area(s) to minimize wait times.
- Keep groups small so there is more opportunity for participation.

Starting Lessons and Activities Smoothly

Effective teachers begin by getting the attention of their students. Sounds simple, but this can be difficult if you do not establish a protocol for this. So teach and use a signal to stop, look, and listen. Call individual students by name if necessary but do not start instructions until all of the students appear ready to receive information. After they appear ready to learn, you should use simple, precise terminology to explain the task they will be learning and offer some idea of what they should be able to do after instruction, that is, the objective. Relate the task to something they already know and can do to provide context for the learning. For example, when you introduce a new circle dance, you can remind the students of other dances they learned using the circle forma-

tion. The following hints set the stage for a successful learning environment:

- Be certain the children understand the goal of the activity; in other words, each child must know what he or she is supposed to do. A question such as, "Can anyone tell me the important points you need to remember to perform the skill correctly?" will help.
- Be explicit about what you want the students to think about during instruction and practice. Select important cues, repeating them several times, have the children repeat the cues aloud, and then remind the children that they should remember the points because each point contributes to success.
- Use part practice as needed, which means that a task that is long or has several parts should be practiced in parts. You might explain the first step, pause, and ask the children to practice that step. Give adequate time for children to practice and think about the first step before introducing the second step using the same process. Usually, then, you should add the second part to the first part for practice.
- Give clear and concise verbal instructions in language the age group can understand. However, do not talk too much. For example, when explaining the basic jump in jump rope, you might simply say, "Twirl the rope overhead and jump over it when it hits the ground."
- Provide a demonstration of the task. You can demonstrate or use a skilled child to demonstrate. For example, a low-skilled child can demonstrate a small segment of a skill and feel encouraged to participate. Limit demonstrations to three repetitions.
- Provide time for the children to think about what you have said. Ask a question to determine if the children understand the activity and wait. Try counting to 10 before calling on a student or assuming there are no questions to allow the children time to formulate responses.
- Explain the "why" as well as the "how" of tasks. Children need to understand how they will use a skill. Knowing this provides prerequisite knowledge and often motivates children during practice drills. For example, explain that crunches (or sit-ups)

improve the endurance of the abdominal muscles and push-ups improve endurance of the arm muscles.

- Help students attach meaning to a verbal description and demonstration of a skill by using good, age-appropriate metaphors. For example, with fifth graders, you could compare the arm position for the forearm pass in volleyball to a platform that is level and firm. This helps students to perceive the movement needed for a successful pattern.

- Help children identify the important parts of the activity that are critical to good performance. Using verbal labels often helps. When teaching them the forehand stroke in tennis, for example, you might say "ready, turn, step, swing" to help children establish good rhythm. Counting can also help students establish the desirable rhythm as well as simply focus their attention better.

- Help children relate new skills to skills they have mastered. For example, say, "Remember how we tossed the Frisbee in our last class? Today we are going to learn the backhand drive in tennis, and the movement is similar."

Staying on Track

During the course of instruction it is your responsibility to guide learning. Managing behavior, asking critical questions so children think about what they are doing, encouraging children to self-correct, and providing specific feedback about performance are ways you should guide learning. In addition, provide children with verbal and nonverbal feedback that will let the child know about acceptable behavior; for example, "Good job—you are all following the rules today" or "I like the way Katie put away her equipment." Deal with unacceptable behavior quickly the first time it becomes evident. Be consistent with rewards and consequences. Set limits for children but always maintain a warm and supportive environment; for example, "I want to hear what you have to say, but don't shout. You must raise your hand." Avoid sarcasm and hostility. Use eye contact and gentle physical touch to send a message that you are serious about your rules for behavior. Never argue with a child, instead making a statement like "I understand, but I need you to . . ." will allow you to repeat what you want the child to do. Do not use threats; for example, rather

than saying "If you don't follow the rules, I will . . ." provide incentives, for example, "If you line up quickly so we can begin on time we will have time to play a favorite game at the end of class."

Another effective way to keep class on track is to spend time teaching the children self-management skills so they do not have to depend upon you every moment. This involves not only teaching protocols for class routines but also consciously preparing students for self-regulated learning. This approach can contribute to more meaningful practice for more students. So help children learn to make self-corrections, as this will allow them to become independent learners. Moreover, encourage children to monitor their own progress and to handle distractions. Specifically, encourage students to ask themselves a series of questions about the task, such as "What is the goal of this task? What am I supposed to do? What are the key elements to remember?" This will help the students who think about what others think of them, rather than thinking about the instructions or the task. This is especially true for students who may consider themselves different from the rest of the class (e.g., girls, low-skilled, or minority students). Some self-rules you may want students to learn to follow include the following (adapt for the vocabulary of younger students):

- Always pay attention to the task I'm working on.
- Avoid students who encourage me to be inattentive.
- Set a goal I want to achieve.
- If I get confused and make errors get help from the teacher.
- When I start to think about other people, I need to stop and think about the task.

Provide positive reinforcement for children who can manage their own behavior and regulate their own learning, as this can be a strong motivator. Likewise, feedback about performances encourages learning. When a child makes a mistake, give the information necessary to do the skill correctly (or at least better) on the next trial. Giving corrective feedback sends the child the message that you care about her learning and that you believe she can learn the skill. Corrective feedback is best given using the "sandwich technique" in which you provide encouragement, corrective information, and encouragement; for example, "Roberto, I can see improvement; next time step further forward; I know you can do it!"

Allow time for children to think about feedback and make corrections before taking another turn.

Watch for early signs of frustration because of lack of success, and help such a child set realistic goals. At times, you may need to break a task down into smaller steps or change the equipment or environment. For example, the child could use a larger-faced racket to practice the forehand drive.

Developing Positive Feelings

An environment that encourages discussion is comfortable and nonintimidating. Children can relate interpersonally without fear of reprimand or judgment. We want children to feel good about themselves and others, creating positive experiences in physical education. The following guidelines create a learning environment that stimulates discussion and critical thinking:

- Demonstrate the behavior so the children can copy you (e.g., say "please" and "thank you"; encourage all children; make mistakes and admit that it is OK and "normal" to make mistakes).

- Recognize that the contributions of each child are important. Send a message that you value each child and are interested in what each child has to say.

- Personalize the lesson whenever possible. Help the children relate new learning to their own experiences. Encourage children to talk about themselves.

- Give each child an opportunity to share. Never allow one or two children to dominate a discussion.

- Be tactful and patient in handling incorrect responses. Try to dignify the answer and get the student back on track. For example, if a child were to say, "I was born able to do this; it is so easy," you might respond by saying, "I am glad that it feels so easy, but I bet you have practiced hard to get so good."

- Encourage children to talk about their favorite things or people (e.g., pets, trips, parents, movies). Ask open-ended questions that cause children to think. For example, questions such as "What do you think about . . . ?"; "Think about a time when . . ."; "What do you do when . . . ?" will open the door to interesting and help-

ful discussions.

- Provide adequate "wait time" for children to respond; 10 seconds is a good rule of thumb. Ask a question, but encourage the children to think before responding.

- Encourage children to laugh *with* each other, but never *at* each other. Do not allow children to make fun of others because of poor or inaccurate responses—or any other reason.

- Watch and listen for signs that children want to include you or have special needs. For example, when a child says, "There is room to sit over here," the child is probably saying, "I want you to sit with me, but I am afraid or embarrassed to ask."

- Stand where you can see all the children, as much of the time as possible. While this is an important safety and instructional concern, your position also reflects how important all of the children are to you. Children positioned behind you or out of your view may feel left out. Some children may prefer this position, while others may move close to you so they can demand your attention. Moving around the outside of the area or formation allows you to see the entire group and share your attention evenly among students.

Keep these teaching tips in mind as you use the lessons. Best wishes for a successful school year!

REFERENCES

Bouchard, C. & Pérusse (1994). Heredity, activity level, fitness and health. In C. Bouchard, R.J. Shepard & T. Stephens (eds), *Physical activity, fitness and health*. Champaign, IL: Human Kinetics.

Greendorfer, S.L., J.H Lewko, & K.S. Rosengren (1996). Family and gender-based influences in sport socialization of children and adolescents. In F.L. Smoll & R.E. Smith (eds), *Children and youth in sport*. Madison, WI: Brown & Benchmark.

Malina, R.M. (1984). Physical growth and maturation. In J.R. Thomas (ed), *Motor development during childhood and adolescence*. Minneapolis, MN: Burgess.

Malina, R.M. (1994). Physical activity: relationship to growth, maturation, and physical fitness. In C. Bouchard, R.J. Shepard & T. Stephens (eds), *Physical activity, fitness and health.* Champaign, IL: Human Kinetics.

Powers, S.K. (1984). Children and exercise. In J.R. Thomas (ed), *Motor development during childhood and adolescence.* Minneapolis, MN: Burgess.

Public Health Service (1991). *Health People 2000.* Washington, D.C.: U.S. Government Printing Office. (Publication No. SN 017001004740).

Roche, A.F. & F. Falkner (1975). Physical growth charts. In W.K. Frankenburg & B.W. Camp (eds), *Pediatric screening tests.* Springfield, IL: Charles C. Thomas.

Welk, G.J. (1999). The youth physical activity promotion model: a conceptual bridge between theory and practice. *Quest,* 51: 5-23.

GRADES **K-1**

GRADES **2-3**

GRADES **4-5**

The purpose of these lessons is to prepare you and your students for the content lessons that follow. For your youngest students, this school year is the first experience with physical education. Thus, one of the objectives of these lessons is to distinguish physical education from recess or other free play. Specifically, we help you introduce skills that enhance class management and therefore learning while distinguishing physical education from recess. Students practice class management aspects, including understanding and following rules, consequences, and signals. Students also learn efficient protocols for making transitions, creating formations, obeying boundaries, and handling equipment.

UNIT ORGANIZATION

Why spend so much precious class time on these issues? Keeping control of the class enhances safety and learning—and therefore enjoyment!

Rules and Consequences

First, help the children identify the need for rules, then give them the opportunity to develop the rules. Next help the group work toward consensus, in which all members (the children and you) agree that the rules are good for everyone and that everyone will abide by the rules. Finally, develop and convey consequences for infractions of the rules, once again involving the children. There are four benefits to this approach. The children

- have greater understanding of the rules,
- have agreed to the rules and consequences,

- learn to work together toward a common goal (e.g., a better learning environment), and
- invest their ideas and emotional commitment in the system.

When teachers make the rules and impose them on children, the children feel powerless and disenfranchised within the system. So take the time and make the effort to guide the children in developing the rules and consequences, ensuring both you and the children can live within the system. Since most children have had little experience with decision making and often little or no control over the events in their lives, this is an important opportunity.

Class Protocols

Next, lay a firm foundation for proper class protocols. Responding to signals promptly, making transitions smoothly, understanding boundaries thoroughly, and handling equipment efficiently and gently are all important aspects of a positive class environment.

Begin by choosing a signal, for example, raising your hand or blowing a whistle, to gain the attention of the students. Some teachers use one signal for everything, often stopping all activity with the signal. Other teachers feel more comfortable with signals that correspond to specific behaviors, for example, raising a hand for silence, a single whistle blow to stop, two whistle blows to start.

Making orderly transitions from one activity (or formation) to another uses time more efficiently and reduces discipline problems. One way to facilitate orderly transitions is to teach a set of formations. Most activities call for a circle, line, scatter, partner, or multiple-line formation, with variations for close or far spacing. When children know these formations, transitions between activities are smoother and faster.

Furthermore, most formations and all activities need boundaries; use the lines in the gymnasium and cones both in the gymnasium and on the field as visual reminders. In addition, personal space can be a boundary; make sure students know what this means. As with knowing signals and formations, practicing observing boundaries can prevent or reduce discipline problems.

Equipment can also be a source of conflict among children and an enemy of efficient use of time. Instruction benefits from clear equipment handling procedures. When possible before class spread equipment around the activity area to prevent congestion. Or designate one child per group to collect and return the equipment for his or her group from a central location. Teach children to handle equipment in a way that extends, rather than reduces, its life. For example, sitting on a playground ball may keep the child from disturbing class, but causes the ball to deflate more quickly. Likewise, "dueling" with rackets between activities can break the rackets, not to mention create serious safety and discipline problems! Instead, teach the children to place unneeded equipment at their feet to one side—and to leave it alone until you direct them to use it again.

Worried these lessons will be too boring? Children enjoy the competence they feel in learning these protocols. Teaching your class these management skills is similar to teaching them a secret code that reveals a way to be successful, to fit in, and to please the teacher. Finally, although, clearly, the lessons focus on rules and class management, your presentation of these also serves as an introduction to cooperative skills among the children. When children know how class is organized and know the rules, they feel included, they know the secrets (of success), and they can avoid being embarrassed by breaking a rule or not knowing what to do. Table O1.1 outlines the content of the organization lessons.

LESSON ORGANIZATION

Like all the other lessons in this book, we have organized each lesson systematically and have included a list of clear objectives and necessary equipment to make planning easier for you. The activities start with a warm-up, progress to skill development, and end with a concluding activity. Unlike the rest of the lessons in this book, however, the content of the lessons and the instructional focus is on management and behavior. Although you may be anxious to teach movement skills and fitness concepts, remember that time spent on organization and class management now is time saved throughout the school year as your classes will run more smoothly.

ADDITIONAL TEACHING HINTS

As we have alluded to, helping the children develop the skills included in these organization lessons is critical to your success as a teacher. View the time spent as a wise investment in good teaching! We recommend that all teachers—novice or seasoned veteran—spend some time on the skills included in these five lessons. Certainly, the content lessons that follow assume that both you and your students have mastered the management skills and have a working rule system in place.

For student teachers, substitute teachers, and teachers taking over part way through the year, we recommend that you at least review these skills. Naturally, you should base the exact amount of time you spend on teaching organizational skills on how the children respond (e.g., Can they get into a circle quickly? Stay in boundaries?) and what your relationship to the students is. A substitute who is there for one day should review her or his rules and signal(s) at the beginning of class, making it clear that the children will use the regular teacher's rules when he or she returns. As the regular teacher, teach your students to cooperate with such changes so that a missed day on your part is less likely to equal missed learning for students. A student teacher who will be working with the class for the semester should, at the minimum, establish rules and signals and review formations.

Sometimes more than one teacher will be responsible for teaching physical education; for example, a physical education specialist and the classroom teacher may alternate or a veteran teacher may gradually give control to a student teacher. It's common sense that when two teachers are regularly sharing the responsibilities for teaching physical education, it is best to have similar management procedures. For example, call the formations by the same name, have similar rules and consequences, and use similar formats for instruction. While of course each teacher's style is unique, basic consistency will facilitate the instruction because the children will know what to expect.

Table O1.1: Unit Plan for Grades K-1: Organization

Week One: discuss rules, signals, and formations

Monday: signals, rules, and boundaries
Tuesday: rules and formations
Wednesday: rules, formations, and groups
Thursday: rules and formations
Friday: rules and formations

LESSON 1
SIGNALS, RULES, AND BOUNDARIES

Student Objectives

- Identify safety and learning as benefits of having and following rules.
- Identify the class signal(s).
- Practice starting and stopping on signal.
- Move into information formation on a signal.
- Move within and around boundaries.

Equipment and Materials

- Chalkboard or flip chart (or poster board, large paper) for writing
- 1 carpet square per child
- 5-10 beanbags

Warm-Up Activities (5 minutes)

Islands in the Ocean Warm-Up

Arrange carpet squares so that there are six or more ft between each square. Each child should be sitting on a carpet square.

1. Explain that each carpet square is an island, so each child has their own island. The islands are small, and the children must try to stay "dry" by staying on the carpet square.

2. Call out the following movements and positions, reminding children to stay on the squares: *stand up, walk, lie down, sit on your knees, sit down and touch your feet, stand up and touch your feet, jump, turn around, and sit down.* You can repeat any of the movements and speed up or slow down the changes in movements, depending upon how successful the children are at each movement.

3. Compliment children who stay on the squares.

Skill-Development Activities (20 minutes)

Physical Education Rules

Arrange the children in a close group sitting on the floor on the carpet squares.

1. Explain the formation: *This is called an "information formation." When I say "information formation," you should move to this close group, sitting on the floor. We will practice this again later.*

2. Ask the children: *What might happen if we did not have rules or laws? For example, how do traffic rules help us?* (If there were no stop signs or cars did not stop at the signs, there would probably be many accidents. Many people could be hurt. Having rules and following rules keeps us safer.)

3. *What rules should we have in physical education so everyone can be safer?* Lead a discussion to rules 1 through 3. Write the rules on the chalkboard or paper:

   • *Rule 1: Hands off. This means we do not put our hands, feet, or other body parts on anyone else, so everyone will be safe.*

   • *Rule 2: Be careful. Do not hurt equipment; do not move wildly so everyone will be safe and so the equipment will stay in good condition for physical education.*

   • *Rule 3: Listen and look for the stop signals. When you hear or see the signal, stop, listen, and look at the teacher.* Demonstrate the stop signal. Say to the children, *Show me the stop signal. Good remembering! Following the stop signal helps everyone hear instructions and stay safe.*

4. *These rules give everyone the same opportunity, or chance, to learn. What other situations should we have rules for?* (When one child does not hear the instructions because another child is talking, when one child keeps a piece of equipment [e.g. a ball] too long so other children do not have the chance to practice, and so on.) Lead the discussion to rules 4 through 6.

   • *Rule 4: Be nice. Do not fight; do not bother others; be helpful. Being nice keeps everyone safe, learning, and having fun!*

   • *Rule 5: Listen and do. When the teacher is talking, you should not talk; when another student has permission to talk, please don't talk; it is OK to talk quietly at other times; do what you are instructed to do.* Some teachers prefer to have a signal for quiet that differs from the stop signal, such as a raised hand or finger over the mouth. If you wish to have a separate quiet signal, explain and demonstrate it now.

   • *Rule 6: Do your best. Always try everything and work hard. This rule makes sure everyone will learn and feel good about physical education.*

5. Continue the discussion about the importance of following rules until you feel the children have a good understanding of acceptable behavior in the physical education setting. Most "rules" the children will come up with will be variations or examples of the six rules already listed. Help the children to categorize these as such. Write any further rules on the chalkboard or paper.

6. *Note:* After class, make a poster of your final version of class rules for future reference.

Moving Within and Around Boundaries

Using the four cones, mark a large rectangle in the playing area.

1. Relate this activity to Rule 5: Listen and do. Tell the children: *Having boundaries helps us to be safe and learn, because if you are too far away, you might not be able to hear what to do or you might be in danger.*

2. Walk the entire class around the sides of the rectangle formed by the four cones.

3. Show them the boundary lines between the cones. Describe the boundary lines: *These are like invisible walls, and the area "inside" is like a room. On the other side of the wall is the "outside."* Scatter the children inside the "room."

4. Signal the children: *Move carefully but freely (randomly) inside.* Signal stop. Compliment those who stop quickly and quietly.

5. *Move along the boundaries on the outside of the line.* Signal stop. Offer compliments.

6. *Move along the boundaries on the inside of the line.* Signal stop. Offer compliments.
7. *Move along the boundaries on the outside.* Signal stop. Offer compliments.
8. Repeat steps 4 through 7 as time permits.

Concluding Activities (5 minutes)

Physical Education Rules

Signal the children to create the information formation.

1. Compliment those who remember the formation and gather quickly and quietly.
2. Repeat the rules that were written earlier and ask: *Can you give a reason for each rule?*
3. *Do you have any questions?* Allow children to raise any concerns they have.
4. If this is your last class, ask one child to gather the cones and two or three others to gather the carpet squares and bring them to you.

LESSON 2
RULES CONSENSUS AND FORMATIONS

Student Objectives

- Recognize the rules.
- Give examples of the rules.
- Reach consensus on the class rules.
- Move from a line to a circle formation.
- Participate in a game.

Equipment and Materials

- Physical Education Rules poster
- 1 carpet square per child plus a few extra
- 4 cones or other markers
- Flour, line chalk, string, or tape circle
- 5-10 beanbags

Warm-Up Activities (5 minutes)

Wild One

Use four cones to define a rectangular play area. Scatter carpet squares and beanbags randomly in the play area, leaving spaces between them. Have each child begin by standing on a carpet square. There should be extra squares.

1. Review and emphasize Rule 2: Be careful before introducing the game.
2. Designate one child as the Wild One ("It") and direct him or her to move randomly about the play area, making faces, waving arms, and generally acting wild while the other children walk from carpet square to carpet square. Tell the children: *Only one child may be on a square at a time. Keep moving all the time from square to square.*
3. After a while, signal stop and select a new Wild One. Stop the game if more than one child ends up on a square to remind them to move to a different square.
4. After the children have learned to moved continuously from square to square, tell them to run between squares.
5. Repeat the game with new Wild Ones, stopping as necessary to remind the children that there is only one Wild One or that only one person may be on each square.

Skill-Development Activities (20 minutes)

Rules Consensus

Gather the children into an information formation.

1. Show the children the rules that were developed in Grades K-1: Organization, Lesson 1, page 7. Ask the children:

Who remembers a rule? Continue until the children have repeated each one.

Why are rules important? (Stay safe; save time.)

2. Give an example of when each rule might apply:

- ***Rule 1: Hands off.*** *If a person is a Wild One, other people may not be able to listen, do, and learn.*

- ***Rule 2: Be careful.*** *If our equipment is broken, no one will learn; a student who is hurt cannot learn.*

- ***Rule 3: Listen and look for the stop signals.*** *Remember yesterday when we practiced moving in and out of our area? If everyone had not stopped when I signaled, some people might not have heard the directions.*

- ***Rule 4: Be nice.*** *People fighting can keep many from learning.*

- ***Rule 5: Listen and do.*** *As a new activity begins, we must listen for instructions, then do them in order to learn as much as possible.*

- ***Rule 6: Do your best.*** *Each of us must try everything, even if we think we are not very good at the activity.*

3. *Do you understand each rule?* Discuss if necessary:

   Are these good rules?

   Can you agree with them? If yes, continue; if no, discuss and resolve any problems or misunderstanding so all children can agree with the rules.

   Can you follow the rules? We are all counting on you.

4. Ask one child to gather the beanbags and two children to gather the carpet squares for you.

Circle and Line

Arrange children in a line between two cones. Mark a large circle with cones, chalk, or flour (for the playground) 20 or 30 ft from the line.

1. Describe the line formation. Tell the children:

   Look at your present location and remember it.

   Look for some special landmark, like a line, clover, or bare spot.

2. Describe and point out the circle.

3. Signal the children: *Move in any way you want to the circle and stand still on the line.* Adjust the children's positions in the circle as necessary. Signal the children: *Move back to your positions on the line.*

4. Repeat several times until the children master the skill.

Moving Within and Around Boundaries

Using four cones, mark a large rectangle in the playing area around the circle. Create the rectangle in a different position from the previous lesson. See Grades K-1: Organization, Lesson 1, page 7.

1. Remind the children what they have learned about boundaries.

2. Ask the children: *Who can show me the boundaries marked by the cones?* Allow one child to demonstrate by running between the four cones marking the boundaries of the rectangle.

Concluding Activities (5 minutes)

Circle Boundaries Game

Arrange half the children in a circle, inside the rectangle formed by the four cones. Scatter the remaining group outside the circle, but inside the rectangle.

1. Explain that there are three places the scattered children can move on your command: *(1) inside the rectangle but outside the circle, (2) inside the circle, and (3) around the boundaries.*

2. Explain the activity: *When I say "rectangle," "boundaries," and "circle," walk or run until I signal for you to stop or change locations.* Repeat several times, then reverse the roles of the two groups.

For additional steps, place a line somewhere in the rectangle.

3. Expand the activity: *Now let's add another word. When I say, "Line!" form a line as quickly as possible.*

4. Have the circle group walk along the circle. Each time you signal for the other group to change locations, have these children change the direction in which they are walking.

5. If this is your last class, ask one to four children to gather the cones.

GRADES

K-1

LESSON 3

FORMATIONS 1 AND GROUPS

Student Objectives

- Participate in two games that use formations and boundaries.
- Demonstrate understanding of scatter, pair, line, and circle formations by moving from one to another on verbal request.
- Point to and move within and around boundaries.

Equipment and Materials

- Physical Education Rules poster
- 4 cones or other markers
- Flour, line chalk, string, or tape circle

Warm-Up Activities (5 minutes)

Circle Boundaries Game

Arrange half the children in a circle, inside the rectangle formed by the four cones. Scatter the remaining group outside the circle, but inside the rectangle. See Grades K-1: Organization, Lesson 2, page 11.

Skill-Development Activities (20 minutes)

Rules Consensus

Call for an information formation. See Grades K-1: Organization, Lesson 2, page 7.

Scatter Formation

Continue in the information formation to begin this segment.

1. Emphasize Rule 1: Hands off. Stress the importance of finding a place with enough space to move without touching others: *Find your own space so everyone will be safe.*
2. Signal the children to move from the line to a scatter formation. Check to make sure each child has free space. Have them move several times from the line to scatter formation and back to the line.
3. With the children in scatter formation, present several movement tasks. Remind the children: *Spread out so no one touches.* Ask them to do the following: *point to the boundary; move to the boundary; move back to your space in scatter formation; move to an empty space; walk in place; march in place, lifting your knees high; point to the circle; move to the circle; move around the circle taking big steps with toes pointing out (with toes pointing in, with knees bent, with hands over your head); and move to your own space in scatter formation.*

Partner Formation

Keep the children in scatter formation.

1. Tell the children: *Find a partner on the signal.*
2. Signal the children to move back to a scatter formation alone. Repeat several times (you can specify same partner or new partner).
3. Tell the children: *On the next signal, find a partner and stand back-to-back.* Repeat this several times, alternating between a partner scatter formation and individual scatter formation.

Moving Within and Around Boundaries

Use the four cones to define a rectangular playing area once again. Ask the children to pick partners, then divide the children into four groups. Line up each group along one side (boundary) of the rectangle.

1. Ask the children: *Walk (or run, hop, gallop) with your partner within the boundaries.*
2. Tell the children: *Move into a scatter formation without your partner.*
3. From the scatter formation, tell the children: *Find a partner again.*
4. Next ask the children: *Walk (or run, hop, gallop) with your partner along the boundaries.*
5. Repeat, mixing steps 1 through 4.

Moving Across the Boundary Lines

Arrange the children in a line outside the rectangle.

1. Ask the children: *Run on the signal across the boundary lines of the rectangle, then stop.* Signal students to return to either a line, scatter, or circle formation. Repeat.

Divide the children into four groups, then assign each group to a boundary line of the rectangle.

2. Signal each group to run to the opposite boundary line. Walk through an example of this for each group first. Begin by explaining the task (e.g., *Run to the opposite side of the rectangle*), then point to a group and demonstrate how they should move. Repeat with another group. Then ask the remaining two groups: *Point to the place where your group will run.*

Concluding Activities (5 minutes)

Fire Engine

Line up the children along one side of the rectangle. Assign each child a number from one to four. Have one child (the Fire Chief) stand in the center of the rectangle.

1. Explain the game:

   The Fire Chief calls, "Fire Engine Number One" (or any number from one to four).

   All the "Ones" run to the opposite side of the rectangle, trying to avoid being caught by the Fire Chief.

   Any children caught must join the Fire Chief and try to catch other engines.

2. Practice the game: Have the children raise their hands when their number is called, then demonstrate running across the rectangle before starting the actual game.
3. Have the Fire Chief begin the game, calling each engine number in turn.

If this is the last class, ask four children to get the cones and bring them to you.

LESSON 4
FORMATIONS 2

Student Objectives

- Move from one formation to another.
- Give examples of the rules.
- Discuss consequences for rules infractions.
- Cooperate with a partner.
- Name and move to four different formations.
- Demonstrate getting and returning equipment.

Equipment and Materials

- Physical Education Rules poster
- 4 carpet squares
- 4 cones or other markers
- Chalkboard or flip chart
- Flour, line chalk, string, or tape circle
- 1 beanbag per child
- Picture signs for tasks at stations

Warm-Up Activities (5 minutes)

Stay With Your Partner

Arrange partners in scatter formation. Number each person in the pair either partner 1 or partner 2. Define the activity area with cones and/or floor markings.

1. Emphasize Rule 3: Listen and look for the stop signals.
2. Describe the game:

    On "Go!" partner 1 runs anywhere in the activity area, and partner 2 tries to stay as close to partner 1 as safely possible.

    On the stop signal, both of you freeze. I will check to see how close each partner 2 is to his or her partner 1.

3. Have the children play Stay With Your Partner. Cue the children: *Remember, partner 2, try to stay as close as you safely can to partner 1.*
4. Repeat several times, and then have partners switch roles.

Skill-Development Activities (20 minutes)

Physical Education Rules

Gather the children into an information formation. Ask the children to state the physical education rules. See Grades K-1: Organization, Lesson 1, page 7.

Consequences

Keep the children in the information formation.

1. Discuss the importance of following the rules with questions such as these:

   What happens if everyone follows the rules? (Everyone is safer and learns.)

   What happens if someone (or several people) break(s) the rules? (Someone may be injured; one or more children may not learn.)

2. Continue the discussion with this question: *If someone does not follow the rules, what should happen?* Discuss the various consequences. Ask children to consider the difference between "just once" and "often."

3. Share these possible consequences for infractions of the rules:

   - First offense: A verbal reminder of the rule.
   - Second offense: 1 minute in time-out.
   - Third offense: 5 minutes in time-out.
   - Fourth offense: Parents are called.
   - Fifth offense: Send to the principal.

4. Record the consequences on a chalkboard or flip chart.

5. *Note:* After class, make a poster of the consequences for future reference.

Stations

Mark four stations with the cones. Divide the class into four groups, and assign each group to a station.
   Each group will perform the specified activity at a station, then move on a signal to the next station. Rotate the groups through the stations. The station activities are on the task cards placed at the stations.

1. Explain the tasks, pointing to the cone at which you wish the children to perform each: *run in place 10 steps; march in place 10 steps; jump 5 times on your left foot, then on your right foot; bend your body.*

2. Explain how station learning occurs: *Each group will do the task at each station. Move to the next station when I signal you.* Define and demonstrate the signal. *Go to the next station this way* (point counterclockwise; walk groups through rotation if necessary).

3. Ask the children to perform the task at their first station.

4. Signal stop. Have the groups move to the next station (point again) and perform the designated task.

5. Continue until the groups have moved through all the stations.

Getting and Returning Equipment

Continue to mark the rectangle and four stations with cones. Place all the beanbags in the center of the rectangle on a carpet square.

1. Emphasize Rule 4: Be nice. Remind the children:

   It's important to share and take care of our equipment.

   When one person in each group passes out and gathers the equipment, we can take care of this chore much more quickly.

2. Have one child from each group come from their station and get enough beanbags for all the children in the group. Then ask a different child from each group to return the beanbags.

3. Next ask the children: *Create a scatter formation. On the way, pick up a beanbag.* After all children are in the scatter formation, ask them: *Move to a line formation, returning your beanbag to the carpet square on the way.*

4. Divide the beanbags evenly among four carpet squares. Tell the children: *Move into a station formation.* Have each group member, in turn, get a beanbag, then return the beanbags to the carpet square.

5. Send each group to a stand along one side of the rectangle. Select one child from each group to get beanbags from a carpet square for all the children in their line.

Concluding Activities (5 minutes)

"How Many Formations Can You Name?" Game

Gather the children into an information formation.

1. Ask the children to name a formation. Repeat the name, and tell the children to move quickly into that formation.

2. Once the children are in the new formation, move to a new location, then signal the children to return to the information formation.

3. Ask them to name a different formation, then to move into that formation. Repeat steps 1 and 2 until the children have practiced all the formations.

Fire Engine

See Grades K-1: Organization, Lesson 3, page 13.

G R A D E S
K-1

ORGANIZATION

LESSON 5
FORMATIONS 3

Student Objectives

- Demonstrate understanding of the formations by moving from one to another on a signal.
- Reach consensus on the consequences for rules infractions.
- Name and describe the formations.
- Relate rules infractions to consequences.
- Demonstrate near and far spacing.

Equipment and Materials

- Physical Education Rules poster
- Consequences poster
- 1 carpet square per child
- 4 cones or other markers
- Flour, line chalk, string, or tape circle

Warm-Up Activities (5 minutes)

Fire Engine

Line up the children along one side of the rectangle. Have one child stand in the center of the rectangle as the Fire Chief. See Grades K-1: Organization, Lesson 3, page 13.

Skill-Development Activities (20 minutes)

Consensus for Consequences

Gather children into an information formation.

1. Read the consequences developed in the previous lesson. Ask: *Does everyone understand the consequences?*

2. Ask the children: *Is there anyone who thinks a consequence is unfair?* Discuss the consequences, helping all the children agree that the consequences are fair.

3. Say: *Can everyone agree with the consequences?* If yes, move to the next lesson. If no, continue the discussion. For example, say to the children, *Julie thinks it may be unfair to call parents as a consequence. Can anyone else explain why this is unfair?* (Children may say parents are busy.) *It does seem unfair to bother a parent when a child makes a mistake. How can we make this more fair?* (Hopefully kids will say "follow the rules.") Consequences 1 through 3, in the previous lesson, involve only the offending child, 4 and 5 involve others.

Organization 17

Near and Far

Gather the children into an information formation closer together than for physical activity, but further apart than for the previous activity, by arranging carpet squares in a scatter formation.

1. Begin the activity by describing personal space—the area around you, that no one else should be in. Tell the children: *If you touch someone else, you have entered their personal space.*

2. Next describe general space—the open areas or everything else that is not personal space. Say to the children: *Sometimes we can be close together, but not touching, like when we are in an information formation or in the classroom.*

3. Ask the children to move into a scatter formation, but not near any carpet squares or other children. Tell the children: *You are in a far scatter formation.*

4. Now ask them to each move onto a carpet square: *You are now in a near scatter formation.*

5. Remind the children that "near" means close but still not in someone else's personal space. Switch back to far scatter formation, then to a near scatter formation. Repeat as often as time permits.

Stations

Mark four stations with the cones in a rectangle or square. Divide the class into four groups, and assign each group to a station. Rotate the children through the stations. See Grades K-1: Organization, Lesson 4, page 15.

Partner Formation

Have the children practice finding a partner quickly and moving in pairs into a scatter formation.

Circle Boundaries Game

See Grades K-1: Organization, Lesson 2, page 11.

Concluding Activities (5 minutes)

Formation Challenge

Arrange the children in scatter formation.

1. Emphasize Rule 6: Do your best.

2. Tell the children: *Move from one formation to another as quickly as possible on the signal.* Signal the following formations: line, circle, partners, stations, and scatter.

3. Repeat and mix the formations with near and far. Remind them: *In a near formation, you should be closer together than in a far formation.* You may have to help them with this for the line, circle, and station formations.

K-1

This section has three parts: the fitness testing lessons, the Fitness Hustles, and the fitness activity lessons. You can conduct fitness testing at the beginning and end of the school year or more often, if you wish. Allow children to practice the tests as test results will be more meaningful if the children are familiar with the procedures. In addition, practicing the tests enhances fitness itself. Don't, however, rely solely on this method of training. Also use and repeat many times the fitness lessons we've provided to keep interest and enthusiasm high through variety. Note, too, that we have designed the lessons to supplement the skills portion of a well-rounded physical education program.

UNIT ORGANIZATION

The first unit consists of the Fitness Hustles, which are similar to aerobic dance routines. Take five class days to teach the warm-up and four routines. Repeat the final Fitness Hustle lesson throughout the school year at your discretion. Next, teach the three one-week units of fitness circuits, fitness challenges, and moderate to vigorous games. We advise that you revisit these lessons throughout the school year, perhaps on Fridays or other designated days.

There are numerous ways to organize these lessons; we suggest two in table I.1. This example includes one week each of Fitness Hustles, moderate to vigorous games, fitness challenges, and circuit training in addition to fitness testing. The activities for each lesson in the section are summarized in table F1.1.

In addition, each unit covers fitness concepts (see table F1.2), fitness activities, and fitness warm-ups. Alternative fitness concept activities are presented for many lessons. Another approach is to assign fitness homework and help the children keep a fitness journal. Homework can be simple activities, such as, "Go for a walk" or "Do crunches while an adult counts for you."

A final note, if you decide not to do fitness testing, you can still do the fitness lessons. The physical activity is good for both you and the children! No matter the lesson or unit, encourage the children to be as active as possible during each lesson and to increase their physical activity levels throughout the school year.

LESSON ORGANIZATION

Note that all lessons have both cognitive and fitness objectives. Each lesson begins with a warm-up activity. Then the skill development activities follow. These are either related to testing or training fitness. Remember that unless you are having the children train the components of health-related fitness at least three days per week, your program will not change fitness levels by itself. In order to do so, encourage children to participate in physical activity outside of class either through fitness contracts or fitness homework. Finally, the concluding activities include a fitness concept, teaching and reinforcing the "whys" behind physical activity.

TEACHING HINTS

These lessons will probably be your kindergartners' and first graders' first exposure to the concepts involved in physical fitness. Bear in mind that most of them are probably already in great shape, given their naturally high physical activity levels. The key is to preserve and enhance their enthusiasm for physical activity through fun and age-appropriate activities in which all are successful. The resulting feelings of competence will help increase the chances that these children will remain physically active as a way of life.

Kindergartners and First Graders

The children in these grades are usually five to seven years old. Your expectations for males and females should be very similar, even though some males may have greater strength than some females.

Children in this age range are usually very active and enjoy the challenges of physical fitness activities. Remember, this unit should be fun, to encourage future participation in physical activities. To this end, do not compare children to each other when you evaluate their fitness levels; instead, compare children to their own previous performances or to a standard that is challenging but attainable. Moreover, encourage participation, improvement, and enthusiasm. For example, children typically enjoy participating with their teacher. So at least some of the time it is important for the children to see you actively involved. Clearly, you are a role model. Furthermore, children will feel more comfortable trying new activities if they see you trying new activities—even if you are having trouble mastering the skill.

Obese and Overweight Students

The most challenging students to teach in a fitness unit are typically the overweight and obese students. Often these students feel frustrated, embarrassed, and incapable. But do not give up on them or allow them to avoid the fitness lessons. Instead, focus on encouraging participation and personal improvement. Allow these children to build their strength and stamina slowly so as not to discourage them altogether. In addition, discussing the value of physical activity may change the behaviors and attitudes of overweight and obese children. Finally, do not allow other children to ridicule anyone for any reason in your classes. Create an environment in which each child can feel safe, competent, and capable.

Safety Considerations

The weather affects children more than adults. For example, if it is hot, children will have more trouble handling the heat than the average adult. So allow them to drink plenty of water and work in the shade (if possible). Encourage them to use sunscreen. Cold weather can also be a problem. Children lose body heat faster than adults. Exercise can make them feel warmer, but their bodies may be less efficient in the cold. Most importantly, be sensitive to their activity patterns. For example, children this age generally stop exercising when their bodies hurt, which is a good sign that they should be allowed to slow down.

Table F1.1: Unit Plan for Grades K-1: Fitness

Week 2: testing	Week 3: Hustles
Monday: introduce backsaver sit-and-reach test and fitness run Tuesday: introduce sit-ups and push-ups Wednesday: practice fitness run, backsaver sit-and-reach test, sit-ups, and push-ups Thursday: testing and self-testing of fitness Friday: testing and self-testing of fitness	Monday: introduce warm-up routine Tuesday: introduce Hustle 1 Wednesday: introduce Hustle 2 Thursday: introduce Hustle 3 Friday: introduce Hustle 4

Week 4: circuit training

Monday: **fitness activity:** circuit training and **fitness concept:** physical fitness and health
Tuesday: **fitness activity:** circuit training and **fitness concept:** physical fitness, physical activity, and health
Wednesday: **fitness activity:** circuit training and **fitness concept:** components of fitness—definitions
Thursday: **fitness activity:** circuit training and **fitness concept:** components of fitness—examples
Friday: **fitness activity:** circuit training and **fitness concept:** components of fitness—measuring

Week 5: moderate to vigorous games

Monday: **fitness activity:** moderate to vigorous games (Leader Ball, Pair Tag, Delivery Relay) and **fitness concept:** components of fitness—training
Tuesday: **fitness activity:** moderate to vigorous games (Follow-the-Leader-Three, Fitness Dodge Ball, Cooperative Relay) and **fitness concept:** cardiovascular endurance
Wednesday: **fitness activity:** moderate to vigorous games (Reveille, Sneaky Tag, Fitness Relay) and **fitness concept:** muscular endurance
Thursday: **fitness activity:** moderate to vigorous games (Buddy Relay, Color Tag, Run-Across) and **fitness concept:** flexibility
Friday: **fitness activity:** moderate to vigorous games (Fitness Go-Around, Crab Relay, Triplet Tag) and **fitness concept:** body composition

Week 6: fitness challenges

Monday: **fitness activity:** fitness challenges and **fitness concept:** muscular strength and endurance
Tuesday: **fitness activity:** fitness challenges and **fitness concept:** cardiovascular endurance and resting heart rate
Wednesday: **fitness activity:** fitness challenges and **fitness concept:** individual differences
Thursday: **fitness activity:** fitness challenges and **fitness concept:** behavior and heredity
Friday: **fitness activity:** fitness challenges and **fitness concept:** risk factors

Week 19: testing	Week 25: Hustles	Week 36: testing
Monday: testing and self-testing of fitness Tuesday: testing and self-testing of fitness Wednesday: testing and self-testing of fitness Thursday: testing and self-testing of fitness Friday: testing and self-testing of fitness	Monday: Fitness Hustles Tuesday: Fitness Hustles Wednesday: Fitness Hustles Thursday: Fitness Hustles Friday: Fitness Hustles	Monday: testing and self-testing of fitness Tuesday: testing and self-testing of fitness Wednesday: testing and self-testing of fitness Thursday: testing and self-testing of fitness Friday: testing and self-testing of fitness

Table F1.2: Fitness Concepts

The following are the 15 fitness concepts presented in the Grades K-1: Fitness lesson plans. Since the lessons can be repeated, we have suggested more than one learning activity for each concept. Thus, when you repeat the lessons, you can use a different learning activity for the fitness concept.

1. Regular exercise helps you develop physical fitness. *Physical fitness* is regular exercise or sport that contributes to health and allows us to do activities throughout the day. Regular exercise means that you exercise at least three times a week.
2. Physical activity, like walking, housework, or yard work, contributes to health. *Physical fitness* is exercise or sport; *physical activity* is moving.
3. Physical fitness has five parts: cardiovascular endurance, muscular strength and endurance, flexibility, and body composition.
4. A physically fit person can exercise for 20 minutes without stopping, do 30 sit-ups, some push-ups or chin-ups, stretch his or her body (e.g., touching toes), and has a healthy amount of body fat.
5. To measure or decide how fit you are you could ride a bike, swim or jog for 20 minutes, do sit-ups and push-ups, and touch your toes. Someone could measure your skinfolds to see how much fat you have.
6. A physically fit person exercises regularly, jogging, cycling, or swimming, doing sit-ups, push-ups, and stretching. These exercises can help our muscles stay healthy and keep our body from storing too much fat. To be physically fit we must exercise at least three times each week for three continuous 10-minute bouts each day.
7. *Cardiovascular fitness*, or heart fitness, is also called *aerobic fitness*. A person who can jog, ride a bike, or swim for 20 minutes is demonstrating aerobic fitness.
8. *Muscular endurance* is when a muscle or group of muscles can make the same movement many times without getting too tired. Sit-ups, push-ups, and chin-ups demonstrate muscular endurance. *Muscular strength* is how much work a muscle can do one time. Muscles get stronger through exercising, for example, moving heavy objects.
9. Flexibility is important to preventing injuries. Slowly stretching our body parts helps us to be more flexible.
10. Too much or too little body fat is not healthy. Body fat can be measured with skinfolds. Our diet, physical activity, and genetics can determine how much fat we have.
11. Muscles become stronger and able to do the same amount of work more times as a result of regular exercise.
12. Resting heart rate is lowered with regular exercise. After you have been lying still for 15 to 30 minutes (or when you first wake up in the morning) the number of times your heart beats is your *resting heart rate.*
13. Each person has to do a different amount of work to become physically fit.
14. Two things decide health and fitness: the characteristics you inherit from your parents (such as height or body type) and your behaviors (what you do every day).
15. Things that may hurt our health and fitness are called *risk factors*. Some risk factors are because of the way we behave; we can change these. Other risk factors are inherited, and we cannot change these.

GRADES
K-1

LESSON 1
FITNESS TESTING 1

Student Objectives

- Practice the backsaver sit-and-reach.
- Practice the fitness run.
- Explain why practice and warm-up before a test are important.
- Demonstrate cooperation when practicing the sit-and-reach.

Equipment and Materials

- 1 carpet square or fitness-type mat per child
- 4 cones
- 1 yardstick per group or 1 sit-and-reach box per group

Warm-Up Activities (5 minutes)

Progressive Walk

Arrange the four cones in a square or rectangular shape with 50 to 100 ft between the cones. Divide the class into four groups, and have each group stand near one cone, on the outside of the rectangle or square.

1. Explain the activity: *On the signal, one group will walk clockwise to the next cone. As soon as the walkers arrive, the group waiting will begin walking to the next cone. This works as though one group is "bumping" the next group away from their cone, on toward the next cone.*

2. Explain further: *Each new group moves faster than the previous group, from walking to fast walking, to jogging to fast jogging, and finally to running.*

3. If desired, repeat the activity counterclockwise, gradually slowing back to a walk.

Warm-Up Stretch

Arrange the children in scatter formation. Begin with slow stretching:

Standing with your feet shoulder-width apart, reach up overhead. Bend to each side and to the front and back, bending your knees slightly. Repeat several times.

Squat, placing your hands on the ground with your arms outside your knees. Keep the knees as straight as possible so the thighs are parallel to the floor.

Slowly stand, keeping your hands on the ground; do not lock knees straight. Be sure to stop if it hurts! Squat again. Repeat several times.

Skill-Development Activities

Backsaver Sit-and-Reach

Set up the backsaver sit-and-reach test stations. Gather the children into an information formation at one station.

1. Explain that before doing the backsaver sit-and-reach test everyone should warm up with gentle stretching. Tell your students: *A warm-up does two things: It reduces the chance of injury and improves your performance on the test.*

2. Explain the test procedure:

   Sit with one leg extended straight out from your body to the front. Do not lock your knees. Place the bottoms of that extended foot against a flat vertical surface, like the backsaver sit-and-reach box or a curb (see the figure below). Bend the other leg at the knee and place that foot by the knee of your extended leg.

   Place one hand on top of the other with your fingers and arms extended forward.

   Reach slowly toward your toes while bending forward.

3. To measure place the yardstick or the sit-and-reach box with the 15-inch mark even with the bottom of the feet and the 0-inch end of the yardstick toward the child's abdomen (the yardstick on a sit-and-reach box should be affixed to the box at the 15-inch mark). This way large numbers indicate more flexibility. Almost everyone should be able to reach the yardstick and therefore score. The score is determined by the number the fingers reach and hold for two to three seconds. This is to discourage "bouncing" and encourage slow stretching. For the test, record the best of three trials.

4. Demonstrate the test.

Arrange the children with partners in small groups so the number of groups equals the number of yardsticks. Place each group at a yardstick or sit-and-reach box.

5. Allow the children to practice with a partner or in small groups of three or four (depending upon the number of yardsticks and sit-and-reach boxes): *One partner does the sit-and-reach, and the other partner measures and makes sure the form is correct.* One partner watches as you present the following instructions for each trial:

   - *Fingers together with one hand on top of the other*
   - *Knees unlocked*
   - *End point held for two or three counts*
   - *No bouncing*

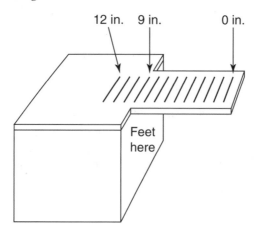

Fitness Run

Gather the children into the information formation. Use cones or other markers to create a running area. The total distance to run is 880 yards (a half mile); a rectangle of 100 by 10 yards fits into most playing fields and can be run four times to complete the half mile.

1. Tell your students: *The fitness run is designed to test cardiorespiratory or aerobic fitness. Most of you are very active. Some of you are more active than others. We are going to practice the fitness run. Then we will work on activities that will help all of us to be in good shape if we aren't already before we take the test again. Practicing the test is important because each person must learn good pacing. Usually, it's best to begin by running slowly and increasing your speed when the finish is near. Today we will all run together slowly, then at the end, anyone who wants to run fast can sprint to the finish.*

2. Spread the group around the outside of the rectangle.

3. Tell the children: *Jog slowly around the outside of the rectangle. Talk to each other and to me! Your pace should allow you to still be able to talk.*

4. *Help me count the laps as we complete each.* On the last lap, remind the children they may run faster if they want to. You should jog, not run, to encourage all skill levels.

5. Make a note of which children are more and less active than the others.

Concluding Activities (5 minutes)

Discussion

Gather the children into the information formation.

1. Discuss the importance of fitness testing. Ask: *Why is practicing the test important before taking a fitness test?* (One reason is to do your best on the test. Second, to learn the "tricks" of the test, like pacing in the fitness run. Third, to understand what you have to do for the test.)

2. Discuss.

3. Ask: *Why is a warm-up important before taking a fitness test?* (One reason is to avoid injury. A second reason is to help you do your best.)

Alternative Learning Activities

Gather the children into an information formation. Discuss the following points:

1. Ask: *Have you ever been so cold that you had trouble moving? How did you move when you were cold?* Allow some children to demonstrate, including moving with stiff limbs.

2. Continue: *Moving in the cold helps us get warm, and as we get warm we become more flexible—less stiff.*

3. Ask: *Have you ever broken a bone or do you know someone who was in a cast because of a broken bone? What happens to the limb (arm, leg)?* (The muscle shrinks and the limb is usually stiff.)

4. Say: *It is important to warm up and exercise to keep our bodies flexible and our muscles strong and healthy.*

FITNESS

LESSON 2
FITNESS TESTING 2

Student Objectives

- Practice performing correct sit-ups.
- Practice performing correct push-ups.
- Cooperate by watching a partner do sit-ups and push-ups.
- List two criteria each for a correct sit-up and push-up.

Equipment and Materials

- 4 cones
- 1 carpet square or mat per child

Warm-Up Activities (5 minutes)

Progressive Walk

See Grades K-1: Fitness, Lesson 1, page 23.

Skill-Development Activities (20 minutes)

Push-Ups

Gather the children into an information formation.

1. Describe and demonstrate a correct push-up:

   Start with the balls of your feet and hands on the ground, hands shoulder-width apart, feet together or comfortably apart.

   Stretch out (extend) your legs so that they and your upper body form a nearly straight line.

   Lower your body toward the ground by bending your elbows, keeping your body straight.

   When your body is nearly to the ground, move back up to the original position.

   Keep your body "stiff as a board."

2. Have the children practice giving you feedback on correct and incorrect push-up form. Emphasize supportive ways to offer feedback.

3. Rearrange the children into partners in scatter formation.

4. Tell the children: *One partner will do push-ups while the other watches to see that the person is performing the push-up correctly.*

5. After a few minutes, have the children switch roles. Circulate, helping children give accurate feedback.

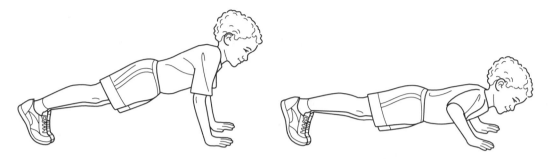

Sit-Ups

Gather the children into an information formation.

1. Describe and demonstrate a correct sit-up:

   The sit-up is really done with a rolling motion.

   Begin by lying on your back with your legs bent slightly at the knees so the bottoms of your feet are flat on the ground.

   Choose one of the two hand-arm positions: You can cross your hands and arms on your chest so that your hands are resting on the opposite shoulders, or you can place your hands on the sides of your head with a finger placed on each ear, keeping your elbows lined up (parallel) with the back of your head (keep them there, not pulling forward past the ears).

   Perform each sit-up slowly, rolling your chin to your chest to lift your head, next your shoulders, then your lower back off the ground. During the movement, you should feel the muscles under your belly button working.

   Once your lower back is off the ground, unroll back down to the start position.

2. Have the children practice analyzing your sit-up form.

Arrange the children in scatter formation, each with a carpet square or mat.

3. As you say, *"Rollllllllll,"* have each child do a sit-up, emphasizing moving slowly.

4. After one sit-up, tell the children: *Point to the muscles that did the work* (the muscles under the belly button). Repeat several times.

5. Have partners check each other's form as with push-ups. Children should practice giving feedback as with the push-up.

Fitness Run

See Grades K-1: Fitness, Lesson 1, page 25.

Concluding Activities (5 minutes)

Discussion

Gather the children into an information formation. Discuss correct form for sit-ups and push-ups:

What are the important things to remember about the sit-up? (Rolling up, going slowly, not pulling on the head and neck.)

What are the important parts of the push-up? (Keeping body stiff as a board, bending the elbows, going close to the ground, but stopping before touching the ground.)

Alternative Learning Activities

Gather the children into an information formation. If available, meet near climbing equipment. Discuss what the children have learned today:

1. Tell the children: *Sit-ups build up our stomach muscles.* If desired or appropriate for the particular class, introduce the word *abdominal.* Ask: *When do you use your stomach (abdominal) muscles?* (Jumping, bending.) *Now lie down and try to stand without using your hands and arms, going directly from lying on your back to standing.*

2. Ask: *What muscles did you use?* (Stomach/abdominal.) *Do it again and think about what your stomach (abdominal) muscles are doing.*

3. Tell the children: *Push-ups help build our arm strength.* Ask: *What does good arm strength help you with?* (Lifting objects, hitting a baseball far, and so on.) Have the children demonstrate different ways to use their arm muscles on climbing equipment. Say: *Even when climbing a ladder, we use our arms to pull us up.*

LESSON 3
FITNESS TESTING 3

Student Objectives

- Warm up for the fitness tests.
- Practice the fitness test.
- Help each other score the fitness test by counting sit-ups and push-ups and measuring the sit-and-reach.

Equipment and Materials

- 1 carpet square or mat per child
- 4 cones
- 1 yardstick per group
- 1 sit-and-reach box per group
- Fitness Assessment Recording Sheet (form F1.1)

Warm-Up Activities (5 minutes)

Progressive Walk

See Grades K-1: Fitness, Lesson 1, page 23.

Skill-Development Activities (20 minutes)

Divide the children into six groups of four or five children each. Set up three stations, one for each of the following: sit-ups, push-ups, and the sit-and-reach.

1. Have three groups practice the fitness run, while the other three groups rotate through the remaining three fitness activities (sit-ups, push-ups and sit-and-reach). Allow about two to three minutes each to complete the sit-ups, push-ups, and sit-and-reach stations. Children should move continuously for the fitness run by walking, jogging, or running. You may want to time the fitness run so you have an idea of how long the children can exercise continuously. A goal for the school year of 10 to 20 minutes of moderate to vigorous, continuous exercise is appropriate.

2. The children should walk after finishing the fitness run until you signal to switch with the other three groups.

3. Switch halves of the class, so all children do all four fitness activities.

Concluding Activities (5 minutes)

Discussion

Gather the children into an information formation.

1. Discuss the fitness testing that will occur during the next two classes.
2. Show the children the recording sheets you will use (see form F1.1) and explain that you will use the scores to show them how their fitness improves and how much they grow during the year.

FORM F1.1 FITNESS ASSESSMENT RECORDING SHEET

Name	Height	Weight	Triceps	Calf	Subscapular	Sum skinfolds

Name	Sit-and-reach, Day 1	Sit-and-reach, Day 2	Run, Day 1	Run, Day 2	Sit-ups Day 1	Sit-ups Day 2	Push-ups, Day 1	Push-ups, Day 2

G R A D E S
K-1

FITNESS

LESSONS 4 AND 5
FITNESS TESTING 4 AND 5

Student Objectives

- Demonstrate their current level of cardio-respiratory fitness, muscular endurance, and flexibility.
- Cooperate by participating in self-testing.
- Participate in skinfolds assessment.

Equipment and Materials

- 1 carpet square or mat per child
- 4 cones
- 1 sit-and-reach box or 1 yardstick per group
- Skinfold calipers
- Scale to measure weight
- Tape, yardstick, or other tool to measure height
- Fitness Assessment Recording Sheet (form F1.1)
- Privacy screen, if possible
- Equipment needed for active game played in Fitness Testing 5, page 32

Warm-Up Activities (5 minutes)

Progressive Walk

See Grades K-1: Fitness, Lesson 1, page 23.

Skill-Development Activities (25 minutes)

Fitness Testing 4

Divide the children into four groups or stations. Set up three stations, one for each of the following: sit-ups, push-ups, and the sit-and-reach. Set up a body composition testing station with the scale, measuring tape, and skinfold calipers. Teachers who have help in testing or supervising the children may want to use a privacy screen for this station.

1. Have three groups rotate through the three fitness activities (sit-ups, push-ups, and sit-and-reach). Allow two to three minutes for each of these stations for a total of six to nine minutes.

2. For the fourth group, you or a helper (parent, assistant) measures and records height and weight of each child, taking each individually. You measure and record skinfolds at the triceps, calf, and subscapular. When the children are with you at station 4, you

should measure them as privately as possible while keeping control of the other three groups. A parent, assistant, or other helper is valuable for either supervising stations 1 through 3 or measuring height and weight. As you record the skinfold measurements, you should ask the children for their scores from station 1 through 3. Your helper can also record these for you as children complete the stations.

3. Send the children in group 4 (at station 4) to station 1, and bring the group from station 1 to station 4. Two groups will repeat rotating through stations 1 through 3.

4. Observe fitness during a vigorous game for the final 10 minutes of class with all the students (see Fitness Testing 5).

5. Repeat this process tomorrow to allow all children to rotate through station 4.

Fitness Testing 5

Set up an active game in the play area.

1. Assess cardiorespiratory fitness by observing the children playing a moderate to vigorous game during the remaining 10 minutes. Remember, if the weather is hot, make sure the children have ample opportunity to drink water. Even in cool weather, children should drink water after exercising.

2. Select one or more games from Grades K-1: Games and Sports, Warm-Ups, pages 90-96, for example, Run and Touch, Midnight, Back-to-Back Tag, Race Around the Moon, or Run, Rabbit, Run.

3. As you observe children play the games (as you did in the fitness runs on previous days), determine if a child is more active than most children, similar to most children, or less active than most children. Less active than most may represent an acceptable level of fitness or may represent poor fitness. Teachers may share this information with parents. Children who cannot play vigorous games with others are of concern. Not keeping up has social, educational, and health implications. Playing is a major source of socialization and testing, so children need to be successful. Testing will take two days (Fitness Testing 3, 4, and 5), so children will have two fitness scores for fitness runs, sit-ups, push-ups, and the sit-and-reach. You can record both scores and send home each best score to parents.

Alternative Fitness Activities

1. Select activities that stress muscular strength and endurance of arms and shoulders, legs, and abdominal area (for example, climbing apparatus, overhead ladders, or chinning bars).

2. Rate the children as more active than other children, similar to other children, or less active than other children for each component (muscular strength, muscular endurance, and cardiorespiratory endurance [running]).

3. Prepare individual feedback recording sheets and the parent's letter. Send these home, requiring students to have them signed and returned (see form F1.2). Encourage children to talk with their parents about the fitness testing.

Lesson 5 is the same as lesson 4 so all children can get through all four stations.

FORM F1.2 FITNESS LETTER AND DATA SHEET FOR PARENTS

Every School
1 Learning Lane
Home Town, USA

Dear Parent/Guardian:

We do fitness testing and assessment of growth in physical education

- to help children understand the relationship between health, fitness, and activity,
- to help the teacher assess the effectiveness of the program, and
- to track growth and fitness in the children.

How the test is scored:

- The number for push-ups and sit-ups represents the number of correct push-ups done without stopping (no time limit).
- The score for the sit-and-reach represents flexibility; a score of 15 represents touching the toes. Scores above 15 represent reaching beyond the toes.
- Cardiovascular fitness is scored as (1) similar to most children, (2) more active than most children, or (3) less active than most children. Children who are less active than most should be encouraged to participate in a variety of activities, especially moderate to vigorous activities.
- Height is in inches; weight is in pounds. Skinfolds represent subcutaneous fat and are the sum of three skinfolds in millimeters (mm).

During physical education we will be working on fitness. So we expect everyone to improve or maintain fitness during the year. Normally children will grow, so both height and weight will also increase. Please sign the form at the bottom, under the most recent fitness scores. Please have your child bring the form to our next physical education class. I will record the next test scores on this form. Then you and your child can see how much growth and fitness improvement occurs during the year. If you have any questions please call (teacher's name) at (teacher's phone number).

Sincerely,

I.M. Fit

— —

I have read the above letter and discussed its contents with my child.

Parent/guardian's signature_____

(continued)

FORM F1.2 *(continued)*

Name_____ Age_____

Test	Date	Date	Date
Sit-and-reach			
Sit-ups			
Push-ups			
Fitness run			
Sum of skinfolds			
Weight			
Height			
Parent signature			

Dear parent or guardian:

LESSON 6
GRADES K-1 FITNESS WARM-UP ROUTINE

Student Objectives

- Demonstrate the steps to a fitness warm-up.
- Perform the Grades K-1 Fitness Warm-Up Routine.
- Identify two reasons warming up is important.
- Work together as demonstrated by not bumping into each other during the activity.

Equipment and Materials

- Record player or tape player
- Music: "Thriller" from *A Thriller for Kids* (Side B), Georgiana Stewart, Kimbo Records (KIM 7065)
- Music: "Good Times, Good Music, Good Friends" from *Stepping Out*, Neil Sedaka, RCA
- 4 cones

Warm-Up Activities (5 minutes)

Progressive Walk

See Grades K-1: Fitness, Lesson 1, page 23.

Skill-Development Activities (20 minutes)

Steps for the Grades K-1 Fitness Warm-Up Routine

Arrange the children in scatter formation.

1. Teach each step of the warm-up routine individually.
2. Combine the steps and have the children perform them to music as indicated.

Standing Body Stretch 1

Standing with feet comfortably apart and arms extended overhead, stretch upward, alternating right and left arms:

> *Count 1, stretch left arm up,*
>
> *Count 2, return to start,*
>
> *Count 3, stretch right arm up, and*
>
> *Count 4, return to start.*

Rag Doll

Standing with feet comfortably apart and arms extended overhead, bend sideways, first to the right and then to the left:

> *Counts 1 and 2, extend to right,*
>
> *Counts 3 and 4, stand straight, and*
>
> *Repeat to left (four more counts).*

Side Lunges

Standing with feet wide apart, toes pointed forward, and hands on hips, lean to right side, bending your right knee and pointing the toes of your right foot in the direction you're leaning. Repeat on the opposite side, extending your left leg and leaning to the left:

> *Counts 1 and 2, lean right,*
>
> *Counts 3 and 4, return to starting position, and*
>
> *Repeat to left (four more counts).*

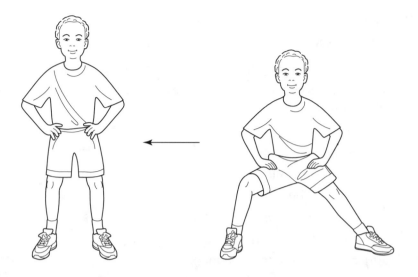

Knee Dips

Standing with feet comfortably apart, heels flat, and hands on hips, bend your knees halfway, keeping your back straight and heels flat, and then extend back to starting position:

Count 1, down, and

Count 2, up.

Airplane Circles

Standing with feet comfortably apart and arms extended to sides, circle your arms forward: Count 1, circle forward (one complete circle for each count).

Grades K-1 Fitness Warm-Up Routine

Keep the children in scatter formation.

1. Play "Thriller," directing the children to listen during a short introduction.
2. After listening to the song, help the children learn, then perform the following sequence of steps:

> *Standing body stretch 1* (16 counts),
>
> *Rag doll* (16 counts),
>
> *Side lunge* (16 counts),
>
> *Knee dips* (16 counts),
>
> *Airplane circles forward* (8 counts),
>
> *Airplane circles backward* (8 counts),
>
> *Airplane circles forward* (8 counts),
>
> *Airplane circles backward* (8 counts),
>
> *Standing body stretch 1* (16 counts),
>
> *Rag doll* (16 counts),
>
> *Side lunge* (16 counts),
>
> *Knee dips* (16 counts),
>
> *Airplane circles forward* (8 counts),
>
> *Airplane circles backward* (8 counts),
>
> *Airplane circles forward* (8 counts),
>
> *Airplane circles backward* (8 counts), *and*
>
> *March in place to the end of the song.*

Alternative Grades K-1 Fitness Warm-Up Routine

1. Play "Good Times, Good Music, Good Friends."
2. After listening to the song, help the children learn, then perform the following sequence of steps, using the cue words provided:

> *Standing body stretch 1* (16 counts),
>
> *Rag doll* (32 counts),
>
> *Side lunge* (32 counts),
>
> *Knee dips* (32 counts),
>
> *Standing body stretch 1* (16 counts),
>
> *Airplane circles* (16 counts),
>
> *Rag doll* (32 counts),
>
> *Side lunge* (32 counts),
>
> *Knee dips* (32 counts),
>
> *March* (8 counts); *Standing body stretch 1* (8 counts); *March* (8 counts); *Standing body stretch 1* (8 counts),
>
> *Airplane circles* (8 counts),
>
> *Rag doll* (8 counts),
>
> *Side lunge* (8 counts),

Knee dips (8 counts),
March in place to end.

Concluding Activities (5 minutes)

Discussion

Gather the children into an information formation.

1. Discuss the warm-up routine: *Why is warming up important?* (To prevent injuries and help achieve the best performance possible.)
2. Divide the class into two groups. Have one group get back into scatter formation and one group sit along one side of the play area as an audience.
3. Have one group demonstrate the warm-up routine to music, with your leading with cues and demonstration. Have the other group watch the performers, saying the steps and counts aloud.
4. Switch group roles.

K-1

LESSON 7
FITNESS HUSTLE 1

Student Objectives

- Demonstrate the individual steps to Fitness Hustle 1.
- Perform Fitness Hustle 1.
- Watch classmates perform Fitness Hustle 1.

Equipment and Materials

- Record player or tape player
- Music: "Thank God I'm a Country Boy" from *Jump Aerobics*, Don Disney, Kimbo Records (KIM 2095)
- Music: "Milkshake" from *Village People*, Polygram Records

Warm-Up Activities (5 minutes)

Grades K-1 Fitness Warm-Up Routine

See Grades K-1: Fitness, Lesson 6, page 38.

Skill-Development Activities (20 minutes)

Steps for Fitness Hustle 1

Arrange the children in scatter formation.

1. Introduce each step of Fitness Hustle 1 individually.
2. Have students perform steps in combinations as indicated.

Jump and Twirl

With feet together, jump in place, twirling both arms in front of your body. Keep your elbows close to your body with your forearms making small circles.

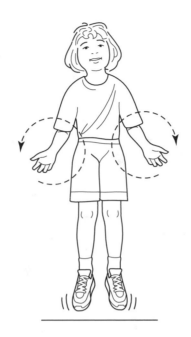

Run Forward and Back Eight

Run forward eight steps and then backward eight steps.

In-and-Out Jump

Jump up moving the feet apart and then jump up with feet together.

Punch

Standing in place, extend one arm and then the other forcefully forward in a punch.

Fitness Hustle 1

Keep the children in scatter formation.

1. Play "Thank God I'm A Country Boy."

2. After listening to the song, help the children learn, then perform the following sequence of steps without and then with the music:

   Listen to the music (8 counts),

   Jump and twirl (16 counts),

   In-and-out jump (16 counts),

   March in place (18 counts),

   Run forward and back 8 (32 counts),

   March in place (18 counts),

   Jump and twirl (16 counts),

   In-and-out jump (16 counts),

   March in place (18 counts), *and*

   Punch (12 counts).

Alternate Fitness Hustle 1

1. Play "Milkshake."

2. After listening to the song, help the children learn, then perform the following sequence of steps, using the cue words provided:

   Do the shake (jump and twirl),

   When they come home (run forward and back 8),

   Just get a glass of milk (in-and-out jump),

   Do the shake (jump and twirl),

   When you're at work (run forward and back 8),

   When it is time (in-and-out jump),

Do it, all right, do the shake (march in place),

Just get some ice cream (punch),

Just do the shake (jump and twirl), *and*

Vanilla (march in place to end of song).

Concluding Activities (5 minutes)

Divide the class into two groups. Have one group get back into scatter formation and one group sit along one side of the play area as an audience.

1. Have one group demonstrate Fitness Hustle 1 to music, with your leading with cues and demonstration. Have the other group watch the performers, saying the steps and counts aloud.

2. Switch group roles.

G R A D E S
K-1

FITNESS

LESSON 8
FITNESS HUSTLE 2

Student Objectives

- Demonstrate the steps to Fitness Hustle 2.
- Perform Fitness Hustle 2.
- Watch classmates perform Fitness Hustle 2.

Equipment and Materials

- Record or tape player
- Music: "Devil Went Down to Georgia" from *Jump Aerobics*, Don Disney, Kimbo Records (KIM 2095)
- Music: "Break My Mind" from *I Guess It Never Hurts to Hurt Sometimes* (1983), Oak Ridge Boys, MCA (C–20 689)

Warm-Up Activities (5 minutes)

Grades K-1 Fitness Warm-Up Routine

See Grades K-1: Fitness, Lesson 6, page 38.

Skill-Development Activities (20 minutes)

Review Fitness Hustle 1

See Grades K-1: Fitness, Lesson 7, page 42.

Steps for Fitness Hustle 2

Keep the children in scatter formation.

1. Introduce each step of Fitness Hustle 2 individually.
2. Have students perform steps in combinations as indicated.

Hop Right and Left

Beginning with the right foot, step in place and hop. Repeat on the left. Cue the students: *Right hop, left hop.*

Jump Eight and Turn

Beginning with feet together and hands on hips, jump in place eight counts. On the last jump, make a quarter-turn to the right. Jump in place again for eight counts, making another quarter-turn on the last jump and continue jumping and turning.

Fitness Hustle 2

Keep the children in scatter formation.

1. Play "Devil Went Down to Georgia."
2. After listening to the song, help the children learn, then perform the following sequence of steps:

Clap for 16 counts during introduction,

Hop right and left (16 counts),

March in place, clapping on the beat (16 counts),

Hop right and left (16 counts),

March in place, clapping on the beat (16 counts),

Jump eight and turn (4 times) (32 counts),

Hop right and left (16 counts),

March in place, clapping on the beat (16 counts),

Hop right and left (16 counts),

March in place, clapping on the beat (16 counts),

Hop right and left (16 counts),

March in place, clapping on the beat (16 counts),

Jump eight and turn (4 times) (32 counts),

Hop right and left (8 counts), *and*

March in place, clapping on the beat (8 counts).

Alternative Fitness Hustle 2

1. Play "Break My Mind."
2. After listening to the song, help the children learn, then perform the following sequence of steps, using the word cues provided:

Knee dips,

Hip right anbd left (16 counts),

Walk in place (16 counts),

Jog in place (32 counts),

Jump 8 and turn (16 counts),

Hop right and left (16 counts),

Walk in place, with arms swinging (16 counts),

Jog in place to end of song.

Concluding Activities (5 minutes)

Divide the class into two groups. Have one group get back into scatter formation and one group sit along one side of the play area as an audience.

1. Have one group demonstrate Fitness Hustle 2 to music, with your leading with cues and demonstration. Have the other group watch the performers, saying the steps and counts aloud.
2. Switch group roles.

LESSON 9
FITNESS HUSTLE 3

Student Objectives

- Demonstrate the steps to Fitness Hustle 3.
- Perform Fitness Hustle 3.
- Watch as classmates perform Fitness Hustle 3.

Equipment and Materials

- Record or tape player
- Music: "Sneakin' Around," *The Aerobic Express* (Side B), Gay Bergman, Kimbo Records (KIM 9092)

Warm-Up Activities (5 minutes)

Grades K-1 Fitness Warm-Up Routine

See Grades K-1: Fitness, Lesson 6, page 38.

Skill-Development Activities (20 minutes)

Review Fitness Hustle 2

Keep the children in scatter formation.

1. Review each step to Fitness Hustle 2 individually.
2. Have students perform steps in combinations as indicated. See Grades K-1: Fitness, Lesson 8, page 44.

Fitness Hustle 3

Keep the children in scatter formation.

1. Play "Sneakin' Around."
2. After listening to the song, help the children learn, then perform the following sequence of steps, using the word cues provided:

    Walk in place, clapping to the beat (16 counts),

    Knee dips (16 counts),

    Walk in place, clapping to the beat (16 counts),

    Knee dips (16 counts),

    Jump eight and turn (32 counts),

    Run forward and back eight (2 times) (16 counts)

In-and-out jump (16 counts),

Hop right and left (16 counts),

In-and-out jump (16 counts),

Hop right and left (16 counts),

Jump eight and turn (32 counts), *and*

Run forward and back eight (2 times) (16 counts).

Concluding Activities (5 minutes)

Divide the class into two groups. Have one group get back into scatter formation and one group sit along one side of the play area as an audience.

1. Have one group demonstrate Fitness Hustle 3 to music, with your leading with cues and demonstration. Have the other group watch the performers, saying the steps and counts aloud.

2. Switch group roles.

LESSON 10
FITNESS HUSTLE 4

Student Objectives

- Perform warm-up routine to music.
- Give and follow directions in Fitness Hustle 4.

Equipment and Materials

- Record or tape player
- Music: *The Aerobic Express*, Gay Bergman, Kimbo (KIM 9092)
- Music: "Thriller" from *A Thriller for Kids*, Georgiana Stewart, Kimbo Records (KIM 7065)
- Music: *Jump Aerobics*, Don Disney, Kimbo Records (KIM 2095)
- 4 cones

Warm-Up Activities (5 minutes)

Grades K-1 Fitness Warm-Up Routine

See Grades K-1: Fitness, Lesson 6, page 38.

Skill-Development Activities (20 minutes)

Steps for Fitness Hustle 4

Keep the children in scatter formation.

1. Introduce each step of Fitness Hustle 4 individually.
2. Have students perform steps in combinations as indicated.

Flys

Begin with your arms extended to your sides at shoulder level, with your elbows bent so your hands are up and palms are facing forward. Lift your right foot, as you step on your left foot, swinging arms forward until your elbows and palms touch. Step on your left foot and return your arms to the starting position. The foot motion is similar to rocking from left to right, as your arms move forward and backward.

Fitness Hustle 4

Arrange children in a circle formation.

1. Allow a child to select the music from your choices (any of the previously used pieces will work).
2. As the music starts, have the children do flys (16 counts).
3. Point to a child, who must then change to another movement for everyone to follow (jump and twist, march in place, punches, in-and-out jump, forward and backward eight, jump eight and turn, hop left and right), for 16 counts.
4. Continue, designating different children to select new movements every 16 counts until the music ends.

Concluding Activities (5 minutes)

Progressive Walk

See Grades K-1: Fitness, Lesson 1, page 23. Have the children do the Progressive Walk, beginning with running and working down to walking as a cool-down. *Note*: This lesson can and should be repeated.

K-1

LESSON 11
CIRCUIT TRAINING 1

Student Objectives

- Demonstrate Fitness Circuit 1.
- Stay on-task.
- Take turns.
- State that, "Regular exercise means exercising three times every week."
- State that, "Physical fitness means having enough energy to move all day and be healthy."

Equipment and Materials

- 6 cones
- 6 identifying signs (numbers and pictures reminding children of what to do at the stations; photos of previous or older students performing the exercises are helpful)
- Tape (to attach signs to cones)
- Music or special signal (e.g., whistle)

Warm-Up Activities (5 minutes)

Pyramid

Arrange children along one side of the play area in a line, facing the other side.

1. Tell the students: *We are going to move across the activity area very slowly. When we come back we will speed up a little. We will continue until we are running as fast as we can. This is called "Pyramid" because we are building from a slow to a fast speed, just like a pyramid is built from low to high. Remember to stay in your own personal space so no one gets hurt.*

2. Move across the area at least six times, each time increasing the speed.

3. Repeat, moving backward, then sideways.

Skill-Development Activities (20 minutes)

Circuit Training: Fitness Circuit 1

Place six cones with either numbers or pictures for identification in a circle with 30 ft between each cone. Divide the children in six small groups, and place one group at each cone.

1. Spend five to six minutes explaining how to use the circuit and how to do each exercise. (When this is a repeat lesson, quickly review the circuit by describing and demonstrating the activities for only one to two minutes.)

2. At first, have the children spend about one minute at each station, with 30 seconds to travel between each station.

3. Over time as the children gain experience and strength and endurance, have them spend two minutes at each station and 15 seconds between. In addition, altering the time frames makes this fun; for example, sometimes go slowly between cones (one minute) and short (5 seconds) at cones.

4. Tell the students:

    At each cone you will do a different exercise until the signal. When the music stops (or the whistle blows) you will run to the next cone and do the exercise for that cone.

    Everyone will run clockwise, in this direction (point).

    When you hear the music, what should you be doing? (Exercising.)

    When the music stops what should you be doing? (Running to the next cone.)

    If you get to the cone and the music has not started, run in place until the music signals for you to start the exercise.

5. Have the children practice running between and stopping at the cones on the signal. Alter the amount of time between the cones by saying: *Change, move s-l-o-w-l-y, at normal speed,* or *fast.* You may want to accompany the verbal instruction with an arm signal. For example, moving your arm in a circle so that the children can judge the amount of time to move between stations by the speed of your arm (e.g., slow arm circle for long times between).

6. Begin the activity, continuing as time permits.

Station 1: Big Swing

Tell and demonstrate for the children: *Stand with your feet shoulder-width apart and knees slightly bent. Bending at the waist and knees, swing both arms between your legs, reaching backward as far as possible. Change directions of the arm swing, moving both arms in front of your body and then up and over your head and back as far as possible. Do this as continuously as possible in a rhythmical motion.This exercise helps your body bend or become more flexible.*

Station 2: Big Steppers

Tell and demonstrate for the children: *Standing and staying in one place, take big marching steps* (exaggerate bringing knees toward chest).

Station 3: Big Curls

Tell and demonstrate for the children: *Standing with feet shoulder-width apart, arms hanging relaxed to the side, look at your belly button by curving your backbone slightly. Tighten your stomach muscles and hold for five counts, then stand straight, relax five counts, and repeat.*

Station 4: Big Jumps

Tell and demonstrate for the children: *Pretend you are standing at the back of an imaginary box. Jump over the box going forward, then jump to the side, backward, and to the other side, in a pattern like you were jumping over the edges of the box.* (Note: A picture of a box may be a good reminder of what to do at this station.)

Station 5: Big Apples

Tell and demonstrate for the children: *Stand with feet shoulder-width apart and hands on waist. Reach with one hand as far to one side as possible, pretend you are picking an apple off of a high branch on a tree beside you. Now move the apple above your head and put it in the pretend basket on the opposite side of your body. Remember to stretch all through the movement. Repeat with the other hand to the other side.* (Note: A picture of an apple may be a good reminder of what to do at this station.)

Station 6: Big Circles

Tell and demonstrate for the children: *Jog in your own circle forward, backward, sideways facing in, sideways facing out. Repeat. Remember to stay in your own space!* (Note: You may need to have groups practice this all at once [spread out through play area] before sending students through the circuit.)

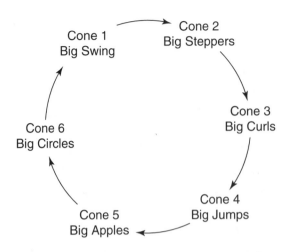

Cone 1
Big Swing

Cone 2
Big Steppers

Cone 3
Big Curls

Cone 4
Big Jumps

Cone 5
Big Apples

Cone 6
Big Circles

Concluding Activities (5 minutes)

Physical Fitness Concept

Gather the children into an information formation.

1. Explain the concept to the students: *Regular exercise helps you develop physical fitness. Physical fitness means that you are healthy and have enough energy to move all day without becoming too tired. Regular exercise means that you do moderate to vigorous exercise at least three times a week for at least 10 minutes at a time, three times each exercise day.*

2. Discuss these concepts: *"Moderate to vigorous" means that the movements make you breathe hard and possibly sweat. Can you name some things you do that are moderate to vigorous exercise?* Allow children to respond, helping them distinguish between moderate to vigorous and sedentary activities.

3. Continue the discussion:

   Do members of your family exercise regularly? How? (Long walks, tennis, jogging.)

   Being healthy and having enough energy to move all day long without becoming too tired probably means you are physically fit.

   Can you name someone from the movies or television who is physically fit? (Michael Jordan, Sylvester Stallone, Mia Hamm.)

   Why do you think these people are physically fit? (They exercise regularly, they look healthy, and they appear to have a lot of energy, so it is a combination of exercise and energy.)

4. Finish the discussion: *Can you walk like a person with a lot of energy?* Encourage children to move about the area with a lot of energy, and point out children who are especially energetic. Ask the children: *Can you move like a person with little or no energy?* Children should move slowly, with poor posture, sad faces, and so on.

Alternative Learning Activities

1. Ask the children to bring in or select from magazines and newspapers you provide pictures of "fit" and "not fit" individuals. The individuals who are fit should be demonstrating high energy. Make a collage of the two types of pictures and draw a large circle with a slash through it on those of "not fit."

2. Ask children to draw pictures of individuals doing moderate to vigorous activities.

3. Invite a parent or individual from the community to talk about their exercise program. (*Hint*: Police and firefighters are good sources.)

LESSON 12
CIRCUIT TRAINING 2

Student Objectives

- Demonstrate Fitness Circuit 2.
- Stay on-task.
- Take turns.
- State that physical fitness is exercise or sport that contributes to health and allows us to do activities throughout the day.
- State that physical activity is any movement that contributes to being healthy.

Equipment and Materials

- 6 cones
- 6 identifying signs (numbers and pictures)
- Tape (to attach signs to cones)
- Music or special signal (e.g., whistle)
- Enough short jump ropes for 1/6 of the class (see station 6 instructions)
- 2 long jump ropes (for crab walk, station 4)

Warm-Up Activities (5 minutes)

Pyramid
See Grades K-1: Fitness, Lesson 11, page 50.

Skill-Development Activities (20 minutes)

Circuit Training: Fitness Circuit 2

Set up the six stations as described, using the cones to mark their locations. Divide the children into six groups, and assign each group to a station.

1. Explain and demonstrate the activities for each station.
2. Rotate the groups through the stations, repeating each station as follows:

Round	Time at each station (in seconds)	Time between stations (in seconds)
1	15 s	15 s
2	20 s	15 s
3	25 s	15 s
4	30 s	15 s

3. As you have students repeat this circuit on other days, you can increase the time at each station, decrease the time between stations, and increase the number of rounds.

Station 1: Jumping Jacks

Tell and demonstrate for the children: *Standing with your feet together and your hands at your sides, bounce up and land with your feet apart while moving your arms and clapping your hands above your head. Then jump back to the starting position. Jumping jacks help to enhance muscle endurance and cardiovascular endurance.*

Station 2: Airplane Circles

See Grades K-1: Fitness, Lesson 6, page 37. Tell the children: *This helps your flexibility and muscle endurance.*

Station 3: Sit-Ups

See Grades K-1: Fitness, Lesson 2, page 27. Tell the children: *This helps make your stomach (abdominal) muscles stronger.*

Station 4: Crab Walk

Tell and demonstrate for the children: *Assuming a back support position with your knees bent and your body straight, walk on your hands and feet from line A to line B and from line B to line A, continuing until the time is up. This helps make your arm muscles stronger.*

Station 5: Push-Ups

See Grades K-1: Fitness, Lesson 2, page 26. *This helps make your arm muscles stronger.*

Station 6: Rope Jump

Tell and demonstrate for the children: *Begin with both feet on one side of the rope, then jump up and sideways so that you land on the other side of the rope moving forward slightly. Repeat, crossing back and forth over the rope. When you reach the end of the rope, turn around and continue until the time is up. This helps make your leg muscles stronger.*

Station 1
Jumping jacks

Station 2
Airplane circles

Station 3
Sit-ups

Station 6
Rope jump

Station 5
Push-ups

Station 4
Crab walk

Line A

30 ft

Line B

Concluding Activities (5 minutes)

Physical Fitness Concept

Gather the children into an information formation.

1. Explain the concept to the students: *Physical activity, like walking, house- or yard work, contributes to health. Physical fitness is a type of physical activity that makes your body work hard; physical activity is moving that helps us be healthier.*

2. Begin the discussion by asking the students: *Can you name some jobs that require physical fitness?* Discuss the answers, identifying jobs that require energy (e.g., construction, farming).

3. Ask the students: *What after-work activities can you think of that are not sport, but are physical activity?* (Housework, gardening.)

Alternative Learning Activities

1. Using magazines and newspapers make two collages, one of physical fitness activities (aerobic dance, weight training, jogging), one of physical activities (e.g., not sport or exercise). Discuss that both physical fitness and physical activities can contribute to health.

2. Make a list of ways people could add physical activity to their lives, for example, taking the stairs instead of the elevator, walking to the store instead of driving (or parking farther from stores).

GRADES K-1

FITNESS

LESSON 13
CIRCUIT TRAINING 3

Student Objectives

- Demonstrate Fitness Circuit 3.
- Stay on-task.
- Take turns.
- Name the five components of health-related physical fitness.
- Define each of the five components of health-related physical fitness.

Equipment and Materials

- 12 cones
- 6 identifying signs (numbers or pictures)
- Tape (to attach signs to cones)
- Music or special signal (e.g., whistle)
- 4 long jump ropes (or lines marked on floor; 2 for station 3 and 2 for station 5—see instructions)
- Mats for station 6 (crunches)

Warm-Up Activities (5 minutes)

Progressive Stretch

Arrange the children in scatter formation. Have the children do the standing body stretch 1, rag doll, side lunge, and knee dips stretches in order. (See Grades K-1: Fitness, Lesson 6, page 35.) Lead one repetition (repeat on both sides as one repetition) the first time through the order, two the second time, three the third time, four the fourth time, and five the fifth time.

Skill-Development Activities (20 minutes)

Circuit Training: Fitness Circuit 3

Set up the six stations as described, using a cone to mark each location. Divide the children into six groups, and assign each group to a station.

1. Explain and demonstrate the activities for each station.
2. Have the children rotate through the stations at least twice. (*Note*: Rotate after everyone in the station 1 group has one turn in the zigzag run. As you repeat this lesson, increase the number of repetitions for the group at the zigzag run before rotating.)

Station 1: Zigzag Run

Arrange the six remaining cones in a zigzag pattern. Tell and demonstrate for the children: *One person at a time, run around the cones and then straight back to the starting line. The next person can start as soon as the first person is at the farthest cone. Just be careful not to run into each other.*

Station 2: Hip Raise

Tell and demonstrate for the children: *Sitting with your upper body supported by your arms, lift your trunk until your body is straight, then return to sitting position.*

Station 3: Line Jumps

Mark two lines (jump ropes or lines on the ground), about 12 in. apart. Tell and demonstrate for the children: *Standing outside the lines, jump sideways over both lines, and then jump back to the starting position. Repeat.*

Station 4: Triceps Push-Ups

Tell and demonstrate for the children: *Sit on the floor (ground) with your legs stretched out in front and your hands on the floor near your hips. Lift your hips to the starting position so that your body is in a straight line. Lower your body by bending your elbows; do not bend your body. Raise your body by straightening your elbows.*

Station 5: Agility Run

Mark two lines (or jump ropes), about 10 ft apart. Tell and demonstrate for the children: *Beginning at the starting line, run and touch the second line, turn around, run back, touch the starting line. Continue running back and forth, touching each line. Repeat as many times as possible.*

Station 6: Crunches

Tell and demonstrate for the children: *Lie on your back on a mat. Cross your legs at the ankle with your knees slightly bent. Bring your knees toward your stomach or chest until your feet are over your hips or chest. At the same time, place your hands near your ears without gripping your head. Start the crunches by lifting your head and shoulders off the floor, pointing your nose toward your knees. Lower your shoulders to the starting position but keep your head slightly off the floor. Repeat, twisting at your waist slightly so the opposite elbow and knee touch. Be sure to twist your upper body, not your elbow. One repetition is one to the left, one to the center, and one to the right.*

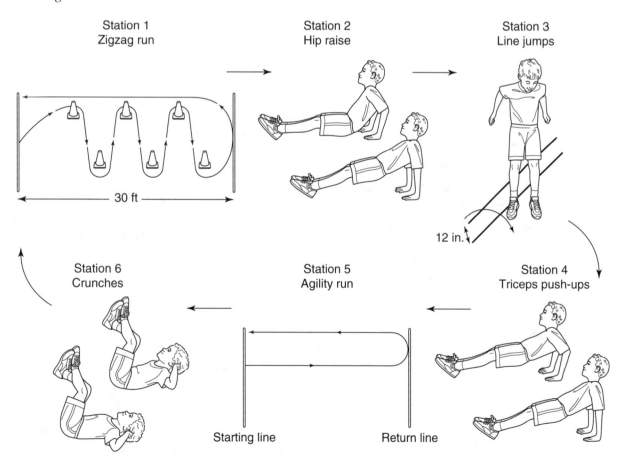

Concluding Activities (5 minutes)

Physical Fitness Concept

Gather the children into an information formation.

1. Explain the concept to the students: *Physical fitness has five parts: cardiorespiratory endurance, muscular strength and endurance, flexibility, and body composition.*

2. Discuss and describe the concepts: *Cardiorespiratory endurance is aerobic fitness, which means the heart is working efficiently (well; without wasted effort). Muscular strength is how much work or force a muscle can produce in one movement. Muscular endurance is how many times a muscle can make the same movement before it gets tired. Muscles move the joints. Some muscles move the same joint many times. For example, when we walk, our knees, hips, and ankles move many times. Flexibility is how far a joint can move safely. Body composition is the amount of fat compared to lean (muscle and bone) tissue in a body. You can feel fat under your skin by pinching, for example, around your waist or above your knee.*

3. Have the children say the five components aloud several times. Emphasize the following ideas by having the children repeat the cue when you say the component:

Component	Cue
Cardiorespiratory endurance	Heart health
Muscular strength	One-time force
Muscular endurance	Many times
Flexibility	Bending
Cardiorespiratory endurance	Aerobic fitness
Body composition	Pinch an inch
Muscular strength	Strong
Muscular endurance	Muscular
Flexibility	Stretching
Body composition	Lean or fat

4. Name one of the five components of health-related physical fitness. Select a child to define each component. Repeat with the other components.

Alternative Learning Activities

1. Make index cards, each listing one of the five components and its definition (or cue). Have the children match the components to the definitions (or cues).

2. Make a set of cards with pairs for the components and definitions (e.g., two identical cards of each) and one "Couch Potato." Play cards, as in "Old Maid" where the Couch Potato is the odd card.

GRADES K-1

LESSON 14
CIRCUIT TRAINING 4

Student Objectives

- Demonstrate Fitness Circuit 4.
- Stay on-task.
- Take turns.
- Give examples of the five components of health-related physical fitness.

Equipment and Materials

- 6 cones
- 6 identifying signs (numbers and pictures)
- Tape (to attach signs to cones)
- Music or special signal (e.g., whistle)
- Station 1: benches, blocks, balance beam, or curb 6-12 in. high
- Station 2: mats for safety
- Station 4: 1 long jump rope (or line marked on floor) per child in group

Warm-Up Activities (5 minutes)

Progressive Stretch

See Grades K-1: Fitness, Lesson 13, page 56.

Skill-Development Activities (20 minutes)

Circuit Training: Fitness Circuit 4

Set up the six stations as described, using the cones to mark their locations. Divide the children into six groups, and place one group at each station.

1. Explain and demonstrate the activities for each station.
2. Rotate the groups so that all children do the six stations in the circuit.

Station 1: Bench Stepping

Tell and demonstrate for the children: *Step up on the bench (box, balance beam, curb, or the like). Step with one leg, then the other, straightening out (extending) both legs and raising up on your toes once you are up on the bench. Step down with the first leg, followed by the other leg. Do this exercise in five counts, up, up, raise, down, down. Repeat with the opposite leg leading. So this goes—up right, up left, raise up, down right, down left, up left, up right, raise up, down left, down right, and so on.*

Station 2: Bridge

Tell and demonstrate for the children: *Start in a push-up position with your back straight. Lift one hand and touch your stomach. Return to starting position and repeat with your other hand. Continue.*

Station 3: Hoop Jump

Arrange four hoops in a pattern for each participant at this station. Tell and demonstrate for the children: *Jump with your feet together through the hoops. When finished, turn around and jump back.*

Station 4: Feet Springs

Mark a line (or use a jump rope) for each participant.

Tell and demonstrate for the children: *Begin in a push-up position with your feet on one side of the line and one hand on each side of the line. Jump your feet across the line, taking weight on your arms. Continue jumping your feet back and forth across the line.*

Station 5: Crunches

See Grades K-1: Fitness, Lesson 13, page 57.

Station 6: Sit and Stand

Tell and demonstrate for the children: *Sit down with your back straight and your legs extended. Stand up straight and sit back down (do not use your hands to push off the ground). Repeat.*

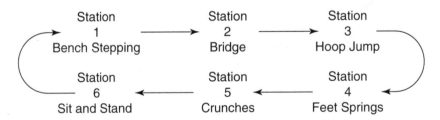

Concluding Activities (5 minutes)

Physical Fitness Concept

Gather the children into an information formation.

1. Explain the concept to the students: *A physically fit person could exercise for 20 minutes without stopping, do 30 sit-ups, some push-ups or chin-ups, stretch their body, and have a healthy amount of body fat.*

2. Discuss the concept. Ask the students: *What activities could a person do for 20 minutes?* (Ride a bike, jog, swim.) *These activities help improve cardiorespiratory fitness. What other activities would show muscular strength or endurance?* (Lifting weights, climbing the jungle gym.)

LESSON 15
CIRCUIT TRAINING 5

Student Objectives

- Demonstrate Fitness Circuit 5.
- Stay on-task.
- Take turns.
- Give an example of a test for each component of health-related physical fitness.

Equipment and Materials

- 6 cones
- 6 identifying signs (numbers and pictures)
- Tape (to attach signs to cones)
- Music or special signal (e.g., whistle)
- Station 1: 1 sit-and-reach box or yardstick per child in group

Warm-Up Activities (5 minutes)

Progressive Stretch

See Grades K-1: Fitness, Lesson 13, page 56.

Skill-Development Activities (20 minutes)

Circuit Training: Fitness Circuit 5

Set up the six stations in a circle as described, using the cones to mark their locations. Divide the children into six groups, and place one group at each station.

1. Explain and demonstrate the activities for each station.
2. Rotate the groups so that all children do the six stations in the circuit, using the following schedule, so that early in the fitness training students use stage 1, later in fitness training they use stage 2, and then stage 3.

Station 1: Backsaver Sit-and-Reach
See Grades K-1: Fitness, Lesson 1, page 24.

Stations 2, 4, and 6: Jog-Around
Have the children in each group line up single file (so there will be three lines starting from three different stations). Tell and demonstrate for the children: *Jog in your group's line around the outside of all the stations. The first person should set a speed (pace) that everyone can keep up with. When you hear the stop signal, return as quickly as possible to your own station. Groups may pass other groups, but be careful, showing me how cooperative and considerate you can be.*

Station 3: Sit-Ups
See Grades K-1: Fitness, Lesson 2, page 27.

Station 5: Push-Ups
See Grades K-1: Fitness, Lesson 2, page 26.

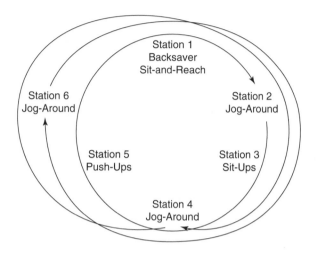

Stage	Time at station (in minutes)	Time between stations (in seconds)
1	1 min	25 s
2	2 min	20 s
3	3 min	15 s

Concluding Activities (5 minutes)

Physical Fitness Concept

Gather the children into an information formation.

1. Explain the concept to the students: *To measure or decide how fit you are, you could ride a bike, swim, or jog for 20 minutes and do sit-ups, push-ups, and the stretches you've learned in class. A trained person could measure your skinfolds to see how much fat your body has.*

2. Ask the students: *What component of health-related physical fitness does each station use?* (Stations 2, 4, and 6 use cardiorespiratory fitness; station 1 uses flexibility; and stations 3 and 5 use muscular strength and endurance.) *What component of health-related physical fitness is not used in today's circuit?* (Body fatness.) *A sign that you have aerobic fitness is that you should be able to jog 20 minutes; today we jogged a total of about* (fill in) *minutes. How many of you can do more than one sit-up?* (Pause.) *How many can do more than one push-up?* (Pause.) *How many of you can* (stretch name)? *As we practice these activities this year, you should get better.*

FITNESS

LESSON 16
MODERATE TO VIGOROUS GAMES 1

Student Objectives

- Demonstrate stretching in a warm-up routine.
- Play a moderate to vigorous game.
- Describe how much exercise is needed to be physically fit.
- Demonstrate cooperation by playing one of the games.

Equipment and Materials

- 4 cones or tape or if outside, flour or chalk
- 1 hoop or carpet square per group
- 1 playground ball
- 1 foam or small playground ball per group

Warm-Up Activities (5 minutes)

Arrange the children in scatter formation.

Shoulder Shrugs

Lift your shoulders to touch your ears, then return to relaxed position.

Side Stretches

Sit with your feet apart and knees slightly bent. Place one hand on your hip and extend the other arm up over your head. Slowly bend to the side toward the hand on your hip. Hold for 10 seconds and relax. Repeat in the opposite direction.

Ankle Rotations

Standing on one leg, make as large a circle with the foot of the opposite leg as possible. Your knee and hip should not move—only your ankle.

Side Lunges

See Grades K-1: Fitness, Lesson 6, page 36.

Stretching Routine 1

Keep the children in scatter formation.

1. Describe and demonstrate the four stretches.
2. Direct students to do the stretches in the following order:

    Eight shoulder shrugs

    Eight side stretches (four each side)

Eight side lunges (four each side)

Eight ankle rotations (four each ankle)

3. Repeat entire sequence.

Skill-Development Activities (20 minutes)

Select one or two games to play. Keep group sizes small to increase participation opportunities.

Leader Ball

Divide the children into groups of four to five children. Each group has a leader and a ball.

1. Describe and demonstrate the game:

    You will take turns being the leader.

    Everyone stand behind the starting line shoulder to shoulder, facing the leader, who should stand about 10 ft away.

    Jog in place all during the activity.

    The leader throws the ball to the first child at one end of the line, who throws the ball back to the leader.

    The leader throws it to the second child, who also throws it back to the leader. This continues until each child has caught and thrown the ball.

    When the leader catches the ball tossed by the last child, the entire group runs to the end line (point to a line parallel to the starting line), and the child who was originally first in line becomes the new leader.

    Keep playing until everyone has had a turn being the leader.

2. Designate a spot to put the ball while the children are running, such as a hoop or carpet square.

3. Have the children play Leader Ball.

Pair Tag

Arrange children, each holding hands with a partner, in equal numbers on two facing lines, 50 to 60 ft apart. One pair (also holding hands) is in the center between the two lines. These two are "It."

1. Describe and demonstrate the game:

    With hands joined, the It pair tries to tag other pairs, who run from It to the opposite side of the play area on the go signal.

    As pairs are tagged they also become It and join the other taggers in the middle.

    When all pairs have been tagged, the last pair stands alone in the center for a new game. Any pair that drops hands must also join the taggers in the middle. Work with your partner so that when you're running one of you doesn't drag the other around.

2. Have the children play Pair Tag.

Delivery Relay

Divide the children into groups of four, and have two groups stand across from each other on each side of two lines, 60 ft apart.

1. Describe and demonstrate the game:

    One child in each group will get a ball (or other small object).

On the signal, that child carries (delivers) the ball to a teammate at the other line. That child returns the ball to a child at the first line and so on until each child has carried the ball over the distance.

Jog in place while waiting for your turn.

2. Have the children play Delivery Relay, repeating as time allows.

Concluding Activities (5 minutes)

Physical Fitness Concept

Gather the children into an information formation.

1. Present the concept to the children: *A physically fit person exercises regularly, jogging, cycling, or swimming, doing sit-ups and push-ups, and stretching. These exercises can help our muscles stay healthy and keep our bodies from storing too much fat. To be physically fit we must exercise at least three times each week. It is best to spread the exercise throughout the week, rather than doing three days in a row. But, if you can, exercising more than three days a week is great! Fun, active games also improve our health-related physical fitness.*

2. Ask: *How could we do this?* Discuss possible scenarios; for example, do fitness Monday, Wednesday, and Friday or Tuesday, Thursday, and Saturday.

3. Discuss activities that the children could do at home in addition to the program at school.

Alternative Learning Activities

1. Make a fitness contract and help the children fill it out.

2. Make a fitness calendar. For the current month, have each child mark days when they have done 30 minutes of total activity (at least 10 minutes at a time). Children may write the actual activities or parents may help.

GRADES K-1

LESSON 17
MODERATE TO VIGOROUS GAMES 2

Student Objectives

- Participate in moderate to vigorous games.
- Define cardiorespiratory fitness.
- Demonstrate cooperation during the game(s).

Equipment and Materials

- 4 cones
- 6, 8-12 in. foam balls
- Signal

Warm-Up Activities (5 minutes)

Stretching Routine 1

See Grades K-1: Fitness, Lesson 16, page 64.

Skill-Development Activities (20 minutes)

Select one or two games to play. Keep group sizes small to increase participation opportunities.

Follow-the-Leader-Three

Arrange children in groups of three with groups in scatter formation.

1. Describe the game and demonstrate several ways to move around the area:

   Form lines of three people. The first person in line is the first leader.

   The leader moves about the area as many ways as possible, for example, by running, walking with hands grasping ankles, or fast walking on all-fours, with both feet and hands touching the ground. The leader changes how he or she is moving as often as he or she wants.

   When you hear the signal, the second child in line becomes the leader.

   When you hear the next signal, the child who hasn't had a turn being a leader becomes the leader.

2. Have the children play Follow-the-Leader-Three.

Fitness Dodge Ball

Arrange half the children in a large circle, and scatter the rest inside the circle. Give foam balls to several of the children forming the circle.

1. Describe and demonstrate the game:

This half of the class (point) will form a circle and throw the balls at the children in the circle, aiming to hit them below the waist.

When children are hit they yell "Hit!" and jog two times around the outside of the circle for fitness.

After completing the jog, they return to the center and continue play.

After several minutes of play, we will switch group roles.

2. You can count hits and see which group had more exercise today (e.g., more hits).
3. Have the children play Dodge Ball.

Cooperative Relay

Divide the children into four groups. Direct each group to stand behind a starting line on one side of a 50- by 60-ft rectangle, defined by the four cones.

1. Describe and demonstrate the activity:

   When you hear the signal, the first child in each line will run across the rectangle to the opposite line. The object is for all four runners (one from each group) to arrive at the same time (even though they may use different speeds). Go as quickly as possible, but you must arrive at the new lines at the same time.

   Once everyone has arrived, they return to their starting positions. While the runners are moving over and back, the other children jump in place 10 times.

   The second child in each line begins as soon as possible after the first child has returned, but this group of four must still arrive on the opposite side at the same time.

   We will repeat this with the other two runners.

2. Have the children run the Cooperative Relay.

Concluding Activities (5 minutes)

Physical Fitness Concept

Arrange the children in scatter formation, allowing them to sit down.

1. Describe the concept by telling the students: *Cardiorespiratory fitness or heart fitness is also called "aerobic fitness." A person who can jog, ride a bike, or swim for 20 minutes without stopping is demonstrating aerobic fitness.*
2. Have the children place a hand on their chest to feel their hearts beating.
3. Have them try to find their pulse at the carotid artery. This is easiest to locate by swallowing while placing fingers gently around the Adam's apple which will move up and down as you swallow. Ask: *How fast is your heart beating?* (Medium to fast; forceful.) *Why?* (From running in Cooperative Relay.)
4. Have the children rest while they share physical activities they enjoy, then have them feel their heart beat again. *How fast is it beating now?* (It should be beating more slowly and less forcefully.)
5. Discuss: *Exercise trains the heart by making it work harder so that it learns to pump more blood in each beat. This means it can beat a little more slowly and do the same job. This is good for it.*

Alternative Learning Activities

Gather the children into an information formation. Make a list of as many aerobic activities as possible (e.g., aerobic dance, rowing, jogging, and so on). Note how much time the children spent today on each moderate to vigorous activity, then find the total.

G R A D E S
K-1

FITNESS

LESSON 18
MODERATE TO VIGOROUS GAMES 3

Student Objectives

- Distinguish between muscular strength and muscular endurance.
- Participate in moderate to vigorous activities.
- Demonstrate cooperation when playing Reveille.

Equipment and Materials

- 4 cones or tape or if outside, chalk
- Horn or other signal (a horn is best, but a whistle, bell, or other noisemaker will work)
- Enough carpet squares or taped or chalked X's for half the class

Warm-Up Activities (5 minutes)

Divide the children into small groups. Have the children do crunches (see Grades K-1: Fitness, Lesson 13, page 57) and push-ups (see Grades K-1: Fitness, Lesson 2, page 26).

Skill-Development Activities (20 minutes)

Select one or two games to play. Keep group sizes small to increase participation opportunities.

Reveille

Arrange children in two groups on parallel lines about 40 ft apart, defined by the four cones.

1. Describe and demonstrate the game:

    On the signal, everyone runs for the opposite line.

    The first group to line up, standing at attention, gets one point.

    Take care and cooperate when running past other children so that no one gets bumped or tripped.

2. Have the children play Reveille, repeating several times.

Sneaky Tag

Use the four cones to define a square playing area. Place the carpet squares on one side of the square. The starting line is opposite the squares. Arrange children in two groups, one group on the starting line, one group on the carpet squares or chalked or taped X's. (On a hard surface mark X's with tape or chalk; on soft ground, carpet squares work well.)

1. Describe and demonstrate the game:

    The children on the start line are the Sneakers, and the children on the X's (or carpet squares) are the Taggers.

On the signal, the Sneakers move through the Taggers trying to get to the endline without being tagged. Sneakers must stay inside the boundaries, and Taggers must keep at least one foot on the X.

If you are tagged, jog around the end boundary during the next round, then rejoin the Sneakers for later rounds.

Sneakers who safely get to the endline use that new line for their starting end for the next round, which will begin on the next signal.

2. Have the children play several rounds. Then have Taggers and Sneakers switch roles.

Fitness Relay

Arrange six groups of children at one end of the play area.

1. Describe and demonstrate the activity:

   The first child in each line will run to the other end of the play area (marked with cones), and do five sit-ups, then run back to the start.

   The second child will do the same thing, and so forth until all of you have had a turn.

   The first group to finish selects the exercise to be done on the next round (e.g., run and do push-ups, crunches, or reverse push-ups, or the like).

2. Play several rounds to practice a variety of fitness tasks.

Concluding Activities (5 minutes)

Physical Fitness Concept

Gather the children into an information formation.

1. Present the concept to the students: *Muscular endurance is when a muscle or group of muscles can make the same movement many times without getting too tired. Being able to do several sit-ups, push-ups, and chin-ups demonstrates muscular endurance. Muscular strength is how much work a muscle can do in one try. Muscles get stronger by exercising, for example, by moving heavy objects.*

2. Begin the discussion: *What activities have we done that call for you to repeat a movement many times?* (Crunches, sit-ups, push-ups, reverse push-ups.) *What about jogging?* (Yes.) *What about throwing a ball?* (No.) *Jumping rope?* (Yes.) *Now, everyone is going to do a muscular endurance activity. Be sure to stay in your own space.*

3. Tell the students: *Everyone switch and do a different endurance activity.* (Do this 30 to 60 seconds.) *Switch again!* (Do this 30 to 60 seconds.) *OK, sit down and relax. Usually muscular endurance activities are done for at least 10 minutes in activities like jogging and in three sets of 10 repetitions for a task like sit-ups. This kind of work helps your muscles develop endurance.*

Alternative Learning Activities

Gather the children into an information formation for this discussion.

1. Loop a rubber band around the blades of scissors. Open and close the scissors as you describe the action.

2. Begin the discussion by saying: *The rubber band is elastic, which means it stretches. When I open the scissors, the joint—the part where the blades are joined—opens wider, and the rubber band stretches. When the scissors are closed, the rubber band contracts (shortens). Your muscles are designed the same way, with muscles on one side of a joint stretching and those on the other side contracting (shortening) to make the bones move.*

3. *Put your hand on the big muscle in the front of your upper arm. This is called the "biceps."*

Bend your arm so that your fist moves toward your shoulder. Do you feel the biceps pulling, tightening to move your arm? Now slowly lower your fist until your arm is straight. Do you feel the biceps relaxing? Muscular strength is the greatest amount of weight a muscle can lift in one try.

4. *To train muscles and help them become stronger and able to work longer (increase endurance), we use the "overload principle." Can anyone guess what "overload" means? The overload principle means you make your body do extra work—by moving either more weight at one time or the same or lower weight more times—to increase the muscle's ability to work. At your age the weight you usually move is your own body weight, so doing a few more of an exercise each time you exercise helps build your muscular strength and endurance.*

G R A D E S
K-1

FITNESS

LESSON 19
MODERATE TO VIGOROUS GAMES 4

Student Objectives

- State that slowly stretching muscles helps flexibility.
- Participate in moderate to vigorous activities.
- Demonstrate cooperation when playing Buddy Relay.

Equipment and Materials

- 4 cones
- Horn or whistle
- One carpet square per child
- Drawing or model of human bones and/ or joints

Warm-Up Activities (5 minutes)

Divide the children into small groups. Have the children do push-ups and crunches. See Grades K-1: Fitness, Lesson 2 (page 26) and Lesson 13 (page 59), respectively.

Skill-Development Activities (20 minutes)

Buddy Relay

Mark an endline parallel to a start line, 40 to 60 ft apart, with the cones. Arrange children in four groups standing behind the endline, with one child from each group on the start line.

1. Describe and demonstrate the activity:

    On the signal, the child on the start line runs to the endline and takes the first child in line by the hand. Now both children run together to the start line.

    The child who began on the start line stays there.

    The other child runs back to the endline and takes the next child's hand. Both of these children run to the start line, and so on, until all of your group is on the start line.

2. Have the children play Buddy Relay.

Color Tag

Arrange the children in scatter formation. Designate boundaries of the playing area either with the cones or another means.

1. Name four colors (e.g., red, green, purple, pink) and designate one "Runner." Describe and demonstrate the game:

    Each of you needs to secretly pick out one of the colors.

    The Runner will then call out one of the four colors.

All children who have selected that color try to tag the Runner while the children who have not chosen that color jog in place. The Runner tries to avoid the children by dodging and running within the marked boundaries.

When the Runner is tagged (or after a reasonable time), the game begins again with the child who tagged the Runner as the new Runner. The new Runner must not choose the color that was just used. Taggers keep the same color choice.

2. Have the children play Color Tag.

Run-Across

Arrange the children in a circle on carpet squares. Assign a number or letter to each child, and then select one child as "It." Set up more circles once the children understand the game to increase participation opportunities.

1. Describe and demonstrate the game:

   The It calls out two or three numbers or letters, and those children try to exchange places before It can take one of the places in the circle they've vacated.

   The one child left over becomes the new It. If unsuccessful after three times, the It picks a new It.

2. Have the children play Run-Across.

Concluding Activities (5 minutes)

Physical Fitness Concept

Arrange the children in information formation.

1. Present the concept to the students: *Flexibility is important to preventing injuries. Slowly stretching our body parts helps us to be flexible.*

2. Discuss flexibility concepts:

   Flexibility is the range or amount of movement in a joint. A joint is a body part that bends, a place where bones join together. Showing a picture or model of the bones of the body or a joint is helpful.

   When a joint is suddenly moved through its range of motion (as when we play) a more flexible joint is less likely to be hurt. A less flexible joint—one with a smaller range of motion—is more likely to be hurt.

   Everyone start with a straight arm and move it slowly until your elbow is bent as much as possible. Now do the same with your knee; now your wrist. What is different about the wrist and elbow? (The wrist can move many directions and the elbow can move one.)

   What other joints can you move? Show me. (Point out different joints, for example, neck, ankle, shoulder, fingers, toes, and so on.)

LESSON 20
MODERATE TO VIGOROUS GAMES 5

Student Objectives

- Name one good thing and one bad thing about fat.
- Cooperate when playing Triplet Tag.
- Demonstrate leadership when playing Fitness Go-Around.
- Participate in moderate to moderate to vigorous activities.

Equipment and Materials

- 6 cones

Warm-Up Activities (5 minutes)

Stretching Routine 1

See Grades K-1: Fitness, Lesson 16, page 64.

Skill-Development Activities (20 minutes)

Fitness Go-Around

Divide the children into six groups, and direct each group to stand at one of six cones arranged in a large circle. Designate a leader in each group.

1. Describe and demonstrate the game:

   On the signal, you and your group will jog clockwise (point) *to the next cone where you will do a fitness exercise chosen by the group leader.*

   On the next signal, begin jogging to the next cone.

   At the new cone, the group leader needs to name a new leader, who will choose the activity at the new cone.

   Continue until everyone in your group has had the chance to choose an activity.

2. Have the children play Fitness Go-Around.

Crab Relay

Use the cones to define an endline and a start line, parallel to each other, 40 to 60 ft apart. Divide the children into six groups. Line up half of each group on the endline, the other half on the start line.

1. Describe and demonstrate the activity:

   To begin the relay, the first child in line at the start line will get into the crab walk position (see Grades K-1: Fitness, Lesson 12, page 54) with his or her hands behind the start line.

   On the signal these first children will crab walk as quickly as possible to the endline.

   As soon as they arrive, the first child in line on that side will crab walk back to the start line.

   We will continue until everyone has had a turn.

2. Have the children perform the Crab Relay.

Triplet Tag

Divide the children into groups of three ("Triplets"), with their inside hands joined. Place half the groups on each of two facing lines, 50 to 60 ft apart.

1. Describe and demonstrate the game:

   This game is played like Pair Tag (Grades K-1: Fitness, Lesson 16, page 65) except that three children hold hands and play as one "Triplet."

   To begin, one Triplet group (designate) *stands in the center area between two lines. Only the two end children in the tagging Triplet can do the tagging, but any child in another Triplet can be tagged.*

   It's important to communicate and agree on where you will run to avoid dragging someone around.

2. Have the children play Triplet Tag.

Concluding Activities (5 minutes)

Physical Fitness Concept

Gather the children into an information formation.

1. Present the concept to the students: *Too much or too little body fat is not healthy. Body fat can be measured by skinfolds, like when you pinch your waist* (or demonstrate a skinfold caliper test on an average-sized child). *Our diet and physical activity are two big reasons why we have the amount of fat we do.*

2. Begin the discussion: *When we eat more food than our body needs to grow, do work, and play, the extra food is stored under our skin as fat, a type of body tissue. Fat can be found under your skin—try pinching yourself to feel the fat—or deep in your body where you can't see or feel it. Fat can also be found in your blood. Does anyone know what this fat is called?* (Cholesterol, triglycerides.) *Fat in the blood can stick to the arteries (blood vessels/tubes) and make the heart work harder because it has to pump harder to squeeze through the narrower arteries. Fat under your skin also makes you work harder because you have to carry this fat around. Think about how tired you would be if you had to carry a brick around all day as you worked and played. We all need some fat: fat helps us stay warm, and your body uses some fat for energy. But too much or too little body fat is not healthy.*

FITNESS

LESSON 21
FITNESS CHALLENGE 1

Student Objectives

- State that regular exercise helps the muscles build endurance (do the same work more times) and strength.
- Participate in locomotor challenges.
- Cooperate when playing the partner challenges.

Equipment and Materials

- 4 cones
- Signal (e.g., whistle)

Warm-Up Activities (5 minutes)

Arrange the children in scatter formation. Have the children do 5 to 10 each of the following exercises: crunches (see Grades K-1: Fitness, Lesson 13, page 57); triceps push-ups (see Grades K-1: Fitness, Lesson 13, page 57); push-ups (see Grades K-1: Fitness, Lesson 2, page 26); sit-ups (see Grades K-1: Fitness, Lesson 2, page 27); and standing body stretch 1 (see Grades K-1: Fitness, Lesson 6, page 35).

Skill-Development Activities (20 minutes)

Locomotor Challenges

Keep the children in scatter formation.

1. Describe the activity: *Run, then when you hear the signal, listen for the challenges. Start running again after completing the challenge until you hear the next signal.*

2. Begin the activity: *It's important to keep your voice quiet so you can hear the signals and the instructions.* Repeat the following instructions as necessary for practice:

   Leap three times.

   Hop three times.

   Hop three times on one foot, then three on the other foot.

   Leap three times, hop three times on one foot, then three times on the other foot.

   Jump three times, then four times, then five times.

   Jump three times forward and three times backward.

   Turn quickly to the right.

   Turn quickly to the left.

Walk in a small circle. Walk in a large circle. Run faster, then slower, then faster, then slower until the next signal.

Travel along a zigzagging path until the next signal.

Arrange partners in scatter formation.

3. Tell the children: *Remember, it's important to stay quiet enough to hear the signals and challenges. You must also be careful not to drag each other around or to run into other pairs.*

4. Have the children try the following challenges:

    Run with one person in front and one person behind (in follow-the-leader style).

    Run beside your partner.

    Run back-to-back with your partner.

    On the signal, partner 1 runs and dodges trying to get away from partner 2 who stays as close as possible to partner 1.

    On the signal, partner 2 runs and dodges trying to get away from partner 1, who stays as close as possible to partner 2.

Concluding Activities (5 minutes)

Physical Fitness Concept

Gather the children into an information formation.

1. Present the concept to the students: *Muscles become stronger and able to do the same amount of work more times as a result of regular exercise.*

2. Begin the discussion: *"Training" is what we call a program of exercise designed and done especially to cause a change in your body's ability to perform. Overload means exercising with more weight than usual or repeating an exercise more times. Overload training is a way to make muscles stronger. You may have seen people walk with weights in their hands or tied to their legs. They are working the muscles to make them stronger. Have you ever seen a weightlifter? Lifting weights to gain strength is based on overload training. As we practice doing crunches, sit-ups, push-ups, and jogging, you will be able to do more, because your muscles will get stronger. Muscles also get stronger as we grow. When you are older you will be stronger than you are now.*

Alternative Learning Activities

Make each child a push-up chart for their portfolio. Record the date and the number of push-ups each child can do by putting stars or X's on their chart, one for each push-up. The next time, make a new line of X's or stars. As each child improves, they will be able to see improvement in the length of the lines. Some children this age may be able to record their own stars or X's once you show them how.

GRADES
K-1

FITNESS

LESSON 22
FITNESS CHALLENGE 2

Student Objectives

- Define resting heart rate.
- Participate in Wand Challenges.
- Cooperate with a partner during Wand Challenges.

Equipment and Materials

- 1 wand per child
- 4 cones

Safety Tips

- Remind the children to use the equipment appropriately and safely.

Warm-Up Activities (5 minutes)

Arrange the children in scatter formation. Have the children do 5 to 10 each of the following activities: crunches, reverse push-ups, push-ups, sit-ups, and standing body stretch 1.

Skill-Development Activities (20 minutes)

Wand Challenges

Keep the children in scatter formation, and give each child a wand.

1. Tell the children: *The Wand Challenges we are going to do enhance endurance and flexibility.*

2. Describe, demonstrate, and have the children practice the following Wand Challenges:

   Put the wand on the ground, run around it three times.

   With the wand on the ground on one side of you, jump back and forth over it sideways.

   With the wand on the ground in front of you, jump over it; turn around and jump over it again.

   With the wand on the ground in front of you, jump over it while clapping your hands.

   With the wand on the ground in front of you, jump over it while clapping your hands and spinning around in the air. Be careful not to slide across the wand and fall.

   With the wand on the ground behind you, jump over it backward.

   With the wand on the ground, jump as far over it as possible (try several times).

   Pick up the wand holding one end of the wand with the other end on the ground, jump over the wand.

Holding the wand overhead with both hands, slowly move the wand backward and downward as far as possible, return to the start position (overhead) and repeat several times (try to get the wand all the way down without letting go).

Divide the children into pairs and arrange again in scatter formation.

3. Offer the following challenges:

   One partner holds one wand about knee-high, the other partner jumps over the wand 10 times.

   Repeat, switching roles.

Concluding Activities (5 minutes)

Physical Fitness Concept

Gather the children into an information formation.

1. Present the concept to the students: *Resting heart rate is lowered by regular exercise. After you have been lying still for 15 to 30 minutes (or when you first wake up in the morning) the number of times your heart beats is "resting heart rate."*

2. Begin the discussion: *Training for aerobic fitness does many important things:*

   It lowers the resting heart rate, because the heart pumps more blood per beat.

   So fewer beats are needed to pump the same amount of blood.

   The body develops more pathways for the blood to travel into and around the heart.

   A person's blood pressure (how hard the blood pushes against the artery walls) can be lowered, which reduces a person's risk of heart-related illnesses.

3. Summarize this information: *So resting heart rate will go down as you train because of more blood pumped per beat, more blood pathways, and lower blood pressure.*

LESSON 23
FITNESS CHALLENGE 3

Student Objectives

- State that physical fitness training is different for everyone.
- Participate in Hoop Challenges.
- Cooperate with a partner during Hoop Challenges.

Equipment and Materials

- 1 hoop per child
- 4 cones to define the play area

Warm-Up Activities (5 minutes)

Arrange the children in scatter formation. Have the children do 5 to 10 each of the following activities: crunches, reverse push-ups, push-ups, sit-ups, and standing body stretch 1.

Skill-Development Activities (20 minutes)

Hoop Challenges

Keep the children in scatter formation, and give each child a hoop.

1. Have the children lay their hoop on the ground and try the following challenges:

   Run around the outside of the hoop.

   Run around the inside of the hoop (be careful not to trip or slide).

   Jump into and then out of the hoop several times.

   Jump up and down 10 times in the hoop.

   Jump around the hoop.

   Jump over the hoop.

   Stand with your feet out of the hoop and your hands on the ground inside the hoop.

   Stand with your feet out of the hoop and your hands on the ground inside the hoop, and walk your feet around the outside of the hoop. Crab walk around the outside of your hoop.

Divide the children into groups of five or six with their hoops. Direct each group to arrange their hoops in a unique pattern.

2. Tell the children: *Play Follow the Leader and move through your group's hoops, jumping,*

running, skipping, and so on. Take turns being the leader.

3. Vary the game in the following ways:

   Each group moves through its own hoops only.

   Each group moves through all the hoops, taking turns.

   Each group follows you as the leader through all the hoops.

Concluding Activities (5 minutes)

Physical Fitness Concept

Gather the children into an information formation.

1. Present the concept to the students: *Each person has to do a different amount of work to become physically fit.*

2. Begin the discussion: *"Training" is another way of saying the amount of work we have to do to be fit. We each have to train to be fit, but the amount of training necessary is different for each person. We are unique—each of us is different. The amount of training is different because we inherit different characteristics from our parents and because we live different lifestyles. For example, if you eat more than you need or too much junk food you may have to train more so you don't add too much fat. People who have jobs that require hard work may not need to train as much as someone who sits at a desk all day. Who can name a job that has lots of physical activity?* (Bicycle messenger, baggage handler.) *What jobs have very little physical activity?* (Secretary, doctor.)

FITNESS

LESSON 24
FITNESS CHALLENGE 4

Student Objectives

- Name the two things that determine health and fitness.
- Participate in Carpet Square Challenges.
- Cooperate with a partner in the Carpet Square Challenges.

Equipment and Materials

- 1 carpet square per child
- Signal or music

Warm-Up Activities (5 minutes)

Arrange the children in scatter formation. Have the children do 5 to 10 each of the following activities: crunches, reverse push-ups, push-ups, sit-ups, and standing body stretch 1.

Skill-Development Activities (20 minutes)

Carpet Square Challenges

Keep the children in scatter formation, and give each child a carpet square.

1. Try the following challenges (to avoid straining the knee ligaments, teach the children to touch their toes with their knees slightly bent):

    Stand on your carpet square and touch your toes.

    While holding your toes, walk staying on your square.

    While holding your toes, walk backward on your square.

    While holding your toes, jump over your carpet square.

    Sit on your carpet square so no body parts are off the square.

    Sit on your carpet square and put your arms and legs in the air.

    Jump over your carpet square.

    Jump sideways and backward over your carpet square.

Pair the children and continue in scatter formation.

2. Offer these challenges:

    Both stand on one carpet square.

    Run from one square to the other holding hands.

One of you jump to the other square.

The other of you jump over the carpet square.

Both of you sit on one carpet square.

Arrange individuals in scatter formation, each child still with a carpet square.

3. On your signal, tell the children: *Move from square to square, taking care not to bump into each other.*

4. Remove one square and then on a signal everyone stops: *Two children will have to share one square.*

5. Give the signal to go, and remove another square. Continue until the remaining squares are crowded with children (only require that one body part be on the square, e.g., a fingertip). Play music (like musical chairs), if desired. Stress cooperation and safety.

Concluding Activities (5 minutes)

Physical Fitness Concept

Gather the children into an information formation.

1. Present the concept to the students: *Two things decide health and fitness: the characteristics you inherit from your parents (such as height or body type) and your behaviors (what you do every day).*

2. Begin the discussion: *Behaviors that influence health and fitness are exercise, rest, diet, stress, smoking, and drug use. The characteristics you inherit affect how easy it is to train your heart, how easy it is for you to get certain diseases, and what body type (shape) you have. How much are you like your parents? Are your eyes and hair the same color? If you have brothers and sisters, are you like them? These similarities are inherited (gotten from our family). People are more alike than different, but we are most like our relatives. Still, all people are unique—no one is exactly like someone else.*

LESSON 25
FITNESS CHALLENGE 5

Student Objectives

- State that risk factors hurt health and fitness.
- Participate in Group Challenges.
- Cooperate in a group to solve the Challenges.

Equipment and Materials

- 1 hoop per group
- 1 carpet square per group
- 4 cones to define the play area

Warm-Up Activities (5 minutes)

Arrange the children in scatter formation. Have the children do 5 to 10 each of the following activities: crunches, reverse push-ups, push-ups, sit-ups, and standing body stretch 1.

Skill-Development Activities (20 minutes)

Group Challenges

Divide the children into small groups, and arrange the groups in scatter formation, each group with a hoop.

1. Ask the groups to try the following hoop challenges:

    Everyone stand in the hoop.

    Put six arms and seven legs in the hoop.

    Make a circle around the hoop.

    Half of you run inside (in place) and half run around the hoop.

    Switch and different children run inside and different children around the hoop.

    Everyone stand under the hoop.

    Everyone stand beside the hoop.

    One person run as far as possible with the hoop, stop; on your signal the rest of the group will follow and run through the hoop, which the first child is holding up (perpendicular to the ground).

Divide the children into new small groups, and arrange the groups in scatter formation, with a hoop and carpet square spaced about 10 ft apart for each group.

2. Ask the children to try the following challenges:

Each person will jump 10 times to move from the carpet square into the hoop (wait for your turn near the carpet square and after your turn near the hoop). Run backward from the hoop to the carpet square.

Jump and clap 10 times moving from the carpet square to the hoop.

Run backward, clapping, from the hoop to the carpet square.

The group runs in a line from the carpet square to the hoop, around the hoop, back to the carpet square as many times as possible before you hear the stop signal. Switch and half of your group runs around the hoop, and half runs backward around the carpet square; switch again.

Concluding Activities (5 minutes)

Physical Fitness Concept

Gather the children into an information formation.

1. Present the concept to the students: *Things that may hurt our health and fitness are called "risk factors." Some risk factors are because of the way we behave, and we can change these. Other risk factors are inherited (gotten from our family), and we cannot change these.*

2. Begin the discussion: *We can do something about some risk factors: how much fat we have (to some degree), the amount of exercise we get, the amount of cholesterol in our diets, how much rest we get, and whether or not we abuse drugs or alcohol.*

3. Continue with: *There are factors we can't change—those we inherit, such as how easily our hearts are trained or how easily we develop disease, and some in the environment, such as the pollution we breathe—but we can still make healthy choices so we are as physically fit as possible.*

Alternative Learning Activities

Gather the children into an information formation for this discussion.

1. Make picture cards portraying the risk factors (e.g., junk food, cigarette advertisement, and so on).

2. Have children pick a card and identify if it is a risk factor that can be changed—whether it is environmental, behavioral (the choices we make), or inherited. Help them as necessary.

3. Note that some risk factors may be partly both behavioral and inherited; for example, a person may have inherited the likelihood that they'll put on excess body fat and may also make poor diet and activity choices.

GAMES AND SPORTS

In kindergarten and first grade the focus is on skill development and games of low organization. We hope that practicing skills like throwing, catching, kicking, running, and jumping will transfer to sport or make learning these skills in sport easier in the future. While there are questions about how much actual skill is transferred, considerable evidence does exist that tells us that early experience can help boost a child's confidence, competence, and skill efficiency. *Confidence* is the child's belief that he or she has the ability to be successful. *Competence* is the actual ability to do motor tasks. *Efficiency* is understanding or demonstrating movement that is smooth and effective and that uses the least amount of energy but is still successful.

UNIT ORGANIZATION

Table S1.1 provides an overview of the lesson content in this unit. Refer to the warm-up games at the beginning of the unit and throughout the unit. The main body of the unit begins with a body parts review lesson, then progresses to several lessons on throwing, catching, and tossing. This is followed by moving objects with the feet (dribbling and kicking). We cover striking next, followed by a manipulative skills review. Then we teach running, dodging, jumping, and other locomotor skills. We visit manipulative skills again, progressing from handling large soft balls in early lessons to tennis balls and Frisbees, and finally to playing games using manipulative skills.

We recommend you repeat all these lessons (many more than once) to enhance skill development. There are numerous ways to organize the lessons. For example, teaching one or two units

of sport skills, lasting three to eight weeks each is one approach. Another is to teach games and sport one or two days each week. As a general rule, the longer the time between lessons, the more often you should repeat the lesson. This is because children forget what was covered in the preceding lesson. So if you teach games and sports two days each week (with gymnastics, rhythmical activities, and fitness the other three days per week), you will probably have to teach the lessons twice. For example, if you teach body parts (Lesson 1) and throwing and catching beanbags (Lesson 2) the first week, you should repeat throwing and catching beanbags (Lesson 2) the second week with Lesson 3 (more catching and throwing a beanbag activities).

LESSON ORGANIZATION

The equipment and materials you'll need are listed at the beginning of each lesson. A warmup game follows. At first, you will have to spend more time teaching these warm-up games, but then the children will be able to quickly organize for and play them the rest of the school year. These warm-up games also make good concluding activities, and we often suggest them as such throughout the games and sports lesson plans. A 20-minute skill development activity section is next; some lessons have several activities, others have just one. Each lesson has one or more concluding activities, bringing closure and often functioning as a cool-down and calm-down time. Note the cognitive objectives, and periodically test these by asking one or two children to perform the objective. Avoid pointing out a child's mistakes in front of others, however.

TEACHING HINTS

Young children judge themselves and others based on movement. Therefore skill development is important to these children. With age, children will be eliminated from or choose not to participate in optional physical activities if they do not have the appropriate skills. Make sure, then, that physical education is a physically and emotionally safe environment for learning the basic movement skills of childhood.

Skill Acquisition

Different skills will be easy or difficult for each child, depending on the individual. Moreover, certain parts of skills will be easier than others. At the same time, children want to answer two questions about their movement: "Am I getting better?" and "Am I normal?" You can help them by pointing out difficult parts of movements where you expect them to have trouble. We have noted some of these in the lessons. Your own experience will also guide you to make statements such as, "When I was learning this skill I had trouble with. . . ." or "I think (name the part) is the most difficult part of this skill." This way, children having trouble will feel "normal," and all children will know what to expect.

Motivate children in positive ways. Learning that improvement takes practice, seeing their own improvement, and receiving feedback (reinforcement, correction, and confirmation) all motivate children. Such awareness is important to the children. Keep in mind that often when they say, "This is stupid!" they are really saying, "I don't think I can do this." In addition, knowing how they might sometimes use a skill can be motivational. Thus, naming sports that or athletes who use similar skills or variations of the skills can motivate children to practice.

Class Management

If you notice problems with transitions or formations, you may need to review one or more of the organization lessons. But stay in tune with your own preferences as well. Some teachers feel more comfortable with noise and disorder than others. A good guideline to help you decide when it is time to restore order is to decide if the problem (e.g., talking, moving) is interfering with learning. As long as the children are learning, you are doing well.

If student behaviors are interfering with learning, however, you must intervene. First decide if the problem is one student or the way you have organized the class and then act accordingly. Often problem students are seeking attention. Two strategies work well in such cases: one is to move them to a place where it is impossible to get attention (e.g., to the back of the class), the other is to move them near you (even "hiring" them as an assistant) and give them all your attention for awhile. If the problem is more general—most or all of the class—try repeating a pertinent organization lesson, reviewing the rules, and moving into each games and sports lesson gradually with a great deal of control at first. For example, have all children sit, then have one child do the skill at a time, while everyone else watches quietly, gradually increasing to two children, then three, until you have the entire class on task and under control. Use volunteers for the first several participants to promote enthusiasm among cooperative children and to avoid humiliating anyone. The activities are on your side, however. They are fun, and the children are going to be excited. Their ongoing enthusiasm means you are doing a good job!

Table S1.1: Unit Plan for Grades K-1: Games and Sports

Week 7: body parts, throwing, and catching	Week 8: throwing, catching, and moving objects
Monday: body parts Tuesday: throwing and catching beanbags Wednesday: throwing and catching beanbags Thursday: tossing and catching beanbags Friday: rolling, tossing, and catching foam balls	Monday: throwing, catching, rolling, and tossing a foam ball Tuesday: throwing, catching, rolling, and bouncing Wednesday: throwing, catching, bouncing, and rolling a tennis ball Thursday: moving objects with the feet Friday: moving a ball with the feet
Week 9: running, kicking, and striking	**Week 10: manipulative skills**
Monday: running and kicking Tuesday: kicking with the inside and outside of the foot, kicking for distance Wednesday: striking balloons with the hand Thursday: striking foam balls with the hand Friday: striking a playground ball with the hand	Monday: moving an object with an implement Tuesday: manipulative skills stations (repeat four days) Wednesday: manipulative skills stations Thursday: manipulative skills stations Friday: manipulative skills stations
Week 20: locomotor skills	**Week 21: locomotor skills**
Monday: throwing and catching Tuesday: kicking a moving ball Wednesday: striking, catching, and volleying Thursday: running and dodging Friday: jumping for distance and height	Monday: running and jumping Tuesday: hopping Wednesday: jumping and hopping with hoops Thursday: Locomotor Skills Obstacle Course 1 Friday: skipping, galloping, and sliding
Week 22: locomotor skills	**Week 23: manipulative skills**
Monday: Locomotor Skills Obstacle Course 2 Tuesday: tossing and catching Wednesday: dribbling and throwing a ball Thursday: stopping and kicking, changing directions, running and kicking, and kicking an elevated ball Friday: striking	Monday: throwing, catching, kicking, and striking with a playground ball Tuesday: throwing, catching, kicking, and striking with tennis ball Wednesday: striking, catching, kicking, and tossing in manipulative games Thursday: striking, tossing, and catching in manipulative games Friday: manipulative skills review and manipulative games

Week 24: Fun and choice games and sports

WARM-UPS

Back-to-Back Tag

Arrange partners in scatter formation. The format is the same as for most tag games, with two or more "Its" trying to tag the remaining children.

1. Describe and demonstrate the game: *A child is safe when "on base"; base in this case is standing with one's back touching another child, but you may stand this way for only 10 counts (each pair counts out loud). Each time you go on base, you must select a new partner. The last two caught become the Its for next game. Caught children become Its as well to help out until all the children are caught.*

2. Have the children play Back-to-Back Tag.

"It"   Base

Captain Kangaroo Creeps and Crawls

Arrange the children in several lines of five to seven.

1. Describe and demonstrate the game:

   Captain Kangaroo (the leader) can run (or jog), creep (walk or jog with hands grasping ankles), or crawl on all fours.

Mr. (Ms.) Green Jeans is the second person in the line. No one may pass Mr. (Ms.) Green Jeans or the Captain.

The group follows Captain, until he or she has done all three movements once (creep, crawl, and run); then Mr. (Ms.) Green Jeans becomes the Captain, and the Captain goes to the end of the line.

2. Have the children play Captain Kangaroo Creeps and Crawls.

3. Substitute other television characters (e.g., Barney), if the children are not familiar with this show.

Circle Pass Ball

Arrange the children in a circle with two or more balls (it is helpful if the balls are different colors).

1. Describe and demonstrate the activity:

   Pass the balls around the circle to the child next to you.

   The object is to keep the balls going as long and as fast as possible without one ball passing the other and without dropping the balls.

2. Have the children play Circle Pass Ball.

Circle Toss Ball

Divide the children into groups of four to six, standing in a circle. Place one child in the middle with a foam ball. Scatter the circles. The first time you play this you will probably want to play as one large group. After the chidren have learned the game, divide into groups to play. *Note*: This is a good game for helping the children get to know each other's names at the beginning of the school year.

1. Describe and demonstrate the game:

   The child in the middle of the circle tosses the foam ball high (and straight up) into the air and calls the name of one of the other children.

   The child whose name is called tries to catch the ball before it hits the ground.

   The tosser joins the circle, and the catcher becomes the tosser.

   Note: If the children do not try to catch the ball, replace the tosser only when the ball is successfully caught.

2. Have the children play Circle Toss Ball.

Circus Animals

Arrange the children on a line facing an open area and designate another line 30 ft away. One student is the Ringmaster and stands in the field (open area), facing the starting line. Assign different animal names (e.g., lions, tigers) to small groups of children. *Note*: Either start with two Ringmasters or choose a fast child so he or she does not have to be the lone Ringmaster for long.

1. Describe and demonstrate the game:

   The Ringmaster calls out the name of an animal group. The children assigned that animal name run to the opposite line and return to the starting line.

   The Ringmaster attempts to tag the animals. Any animal that is tagged helps the Ringmaster. We will keep playing until everyone is caught. The last animal caught becomes the new Ringmaster.

2. Have the children play Circus Animals.

I See

Arrange the children in scatter formation.

1. You begin by saying *I see*. The students respond with, "What do you see?"

2. You give a movement command such as *I see everybody running in place*. The children run in place.

3. After a short time you begin again with *I see*. The students freeze and respond with, "What do you see?" and so on.

4. Some other activities are clowns marching, children running fast, children jumping, children chopping wood, horses galloping, and children skipping.

Midnight

Arrange the children in a line on one end of the play area, with one child standing in the middle of the play area. This tag game begins with one child as a Fox (the tagger) and the rest of the group as Rabbits. *Note:* Either start with two Foxes or choose a fast child so he or she does not have to be the lone Fox for long.

1. Describe and demonstrate the game:

   The Fox begins at the middle of the play area with his or her back to the Rabbits and eyes closed.

   The Rabbits ask the Fox what time it is as they sneak up trying to get past to the other end of the play area.

   The Fox answers, "One o'clock," "Eight o'clock," "very late," and so on, and nothing happens.

   But when the Fox says "Midnight," the Fox turns, eyes suddenly open, and tries to tag as many children as possible. Those who are tagged become Foxes too. We will keep playing until you are all caught. The last one (two) caught become(s) the new Fox(es).

2. Have the children play Midnight.

Race Around the Moon

Arrange the children along one line, facing a second line about 20 ft away. One child stands between base (the start line is earth) and the endline (the moon). This child is the Launcher.

1. Describe the game:

   The Launcher calls out, "Five, four, three, two, one, blast off"; upon "blast off," the rest of you run to the moon and back.

   The first child back from the moon gets to be the Launcher on the next turn.

2. Have the children play Race Around the Moon.

3. If necessary, place groups of children on different starting lines. The "handicap" system equalizes play by having faster children run further.

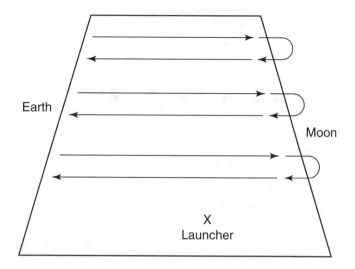

Earth

Moon

X
Launcher

Run and Touch

Arrange the children in a widespread scatter formation.

1. Explain the activity:

   I will call a body part, and each of you must run to another child and touch those body parts together. For example, when I call "knees," you run and touch your knees to a partner's knees.

   On each call, you must find a new partner, never repeating partners.

2. Have the children play Run and Touch.

Run, Rabbit, Run

Arrange the children on a line facing a large open area (at least 50 by 100 ft). Define a smaller area at one end of the open area. This is the Rabbits' "home." Call the remainder of the area "woods." Make three-fourths of the players Rabbits, and the rest Foxes.

1. Describe and demonstrate the game:

   The Foxes hide in the woods (the large area) and the Rabbits leave their home (the small area) in search of food. Beanbags are scattered in the woods as food for the rabbits to gather.

   When I call, "Run, Rabbit, run," the Foxes chase the Rabbits back to their home, tagging as many as possible. The tagged Rabbits become Foxes and play continues until all but one-fourth of the class is a Fox. Then, the roles are reversed.

2. Have the children play Run Rabbit Run.

3. Variation: The children must gallop or skip.

Run With the Roadrunner

Arrange the children in a single line (you can use multiple lines after the children have learned the game). Designate one child as the leader (Roadrunner), and have the other children follow.

1. Describe and demonstrate the game:

   Roadrunner calls out, "All clear" and jogs around the area.

   After a time Roadrunner calls out, "Wile E. Coyote," and everyone runs faster, still following the leader until she or he calls out "All clear," to tell you to slow to a jog again.

   I will call out, "Beep, beep" every minute to tell the Roadrunner to choose a new Roadrunner.

2. Have the children play Run With the Roadrunner.

Spidey Stretches

Arrange the children in a large circle (10 ft between children), with one child in the center. This is Spider Man or Spider Woman.

1. Describe and demonstrate the activity:

   Spider Man (Woman) thinks of different ways to stretch (touch toes with knees slightly bent, overhead, to the side, and so on), while the rest of the group jogs around the circle.

   When Spidey calls out, "Spidey stretches," you all stop and copy the stretch Spidey is demonstrating.

   Then Spidey joins the circle, and you all start to jog again; as Spidey joins the circle, he or she chooses a new Spidey who gets to choose a new stretch.

   We will continue playing for about five minutes.

2. Have the children play Spidey Stretches.

Stop and Go

Arrange the children in a line, side-by-side, facing a goal line 50 to 60 ft away.

1. Describe the activity:

   On the signal, run toward the goal line.

   On the second signal, run in the opposite direction.

   We will continue until a player reaches the goal line. Then the game starts again.

2. Have the children play Stop and Go. Signal at various intervals.

Teacher Ball

Divide the children into small groups, arranged in circles. For each group, select a Teacher to stand in the middle with a beanbag.

1. Describe and demonstrate the activity:

   The Teacher tosses the beanbag to one of the other children, who in turn tosses it back to the Teacher.

   Continue until each child in your group has one turn.

   Then the Teacher chooses a new Teacher.

2. Have the children play Teacher Ball.

Throw and Fetch

Arrange the children in a line facing a long open area, each child with a beanbag.

1. Describe the activity:

   Throw your beanbag as far as possible.

   Then on the signal, run to the beanbags, pick one up, and return to the line. It doesn't matter which beanbag you get.

   We will continue this several times as quickly as possible.

2. Have the children play Throw and Fetch.

Tortoise and Hare

Arrange the children in scatter formation.

1. Describe the activity:

   Run very slowly when I say, "Tortoise" and very fast when I say, "Hare."

   We will start with running in place, and move on to running in general space.

2. Have the children play Tortoise and Hare.

Zigzag Toss

Arrange small groups of students in pairs of lines, facing each other, each line with a beanbag. For kindergarten or the first time you play, one group works better.

1. Describe and demonstrate the activity:

   The first child in line 1 tosses the beanbag to the first child in line 2.

   The first child in line 2 tosses to the second child in line 1, and so on until the beanbag gets to the end of both lines.

2. Have the children play Zigzag Toss, going up and down the lines as time allows.

GAMES AND SPORTS

LESSON 1
BODY PARTS

Student Objectives

- Demonstrate various relationships between beanbags and their bodies (high, behind, on knees).
- Balance the beanbag on various body parts when moving.
- Participate in a simple game using beanbags.
- Cooperate when playing Over and Under.

Equipment and Materials

- 1 beanbag per child, minimum
- Signal

Safety Tips

- For the warm-up game stress touching body parts gently, not bumping, banging, or hitting.
- Remind the children to respect other children's personal space (space they can be in without touching anyone else).

Warm-Up Activities (5 minutes)

Run and Touch

See Grades K-1: Games and Sports, Warm-Ups, page 93.

Skill-Development Activities (15 minutes)

Movement Challenges

Arrange the children in scatter formation, each with a beanbag.

1. Tell the students: *Put your beanbag up high. (Child's name)'s beanbag is really high (low)!*
2. Ask the students: *How low can you hold your beanbag? Can you hold it in front of you (behind you, under you, beside you, between high and low)?* Tell the students: *Touch your foot (head, neck, knee, ankle, shoulder, elbow, calf, chest, shin, forearm, wrists, hip, stomach, back, chin) with your beanbag.*
3. Discuss any body parts that the children have trouble recognizing, such as shin, chin, or forearm.
4. Tell the students: *Balance your beanbag on your forearm (head, elbow, knee, shoulder, wrist, ankle, chest, foot). Balance your beanbag on your hand (arm, thigh, head, shoulder, chest) and walk slowly.*

Concluding Activities (10 minutes)

Over and Under

Arrange the children in a circle facing counterclockwise. Give a beanbag to each of three to six children spaced around the circle so that approximately the same number of children are between each beanbag.

1. Describe and demonstrate the game:

   On the start signal, you will pass the beanbags alternately over one child's head and between (or under) the next child's legs.

   Do not drop any beanbags, never go over or under two children in a row, and try to move as many beanbags as quickly as possible around the circle.

   I will gradually increase the number of beanbags and the speed. When you make mistakes (drops or two overs or unders), I will stop the game and slow down the speed and/or take away one or more of the beanbags.

   I am looking for you to really cooperate with each other.

2. Have the children play Over and Under.

LESSON 2
THROWING AND CATCHING BEANBAGS

Student Objectives

- Toss a beanbag above their heads and catch it, toss a beanbag from hand to hand successfully, and toss and catch a beanbag with the same hand.
- Demonstrate a high and low toss and throw.
- Practice tossing into a hoop from varying distances (kindergarten children).
- Toss a beanbag into a hoop from 10 ft away (first grade children).
- Demonstrate cooperation when playing Beanbag Rope Toss.
- Correctly identify five body parts (wrist, elbow, arm, chest, head) by placing the beanbag on the part during Movement Challenges.

Equipment and Materials

- 1 beanbag per child, plus extra beanbags
- 1 hoop per group (30-36 in.)
- 1 rope (at least 20 ft long)
- 1 foam ball per group (1st grade)
- 2 standards per rope

Safety Tip

- Remind the children to respect other children's personal space.

Warm-Up Activities (5 minutes)

Throw and Fetch

See Grades K-1: Games and Sports, Warm-Ups, page 95.

Skill-Development Activities (20 minutes)

Movement Challenges

Arrange the children in scatter formation, each with a beanbag.

1. Ask the students: *Can you walk and balance the beanbag on your head?*
2. Have the students practice balancing the beanbag on their shoulder, wrist, arm, or chest.

Tossing a Beanbag

Keep the children in scatter formation, each with a beanbag.

1. Ask the students: *Can you toss the beanbag up and catch it, like this?*
2. Demonstrate. Cup a beanbag in both hands and toss it four to six in high.
3. Tell the students: *Keep it low! Now try a little higher.* Look for tosses above the children's heads. They should still be tossing, using both hands. *This is harder. Try with one hand, start low! Put the other hand behind your back. Try throwing above your head with one hand.*
4. Stop the children. Demonstrate tossing from hand to hand. Tell the students: *You try! Can you make the beanbag arch up high?*

Beanbag Rope Toss

Arrange partners in two lines, facing each other 6 to 10 ft apart, with a rope suspended in the air midway between the lines at the children's eye level (use two standards to hold the rope). Give each pair a beanbag.

1. Describe the game: *Partners toss one beanbag back and forth over the rope for four or five minutes. Try to toss so it is possible to catch and try hard to catch.*
2. Have the children play Beanbag Rope Toss. If this is too easy, raise the rope or move the children further from the rope (or move pairs who are successful further apart or move the rope at one end higher to make more challenging).

Beanbag Hoop Toss

Divide the children into groups of four or five, each group around a hoop laid on the ground.

1. Have the children practice tossing beanbags into the hoops for four or five minutes.
2. Ask the children: *How far can you toss and hit inside the hoop?*

Concluding Activities (5 minutes)

Play either Teacher Ball or Circle Toss Ball depending on the age group.

Teacher Ball (kindergarten)

See Grades K-1: Games and Sports, Warm-Ups, page 95. Use a beanbag.

Circle Toss Ball (first grade)

See Grades K-1: Games and Sports, Warm-Ups, page 91. Use a foam ball.

GAMES AND SPORTS

LESSON 3
CATCHING AND THROWING A BEANBAG

Student Objectives

- Catch a beanbag tossed from 10 ft that descends at an approximately 45-degree angle.
- Catch and toss a beanbag in group play.
- Practice foot-launching and catching a beanbag (kindergarten).
- Successfully foot-launch and then catch a beanbag (first grade).
- Work independently during practice.

Equipment and Materials

- 1 beanbag per child
- 1 launcher per pair
- 1 hoop (30-36 in.) per pair
- 1 foam ball per group

Safety Tips

- When the children are tossing beanbags through hoops, caution them to toss gently.
- Encourage children holding the hoops to hold them away from their bodies.

Warm-Up Activities (5 minutes)

Teacher Ball (kindergarten) or Circle Toss Ball (first grade)

See Grades K-1: Games and Sports, Warm-Ups, page 95 or 91. Between each throw, have the children run counterclockwise around the circle, back to their original locations.

Skill-Development Activities (20 minutes)

Beanie Launchers

Have partners stand near each other with one partner three to four ft from the end of the beanie launcher. Give each pair a beanie launcher and beanbag.

1. Describe and demonstrate how to use the beanie launcher: *Place a beanbag on the long end and step forcefully on the other end. Change where you place the beanbag or how hard you step on the launching end. See how these changes change how high the beanbag goes.*

2. Have the partners take turns practicing using the beanie launcher. The child not launching helps retrieve the beanbag: *Be careful of others when you're retrieving a beanbag.*

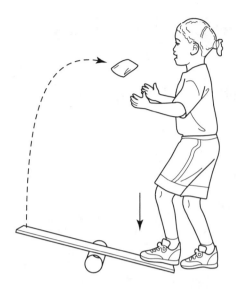

3. Ask the students:

    Can you launch your beanbag and catch it with both hands?

    Can you make the beanbag go higher (lower) and catch it with both hands?

    Can you launch and catch the beanbag with one hand (the other hand)?

    Can you launch the beanbag, clap three times, and catch the beanbag?

    Can you launch the beanbag, turn around once, and catch the beanbag?

Hoops and Beanbags

Now give one child per pair a hoop and have that child hold the hoop. Have the other child turn in the beanie launcher but keep the beanbag.

1. Describe and demonstrate how to toss the beanbag through the hoop.

2. Ask the students: *Can you toss the beanbag through your partner's hoop? Hold the hoop higher (lower, further away) and try again. Take turns practicing.*

3. Demonstrate how they can hold the hoop at different angles.

4. Challenge the students: *Can you toss the beanbag through the hoop when it's held at different angles?*

Concluding Activities (5 minutes)

Zigzag Toss

See Grades K-1: Games and Sports, Warm-Ups, page 95.

LESSON 4
TOSSING AND CATCHING BEANBAGS

Student Objectives

- Catch a self-tossed beanbag.
- Play one game that uses tossing and catching with a foam ball or playground ball.
- Cooperate with a partner during Rope Toss.
- Cooperate during Circle Pass Ball.
- Distinguish between tossing (underhand) and throwing (overhand).

Equipment and Materials

- 1 beanbag per child
- Several foam or playground balls
- 1 long rope (at least 20 ft long)
- 2 standards per rope

Safety Tip

- Remind the children of personal space.

Warm-Up Activities (5 minutes)

Teacher Ball (kindergarten) or Circle Toss Ball (first grade)

See Grades K-1: Games and Sports, Warm-Ups, pages 95 and 91. Have the children run around the circle after each turn.

Skill-Development Activities (20 minutes)

Beanbag Tasks

Seat the children in scatter formation or a large circle. Allow as many or as few turns as necessary for most of the children to successfully complete the task before going on to the next task. The tasks are ordered by difficulty, although some children who cannot do early tasks may succeed at later tasks. Encourage children to focus on tasks for which they need practice. If they are successful, have them go on; if not, have them repeat.

1. Tell the students: *Sitting on the ground, toss and catch the beanbag.* Have them stand up and continue with:

   Toss and catch with your favorite hand.

   Toss and catch with your other hand.

   Toss and catch on the back of your hand.

   Toss from hand to hand, gradually moving your hands farther apart.

   Staying in your personal space, toss your beanbag and jump to catch it.

2. Continue with harder tasks for those who are ready:

   Toss the beanbag in front of you and run to catch it.

Toss, clap as many times as you can, and catch.

Toss, turn around, and catch.

Beanbag Rope Toss

Line up partners opposite each other along each side of a rope strung about five ft off the ground.

1. Have the partners toss the beanbags to each other over the rope and catch the beanbags. When they are successful, have them move further back from the rope.

2. To use this task again, raise the rope or set up two parallel ropes about five ft apart to throw over.

Over-the-Rope Tasks

Keep partners across from each other on either side of the rope.

1. Tell the students:

   Toss and catch your beanbag with both hands.

   Toss and catch your beanbag with your favorite hand.

   Toss and catch your beanbag with the other hand.

   Toss your beanbag with your back to the rope.

   Toss your beanbag between your legs with your back to the rope.

2. Describe and demonstrate the overhand throw.

3. Have them repeat the tasks, throwing overhand instead of tossing.

Concluding Activities (5 minutes)

Circle Pass Ball

See Grades K-1: Games and Sports, Warm-Ups, page 91.

LESSON 5

ROLLING, TOSSING, AND CATCHING FOAM BALLS

Student Objectives

- Practice rolling, tossing, and catching a foam ball.
- Learn a new game.
- Adapt and play a beanbag game with a ball.

Equipment and Materials

- 1 foam ball per child
- 6 or more cones
- 1 empty 2-liter plastic bottle (or bowling pin) per group

Safety Tips

- Use only foam balls.
- Remind the children to watch out for others when retrieving balls.

Warm-Up Activities (5 minutes)

Midnight

See Grades K-1: Games and Sports, Warm-Ups, page 92.

Skill-Development Activities (15 minutes)

Chase Ball

Arrange the children in a long line along one side of the play area, each with a ball.

1. Tell the children: *Roll your ball forward* (if you are crowded, count off and have one half or one third roll at a time).
2. *On the signal, go get a ball and return to the start. Watch out for others! Repeat.*
3. *Now roll your ball, chase after it, and catch it. Repeat.*
4. Ask the students: *Can you toss the ball high (low) and catch it? Can you walk and gently toss and catch the ball?*

Scatter the children again.

5. *Throw your ball anywhere as far as you can* (do this only with foam balls!). *Retrieve the ball and repeat.*

Tunnel Ball

Use four cones to define the boundaries of a large rectangle. Place three target cones near the end of the rectangle, about 10 ft apart. This forms two target zones. Arrange four small groups standing in lines at the opposite end of the rectangle from the target cones (two groups across from each target zone).

1. Describe and demonstrate the game:

   One child at a time from each line will run a few steps and roll his or her ball, aiming to roll the ball between the two target cones on his or her side of the play area.

   Chase and capture your ball, then return to the end of the line.

   We will keep going until all children have had a turn.

   Then we'll repeat, tossing the balls instead of rolling them.

2. Have the children practice these challenges.

Have four children serve as catchers, standing between the target cones, two per target zone.

3. Offer these new challenges:

   The first people in line will roll their balls, aiming at the catchers, who will try to catch the balls.

   The throwers will run to replace the catchers, who will carry the balls to the end of the line.

   Repeat, tossing the balls to the catchers instead of rolling them.

4. Have the children practice these challenges.

Concluding Activities (10 minutes)

Circle Pin Ball

For kindergarten, arrange the children in one circle. For first grade, divide the children into groups of six to eight and arrange each group in a circle with one pin and one child in the middle. Give one child per group a foam ball; this child begins play.

1. Describe the game: *The children in the circle try to knock down the pin, and the child in the middle tries to protect the pin. When the pin is knocked down, the child in the middle switches places with the child who knocked the pin down.*

2. To play this game with other types of balls, change the weight of the pin (e.g., for a playground ball, fill the bottle halfway with water or sand; for a tennis ball, fill the bottle about two inches with water or sand; first graders who are skilled might play this with a playground ball and a plastic bottle that has some water or sand inside).

3. As children increase in skill, use more than one ball at a time.

LESSON 6

THROWING, CATCHING, ROLLING, AND TOSSING A FOAM BALL

Student Objectives

- Roll a ball to a partner.
- Catch a ball rolled toward him or her.
- Roll a ball toward a target.
- Toss a ball at a wall.

Equipment and Materials

- Wall or solid fence
- 1 foam ball per child
- 1 2-liter bottle (or bowling pin) per group

Warm-Up Activities (5 minutes)

Midnight

See Grades K-1: Games and Sports, Warm-Ups, page 92.

Skill-Development Activities (20 minutes)

Rolling a Ball

Arrange partners in scatter formation, each child with a ball, standing about 10 ft from the partner.

1. Describe and demonstrate the skill:

    Hold the ball in one hand and swing backward then forward with a step forward on the opposite foot.

    Your torso is bending as you release the ball with a reaching motion toward the target (your partner).

    The ball should be as close to the ground as possible at release. Do not drop the ball.

2. Have them roll the balls back and forth to each other. As they become successful, move them farther apart.

3. Cue the students: *Reach after the ball with your hand.*

Tossing a Ball

Arrange partners in scatter formation, each pair with a ball. The partners should start 10 ft apart from each other.

1. Describe and demonstrate the skill:

   With one (or both; one hand for small balls, both for large balls) hand(s) on the ball, begin the toss with the ball to the side and behind ([for one hand]; or close to your body [for both hands]).

   Your arm(s) move(s) forward and upward, adjusting the point of release for the desired angle of flight.

2. Have the children practice tossing. If the children practice tossing successfully from the starting distance, have them step farther back.

Catching a Ball

Keep partners in scatter formation, each pair with a ball, partners standing 10 ft apart.

1. Describe and demonstrate the skill:

   Keep your thumbs together to catch medium and high balls.

   Keep your pinkies together to catch low balls.

   Use your hands to catch the ball; have good hand control. Do not trap the ball against your chest (see Checklist for Fundamental Patterns: Catching in Evaluation section in the appendix).

2. Have partners practice tossing and catching. If the children practice tossing and catching successfully from the starting distance, have them step farther back.

High Medium Low

Throwing a Ball Overhand

Keep partners in scatter formation, each pair with a ball. The partners should be spaced 10 ft apart.

1. Describe and demonstrate the skill: *Step forward with the foot opposite your throwing arm as you throw. Turn your body and throw as hard and fast as you can* (see Checklist for Fundamental Patterns: Overhand throwing in Evaluation section in the appendix).

2. Have the children practice the overhand throw. Move children who are catching well farther apart.

3. Ask the students: *Can you throw your ball to your partner?*

Move the children near the wall (or fence) in a line, each child with a ball.

4. Offer the following tasks:

   Throw at the wall as hard as possible.

Throw high.

Throw low.

Now roll the ball.

Throw softly so the ball barely gets to the wall.

Extension Activities (5 to 10 minutes)

Keep the children in a line facing the wall, paired off.

Have partners roll, toss, and throw the ball against the wall at an angle so their partners can catch the ball on the rebound. (*Note*: New balls rebound better than old ones.)

Concluding Activities (5 minutes)

Circle Pin Ball

See Grades K-1: Games and Sports, Lesson 5, page 108.

LESSON 7
THROWING, CATCHING, ROLLING, AND BOUNCING

Student Objectives

- Practice throwing, catching, bouncing, and rolling a playground ball.
- Roll a ball and catch a rolled ball.
- State the hand position for catching high, medium, and low balls.
- Cooperate with a partner when practicing catching.

Equipment and Materials

- 1 playground ball (8+ in.) per pair
- 1 2-liter bottle (or bowling pin) per group

Warm-Up Activities (5 minutes)

Midnight

See Grades K-1: Games and Sports, Warm-Ups, page 92.

Skill-Development Activities (20 minutes)

Catching a Ball

Arrange partners in scatter formation, each pair with a ball. The partners should be spaced 10 ft apart from each other.

1. Emphasize pinkies together for low balls and thumbs together for medium and high balls. See Grades K-1: Games and Sports, Lesson 6, page 111.
2. Give the children the following tasks:

    Bounce and catch the ball.

    Toss and catch the ball.

    Toss, let it bounce, and catch the ball.

3. Repeat many times.

Rolling, Tossing, and Catching a Ball

Arrange pairs in scatter formation, standing about 10 ft apart. See the various related activities in Grades K-1: Games and Sports, Lesson 6, page 110.

1. Roll (toss, bounce) ball to their partners with the partners catching.
2. Plan enough time for many practice trials per skill.

Concluding Activities (5 minutes)

Circle Pin Ball

See Grades K-1: Games and Sports, Lesson 5, page 108. Give each group a playground ball instead of a foam ball. Fill the two-liter bottle with sand or water.

LESSON 8

THROWING, CATCHING, BOUNCING, AND ROLLING A TENNIS BALL

Student Objectives

- Practice throwing, catching, bouncing, and rolling a tennis ball.
- Cooperate with a partner when practicing catching.

Equipment and Materials

- 1 tennis ball per child
- 1 2-liter plastic bottle (or bowling pin) per group, filled 2 in. with sand or water
- Playground balls (optional)

Warm-Up Activities (5 minutes)

Midnight

See Grades K-1: Games and Sports, Warm-Ups, page 92.

Skill-Development Activities (20 minutes)

Tossing and Catching a Ball

Arrange the children in scatter formation, each child with a ball.

1. Tell the students: *Toss the ball and catch it (high, low). Toss it from hand to hand. Bounce and catch the ball.*

2. Watch the children, giving encouragement. Help set goals (e.g., *Can you toss and catch the ball five times in a row without missing?*). Move around so that you observe and speak to each child at least once.

Rearrange the children with partners, each pair with one ball, standing about 10 ft apart.

3. Tell the students: *With your partner, roll (toss) and catch the ball.*

4. Give a playground ball instead of a tennis ball to children having trouble with this activity.

Concluding Activities (5 minutes)

Circle Pin Ball

See Grades K-1: Games and Sports, Lesson 5, page 108. Use a tennis ball if a group of children is ready for this level of difficulty. If necessary, allow one or more groups to play with a playground ball, so that all children can participate successfully.

GAMES AND SPORTS

LESSON 9
MOVING OBJECTS WITH THE FEET

Student Objectives

- Practice moving various objects with their feet.
- Kick a ball with either foot.
- Work together in the jump rope straddle tasks and the Jump the Knot game.

Equipment and Materials

- 1 beanbag (on a smooth surface only), foam ball, balloon, crumpled up paper bag or carton, and playground ball per child
- 2-3 cones (or 2-3 1-liter plastic bottles, weighted with sand or water) per group
- 1 long jump rope per group

Warm-Up Activities (5 minutes)

Back-to-Back Tag

See Grades K-1: Games and Sports, Warm-Ups, page 90.

Skill-Development Activities (20 minutes)

Obstacle Ball Walk

Divide the children into small groups, and arrange each group in a line with a set of two or three cones (or bottles). Give each child a balloon. See figure on page 118.

1. Describe, demonstrate, and have the children try these tasks:

   The first child in line puts the balloon on the ground and pushes it with feet through the cones (or bottles).

   When the first child starts the return trip, the second child in line starts, and so on down the line.

2. Repeat with each additional manipulative object: beanbag (only on a smooth surface, not on grass), foam ball, milk carton and/or crumpled-up paper bag, and playground ball.

3. Discuss the preceding activities with the children: *Which was the easiest to keep close?* (Milk carton.) *Which was the hardest to control?* (Balloon.)

4. Allow each child to select one of the objects. Have the children kick their object, keeping them under control, as they play Follow the Leader with their group.

5. Variations: Repeat the lesson, or parts of it, on different surfaces (grass, wood, concrete, dirt). Repeat the activities running instead of walking.

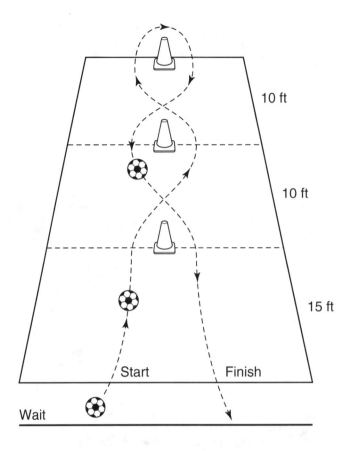

10 ft

10 ft

15 ft

Start

Finish

Wait

Concluding Activities (5 minutes)

Jump Rope Straddle

Divide the children into small groups, and give each group one long rope.

1. Describe and demonstrate the activity:

   Two children hold the long jump rope several inches off the ground.

   The rest of you move from one end of the rope to the other in various patterns: one leg on each side of the rope, jumping from one side to the other with both feet while moving forward (similar to actual jump rope rebounding), jumping with one leg in a hopping motion over the rope (repeat on the opposite side), and a crossover jump where you take off and land on the leg nearest the rope (start with the right leg and land on left, start on left and land on right).

   People holding the rope, be careful to hold it steady so people don't trip. Lower the rope if someone is having trouble.

2. Have the children practice the jump rope straddle tasks.

Jump the Knot

Tie a knot in one end of a long rope. One child or the teacher holds the knot-less end of the jump rope (the shorter the rope, the more difficult the task because the rope moves faster). Arrange the children in a large circle (defined by the path the knot will take) around the center person.

1. Describe the game:

   The center person will move the rope at ground level (or as close as possible) in a circle.

   The rest of you jump over the rope as its sweep reaches your feet.

2. Have the children play Jump the Knot.

LESSON 10
MOVING A BALL WITH THE FEET

Student Objectives

- Run and kick a stationary ball 10 ft.
- Kick a rolled ball 10 ft.
- Work cooperatively with a partner to practice kicking.

Equipment and Materials

- 1 playground ball per child

Warm-Up Activities (5 minutes)

Back-to-Back Tag

See Grades K-1: Games and Sports, Warm-Ups, page 90.

Skill-Development Activities (20 minutes)

Kicking

Arrange the children in scatter formation at least 10 ft apart, each child with a ball placed on the ground in front of him or her.

1. Describe and demonstrate the skill: *Point in front of you with your right hand. Now point in front of you with your right foot. Kick the ball straight ahead (in front of you) with your right foot. Look at the ball.*

2. Have the children retrieve their balls after each turn. Have them repeat several times, then repeat, using the left foot.

3. Repeat alternating right and left feet.

4. Tell the students: *Point to the right with your right foot and kick the ball to your right. Now try to kick it to the right with your other (left) foot.*

5. Have them repeat, kicking to the left with the left foot, then kicking to the left with the right foot. Have them continue alternating their feet and the directions of the kicks.

Kicking Game

Keep the children in scatter formation, at least 10 ft apart, each with a ball on the ground in front of him or her.

1. Describe and demonstrate the game:

    I will call out a foot (right or left), then point up (for straight ahead) or to the side (left or right).

    Kick your ball with the correct foot (the one called out) in the direction I pointed to.

    After kicking, quickly move to where your ball stopped, and I will quickly call out another set of instructions.

2. Have the children play the game.

Kicking to a Partner

Arrange partners in two lines 10 ft apart, facing each other, each pair with one playground ball. Spread the lines out so that the children also have 10 ft on either side of them.

1. Tell the students: *Roll your ball to your partner, who will try to kick the ball back to you. Repeat.*

2. Reverse what the partners do; repeat. Move partners closer and farther apart.

3. Describe and demonstrate kicking hard and kicking softly. Then challenge the children: *Kick hard to your partner. Kick softly to your partner.*

Concluding Activities (5 minutes)

Circle Kickball

Divide the children into groups of four to six, and arrange each group in a circle with about 10 ft between children. Give each group one playground ball.

1. Describe the game:

    Kick the ball from person to person clockwise (point) *around the circle.*

    When the ball gets back to the first person, switch and go around the circle in the opposite direction.

2. Have the children play Circle Kickball.

LESSON 11
RUNNING AND KICKING

Student Objectives

- Run and kick a stationary ball (kindergarten).
- Run and kick a moving ball (first grade).

Equipment and Materials

- 1 playground ball per pair

Warm-Up Activities (5 minutes)

Back-to-Back Tag

See Grades K-1: Games and Sports, Warm-Ups, page 90.

Skill-Development Activities (20 minutes)

Partner Line Kick

Mark two parallel lines 20 to 30 ft apart on each long side of the field or play area. The lines nearer the center of the field are the ball lines; the outer lines are the baselines. Divide the children into two groups and line them up along the baselines facing each other, with partners directly opposite each other. For each pair, place one ball on one of the ball lines in front of one of the partners.

1. Describe and demonstrate the drill:

   The partner with the ball runs and kick the ball toward their partner, who catches the ball.

   After placing the ball back on the ball line and returning to the baseline, the partner with the ball runs and kicks the ball back to their partner.

2. Have the children practice the drill.

Partner Line Kick With a Rolling Ball

Keep the children in the same formation as for the previous drill.

1. Describe and demonstrate the drill:

   Now in this game, the partner with the ball rolls the ball from their ball line toward their partner.

   The receiver tries to kick the ball when the ball reaches their ball line.

   Their partner catches the kicked ball and rolls it back.

2. Have the children practice the drill. Repeat as time allows.

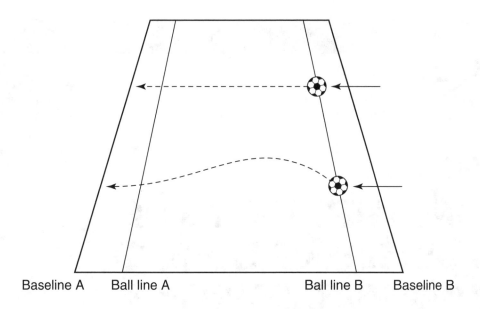

Baseline A   Ball line A   Ball line B   Baseline B

Concluding Activities (5 minutes)

Zigzag Kickball

Arrange the children in two facing, but staggered, lines (children should not be directly across from each other) with about 20 ft between lines and 10 ft between line members. Set up two games if space permits to increase participation opportunities.

1. Describe and demonstrate the game:

    The first person in line 1 kicks the ball to the first person in line 2, who kicks it to the second person in line 1, and so on.

    When the ball reaches the end of the lines, the last person picks it up, runs to the head of the line, and begins again.

    This continues until each of you has been at the head of the line.

2. Have the children play Zigzag Kickball.

LESSON 12

KICKING WITH THE INSIDE AND OUTSIDE OF THE FOOT, KICKING FOR DISTANCE

Student Objectives

- Move a beanbag (or foam ball) with the inside and outside of each foot.
- Move a playground ball with the inside and outside of each foot.
- Kick a playground ball for distance using correct form.

Equipment and Materials

- 1 beanbag (smooth surface; or foam ball, for grass surface) per child
- 1 playground ball per child

Warm-Up Activities (5 minutes)

Back-to-Back Tag

See Grades K-1: Games and Sports, Warm-Ups, page 90.

Skill-Development Activities (20 minutes)

Kicking With the Inside and Outside of the Foot

Arrange the children in a long line with at least five ft between children, one beanbag or ball per child.

1. Describe and demonstrate kicking with the inside and outside of the foot.
2. Have the children practice the skills, moving across the play space, doing the following:

   Push the beanbag (or ball) with the outside of your left foot only.

   Use the outside of your right foot only.

   Push with the inside of your left foot only.

   Use the inside of your right foot only.

   Push with the outside of both feet alternately (have your feet take turns).

   Use the inside of both feet alternately.

Use the inside then outside of your left, then the inside then outside of your right foot alternately.

Use the inside of your right, inside of your left, outside of your right, outside of your left foot.

3. Ask the students: *Can you think of any other ways we have not tried?*

4. Allow a child to demonstrate, then all try.

Inside   Outside

Kicking for Distance

Keep the children in a long line with at least five ft between children, one ball per child. Provide a supply of beanbags to mark kick distances.

1. Describe and demonstrate the skill:

    To kick with your right leg, begin with a step onto your left foot, just behind and to the left of the ball.

    At the same time, your right arm goes forward and your right leg goes backward.

    Your body leans slightly forward, too.

    As your right leg swings forward to kick, your left arm moves forward and your right arm moves back. This is for balance. The kicking leg follows the line of flight; this is called "follow-through." (Reverse for the left-footed kicker; you may need to have children try each foot and tell you which feels best to use.)

2. Have the children practice kicking for distance by trying the kicking motion without, then with, the ball.

3. Have the children start at the line each time and use a beanbag to mark the distance of each kick, so the children can see whether or not their kicks are getting longer.

Concluding Activities (5 minutes)

Keep It Moving

Divide the children into groups of six to eight, and arrange each group in a circle with three to five ft between children and one to five balls per circle.

1. Describe the game:

   Stay in your position in the circle and try to keep the ball(s) moving around the circle by kicking each on to the next person.

   The child who receives a kick in turn tries to kick the ball on to the next without moving from position. (Of course, slight movement from the child's place is expected, but the object is to show control of the ball.)

2. Have the children play Keep It Moving.

LESSON 13
STRIKING BALLOONS WITH THE HAND

Student Objectives

- Strike a balloon 5 (10 for first grade) consecutive times, keeping the balloon in the air.
- Strike a balloon from three or more different positions (standing, sitting, kneeling, lying down, and so on).
- Strike a balloon with two or more body parts.

Equipment and Materials

- 1 balloon per child (have a few extra in case some burst)

Safety Tips

- Do not overinflate the balloons.
- Remind students to stay in personal space.

Warm-Up Activities (5 minutes)

Race Around the Moon

See Grades K-1: Games and Sports, Warm-Ups, page 92.

Skill-Development Activities (20 minutes)

Striking Balloons

Arrange the children in scatter formation, each child with a balloon.

1. Have the children strike the balloons with different body parts from different levels.
2. Encourage them to try the most difficult parts (back, stomach, hip, shoulder, ankle).
3. Ask the students:

   Can you hit the balloon up?

   What other body parts can you use? Head? Knee? Elbow?

   Can you hit the balloon down?

   Make it go from hand to hand?

   Can you kneel and hit the balloon? Can you get lower and hit the balloon? Lie all the way down? How high can you hit the balloon from down there?

   What other positions can you think of? Lying on your stomach?

Watch out for others if the balloon gets away from you.

Can you hit the balloon from one body part to another? Keep going!

Can you hit the balloon to someone near you? Keep hitting it to your partner!

Concluding Activities (5 minutes)

Keep It Up

Arrange the children, each with a balloon, in a circle with three to five ft between children.

1. Tell the children: *Work together to keep all the balloons in the air at the same time; no balloon should touch the ground.* It is more challenging if there are more balloons than children.

2. You can also have older or more skilled children play with foam or playground balls, but use fewer balls than children.

LESSON 14
STRIKING FOAM BALLS WITH THE HAND

Student Objectives

- Hit a foam ball held in one hand with the other hand.
- Hit a stationary foam ball to different levels.
- Identify body parts correctly when asked to strike a balloon with various body parts.

Equipment and Materials

- 1 foam ball per child
- 1 balloon per child
- 1 long rope per group
- 2 standards per rope (optional)
- Cones, tape, chalk, or flour (outdoors only) to define lines

Warm-Up Activities (5 minutes)

Race Around the Moon

See Grades K-1: Games and Sports, Warm-Ups, page 92.

Skill-Development Activities (20 minutes)

Striking From Various Positions With Different Body Parts

Arrange the children in scatter formation, each with a foam ball.

1. This is similar to the balloon activity, Keep It Up (see previous lesson), but using a ball demands that the children move more quickly and strike harder. Let any child who is having great difficulty use a balloon instead of a ball.

2. Challenge the children:

    Can you hit the ball up with your hand (foot, knee, wrist)?

    Can you hit it up while you are on your knees?

    Can you hit it up while lying down?

    Can you hit it up several times in a row?

    You can stand up!

Striking From the Hand

Keep the children in scatter formation, each with a foam ball.

1. Describe and demonstrate the skill: *Hold the ball on an open palm, to the side of your body toward your striking arm. Swing your striking arm backward and, with a fist or an open palm, hit the ball off your other hand.*
2. Have the children strike the ball, run after it, and then strike again from where they pick it up. Repeat as time allows.

Striking Over and Under a Rope

Arrange the children in lines facing ropes five ft off the ground. Assign six to eight children per rope. The children should stand 5 to 10 ft from the rope. If available, use standards to hold the ropes.

1. Tell the children: *Strike the foam balls upward with your hand so they go over a rope, and then downward so they bounce under the rope.*
2. Ask the children: *Can you hit the ball over the rope?* Have the children chase the ball to the other side of the rope and then strike it back. Use foam balls for safety. Repeat.
3. Ask the children: *Can you hit the ball under the rope?*
4. Move the successful children farther back from the rope and repeat; allow those still needing practice to continue from the original position.

Run and Strike

Place all balls on the ground on a line marked with a rope, with the children lined up parallel to the rope and about 10 ft away.

1. Tell the children: *Run to the balls and bend down low as you strike the ball with your hands.*
2. Ask the children: *Can you run and hit your ball toward me? Run and get your ball, bring it back to the line, and repeat. Watch out for others when retrieving your ball!*

Concluding Activities (5 minutes)

Hit-and-Run Relay

Arrange the children into relay teams of four to six, each team with a foam ball. Line teams up at a start line, about 20 ft away from an endline.

1. Describe and demonstrate the game:

    The first child in each team hits the foam ball off his or her hand as far as possible.

    The second child in the team runs to where the ball lands and hits the ball as far as possible. Continue until the ball has reached the endline and then send it back to the starting line. You might have more than one turn to complete the distance.

2. Have the children do the Hit-and-Run Relay. Emphasize and praise the skill of hitting for distance rather than the competition.

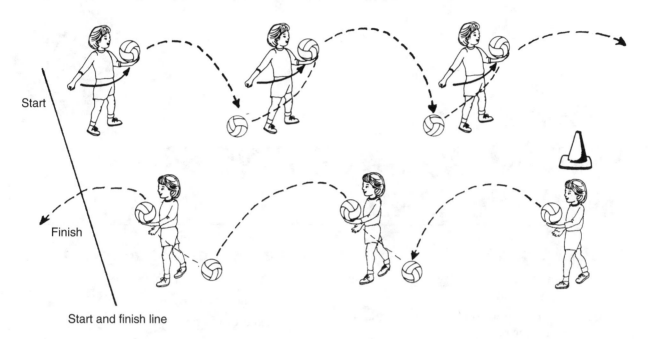

Start

Finish

Start and finish line

LESSON 15
STRIKING A PLAYGROUND BALL WITH THE HAND

Student Objectives

- Strike a playground ball with a hand at two levels (high and low).
- Strike a playground ball with a hand after dropping the ball.
- Practice striking a dropped ball (kindergarten).
- Strike a playground ball with a hand after bouncing the ball (first grade).

Equipment and Materials

- 1 playground ball per child
- 1 long rope per group
- 2 standards per rope
- Wall or solid fence

Warm-Up Activities (5 minutes)

Race Around the Moon

See Grades K-1: Games and Sports, Warm-Ups, page 92.

Skill-Development Activities (20 minutes)

Striking From the Hand

Arrange the children in two lines, one on each side of the rope(s) about 10 ft from the rope.

1. Ask the following questions:
   Who remembers what makes the ball go high (swinging upward)?
   Can you strike the ball and make it go up?
2. Repeat. *Can you make the ball go low?*
3. Have the children practice hitting under the rope.
4. Have them alternate hitting over, then under, the rope. See Grades K-1: Games and Sports, Lesson 14, Striking Over and Under the Rope, page 130.

Drop and Strike

Arrange the children in scatter formation with one ball per child.

1. Describe and demonstrate the Drop and Strike, using an underhand striking motion:

   This begins as with striking off the palm, but you drop the ball by turning (rotating) your palm to the side.

   Swing your striking arm back with an underhand motion.

   Then swing your arm forward and make contact with the ball as you drop it.

2. Have the children practice the Drop and Strike: *Chase the ball after striking and practice again from where you get it. Stay in personal space when striking.*

3. As a variation, describe and demonstrate the Drop and Strike, using a sidearm striking motion: *For a sidearm hit, swing your arm back in a sideways motion and strike the ball as you drop it.*

4. Have the children practice the sidearm Drop and Strike: *Chase the ball after striking and practice again from where you get it.* Repeat.

Bounce and Strike

Keep the children in scatter formation.

1. Describe and demonstrate the Bounce and Strike using an underhand striking motion: *This is the same as the Drop and Strike, except that the ball is moving faster because you force the ball downward to rebound from the ground before striking it.*

2. Have the children practice the Bounce and Strike: *Chase the ball after striking and practice again from where you get it. Stay in personal space when retrieving.*

3. Describe and demonstrate the Bounce and Strike using a sidearm striking motion. Tell the children: *Bounce and hit.*

4. Have the children practice the Bounce and Strike with sidearm striking motion.

Concluding Activities (5 minutes)

Wall Ball

Arrange the children facing a wall and about 10 ft away from it, each with a playground ball.

1. Tell the children: *Strike the ball against the wall, catch the rebound, and repeat.*

2. As they improve have them strike, watch the rebound, and strike again without catching.

LESSON 16
MOVING AN OBJECT WITH AN IMPLEMENT

Student Objectives

- Move an object with an implement.
- Control a ball on the ground with an implement (the degree of success should improve toward the end of first grade).

Equipment and Materials

- 1 beanbag per child (for smooth, hard surfaces; use a crumpled newspaper ball for a grassy or clay surface)
- 1 stick per child (broomstick handle or dowels, 1/2-1 1/2 in. diameter, 24-36 in. length)

- 1 rolled-up newspaper (held together with masking tape) per child
- 1 foam ball per child
- 4 or more cones or plastic bottles per group

Safety Tip

- Remind the children that anyone who touches another child with her or his stick will have to go to time-out.

Warm-Up Activities (5 minutes)

Race Around the Moon

See Grades K-1: Games and Sports, Warm-Ups, page 92. Make sure that all children have been the Launcher. If necessary, handicap the race to give all a chance by placing groups of children on different starting lines. The "handicap" system equalizes play by having faster children run further.

Skill-Development Activities (20 minutes)

Stick Beanbag

Place four or more markers (cones, bottles) per group on the field as shown in figure on page 136. Divide the children into small groups. Line each group up at the start line, each child with a beanbag and a stick.

1. Demonstrate how to push a beanbag around a cone using a broomstick. Tell the students: *Walk, pushing your beanbag around the first cone.*

2. Tell the children: *Go one at a time on the signal. The second child may begin as soon as the first child passes the first cone.*

3. Ask the children: *Can you weave in and out, pushing your beanbag around the cones, like this?* Demonstrate.

4. Have the children practice the skill.

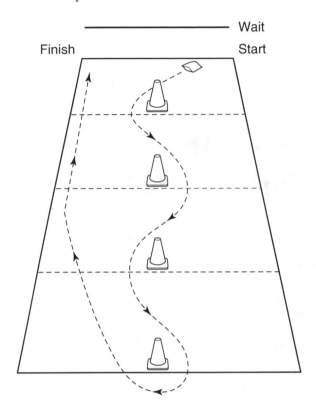

Collect the sticks and beanbags. Have the groups line back up at their start lines. Give each child a rolled-up newspaper and a foam ball.

5. Ask the children: *Can you push the ball with your feet to the endline? Can you go in and out of the cones?*

Arrange the children in pairs, each pair with a foam ball.

6. Tell the children: *Practice striking the foam balls from your hands to your partner's hands so your partner can catch and strike again.* Move the partners farther apart as necessary.

Concluding Activities (5 minutes)

Push Relay

Divide the children into teams of four, and place the teams in relay lines.

Have each child on a team do one of the four pushing activities to the endline (push beanbag or paper ball with stick, weave in and out of cones pushing beanbag or paper ball with stick, strike with rolled-up newspaper to endline, and use newspaper roll to strike foam ball and weave in and out of cones). To emphasize skill development have the children take turns in the relay until the time is up, rather than competing between teams.

LESSON 17
MANIPULATIVE SKILL STATIONS

Student Objectives

- Practice independently.
- Record own progress.
- Improve performance in the six tasks as a result of practice.

Equipment and Materials

Plan to set up two complete sets of stations.

- Station 1: tennis balls, targets, rope, 2 standards (or other supports to suspend the rope from 5 to 15 ft high)
- Station 2: bowling pins or weighted plastic bottles, playground balls
- Station 3: 4 barrels, 5 hoops, rope, beanbags, tennis balls, foam balls, 2 standards (or other supports to suspend the rope 5 ft high)

- Station 4: playground balls, launchers, beanbags
- Station 5: playground balls, rope and 2 standards, wall or fence
- Station 6: balloons, foam balls, playground ball, wall or fence
- 4 student progress sheets per child (see end of this lesson for sample)
- Tape, flour (outside only), cones, or chalk to mark lines as needed
- Signal

Safety Tip

- Remind children of the signals that will be used to stop activity, change stations, and so on.

Warm-Up Activities (5 minutes)

Slap Tag

Arrange the children into two equal groups on two parallel lines, about 50 ft apart. Designate one group as the Runners and the other as the Chasers. Have the Chasers stand with their backs to the play area and their hands stretched out behind.

1. Describe the game:

   The Runners sneak across and slap the hands of the Chasers.

   As soon as the hands are slapped, both the Runners and the Chasers turn and run for the Runners' baseline at the other side of the play area.

   The Chasers try to tag the Runners before they reach base.

   Every Runner who is tagged moves to the other side and joins the Chasers.

   Each round we will switch who starts as the Runners and Chasers.

2. Have the children play Slap Tag.

Skill-Development Activities (25 minutes)

Ball Stations

Set up two complete sets of stations. Arrange the children into 12 groups of two or three. You may want to group the children in the classroom (e.g., red, blue, gold, silver, orange, and green stars); this will help you send groups to their starting stations quickly (red stars to station 1, blue stars to station 2, and so on).

1. Spend six to seven minutes explaining stations. Then send the children to the stations the first day.

2. Rotate each group to a new station after six minutes the first day (eight or nine min. on subsequent days). Rotate the children through three stations each day.

Station 1

Mark lines 10, 15, 20, 30, 40, 50, and 60 ft from the wall. Suspend a rope 5 ft above the ground at 30 ft back from the wall.
Throw tennis balls at the wall. Throw tennis balls over the rope from the different distances.

Station 2

Set up a bowling pin and mark lines 5, 10, and 15 ft from the pin.
Play one-pin bowling (from increasingly difficult distances of 5, 10, and 15 ft) *using a playground ball.*

Station 3

Place ice cream barrels (marked a, b, c, and d) 2 ft apart with the nearest one 5 ft away. Place hoops (marked a, b, c, d, and e) 5 ft apart with the nearest hoop 5 ft away. Mark lines 5 and 10 ft away from the hoops and barrels. Suspend a 5-ft-high rope and mark a line 10 ft away.
Toss balls into the barrels. Toss foam balls into five hoops. Toss over and under a 5-ft-high rope from 10 ft away.

Station 4

Mark lines 5, 10, and 15 ft from a wall.
Bounce the ball to the wall, let it rebound, and catch it from 5, 10, and 15 ft. Launch the beanbag and catch it with both hands (same hand as launching foot, opposite hand as launching foot). Toss the beanbag in the air and catch it.

Station 5

Mark lines 10, 20, 30, and 40 ft from a wall. Suspend a rope 3 ft above the ground in front of the wall.
Kick the ball to the wall from each line. Kick the ball above the rope from the 10-ft line. Kick the ball under the rope from 10-ft line.

Station 6

Mark lines 5, 10, and 15 ft away from a wall.
Hit the balloon up as many times as possible. Hit the foam ball from your palm. Hit the playground ball on a bounce from the ground to the wall from the lines.

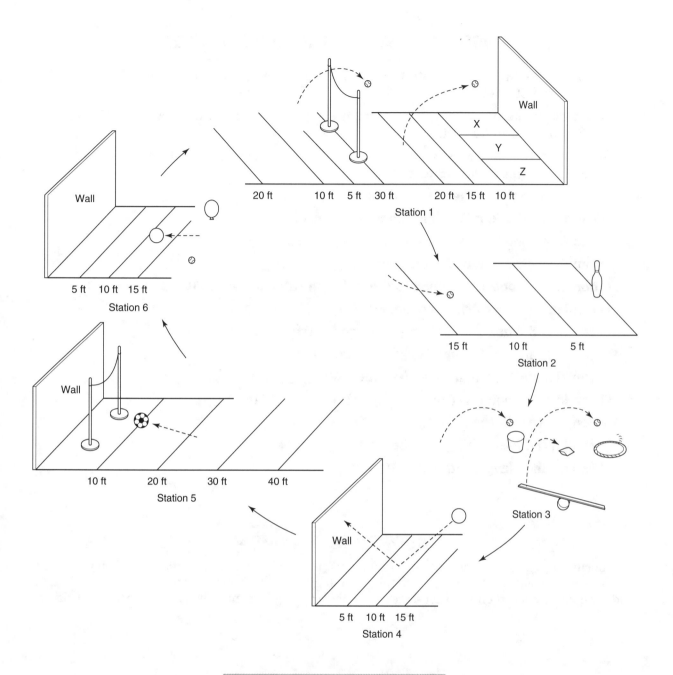

Station 1

Station 2

Station 3

Station 4

Station 5

Station 6

Student Progress Sheet

Have one sheet per child to use each day. Have a red pencil at each station the first two days, and a blue pencil the second two days. Have or help each child circle her or his best score for the day at each station. Using the different-colored pencils allows you, the children, and their parents to see progress.

FORM S1.1 STUDENT PROGRESS SHEET

Station 1: I can hit the wall with the ball standing on the line marked 10, 15, 20, 30, 40, 50, and 60 feet.

I can throw the ball over the rope to zone x, y, z, from the line marked 10, 15, 20, 30, 40, 50, and 60 feet.

Station 2: In 10 rolls I hit the pin _____ times from 5 feet; _____ times from 10 feet; and _____ times from 15 feet.

Station 3: I can throw the foam ball into hoop a, b, c, d, e.

I can throw the tennis ball into barrel a, b, c, d.

I can throw the ball over the rope: Yes _____ No _____

I can throw the ball under the rope: Yes _____ No _____

Station 4: I can bounce the ball to the wall and catch it from 5, 10, 15 feet.

I can launch and catch the beanbag: Yes _____ No _____

I can toss the beanbag over my head and catch it: Yes _____ No _____

Station 5: I can kick the ball 10, 20, 30, and 40 feet.

I can kick the ball high (over the rope): Yes _____ No _____

I can kick the ball low (under the rope): Yes _____ No _____

Station 6: I can hit the balloon _____ times.

I can hit the foam ball _____ times.

I can hit the playground ball 5, 10, 15 feet.

Concluding Activities

No concluding activity, as the children should spend all their time at the stations. As you rotate students to the last station, however, tell them you will give a three-minute warning that class is ending and for them to circle their last best score and replace the equipment so it is ready for the next class.

LESSON 18
THROWING AND CATCHING

Student Objectives

- Toss and catch a foam or playground ball with a partner.
- Throw and catch a foam or playground ball with a partner.
- Run and throw to a partner.
- Run, toss, and catch with a partner.

Equipment and Materials

- 1 foam ball per child
- 1 playground ball per child
- 10 cones

Safety Tip

- Remind children to be certain their partner is looking at them before throwing the ball.

Warm-Up Activities (5 minutes)

Midnight

See Grades K-1: Games and Sports, Warm-Ups, page 92.

Skill-Development Activities (20 minutes)

Toss-Across Five

Arrange partners in scatter formation, each pair with a foam and playground ball. The partners stand about 10 ft apart.

1. Demonstrate tossing (underhand).
2. Tell the students: *Toss the foam ball underhand to your partner, counting each time you toss and catch without missing. Start counting over if you miss! Toss and catch five times each without missing.*
3. Repeat with the playground ball: *Toss the playground ball to your partner, aiming at their chest. Count until each of you has caught the ball five times in a row!*
4. Repeat steps 1, 2, and 3 with the overhand throw.
5. Ask the students: *Who can name some sports where throwing and catching are important?* (Football, softball, baseball, and basketball.)

Running Toss-Across

Define a 40- by 60-ft rectangle with four of the cones. Along each of the long sides place three cones about 15 ft apart, so there will be a cone every 15 ft. Divide the students into three groups and pair up the children in each group. Have the groups stand about 10 ft apart in three lines along one of the short sides of the rectangle. The children are going to move 60 ft to the opposite end of the rectangle with their partner so that six children are moving at one time.

1. Describe and demonstrate the game:

    The object is for each pair of children to move from one end of the rectangle to the other, exchanging the ball at each cone (so it will be "passed" every 15 ft).

    Pairs begin on the signal. We will allow the first three pairs to finish before starting the second set of pairs, and so on.

    Pairs should form a new beginning line at the end (or return to the end of the line at the start after each turn by jogging around the outside of the rectangle).

    Walk, tossing your foam ball to your partner at the first cone. Walk to the second cone, and your partner will toss the ball to you again. Walk to the third cone and toss the ball back to your partner. Walk to the endline.

2. Have the children play Running Toss-Across.

3. Repeat, jogging and tossing, five times per pair. Repeat, walking with the playground ball, five times per pair. Repeat, jogging with the playground ball, five times per pair, jogging from start line to endline.

4. Describe and demonstrate: *Partner 1, run to the line at the first cone. Partner 2, toss the foam ball to partner 1. Partner 2, run to the second cone; partner 1, toss the ball to your partner. Partner 1, run to the fourth cone; partner 2 toss the ball to your partner. Now both of you run to the endline.* Repeat several times. Repeat with the playground ball.

Concluding Activities (5 minutes)

Line Toss-Across

Line up all the children along one endline. Begin with one foam ball.

1. Tell the children: *Walk toward the other endline, tossing the ball from one end of the line to the other* (the children will be close together and the tosses will be short). Repeat, jogging. Repeat with a playground ball.

2. As skill increases, you can have the students play with more than one ball at a time, so balls will be moving in both directions. Challenge the children to see how few times they can drop the ball and how many balls they can keep going at once.

LESSON 19
KICKING A MOVING BALL

Student Objectives

- Practice kicking short and long kicks.
- Practice kicking to the left and right.
- Kick a moving ball.
- Work with a partner kicking a ball.
- Identify short and long kicks.
- Name one sport that uses kicking.

Equipment and Materials

- 1 playground ball per child
- 8 cones

Safety Tip

- Remind children to be considerate of others; point out that one way to do this is to keep the balls under control.

Warm-Up Activities (5 minutes)

Back-to-Back Tag

See Grades K-1: Games and Sports, Warm-Ups, page 90.

Skill-Development Activities (20 minutes)

Kicking Tasks

Use four cones to define a large rectangle. Arrange children in a line, each with a ball along one long side of the rectangle. Use cones or a line to mark a short and long distance from the long side of the rectangle.

1. Introduce the purpose of the skill: *Kicking is used in many sports; can you name some?* (Soccer, football, and rugby.)
2. Describe, demonstrate, and have the children try the following kicking tasks:

    Using your right foot, kick your ball to the first line. This is a short distance.

    On the signal, walk (or jog) to the short line and pick up your ball and place it on the short line.

    Using your left foot, kick the ball back to the starting line—try to make your ball stop on the line! Repeat several times.

    Using your right foot, kick your ball to the second line; this is a long distance.

    On the signal, jog to the long line and pick up your ball and place the ball back on the long line. Remember, try to make the ball stop on the line.

Using your left foot, kick your ball back to the starting line. Repeat several times. Repeat alternating among short and long distances and left and right feet. Stand sideways on the line, so your right foot is toward the short line. Kick your ball with your left foot to the short line.

On the signal, get your ball from the short line. Stand sideways on the short line, so your left foot is toward the starting line. Kick your ball with your right foot to the starting line. Repeat several times.

Be sure to praise students who stop their ball on the line, help others find their ball, and improve.

Rearrange children with partners. Have one partner stand on the starting line with a ball, the other on the short line.

3. Describe, demonstrate, and have the children try: *Roll your ball to your partner; your partner will try to kick the ball back to you. Repeat several times.*

4. Gradually have the children kick, stop, and return kick continuously. Repeat with the partners on the starting and long lines.

Concluding Activities (5 minutes)

Zigzag Kickball

See Grades K-1: Games and Sports, Lesson 11, page 123.

GAMES AND SPORTS

LESSON 20
STRIKING, CATCHING, AND VOLLEYING

Student Objectives

- Demonstrate an underhand strike.
- Catch a ball that was hit underhand.
- Practice striking a ball that was hit underhand.
- Work with a partner to volley a ball.
- Count the number of consecutive volleys.

Equipment and Materials

- 1 playground ball per child
- 1 hoop per pair

Warm-Up Activities (5 minutes)

Race Around the Moon

See Grades K-1: Games and Sports, Warm-Ups, page 92.

Skill-Development Activities (20 minutes)

Striking From the Hand

Arrange the children in scatter formation.

1. Ask the children: *Who can name a sport where a ball is hit from a player's hand?* (Volleyball.)
2. Review the skill: *Hold the ball on an open palm, to the side of your body toward your striking arm. Swing your striking arm backward and, with a fist or an open palm, hit the ball off the other hand.*
3. Have the children practice the skill: *Strike the ball, run after it, and then strike again from where you pick it up.* Repeat.

Strike and Catch

Arrange partners in scatter formation, each pair with a ball, standing about 10 ft apart, facing each other.

1. Tell the children: *The partner with the ball strikes it from the hand toward the partner who tries to catch the ball.*

2. *Then the catching partner strikes the ball to the first partner who will now try to catch the ball.* Repeat.

Bounce the Hoop

Arrange the pairs in a line, one partner standing behind the other, each child with a ball. Place a hoop on the ground in front of each pair of children, about five ft from the first child.

1. Describe and demonstrate the activity:

   The first partner strikes the ball from the hand trying to make the ball land (bounce) in the hoop. This means that you must hit the ball gently and with your arm traveling down slightly toward the hoop.

   Then the other partner gets a turn.

2. Have the partners do this activity in rounds, sending the children all at once to each retrieve a ball.

Partner Hoop Volley

Arrange the pairs in two lines 10 ft apart, with partners facing each other, a hoop midway between the two children, one ball per pair.

1. Describe and demonstrate the game:

   The object is to strike the ball from your hand, have it bounce in the hoop and on to your partner so that your partner can strike the ball back into the hoop and back toward you.

   To begin, toss the ball into the hoop and allow your partner to strike it with one hand.

   Go back and forth several times.

2. Have the children play Partner Hoop Volley.

3. As skill develops, describe and demonstrate striking rather than tossing the ball. Children should attempt to strike the ball into the hoop and to their partner. Tossing the ball is a good way to get started for the first strike.

4. As children are able to volley, have them count the number of continuous strikes; encourage each pair to improve.

Concluding Activities (5 minutes)

Loop-de-Hoop

Arrange small groups of children around one hoop with one ball.

1. Describe and demonstrate the game:

   The object is to strike or toss and bounce the ball in the hoop continuously.

   You can strike with one or both hands but you must use an underhand motion to move the ball into the hoop. Only one bounce of the ball is OK.

   When your group misses the ball (it touches the ground more than once before being hit back into the hoop) your group jogs in place.

2. Have the children play Loop-de-Hoop.

3. When only one group remains, stop the game, move all but one of the standing children to other hoops, replacing them at their hoop with a child from one of the other groups. Repeat several times.

GAMES AND SPORTS

LESSON 21
RUNNING AND DODGING

Student Objectives

- Run and dodge using a relaxed, rhythmical pattern.
- Follow visual and verbal signals which indicate movement direction.
- Cooperate with a partner during the partner run.

Equipment and Materials

- None

Warm-Up Activities (5 minutes)

Tortoise and Hare

See Grades K-1: Games and Sports, Warm-Ups, page 95.

Skill-Development Activities (20 minutes)

Running and Dodging Tasks

Make sure the children are still in scatter formation.

1. Ask the students: *What kind of athletes use dodging when they run?* (Football running backs, basketball players, soccer players.)

2. Challenge the children with these tasks:

    Run and turn quickly to the right.

    Run and turn quickly to the left.

    Run and make a small and then a large circle.

    Run and alternate fast and slow movements.

    Run and make a zigzag pattern.

3. Tell the students: *Watch my hand. When I point move (dodge) quickly in that direction; begin by running toward me.* Alternate pointing right, left, back, and so forth. You can also move your hand in a circle to indicate running in a small circle.

Arrange partners in scatter formation.

4. Tell the students: *Run with one partner in front and one behind (follow-the-leader style). Run beside your partner. Run back-to-back with your partner (one going forward and one going backward).*

5. Repeat, using hand signals: *The partner who can see me needs to tell the other partner about the signal.*

6. *In each pair, decide who will be "1" and who will be "2."*

7. *On the signal partner 1 runs and dodges, trying to get away from partner 2. Partner 2 tries to stay as close to partner 1 as possible.*

8. *Now trade positions, and partner 2 runs and dodges, while partner 1 tries to stay close to partner 2.*

Concluding Activities (5 minutes)

Squirrels in the Trees

Arrange groups of three in scatter formation. In each group, have two children stand facing each other and form an arch by joining hands above their heads; the third stands under their raised hands. You need to have two "spare" children. If you have an extra pair, you fill in as the third person. If you have one extra child, he or she will be an extra Fox. Once the children know the game, create two or more simultaneously running games or designate more Squirrels Without a Tree and Foxes to increase participation opportunities.

1. Describe and demonstrate the game:

    The players holding hands over their heads are "Trees," and the center players are "Squirrels."

    To begin the game, (designate one of the spare children) *is a Squirrel Without a Tree and* (the other spare child) *is a Fox. The Fox chases the Squirrel Without a Tree. To avoid being caught, the Squirrel Without a Tree may run under a Tree, and the Squirrel originally under the Tree must leave that Tree and run away from the Fox.*

    When a Squirrel Without a Tree is tagged by the Fox, that Squirrel becomes the Fox, and the Fox becomes the Squirrel Without a Tree.

LESSON 22
JUMPING FOR DISTANCE AND HEIGHT

Student Objective

- Take off and land with both feet simultaneously in a controlled jump.

Equipment and Materials

- Chalk or tape (or 1-2 long rope[s] per group)

Warm-Up Activities (5 minutes)

Circus Animals

See Grades K-1: Games and Sports, Warm-Ups, page 91.

Skill-Development Activities (20 minutes)

Jumping Tasks

Arrange the children in scatter formation.

1. Tell the students: *Jump as far as you can. Land on both feet. Swing your arms forward. Bend your knees before you land.* Repeat.

2. Challenge the students with the following tasks:

   Jump and land with your feet wide apart. Make sure your feet work together.

   Now try landing with feet close together.

   Jump from both feet and land on one foot.

   Jump from one foot and land on both feet.

   Jump as high as you can.

   Jump high and make your body straight.

   Jump and land on the same spot.

   Jump high and land with feet apart (together).

Arrange partners in scatter formation.

3. Tell the students: *Standing beside your partner, jump five jumps forward, five backward, and five sideways. Repeat.*

4. *Now play a jumping game with your partner; see who can think of the most ways to jump, such as long and high.*

Jumping for Distance

Assign each group of three or four to a jumping area. Use chalk, masking tape, or ropes to mark a "V" shape to create each jumping area.

1. Describe the activity:

   Start at the narrow end, taking turns jumping from one side of the V to the other.

   Each time you jump across, take a step to the next wider part of the V and jump again.

2. Have the children jump for distance.

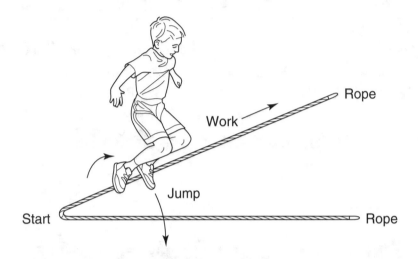

GAMES AND SPORTS

LESSON 23
RUNNING AND JUMPING

Student Objectives

- Run and jump through space with control and coordination.

Equipment and Materials

- Cones for marking lines
- 1 foam ball per child

Warm-Up Activities (5 minutes)

I See

See Grades K-1: Games and Sports, Warm-Ups, page 92.

Skill-Development Activities (20 minutes)

Running and Jumping Tasks

Keep the children in scatter formation.

1. Challenge the children with these running and jumping tasks:

    Run in place, lifting your knees high.

    Run in a circle with short (long) steps.

    Run quickly (slowly).

    Run 10 steps away and 10 steps back. Do not bump into others.

    Run and change directions on a signal.

    Run with a partner.

    Jump in place with your body high (low).

    Jump lightly (heavily).

    Jump three jumps forward and three jumps backward.

    Jump three jumps to the side.

    Jump as far as possible.

    Jump with your feet apart (together).

2. Give each child a ball to place on the ground. Challenge the children with these tasks:

    Run and jump over the ball.

    Stand near the ball and jump over the ball.

How far away can you stand and still jump over the ball? Allow several tries.

Stand next to the ball and jump sideways over the ball.

Jump back with the other side first over the ball. Repeat several times. Keep going back and forth.

Can you jump (hop) over the ball using only one leg?

Run, jump over the ball and clap while you are in the air.

Concluding Activities (5 minutes)

Hill Dill

Define two lines 50 ft apart with cones. Arrange the children along one line, facing the other line. Have one or more player(s) stand midway between the two lines.

1. Describe the game:

   The player(s) in the middle call(s) "Hill Dill, come over the hill." At this signal all players run across from the one line to safety at the other line.

   The center player(s) tag(s) as many players as possible as they run across. Those who get tagged become center players.

   We will continue until everyone gets tagged. The last player(s) caught get(s) to be the new "It(s)."

2. Have the children play Hill Dill.

GAMES AND SPORTS

LESSON 24
HOPPING

Student Objectives

- Hop in place three times on right foot and left foot.
- Demonstrate hopping (one foot) and jumping (two feet).
- Take turns playing Hopscotch.

Equipment and Materials

- 1 Hopscotch diagram on ground, carpet, or hard surface (use tape or chalk or have already painted) per group
- Cones to mark lines

Warm-Up Activities (5 minutes)

Stop and Go

See Grades K-1: Games and Sports, Warm-Ups, page 94.

Skill-Development Activities (20 minutes)

Hopping Challenges

Arrange the children in scatter formation.

1. Challenge the students with the following tasks:

    Hop in place on your right foot.

    Hop in place on your left foot.

    Hop forward, backward, and sideways on your right (left) foot.

    Hop forward and back on your right (left) foot.

    Hop side-to-side on your right (left) foot.

    Hop high (low) on your right (left) foot. Use your arms to lift you up.

    Hop, taking long (short) hops on your right (left) foot.

    Hop in a circle (square, triangle) on your right (left) foot.

    Hop in a zigzag pattern on your right (left) foot.

    Fold your arms across your chest while you hop on your right (left) foot.

2. Continue with these challenges:

    Hop 3 times away from me and 3 times toward me.

    Hop 10 times in a circle and 10 in a line.

Hop 4 little (short) hops and 5 big (long) hops.

Hop 3 times, jump (both feet) 3 times, hop 3 times on the other foot.

Can you do 2 right hops and 3 left hops (4 forward on right and 5 backward on left, 2 right and 4 left)?

Concluding Activities (5 minutes)

Hopscotch

Divide the children into small groups, and place each group at a Hopscotch pattern.

1. Describe and demonstrate the game:

    Hop through the diagrams first on your right foot and then on your left.

    If you step on a line or lose your balance you must start again, but keep track of how far into the pattern you got.

2. Have the children play Hopscotch.

GAMES AND SPORTS

LESSON 25

JUMPING AND HOPPING WITH HOOPS

Student Objectives

- Demonstrate jumping and hopping with good control.
- Work cooperatively with a group on hopping and jumping tasks.

Equipment and Materials

- 1 hoop (30-36 in.) per child

Warm-Up Activities (5 minutes)

Tortoise and Hare

See Grades K-1: Games and Sports, Warm-Ups, page 95.

Skill-Development Activities (17 minutes)

Tasks for Hoops

Keep the children in scatter formation, and give each child a hoop.

1. Challenge the children with the following hoop tasks:

    Balance on your right (left) foot in the center of your hoop.

    While balancing on one foot, try to stretch your body tall (bend over and touch the ground, stretch your arms wide, swing your free leg).

    Jump around your hoop, forward (backward).

    Jump in and out of your hoop.

    Jump forward into your hoop. Jump backward out of your hoop.

    With one foot inside the hoop and one foot outside the hoop, jump around the hoop. Repeat, going backward.

    Hop inside your hoop five times on your right (left) foot.

    Hop forward around the outside of your hoop.

Hop in and out of your hoop.

Jump around the outside of your hoop, jump into the hoop and balance on one foot.

Rearrange children in groups of three or four, each group with one hoop.

2. Challenge the groups with the following tasks:

Jump around the hoop with your right side toward the hoop (clockwise).

Take five giant steps away from the hoop, then hop back toward the hoop.

Everyone stand in the hoop. (Combine groups to see how many children can fit into one hoop!)

Concluding Activities (8 minutes)

Jumping and Hopping Through Hoop Patterns Stations

Set up the four stations as shown in figure on page 157. Divide the children into four groups, and place each group at one of the four stations.

1. Briefly describe and demonstrate each station.
2. Have the children perform the tasks.
3. Rotate the children to a new station every two minutes.

Station 1

Jump forward and backward through the hoops. Hop forward and backward through the hoops.

Station 2

Straddle jump (one foot in each hoop) forward and backward through the hoops. Hop through the hoops, creating a pattern.

Station 3

Hop forward and backward through the hoops. Jump through the hoops.

Station 4

Jump sideways through the hoops. Hop sideways through the hoops.

Station 1

Station 2

Station 3

Station 4

LESSON 26
LOCOMOTOR SKILLS OBSTACLE COURSE 1

Student Objectives

- Walk, run, crawl, hop, and jump through a beginning-level obstacle course with control and coordination.

Equipment and Materials

List is an example only. Use similar items you already have to create an age-appropriate obstacle course (see also figure on page 159). If possible, set up more than one course to increase participation opportunities.

- 5 cones
- 10 hoops
- 1 wooden ladder and wall
- 1 walking board
- 3 geometric shapes
- 3 pairs of jumping standards
- 3 jumping boxes
- Chalk, flour, or tape to mark starting line
- Wands to lay across jumping standards

Warm-Up Activities (5 minutes)

Circus Animals

See Grades K-1: Games and Sports, Warm-Ups, page 91.

Skill-Development Activities (20 minutes)

Locomotor Skills Obstacle Course 1

Arrange the obstacle course as shown in figure on page 159. If possible set up more than one course so you can divide the class. Have the students line up at the beginning of the course(s).

1. Briefly explain and demonstrate each part of the obstacle course.
2. Have the students begin the course at safe intervals until all students are rotating through it.
3. Each round, present the following obstacle course challenges:

    Run through the course twice.

    Walk through the course once.

    Hop through the course once.

    Jump through the course once.

4. Repeat the entire sequence.

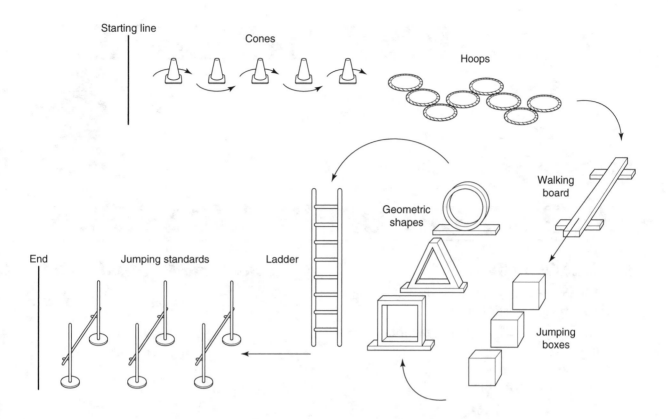

Starting line

Cones

Hoops

Walking board

Geometric shapes

End

Jumping standards

Ladder

Jumping boxes

Concluding Activities (5 minutes)

Firefighter

Divide the children into four or five groups, and have them stand along a start line facing a baseline 50 ft away. Designate one student as the Fire Chief and have this child stand about 10 ft from the others. Assign each group a number, one to five.

1. Describe the game:

   The Fire Chief calls out groups by number, saying, for instance, "Fire Station Number 2." All students in group 2 run to the baseline and back.

   The first person to reach the start line becomes the new Fire Chief and play continues.

   The Fire Chief may call "General alarm!" at which time all groups run.

2. Have the children play Firefighter.

LESSON 27
SKIPPING, GALLOPING, AND SLIDING

Student Objectives

- Demonstrate the step pattern for skipping, galloping, and sliding.
- Correctly identify skipping, galloping, and sliding.
- Cooperate when skipping, galloping, and sliding with a partner.

Equipment and Materials

- Signal

Warm-Up Activities (5 minutes)

I See

See Grades K-1: Games and Sports, Warm-Ups, page 92.

Skill-Development Activities (20 minutes)

Galloping

Keep the children in scatter formation or arrange them in a semicircle.

1. Describe and demonstrate the skill: *Galloping is walking, leaping (one leg leads, the other joins). You push off with the back foot.*
2. Challenge the children with the following galloping tasks:

    Walk, keeping one foot in front and the other behind.

    Go a little faster. Be sure to keep one foot in front.

    Put your other foot in front and walk.

    Go a little faster.

    Gallop around the playground in any direction, and stop on the signal.

    Gallop with a partner.

Skipping

Keep the children in scatter formation or in a semicircle.

1. Describe and demonstrate the skill: *To skip is to step-hop.*

2. Challenge the children with the following skipping tasks:

Move forward, hopping on one foot and then on the other foot.

Try again, going faster—step-hop, step-hop.

Skip around the playground.

Skip with a partner.

Sliding

Keep the children in scatter formation or in a semicircle.

1. Describe and demonstrate the skill: *Sliding involves a step-close going sideways. Step, close to the side.*

2. Challenge the children with the following sliding tasks:

Take a step to the side with one foot, and slide the other foot to bring your feet together. Repeat.

Try going in the opposite direction.

Slide around the playground. Bend your knees.

Slide with a partner. The sliding is like galloping sideways.

Concluding Activities (5 minutes)

Firefighter

See Grades K-1: Games and Sports, Lesson 26, page 159. Have the children skip or gallop instead of run.

GAMES AND SPORTS

LESSON 28

LOCOMOTOR SKILLS OBSTACLE COURSE 2

Student Objectives

- Jump, hop, skip, gallop, and slide through a beginning-level obstacle course with control and coordination.
- Take turns doing the obstacle course.
- Follow the rules playing Run, Rabbit, Run.

Equipment and Materials

List is an example only. Use similar items you already have to create an age-appropriate obstacle course (see also figure on page 163). If possible, set up more than one course to increase participation opportunities.

- 11 cones (6 in pairs with 3 wands across them)
- 11 hoops
- 4 ropes
- Chalk, flour, or tape to mark starting line

Warm-Up Activities (5 minutes)

Stop and Go

See Grades K-1: Games and Sports, Warm-Ups, page 94.

Skill-Development Activities (20 minutes)

Locomotor Skills Obstacle Course 2

Arrange one or more obstacles as in figure on page 163. If possible, set up more than one course, so you can divide the children. Have the children line up at the starting line.

1. Describe and demonstrate the course, pointing out where they will be jumping, hopping, skipping, galloping, and sliding.
2. Have the students begin the course at safe intervals until all students are rotating through it.
3. Repeat several times.

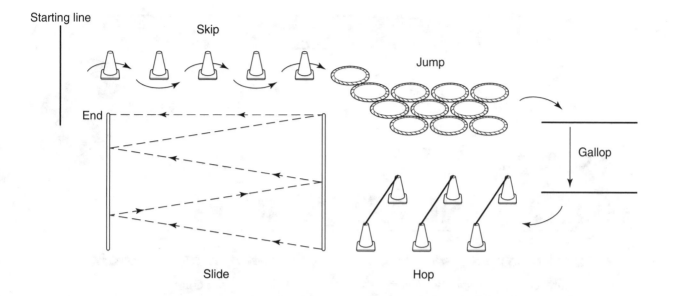

Starting line

Skip

Jump

End

Gallop

Slide

Hop

Concluding Activities (5 minutes)

Run, Rabbit, Run

See Grades K-1: Games and Sports, Warm-Ups, page 93. Use the variation, having the children gallop or skip.

LESSON 29
TOSSING AND CATCHING

Student Objectives

- Toss and catch a Frisbee with a partner and/or with the teacher.
- Toss and catch a ball with speed and accuracy in a game situation.

Equipment and Materials

- 1 Frisbee per child
- 1 playground ball per pair
- 1-3 beanbags per group
- Signal

Safety Tip

- Remind the children of personal space and how this applies to partner activities.

Warm-Up Activities (5 minutes)

Run With the Roadrunner

See Grades K-1: Games and Sports, Warm-Ups, page 94. Remember, you can use multiple lines after the children know the game. Variation: Have the children try galloping or skipping instead of jogging.

Skill-Development Activities (20 minutes)

Movement Challenges

Arrange partners in scatter formation, standing about 10 ft apart, each pair with a ball.

1. Challenge the pairs with the following tasks:

   Play catch with your partner using the ball.

   Toss the ball high. Make it go higher than you.

   Toss the ball in a straight line. Aim for your partner's chest.

   Toss the ball low—below the waist. Aim for your partner's knees.

   Who can jump and then throw to their partner? Throw while you're in the air.

   Now try jumping when you are catching the ball. In the air, toss it high.

2. If the children are successful at these tasks, have them try jumping while throwing and catching. *See how many you can do without missing.*

3. Ask the students: *Can you show me any other jumping, throwing, and catching combinations?*

Tossing the Frisbee

Arrange the children in scatter formation, each with a Frisbee.

1. Describe and demonstrate how to hold a Frisbee: *Hold the Frisbee so the open side of the disc is toward the ground. Grip it on the side of the Frisbee toward where you are going to throw it. Let the rim of the Frisbee rest on the inside of your wrist, with your fingers wrapped under the rim, and your thumb along the top.*

2. Check each child's grip.

3. Describe and demonstrate how to toss a Frisbee: *Toss your Frisbee with a wrist motion, moving the Frisbee toward your body (and away from the target) and then flicking the Frisbee toward the target and releasing your grip.*

4. Have the children practice tossing a Frisbee.

Teacher Ball

Play Teacher Ball with the Frisbee. See Grades K-1: Games and Sports, Warm-Ups, page 95.

Frisbee Tasks

Scatter partners, standing about 10 ft apart from each other, each pair with a Frisbee. Challenge the students with the following tasks:

> *Toss and catch at chest level.*
>
> *Toss and catch high.*
>
> *Move farther apart, toss, and catch.*
>
> *Toss so that your partner has to run (jump, bend) to catch.*

Concluding Activities (5 minutes)

Hot Potato

Arrange the children in small groups, each group sitting in a small circle, four to six ft between children. Give each group one to three beanbags, balls, or for advanced children, Frisbees.

1. Describe the game:

   On the signal toss the objects as quickly as possible from child to child. Moving the object quickly around the circle is the object of the game. Be alert and accurate in your catching and tossing.

   On the next signal the action stops, and I will give a funny task to the children who are holding the hot potatoes, such as doing a stunt for the class or making a face.

2. Have the children play Hot Potato.

3. As the children's skills increase, add to the number of objects each group is tossing.

GAMES AND SPORTS

LESSON 30
DRIBBLING AND THROWING A BALL

Student Objectives

- Combine self-paced dribbling around a target with throwing to a target.
- Combine self-paced dribbling with jumping and throwing to a target.
- Cooperate with a partner to complete movement challenges.
- Discuss the differences between one- and two-handed bouncing.
- Name a sport in which dribbling is used.

Equipment and Materials

- 1 hoop (30-36 in.) per pair
- 1 playground ball (8 1/2 in.) per pair
- 3 carpet squares for bases

Warm-Up Activities (5 minutes)

Spidey Stretches

See Grades K-1: Games and Sports, Warm-Ups, page 94.

Skill-Development Activities (20 minutes)

Movement Challenges

Arrange partners in scatter formation. Have one partner stand in a hoop with a ball with the other partner standing 15 to 20 ft away.

1. Describe and demonstrate bouncing the ball with both hands, then one hand.
2. Challenge the children with the following tasks:

    Partner with the ball, bounce it with both hands while walking from the hoop to your partner, around the partner, and back to the hoop. Trade places and repeat.

    Now take turns dribbling (bouncing with one hand).

    Repeat, trying with the other hand.

    Partner in the hoop, bounce the ball around the outside of the hoop, then throw to your partner, who returns the ball by throwing. Try again, then let your partner try two times.

Partner near the hoop, bounce the ball around the outside of the hoop, jump up trying to land in the hoop, and at the same time throw to your partner. Other partner, return the ball by throwing. Do this again, then trade places and try two more times.

3. If the children are successful with these skills, go on:

   Using the same format, have the children dribble, jump, and throw to a moving target (a walking partner). Adjust the distance between partners as necessary.

   Using the same format, have the children dribble, jump, and throw, but when the ball is caught the catcher dribbles back to the hoop, jumps, and throws to his or her partner, who has moved to a new location about 15 ft away.

4. Ask the children:

   Which is easier, bouncing with two hands or dribbling with one hand? Which is faster? (Two hands is easier at first, but after practice, dribbling with one hand will be as easy as bouncing. Bouncing is usually slower than dribbling.)

   Who can name a sport in which or an athlete for whom dribbling is important? (Basketball, Michael Jordan, Grant Hill, Jason Kidd.)

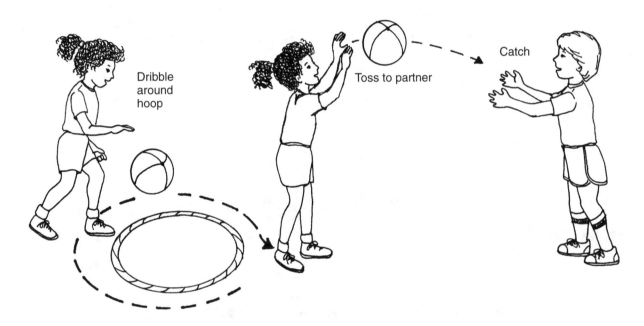

Dribble around hoop

Toss to partner

Catch

Concluding Activities (5 minutes)

Stop

Divide the children into three groups, standing in a circle with one child in the center on a base, each group with one playground ball.

1. Describe and demonstrate the game:

    The Leader (child in the center) tosses the ball high into the air and calls the name of another player.

    The Leader and all other players scatter quickly. The named player tries to catch the ball (or chase it, if necessary, until control is gained).

    When the named player has the ball, he or she yells "Stop!" All other players must freeze.

    Then the player with the ball throws the ball at any one of the frozen players. Whoever catches the ball becomes the Leader.

2. Have the children play Stop.

LESSON 31

STOPPING AND KICKING, KICKING AND CHANGING DIRECTIONS, RUNNING AND KICKING, KICKING AN ELEVATED BALL

Student Objectives

- Stop a moving ball and then kick it.
- Kick a ball and then move in another direction.
- Run and kick a ball.
- Kick a ball that is not on the ground.

Equipment and Materials

- 1 playground ball (8 1/2 in.) per child
- Foam balls
- Cones, rope, tape, or chalk to mark lines

Warm-Up Activities (5 minutes)

Captain Kangaroo Creeps and Crawls

See Grades K-1: Games and Sports, Warm-Ups, page 90.

Skill-Development Activities (20 minutes)

Movement Challenges

Arrange the children in one or two lines, 10 ft between children, each child with a playground ball. Allow children who are having trouble with these activities to use foam balls because these are easier to control.

Challenge the children with the following tasks:

> *Put the ball in front of you on the ground, take three giant steps backward, run and kick the ball so that it rolls about as far as you went in three giant steps. Not too hard.*
>
> *Retrieve the balls and repeat.*
>
> *From the starting line, roll the ball forward, run after it, and kick it to the right (left).*

Stopping a Ball With the Foot

Continue in the same formation. The object is to control the ball with the foot but not to put body weight on the rolling ball (this may cause the child to fall).

1. Describe and demonstrate the skill:

    With your heel down and toes up, place your foot on the ball so there is enough pressure to keep the ball from rolling away.

    If the ball is moving so that you have to change your body position, hop (not step) to the ball.

    Now watch how I trap the ball with one foot. In which sport would you need this skill? (Soccer.)

2. Have the children practice these skills:

    Walk to a stationary ball and put your foot (heel down, toes up) on the ball.

    Working with a partner for just this task, stop a ball rolled directly to you from the front with your foot.

    Hop to a stationary ball and put your nonsupporting foot on the ball.

    From the starting line, roll the ball to the right, run to intercept it, stop it with your foot, and kick it to the left. Repeat.

    Reverse and repeat, rolling to the left and kicking right.

    Try rolling right, stopping, and kicking right, then left.

Kicking an Elevated Ball

Make sure the children are still along the start line, at least 10 ft apart.

1. Demonstrate bouncing the ball in front and kicking it.
2. Challenge the children with the following tasks:

    Bounce your ball in front of you, then kick it forward.

    Bounce your ball in front of you, stop it, and kick it.

    Roll the ball, run after it, kick it right, and run left.

3. Repeat all, having them use the opposite foot.

Free Ball

Use rope, tape, or chalk to mark lines. Arrange the children in several groups of four to six along a line. For each group, have one child stand about 20 ft from the others, facing them.

1. Describe and demonstrate the game:

    The player who stands facing the group is "It." She or he kicks a playground ball to a player in the line while calling out that player's name.

    That player stops the ball and kicks the ball back.

    Once the ball has been kicked to all other players in this way, It kicks the ball and calls "Free ball!"

    The first player to gain control of the ball by trapping it is the new It, and a new round begins. Hint: Remind the children to keep the ball low when kicking.

2. Have the children play Free Ball.

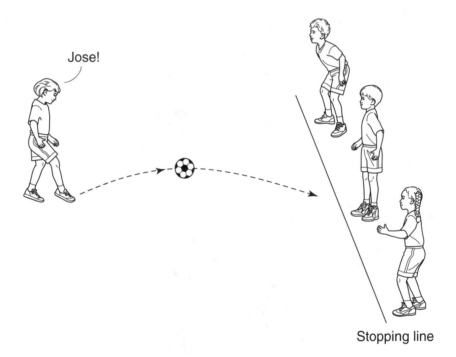

Jose!

Stopping line

LESSON 32
STRIKING

Student Objectives

- Catch, then strike, a ball.
- Strike a ball, then run.
- Catch and strike a ball, and then run (first grade).
- Name a sport in which striking is used.

Equipment and Materials

- 1 playground ball (8 1/2 in.) per child
- Foam balls (optional)
- Chalk, tape, or flour to mark lines

Warm-Up Activities (5 minutes)

Run With the Roadrunner

See Grades K-1: Games and Sports, Warm-Ups, page 94.

Skill-Development Activities (20 minutes)

Movement Challenges

Arrange the children in scatter formation. Each child should begin with a playground ball. Any child who has difficulty may use a foam ball.

1. Challenge the children with the following tasks:

    Holding the ball on a flat palm, strike it with the fist of your other hand.

    Bounce the ball and strike it on the rebound with a flat palm.

2. Have the children repeat the first two challenges with the other hand, then perform these challenges:

    Strike the ball from the palm and run and retrieve it.

    Strike the ball from a bounce and run and retrieve it.

    Strike the ball from a bounce and run and retrieve it.

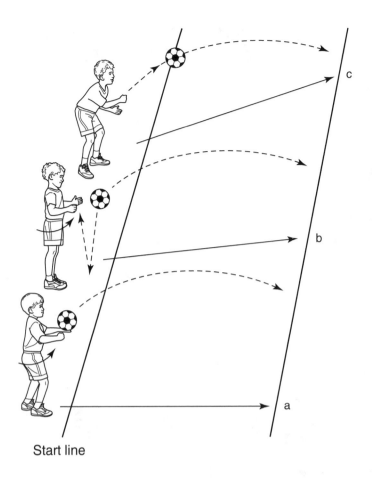

Start line

Rearrange the children with partners. One partner stands on line a-c with a ball, the other stands on the start line.

3. Describe the task: *The child with the ball strikes it from the open palm to her or his partner on line a-c who catches it and throws it back. Change jobs.*

4. Repeat, except have them bounce and strike.

5. For first grade children, repeat, but after striking the ball the child runs to line a-c and back.

6. Ask the children: *Who can name a sport in which striking is used?* (Baseball, softball, tennis, badminton, and the like.) Discuss the various types of strikes, for example, batting, serving, and volleying.

Concluding Activities (5 minutes)

Free Ball

See Grades K-1: Games and Sports, Lesson 31, page 172. Have the children strike instead of kick.

LESSON 33
MANIPULATIVE SKILLS–THROWING, CATCHING, KICKING, AND STRIKING

Student Objectives

- Practice using manipulative skills.
- Name a sport that uses each manipulative skill (throwing, catching, kicking, and striking).

Equipment and Materials

- 1 playground ball (8 1/2 in.) per child
- 1-3 beanbags or, for advanced students, Frisbees, per group

Warm-Up Activities (5 minutes)

Spidey Stretches

See Grades K-1: Games and Sports, Warm-Ups, page 94.

Skill-Development Activities (20 minutes)

Movement Challenges

Keep the children in scatter formation, and give each a playground ball.

1. Ask the children:

    What sports use throwing and catching? (Football, baseball, basketball.)

    Who can name a sport that uses kicking? (Football, soccer.)

    What sports use striking? (Tennis, baseball, softball.)

    What other sports can you name that use skills like dribbling, foot stopping, and bouncing? (Volleyball, soccer, badminton.)

2. Have the children do the following:

    Bounce and catch.

    Bounce hard so the ball goes over your head and falls before you can catch it.

    Toss and catch.

    Toss high (overhead) and catch.

    Toss overhead, let bounce, and catch.

    Toss, clap hands as many times as possible, and catch.

Bounce, clap, and catch. Add more claps each time.

Drop the ball, let it bounce twice, and catch it.

Bounce three forward, three backward, three in place.

Bounce in a circle right, then circle left.

Bounce the ball and stop it with your foot.

Bounce the ball, stop it with your foot, and kick it (foot-dribble) in a circle.

Kick the ball to the right, then stop it with your foot.

Roll the ball left, run after it, and kick it to the left.

Bounce the ball and kick it.

Strike the ball from the palm of your right (left) hand with your left (right) hand.

Bounce and strike the ball underhand.

Toss the ball, let it bounce, and strike it underhand.

Toss the ball and try to hit it before it hits the ground.

Concluding Activities (5 minutes)

Hot Potato

See Grades K-1: Games and Sports, Lesson 29, page 165.

LESSON 34
MANIPULATIVE SKILLS–THROWING, CATCHING, KICKING, AND STRIKING

Student Objectives

- Practice manipulative skills, using a tennis ball.

Equipment and Materials

- 1 tennis ball per child
- 1, 8 1/2 in. playground ball per group
- 3 bases

Warm-Up Activities (5 minutes)

Captain Kangaroo Creeps and Crawls

See Grades K-1: Games and Sports, Warm-Ups, page 90.

Skill-Development Activities (20 minutes)

Movement Challenges

Arrange the children in scatter formation, each with a tennis ball.

1. Challenge the children with the following tasks:

   Bounce and catch.

   Bounce hard so the ball goes over your head and falls before you catch it.

   Toss and catch.

   Toss high (overhead) and catch.

   Toss overhead, let bounce, and catch.

   Toss, clap hands as many times as possible, and catch.

   Bounce, clap, and catch. Add more claps each time.

   Drop the ball, let it bounce twice, and catch it.

   Bounce three bounces moving forward, two bounces moving backward, three in place. Bounce in a circle to the right, then circle to the left.

   Strike the ball from the palm with the left (right) hand.

   Bounce and strike the ball underhand.

Toss the ball, let it bounce, and strike it underhand.

Toss the ball and try to hit it before it hits the ground.

Arrange pairs in scatter formation, each pair with one tennis ball.

2. Challenge the children with the following tasks:

Play catch with one ball.

Bounce the ball to your partner.

Toss it high, let it bounce, and then have your partner catch it.

Hit it off your palm to your partner.

Bounce it and strike it to your partner.

Concluding Activities (5 minutes)

Stop

See Grades K-1: Games and Sports, Lesson 30, page 169.

LESSON 35
STRIKING, CATCHING, KICKING, AND TOSSING

Student Objectives

- Practice manipulative skills of throwing, catching, striking, and kicking.
- Use tossing, throwing, and catching in a game situation.

Equipment and Materials

- 1 playground ball (8+ in.) per group (may need more for Over and Under)
- Foam balls (optional)
- 3 bases

Warm-Up Activities (5 minutes)

Firefighter

See Grades K-1: Games and Sports, Lesson 26, page 159.

Skill-Development Activities (20 minutes)

Teacher Ball

See Grades K-1: Games and Sports, Warm-Ups, page 95. Use playground balls.

1. Present the following challenges for the "Teacher" and children:

   Bounce the ball.

   Bounce and catch, then toss.

   Kick the ball with the inside (outside) of the foot.

   Strike the ball with both (one) hands underhand.

2. Let them play freestyle: allow each child to select the method of projecting the ball to the Teacher.

3. Stress that accuracy counts, no matter how they send the ball.

Stop

See Grades K-1: Games and Sports, Lesson 30, page 169.

Concluding Activities (5 minutes)

Over and Under

See Grades K-1: Games and Sports, Lesson 1, page 98. Use balls instead of beanbags.

GAMES AND SPORTS

LESSON 36
STRIKING, TOSSING, AND CATCHING

Student Objectives

- Practice striking, catching, and tossing.
- Use striking, catching, and tossing in a game situation.
- Work cooperatively to play Circle Pass Ball.

Equipment and Materials

- Several playground balls (8+ in.)
- Foam balls (optional)
- Several tennis balls
- Chalk, tape, ropes, or flour to mark lines

Warm-Up Activities (5 minutes)

Run, Rabbit, Run

See Grades K-1: Games and Sports, Warm-Ups, page 93. Have the children gallop or skip instead of run.

Skill-Development Activities (20 minutes)

Hot Potato

See Grades K-1: Games and Sports, Lesson 29, page 165.

Free Ball

See Grades K-1: Games and Sports, Lesson 31, page 172. Have the players strike, instead of kick, the balls.

Concluding Activities (5 minutes)

Circle Pass Ball

See Grades K-1: Games and Sports, Warm-Ups, page 91.

RHYTHMIC ACTIVITIES

The activities in this section fall into two categories: lessons that reinforce more general movement concepts, for example, personal and general space, and lessons that focus on movements executed to external timing, such as songs, chants, or beats. Classroom teachers will be familiar and comfortable with many of these activities. Physical education teachers will enjoy teaching these activities as well.

UNIT ORGANIZATION

These lessons can be taught as a six-week unit, or spread out through year. You can repeat all of the lessons to help students attain mastery, but it is especially important to repeat the rope jumping lessons to allow enough practice time. The skills introduced in these lessons include locomotor and nonlocomotor skills; keeping a beat; moving to songs, action words, and poems; using rhythm sticks; and jumping long and short jump ropes. These activities introduce the basic skills students will apply later in folk dance, advanced jump rope, cheerleading, gymnastics, aerobic dance, and fitness activities. Several of these activities make excellent presentations for parents' groups or school programs, for example, "Baa, Baa, Black Sheep," rhythm sticks routines, and the Grand

March or Grand Circle March. Table RA1.1 summarizes the content included in this section.

LESSON ORGANIZATION

Each lesson begins with a warm-up, which is typically tailored to the main objective of the lesson. The skill development activities assume students have had little or no experience with rhythmic activities. The lessons end with concluding activities, which usually involve assessment of the lesson or applying the skills in some way.

TEACHING HINTS

Children may demonstrate a variety of skill levels for certain tasks, such as jumping rope. Encourage the children who have trouble to practice, and modify the activity to increase success rates, for example, substituting a hoop for the short rope may help some children get the idea of jumping rope. Finally, children will enjoy moving to songs, action words, and poems even more if you participate with them. Children this age enjoy repeating favorite activities like these, and enjoy performing the songs and dances. Young children respond well to the routine of repeating what is familiar.

Table RA1.1: Unit Plan for Grades K-1: Rhythmic Activities

Week 11: body shapes and locomotor skills

Monday: body shapes and personal and
  general space
Tuesday: stretch and curl
Wednesday: locomotor skills with directions
Thursday: twisting and shaking
Friday: review locomotor and nonlocomotor
  skills

Week 12: moving to a beat and singing games

Monday: keeping time to a beat
Tuesday: pretending
Wednesday: "Baa, Baa, Black Sheep" and
  "Mulberry Bush"
Thursday: "Looby Loo" and "Muffin Man"
Friday: review four singing games and move to a
  beat

Week 13: movements to lyrics and action words

Monday: "Farmer in the Dell" and
  "Go Round and Round the Village"
Tuesday: movement to action words
Wednesday: movement to a rhyme
Thursday: movement to a poem
Friday: review movements to a poem, a rhyme,
  and song, and move to action words

Week 14: rhythm sticks

Monday: rhythm sticks (stick positions and taps)
Tuesday: rhythm sticks (march and tap and tap
  rhythmically)
Wednesday: rhythm sticks with a partner
Thursday: rhythm sticks (create a routine)
Friday: rhythm sticks (new routines)

Week 26: rope activities

Monday: rope activities
Tuesday: jumping long ropes
Wednesday: jumping long ropes to a chant
Thursday: jumping long ropes
Friday: jumping short ropes

Week 27: rope activities and marches

Monday: short rope routines
Tuesday: jumping short ropes
Wednesday: Grand March
Thursday: Circle March and Circle Grand March
Friday: review marches

RHYTHMIC ACTIVITIES

WARM-UPS

Fitness Circle

Arrange the children in a large circle.

1. Have the children move continuously in a large circle, counterclockwise, changing movements on a drumbeat or other signal. Cue the children, for example: *walk with big steps, walk with tiny steps, run, walk on all-fours, jump, hop, run lifting knees high, skip, leap.*
2. Use a drumbeat to set the pace, once the children have the idea of keeping a beat.
3. You can speed up the movement by speeding up the drumbeat.
4. Stop the drum, stopping the movement to change movement patterns.

In, Out, and Around

Arrange the children in scatter formation around you.

1. Use the commands *in, out,* and *around* to cue the children. Explain the actions: *On "in," run toward me. On "out," run away from me toward (a fence or building). On "around," run in a circle around me.*
2. Repeat several times.
3. Variation: Specify a locomotor movement.

I See

Arrange the children in scatter formation.

1. You begin by saying, *I see.* The students respond with, "What do you see?"
2. You give a movement command such as, *I see everybody running in place.* The children run in place.
3. After a short time you begin again with, *I see.* The students freeze and respond with, "What do you see?" and so on.
4. Other examples of movement commands are jumping in place, hopping in a circle, skipping forward, balancing on three body parts, walking backward.

Jumping Patterns With Long Ropes

Arrange the children along long ropes laid out parallel to each other.

Tell the children: *Jump over the ropes and into the spaces between the ropes, first going forward and then going sideways.*

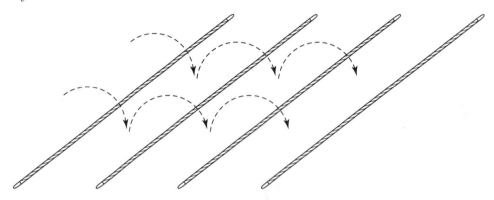

Jumping Patterns With Short Ropes

Arrange the students in scatter formation, each student with a short rope laid on a hard surface.

Tell the children: *Practice jumping and hopping back and forth over the rope.*

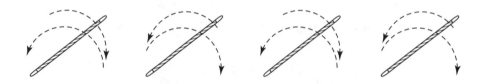

Move and Freeze

Arrange the children in scatter formation.

1. Tell the children: *Walk freely around the area to a drumbeat and freeze when the drumbeat stops.*

2. *When the drum starts again, find another way to travel (backward, sideways, in a circle, with a jump, hop, leap, [or the like]).*

Moving Different Directions

A leader (you, at first) faces the class, which is in scatter formation.

1. The leader chooses and calls out a locomotor skill.
2. The leader beats a drum, and after eight beats signals a change in direction for the class, using the signal cards shown.

⬜ ⟶ = Move sideways right.	⬜ ↓ = Move in place.
⬜ ⟵ = Move sideways left.	⬜ ◯ = Move in a circle.

One, Two, Three

Arrange the children in scatter formation, each with a carpet square.

1. Describe the warm-up:

    On "one," run freely around the carpet square.

    On "two," make bridges over the carpet square with your body.

    On "three," jump in place on the carpet square.

2. Have students warm up.
3. Variations: Instead of running, have them leap, skip, gallop, or slide. Specify the direction of the movement (forward, backward, sideways, in a circle). Specify the type of bridge (front, back, high, low, narrow, wide). Have them hop instead of jump.

Run around   Make a bridge   Jump in place

Traffic Lights

Arrange the children in scatter formation. A leader (you, at first) faces the class, holding movement cards.

1. Describe the warm-up:

   The leader chooses and calls out a locomotor skill.

   The leader holds up a red card indicating "freeze," a green card indicating "run," and a yellow card indicating "walk slowly." You perform the movements at the right speeds.

2. Have the children warm up.

3. Variation: You can select other movements for yellow and green, such as walking in place or walking backward and running sideways or leaping forward.

GRADES K-1 RHYTHMIC ACTIVITIES

LESSON 1
BODY SHAPES

Student Objectives

- Define personal and general space.
- Create movements in personal and general space.
- Work cooperatively with a small group to demonstrate the boundaries of general space.

Equipment and Materials

- 4 cones
- 1 carpet square per child
- Shape cards (8+ in. × 11 in. cards with letters and shapes)

Shape cards

Warm-Up Activities (5 minutes)

One, Two, Three

See Grades K-1: Rhythmic Activities, Warm-Ups, page 187.

Skill-Development Activities (20 minutes)

Personal Space

Keep the children in scatter formation, each with a carpet square.

1. Explain to the students: *Personal space is the area around your body.*
2. Present the following movement challenge: *Put one foot on your carpet square and see how far you can reach. Stretch to one side and then the other.*
3. Repeat and demonstrate interesting alternatives:
   Try reaching in other directions.
   Put a hand on your carpet square and reach.
   Sit on your carpet and move your arms different ways.
   Try circles with your arms. Now try from a kneeling position.
   Reach up high.

Try from a standing position.
Reach to the side.

Shape Cards

Keep the children in scatter formation.

1. Hold up a card.
2. Tell the children: *Use your body to make the shapes on the cards. Use different body parts. Try using your whole body.*

General Space

Keep the children in scatter formation. Define the boundaries of general space with the four cones.

1. Tell the children: *General space is all the space on the playground (or inside the cones).*
2. Hold up a shape card: *Make the shape on the card and move in general space. Watch where you are going. We do not want collisions.*

Rearrange the children in groups of four in close scatter formation.

3. Tell the children: *When I show you a shape card, one person from each group should move to a different place in general space, get as far away from each other as possible (the children will move toward the cones). Make the shape on the card, and once everyone is making the shape, I will signal for you to return to the place you are now standing.*
4. Repeat with different shapes. Encourage the children to run to different areas of general space on each repetition.

Extension Activities (10 to 20 minutes)

Keep the children in scatter formation.

1. Use other letters and shapes. Have the children make shapes with partners or in small groups.
2. Add color; for example, red means large shape, blue means small shape.

Concluding Activities (5 minutes)

Copycat

Arrange partners in scatter formation.

1. Describe the game:

    One of you makes a shape, and the partner must copy the shape.
    After several movements, the other child leads.

2. Have the children play Copycat.

RHYTHMIC ACTIVITIES

LESSON 2
STRETCH AND CURL

Student Objectives

- Create stretch and curl movements with and without hoops.
- Cooperate with a partner during the Opposite Game.

Equipment and Materials

- 1 hoop (30 in.) per child
- 1 drum

Warm-Up Activities (5 minutes)

One, Two, Three

See Grades K-1: Rhythmic Activities, Warm-Ups, page 187. Give each child a hoop instead of a carpet square. Use the following movements:

On "one," run around the hoop.

On "two," balance on three body parts in the hoop.

On "three," jump up and down in the hoop.

Run around hoop

Balance on body parts

Jump in hoop

Skill-Development Activities (20 minutes)

Movement Challenges

Arrange the children in scatter formation, each child standing in a hoop.

1. Tell the children: *Stretch one body part (two parts, three parts, your whole body). Now make yourself small.*
2. Have them repeat, sitting down.
3. Have them repeat, lying down.
4. Have the children perform the following stretches:

    Stretch while balancing on one (two, three, four) body parts.

    Stretch and curl arms (legs, neck, trunk).

    Make a long bridge over your hoop.

    Make a short, high bridge in your hoop.

    Pick up your hoop and stretch with the hoop overhead.

    Holding your hoop, stretch to one side and then the other.

    Sit on the floor and stretch with your hoop.

    Make a curled shape with your body and your hoop. Show me your shape.

    Try different shapes: big, small, wide, narrow.

5. Repeat several times, going from stretch to curl.

Extension Activities (5 to 20 minutes)

Keep the children in scatter formation, each with a hoop.

1. Have the children experiment with making stretch and curl shapes while in the air, moving across the floor, moving over a hoop, and going through a hoop.
2. Have the children create a stretch and curl sequence to a drumbeat.
3. Have them create a shape dance with stretch and curl movements.
4. Have them stretch and curl on playground equipment.

Concluding Activities (5 minutes)

Opposite Game

Arrange partners in scatter formation.

1. Describe the game:

    On the drumbeat one of you makes a stretched shape. The other child must respond with a curled shape.

    Then you will trade jobs.

2. Have the children play the Opposite Game.

LESSON 3
LOCOMOTOR SKILLS
WITH DIRECTIONS

Student Objectives

- Imitate real and imaginary people.
- Interpret feeling words through movement.
- Control locomotor movements: walk, run, and jump, going forward and backward.
- Take turns when doing the obstacle course.

Equipment and Materials

- 1 carpet square per child
- 1 tambourine
- 8 or more hoops (30-36 in.)
- 4 cones
- Tape, chalk, or flour (outdoors) to mark lines

Warm-Up Activities (5 minutes)

One, Two, Three

See Grades K-1: Rhythmic Activities, Warm-Ups, page 187. Give each child a carpet square. Use the following movements:

> On "one," run backward around the carpet square.
>
> On "two," make high bridges over the carpet square.
>
> On "three," hop in place on the carpet square.

Skill-Development Activities (20 minutes)

Personal Space

Keep the children in scatter formation, each with a carpet square.

1. Remind the children: *Personal space is the area around your body.*
2. Ask the children to perform the following tasks:

   > *Walk around your carpet square on tiptoe (backward, sideways with bent knees, walking five steps forward and five steps backward).*

Walk like a soldier (rag doll, clown, robot, drummer, giant, troll).

Think of other ways to walk.

Walk like you're happy (sad, angry, scared, cold, shy, bored, disappointed, brave).

General Space

Keep the children in scatter formation with the carpet squares.

1. Tell the children: *General space is all the space on the playground.*
2. Ask the children to perform the following tasks:

    Run forward (backward, sideways, turning, fast, slow, with knees high) and stop on a tambourine signal.

    Jump in place.

    Jump four jumps forward (backward, sideways, in a circle).

Concluding Activities (5 minutes)

Obstacle Course

Set up an obstacle course as shown in figure on page 195. Gather the children into an information formation.

1. Explain each movement in the obstacle course and the direction of the movement (see figure).
2. Line the children up at the starting line.
3. Have the first child begin walking sideways.
4. When the first child gets to the hoops, have the second child begin, and so on.

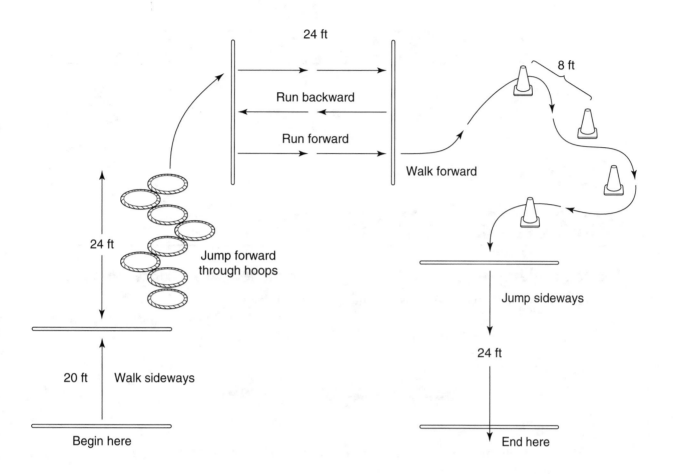

24 ft

Run backward

Run forward

8 ft

Walk forward

24 ft

Jump forward
through hoops

Jump sideways

20 ft   Walk sideways

24 ft

Begin here

End here

LESSON 4
TWISTING AND SHAKING

Student Objectives

- Create body shapes using the twist and the shake.
- Create a twist-and-shake dance.

Equipment and Materials

- 1 drum
- Music: "Funky Penguin" from *Movin'*, Hap Palmer (EA 546)

Warm-Up Activities (5 minutes)

One, Two, Three

See Grades K-1: Rhythmic Activities, Warm-Ups, page 187. Give each child a carpet square. Use the following movements:

> *On "one," run forward around the carpet square.*
>
> *On "two," make wide bridges over the carpet square.*
>
> *On "three," jump in place on the carpet square.*

Skill-Development Activities (20 minutes)

Twisting

Keep the children in scatter formation, each with a carpet square.

1. Describe and demonstrate the skill: *"Twisting" is a turning (rotation) of the body or a body part.*
2. Have the children perform the following twisting motions:
   > *Twist one body part (two parts, three parts).*
   > *Twist your trunk (shoulders, hips).*
   > *Twist your whole body.*

The "Funky Penguin"

Keep the children in scatter formation, each child with a carpet square.

1. Have the children twist one body part to the music, then two body parts, three body parts, and finally many body parts.
2. Have them repeat, shaking or moving instead of twisting.

3. Play the "Funky Penguin" music.

4. Tell the children: *Twist one body part.*

5. Continue with remaining parts.

6. Have them repeat, shaking or moving one to all body parts.

Extension Activities (5 to 10 minutes)

Keep the children in scatter formation, each child with a carpet square.

1. Have the children explore making twist-and-shake movements at different levels.

2. Have them move across the floor (kindergarten: walk, run; first grade: leap, gallop) while twisting and shaking.

Concluding Activities (5 minutes)

Twist and Shake

Arrange the children in a circle formation, each child with a carpet square.

1. Have the children start with a twisted shape.

2. When music starts, have them twist for eight counts and then alternate between twisting and shaking.

LESSON 5
REVIEW

Student Objectives

- Demonstrate five or more body shapes (letters, numbers, curved, straight).
- Demonstrate moving in various directions using different locomotor skills.

Equipment and Materials

- 1 carpet square per child
- Shape cards (8+ in. × 11 in. cards with letters and shapes)
- 1 drum
- Music: "Funky Penguin" from *Movin'*, Hap Palmer (EA 546)

Warm-Up Activities (5 minutes)

One, Two, Three

See Grades K-1: Rhythmic Activities, Warm-Ups, page 187. Use any variation.

Skill-Development Activities (20 minutes)

Shape Cards

Keep the children in scatter formation, each child with a carpet square.

1. Hold up each card in turn.
2. Ask the children to do the following tasks:

   Use your body to make the shapes on the cards. Use different body parts. Try using your whole body.

   Make the shape on the card and move in general space. Watch where you are going. We do not want collisions.

Copycat

See Grades K-1: Rhythmic Activities, Lesson 1, page 190.

Stretching Tasks

Arrange individuals in scatter formation, each child with a carpet square.

1. Have the students perform the following stretching tasks:

   Stretch one body part (two parts, three parts).

> *Stretch your whole body.*
>
> *Become small.*

2. Remind the children of personal space. Ask the children: *Walk like a soldier (rag doll, clown, robot, drummer, giant, troll) or other ways.*

3. *Walk like you're happy, (sad, angry, scared, cold, shy, bored, disappointed, brave).*

The "Funky Penguin"

See Grades K-1: Rhythmic Activities, Lesson 4, page 196.

Concluding Activities (5 minutes)

Obstacle Course

See Grades K-1: Rhythmic Activities, Lesson 3, page 194.

LESSON 6
KEEPING TIME TO A BEAT

Student Objectives
- Move body parts to a beat.
- Step in place to a beat.
- Tap rhythm sticks to a beat.

Equipment and Materials
- 1 drum
- Music: "Sunshine" from *Modern Tunes for Rhythm and Instruments*, Hap Palmer (AR 523)
- 2 rhythm sticks per child

Warm-Up Activities (5 minutes)

Fitness Circle

See Grades K-1: Rhythmic Activities, Warm-Ups, page 185.

Skill-Development Activities (20 minutes)

Keeping Time to a Beat

Have the children sit down, still in a large circle.

1. Play a rhythmic pattern on the drum as follows, providing a continuous sound so that the underlying beat is evident and varying the tempo (speed):

    Clap your hands to keep the beat.

    Tap your hands on your thighs (your shoulders, the floor) to keep the beat.

    Tap your feet on the floor.

    Move your head (shoulders, elbows, fingers) to the beat.

    Make punching movements overhead (in front of your body, to the side of your body) with your arms to the beat.

2. Keep the rhythmic pattern going on the drum.
3. Keep encouraging the children to keep the beat.
4. Repeat all methods of keeping the beat to the song "Sunshine."

Extension Activities (5 to 10 minutes)

Keep the children in a large circle.

1. Tell the children: *Walk in a circle to the beat, creating body movements to the beat of the music.*

2. Ask the children to create other ways to keep time to the beat.

Concluding Activities (5 minutes)

Movement to a Beat

Arrange the children in a large circle.

1. Play "Sunshine" and have the children perform the following sequence:

   Eight steps in place,

   Eight claps,

   Four punch movements overhead, and

   Four punch movements forward.

2. Repeat four punches overhead and four punches forward.

3. Repeat the entire sequence.

RHYTHMIC ACTIVITIES

K-1

LESSON 7
PRETENDING

Student Objectives

- Create unique movements to represent objects, animals, and things.
- Cooperate with a partner to create a movement for the other to guess what the movement is.

Equipment and Materials

- None

Warm-Up Activities (5 minutes)

Fitness Circle

See Grades K-1: Rhythmic Activities, Warm-Ups, page 185.

Skill-Development Activities (20 minutes)

Creating Movements

Arrange the children in scatter formation.

1. Tell the children: *Pretend you are a witch (a scarecrow, a rag doll, a giant, a dragon, a monster, an elephant, a duck, a giraffe, a kangaroo, a snake, a seal, a rabbit, the wind, lightning, rain, clouds, the sun, snowflakes).*
2. *Pretend you are playing tennis (football, soccer, swimming, skiing, riding a bike).*
3. *Now pretend you are walking on ice (in hot sand, in a strong wind, through the jungle).*

Partner Guessing

Arrange partners in scatter formation.
    Challenge the children with the following tasks:

One partner, pretend to be something; the other partner, try to guess what it is. Take turns.

One partner, pretend to do a household chore; the other partner, try to guess the chore. Take turns.

One partner, pretend to be something that moves but is not alive (like a car or a clock); the other partner, try to guess what it is. Take turns.

Concluding Activities (5 minutes)

Guessing Game

Gather the children into an information formation.

1. Select five children to pretend to be doing something. Encourage the other children to try to guess what each is.
2. Repeat several times.

GRADES K-1 RHYTHMIC ACTIVITIES

LESSON 8
"BAA, BAA, BLACK SHEEP" AND "MULBERRY BUSH"

Student Objectives
- Remember the words to the songs.
- Perform the movement sequences to the words of the songs.

Equipment and Materials
- 1 tambourine
- Music (optional): "Baa, Baa, Black Sheep" (Folkraft 1191, Victor E-83) and "Mulberry Bush" (Folkraft 1183, Victor 20806)

Warm-Up Activities (5 minutes)

Fitness Circle

See Grades K-1: Rhythmic Activities, Warm-Ups, page 185. Use leap, walk, hop right, skip, walk on all-fours, hop left.

Skill-Development Activities (20 minutes)

"Baa, Baa, Black Sheep"

Arrange the children in a circle, facing center.

1. Describe and demonstrate the following steps, based on the lyrics:

    Baa, baa, black sheep (three claps),
    Have you any wool (three stamps)?
    Yes sir, yes sir (nod two times),
    Three bags full (hold up three fingers).
    One for my master (turn and bow right),
    One for my dame (turn and bow left),
    One for the little boy (turn in place once),
    Who lives down the lane (bow forward).
    Baa, baa, black sheep (three claps),
    Have you any wool (three stamps)?

Yes sir, yes sir (nod two times),

Three bags full (hold up three fingers).

2. Sing "*Baa, baa, black sheep*" (line 1).
3. Repeat as the children sing with you.
4. Continue with each line until you complete the song.
5. *Now we will sing the entire song.* (Sing the whole song with the children.) Have the children practice the movements: *When we sing "Baa, baa, black sheep," we will clap three times, like this.* Sing and clap each part of the song.
6. Tell the children: *Now let's do all the movements.*

"Mulberry Bush"

Keep the children in a circle, facing center.

1. Describe and demonstrate the following steps, based on the lyrics:

    Here we go 'round the mulberry bush (walk or skip to the right),

    The mulberry bush, the mulberry bush,

    Here we go 'round the mulberry bush,

    So early in the morning.

    This is the way we wash our clothes (stop, drop hands, and turn in place once),

    Wash our clothes, wash our clothes (pantomime washing clothes on a washboard),

    This is the way we wash our clothes,

    So early Monday morning.

2. Repeat, having the children use the following actions:

    Iron our clothes (Tuesday)

    Mend our clothes (Wednesday)

    Sweep our floor (Thursday)

    Make a cake (Friday)

    Build a house (Saturday)

    Bake our bread (Sunday)

3. Sing "Mulberry Bush," having the children practice each action with the song.

Concluding Activities (5 minutes)

"Baa, Baa, Black Sheep" or "Mulberry Bush"

Repeat, going through the words and movements several times.

LESSON 9
"LOOBY LOO" AND "MUFFIN MAN"

Student Objectives

- Remember the words to the songs.
- Correctly identify the right and left sides of the body.
- Perform the sequences of movements to the songs.

Equipment and Materials

- 1 whistle
- Music (optional): "Looby Loo" (Folkraft 1102, Victor 20214) or "Muffin Man" (Folkraft 1188)

Warm-Up Activities (5 minutes)

Whistle Stop

Arrange the students in a large circle.

1. The students run in the circle, and on a signal (the whistle) they freeze and make a shape as directed by you.
2. Use a letter of the alphabet (L, P, S, and so on), or an animal (elephant, giraffe, and so forth).

Skill-Development Activities (20 minutes)

"Looby Loo"

Keep the children in a circle.

1. Use the following word cues to direct the children to perform each step:

   Here we go Looby Loo (walk eight steps right),

   Here we go Looby Light,

   Here we go Looby Loo (walk eight steps back to left),

   All on a Saturday's night.

   I put my right hand in (pantomime by putting right hand into center of circle),

   I take my right hand out (take right hand back),

   I give my right hand a shake, shake, shake, and I turn myself about (shake right hand three times and turn in place).

2. Repeat the entire dance, using left hand (*I put my left hand in*), right foot (*I put my right foot in*), left foot (*I put my left foot in*), head (*I put my head in*), whole body (*I put my whole body in*).

"Muffin Man"

Keep the children in a circle. Have one child, the Muffin Man, stand in the center.

1. Have the children sing "Muffin Man."
2. Select a child to be the Muffin Man.
3. Demonstrate and practice the actions with the song:

   Oh, do you know the Muffin Man (the Muffin Man walks [or for first grade, skips] around the inside of the circle while the children in the circle stand still, sing, and clap),

   The Muffin Man, the Muffin Man?

   Do you know the Muffin Man, (Muffin Man selects a partner and brings them into the center of the circle),

   Who lives on Drury Lane?

   Oh, yes we know the Muffin Man (the actions are the same except that the first Muffin Man chooses a partner to walk or skip around the inside of the circle; then these two each choose a partner),

   The Muffin Man, the Muffin Man.

   Yes, we know the Muffin Man,

   Who lives on Drury lane.

   Four of us know the Muffin Man (the actions are repeated with four children and so on, doubling the number of Muffin Men each round). . . .

4. Continue, repeating the song until all the children are in the center.
5. Lead the last verse with the children walking or skipping around the room: *All of us know the Muffin Man.* . . .

Concluding Activities (5 minutes)

"Looby Loo" or "Muffin Man"

Have the children perform the entire sequence, going through the words and movements several times.

LESSON 10
REVIEW

Student Objectives

- Remember the words and actions for four singing games and a movement dance.
- Demonstrate three songs with movements.
- Move to a beat.

Equipment and Materials

- 1 drum
- 1 tambourine
- Music: "Sunshine" from *Modern Tunes for Rhythm and Instruments*, Hap Palmer (AR 523)
- Music (optional): "Baa, Baa, Black Sheep" (Folkraft 1191,Victor E-83) and "Mulberry Bush" (Folkraft 1183, Victor 20806); "Looby Loo" (Folkraft 1102, Victor 20214) and "Muffin Man" (Folkraft 1188)

Warm-Up Activities (5 minutes)

Fitness Circle

See Grades K-1: Rhythmic Activities, Warm-Ups, page 185. Use one of the variations.

Skill-Development Activities (20 minutes)

Movement to a Beat: "Sunshine"

See Grades K-1: Rhythmic Activities, Lesson 6, page 201. Review, then have the children practice, repeating the actions twice.

"Baa, Baa, Black Sheep"

See Grades K-1: Rhythmic Activities, Lesson 8, page 204. Review, then have the children practice, repeating the actions twice.

"Mulberry Bush"

See Grades K-1: Rhythmic Activities, Lesson 8, page 205. Review, then have the children practice once.

"Looby Loo"

See Grades K-1: Rhythmic Activities, Lesson 9, page 206. Review, then have the children practice, repeating the actions twice.

"Muffin Man"

See Grades K-1: Rhythmic Activities, Lesson 9, page 207. Review, then have the children practice once.

Concluding Activities (5 minutes)

Rhythmic Activities

Divide the children into two groups. Arrange one group in a circle, and gather the other group into an information formation.

1. Allow the two groups to decide which rhythmic activity they would like to perform.
2. Have the children in the circle repeat their favorite rhythmic activities, with the other half of the class watching.
3. Reverse groups and repeat with the other group's favorite rhythmic activities.

LESSON 11

"FARMER IN THE DELL" AND "GO ROUND AND ROUND THE VILLAGE"

Student Objectives

- Remember the words to the songs.
- Participate in simple singing games.

Equipment and Materials

- 1 whistle
- Music (optional): "Farmer in the Dell" (Folkraft 1182, Victor 45-5066) and "Go Round and Round the Village" (Folkraft 1191)

Warm-Up Activities (5 minutes)

Whistle Stop

Use these variations: Have the children freeze in the shapes of play objects (ball, yo-yo, swing, slide) and machines (bulldozer, elevator, cement mixer). See Grades K-1: Rhythmic Activities, Lesson 9, page 206.

Skill-Development Activities (20 minutes)

"Farmer in the Dell"

Arrange the children in a circle, facing the center. Choose one child to stand in the center as the Farmer.

1. Sing the words to the song while demonstrating the movements for each part of the activity.
2. Have the children practice the movements with the song:

    The Farmer in the dell (walk to right),

    The Farmer in the dell,

    Hi, ho, the dairy oh,

    The Farmer in the Dell.

    The Farmer takes a Wife, (continue to walk right; Farmer chooses a second child as a Wife),

    The Farmer takes a Wife,

Hi, ho, the dairy oh,

The Farmer takes a Wife.

3. Direct the remaining children to continue to walk right. Each child chosen moves to the center. Repeat the verse with each of the following, each time having another child selected:

    The Wife takes a Child.

    The Child takes a Nurse.

    The Nurse takes a Dog.

    The Dog takes a Cat.

    The Cat takes a Rat.

    The Rat takes the Cheese.

    The Cheese stands alone.

4. Have all the children return to the circle except the Cheese, who becomes the new Farmer.

"Go Round and Round the Village"

Arrange the children in a circle. Select four children to stand outside the circle in scatter formation around the circle.

1. Sing the words to the song while demonstrating the movements for each part of the dance.

2. Have the children practice the movements with the song:

    Go round and round the village (children in the circle walk to the right),

    Go round and round the village,

    Go round and round the village (children on the outside of the circle walk the opposite direction),

    As we have done before.

    Go in and out the windows (children in the circle stop and lift joined hands—forming "windows"),

    Go in and out the windows,

    Go in and out the windows (children on the outside of the circle walk in and out the windows),

    As we have done before.

    Now stand and face your partner (children going in and out the windows select partners by standing in front of them),

    Now stand and face your partner,

    Now stand and face your partner,

    As we have done before.

    Now follow me to London (children who have chosen partners take their partners to the center of the circle and any direction),

    Now follow me to London,

    Now follow me to London,

    As we have done before (children in the circle walk to the right).

3. Have every child return to the circle and then select four new children. Repeat the activity.

Concluding Activities (5 minutes)

"Farmer in the Dell"

Have the children perform "Farmer in the Dell," allowing them to change the words. For example, use Husband, Fox, Bear, and Duck for Wife, Nurse, Dog, and Cat.

RHYTHMIC ACTIVITIES

LESSON 12
MOVEMENT TO ACTION WORDS

Student Objectives

- Create individual movements expressing action words.
- Create a sequence of movements.
- Cooperate with a group to select and demonstrate an action word.

Equipment and Materials

- Picture cards (8 1/2 in. × 11 in.)

Picture cards

Warm-Up Activities (5 minutes)

Whistle Stop

See Grades K-1: Rhythmic Activities, Lesson 9, page 206. Use giant, fairy, elf, monster, dragon, troll.

Skill-Development Activities (20 minutes)

Action Words 1

Arrange the children in scatter formation.

1. Present the following words to the class and ask the children to respond with a movement: *sizzle, pour, melt, spin, sneak, grab, twist, swim, hammer, kick, prance, stretch, reach, dive, splash, squeeze, fall.*

2. Repeat, telling the children: *Move in general space with your movement. Make a movement for each of these words* (movements should be in order and continuous): *pour, sneak, melt, sizzle, splash, squeeze, reach, spin, stretch, hammer, fall, twist, dive, swim, grab.*

Concluding Activities (5 minutes)

Action Words 2

Divide the children into groups of four to six.

1. Have each group select an action word.
2. Give them a minute to decide how they will work together to act out their word.
3. Allow one group at a time to demonstrate their action word.
4. Encourage the other groups to try to guess the action word, based on the demonstration.

LESSON 13
MOVEMENT TO A RHYME

Student Objectives
- Create movements that express a rhyme.

Equipment and Materials
- None

Warm-Up Activities (5 minutes)

In, Out, and Around
See Grades K-1: Rhythmic Activities, Warm-Ups, page 185. Use the commands *in*, *out*, and *around* several times.

Skill-Development Activities (20 minutes)

"Jack Be Nimble"
Seat the students in a semicircle. *Note*: Each syllable represents one beat. The lines under the words show the beats.

1. Say the chant aloud, clapping the beat:

   Jack be nimble, Jack be quick,

   – – – – – – –

   Jack jumped over the candle stick.

   – – – – – – – –

2. Have the children clap to each syllable or beat.
3. Select a movement, and have the children move to the beat. Some examples of movements are: punch, tap, nod, shoulder twist, and the like.
4. Repeat, varying the movements.
5. Have the children combine a step forward with a movement (such as a nod or a punch) to the beat.

Concluding Activities (5 minutes)

"Jack Be Nimble"

Keep the children seated in a semicircle. Have the children each create an individual movement pattern to interpret the rhyme. Select several volunteers to show their patterns.

LESSON 14
MOVEMENT TO A POEM

Student Objectives

- Create movement to an action phrase.
- Create movement as a result of feeling created by hearing a poem.

Equipment and Materials

- None

Warm-Up Activities (5 minutes)

In, Out, and Around

See Grades K-1: Rhythmic Activities, Warm-Ups, page 185. Use the following variation: On *in*, the students jump forward toward you. On *out*, the students gallop away. On *around*, the students slide in a circle around you.

Skill-Development Activities (20 minutes)

"The Silly Swans From Snowlake"

Arrange the children in scatter formation.

1. Read the poem to the class:

   The silly swans from Snowlake
   Loved to splash and play,
   Dipping and diving, swimming, and gliding,
   Happily filled most of the day.
   The silly swans from Snowlake
   Churned and thrashed a lot,
   Graceful they could be if they would be,
   But those silly swans would not.

2. Discuss the movement words: *splash, play, dipping, diving, swimming, gliding, churning, thrashing.*

3. Have the children create movements for the movement words as you repeat the poem.

4. Present the following ideas to help the children with the interpretation:

Swimming in an ocean with large waves

Diving from a high board

Reaching up and dipping to the ground

Gliding like a magic carpet

Churning like a cement mixer

Thrashing like a small bird taking a bath

5. Have the children discuss and create their own movements to represent each idea.

Extension Activities (10 to 30 minutes)

1. Select other poems for the children to interpret.
2. Work with the classroom teacher to have all the children write (or dictate) original poems for movement interpretation.

Concluding Activities (5 minutes)

Moving to a Poem

Arrange the children in a semicircle. Select several students to demonstrate their movements to the poem.

GRADES K-1 RHYTHMIC ACTIVITIES

LESSON 15
REVIEW

Student Objectives

- Create and demonstrate movements for a poem.
- Demonstrate one song with movements.
- Move to a rhyme.
- Demonstrate movements for action words.

Equipment and Materials

- Picture cards (optional; at least 8 1/2 in. × 11 in.)
- A poem that includes action words
- Music (optional): "Farmer in the Dell" (Folkraft 1182, Victor 45-5066)

Warm-Up Activities (5 minutes)

In, Out, and Around

See Grades K-1: Rhythmic Activities, Warm-Ups, page 185. Use any variation.

Skill-Development Activities (20 minutes)

"Farmer in the Dell"

Keep the children in scatter formation, but in front of you. See Grades K-1: Rhythmic Activities, Lesson 11, page 210. Review and have the children practice the song and movements.

Action Words

Keep the children in scatter formation.

Have the children create movements for the following words: *sizzle, pour, melt, spin, sneak, grab, twist, swim, hammer, kick, prance, stretch, reach, dive, splash, squeeze, fall.*

Moving to a Rhyme

Keep the children in scatter formation.

Have the children recite and clap to "Jack Be Nimble."

Movement to a Poem

Keep the children in scatter formation. Use a different poem. See example of this type of activity in Grades K-1: Rhythmic Activities, Lesson 14, page 217.

1. Read the poem.
2. Help the children identify the action words.

3. Have the children create new movements to go with the action words.

Concluding Activities (5 minutes)

Movement to a Poem

Arrange the children in a semicircle. Select two or three volunteers to demonstrate their movements.

1. Read the poem while the children simultaneously demonstrate their movements.
2. Repeat with other volunteers.

RHYTHMIC ACTIVITIES

LESSON 16
RHYTHM STICKS

Student Objectives

- Demonstrate the stick positions for tap down, tap together, tap front, tap side, and cross tap.
- Tap a stick sequence rhythmically.
- Be safe when using the sticks.

Equipment and Materials

- 2 rhythm sticks per child
- Music: "Happy Mechanical Man" from *Modern Tunes for Rhythm and Instruments*, Hap Palmer (AR 523)

Warm-Up Activities (5 minutes)

In, Out, and Around

Use these movements: hop forward, run away backward, and skip forward around you. See Grades K-1: Rhythmic Activities, Warm-Ups, page 185.

Skill-Development Activities (20 minutes)

Rhythm Sticks

Have the children sit in scatter formation facing you, each child with two rhythm sticks.

1. Describe and demonstrate the following rhythm motions to the children:

   Stick grip—*Hold the sticks vertically* (demonstrate clearly), *with your thumb and fingers slightly below the midpoint.* Have the children practice the stick grip.

   Tap down—*Tap the bottom ends of the sticks by touching the upright sticks to the floor.* Have the children practice tap down.

   Tap front—*Tap the top ends of the sticks by tilting the sticks forward and touching the opposite ends to the floor.* Have the children practice tap front.

   Tap together—*Hold the sticks parallel* (demonstrate clearly) *and touch them together.* Have the children practice tap together.

   Side tap—*Touch the sticks to the floor on each side of your body (right to right and left to left).* Have the children practice side tap.

   Cross tap—*Cross your arms in front of your body, and tap the top ends of the sticks on the floor.* Have the children practice cross tap.

2. Have the children tap the following sequence:

   Tap down (eight counts),

Tap together (eight counts),
Tap the floor, then together (eight counts),
Tap side (eight counts),
Tap together (eight counts),
Tap side, then together (eight counts),
Cross tap, right over left (eight counts),
Cross tap, left over right (eight counts).

3. Allow the children to create additional stick movements to add to the routine.

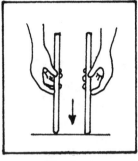

Tap front

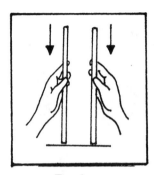

Tap down

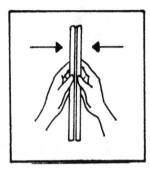

Tap together

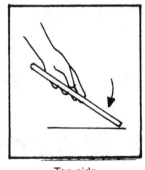

Tap side

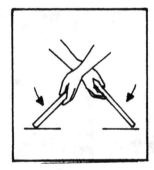

Cross tap

Concluding Activities (5 minutes)

Rhythm Sticks

Keep the children in scatter formation.

1. Have the children perform the entire sequence to "Happy Mechanical Man":
   Tap down (eight counts),
   Tap together (eight counts),
   Tap the floor, then together (eight counts),
   Tap side (eight counts),
   Tap together (eight counts),
   Tap side, then together (eight counts),
   Cross tap, right over left (eight counts),
   Cross tap, left over right (eight counts).

2. Repeat several times.

GRADES K-1

RHYTHMIC ACTIVITIES

LESSON 17
RHYTHM STICKS

Student Objectives

- Tap a stick sequence rhythmically.
- March to a beat.

Equipment and Materials

- 2 rhythm sticks per child
- Music: "Frere Jacques" from *Modern Tunes for Rhythm and Instruments*, Hap Palmer (AR 523)

Warm-Up Activities (5 minutes)

I See

See Grades K-1: Rhythmic Activities, Warm-Ups, page 185. Have the children use movements such as jumping in place, hopping in a small circle, and skipping forward.

Skill-Development Activities (20 minutes)

Rhythm Sticks

Arrange the children in a straight line allowing them enough space to move around, but also close enough so they are able to touch the rhythm sticks of the child on either side of them. See Grades K-1: Rhythmic Activities, Lesson 16, page 221, and have the children practice the following sequence, reminding them of safety rules:

> *March in place* (eight counts),
>
> *March and tap the sticks together in front, waist-high* (eight counts),
>
> *March in place* (eight counts),
>
> *March and tap the sticks in front, waist-high* (eight counts),
>
> *Standing straight, tap sticks together overhead* (four counts),
>
> *Tap sticks low to the floor* (four counts),
>
> *Extend (stretch) your arms out to your sides and tap the sticks of the children on each side* (four counts),
>
> *Tap your own sticks together in front, waist-high* (four counts),
>
> *While marching, extend your arms out to sides at shoulder level* (count 1), *and then bring arms back, and tap sticks in front* (count 2),
>
> *Continue for 16 counts.*

Concluding Activities (5 minutes)

Rhythm Sticks

Keep the children in the same formation.

1. Have the children listen to the tune "Frere Jacques" and clap to the music.
2. Have them perform the stick sequence to the music.

GRADES K-1 RHYTHMIC ACTIVITIES

LESSON 18
RHYTHM STICKS

Student Objectives

- Tap a stick sequence rhythmically.
- Cooperate with tapping sticks with a partner.

Equipment and Materials

- 2 rhythm sticks per child
- Music: "Small, Small World" from *Simplified Lummi Stick Activities*, Laura Johnson (Kim 2015)

Warm-Up Activities (5 minutes)

I See

See Grades K-1: Rhythmic Activities, Warm-Ups, page 185. Have the children use movements such as walking backward, galloping in a circle, marching in place, jumping forward, and balancing on one foot.

Skill-Development Activities (20 minutes)

Stick Sequences

Arrange partners in scatter formation. Have each child sit cross-legged with sticks, facing his or her partner. Remind students of safety rules.

1. Have the children practice the following sequence, with each tap receiving one count:

   Tap down in front (8 counts),

   Tap sticks together (8 counts),

   Tap down in front (count 1), *tap own sticks together* (count 2), *tap partner's right* (count 3), *tap partner's left* (count 4).

   Repeat three more times for 16 counts.

   Cross forearms (right over left) *in front of body and tap up* (8 counts),

   Tap down in front (count 1), *tap own sticks together* (count 2), *tap both sticks with partner's sticks twice* (counts 3 and 4). (Repeat three more times for 16 counts.)

Concluding Activities (5 minutes)

Stick Sequences

Keep partners in scatter formation, facing each other. Have the children perform the entire sequence to "Small, Small World."

LESSON 19
RHYTHM STICKS

Student Objectives

- Refine the rhythm stick routines.
- Create an original rhythm stick routine.

Equipment and Materials

- 2 rhythm sticks per child
- Music: "We All Live Together" from *We All Live Together*, Vol. I (YM1 or YM1C, Kimbo); other music with a 4/4 beat (if desired, allow children to bring in their own music; review for appropriateness ahead of time)

Warm-Up Activities (5 minutes)

I See

See Grades K-1: Rhythmic Activities, Warm-Ups, page 185. Have the children use new movements such as leaping forward, running backward, balancing on three body parts, and jumping high and landing softly.

Skill-Development Activities (20 minutes)

Creative Stick Routines

Arrange the children in a circle, each with two rhythm sticks.

1. Play a piece of music.
2. Repeat the music, suggesting possible stick patterns.
3. Play a different piece of music.
4. Repeat the music, and ask the children to suggest possible stick patterns.

Divide the children (with rhythm sticks) into small groups or allow children to work alone. Scatter the children and groups as widely as possible.

5. Have the children create routines, using music or self-generated beats.
6. Allow the children to bring in their own music to use as accompaniment. Be sure the music is in 4/4 meter and has a strong underlying beat. Provide a variety of music for children to experiment with before selecting their piece.

Concluding Activities (5 minutes)

Follow the Leader

Arrange partners in scatter formation, each child with two sticks. Designate one child in each pair as the leader.

1. Explain the activity: *The leader selects a sequence to tap, and the partner taps the same sequence. For example, the sequence might be*:

   Tap down (four counts),

   Tap together (four counts),

   Tap side (four counts),

   Tap together (four counts).

2. Tell the children: *Change leaders after each sequence.*

GRADES K-1 RHYTHMIC ACTIVITIES

LESSON 20
RHYTHM STICKS

Student Objectives

- Demonstrate a new stick routine.
- Present an original stick routine.
- Be considerate of other students as routines are presented.

Equipment and Materials

- 2 rhythm sticks per child

Warm-Up Activities (5 minutes)

Routine Practice

Divide the children into small groups or allow children to work alone. Hint: Keep the same groups as in Lesson 19. Scatter children and groups as widely as possible. Allow the children to practice their routines.

Skill-Development Activities (20 minutes)

Stick Routines

Arrange the children in a circle, each with two rhythm sticks.

1. Select an individual or group to present a routine to the class (ask for volunteers, allowing them to go first).
2. Repeat until all the children and/or groups have presented routines.

Concluding Activities (5 minutes)

Stick Routines

Keep the children in a circle, each with two rhythm sticks.

1. Select a unique, especially good, or favorite routine.
2. Have all the children practice that routine.

RHYTHMIC ACTIVITIES

LESSON 21
ROPE ACTIVITIES

Student Objectives

- Create letters and shapes with a rope.
- Jump rhythmically back and forth over a rope on the floor.

Equipment and Materials

- 1 small (6 ft) jump rope per child
- 1 drum
- Music: "Sunshine" from *Modern Tunes for Rhythm and Instruments*, Hap Palmer (AR 523)
- Color cards: 1 red, 1 green, and 1 yellow

Warm-Up Activities (5 minutes)

Traffic Lights

See Grades K-1: Rhythmic Activities, Warm-Ups, page 188. Repeat several times.

Skill-Development Activities (20 minutes)

Jump Rope Activities

Make sure the children are still in scatter formation, and give each a jump rope.

1. Challenge the children with the following tasks:

    Can you make a circle (square, triangle) with your rope?

    Can you walk (jump, hop) around your triangle?

    Can you make a letter with your rope?

    Can you jump (leap, hop) over your letter?

    Can you think of another way to move over your letter?

    Can you put your rope in a straight line? Now with your side to the rope, jump from side-to-side over the rope (facing the rope, jump over the rope and back).

2. Repeat the challenges several times.

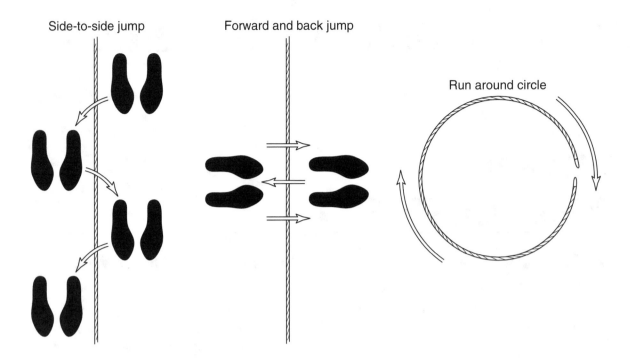

Side-to-side jump   Forward and back jump   Run around circle

Concluding Activities (5 minutes)

Rope Tasks

Have the children stand beside their ropes, which are laid out straight on the ground.

1. Tell the children: *Jump side-to-side (forward, backward) to a drumbeat (to music)* over the rope.
2. Repeat several times.

K-1

LESSON 22
JUMPING LONG ROPES

Student Objectives

- Coordinate the jumping pattern to jump a long rope.
- Jump a long rope to a simple chant.

Equipment and Materials

- 1 long jump rope (12-16 ft) per group

Warm-Up Activities (5 minutes)

Traffic Lights

Arrange the children along a line on one side of a rectangular area. See Grades K-1: Rhythmic Activities, Warm-Ups, page 188. Call out color cues until all the children are across.

Skill-Development Activities (20 minutes)

Long Rope Activities

Arrange the children in groups of four or five in scatter formation, each group with a long rope. Establish a rotation system for each group, with two turning the rope and two or three jumping in turn. Demonstrate and describe each action:

Swinging—*Turners swing the rope slightly from side-to-side. Jumpers stand next to the rope and jump as it swings.* Have the children practice swinging, rotating so everyone gets a chance to practice.

Swing and turn—*Turners swing the rope over the head of the jumper. Jumpers jump over the rope.* Have the children practice swing and turn, rotating turns.

Two-footed double jump—*With two feet together, the jumper jumps with a rebound (heavy jump, light jump) for each turn of the rope.* Have the children practice the two-footed double jump, rotating turns.

Two-footed single jump—*With two feet together, the jumper jumps once for each turn of the rope.* Have the children practice the two-footed single jump, rotating turns.

Running in the front door—*Turn the rope toward the jumper. The jumper runs under the turning rope (runs in the front door), jumps once, and runs out.* Have the children practice running in the front door, rotating turns.

Running out the back door—*Turn the rope away from the jumper. The jumper runs through the turning rope (runs in the back door), jumps once, and runs out.* Have the children practice running out the back door, rotating turns.

Concluding Activities (5 minutes)

Coffee

Keep the children in the same groups, each group with a long jump rope.

1. Recite the chant: *I like coffee, I like tea, how many kids play with me?*
    1, 2, 3, 4, (up to 20, or until a miss).
2. Have the children say the chant, allowing one child in each group to jump.
3. Repeat until all have had a turn.

LESSONS 23 AND 24
JUMPING LONG ROPES

Student Objectives

- Jump a long rope five times consecutively.

Equipment and Materials

- 5-6 long jump ropes (12-16 ft) per group (plan for at least 2 groups)

Warm-Up Activities (5 minutes)

Long Ropes

Place the long ropes on the floor or ground, making two parallel patterns (see figure below). Divide the students into two groups, and place each group at the beginning of a rope pattern. If space, set up more than two patterns to reduce group size.

1. Direct the students: *Jump over the ropes and into the spaces between the ropes, first going forward and then going sideways.*
2. Have them repeat several times, hopping on the right foot, hopping on the left foot, and then leaping.

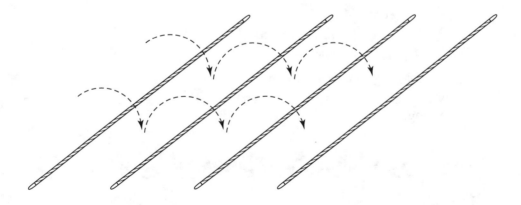

Skill-Development Activities (20 minutes)

Jumping Rope

Arrange groups of four or five in scatter formation, each group with a long jump rope.

1. Have the jumpers practice the following jump rope activities: swinging, swing and turn, running in the front door, running out the back door, two-footed double jump, two-footed single jump.
2. Have the children repeat, switching jumpers and turners. See also Grades K-1: Rhythmic Activities, Lesson 22, page 231.

Jumping and Chanting

Keep the same formation.

1. Work on one or two chants per day:
    *   Chant 1: "Chickety, Chickety"
        Chickety, chickety, chickety, chop,
        How many times before I stop?
        One, two, three, four (and so on).
    *   Chant 2: "Bobby, Bobby"
        Bobby, Bobby, at the gate,
        Eating cherries from a plate.
        How many cherries did he eat?
        One, two, three, four (and so on).
    *   Chant 3: "Down in the Valley"
        Down in the valley,
        Where the green grass grows,
        Sat little rabbits all in rows.
        Along came Mary,
        and she touched them on the nose.
        How many noses did she touch?
        One, two, three, four (and so on).
2. Say each chant, and then have the children practice each chant while taking turns jumping.

Concluding Activities (5 minutes)

Jumping and Chanting

Keep the same formation.

1. Have the groups continue practicing jumping rope and chanting.
2. Have the children practice running in the front door and running out the back door.
3. Have them practice jumping with two-footed single and double jumps.

RHYTHMIC ACTIVITIES

LESSON 25
JUMPING SHORT ROPES

Student Objectives

- Jump rhythmically in place without a rope.
- Swing a rope in circles overhead and to the side of the body to a drumbeat.

Equipment and Materials

- 1 short jump rope (6 ft) per child
- 1 drum

Warm-Up Activities (5 minutes)

Jump the Line

Arrange the students in scatter formation, each child with a short rope laid out in a straight line on the floor or ground.

1. Have the students practice jumping and hopping back and forth over the rope to a drumbeat.
2. Begin at a slow tempo and gradually increase the speed.

Skill-Development Activities (20 minutes)

Helicopter

Keep the children in scatter formation, each with a jump rope.

1. Describe and demonstrate the activity: *With both ends of the rope in one hand, swing the rope in a circle overhead. Be sure you stay in your own space and hold the rope tightly, so no one gets hurt.*
2. Have the children practice the helicopter with each hand.

Single-Sided Taps

Keep the children in scatter formation, each with a jump rope.

1. Describe and demonstrate the activity: *Holding both ends of the rope in one hand, swing the rope in a circle on one side of your body.*
2. Provide a drumbeat, and have the students practice single-sided taps to the drumbeat with each hand.

Double-Sided Taps

Keep the children in scatter formation, each with a jump rope.

1. Describe and demonstrate the activity: *Holding both ends of the rope in one hand, swing the rope in a circle once on one side of your body and once on the opposite side of your body.*
2. Provide a drumbeat, and have the students practice double-sided taps to a drumbeat with each hand.
3. Have the students practice jumping in place to a drumbeat while doing double-sided taps.

Basic Jump Forward and Backward

Keep the children in scatter formation, each with a jump rope.

1. Describe and demonstrate the skill: *Turn the rope forward overhead and jump over it with both feet together as it comes over to hit the floor. You can also do this backward.*
2. Have the students practice the basic jump forward.
3. Have them practice the basic jump backward.

Concluding Activities (5 minutes)

Jump Rope Routine 1

Arrange the children in a large circle or semicircle, each with a jump rope.

1. Have the children perform the following sequence:
   Eight helicopters
   Eight single-sided taps with right hand
   Eight single-sided taps with left hand
   Eight double-sided taps
2. Repeat.

RHYTHMIC ACTIVITIES

LESSONS 26 AND 27
JUMPING SHORT ROPES

Student Objectives

- Jump a short rope five times consecutively without missing.
- Create a simple routine using helicopter, single-sided taps, and double-sided taps.

Equipment and Materials

- 1 short jump rope (6 ft) per child

Warm-Up Activities (5 minutes)

Rope Challenges

Arrange the children in scatter formation, each child with a short rope placed in a straight line on the floor or ground. Have the children perform jumping and hopping activities back and forth over the rope. For example: *Try walking forward on top of the rope (running around the rope, leaping over the rope, galloping around someone else's rope).*

Skill-Development Activities (20 minutes)

Jump Rope Skills

Keep the children in scatter formation, each with a jump rope.

1. Review the jump rope skills they have learned: basic jump (helicopter, single-sided taps, double-sided taps).
2. Have the children practice the jump skills.

Creative Jump Rope Routines

Keep the children in scatter formation, each with a jump rope.

1. Have a child name one of the jump rope skills just reviewed.
2. Have another child pick a number (4, 8, or 16), and have the children perform the skill for that number of counts.
3. Repeat, but each time have the children perform all previous skills in addition to the newly selected skill.

Concluding Activities (5 minutes)

Rope Routines

Keep the children in scatter formation, each with a jump rope.

1. Have each child create a routine using the skills learned.
2. Select a volunteer to demonstrate his or her creative routine.
3. Repeat as time allows.

RHYTHMIC ACTIVITIES

LESSON 28
FORMATION MARCHING

Student Objectives

- Cooperate to make formations.
- Follow verbal directions.
- Remember a movement sequence.

Equipment and Materials

- Marching music
- 6 cones
- 1 small flag (or streamer or wand) per child

Warm-Up Activities (5 minutes)

Fitness Circle

See Grades K-1: Rhythmic Activities, Warm-Ups, page 185. Use one variation.

Skill-Development Activities (20 minutes)

Grand March

Use the cones to define a large (40- by 60-ft) rectangle. Have the children line up single file, perpendicular to one end of the rectangle (see figure on page 240).

1. As the music begins, help the children clap to the beat.
2. Explain the activity:

    You will do three skills: clapping to the beat, marking time (marching in place) to the beat, and walking in a formation to the beat.

    The "formation" is marching around the outside of this large rectangle. I will stand near the turning point and I will tell you by pointing if you should turn right or left, showing you which half of the rectangle you will march around.

2. Describe and demonstrate each skill.
3. Tell the children: *First, though, let's clap to the music. Now walk in place to the beat.*
4. Have the children practice the Grand March:

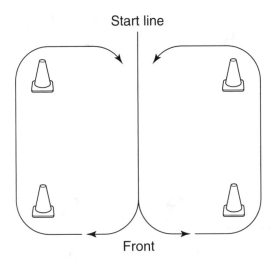

Start line

Front

- *With the beat, the first person in line will begin walking (marching), followed a few beats later by the next person in line, and so forth. (Name) begin walking to the beat toward me, (wait several beats). (Name) now you begin walking (and so forth until all children have moved around the rectangle).*

- *Now let's make this trickier. We will double the number of marchers in a row on each round. Watch where I point so you will know what to do. We will try this without the music first. (Name) begin marching now.* This begins as before, however when the children arrive at the starting position they will match up with a partner and repeat the pattern. As a pair approaches you, both children will turn to one side. When the pair reaches the starting place each pair will match with another pair, doubling the number in a row. Eventually all children will march in one row from the back line to the front.

5. Walk the children through the formation, first without, then with the music.

Concluding Activities (5 minutes)

Flag Grand March

Line up children as in the Grand March, one child with a flag (or streamer or wand). Place enough flags (or streamers or wands) for the rest of the class near the starting position.

1. Describe and demonstrate the activity:

   The first child begins the march carrying a flag (or streamer or wand), which he or she waves in time to the music as he or she marches.

   At the end of the first round, the partner joining the flag bearer picks up a flag.

   The two children wave these in unison (to the same side, at the same pace to the beat) making a figure eight in front of their bodies.

   The flag should make a complete "8" every two steps (for faster marches every four steps).

   The first row will all have flags, so each time the row size is doubled the new additions must pick up a flag at the starting position.

2. Have the children practice the Flag Grand March.

G R A D E S RHYTHMIC ACTIVITIES
K-1

LESSON 29
FORMATION MARCHING

Student Objectives

- Cooperate to make formations.
- Use equipment while marching.
- Remember a movement sequence.

Equipment and Materials

- Marching music
- Streamers
- Banners or sticks
- 4 cones to mark a rectangle or square
- Signal

Warm-Up Activities (5 minutes)

Fitness Circle

See Grades K-1: Rhythmic Activities, Warm-Ups, page 185. Use one variation.

Skill-Development Activities (20 minutes)

Circle March

Arrange the children in lines of four to six, standing shoulder-to-shoulder.

1. Describe and demonstrate the activity:

    The goal is to have your group keep a straight line while marching in a circle with one end of the line used as the anchor. This is easiest to learn by beginning with each child placing his or her right arm around the shoulder of the child to their immediate right (point).

    The child with no one to the right is the Anchor. That child will stay in one location, marching in place (marking time) as the line rotates (turns) around the Anchor in time to the beat.

2. Have the children practice the Circle March.

3. Repeat several times, varying who functions as the anchor.

4. Tell the children: *Reverse by placing your left arm over the person to your left. The child on the left end of the line becomes the anchor.*

5. Repeat several times, varying who functions as the anchor.

6. Combine groups to make the line longer, and have the children practice going to the right and to the left several times.

7. Variation: You can also have students practice this skill with their arms dropped to the side rather than over the shoulder of the adjacent child.

Circle Grand March

Arrange children for the Grand March. See Grades K-1: Rhythmic Activities, Lesson 28, page 239.

1. Begin by doing the Grand March until the rows contain four children.
2. Explain the activity: *On the signal the rows of four will circle to the right, with the child on the right as Anchor.*
3. Have the children practice the Circle Grand March. The best time to do this is when all the groups of four that have been formed are marching forward. With practice you can give the circle signal any time during the Grand March.
4. Repeat circle signals until all of the children are in one large circle. Stop the march and the music if the children have trouble and correct problems.

Concluding Activities (5 minutes)

Circle Grand March

Use the cones to define a large (40- by 60-ft) rectangle. Have the children line up single file, perpendicular to one end of the rectangle.

1. Complete the routine several times, allowing different children to be the leader.
2. Variation: Have the children do the march from the corners diagonally across the square (use a square rather than a rectangle for this variation), with two single lines to begin. Have these lines cross in the middle, then each line split and join the partner line in the adjacent corner. Children must anticipate and time when the lines will cross so no one has to wait and no one bumps into another marcher.

GRADES K-1

GYMNASTICS

Gymnastics lessons can enhance many other areas of a child's movement education and experiences. It promotes fitness, for example, especially flexibility and muscular strength and endurance. Moreover, tumbling is a valuable and fun activity as well as the foundation for floor exercise, an Olympic gymnastics event. Students may also have opportunities to use tumbling in other venues, such as cheerleading and dance. Partner stunts promote cooperation, trust, and fun. Children use many of the skills included in the large equipment lessons on the playground, without instruction.

However, some teachers may feel uncomfortable teaching some skills. For example, you may feel rope climbing is too difficult for you to supervise or handstands too difficult to spot. And some schools may not have the large equipment. In either case, do what is possible in terms of equipment and your comfort level, including all or part of the lessons as you deem appropriate. You know your students and situation better than anyone; therefore, your judgment is critical to the success and safety of your students.

UNIT ORGANIZATION

The early lessons in this unit cover awareness of body parts, understanding directions, and practicing locomotor skills. Next, several lessons explore pretumbling and tumbling skills. Then we cover partner stunts and small equipment (similar to European, Danish, and rhythmic gymnastics, including balls and streamers). The final lessons allow students to explore large equipment, such as the balance beam and vaulting box. See tables G1.1, G1.2, and G1.3 for sample unit plans.

We have organized these lessons so that the easier or prerequisite skills come first, progressing to more difficult skills within each lesson and from lesson to lesson. Kindergarten students may not master all of the skills in a lesson, so plan to repeat such lessons until most students master the skills. Remember, however, we intend the lessons to be repeated in first grade, so you can wait and introduce more difficult skills then when mastery is likely to be easier.

LESSON ORGANIZATION

For safety reasons, we have structured the lessons in this unit more tightly and have often suggested that fewer children participate at one time than in the other units. This is especially true of the tumbling, partner stunts, and large equipment lessons. Children may need spotting—your physical guidance—in a task. Furthermore, a child who is out of control can hurt him- or herself or others. Your close supervision can help ensure all children remain calm and focused appropriately. While this is true of any instructional setting, it seems to apply more in gymnastics settings. One reason to teach gymnastics is that children will try most of these activities, and it is clearly safer to do so with supervision, proper equipment, and expert instruction than without them. We believe that gymnastics is both safe and fun when the instruction and supervision is appropriate.

Immediately following this introduction are the warm-ups for this section. The lessons refer to this core of activities. Feel free, however, to vary these warm-ups, remembering that stretching is important before participating in any gymnastics lesson.

Since many of the tasks demand skill and fitness considerable practice is necessary. This means you can and should repeat the lessons to help students master the skills. Within the lessons, have students repeat tasks until they achieve mastery. Repeating a task two or three times consecutively, moving on to another task, revisiting the first task, then moving on to another task, and so forth works well. Revisiting skills from the previous lesson is also helpful, as is repeating the lessons we have designated for repetition.

Encourage and motivate children by telling them that these skills take time to learn, which means practicing or repeating the skill. One way is to simply help the children appreciate effort, practice, and individuality. Some children will have had more experience and find the skills easier to master. Others will struggle more. Tell students that the sport of gymnastics is judged on two characteristics: correct execution and difficulty, and "doing each skill right" is the most important factor. Fortunately, correct execution is also safe execution.

There are numerous ways to organize these lessons. Table G1.3 summarizes the content of our gymnastics lessons. To cover this content, you could designate one day per week as "gymnastics day" or teach an eight-week gymnastics unit as presented in table G1.2. You could use table G1.1 as written to create a six-week gymnastics unit. Or you could scatter each week of the six- or eight-week plan throughout the school year.

TEACHING HINTS

As you well know, practicing skills allows students to master the skill, and repetition is an essential part of practice. Indeed, most children want many turns and do not want to stop at the end of class. You may want to vary practice by introducing a skill, practicing that skill several times for each child, then either introducing a new skill or reviewing a previous skill. Then alternate the two skills for several turns. You can continue this process, adding a new skill and practicing that with previous skills so that you do one turn of four or five skills with one child per group, then repeat the sequence with the next child in line. This type of practice is interesting. You may want to encourage the children in line to watch by asking them the order of the skills before their turn.

Encourage, recognize, and praise good skill execution. Rather than focusing on learning new and difficult skills, help children focus on mastering and executing skills correctly. This encourages all children to participate fully as well as promotes safety.

SAFETY CONSIDERATIONS

You must establish clear rules for practicing gymnastics. For example, practice only on the mats, have only one person on a mat at a time (unless specifically told otherwise by the teacher), and use equipment only as intended. We recommend dividing the children into as many groups as you have mats and space, keeping groups as small as possible to increase participation opportunities. Have each group sit in a line near the mat, waiting for turns and specific instructions. You may find it helpful to have a carpet square for each waiting child to sit on.

When starting each stunt, call the first child in each group to the mat. Do not allow children to stand on the floor at the end of the mat to begin a task. Instead, as you give instructions, children should stand (sit or lie) on the mat, beginning their turn when you say "Begin." You may want to use cues to regulate the movement; for example "bend, hands down, look at your tummy, roll." Stand so that you can see all children. If the activity requires spotting, you should

Table G1.1: Using the Gymnastics Lessons in a Six-Week Gymnastics Unit

Week	Content	Number of different lessons	Lessons that should be repeated
1	Body parts, directions, locomotor skills	5 (1-5)	1, 4
2	Pretumbling and tumbling	5 (6-10)	9, 10
3	Tumbling	5 (11-15)	14
4	Partner stunts	4 (16-19)	18, 19
5	Small equipment	5 (20-24)	23
6	Large equipment	5 (25-29)	29

spot the children. While this means more waiting for turns, it greatly increases safety. When children have learned to take turns, however, you can assign different skills to each mat, assigning one skill that you must spot, while having the children at the other mats do skills that do not require spotting. Remember to place yourself so you can see the other mats while spotting to monitor behavior. Efficient organization allows for maximum practice and safety.

Finally, it is your responsibility to see that you or another responsible adult maintains the gymnastics equipment in good order. You should check the mats and equipment to make sure everything is in good repair each day. In addition, make sure mats are cleaned regularly.

Table G1.2: Using the Gymnastics Lessons in an Eight-Week Gymnastics Unit

Week	Monday	Tuesday	Wednesday	Thursday	Friday
1	Lesson 1	Lesson 1	Lesson 2	Lesson 3	Lesson 4
2	Lesson 4	Lesson 5	Lesson 6	Lesson 7	Lesson 8
3	Lesson 9	Lesson 9	Lesson 10	Lesson 10	Lesson 11
4	Lesson 12	Lesson 13	Lesson 14	Lesson 14	Lesson 15
5	Lesson 16	Lesson 17	Lesson 18	Lesson 18	Lesson 19
6	Lesson 19	Lesson 20	Lesson 21	Lesson 22	Lesson 23
7	Lesson 23	Lesson 24	Lesson 25	Lesson 26	Lesson 27
8	Lesson 28	Lesson 29	Lesson 29	Lesson 29	Choose one lesson: 1, 4, 9, 10, 14, 18, 23, 29

Table G1.3: Unit Plan for Grades K-1: Gymnastics

Week 15: locomotor skills	Week 16: warm-up routine and pretumbling	Week 17: tumbling
Monday: body parts, positions in space, directions, Hokey Pokey Tuesday: fundamental locomotor patterns Wednesday: locomotor patterns and combinations Thursday: combining locomotor skills and body awareness Friday: evaluating the locomotor skills, body awareness, and spatial abilities of the children	Monday: introduction to gymnastics Tuesday: animal walks Wednesday: pretumbling Thursday: pretumbling and animal walks Friday: animal walks and locomotor skills	Monday: introduce locomotor and balance combinations, continue basic tumbling Tuesday: balance stunts, balance combinations, and tumbling Wednesday: tumbling Thursday: tumbling Friday: tumbling checklist

Week 18: partner stunts	Week 30: small equipment	Week 31: large equipment
Monday: partner stunts Tuesday: partner stunts Wednesday: partner stunts Thursday: partner obstacle course Friday: review	Monday: small equipment Tuesday: foam balls and wands Wednesday: hoops and streamers Thursday: small apparatus Friday: small apparatus	Monday: large apparatus Tuesday: large apparatus Wednesday: large apparatus Thursday: large apparatus Friday: large apparatus

Week 32: gymnastics review

WARM-UPS

Body Parts Runaround

Arrange the children in scatter formation.

1. Call out a movement and a body part.
2. Have the children touch the body part and execute the movement until you signal them to stop.

   Some example movements include the following:

   Run in a circle; touch your foot (head, toes, neck, back, ankle, feet).

   Hop forward; touch your knee (arms, front, side, chest, shoulder).

   Jump up and down; touch your hip (elbow, thigh, calf, bottom or seat, stomach).

3. Discuss any problems children had with body parts or directions.
4. Variation: Make new combinations of body parts and movements.

Circle Challenges

Arrange the children in a large circle, 5 to 10 ft between children, right shoulders toward the center of the circle. Challenge the children with the following tasks (warn them not to pass or bump the person in front of them in the circle):

Walk quickly while swinging your arms.

Walk slowly on tiptoe.

Hop on your right foot.

Hop on your left foot.

Stop. Turn around so your left shoulder is in the center of the circle.

Skip, swinging your arms and lifting yourself as high as you can.

Walk, rocking as far to each side as possible with each step.

Point and Run

Arrange the children in scatter formation; stand at the front of the area facing the children.

1. Have the children run through general space. Have the children continue to run in one direction until you signal them to change direction.
2. Whistle to call their attention, then use a hand signal to indicate a change in direction: signal with the thumb (toward you so the thumb points in the direction the children are to move—front) or finger (left, right, or away from you so the finger points in the direction the children are to move—back).
3. Remind the children not to bump into each other.

Steps for Grades K-1 Warm-Up Routine

Arrange the children in a large circle facing the circle.

Locomotor Component: Run and Slide

1. Describe and demonstrate this component:

   With arms spread to the side, slide to the right for 16 counts.

   Then repeat 16 counts to the left.

   Turn your right shoulder toward the center of the circle and run, taking large and high steps, for 32 counts.

   Turn and repeat 32 counts to the left.

2. Have the children perform this component.

Stretching Component: Legs, Torso, Arms

1. Describe and demonstrate this component:

   Standing with your arms together and straight, feet together, legs straight, and facing the center of the circle, reach overhead, keeping your feet flat on the floor (eight counts).

   Bend at the waist, reaching forward, with your knees slightly bent (eight counts).

   Stand straight, bend right (eight counts).

   Repeat to the left.

   Touch toes, bending forward and downward, knees slightly bent (eight counts).

   Do waist circles: Bend left, back, right, and front (eight counts each); *repeat to the right.*

   Sit facing the center of the circle with your legs straight and spread apart (straddled) and stretch forward, left, forward, right (eight counts each); *repeat. Rolling onto your tummy facing the center of the circle with your arms in front and looking up at the ceiling, arch back as far as possible* (eight counts each); *repeat.*

2. Have the children perform this component. Cue the children: *Stretch up, two, three, four, five, six, seven, eight; forward, two, three, four, five, six, seven, eight; up and right, two, three, four, five, six, seven, eight; to the left, two, three, four, five, six, seven, eight; toe touch, two, three, four, five, six, seven, eight; circle left, back, right, forward, reverse, right, back, left, forward; sitting reach forward, left, forward, right, reach forward, left, forward, right; roll over and stretch back, two, three, four; relax, stretch back two, three, four.*

Standing stretches

Straddle stretches

Back arches

Endurance Component: Abdomen and Arms

Do up to 10 sit-ups with arms crossed on chest, knees bent, and feet flat on floor, and then up to 10 regular push-ups. See Grades K-1: Fitness, Lesson 2, pages 26 and 27.

Grades K-1 Warm-Up Routine

Arrange the children in a large circle facing the center.

1. Teach all parts of the warm-up as a routine.
2. Have the children perform the following sequence of steps:

   Slide right (16 counts),
   Slide left (16 counts),
   Run clockwise (32 counts),
   Run counterclockwise (32 counts),
   Stretch upward (8 counts),
   Stretch forward (8 counts),
   Stretch right (8 counts),
   Stretch left (8 counts),
   Stretch downward (8 counts),
   Two waist circles (4 counts),
   Two straddle stretches (4 counts),
   Two back arches (8 counts), *and*
   Sit-ups and push-ups.

LESSON 1
BODY PARTS, POSITIONS IN SPACE, DIRECTIONS

Student Objectives

- Identify body parts and spatial directions.
- Explain the signals per direction.
- Participate in gymnastics activities.
- Follow instructions.
- Cooperate when playing Identify the Body Part.

Equipment and Materials

- Whistle
- 1 hoop (30-36 in.) per child or pair
- Music: "Hokey Pokey" (with and without words) from *Hokey Pokey*, Melody House (MHD 33)

Warm-Up Activities (5 minutes)

Point and Run

See Grades K-1: Gymnastics, Warm-Ups, page 247.

Skill-Development Activities (20 minutes)

Movement Challenges

Arrange the children in scatter formation or in a semicircle, with all children visible to you.

1. Tell the children: *Touch your foot (head, chest, knees, toes, elbows, legs, thighs, calf, back, shoulder, arm, hip, wrist, ankle, finger, front, bottom, neck, stomach, forearm, face) with both hands.*

2. Repeat step 1 with: *Wiggle (or move) your foot.* Continue with the remaining body parts.

Give each child or pair of children a hoop. Keep the children in scatter formation or in a semicircle, standing near their hoops.

3. Have the children perform the following challenges:

   Put your elbow (leg, knee, head, foot) inside your hoop.

   Get inside the hoop (in front of the hoop, beside the hoop, part in and part out of the hoop, under the hoop).

   Walk around the hoop.

   Move the hoop around you.

Next, arrange partners in scatter formation.

4. Tell the children: *Touch your partner's foot.* Continue with the body parts previously listed. Continue with modified formations: *Stand beside (back-to-back with, elbow-to-elbow with) your partner.*

Identify the Body Part

Keep partners in scatter formation. Designate one partner as the caller and the other as the mover.

1. Describe the activity: *The mover moves a body part, and the caller says the name of the part out loud. We will repeat this several times, then switch caller and mover.*
2. Have the children play Identify the Body Part.

Movement Challenges

Arrange individuals in scatter formation. Challenge the children with the following tasks:

Raise your right (left) hand.

Move your left (right) foot.

Walk to your right (backward to the left).

Concluding Activities (5 minutes)

Hokey Pokey

Arrange the children in a circle, facing center.

1. Play a record or tape of the music. Try the first few times with a voice singing the words, then let the children sing to an instrumental version. As they follow the directions, have the children rock, or move back and forth as one would in a rocking chair, with the music.
2. On the chorus (*You do the hokey pokey and you turn yourself around, that's what it's all about!*), direct the children to turn in individual circles while pointing fingers to the sky and shaking hands. Then (*You do the hokey pokey, h-o-o-key p-o-o-key*) have the children get on their knees and bow with their arms extended and hands wiggling.

Turn yourself around   (H-o-o-k-e-y P-o-o-k-e-y)

LESSON 2
FUNDAMENTAL LOCOMOTOR PATTERNS

Student Objectives

- Practice the fundamental patterns of walking, running, jumping, hopping (left and right), galloping (left and right), and skipping.
- Identify hopping and galloping.
- Cooperate with a partner during partner matching parts game.

Equipment and Materials

- None

Safety Tip

- Remind the children not to bump into each other.

Warm-Up Activities (5 minutes)

Body Parts Runaround

See Grades K-1: Gymnastics, Warm-Ups, page 246. Be sure to discuss any problems the children have with body parts or directions.

Skill-Development Activities (20 minutes)

Movement Tasks

Keep the children in scatter formation.

1. Tell the children: *Walk in a straight line (a circle, along a zigzagging path).*
2. Repeat with running. Tell the children: *Run fast (slowly).*

Hopping

Keep the children in scatter formation.

1. Describe and demonstrate the skill: *This is a series of small jumps where the same foot touches the ground as your body moves from one place to another. Use your hands for balance.*
2. Have the children practice hopping on the right foot.
3. Have them repeat on the left foot.
4. Challenge the children: *Who can hop sideways (backward)?*

Jumping in a Series

Keep the children in scatter formation.

1. Describe and demonstrate the skill:

   Put your feet together and use your arms to make your body move forward and upward.

   Take off and land from both feet to both feet.

   Keep doing this to move your body from one place to another.

2. Ask the children: *What is the difference between this and hopping?*

3. Have the children practice jumping in a series. Tell the children: *Show me jumping. Now hopping.*

Galloping

Keep the children in scatter formation.

1. Describe and demonstrate the skill: *Step-together-step, with the same foot leading all the time.*
2. Have the children practice galloping with one foot leading.
3. Have them repeat with the opposite foot leading.

Skipping

Keep the children in scatter formation.

1. Describe and demonstrate the skill: *Step-hop, step-hop. The faster you can go, the higher you can go. Use your arms to generate force (create power).*
2. Have the children say "Step-hop, step-hop."
3. Have them practice skipping.

Concluding Activities (5 minutes)

Partner Matching Parts Game

Arrange partners in scatter formation.

1. Describe and demonstrate the game:

   I will call out the name of a body part.

   Partners touch those body parts to each other (see figure).

   For instance, I might call out "hand," and you and your partner should touch hands.
2. Have the children play the Partner Matching Parts Game.

GYMNASTICS

LESSON 3
LOCOMOTOR PATTERNS AND COMBINATIONS

Student Objectives

- Demonstrate various locomotor patterns and at least one combination of two patterns.
- Distinguish between personal and general space.
- Cooperate while playing Partner Follow the Leader.

Equipment and Materials

- None

Safety Tip

- Remind the children of personal and general space.

Warm-Up Activities (5 minutes)

Point and Run

See Grades K-1: Gymnastics, Warm-Ups, page 247.

Skill-Development Activities (20 minutes)

Movement Challenges

Keep the children in scatter formation.

1. Tell the children: *Walk from your space to another space.*
2. Describe the route taken, for example, from your classroom to the physical education area. Call it a "pathway," "pattern," or "route."
3. Describe an alternate route from your classroom to the physical education area. Call it a pathway, pattern, or route, too.
4. Tell the children: *Walk back to your space a different way, using a different route or pathway.*

   Are there more ways to travel between spaces differently, other than a different route or path? We might use different levels (high, low) or walk backward.
5. *Walk backward on your toes (on heels, bent over, sideways).*

Sliding

Keep the children in scatter formation.

1. Describe and demonstrate the skill: *Sliding is a kind of walking in a sideways direction with a slight hop in the middle, in which the following foot never passes the leading foot.*
2. Have the children practice sliding. Add: *Slide with your arms out.*
3. Have them practice sliding at various speeds in both directions.

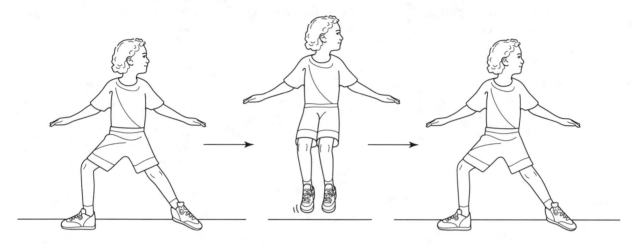

Galloping

Arrange the children in scatter formation. See Grades K-1: Gymnastics, Lesson 2, page 254 for basic instructions.

1. Ask the children: *What is the name for the kind of running a horse does?* (Galloping.) *Galloping is like sliding. Can you tell me how? Can you show me galloping?*
2. Have the children practice leading with each foot.
3. Ask the children: *Who can gallop with one foot leading, then switch to the other foot leading?*
4. Discuss and demonstrate "right," "left," "front," and "back."
5. Challenge the children with the following tasks:

    Slide right.

    Gallop forward.

    Run backward.

    Slide to the right.

    Gallop with your left foot leading.

Movement Challenges

Arrange partners in scatter formation.

1. Tell the children: *One partner stands still, the other partner walk around your partner. Stop!*
2. Have the pairs switch standing-still partner and moving partner.
3. Repeat; then continue with: *Move until you are in front of your partner.*

Concluding Activities (5 minutes)

Partner Follow the Leader

Keep partners in scatter formation.

1. Have partners alternate being leader every one minute.
2. Direct the leader to use one of today's locomotor patterns to move about the area with the partner following using the same pattern: *Leaders, you can walk, slide, or gallop. Change which foot you lead with. Partners, follow the leader!*

GRADES K-1

LESSON 4
COMBINING LOCOMOTOR SKILLS AND BODY AWARENESS

Student Objectives

- Demonstrate a locomotor skill while identifying a body part.
- Perform movements in three or more directions.
- Cooperate while doing movement challenges.
- Take turns while doing show-offs.

Equipment and Materials

- None

Warm-Up Activities (5 minutes)

Body Parts Runaround

See Grades K-1: Gymnastics, Warm-Ups, page 246.

Skill-Development Activities (20 minutes)

Movement Challenges

Keep the children in scatter formation.
 Challenge the children with the following tasks:

> *Walk forward, touch your nose.*
>
> *Wave your left hand. Keep walking. Touch your knees (toes).*
>
> *Jump backward, wave both arms overhead. Hands on hips. Keep jumping. Put one hand on your head, the other on your knee.*
>
> *Gallop in a circle, arms in front of you. Tip your head from side-to-side. Keep galloping. Clap your hands behind you.*
>
> *Hop on your right foot, hands on hips. Touch your chest. Keep hopping. Put both hands on your head. Touch your wrist (elbow, shoulder).*

Movement Directions

Gather the children into an information formation.

1. Discuss the meanings of "forward," "front," "in front of." Have two children demonstrate these relationships.
2. Discuss "backward," "back," "in back of." Have two different children demonstrate these.
3. Discuss "beside," "next to," "left," "right." Have two different children demonstrate these relationships.
4. Discuss "straight," "curved," "zigzag." Have one child demonstrate each.

Movement Challenges

Arrange the children in four parallel lines facing you. In each line, space the children about three ft apart.

Challenge the children with the following tasks:

Walk in your own small circle.

Hop the opposite direction in your own small circle.

Jump in a straight line toward me.

Run backward in a straight line. Be sure you look over your shoulder, so you don't bump into anyone.

Each line walk in your own circle, so we have four circles.

Make your circles into lines again.

Hop in a zigzag pattern in general space.

Concluding Activities (5 minutes)

Show-Offs

Arrange the children in a circle, sitting.

1. Have one child at a time demonstrate a movement sequence that uses two locomotor skills (e.g., run and hop) and two spatial patterns (e.g., straight and zigzag).
2. As the child performs the sequence, encourage the remaining children to identify the skills and patterns out loud.
3. Allow as many children as possible to demonstrate their sequences.

GYMNASTICS

LESSON 5

EVALUATING THE LOCOMOTOR SKILLS, BODY AWARENESS, AND SPATIAL ABILITIES OF THE CHILDREN

Student Objectives

- Name the skills of sliding, galloping, and skipping when demonstrated.
- Work cooperatively as a group when moving across the floor in Checklist Skills.

Equipment and Materials

- 1 copy of the Grades K-1: Locomotor Skills checklist for gymnastics per each group (see appendix)

Warm-Up Activities (5 minutes)

Point and Run

See Grades K-1: Gymnastics, Warm-Ups, page 247. First grade classes completing the evaluation checklist may choose to delete the warm-up activity for today.

Skill-Development Activities (20 minutes)

Locomotor Skills Checklist

Arrange the children in small groups (corresponding to your checklist order). Assign each group to a space along an edge of the play area. Appoint one child as leader in each group; direct the other children to stay in checklist order.

1. Ask one group to move across the area doing a locomotor pattern.
2. Observe each group. If necessary, demonstrate, or have a child demonstrate, the pattern.
3. Note individual performances on your checklist.
4. Complete each pattern with each group. Give additional turns to children who have trouble.
5. Observe these patterns:

    Walking in patterns

    Running (fast and slow)

Sliding
Jumping in a series
Hopping (each foot)
Galloping (each side leading)
Skipping

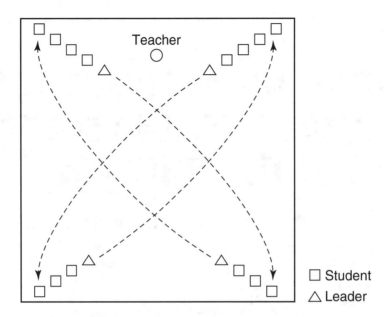

Concluding Activities (5 minutes)

Follow the Leader

Keep the children in the same groups with the same leaders in the same areas.

1. Tell the leaders to execute various locomotor skills in varying patterns as the remaining children in the groups copy their leader's movements.
2. After a period of time switch leaders, trying to allow each child a turn at being leader.

Name the Skill

Continue with the same setup.

1. Ask the leader to demonstrate a locomotor skill.
2. Select one of the three groups to name the skill. Repeat with each leader.

GRADES K-1

GYMNASTICS

LESSON 6
INTRODUCTION TO GYMNASTICS

Student Objectives

- Follow cues during warm-ups.
- Recognize safety rules.
- Complete the warm-up routine.

Equipment and Materials

- 1 mat (4 ft × 8 ft) per group
- Background music (optional)

Safety Tip

- Keep the children in a semicircle or scattered groups where you can see them all.

Warm-Up Activities (5 minutes)

Circle Challenges

See Grades K-1: Gymnastics, Warm-Ups, page 246. Remember to warn the children that they are not to pass the students in front of them in the circle.

Skill-Development Activities (20 minutes)

Rules

Gather the children into an information formation.

1. Tell the children: *Remember, we have an important rule: Do not put your hands on anyone else. Why is it dangerous to break this rule?* (We might hurt someone, or they could hurt us.)

2. *Another rule is that we only allow one person on the mat at a time. Wait until the person in front of you finishes before getting on the mat. What might happen if you take your turn too soon?* (Might bump into each other.)

3. *If you need help, ask the teacher. You must try everything, but you can have help!*

4. *Sit and do not talk while waiting for your turn. How will this help us learn?* (Everyone can still hear the teacher and no one is getting in the way moving around.)

5. Ask the children to tell you a rule, until all the rules have been repeated.

   - *Rule 1: Do not touch anyone else.*
   - *Rule 2: One person on the mat at a time.*
   - *Rule 3: Ask for help.*
   - *Rule 4: Sit quietly while waiting for your turn.*

Grades K-1 Warm-Up Routine

Arrange the children in circle formation, everyone facing center.

1. Ask the children: *Can everyone see me? Today we are going to learn a warm-up routine that we will use for the next few weeks.*

2. Describe and demonstrate each component of the warm-up routine, one by one. See Grades K-1: Gymnastics, Warm-Ups, page 246 for full descriptions.

3. Have the students practice each component, using the hints and sequences listed in the sections for each component of the routine.

4. Lead the children in doing the entire routine straight through.

Concluding Activities (5 minutes)

Elephant Walk

Arrange small groups at each mat.

Challenge the children with the following movement tasks, while emphasizing the rules:

With your arms straight and hands clasped together, bend at the waist and walk slowly, swinging your arms and swaying your whole body. Who can walk across the mat like an elephant walks?

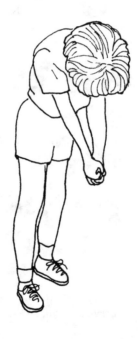

Camel Walk

Keep the same groups, each at a mat.

1. Challenge the children with the following movement tasks:

   With hands behind hips or waist and the elbows together, bend at the waist. Make your arms into the camel's hump.

   Move your body up and down by going onto your toes then bending your knees.

2. Remember to praise those who follow the rules.

GRADES K-1

GYMNASTICS

LESSON 7
ANIMAL WALKS

Student Objectives

- Demonstrate at least four different animal walks.
- Do five different warm-up activities.
- Explain two safety rules.

Equipment and Materials

- 1 mat (4 ft × 8 ft) per group

Safety Tip

- Occasionally have the children sit down, to calm them and make sure they're with their groups.

Warm-Up Activities (10 minutes)

Grades K-1 Warm-Up Routine

See Grades K-1: Gymnastics, Warm-Ups, page 249.

Skill-Development Activities (15 minutes)

Movement Challenges

Arrange small groups, each at a mat.

Crocodile Walk

1. Ask the children: *How would a crocodile walk?* (Lying on its tummy and alternating moving right leg and arm, then left leg and arm, it pulls its body forward.)
2. Have the children do the crocodile walk.

Kangaroo Walk

1. Ask the children: *Can you guess which animal this is?*
2. Describe and demonstrate the stunt: *With your hands cupped and palms down and touching chest, jump with both feet.*
3. Have the children practice the kangaroo walk. Ask: *Can you walk like a kangaroo?*

Giraffe Walk

1. Ask the children: *What is so special about a giraffe?* (It is very tall.)
2. Describe and demonstrate the stunt: *With hands cupped together and the arms extended overhead, walk on tiptoe, using your arms as the giraffe's head.*
3. Have the children practice the giraffe walk. Ask: *Can you walk like a giraffe?*

Frog Jump

1. Ask the children: *Can you name this animal?*
2. Describe and demonstrate the stunt: *Squatting with your hands between your legs, jump all at once, landing on your hands and feet at the same time.*
3. Have the children practice the frog jump. Ask: *Can you jump like a frog?*

Extension Activities

1. Bring pictures of various animals. When you hold up a picture, have the children respond with the appropriate animal walk.
2. Ask the children to name and walk like an animal that they have not done in class (e.g., snake, monkey, and so on). Let the children take turns demonstrating for the class, then have everyone try the new animal walks.

Concluding Activities (5 minutes)

Animal Walks

Arrange the children in a semicircle around one mat.
   Allow the children to demonstrate their favorite animal walks.

Rules

Keep the children in the semicircle.
   Ask the children to tell you a rule, until all the rules have been repeated.
   • *Rule 1: Do not touch anyone else.*

   • *Rule 2: One person on the mat at a time.*

   • *Rule 3: Ask for help.*

   • *Rule 4: Sit quietly while waiting for your turn.*

LESSON 8
PRETUMBLING

Student Objectives

- Demonstrate one balance, one roll, one flexibility skill, and one locomotor skill.
- State the most important safety rule for gymnastics.
- Cooperate with other children during balance challenge.

Equipment and Materials

- 1 mat (4 ft × 8 ft) per group
- Background music (optional)

Safety Tips

- Because this is the first day of tumbling, emphasize safety, especially the rule that there be only one person at a time on the mat.
- Allow only one child on the mat at a time, unless the instructions specifically state that more than one child should practice on the same mat.

Warm-Up Activities (7 to 10 minutes)

Grades K-1 Warm-Up Routine

See Grades K-1: Gymnastics, Warm-Ups, page 249.

Skill-Development Activities (15 to 20 minutes)

Basic Leap

Arrange small groups, each at a mat. The children will have to take turns practicing, so line up the children to emphasize that only one child goes at a time.

1. Describe and demonstrate the stunt:

    Run and take off on one foot, travel through the air, and land on the opposite foot.

    Stretch out your arms at shoulder height, slightly in front of your body.

    Practice so you can go farther and higher.

2. Upon your verbal cue, have one child from each group run across the area. Continue until all the children have had a turn.

3. Then ask the children: *Can you run using giant steps? Take as few steps as possible to travel the distance.* Have each child practice using giant steps, several times. Tell the children: *Count your steps. Let's see who can use the fewest steps.*

4. Have the children run a few little steps, then a giant step. Ask the children: *Can you make the giant step go high into the air?*

5. Describe and demonstrate the leap again. Tell the children: *"Leap" is the name of the skill I just performed—several small steps and a high giant step.*

6. Have the children practice leaping, moving their arms to the sides if necessary.

Log Roll

Continue with the same setup, reminding the children to take turns practicing one at a time.

1. Describe and demonstrate the stunt:

    Lying on one side with your arms and legs together and stretched out (extended), roll onto your stomach and quickly over onto your other side, continuing rolling over until you reach the other end of the mat.

    You start the rolling motion by turning your head and shoulders, then your trunk and legs. Your hands and feet should not push to turn your body.

2. Have the children practice the log roll with their heads all in the same direction.

3. Have the children repeat, rolling the opposite direction. Cue the children: *Keep your arms and legs straight.*

Rocker

Keep the same setup.

1. Describe and demonstrate the skill:

    Beginning in a tight tuck while sitting with hands and arms tightly holding knees, chin on chest, and forehead against knees, roll backward onto your back.

    While your body weight is on your shoulders, change the direction of the roll and rock back toward your feet until your bottom and feet are the only parts touching the ground. Continue rocking from your bottom and feet to your shoulders, and then reverse.

2. Have the children practice the rocker. Cue the children: *As you rock, try to get your shoulders off the mat, then your legs and hips off the mat.*

Straddle Scale

Continue with the same setup.

1. Describe and demonstrate the skill:

    Standing with feet together, slowly slide your feet out to each side with either your toes pointing in the direction of the slide or your feet parallel to each other (demonstrate "parallel" very clearly).

    As your feet move apart, lower your torso (define) so that when your feet have stretched as far sideways as is comfortable, your torso is parallel to (flat as) the ground.

    Stretch your arms out to the sides shoulder-high, so you can't see your hands when you are looking straight forward.

    Balance in this position for five counts, then reach to the floor with your arms, put your body weight on your arms, lower your chest to the floor, and gradually move your feet and legs together. Your body will end up flat on the floor.

2. Have the children practice the straddle scale.

One-Legged Balance

Continue with the same setup.

1. Describe and demonstrate the skill:

    Standing with your hands on your hips or waist, lift your left foot and place it against your right knee.

    Stand in this position as long as possible.

    Then repeat, touching your right foot to your left knee.

2. Have the children practice the one-legged balance. Give the children this tip: *Try looking at a place on the wall to maintain your balance.*

Balance Challenge

Continue with the same setup.

1. Have the first child in each group move onto the mat.
2. Name one of the balance activities learned today. Have all the first children do the balance activity, holding the position until all are balanced. (Use the cue "Look at me," and stand in one place while the children balance.)
3. Repeat with a different balance challenge for each new child in line.

Concluding Activities (5 to 8 minutes)

Movement Challenges

Gather the children into an information formation.
  Discuss what the children have learned today:

    What were you best at? A few at a time, everyone show me your best skill.

    Which was your worst? Practice your worst.

Discussing the Importance of Warming Up

Gather the children into an information formation.

1. Begin the discussion: *Warming up is important for three reasons. First, to help our bodies prepare for gymnastics so there is less chance of injury. Second, to help our bodies become more flexible, which will allow us to do more and better gymnastics skills. Third, to increase our flexibility as part of physical fitness. Point to a body part that we stretched today.* (The lower back, legs, and shoulders.)

2. Ask the children: *How can you tell when you are stretching a body part?* (Sometimes it begins to hurt, other times it may feel warm.) *To be safe when stretching, move slowly and do not allow someone to push on your body to make a body part bend more than you can make it bend. When you feel pain during stretching you should stop. As you practice stretching, your body parts will be able to stretch farther or more easily.*

3. Ask the children for questions or comments.

GYMNASTICS

LESSON 9
PRETUMBLING AND ANIMAL WALKS

Student Objectives

- Take turns practicing.
- Follow the safety rule of waiting for a turn.
- Perform one additional animal walk and one new balance activity.
- State the cues for the forward roll.

Equipment and Materials

- 1 mat (4 ft × 8 ft) per group
- 1 jump rope per mat
- Background music (optional)

Safety Tip

- During practice time, stop the music as a signal to sit and get organized.

Warm-Up Activities (7 minutes)

Grades K-1 Warm-Up Routine

See Grades K-1: Gymnastics, Warm-Ups, page 249. If possible, encourage all to do at least 10 sit-ups and increase the number of push-ups to 5 or 10.

Skill-Development Activities (18 minutes)

Bear Walk

Arrange small groups, each at a mat. Remind the children that there should be only one child practicing at a time on each mat.

1. Describe and demonstrate the stunt: *With your hands on the floor and arms and legs straight, move one hand, then the foot on that side, then the other hand, then the foot on that side, rolling your body and "lumbering" while walking.*
2. Have the children practice the bear walk.

Puppy Run

Keep the same setup.

1. Describe and demonstrate the skill:

    Bend your knees, crouching down on all-fours.

    Let your hands support some of your body weight, look forward, and run.

    Now try sitting and lying on the floor like a dog.

2. Have the children practice the puppy run.

Animal Walk Game

Have groups of four to six line up.

1. Describe and demonstrate the game:

    The first child in each line begins to walk like an animal. The rest of the children in the group follow.

    The leader changes to another animal walk, and each child in that line follows.

    I will surprise you and (at random times) *call out the name of the animal walk a group is doing. When a group's animal walk is called out, the first child in that line goes to the end of the line, and the second child becomes the leader.*

2. Have the children play the Animal Walk Game.

3. Variations: *Does a cat move the same way as a dog?* Cue the ideas of stretching, moving quietly, dragging the feet a bit pigeon-toed. Have the children move like cats. Then have half of the children be cats, the other half dogs. *How do cats and dogs play together? How does an injured dog move? Sometimes they run on three legs or limp on one of the four.* Have the children move like an injured dog.

Rocker, One-Legged Balance, Log Roll

See Grades K-1: Gymnastics, Lesson 8, pages 270 and 271.

Forehead Touch

Continue with the same setup.

1. Describe and demonstrate the stunt: *Kneeling with hands joined behind your back, slowly lower your head and chest until your forehead touches the mat. Keep your hands behind your back. Keep your knees and feet together throughout the whole movement.*

2. Have the children practice the forehead touch.

3. If children are having trouble with this, especially overbalancing to avoid hitting their heads, allow them to practice a few times with one hand behind their backs and the other in front of them on the mat—but allow them to support their weight with one finger only!

4. Remind the children: *Be sure that your knees and feet are together throughout. Be sure to keep your hands behind you. Go slowly!*

Tightrope

Keep the same setup, but place one jump rope at each mat.

1. Describe and demonstrate the skill, relating it to the circus tightrope-walking with which some children may be familiar: *Walk on the jump rope as though it were above the ground, trying not to step off.* Ask the children: *What helps us balance?* Demonstrate balancing by using arms, looking at a spot, and watching the rope about 18 in. in front of your feet.

2. Have the children practice walking on a "tightrope." Remind students to use their arms to balance.

3. Variation: You can expand the activity making the rope curved, wiggly, and other shapes.

Forward Roll

Keep the same setup.

1. Describe and have a child demonstrate the skill:

   Begin in a squat with your hands on the mat shoulder-width apart, chin on chest, looking at your stomach.

   Bend your arms to bring your shoulders closer to the mat, overbalance, roll onto your shoulders, and continue to roll with your legs tucked.

   Keep your heels close to your bottom and your knees close to your chest, until your feet touch the ground and you are squatting again. (Variations will be presented later for the takeoff, roll, and landing phases.)

2. Have the children practice the forward roll. Cue each child in line: *Bend, hands on mat. Look at tummy. Straighten legs and roll onto your back. Stand up.* Or: *Hands on mat, chin on chest, bend arms, and straighten legs. Roll.*

3. Remind the children: *Land on your back.*

4. Don't worry if the children do not get all the way around to their feet. Stress the shoulder landing and keeping their heads out of the way.

Concluding Activities (5 minutes)

Regroup the children on mats according to what they need to practice (e.g., put those practicing the tightrope on one mat, the log roll on another, and the rocker on another).

Use this time to observe skills and offer individual instruction.

LESSON 10
ANIMAL WALKS AND LOCOMOTOR SKILLS

Student Objectives

- Practice locomotor skills and animal walks.
- Cooperate when playing Zoo.
- Demonstrate two or more animal walks when the animals are named.

Equipment and Materials

- Pictures of animals (perhaps the children could color these or find them in magazines)
- Animal word cards (optional, instead of pictures for children who can read)
- 1 mat (4 ft × 8 ft) per group

Safety Tip

- Remind the children of personal space and to keep their hands off other children.

Warm-Up Activities (5 minutes)

Grades K-1 Warm-Up Routine

See Grades K-1: Gymnastics, Warm-Ups, page 249.

Skill-Development Activities (20 minutes)

Animal Pictures

Arrange small groups, each at a mat.

1. Show animal pictures (chicken, pig, deer, tiger, shark, monkey, and so on).
2. Ask the children: *Can you walk like the animal in the picture?*
3. For classes who are able to read, you can use cards with the names instead of pictures. Hold up a picture or card, and have the children respond with the appropriate animal walk. You may want to repeat some of the animals; try changing cards rapidly or using the same animal twice in a row.

Animal Walk Game

Gather the children into an information formation.

1. Ask the children to name the animal walks that have been done in physical education class (bear, puppy, crocodile, kangaroo, frog, elephant, camel). Ask the children to name additional animals (e.g., porpoise, hamster, rooster, tiger).

2. Review the Animal Walk Game (see Grades K-1: Gymnastics, Lesson 9, page 274; see also animal walk descriptions in Lessons 6 and 7, pages 264-267).

3. Have individuals who name new animals demonstrate how those animals walk. If the children are having trouble thinking of animals, ask them about pets, farm animals, things in the ocean, animals from Africa, and so on. After one child demonstrates, have the rest of the class try.

Arrange the children in four groups. Each group should form a line.

4. Have the children play the Animal Walk Game.

5. You can expand this further by discussing the animals' homes, food, and so on.

Doggie Day Game

Keep the children in the same setup.
  *For many children, dogs are more familiar than other animals.

1. Ask the children to name different breeds, then to show differences in how those dogs move. For example, tell the children: *Hound dogs (bassets, bloodhounds) are usually lazy and lie around like a bag of bones, and small dogs (poodles, schnauzers, Benji-types) bounce as they move and seem ready to pounce and play even when lying down. The size of the dog also influences how it moves: large dogs like the German shepherd (a police dog) move differently from dachshunds (hot dogs).*

2. Ask the children: *How do dogs move when they are injured?*

3. Have the children demonstrate. *Walk like your leg is hurt. How would a dog walk if she were hurt?*

4. Ask the children: *How does a poodle (St. Bernard) walk? Do dogs and cats move the same way? No! Cats move quietly; they stretch, walk pigeon-toed, and often crouch ready to pounce on their prey.*

5. Have the children demonstrate these behaviors.

Allow the children to select partners. Have one of the pair pretend to be a dog, the other a cat.

6. Have them demonstrate how dogs and cats play together: *Sometimes the dog tries to get the cat to play while the cat ignores the dog; other times the cat hisses and bats its paw at the dog. Sometimes they chase each other, but they do move differently. Be careful you don't hurt your partner.*

Concluding Activities (5 minutes)

Zoo

Assign small groups to their own spaces, and assign an animal type to each group.

Circulate, posing as the Zookeeper. Talk to the animals, pretend to feed them, and show them off to the pretend zoo visitors—or a real visitor, if possible!

LESSON 11

INTRODUCE LOCOMOTOR AND BALANCE COMBINATIONS, CONTINUE BASIC TUMBLING

Student Objectives

- Maintain balance in various positions after executing one or more locomotor patterns.
- Name two or more positions for balancing.
- Follow the rules when playing Freeze.

Equipment and Materials

- 1 mat (4 ft × 8 ft) per group
- Signal

Safety Tip

- Discuss personal space and the need to respect others' space by not running into them.

Warm-Up Activities (5 minutes)

Grades K-1 Warm-Up Routine

See Grades K-1: Gymnastics, Warm-Ups, page 249.

Skill-Development Activities (20 minutes)

Tasks

Arrange the children in scatter formation. Define a signal (a whistle, music stopping, a certain word, or the like).

1. Review the one-legged balance.
2. Challenge the children with the following tasks:

    Hop in any pattern; on the signal, do a one-legged balance.

    Run in any pattern; on the signal, do a one-legged balance.

    Skip in any pattern; on the signal, do a one-legged balance.

    Gallop in any pattern; on the signal, do a one-legged balance.

Freeze

Keep the children in scatter formation. Remind them of the signal.

Explain the game: *In this game, you move around the floor until the signal, then you must freeze and stay in the same position until the "Go!" signal.*

Two-Knee Balance

Arrange small groups, each at a mat. Remind them that only one child is permitted on the mat at a time.

1. Describe and demonstrate the stunt: *While kneeling, hold both your feet off the floor while stretching (extending) your arms to the sides. Hold this position.*
2. Have the students practice the two-knee scale.

Rocker, Log Roll, Forward Roll

See Grades K-1: Gymnastics, Lessons 8 and 9, pages 270 and 275.

Concluding Activities (5 minutes)

Balances

Continue with the same setup.

1. Ask the children to demonstrate the funniest (easiest, most difficult) balance position they saw or did today.
2. Ask the children: *What can we do to help us to balance?* (Look at a spot on the wall or on the ground.)

LESSON 12
BALANCE STUNTS, BALANCE COMBINATIONS, AND TUMBLING

Student Objectives

- Master new balance stunts.
- Balance on the number of body parts stated.
- Follow the rules playing Freeze.

Equipment and Materials

- 1 mat (4 ft × 8 ft) per group
- Background music (optional)

Safety Tip

- Review the safety rules. Make sure that heads stay tucked for rolls (chin on chest).

Warm-Up Activities (5 minutes)

Grades K-1 Warm-Up Routine

See Grades K-1: Gymnastics, Warm-Ups, page 249.

Skill-Development Activities (20 minutes)

Movement Challenges

Arrange small groups, each at a mat.

Present the following challenges to the first child in each group, and then in turn to the remaining children:

> Walk onto the mat, stop, and stand on one foot. Hold! Hop to the end of the mat.
>
> Hop, stop, and balance on three body parts. Crawl off the mat.
>
> Skip, balance on one foot, hands on hips! Hold still! Gallop off.
>
> Jump, stop, run off the mat.

Forward Roll

Keep the children in small groups, each at a mat.

1. Select a student who is able to roll over onto the shoulders and recover to her or his feet.
2. Have this child demonstrate the forward roll.

3. Tell the children: *Now everyone try the forward roll again. Land on your back—don't allow your head to touch the mat—and try to roll all the way over to your feet! Push with your hands under your seat if you have to.*

Backward Roll

Keep the same setup.

1. Describe and have one child demonstrate the skill:

    Squat with your back toward the long way of the mat. Put your hands on your shoulders with your palms turned upward. Tuck your chin tightly to your chest, looking at your tummy.

    Rock forward slightly onto your toes, then push backward with your toes so that your weight shifts (moves) to your heels and overbalances until your bottom touches the mat.

    Keep rolling so your back touches the mat. Stay tightly tucked in a ball (chin on chest and knees against chest).

    Continue rolling so your hands touch the mat (your hands are still on the shoulders). Now push with your hands, and begin to stretch (extend) your arms.

    As your body passes over your head, so that only your hands are touching the mat, you can let your chin leave your chest.

    Recover (land) on your feet. (Young children will usually recover on their knees, but with practice they can learn to push very hard with their hands and then land on their feet.)

2. Have another child demonstrate as you give the cues: *Rock forward, get your face close to your knees, roll backward keeping your chin on your chest, and push with your hands as they touch the mat. Lift your legs up and over until your feet are on the mat behind you.*

3. Have one child from each group sit on the mat facing his or her group, legs extended to the front, and hands on shoulders with palms up. Repeat the cues.

4. Repeat for the remaining children in the groups.

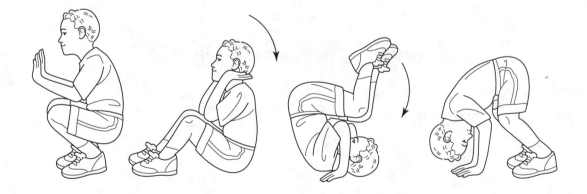

Elbow-Knee Balance

Keep the children in small groups at the mats.

1. Describe and demonstrate or have a child demonstrate the stunt:

    Begin in a squat, with your hands placed on the mat. Keep your arms inside your legs with your knees touching your elbows. Hold your head up; looking straight ahead helps.

Shift your weight from your feet to your hands, and rest your knees on your elbows.

Keep your balance with only your hands supporting your body weight.

2. Have the children practice the elbow-knee balance.

Tripod

Keep the children in small groups at the mats.

1. Describe and demonstrate (or have a child demonstrate) the skill:

   Begin in a squat, with your hands and arms placed on the mat outside your knees and legs.

   Bend forward until your forehead (at the hairline) touches the mat. Your head will serve as a balance point but will support very little weight.

   Bend your arms and make your knees touch your elbows. Support most of your body weight with your arms.

   Stop moving when your knees are resting on your elbows, your head is touching the mat, and your feet are off the mat.

   Remember, support most of your weight on your arms. Your head touches the mat but does not support much body weight.

2. Have the children practice the tripod.

Concluding Activities (5 minutes)

Freeze

See Grades K-1: Gymnastics, Lesson 11, page 279.

GRADES K-1

GYMNASTICS

LESSONS 13 AND 14
TUMBLING

Student Objectives

- Attempt the inchworm and the donkey kick.
- Practice forward and backward rolls and balances.
- Demonstrate the relationship between practice and learning by practicing the most difficult stunts.
- Take turns practicing.

Equipment and Materials

- 1 mat (4 ft × 8 ft) per group
- Background music (optional)

Safety Tip

- Have children look at the mat when doing the donkey kick and inchworm. Spotting may be helpful for some children on the donkey kick. Children who are risk takers (i.e., who will kick wildly) or children who have low upper body strength will need spotting.

Warm-Up Activities (5 minutes)

Grades K-1 Warm-Up Routine

See Grades K-1: Gymnastics, Warm-Ups, page 249.

Skill-Development Activities (20 minutes)

Tumbling Activities (5 minutes)

Arrange small groups, each at a mat.
   Have the children practice the following skills: forehead touch, two-knee balance, tripod, log roll, backward roll.

Inchworm

Keep the same setup.

1. Describe and demonstrate the skill:

   The object of this activity is to move forward while demonstrating flexibility.

   Stand and bend forward and place both hands on the mat.

   Walk your hands forward until your body is stretched (extended) and parallel to (flat as) the ground.

Now move your feet forward (in a walking motion, but with small steps) until your feet are as close as possible to your hands.

Repeat several times.

2. Have the students practice the inchworm.

Donkey Kick

Keep the children in small groups at the mats.

1. Describe and demonstrate (or have a child demonstrate) the stunt:

   The object of this task is to get both feet off of the mat at the same time and to support all of your body weight with your hands.

   Begin by standing in the middle of the mat, facing the length of the mat. Place both hands on the mat, about shoulder-width apart.

   Keep your arms straight, but bend your legs slightly. Let your hands carry some of your body weight.

   As you kick your feet up and back, take all your weight on your hands. Look at the mat, directly between your hands.

   Be careful not to kick very hard, as this may cause overbalancing, and you may flip over onto your back. (Have the children begin with small kicks and gradually increase the force and angle so that eventually the kick is just below 45 degrees.)

2. Have the children practice the donkey kick.

3. Have each child in each group take a turn practicing the following skills: forward roll, backward roll, donkey kick, inchworm, tripod, log roll, elbow-knee balance.

Spotting the Donkey Kick

1. The spotter stands facing the side of and just in front of the performer, with a hand (left if on the performer's left, right if on her or his right) on the shoulder of the performer.

2. The fingers should be facing forward with the thumb pointing down the back of the performer.

3. As the performer kicks upward, the spotter bends and uses the hand on the shoulder to support part of the performer's weight.

4. The opposite hand goes upward to keep the performer's legs from going past vertical.

Concluding Activities (5 minutes)

Discussion and Practice

Gather the children into an information formation. Keep the mats ready to use.

Ask several children which is their best skill. Ask all children to think about those skills they performed least well. Name a skill at which you noticed several children having trouble. Designate a mat for that skill, and tell those who need to practice that skill to move to that mat. Continue this until all children are at a mat, practicing their weakest skills.

LESSON 15
TUMBLING CHECKLIST

Student Objectives

- Evaluate one's own performances of the various skills.

Teacher Objectives

- The teacher will observe and evaluate the children's performance, using either the checklist or informal observation.

Equipment and Materials

- 1 mat (4 ft × 8 ft) per group
- Background music (optional)
- 1 copy of the Grades K-1: Checklist for Tumbling per group (see appendix)

Warm-Up Activities (5 minutes)

Grades K-1 Warm-Up Routine

See Grades K-1: Gymnastics, Warm-Ups, page 249.

Skill-Development Activities (20 minutes)

Skills Checklist

Arrange the children at the mats in small groups corresponding to the order on your checklist. See Grades K-1: Checklist for Tumbling, page 1142 in the appendix.

Repeat one at a time the following skills: log roll, rocker, two-knee balance, forward roll, backward roll, one-leg balance, forehead touch, donkey kick, tripod, and elbow-knee balance.

Extension Activities

Set up the mats as described for the checklist. Invite another teacher, your principal, or other "honored" guest to observe the children.

1. Have the children run through the tumbling activities. You could also review the animal walks and locomotor skills.

2. Have each group of children select a stunt per member of their group and decide the order in which their group will present the stunts.

3. Allow each group to demonstrate for the rest of the class.

Concluding Activities (5 minutes)

Keep the children with their groups at their mats. Tell the students: *Show your group the one skill you did the very best today!*

GRADES K-1

GYMNASTICS

LESSON 16
PARTNER STUNTS

Student Objectives

- Work cooperatively while practicing partner stunts.
- Successfully complete one locomotor partner activity.

Equipment and Materials

- 1 mat (4 ft × 8 ft) per group
- Background music (optional)
- Signal

Safety Tip

- Supervision of the children is important, so only have a third or a half of the pairs work at any one time.

Warm-Up Activities (5 to 10 minutes)

Grades K-1 Warm-Up Routine

For variety and in keeping with the partner activities of this week, you could have the children perform the routine in a different formation, for example, two long lines with partners across from each other or two circles, one inside the other, with partners matched one on the inside circle and the other on the outside circle. For older children it can be fun (but it takes longer!) to do the warm-up as a "round," where one pair begins, four counts later the next pair begins, and so on.

See Grades K-1: Gymnastics, Warm-Ups, pages 247-249 for steps and routine.

Skill-Development Activities (20 minutes)

Locomotor Tasks

Arrange pairs in scatter formation.

1. Tell the children: *Walk as close behind your partner as possible.*
2. Repeat with the other partner in front: *Hop, facing each other, standing arm's-length apart with hands on each other's shoulders. Take off and land together. Skip, holding hands and facing the same direction. Make the same size steps.*

Partner Walk

Designate one partner as the leader in each pair.

1. Describe and demonstrate the stunt:

The leader stands with feet shoulder-width apart, facing his or her partner. The follower (the other partner) stands close to the leader with his or her toes on top of the leader's feet. The partners place their arms on each other's shoulders.

The leader begins to walk (forward, sideways, or backward). The object is to keep your feet joined at all times.

2. Have the children practice the partner walk. Verbal cues are helpful.

3. Variation: Have everyone change partners on signal (music stopping, a whistle, or a hand signal). Continue, then change again.

Leapfrog

Keep the pairs in scatter formation.

1. Describe and demonstrate the stunt:

   One partner squats, with hands placed firmly on the floor, arms between the legs, head tucked against the chest.

   The other partner places both hands on the shoulders of her or his partner from behind, and jumps (with legs spread apart) over the squatting child.

   The jumping partner immediately gets into a squatting position, and the squatting partner becomes the leaping partner. Keep trading off.

2. Have the children practice leapfrog.

3. Once the children have mastered leapfrog with their partners, join two pairs of partners, so that the leaping partner jumps three children successively, then squats, and the last child in line becomes the leaper, and so on.

4. Variations: Have the children leapfrog with the entire class in a long line! The first leaping child leaps the entire line, the second child in line begins when the first leapfrog has leapt five or more children. The game continues until everyone has had a turn leaping the line.

Concluding Activities (5 to 10 minutes)

Mirror Game

Keep pairs in scatter formation. Designate one partner as the leader in each pair.

1. Describe and demonstrate the game:

    The Leader does various movements while facing his or her partner.

    The other child is the Mirror and tries to do whatever the Leader is doing while the Leader does it.

    Leaders, move slowly and stay in one small area.

    On signal, Leaders and Mirrors switch.

2. Have the children play the Mirror Game.

LESSON 17
PARTNER STUNTS

Student Objectives

- Learn two partner stunts.
- Cooperate with a partner.

Equipment and Materials

- 1 mat (4 ft × 8 ft) per group
- Background music (optional)

Safety Tip

- For back-to-back get-up, limit practice to the mats.

Warm-Up Activities (5 to 10 minutes)

Grades K-1 Warm-Up Routine

For variations, see Grades K-1: Gymnastics, Lesson 16, page 287 and Grades K-1: Gymnastics, Warm-Ups, page 249.

Skill-Development Activities (20 minutes)

Partner Walk and Leapfrog

See Grades K-1: Gymnastics, Lesson 16, pages 287 and 288.

Wring the Dishrag

Keep pairs in scatter formation.

1. Describe and demonstrate the stunt:

   Begin facing each other with hands joined. Lift both arms on one side (one partner's right arm, the other's left arm).

   Rotate (turn) your bodies, turning in the direction of the lifted arms but keeping your hands joined.

   Keep turning so your backs are to each other, then return to the starting position.

2. Have the children practice wring the dishrag.

3. Variations: This stunt looks quite nice when the class (or half the class) stands in two lines with partners facing each other. The first pair in line begins to wring the dishrag; when they have lifted their lead arms, the next pair begins, and so on. You can also arrange students in a circle (one partner facing in, the other facing out), so that when the last pair finishes, the first pair begins again.

Back-to-Back Get-Up

Arrange small groups of children, in pairs, at the mats.

1. Describe and have two children demonstrate the stunt:

   Stand on the mat with your partner, with your backs together and arms hooked at the elbows. Place your feet at about shoulder-width apart.

   Sit down together slowly. Press your backs against each other in order to prevent bumping your heads or backs.

   You should end up sitting with your legs tucked up to your body and your feet flat on the floor, arms still locked at the elbow, and backs pressed together.

   Now push with your feet and slowly straighten your legs to stand up again.

2. Have the children practice back-to-back get-up.

Concluding Activities (5 to 10 minutes)

Simon Says

Arrange pairs of children in scatter formation.

1. Describe the game:

   Each pair, working together, does what Simon says, and tries not to do the task if Simon doesn't "say" to.

   For example, suppose Simon says, "Simon says partner walk forward four steps, Simon says wring the dishrag, Simon says hop three steps backward with your partner, do leapfrog with your partner." Partners would not do leapfrog, because "do leapfrog" did not start with "Simon says."

   If you make a mistake carefully move to the front of the play area and continue playing.

   Help your partner be a good listener!

2. Have the children play Simon Says.

GYMNASTICS

LESSON 18
PARTNER STUNTS

Student Objectives

- Demonstrate two partner stunts (wheelbarrow, partner rock, leapfrog).
- Cooperate with a partner.

Equipment and Materials

- 1 mat (4 ft × 8 ft) per group
- Background music (optional)

Safety Tip

- If the children have difficulty with the tasks, have one group at a time try each of the group stunts so you can watch and control activity. Or set up stations so that most groups are working on more familiar tasks while you work with one group.

Warm-Up Activities (5 minutes)

Grades K-1 Warm-Up Routine

For variations for partners, see Grades K-1: Gymnastics, Lesson 16, page 287. See also Grades K-1: Gymnastics, Warm-Ups, page 249.

Skill-Development Activities (20 minutes)

Leapfrog

See Grades K-1: Gymnastics, Lesson 16, page 288.

Bunny Line

Arrange the children in small groups. Have each group form a single file line, standing close together, each child with both hands on the waist of the child in front of her or him.

1. Describe and have several children demonstrate the stunt: *The entire line jumps forward on command, in a series of small continuous jumps. Work at making your jumps equal in length. All of you should jump at the same time (simultaneously).*
2. Have the children practice bunny line.

Wheelbarrow

Arrange pairs in scatter formation.

1. Describe and demonstrate the stunt:

   One partner lies on his or her stomach on the floor. The other partner stands behind the feet of the first partner.

   As the first partner lifts his or her chest off the floor and supports most body weight with hands and arms, the second partner grasps (takes hold of) the legs (near the ankle) of the first partner and lifts.

   Once each partner is balanced, the first partner begins walking forward on both hands. The second partner follows, supporting the legs.

2. Have the children practice the wheelbarrow.
3. Repeat so each partner has the opportunity to try both positions.

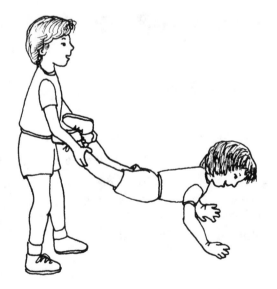

Partner Rock

Keep pairs in scatter formation. Have partners sit on the floor facing each other, with their legs extended out to each side (straddle position), feet touching and hands grasped. Try to pair students with legs of approximately the same length.

1. Describe and demonstrate the stunt:

   One partner leans forward, the other leans back. Then change positions, pulling gently to help stretch each other.

   When it's your turn to lean forward, your chest should be as near to the floor as possible. When it's your turn to lean back, your back should go as near to the floor as possible. Your legs stay straight at all times, and the partner leaning forward determines the amount of stretch.

2. Have the children practice the partner rock.

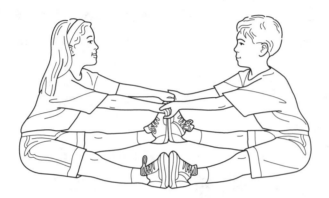

Concluding Activities (5 minutes)

Stunt Practice

Keep pairs in groups in scatter formation.

1. Ask each pair of partners to decide which is their worst partner stunt (leapfrog, bunny line, or wheelbarrow).
2. Have each pair practice that stunt.
3. Ask each pair to decide which is their best partner stunt (or favorite) and to demonstrate that to the group.

GYMNASTICS

K-1

LESSON 19
PARTNER STUNTS

Student Objectives

- Complete an obstacle course with a partner.
- Demonstrate cooperation and helping skills working with a partner to succeed.

Equipment and Materials

- 2 mats (4 ft × 8 ft) per obstacle course
- Cones
- 3 large hoops (30-36 in.) per obstacle course
- Background music (optional)
- Task cards

Safety Tip

- Tell the children not to pass the pair in front of them.

Warm-Up Activities (5 minutes)

Grades K-1 Warm-Up Routine

For variations for partners, see Grades K-1: Gymnastics, Lesson 16, page 287. See also Grades K-1: Gymnastics, Warm-Ups, page 249.

Skill-Development Activities (20 minutes)

Partner Obstacle Course

Set up one or more obstacle courses as shown in figure on page 297. Arrange partners at the beginning of the obstacle course(s). Place task cards at each obstacle illustrating what task is to be done.

1. Describe the obstacle course to the children, demonstrating for them which activities are done in each place:

    Back-to-back get-up

    Wheelbarrow around the cones

    Wring the dishrag

    Partner walk around the cones

    Alternate partner through the hoops (one partner holds the hoop, while the other partner climbs through and then walks to the next hoop, holding it for the first partner, and so on)

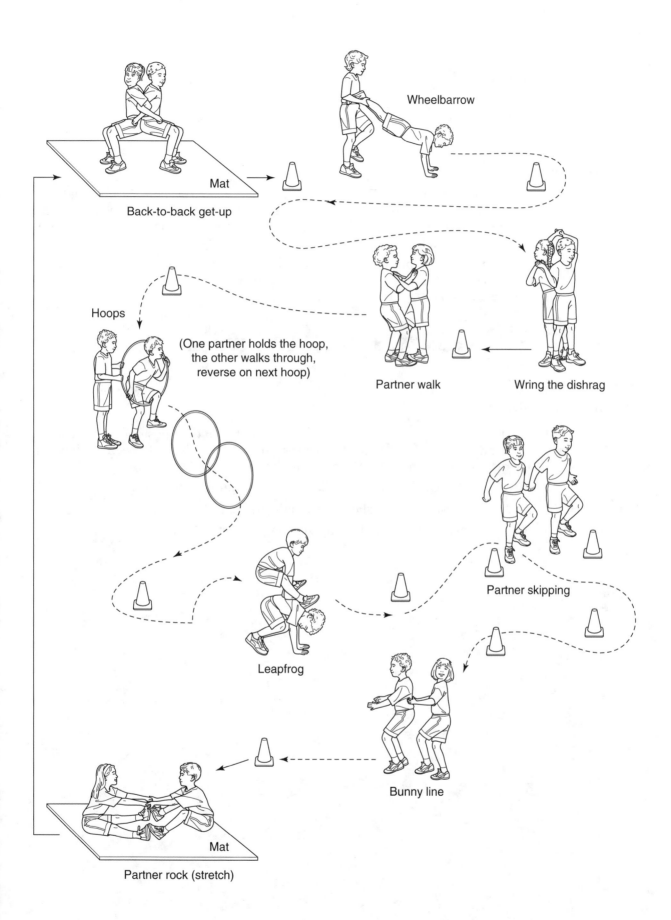

Back-to-back get-up

Mat

Wheelbarrow

Hoops

(One partner holds the hoop, the other walks through, reverse on next hoop)

Partner walk

Wring the dishrag

Partner skipping

Leapfrog

Bunny line

Partner rock (stretch)

Mat

Leapfrog

Partner skipping through cones

Bunny line

Partner rock

Back-to-back get-up

Spread the pairs around the course.

2. Signal for them to begin. Tell the children: *This is called a shotgun start.* All partners follow the same order through the course, simply beginning and ending in different locations. This means there will be little waiting and lots of activity. Do not pass or crowd the pair in front of you.

3. Have each pair go through the course twice. The purpose is to encourage the children to cooperate. Tell the children: *The object is not to complete the activities quickly but to complete them correctly, working together!*

Concluding Activities (10 minutes)

Partner Obstacle Course

Designate one child in each pair as the leader.

1. Use the same obstacle course, but alter the activities at each position on the course. For example, instead of doing partner get-up first, the pair might begin with wring the dishrag and then partner hop through the hoops, and so on.

2. Have the other child in the pair follow the leader through the course.

3. As one pair clears the first station, begin the next pair.

4. Repeat, with leaders and followers exchanging roles.

GRADES K-1

GYMNASTICS

LESSON 20
SMALL EQUIPMENT

Student Objectives

- Execute locomotor, balance, tumbling, flexibility, and other motor tasks while interacting with small equipment.
- State the safety rule that walking cans and balance boards must be used on the mat.
- Demonstrate cooperation by working independently at stations and making quick transitions between stations.

Equipment and Materials

Divide class into three groups. Have one of each item per child in each third of the class.

- Mats (4 ft × 8 ft) as needed for safety
- Station 1: 1 balance board and 1 beanbag per child
- Station 2: 1 pair of walking cans per child
- Station 3: 1 short jump rope (approximately 6 ft) and 1 beanbag per child
- Background music (optional)
- Signal

Safety Tip

- Use the walking cans and balance boards on mats or grass, as they tend to be slippery.

Warm-Up Activities (5 minutes)

Grades K-1 Warm-Up Routine

See Grades K-1: Gymnastics, Warm-Ups, page 249.

Skill-Development Activities (24 minutes)

Small Equipment Stations

Arrange the children in three groups, one group at each station. Have the groups spend five to six minutes at each station (the rest of the allotted time is for explaining the stations).

1. Describe and demonstrate each station.
2. Describe and demonstrate the signal to stop activity and be silent.
3. Describe and demonstrate the rotation order.

Station 1: Balance Boards

Try to keep your balance on the board while standing on one leg with a beanbag on your head and with hands on hips.

Station 2: Walking Cans

Walk the length of the mat on the cans, then practice turning right and left and walking backward and sideways.

Station 3: Ropes

Walk on the rope, trying not to step off, and then try walking backward on the rope, with a beanbag balanced on your head.

Concluding Activities (1 minute)

Clean-Up

Use the last minute for children to clean up.

GYMNASTICS

LESSON 21
FOAM BALLS AND WANDS

Student Objectives

- Execute one partner task and one locomotor task using a foam ball and one individual stunt using the wand.
- State the rule and consequence for wands.
- Work cooperatively when practicing partner toss with the ball.

Equipment and Materials

- 1 wand per child
- 1 playground ball (8 1/2 in.) or foam ball (4-6 in.) per child

Safety Tip

- Make a rule that anyone who touches another student or swings his or her wand at another child will have to go to time-out. Then enforce the rule!

Warm-Up Activities (5 minutes)

Grades K-1 Warm-Up Routine

See Grades K-1: Gymnastics, Warm-Ups, page 249.

Skill-Development Activities (23 minutes)

Around the Wand

Arrange the children in scatter formation, each with a wand.

1. Describe and demonstrate the stunt:

   Put one end of the wand on the ground.

   Hold the other end with a finger, and walk around the wand (as though it were a cane and you are wearing a top hat).

   Then repeat in the opposite direction.

2. Have the children practice around the wand. Tell the children: *Use just your finger to hold the wand!*

3. Have them repeat in the opposite direction.

Thread the Needle

Keep the children in scatter formation, each with a wand.

1. Describe and demonstrate the stunt:

   The key to this is to keep your hands as far apart as possible on the wand with your arms straight.

   Step through the opening between your arms and over the wand with one leg and then the other leg.

   Then swing the wand behind your back and over your head, as your wrists turn (rotate), and back to the front of your body.

2. Have the children practice thread the needle. Cue the children: *Put your hands as close to the ends of the wand as you can, bend over, step through with one leg, now the other. Swing the wand over your head.*

Ball Toss

Keep the children in scatter formation, but collect the wands and give each child a foam ball.

1. Describe and demonstrate the stunt:

   Toss and catch the ball by yourself.

   Stretch (extend) your arms overhead and hold the ball in your fingertips. Move your arms down and then smoothly upward, tossing the ball gently into the air.

   Your arms wait extended for the ball to fall. As the ball reaches your hands, your hands grasp the ball and begin moving downward with the ball.

2. Have the children practice ball toss. Cue the children: *Keep your arms straight and feet still!*

Rolling Ball

Keep the children in scatter formation, each with a foam ball.

1. Describe and demonstrate the stunt:

   Roll the ball, run beside it, pass it, stop, and wait for the ball to catch up so you can catch it.

   Begin by taking two or three steps while bending to a semisquat position (demonstrate clearly). The backswing happens during the first one or two steps; the roll begins on the last one or two steps.

   Let go of the ball (this is similar to bowling) and continue to move forward with the ball, standing back up.

   As the ball slows down, bend and squat to pick up the ball. This is easier if you roll the ball at the same speed that you run.

2. Have the children practice rolling ball. Cue the children: *Stay next to your ball!*

Partner Toss

Arrange pairs in scatter formation. Have partners stand facing each other, 5 to 10 ft apart, one child in each pair with a foam ball.

1. Describe and demonstrate the stunt:

   Stretch (extend) your arms for the catch and toss. Tossers, make the ball go in a high arc (demonstrate path with your hand).

   As you toss and catch, you should appear to never stop moving.

2. Have the children practice partner toss. Tell the children: *Make the ball go high!*

3. Have them repeat, tossing back and forth.

Concluding Activities (2 minutes)

Movement Challenges

Arrange individuals in scatter formation. Either collect the balls or have the children set them aside. Give each child a wand to lay on the ground.

Challenge the children with the following tasks:

Walk around your wand.

Walk with one foot on each side of the wand.

Jump over your wand.

Jump sideways over your wand.

Jump backward over your wand.

Stand behind your wand.

Stand beside your wand.

Hop around your wand.

Put your wand (and ball) away!

GYMNASTICS

LESSON 22
HOOPS AND STREAMERS

Student Objectives

- Execute one locomotor task and one stunt using a hoop and a streamer.
- Define personal space.
- Demonstrate respect for others and equipment.

Equipment and Materials

- 1 streamer per child
- 1 large hoop per child (30-36 in.)

Safety Tip

- Emphasize staying in personal space.

Warm-Up Activities (5 minutes)

Grades K-1 Warm-Up Routine

See Grades K-1: Gymnastics, Warm-Ups, page 249.

Skill-Development Activities (20 minutes)

Hoop and Streamer

Arrange the children in scatter formation, each with a hoop and a streamer.

1. Ask the children to perform the following activities, after reminding them not to touch anyone:

   Put the hoop on the ground.

   Put the streamer in the hoop.

   Walk around the hoop.

2. Move the children farther apart where necessary.

Figure Eight

Keep the children in scatter formation, each with a streamer, but have them set their hoops aside.

1. Describe and demonstrate the stunt: *Holding the streamer, stretch (extend) your arm forward and draw an eight with the streamer in the air in front of you. Keep your streamers in the air at all times.*

2. Have the children practice making figure eights. Tell the children: *Move the streamer slowly, so there is no noise. Move the streamer quickly, so there is noise.*

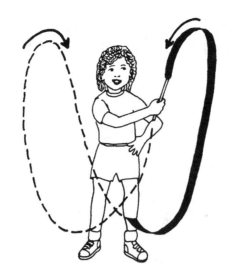

Circles

Continue with the same setup.

1. Describe and demonstrate the stunt: *Moving your entire arm, not just your hand, make circles with the streamer. The streamer should seem to make your arm longer* (be an extension of the arm).
2. Have the children practice making circles.

Draggin'

Continue with the same setup.

1. Describe and demonstrate the stunt: *Drag your streamer on the ground in a circle around yourself. Let your hand with your arm extended lead the way.*
2. Have the children practice draggin'.

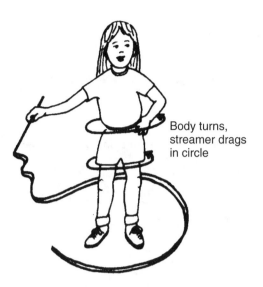

Body turns,
streamer drags
in circle

Hoop Challenges

Keep the same setup, but have the children set aside their streamers and pick up their hoops.

1. Tell the children: *Hold the hoop in both hands (over your head, to the side with one or both hands, behind you, under you).*

2. Ask: *Who can "jump rope" with their hoop (using both hands)?*

"Jump Rope" With a Hoop

Continue with the same setup.

1. Describe and demonstrate the skill, using a volunteer:

   Grip the hoop with your hands near the top center while holding the hoop in front of your body, with the bottom of the hoop's circle near your feet.

   Jump through the hoop and swing it behind your back and over your head. Repeat the process to make the hoop move back in front of your body to the starting position.

2. Have the children try to jump rope with a hoop.

3. Ask the children: *Who can hula-hoop?*

4. Have the children spin the hoop on various body parts, keeping the motion going by

moving with the hoop. Challenge the children: *Try it on your neck (leg, arm).*

Concluding Activities (5 minutes)

Hoop Activities

Gather the children into an information formation.

1. Ask the children: *Who will show me their favorite hoop activity?*
2. Select volunteers and allow them to demonstrate, one at a time, as time allows.

LESSONS 23 AND 24
SMALL EQUIPMENT

Student Objectives

- Practice previously introduced activities and experiment with the equipment.
- Demonstrate cooperation when working at stations.
- State a small equipment safety rule.

Equipment and Materials

- Station 1: 1 wand and 1 streamer per child
- Station 2: 1 large hoop (30-36 in.) per child
- Station 3: 1 balance board and 1 beanbag per child
- Station 4: 1 foam ball (8 1/2 in.) per child

- Station 5: 1 short jump rope and 1 beanbag per child
- Station 6: 1 pair of walking cans per child
- Picture instruction cards for each station
- Tape or 6 sign holders for picture instructions at stations
- Signal

Safety Tip

- Remind the children of the wand rule: The children must not touch other children or equipment with their wands or they will serve a time-out.

Warm-Up Activities (5 minutes)

Grades K-1 Warm-Up Routine

See Grades K-1: Gymnastics, Warm-Ups, page 249.

Skill-Development Activities (24 minutes)

Stations

Gather the children into an information formation. On the first day (Lesson 23) use one to two minutes to explain each station. Arrange small groups at the stations.

1. Describe and demonstrate each station.
2. Have the children do the station activities.
3. Rotate every four minutes the first day (Lesson 23) and every six minutes the second day (Lesson 24).

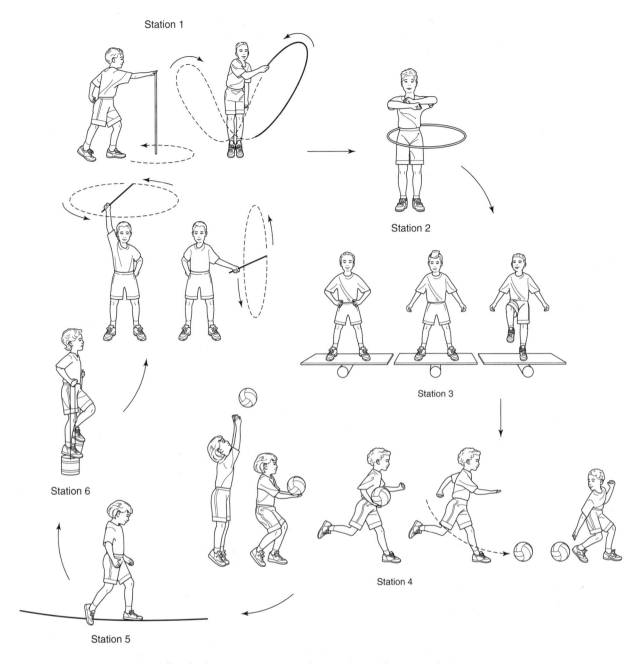

Station 1

Station 2

Station 3

Station 4

Station 5

Station 6

Station 1: Wands and Streamers

Describe and demonstrate these activities:

- *Thread the needle*
- *Around the wand*
- *Figure eight*
- *Circles*
- *Draggin'*

Station 2: Hoops

Describe and demonstrate these activities:

- *Jump rope with a hoop*
- *Hula hoop on various body parts*

Station 3: Balance Boards

Describe and demonstrate the activities: *Maintain balance on the board with a beanbag on your head (on one leg, with hands on hips).*

Station 4: Foam Balls

Describe and demonstrate these activities:

- *Ball toss*
- *Rolling ball*
- *Partner toss*

Station 5: Short Jump Ropes

Describe and demonstrate these activities:

- *Walk on the rope, trying not to step off.*
- *Repeat on a curved rope.*
- *Walk backward on the rope (with a beanbag on your head).*

Station 6: Walking Cans

Describe and demonstrate these activities:

- *Walk the length of the mat on the cans.*
- *Practice turning right and left (walking backward, sideways).*

Concluding Activities (1 minute)

Have the children either help put the stations back in order for the next class or put the equipment away.

LESSON 25
LARGE EQUIPMENT

Student Objectives

- Walk eight ft on a four-in-wide beam without help.
- Jump down from cubes and land with at least one foot on a target.
- Climb over a vault cube.
- Climb a ladder and hang suspended for 10 seconds.
- Negotiate through a large object, using various locomotor patterns.
- Work independently, taking turns and following directions.

Equipment and Materials

- Station 1: 1 low balance beam (e.g., 2 each: 2 in. × 4 in.; 4 in. × 4 in.; 4 in. × 6 in.) and 1 foam ball per child
- Station 2: 1 jumping cube (24 in.) per child
- Station 3: 1, 2-in.-diameter climbing rope (10 ft-20 ft) attached to the wall (12-18 in. high)

- Station 4: 1 tunnel, or 2 or 3 other shapes
- Station 5: 1 vaulting cube (wider at top than bottom, 24-30 in. high, or large paper boxes stuffed with paper) per child
- Station 6: 1 wooden climbing ladder and a wall, mats
- Mats (4 ft × 8 ft) as needed for safety
- Masking tape or chalk for marking targets
- Signal
- Carpet squares (if too many children than spots at the stations)

Safety Tips

- Use mats under the equipment. Have the children sit calmly before rotating to the next station.
- Stand where you can see the entire area and all activities.

Warm-Up Activities (5 minutes)

Grades K-1 Warm-Up Routine

See Grades K-1: Gymnastics, Warm-Ups, page 249.

Skill-Development Activities (24 minutes)

Safety and Management Rules

Gather the children into an information formation. Discuss the safety rules:

Do not put your hands on anyone else.

Wait until the person in front of you has finished her or his turn before getting on the equipment.

Sit on a carpet square while you wait. (This is only necessary if you have more children than "spots" at the stations.)

Put all equipment back as you found it, when the whistle blows (at my signal).

Stations

Set up the stations as described in the text and shown in the figures that follow. Arrange small groups at the six stations.

1. Use six minutes to describe and demonstrate the six stations.
2. Review the stop and rotate signal.
3. Have the children practice at each station three minutes, then rotate. (When revisiting this lesson, you will be able to use more time at each station, as explanations will take less time.)
4. Observe as many children at each station as possible, but spend most of the time with the children who are needing or requesting spotting.

Station 1: Balance Beams

As the spotter, face the child for the balance beam (and most other apparatus). Walk backward if necessary. It is better to hold the child's hand or wrist rather than letting them hold yours because then you are in control. Always tell the truth! Never tell children you will spot them, hold their hands, or catch them, and then not do it! Negotiate with the children to get them to try more difficult tasks, but always do exactly as you say you are going to do!

Have the children practice the following activities: *walk forward, walk backward, walk forward carrying a foam ball.* Wands (broomsticks) make good aids for children who are having trouble on the beam. Allow children to use them like canes (one in each hand) to facilitate balance.

Station 2: Jumping Cubes

Climb up on one side and jump off the opposite side. The direction of movement should always be the same. Land on the mat (soft grass, sand). Try to jump to a square target (jump high, jump long).

Station 3: Climbing Rope

Tie (or attach) the climbing rope so that it runs parallel to the ground, 12 to 18 in. from the ground. *Pull yourself along the ground while lying on your back. You can move in either a headfirst or a feetfirst direction.*

Station 4: Shapes or Tunnel

Any box, barrel, shape, or other object that is large enough for children to move through safely but small enough to make the child bend, crawl, or creep is appropriate. *Walk and crawl through the shapes (tunnel).*

Station 5: Vaulting Cubes

Make sure these cubes are wider on the bottom than on the top and 24 to 30 in. high. (If necessary a large box stuffed with newspaper will substitute.) Have the children begin with easier lead-up skills and progress to vaulting: *The object is to run to the cube, place both hands on it, and jump over it in various ways, landing on your feet. The idea is similar to leapfrog, but you leap over the cube instead of another child.*

Have the children practice the following activities: *climb over the cubes, climb over headfirst (feetfirst, sideways).*

Station 6: Climbing Ladder

Lean the ladder against a wall at an angle of 45 to 60 degrees from horizontal. Place mats under the ladder. The ladder works like a "low" horizontal ladder; the kids climb hand-over-hand, and they are not able to get very far off of the ground.

Climb the ladder on the topside (in the usual way of climbing a ladder) or the underside (don't use your feet).

Concluding Activities (1 minute)

Discussion

Have the children either help set the stations in order for the next class or help put the equipment away. Gather the children into an information formation.

Briefly discuss with the children how things went today, what you liked, and what concerned you. Emphasize safety, taking turns, practicing, and creativity.

GYMNASTICS

LESSONS 26 AND 27
LARGE EQUIPMENT

Student Objectives

- Practice independent work.
- Practice following rules.

Equipment and Materials

- Station 1: 1 low balance beam (e.g., 2 each: 2 in. × 4 in.; 4 in. × 4 in.; 4 in. × 6 in.) and beanbags or 1 rope per child (optional: 2 wands per child)
- Station 2: 1 jumping cube (24 in.) per child
- Station 3: 1, 2-in.-diameter climbing rope (10-20 ft) attached to the wall
- Station 4: 1 tunnel, or 2 or 3 other shapes, several beanbags
- Station 5: 1 vaulting cube (wider at bottom than top, 24-30 in. high, or large paper boxes stuffed with paper) and 1 beanbag per child
- Station 6: 1 wooden climbing ladder, a wall, mats, and several beanbags
- Mats (4 ft × 8 ft) as needed for safety
- Carpet squares (if too many children per spot at stations)

Safety Tip

- Emphasize following the rules. Sit all the children on carpet squares before rotating and as necessary to calm them.

Warm-Up Activities (5 minutes)

Grades K-1 Warm-Up Routine

See Grades K-1: Gymnastics, Warm-Ups, page 249.

Skill-Development Activities (24 minutes)

Stations

Set up the stations as described in the text and shown in figures on pages 317-319. Arrange small groups at the six stations.

1. Use six to seven minutes to describe and demonstrate the six stations.
2. Review the stop and rotate signal.
3. Have the children practice at each station three minutes, then rotate. (When revisiting this lesson, you will be able to use more time at each station, as explanations will take less time.)
4. Move from station to station spotting, observing, and managing.

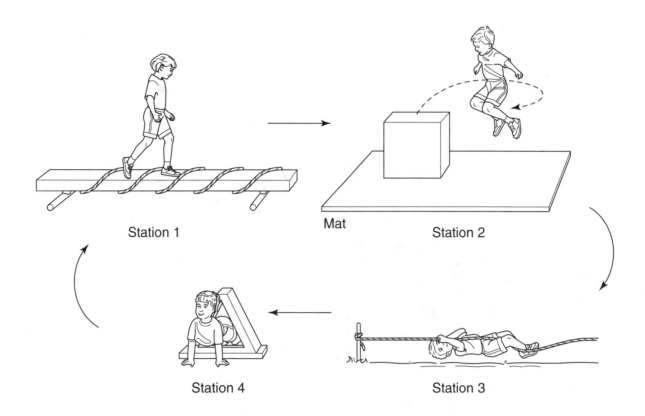

Station 1

Mat Station 2

Station 4

Station 3

Station 1: Balance Beams

Step over the objects on the balance beam (beanbags spaced on a beam or a rope wound around the beam). Wands (broomsticks) make good aids for children who are having trouble on the beam. Allow children to use them like canes (one in each hand) to facilitate balance.

Station 2: Jumping Cubes

Perform the following activities while jumping from the cubes:

> *Clap hands in flight.*

> *Spin all the way around (360 degrees) in the air.*

> *Jump higher.* (Someone can hold their arm up as a target or barrier.)

Station 3: Climbing Rope

Practice climbing the rope:

> *Go feetfirst.*

> *Go no-legs (hold them in the air).*

Station 4: Shapes or Tunnel

Try these tasks while navigating the shapes:

> *Carry an object (a beanbag).*

> *Go with your eyes closed.*

Station 5: Vaulting Cubes

Practice the following vaulting skills:

> *Use only one arm.*
>
> *Use no arms.*
>
> *Carry an object (a beanbag).*

Mat

Station 6: Ladder

Practice ladder-climbing skills:

> *Carry an object (a beanbag).*
>
> *Climb at a steeper angle (by raising the ladder).*

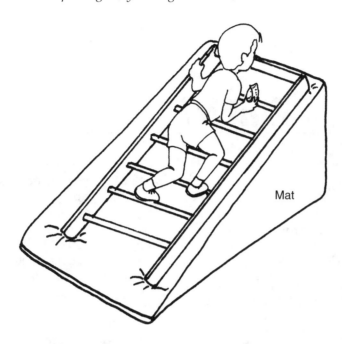

Mat

Concluding Activities (1 minute)

Have the children either help set the stations in order for the next class or help put the equipment away.

LESSON 28
LARGE EQUIPMENT

Student Objectives

- Practice skills on large apparatus.
- Follow other children.
- Cooperate with a large group.

Equipment and Materials

List is per obstacle course you set up. Try to keep group sizes small to increase participation opportunities.

- 1 jumping cube (24 in.)
- 3 balance beams (2 in. × 4 in.; 4 in. × 4 in.; 4 in. × 6 in.; 8-14 ft long)
- 2 vaulting cubes (wider at top than bottom, 24-30 in. high, or large paper boxes stuffed with paper)
- 1 tunnel, or 2 or 3 other shapes
- 1 wooden climbing ladder
- 1, 2-in.-diameter climbing rope (10-20 ft) attached to the wall
- 1 triangle mat
- Mats (4 ft × 8 ft) as needed for safety
- Carpet squares (if children must wait turns)

Warm-Up Activities (5 minutes)

Grades K-1 Warm-Up Routine

See Grades K-1: Gymnastics, Warm-Ups, page 249.

Skill-Development Activities (24 minutes)

Obstacle Course

Set up the course(s) as shown on page 321. Divide the children into the same number of groups as obstacle courses. Try to keep groups small to increase participation opportunities.

1. Describe and demonstrate the obstacle course.
2. Have the children go through the obstacle course using the skills shown in the figure.
3. Send one child at a time (or space the children so no child catches another).
4. Repeat for all the children as many times as possible.

Start

Concluding Activities (1 minute)

Have the children either help set the stations in order for the next class or help put the equipment away.

LESSON 29
LARGE EQUIPMENT

Student Objectives

- Walk an 8-ft-long, 4-in.-wide beam without help.
- Jump down from a 24-in. cube and land on a self-selected target.
- Get over a 24-in. cube without assistance.
- Climb a slanted ladder (45 to 75 degrees) without help.
- Hang suspended from the underside of a ladder for 10 seconds.
- Move 10 ft by making climbing motions and pulling self along the ground while lying under a 2-in.-diameter horizontal rope.
- Move forward and backward through a tunnel or shapes without touching the obstacles.

Equipment and Materials

Same as for Lessons 26 and 27; see page 316, plus masking tape or chalk to mark targets.

Warm-Up Activities (5 minutes)

Grades K-1 Warm-Up Routine
See Grades K-1: Gymnastics, Warm-Ups, page 249.

Skill-Development Activities (24 minutes)

Skills Checklist
Arrange small groups at the stations. This works best if they are grouped as they appear on your checklist. Mark target squares for jumping cubes with tape or chalk.

1. Have the children perform the following skills at the stations:

    Station 1: Balance beam—*Walk forward from one end to the other.*

    Station 2: Jumping cubes—*Jump forward, landing on the square target.*

    Station 3: Climbing rope—*Pull yourself from one end to the other. Don't put your feet on the ground!*

    Station 4: Tunnel or shapes—*Go through the shapes forward and backward.*

    Station 5: Vaulting cubes—*Climb over the cube headfirst.*

    Station 6: Climbing ladder—*Climb up the outside; climb the inside and hang.*

2. Record student performances on your checklist.

Concluding Activities (1 minute)

Have the children either help set the stations in order for the next class or help put the equipment away.

HEALTH

Although some schools have a dedicated health instructor, such as the school nurse, to teach basic health concepts, many physical education teachers find themselves faced with the task of teaching this part of the school curriculum. Take advantage of such an opportunity to show children the connections among fitness, lifestyle choices, and health. We designed this unit to give you an overview of appropriate content for this age level to help you get started.

UNIT ORGANIZATION

You can use the following lessons as a two-week health unit or individually as appropriate. You can also expand each lesson into a unit of its own. The topics include personal health, relationships, living happily, people problems, nutrition, body growth, substance use and abuse, water safety, transportation safety, and physical activity.

LESSON ORGANIZATION

We have organized each lesson in a manner similar to all other types of lessons in this book: student objectives, equipment and materials, health concept (skill development). As it enhances student learning, most lessons include a hands-on activity to reinforce the main health concept. We have suggested times for each lesson. These apply if you were teaching the lesson as it is written; you may expand each lesson or parts of lessons as appropriate in your situation.

TEACHING HINTS

As with any lesson, being well-prepared makes for more effective teaching. Read the lesson carefully before presenting the concept to the students. Allow plenty of time for discussion and application of the concept to promote learning.

Kindergartners and First Graders

Children this age are just beginning to be aware of simple connections between lifestyle choices and health; for example, too much sugar can harm your teeth and cause you to have too much body fat. Make sure the language you plan to use is age-appropriate and accompanied by visual aids whenever possible, such as bright posters, models, and everyday objects such as a bin full of personal care products (e.g., toothbrush for brushing teeth, bar of soap for washing, and so on) when discussing personal health in Lesson 1.

Encourage discussion and participation from each child. One way to encourage discussion is to be sure to wait at least 10 seconds before calling on a child to answer your question. Encourage participation by asking for group responses, such as having the children give you "thumbs up" for "yes" and "thumbs down" for "no."

Collaboration Strategies

Inviting parents and other community members to class can greatly enhance health lessons. Parents from various health professions may serve as guest speakers. You should also include parents by asking them to help complete and/or sign health contracts, sending home information about the concepts with discussion questions, or simply inviting them to attend class. Community experts, such as pediatricians, police, health care professionals, and representatives from awareness groups (e.g., American Heart Association), are often willing to make presentations at schools free of charge. Tap into such resources whenever possible not only to supplement your curriculum but also to raise awareness among students of the many resources available to them in the community.

GRADES
K-1

HEALTH

LESSON 1
PERSONAL HEALTH

Student Objectives

- Identify three daily health habits.
- Name one benefit and one risk for each habit.
- State that personal health is each individual's responsibility.

Equipment and Materials

- Chalkboard
- Flip chart or poster board
- Chalk or marker

Health Concept (30 minutes)

Gather the children into an information formation for the entire discussion.

Healthy Habits

1. Introduce the concept: *Things that we do every day are called "routine." We do these behaviors no matter where we are. Can you name some things you do every day?* (Eat, sleep, go to the bathroom, and so on.)

2. Ask the children: *What should we do every day to help ourselves be healthy?* Write the answers in large print on the board:
   Brush teeth.

   Wash hands and bathe body.

   Eat properly.

   Sleep.

   Get exercise.

   Go to the bathroom.

3. Review each behavior, and discuss why it is important.

Brushing Your Teeth

Tell your students: *Brushing teeth promotes dental health. Unhealthy teeth can interfere with eating, produce bad breath, and cause other health problems. When should you brush your teeth?* (After meals and snacks, before bedtime.)

Washing Your Hands and Bathing Your Body

Remind your students: *Washing hands and bathing help your skin to be healthy and can prevent diseases. Germs can get on your hands, so washing your hands—especially rubbing vigorously with soap—can remove germs and reduce your chances of getting illnesses caused by those germs. When should you wash your hands?*

(Before meals, after using the bathroom, and after sneezing, blowing your nose, or coughing into your hands.)

Continue: *Dirty skin can smell bad and become infected. Keeping the skin and hair clean by regular bathing is important to good health. Do you think it would be bad for you to take a bath and wash your hair every day?* (No, most people need to bathe every day and wash their hair regularly. Some days it is OK to wash carefully and not take a bath.)

Eating Properly

Tell your class: *Eating properly usually means three meals per day with limited and healthy snacks. The food should represent the four food groups and have five or more servings of fruits and vegetables. Grains like bread and pasta should also be a large portion of our diets. Poor nutrition can allow us to become sick or make us feel tired. Good nutrition helps us grow, be healthy, and maintain our routine (sleeping, exercising, and going to the bathroom).*

Ask: *What would we serve at a healthy breakfast?* (Cereal, fruit, bagels, milk, and so on.)

Sleeping

Remind your students: *Sleep is important for everyone. All people sleep, but some of us need more sleep than others. Children usually sleep 8 to 10 hours at night and often take a nap. Who can describe someone who has had too little sleep?* (Grumpy, slow, sometimes sick, makes many mistakes, sleepy, and so on.) *Several things help us to sleep; can you name any?* (Keeping a routine, eating healthy meals on a schedule, exercise, having a regular bedtime, and sleeping in the same place each night all help us to sleep.)

Getting Exercise

Tell your students: *Exercising helps us to grow healthy bones and muscles, sleep better, have a healthy heart, and feel happier and more confident. What is regular exercise?* (Doing some physical activity every day. Sometimes we might go for a walk; other times we might play a vigorous game like football or soccer. "Regular" means every day, and "exercise" means vigorous so that you breathe hard, sweat, and your heart beats faster.)

Going to the Bathroom

Remind your class: *Going to the bathroom is the body's way of getting rid of the waste produced from the things we eat and drink. The things we eat and drink are the fuels that give us energy for our body. It is important to go to the bathroom regularly so the waste can leave our body. Usually our body develops a schedule or routine so that we need to go at about the same time each day. Drinking plenty of water, eating healthy foods, exercising, and sleeping on schedule all help our body to have a good bathroom routine. When we don't have good habits, we can get an ache in our stomach or even an infection in our kidney or bladder.*

4. Ask the children: *Who can name four things we should have in our personal health routine?* (Rest, eat healthy food, drink water, and exercise.) *Who can name some more things we can do to be healthy?* (Cover our mouths when we sneeze, wash hands often, go to the doctor.)

Expansion Activities (10-30 minutes each)

1. Draw pictures of healthy habits.
2. Make a clock that shows healthy habits throughout the day.
3. Write a healthy habits contract, which children sign, indicating a promise to make healthy choices and be responsible for their personal health.
4. Children cut pictures of healthy habits and related products from magazines.
5. Practice washing hands, brushing teeth, and selecting healthy foods.
6. Invite a guest such as a dentist to discuss one of the healthy habits.

LESSON 2
RELATIONSHIPS

Student Objectives

- Give an example of a relationship.
- Name the steps in making a decision.
- List the five basic human needs.

Equipment and Materials

- None

Health Concept (30 minutes)

Gather the children into an information formation for the entire discussion.

Relationships

Introduce the concept: *A "relationship" is a connection made by marriage, family, circumstances, or choice. Name some people with whom you have a relationship.* (Neighbor, relative, friend, teacher, or the like.) *Why is this person important to you? How are you related to him or her?*

Friendships

1. Introduce the concept: *Friendships are special relationships. Friendships are built. Three ways to build a friendship are doing favors, keeping promises, and respecting the other's property.*

2. *What other things can you do to be a good friend?* (Give a hug, praise, smile, help, keep a secret, be friendly.) *Being a friend also means helping your friend to make healthy decisions and supporting those healthy decisions.*

Making Decisions

Introduce the concept: *Making decisions influences our relationships. Decision making has five steps:*

1. *Name the problem(s).*
2. *Look at the facts.*
3. *Think about the choices.*
4. *Consider how the decision will affect others. Will it help, hurt, or bother them?*
5. *Review the decision afterward. See how your choice works to be sure it was the right one.*

Discuss decision making with the children: *Problems can be things like following the rules, having fun, or doing what someone wants you to do. The facts are things that you can touch, see, or prove in some way. Choices are possible actions you can take. Each choice will affect others differently, so think about how each choice might work out. After the decision, think about how it worked out. Would you change the decision next time? Every day you are asked to wait in line. The problem is that you are not first. The fact is that everyone can not be first. Your choice is to follow the rules and wait in line or push to the front of the line trying to be first. If you push, you can hurt someone else or hurt someone's feelings. Waiting your turn in line will make you and everyone else happier. After you follow the rules, by taking turns, you feel better.*

Basic Human Needs

1. Introduce the concept: *There are five basic human needs:*
   - *Survival (food, shelter, water, protection)*
   - *Belonging to a group*
   - *Love*
   - *Having respect*
   - *Becoming independent (learning to take care of yourself)*

2. Discuss basic human needs with the children: *When a person's survival needs are not met, people can become sick or even die. For example, when someone tries to hurt a child, the child needs protection or a person lost in a boat needs water and food. People belong to groups, for example families, classes at school, and sport teams. Our families help us to survive, allow us to belong to a group, and provide love. Family and friends should respect each other. Our groups also help us to grow independent, so we can take care of ourselves. So, relationships are important because these provide basic human needs for love, respect, independence, survival, and belonging. Friendships are important relationships. Good decisions help us to make and keep friendships to be healthy.*

Expansion Activities (10-30 minutes each)

1. Have each child draw a picture of the people with whom they have relationships. Encourage them to show something unique or important about each person in the picture (e.g., their favorite food, a sport or pet they love).

2. Have one child name some things that he or she likes. Try to find at least one thing that everyone in the class also likes. Continue this with several or all the children, making the point that people have some things in common but are also different. Tell the children: *Friends are like this; they don't always like exactly the same things but they can still be friends. We must learn to appreciate the differences in people. All people are more alike than different, but each of us is still unique.*

3. *As homework, ask a parent or sibling how they make decisions.*

4. *Watch a movie or television program and identify the issues, facts, and choices. Identify the things that we learn to do for ourselves from birth to first grade (feeding, dressing, walking, and so on).*

LESSON 3
LIVING HAPPILY

Student Objectives

- Name five emotions.
- Use the seven steps to solve a problem.
- Give one way to reduce stress.

Equipment and Materials

- None

Health Concept (30 minutes)

Gather the children into an information formation for the entire discussion.

Emotions

Introduce the concept: *A person can express all emotions in a positive way. Emotions are feelings, like happy, sad, angry, worry, afraid, love, jealousy, and surprise. Talking about feelings or emotions is good, acting on emotions can be a bad choice. For example if someone hurts your feelings, telling them is good, but hitting them is a bad choice. Difficult emotions can lead to good; for example, sometimes when we worry we try harder.* Ask each child to name something that might worry, anger, or scare him or her.

Love

1. Introduce the concept: *We all have needs and sometimes have to wait for those needs to be met. Love is an important need and emotion. When we need love one way to get it is to love first. We can show love by doing something special for the person we love, saying something nice to them, or giving them something. Sharing with others is important and makes us feel good.*

2. Ask each child to say something nice to the child next to them. Say something nice to and about the class. *All people need to be with other people; this is called "socializing." What do you like to do with other people?* (Allow time for responses.)

Solving Problems

Introduce the concept: *Solving problems is an important part of being happy. All people have problems. We usually think about problems until we solve them. And we should try to solve problems. The steps to solving a problem are:*

1. *Be calm and think about what has happened.*

2. *Decide who owns the problem. Do not blame someone else for your problems.*

3. *Decide how you will solve the problem. Think about things that will solve the problem.*

4. *Talk with someone who will be able to help you solve the problem like a parent, teacher, or friend.*

5. *Choose your best solution and try it.*

6. *Later, ask yourself if the problem is solved; if not try another solution.*

7. *Do not rush; solving problems takes time and effort.*

Select a problem (children can suggest some). Go through the steps and practice problem solving.

Stress

Introduce the concept: *Stress can hurt us. Stress is when something bothers us. Stress often comes from un-solved problems.Reduce stress by*

1. *talking about the problem,*

2. *trying to relax and reduce the amount of stress,*

3. *exercising regularly, and*

4. *being prepared, organized, and keeping up with tasks (like schoolwork or chores).*

Solving problems, reducing stress, and handling our emotions positively can help us live more happily.

LESSON 4
PEOPLE PROBLEMS

Student Objectives

- Change a command into a positive "I" statement.
- Identify ways to fight peer (or other) pressure.

Equipment and Materials

- None

Health Concept (30 minutes)

Gather the children into an information formation for the entire discussion.

Communication

Introduce the concept: *Communication is important to prevent problems with people. "Communication" is sharing information; usually we do this when we talk and listen. There are other ways we send information, especially about our feelings. Some things make communication better.*

1. *Being a good listener. "Body language" can tell a person we don't care about what he or she is saying. Who can show this body language?* (Hands on hips or arms crossed, no eye contact.) Tell them: *In order to be a good listener, we should hear and think about what the person is saying. Sometimes it helps to repeat what they said as a question, to be sure we understood. Who can show body language that seems to be listening carefully?* (Hands at sides, good eye contact, friendly look, and so on.)

2. Continue: *Positive "I" statements also create good communication.* Explain: *Begin a sentence with "I," then tell how you feel. This is better than giving an order or command to someone else. For example rather than "Don't play with the ball in the house" say "I think we should go outside to play with the ball."* Give another command statement and ask the children to change it to a positive "I" statement.

3. Tell your students to be assertive: *You also need to stand up for yourself without being mean. For example, if someone wants you to do something that feels uncomfortable to you, especially if they try to bully you (physical, verbal, or emotional threat), be "assertive," which means stand up for yourself. Several things work:*

   Tell the person your parents won't let you.

   Say "I don't want to," then change the subject.

   Say "no" quickly.

   Ask a trusted adult for help.

   Keep saying "no" to yourself or keep repeating what you should do.

4. Read the following situations, and ask a child to respond with one of the strategies previously listed:

A friend wants you to play in a vacant lot rather than going straight home from school.

A stranger asks you to get in his car.

A neighbor shows you a gun and wants you to touch it.

A teammate tells you to call a person on the other team a bad name.

Your cousin kicks a dog and encourages you to do it too.

The student in the desk next to you asks you for an answer on a test.

K-1

HEALTH

LESSON 5
BODY GROWTH

Student Objectives

- State that the musculoskeletal system is made up of bones and muscle.
- Recognize their own growth since birth.

Equipment and Materials

- One 30-inch-long paper per child
- Skeletal system drawing/diagram

Health Concept (30 minutes)

Gather the children into an information formation for the entire discussion.

The Skeleton

1. Introduce the concept: *Your skeleton is made up of bones. Your muscles move your bones. Tendons attach your muscles to your bones. Together these parts make up the "musculoskeletal system."*

2. *You cannot see your bones, but in some places on your body you can feel your bones. Where can you feel bones through the skin?* (Elbow, knee, ribs, face and head, shin.) *Your bones are covered with muscle, fat, and skin. That is why in some body parts it is difficult to feel the bones. Without bones we would be like jellyfish or Jell-O, and we would not be able to stand or move. Without muscles, bones would be like pencils or logs. Bones cannot move themselves; muscles move bones. Your muscles and bones are growing. The bones grow longer, then thicker. The muscles grow longer, then if you exercise, the muscles also get larger when you are an adult. What happens to a muscle that does not exercise?* (For example, after breaking a bone, the muscle atrophies, or shrinks.) *How old do you think you will be when your bones stop growing?* (Around 20 years old.)

3. Display the skeletal system diagram and have the children touch the body part you point to on the drawing.

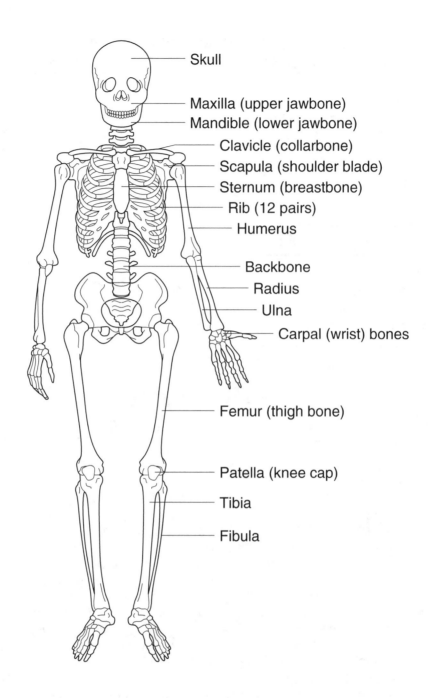

Skull

Maxilla (upper jawbone)

Mandible (lower jawbone)

Clavicle (collarbone)

Scapula (shoulder blade)

Sternum (breastbone)

Rib (12 pairs)

Humerus

Backbone

Radius

Ulna

Carpal (wrist) bones

Femur (thigh bone)

Patella (knee cap)

Tibia

Fibula

Growth

1. Introduce the concept: *Growth is a continuous process. To grow means to get bigger. As we get older we get taller and heavier. All of our body grows. What body parts grow?* (Arms, legs, head, fingers, and so on.)

2. *Name some body parts that grow, but that we cannot see.* (Heart, lungs, muscles, and bones.) *Do you wear a larger shoe that you did last year? What about pants and shirts? That means you have grown. Does anyone know how much they weighed or how long they were when they were born?* (Allow a few children to share.)

3. Make a drawing (outline) of each child's hand and foot on a paper at least 30 in. long. Line up the children with one foot on each child's section of paper. Outline each foot. Go through the line again to do the hand. Send these home and ask the parent to mark the length of the child at birth on the paper to show how much the child has grown in height.

GRADES K-1

HEALTH

LESSON 6
PHYSICAL ACTIVITY AND FITNESS

Student Objectives

- Name a benefit of physical activity.
- Name two or more components of health-related physical fitness.

Equipment and Materials

- Magazines, scissors, glue, paper, markers/crayons for collages

Health Concept (30 minutes)

Gather the children into an information formation for the entire discussion.

Physical Activity

1. Introduce the concept: *Physical activity is a part of a healthy life; physical fitness means being able to do a specific amount of physical activity.* Introduce the following definitions:

   A "sedentary person" is one who sits and rests most of the time.

   A "physically active person" is one who walks or moves around. For example, a "physically active person" may have three 10-minute bouts of activity each day. A physically fit person is one who trains his or her body so it can do certain physical tasks, including everyday living tasks. Physical fitness has five parts: cardiovascular (aerobic) fitness, muscular strength and endurance, flexibility, and a healthy amount of body fat.

2. Ask the children: *Can you name some jobs that are sedentary?* (Typist, bus driver, cashier.) *Can you name some jobs that are physically active?* (Construction worker, train conductor, janitor.) *Who can you name that is physically fit?* (Michael Jordan, Tiger Woods.) *How do you know?* (They are able to perform well in their sports because they have trained their bodies.)

Identify Sedentary Versus Active Activities

1. Tell the children: *For each activity listed, say "active" or "sedentary":*

   Using the elevator

   Riding the bus

   Cleaning the house

   Watching television

   Taking the stairs

   Walking to school

   Playing basketball

Health   335

Taking a nap

Mowing the grass

2. Ask the children: *Can you name some ways you could be more physically active?* (Take several responses, making sure the children understand that chores and other nonsport and nonplay activities, such as yard work and house cleaning, can be good for health.)

Physical Fitness and Health

1. Introduce the idea: *A physically fit person should be able to:*

   jog (or any other combination of aerobic activity) for three 10-minute continuous segments three days each week, do 10 sit-ups and 10 push-ups,

   touch his or her toes (with knees slightly bent for safety), and have some body fat, but not too much fat.

2. Tell your students: *Being physically active regularly leads to being physically fit, reducing health risks. People who are sedentary are often sick and sometimes die when they are young. What could a person with a sedentary job do to be healthier?* (Exercise after work to be more physically active.)

3. Have the children draw or cut pictures out of magazines to make a collage of sedentary and active people.

HEALTH

LESSON 7
SUBSTANCE USE AND ABUSE

Student Objectives

- Identify substances that can be abused.
- Give a reason why people may abuse substances.

Equipment and Materials

- None

Health Concept (30 minutes)

Gather the children into an information formation for the entire discussion.

Misuse of Drugs and Medicines

1. Introduce the concept: *Drugs and medicines are often misused. Drugs are for sick people. Drugs can help us when we are sick. Can you name some ways drugs help us?* (Reduce fever, fight infections, reduce pain.) *Medicines, even from the doctor, can hurt us too; for example, if you take someone else's medicine, if you take medicine without parent or physician's supervision, if you mix medicines, or if you take too much of a medicine.*

2. *Some drugs are illegal, or forbidden, by law. Why do people take these?* (They are uneducated, they are daredevils, they are insecure [they have poor self-concepts and don't think they will have friends unless they do what their friends want them to], they are trying to be popular, or they are trying to escape from the way they live.) *Besides drugs, are there other substances that people use that can be dangerous?* (Alcohol; caffeine; or hair spray, glue, or paint [inhalants].)

Expansion Activity

Have children and parents do a safety check at home. The object is to identify any drugs or other dangerous substances and make sure these are in safe places.

HEALTH

LESSON 8
NUTRITION

Student Objectives

- Name the six groups of nutrients.
- Give examples of foods in each level of the food pyramid.

Equipment and Materials

- Poster board or chalkboard
- Marker or chalk

Health Concept (30 minutes)

Gather the children into an information formation for the entire discussion.

Balanced Diet and Good Health

1. Introduce the concept: *A balanced diet is important for good health. Nutrients are found in food. There are six groups of nutrients: carbohydrates, fats, proteins, vitamins, minerals, and water. Each nutrient provides something important. Most foods provide more than one nutrient.*

2. Have the children name favorite foods; write those on one side of the board. Write the nutrients on the other side of the board. Identify, by drawing lines between the two sides, which foods provide various nutrients. Remember that one food can provide more than one nutrient.

The Food Pyramid

Introduce the concept: *A balanced diet includes foods from each food level, with more servings from the bottom of the pyramid. For example, people should eat 5 or more servings per day of fruits and vegetables. The food groups are*

> *bread (breads and cereals [grains]), 6-11 servings;*
>
> *fruits and vegetables, 5 or more servings;*
>
> *meats (meat, nuts, and fish [proteins]), 1-2 servings; and*
>
> *dairy (milk, cheese and other products made from cheese), 2-3 servings;*
>
> *fats (butter, oil), use sparingly.*

Draw the pyramid on the board. Have children name foods to fill in the pyramid.

K-1

LESSON 9
WATER SAFETY

Student Objectives

- State that no one should be in the water alone.
- Name one dangerous water situation.

Equipment and Materials

- PFD (Personal Flotation Device) (optional)
- 1-gallon empty plastic jug
- Large empty coffee can

Health Concept (30 minutes)

Gather the children into an information formation for the entire discussion.

Do Not Swim Alone

1. Introduce the concept: *Never swim or go near the water alone. This is the first and most important water safety rule.* Who is responsible for water safety? (Lifeguards, parents, friends, and **you**!) *Always tell an adult and get permission before swimming. When you go swimming, make sure there is a guard or another adult who will watch you. Many swimming facilities use the buddy system. Each swimmer has a partner, and on a signal, the partners check on each other.* When you go swimming, what should you make sure of? (That you have an adult's permission, someone is watching out for you [a buddy, parent, the lifeguard], and that you take responsibility for your own safety by making sure you are not alone.)

2. Tell the children: *You must make good decisions about when, where, and with whom to swim. If a situation does not feel safe, don't swim. Make sure a responsible adult is watching you. Having a backup is a good idea, too, like a buddy who also watches you. Remember, never swim or go near the water alone.*

Stay Away From the Edge

Introduce the concept: *Stay away from the edges of pools, lakes, ponds, rivers, and other places that have water. Children often play in places that are not safe.* Can you name some dangerous places children play? (Where the water is dark or cloudy, near a pond, lake or river, on a pool deck, in or near a canal—also vacant lots or empty buildings.) *It is just as dangerous to fall in the water by accident as it is to swim there alone on purpose.*

Use a Personal Flotation Device

1. Introduce the concept: *When in a boat or on the dock or near water, use a PFD. A PFD is a personal flotation device. These should fit you properly and be approved by the Coast Guard. Do not go in a boat without wearing a PFD. If you play near the water and do not intend to swim, you should wear a PFD. For example, if you are fishing with a parent on a pier or dock, wear a PFD.*

2. Ask the children: *Can you name some things that float that you could use in a water emergency?* (A PFD, a one-gallon empty plastic bottle, a large upside-down empty can, or the like.) Demonstrate how the gallon bottle or coffee can work. *You can use these in an emergency, but a PFD works better.*

Water Emergencies at Home

Introduce the concept: *Water emergencies can happen at home, too. Children can drown in the bathtub, toilet, dog's water dish, and home swimming pools and spas. Homes flood too. Children should not go near or in the water alone. Remember, even at home water safety is important.*

GRADES K-1

HEALTH

LESSON 10
TRANSPORTATION SAFETY

Student Objectives

- Describe crossing the street safety.
- Name a rule of bicycle safety.
- Select the safest place in the vehicle for him or her to ride.

Equipment and Materials

- None

Health Concept (30 minutes)

Gather the children into an information formation for the entire discussion.

Crossing the Street

1. Introduce the concept: *Crossing the street is part of transportation safety. Children should try to cross streets where there are crossing guards or parents. The second choice is at a traffic light. The last choice is at a crosswalk. Everyone should cross at corners, not in the middle of the block.*

2. Ask the children: *What should you do first when crossing the street?* (Decide where to cross.) *Even when there is a crossing guard, what should you do next?* (Look both ways for traffic.) *Is it safe to cross at a light when the "walking person" signal comes on?* (Only after looking in all directions for cars and trucks. A car may be turning right or may ignore the signal to stop.)

3. If possible go out to the streets near the school and practice crossing at a crosswalk, with a light, and with a guard.

Bicycle Safety

1. Introduce the concept: *The bicycle rider must be careful. Cars cannot always see bicycles. So the rider must watch for cars. Bicyclists should travel in the same direction as the cars. This makes it easier for car drivers to see the bike. Use intersections either like cars when you're on your bike or get off the bike and use the intersection like a pedestrian (someone walking). Bike riders should follow the same rules as car drivers, so bikes should not go into the road when a car is already using the road (yield to car traffic).*

2. If possible, go to the parking lot with a bike. Demonstrate how difficult it is for a car to see a bike that is on the opposite side of another car.

Vehicle Safety

1. Introduce the concept: *Passengers are responsible for safety when riding in a vehicle.*

   What should passengers do to make riding in a car safer? Bring out the following points:

Wear seat belts.

Children sit in the back seat with seat belts on.

Do not distract the driver with noise.

Do not block the rearview mirror.

Do not play in the car; for example, don't throw objects that could hit or distract the driver.

Most states have laws that require young children (e.g., five years and younger) or small children (e.g., 40 pounds and less) to ride in a car seat.

No one, especially children, should ride in the back of a pickup truck.

2. The police are often willing to discuss car safety with children. Check on local laws regarding passenger safety.

There will be times when the gymnasium or all-purpose areas are unavailable and when the weather prohibits outdoor classes. These lessons give you specific plans for making the most of these times.

UNIT ORGANIZATION

The lessons in this unit cover body parts, fitness, rhythmic activities, manipulative activities (throwing, catching, and striking), games, and creative movement. Feel free to pick and choose among the lessons, repeating them as desired.

LESSON ORGANIZATION

These lessons are structured as the lessons intended for the gymnasium or playing field with clearly stated objectives, equipment and materials lists, and specific activity instructions. Be especially careful to adapt setup instructions to fit the particular venue you're using.

TEACHING HINTS

Teaching in a classroom setting can be a pleasure or a disaster—depending on how well-prepared you and your students are. Plan now for how you'll adapt your rules and protocols to the classroom setting, keeping student ages and abilities and safety considerations in mind. When the day comes where you must teach in the classroom, try to select a lesson that will fit in with what students have been working on in the gymnasium setting. For example, a review of body parts (Lesson 1) may serve to improve gymnastics responses in the gymnasium.

Adapting Rules and Protocols

As at the beginning of the school year when you took the time to teach basic rules and protocols, it is well worth making time for training students to behave appropriately when you must hold physical education class in such a confined space. So the first lesson a particular class experiences in the classroom setting should consist primarily of showing the children how you wish to adapt the gymnasium rules and protocols to the classroom. Then each time you find yourself in the same situation, briefly but clearly review these adaptations with each class. The children will appreciate knowing what is expected of them and will respond more appropriately to the lesson.

Pay particular attention to teaching children how to make smooth transitions. At the beginning and the end of each lesson, you must find a way to set physical education apart from other curricular activities to help students focus. You might, for example, request that all other learning materials be put away, then after reviewing the rule and protocol adaptations, ask a question or two leading into the day's physical education topic, such as, "Does anyone remember what skill we worked on during our last class? What was the most important part of that skill to remember? Today we will work on a part of that skill that we can do safely in the classroom." Such an opening will draw students into the day's lesson. At the end, putting away equipment and sitting quietly doing relaxation or deep breathing exercises for two or three minutes may facilitate the transition back to academic work. You might allow the first group or row the privilege of getting a drink of water first. Children appreciate knowing what will happen and what is expected of them.

Kindergartners and First Graders

One advantage of teaching this age group in the classroom is that there may be an open space already available in which several of the children may work; perhaps a carpeted area used for "show and tell" will do for several activities. It is also quicker to move aside a few large tables than several small desks. Ask the children to sit quietly off to the side while you and their classroom teacher quickly make such changes. A classroom teacher who is willing to have the chairs stacked out of the way and the children already settled on the floor can be a real boon. Always, however, try to respect the classroom teacher's needs so that he or she will be able to move quickly into the next activity after your lesson. Sing with the children or ask questions relevant to the lesson during this transition time to keep them appropriately occupied.

Safety Considerations

You must select activities that take into account crowded conditions, low ceilings, electrical cords, and breakable objects. Then always take time to review your adaptations of your regular rules and protocols to help prevent injuries.

An important point to remember with this age group is that they will not anticipate hazards when playing in the classroom setting. You must be sure to warn them of specifics, such as, "Be careful not to trip over table legs as you move toward the edges of the room" or "We usually run during this game, but today we need to walk only. Can anyone tell us why?"

Making the Most of the Situation

It is important to keep in mind that classroom days are not "throw-away" days. With a little extra effort and planning they can be wonderful extensions of your gymnasium and outdoor time with the children. You may even gain some insights into individual children as you see them in the setting in which they spend most of their school days. Such insights may help you meet their needs throughout the rest of the year. You may also be able to forge a closer relationship with their teachers, enhancing collaboration opportunities.

LESSON 1
IDENTIFYING BODY PARTS

Student Objectives

- Correctly identify 26 body parts.
- Move 12 body parts on verbal request.
- Correctly identify five body surfaces.

Equipment and Materials

- None

Skill-Development Activities (30 minutes)

Identifying Body Parts

Arrange the children in a circle or scatter formation among the desks.

1. Tell the children: *Names help other people understand what we are talking about. Body part names are names that allow us to follow instructions, remember, and understand. Touch a part of your own body and name the part.* Have a few children share.
2. Tell the children: *Name and touch your head (neck, back, shoulder, hip, toe, leg, nose, finger, wrist, elbow, ankle, knee, foot, calf, thigh, shin, stomach, chest, chin, ear, eye, mouth, forehead, eyebrow, bottom).*
3. Repeat this activity, having the children keep their eyes closed.

Movement Challenges

Continue with the same setup.

1. Have the children perform the following challenges, demonstrating as necessary:

   Open and shut your eyes.
   Wiggle your ears.
   Shake your hands.
   Tap your toes.
   Snap your fingers.
   Bend your knees.
   Clap your hands.
   Make a fish mouth.
   Turn at your waist.
   Stamp your feet.
   Roll your shoulders.

Raise your eyebrows.

Circle your arms.

Rotate (turn) your wrists.

2. Ask the children: *Touch a foot to your other knee, (thumb to thumb, chin to chest, chin to shoulder, head to knee, ear to shoulder, heel to toe, elbow to knee, nose to knee, hand to ear, wrist to ankle, hands to hips).*

3. *Put both hands on your front (back, side, top, bottom) surfaces.*

4. Repeat this activity with the children sitting in chairs.

5. If desired, repeat with the children lying down.

LESSON 2
IDENTIFYING BODY PARTS

Student Objectives

- Correctly identify 26 body parts on another individual.
- Correctly identify five body surfaces on another individual.
- Correctly identify "right" and "left."

Equipment and Materials

- None

Skill-Development Activities (30 minutes)

Identifying Body Parts

Arrange partners in a circle or standing near their desks.

1. Ask the children to touch their head (neck, back, shoulder, hip, toe, leg, nose, finger, wrist, elbow, ankle, knee, foot, calf, thigh, shin, stomach, chest, chin, ear, forehead) to their partner's.

2. On your signal, have one child in each pair stand, sit, or lie down. Have the other child point to the body surface called. Use the following surface areas: front, top, side, back, bottom.

3. Repeat, reversing the partners' roles.

4. Continue the activity by asking the children to identify, by touching or lifting: *the left leg (right hand, right hip, left shoulder, left ankle, right elbow, left thumb, right ear).*

5. Turn the children to face another direction and continue: *Touch your left knee (right thigh, left arm, left wrist, right eye, right leg).*

Assign each child a new partner.

6. Ask the children to stand facing their partners. Present the following challenges:

   Touch your partner's right arm.

   Point to your partner's left foot.

   Touch left knees with your partner.

   Stand beside your partner (to the right of your partner).

   Point to the top of your partner.

   Touch the back of your partner (your partner's left shoulder, your head to the floor, your hands to a wall, your wrist to a desktop, your nose to a window, your knee to a chair, your ankle to a friend's ankle).

LESSON 3
IDENTIFYING BODY PARTS

Student Objectives

- Move body parts appropriately on request.
- Indicate understanding of size concepts (big, small, wide, narrow) by responding appropriately on request.
- Mirror a partner's movement.

Equipment and Materials

- None

Skill-Development Activities (30 minutes)

Movement Challenges

Arrange the children in scatter formation or in a circle.

1. Ask the children to respond with eyes closed:

   Nod your head.

   Open and close your mouth.

   Snap your fingers.

   Wiggle your toes.

2. Have the children respond with eyes open: *How big (small, wide, narrow, tall, short) can you make yourself?*

Assign each child a partner.

3. Present the following challenges. The children must respond in pairs: *How big (small, wide, narrow, tall, short) can you make yourselves?*

Mirror Game

Arrange pairs facing each other, and have the children choose one partner as the first leader.

1. Explain the activity: *The leader moves his or her body (staying in own personal space) into various positions. The other partner follows to make a mirror image of the leader.*
2. To demonstrate, have a child move while you mirror his or her movements.
3. Have the partners play the Mirror Game.
4. After the children play for two or three minutes, select a pair to show their movements to the class.
5. Have the partners reverse roles and continue playing.

K-1

LESSON 4
IDENTIFYING BODY PARTS

Student Objectives

- Correctly complete a three-part movement sequence in response to verbal cues.
- Move one or more body parts in isolation (while holding the other body parts still) to music.
- Practice two direction concepts (right and left).

Equipment and Materials

- Picture, color, and key cards (see figure below
- Record: Herb Alpert's "Herb Alpert and Tijuana Brass Vol. 2," Jack Capon's "Isolations," or any machine-like music (A break-dance piece or the like would be perfect.)

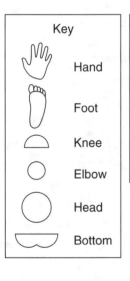

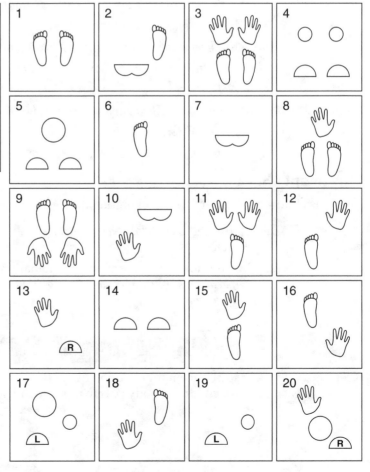

Skill-Development Activities (20 minutes)

Picture Cards for Balance

Arrange the children in scatter formation among the desks. Have cards available. Each card identifies one, two, or three body parts (see key card) and indicates right or left (see color card instructions in figure on page 351). Post the key card where all can see.

1. Have the children look at each card and balance with the correct parts (right or left) in the position shown. No other body parts should touch the floor.
2. Hold up the key card and explain the symbols for body parts.
3. Hold up the color card and explain the colors for right and left.
4. Hold up each picture card, allowing the children time to balance on the body parts in the picture.

Movement Activities

Keep the children in scatter formation among the desks.

1. For each of the following sequences, state the sequence, wait 2 to 10 seconds, and then give a "Go!" signal.
2. On the signal, have the children perform each sequence:

   Stand on one foot for five counts, then hop five times on the other foot.

   Raise your arms up high, bend your knees, lean to the side.

   Walk forward six steps; walk backward four steps.

   Turn around and jump three times.

   Touch your toes, stand on tiptoe, and hop on your right foot three times.

   Jump two times, hop on your left foot two times, and skip two steps.

   Walk in a circle, touch your toes, jump one time, and hop in a circle.

   Balance on one hand and one knee, balance on both knees, stand up, and jump backward.

   Touch your right shoulder, touch your left knee, touch your back, and touch your tummy.

   Jump up, touch your toes, hop in a circle to the left, and walk backward three steps.

Movement Challenges

Keep the children in scatter formation among the desks.

1. Tell the children: *Move the body parts I name with the music. Move only the body parts I mention—and only as I name them.*
2. Give the following parts and combinations of parts at 10- to 45-second intervals: *right arm, hips only, fingers and left leg, head, head and left arm, right leg and hips, right and left arms, thumbs only.*

Extension Activities (8 to 10 minutes)

Keep the children in scatter formation among the desks.

Assign each group of children a body part to move to music. All groups should move different body parts.

LESSON 5
PHYSICAL FITNESS

Student Objectives

- Perform flexibility, muscle endurance, and cardiovascular endurance exercises.

Equipment and Materials

- Recorded music (5 or more selections—any children's songs will work)
- 1 child-size chair per student

Skill-Development Activities (30 minutes)

Moderate to Vigorous Exercise to Music

Arrange the children in scatter formation among the desks.

1. Play a selection of music, and have the children run (hop on right foot, jump, march, hop on left foot) in place.
2. Each time the music changes to another selection, call out a new locomotor skill.

Chair Stretching

Arrange the chairs so that each child has a chair and enough room to stretch without touching others.

1. Describe and demonstrate the activity:

   Sitting in a chair with both feet flat on the floor, reach forward, extending both your arms as far as possible to the sides.

   Now touch the floor on the right, return to sitting, and touch the floor on the left.

   Move both your arms overhead and look backward, reaching backward as far as possible.

   Don't lift your feet from the floor or your bottom from the chair.

2. Have the children practice chair stretching. Cue the children: *Reach forward, sit up, arms out, reach right, sit up, reach left, sit up, arms up and together, look back, and stretch.*

3. Repeat five times.

Chair Leg Stretching

Keep the children in scatter formation, each with a chair.

1. Describe and demonstrate the activity:

   Sitting in normal position, grasp one knee with both hands, bend that knee, pulling your thigh to your chest (do not lean forward).

   Now lift the leg, relax, lower the leg slightly, grasp (grab/hold) the leg on the backside of the knee, straighten the leg, keeping your back against the back of the chair.

   With your toes pointed, flex your toes and hold, bend knee, and return to normal sitting position.

2. Have the children practice chair leg stretching. Cue the children: *Grasp, pull, relax, regrasp, stretch toes and point, bend ankle and hold, bend knee, and stop.*

3. Have them repeat five times with each leg (alternating legs).

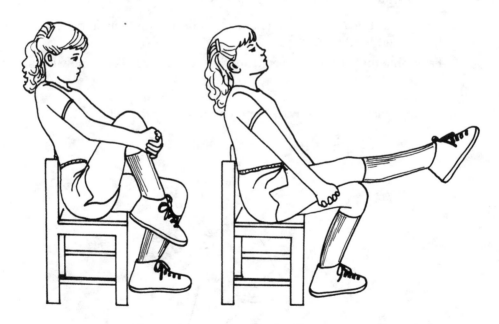

Chair Busters

Keep the children in scatter formation, each with a chair.

1. Describe and demonstrate chair busters, part 1: *Standing behind the chair with your arms extended (stretched) and hands on the back of the chair and keeping your body straight, lower your weight onto your arms until your chest touches the back of the chair; hold, then return to the starting position.*

2. Have the children practice chair busters, part 1, repeating 5 times. Cue the children: *Lower slowly, bending arms, and hold, two, three, four, five; push up, arms straight.*

3. Describe and demonstrate chair busters, part 2: *Sitting on the chair, holding on to the chair seat with both hands, bring your knees to your chest; keeping your legs bent, hold, and then return to start.* Cue the children: *Lower slowly, bending arms, and hold, two, three, four, five; push up, arms straight.*

4. Have the children practice chair busters, part 2, repeating 10 times. Cue the children: *Legs up, hold two, three, four, five; legs down.*

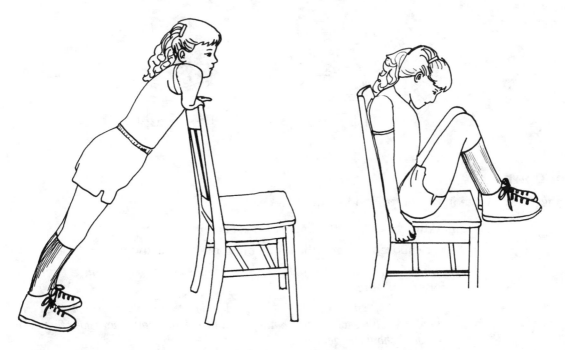

High Steppers

Keep the children in scatter formation, each with a chair.

1. Describe and demonstrate the activity:

    Stand facing the chair, and place your right leg on the chair seat.

    Step up on your right leg, lifting your body into standing position on the chair.

    Stand with weight on both feet on the chair, then step down on the right foot.

    Repeat, starting with the left foot.

    Keep repeating, alternating feet.

2. Have the children practice high steppers at a rate of 30 in 60 seconds. Cue the children: *Up-and-down, and up-and-down, and. . . .*

Cool-Down

Arrange the children in scatter formation with their chairs.

1. Remind the children of the importance of cooling down.
2. Have the children perform the following cool-down activities:

   Walk slowly around the room, taking deep breaths and slowly exhaling. (Continue this for one minute.)

   Sit in a chair with your eyes closed, take a deep breath, breathe out slowly, and relax your shoulders. Think about your shoulders, let them hang; don't move your fingers or arms; feel your shoulders get heavy.

   Take another breath and relax your legs. Your legs are so heavy you can't pick them up; they are going to sleep.

   Take another breath, and as you breathe out slowly, relax your head and neck. Hold very still so your head doesn't bounce forward. Relax your hands and arms. Make a fist with your hands, and hold it! (Wait 10 seconds.)

   Now let go, relaxing your arms and hands. (Keep quiet for a few seconds.) *Now stand up and gently shake your whole body. Everyone sit in your own chairs quietly.*

LESSON 6
PHYSICAL FITNESS

Student Objectives

- Perform flexibility, muscle endurance, and cardiovascular endurance exercises.
- Work with a partner or small group.

Equipment and Materials

- Recorded music (5 or more selections—any children's songs will do)

Skill-Development Activities (30 minutes)

Moderate to Vigorous Exercise to Music

See Grades K-1: Classroom Activities, Lesson 5, page 353.

Partner Pushing

Arrange partners in scatter formation.

1. Describe and have two children demonstrate the activity:

   Partners stand back-to-back with arms hooked at elbows and legs stretched (extended) slightly to the front.

   Push against each other for five counts, and then relax, staying in the same position.

   Repeat this five times for five counts each.

2. Have the children practice partner pushing.

Partner Pulling

Keep partners in scatter formation.

    1. Describe and have two children demonstrate the activity:

> *Sit on the floor, facing each other with feet touching and holding hands. One partner has legs bent at the knees, and the other partner has legs straight at the knees.*

> *By gently pulling the arms and pushing with the legs, change roles so the opposite child has legs bent and straight.*

> *Repeat this five times.*

    2. Have the children practice partner pulling.

Partner Stretching

Keep partners in scatter formation, still facing each other. Have each pair choose a leader.

    1. Describe and demonstrate the activity: *The leader stretches left, front, right, or back, and the other partner must do the opposite (for example, if the leader goes forward the other partner goes backward). Leaders, stretch at least once in each direction.*

    2. Have the children practice partner stretching.

    3. Have the pairs change leaders and continue practicing.

Partner Treadmill

Keep partners in scatter formation, with partners on all-fours, facing each other.

    1. Describe and have two children demonstrate the activity:

> *The first partner brings one leg up between the arms, then quickly extends that leg and brings the other leg forward (this is like running in place but with hands on the floor).*

> *The first partner repeats this 10 times, then the second partner does this 10 times, then the first repeats 10, and so on, until each child has had five turns.*

    2. Have the children practice partner treadmill.

Wiggle Worms

Keep partners in scatter formation, lying on their stomachs beside each other, facing opposite directions.

    1. Describe and have two children demonstrate the activity:

> *Stretch (extend) your arms and legs.*

One partner lifts arms and legs off the floor and holds for five counts, while the other partner lies very still.

Change roles and repeat.

2. Have the children practice wiggle worms. Cue the children: *Up, two, three, four, five; switch two, three, four, five; switch, two, three, four, five.*

Partner Moving Parts

Keep partners in scatter formation, and have each pair choose a leader.

1. Describe and have two children demonstrate the activity:

   The leader moves a body part slowly (for example, making slow circles with the arms), and the other partner copies the leader.

   After a short time, I will tell you to switch, and the other partner will become the leader.

   When you and your partner have moved all your body parts and can think of no other parts to move, go sit down.

2. Have the children practice partner moving parts.

3. When only one pair remains standing, ask all the children to stand and copy the last pair until they have finished going through all the body parts.

LESSON 7
RHYTHMS

Student Objectives
- Copy a rhythmic pattern.
- Move to a rhythmic pattern.
- Create a rhythmic pattern.

Equipment and Materials
- 2 wooden blocks or a drum (to help children beat the rhythm)
- 1 pair of rhythm sticks per child
- Marching music (any march)

Skill-Development Activities (30 minutes)

Clapping a Rhythmic Pattern
Arrange the children in a long line, arm's distance apart. Suggested symbols:
- – means beat (clap)
- ! means accented beat

1. Clap the following patterns while the children listen:
   - (– – – –) even ("one, two, three, four")
   - (– – – !) accent on last beat of four beats ("one, two, three, four")
   - (– – !) accent on last beat of three beats ("one, two, three")
2. Ask the children: *Could you hear a difference in those patterns?*
3. Repeat the patterns with the children clapping the pattern after you clap the pattern.
4. Repeat each pattern several times, clapping with the children and counting aloud.

Walking Patterns
Arrange the children in scatter formation among the desks.

1. Lead the children through each pattern:

   Step-clap, step-clap, step-clap, step-clap, pause, repeat.

   Three small step-claps, one large step-clap, pause, repeat.

   Two small step-claps, one large step-clap, pause, repeat.

   Two small step-claps, two large step-claps, pause, repeat.

   Two large step-claps, three small step-claps backward, pause, repeat.

2. Repeat as time allows.

Marching in a Pattern

Keep the children in scatter formation among the desks, and give each child a pair of rhythm sticks. Caution the children to behave responsibly with the sticks.

1. To marching music, have the children follow the marching patterns with walking steps and tapping the beat with rhythm sticks.
2. Describe the marching pattern. Have several children demonstrate.
3. The children march to the front, down the center line as shown in figure below.
4. Direct alternate children to go right and left, following the line to the back of the room.
5. Once at the back of the room, have the children pair up coming down the center line, with alternate pairs going right or left, creating groups of four at the back of the room.

Stop the music and have the children set their sticks on their desks.

6. Have the children practice the marching pattern without music or sticks. Stand at the front of the center line and point the direction for each child to turn.

Have the children retrieve their sticks.

7. Practice with music and sticks.
8. Stop when all children make one line.

Ask children to return to their desks.

9. Ask each child to work on a new rhythmic pattern with the rhythm sticks.
10. Select a child to present his or her pattern to the class.
11. Ask the class to copy the pattern.
12. Repeat with as many children as possible.

Back of classroom

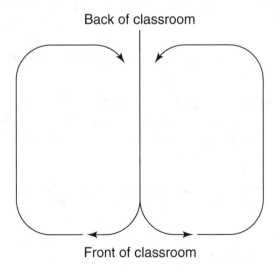

Front of classroom

LESSON 8
THROWING, CATCHING, AND STRIKING

Student Objectives

- Practice throwing, catching, and striking an object.

Equipment and Materials

- Station 1: 1 chair and 4 rings (rope or rubber) per child
- Station 2: 1 beanie launcher and 2 beanbags per child
- Station 3: 2 beanbags per child and 1 wastebasket
- Station 4: 4 colors of modeling clay, 1 large piece of paper with target drawn in pencil, tape
- Station 5: 1 ring stick game per child or rings to throw over chair legs (can throw unbreakable cups instead)
- Station 6: 1 yarn or soft foam ball and 1 stocking paddle (or other paddle) per child

Skill-Development Activities (30 minutes)

Stations

Divide the children into six groups of four (adjust equipment for different-size groups). Assign each group to a station.

1. Describe and demonstrate each of the stations.
2. Allow groups to practice at their stations for four minutes.
3. Rotate until all the children have been at all the stations.

Station 1: Ring Toss

Turn one chair per child upside-down. Place a supply of rings at this station.
 Toss the rings onto the legs of the chairs.

Station 2: Beanie Launchers

Set up one beanie launcher and two beanbags per child.
 Practice stepping (launching) and catching one, and then two, beanbags.

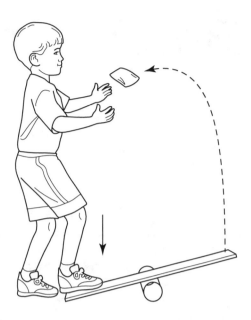

Station 3: Wastebasket Toss

Arrange the children in a circle around the wastebasket, approximately five ft from the wastebasket.

Toss the beanbags into the wastebasket. Once successful at that, toss over the head of a child standing between you and the wastebasket until you can toss over all the children at your station into the wastebasket. As the children become successful, have one child throw at a time.

Station 4: Modeling Clay Throw

Tape a large sheet of paper to the wall on which you have drawn a target with a pencil (do not draw with crayons, as the clay will not stick as well to crayon markings). Use a different color of clay for each group member.

Throw modeling clay at the paper, trying to hit a target. You will have to throw very hard to make the modeling clay stick. As you are successful, move further back from the paper.

Station 5: Ring Stick Games

Place the ring toss games approximately five ft from each child, with the children spread at least two ft apart from each other.

Make a ring (or cup) go over the stick.

Station 6: Fluff Balls and Paddles

Arrange the children in a scatter formation in a designated area.

See how many times you can bounce the fluff ball on the paddle without stopping or dropping the ball. As you do better, try to make the ball go higher between hits.

LESSON 9
GAMES

Student Objectives

- Play a game in the classroom, following the rules.

Equipment and Materials

- 6 erasers

Skill-Development Activities (30 minutes)

Eraser Relay

Divide the children into six groups, with half of each group at opposite ends of the classroom.

1. Explain the activity:

   The first child in line places an eraser on her or his head and walks as quickly as possible to the other half of the group.

   The first child in that line takes the eraser and places it on her or his own head, and walks back to the other half of the group. We will continue until all children have had a turn.

   Sit in line after your turn.

   If the eraser falls off your head, or if you touch the eraser once you have begun walking, you have to go back to the starting place and repeat the turn.

2. Have the children do the Eraser Relay.

Frog

Choose one child to be the "Frog." Remove the Frog's chair from the playing area; you can mark it with a book, or move it to the side, along with any empty chairs in the room.

1. Describe and demonstrate the activity:

   The Frog squats at the front of the room like a frog, while the rest of you form a circle around the Frog.

   Join hands and walk around the Frog, singing "Frog, frog, in the sea."

   Continue until the Frog hops out of the circle and goes to an empty seat.

   Once the Frog is seated, the rest of you try to get an empty seat; the child without a seat is the new Frog, and the game begins again.

2. Have the children play Frog.

LESSON 10
CREATIVE MOVEMENT

Student Objectives

- Respond appropriately to challenges.
- Create their own movement patterns to a beat set by the teacher.

Equipment and Materials

- 1 drum or 2 wooden blocks

Skill-Development Activities (30 minutes)

Movement to a Beat

Arrange the children standing in scatter formation.

1. Use the drum or blocks to make an even beat, one beat per second.
2. Using the appropriate movement, direct the children to respond to the beat until the drum stops. Begin with the children standing:

   Moving down, down, down (16 beats)

   Moving up (8 beats)

   Moving in a circle in your own space (30 beats)

   Moving to someone else's space (8 beats)

   Moving back to your space (8 beats)

   Making small movements (16 beats)

   Making fast movements (8 beats)

   Making big movements (4 beats)

Movement Challenges

Arrange the children in small groups (by tables or rows is an easy way to do this).

1. Have the children perform the following challenges:

   Everyone in the group must find a different level (at the same high level, at the same medium level, at the same low level, at a different level while balancing on one body part, at the same level while balancing on two body parts).

   Make yourselves curved and touching someone in your group (straight and touching someone in your group).

   Some people in each group balance at a low level. The rest of the group balance over them at a high level.

Within each group, number the children.

2. Tell the children: *Child 1 moves for the first eight beats* (emphasize last beat), *child 2 follows for eight counts, and so on. When the last child finishes moving eight counts, the first child continues. Change levels each time child 1 moves (change speed, change direction, make big movements, make small movements).*

GRADES 2-3

ORGANIZATION

The purpose of the five lessons in this unit is to practice the routines you want your students to follow in the instructional units. When students understand the routines, you'll have fewer discipline problems, lose less time on management, and become a team with your students, working from the same plan. Ultimately, this means you'll have more time for instruction. The skills we present in this unit are more advanced, but they are based upon the skills we presented in Grades K-1: Organization. These lessons, however, can stand alone.

UNIT ORGANIZATION

The lessons review or introduce the following organizational tasks:

- Signals and receiving information
- Formations and boundaries
- Equipment and spacing
- Stations and rotations
- Rules and consequences

The lessons are a fun way to introduce and/or review important skills; repeat them as needed throughout the year. For children who have experienced Grades K-1, some of these lessons will be a review. Do not, however, assume the children know or remember the content of the lessons; some will, and some won't. Even if you're sure they know these routines, it is important to review what you expect of them and to remind them that you will be using these routines. Moreover, repeating something that the children know builds confidence right from the start of the school year, helping to create an enjoyable and comfortable learning environment. Table O2.1 outlines the content of the lessons.

LESSON ORGANIZATION

Like all the other lessons in this book, we have organized each lesson systematically and have included a list of clear objectives and necessary equipment to make planning easier for you. The activities start with a warm-up, progress to skill development, and end with a concluding activity. Unlike the rest of the lessons in this book, however, the content of the lessons and the instructional focus is on management and behavior. Although you may be anxious to teach movement skills and fitness concepts, remember that time spent on organization and class management now is time saved throughout the school year, as your classes will run more smoothly.

TEACHING HINTS

Feel free to modify certain aspects of the lessons. For example, some schools or districts have uniform consequences for rules infractions that may be different from those presented in these lessons. Further, use your individual preferences for signals and formation names. Use the lessons as presented or modify them to suit your individual situation and preferences. The key is to take a few days and cover the topics until you and your students are comfortable with the routines. This is a worthwhile investment of time, one we observe in expert teachers and know helps novice teachers be more effective.

See also Grades K-1: Organization, pages 3-18 for more information on why and how to use the organization lessons.

Table O2.1: Unit Plan for Grades 2-3: Organization

Week 1: teach and review rules

Monday: signals and information and line and scatter formations
Tuesday: formations and boundaries
Wednesday: signals, formations, and boundaries
Thursday: equipment and spacing
Friday: stations and rotations and rules and consequences

LESSON 1
RULES, SIGNALS AND INFORMATION, LINE AND SCATTER FORMATIONS

Student Objectives

- Recognize class rules.
- Cooperate when developing class rules.
- State one reason for each rule.
- Move into scatter, information, and line formations.
- Define personal and general space.
- Stop and look on signal.

Equipment and Materials

- Poster board or chalkboard
- Chalk or marker
- 4 cones
- Whistle

Warm-Up Activities (5 minutes)

Circle Stop

Arrange children in a large circle with 5 to 10 ft between children. Designate a signal (whistle, bell, clap, or the like) as the start and stop signal.

1. Have the children jog around the circle on the signal.
2. Signal stop and either have them continue jogging in the same direction or reverse directions upon your softly spoken instructions. Repeat several times.

Skill-Development Activities (20 minutes)

Signals

Arrange the children in a close group, sitting on the floor.

1. Ask the children: *Does anyone remember what this is called?* (An "information formation.")
2. Explain and demonstrate the start/stop signal. You may have more than one signal, so you may develop any additional signals you feel you need.
3. *Note*: Signals, rules, and formations were presented in Grades K-1: Organization; these are reviewed here in Grades 2-3.

Signal Game

Keep the children in the information formation.

1. Direct the children to begin talking to each other. To encourage this you may want to whisper a secret to one child and tell him or her to pass it on to another child.

2. Signal for quiet. Tell the children: *You should be quiet and watch for instructions when you hear that signal.* Try giving the signal quietly or in a sneaky way to "trick" the students. Praise them when they become quiet quickly: *Good listening and following the signal!*

3. Repeat several times.

Class Rules

Gather the children into an information formation.

1. Introduce the idea that rules are important. Tell the children:

   Rules help everyone have a chance to learn.

   Rules help us to know what to expect.

   Rules make physical education (and life) safer.

2. Give and ask for examples of rules that protect us, and explain that when broken, people often get hurt: *What happens when drivers run a red light?* (It makes it hard or impossible for the other drivers to stay safe.) *In addition to being safer, traffic rules prevent chaos.* (Define chaos.)

3. Ask the children to help develop class rules:

   What makes you mad during class or recess?

   How might a rule help, for example, when you're pushed by another student or when you have a ball taken away by another student?

   Can you make up a rule that would help for each of these examples?

4. Lead a discussion of the following list of rules:

   - *Rule 1: Follow directions. When the teacher is talking, do not talk; when another student has permission to talk, do not talk; it is OK to talk at other times; do what you are asked to do.*

   - *Rule 2: Hands off other students. Do not put your hands, feet, or other body parts on anyone else.*

   - *Rule 3: Be careful of equipment and others. Do not handle equipment roughly; do not move wildly.*

   - *Rule 4: Stop, look, and listen on the signal. Do not move or talk after the stop signal; listen for directions.*

   - *Rule 5: Do not fight or stop practice or play. Do not try to make others angry or hurt their feelings; do not disrupt the game or practice.*

5. As the students suggest rules that are appropriate, write them on the board.

6. Review the rules, reading them first, then going over each rule and asking why it is important.

   - *Rule 1: Follow directions.* (If you follow directions, everyone will learn.)

   - *Rule 2: Hands off other students.* (This way everyone will be safe.)

   - *Rule 3: Be careful of equipment and others.* (If we take good care of equipment, everyone will be safe and there will be enough equipment for physical education class.)

- *Rule 4: Stop, look, and listen on the signal.* (Everyone can learn, play, be safe, and have fun.)
- *Rule 5: Do not fight or stop practice or play.* (This way everyone can learn, play, be safe, and have fun.)

7. Note: After class, prepare a poster of your rules for future reference.

Scatter Formation

Arrange the children in scatter formation. (See Grades K-1: Organization, Lesson 3, page 12.)

1. Ask the children: *Spread your arms out. If you can touch someone, you need to move out of reach.*

2. Introduce or review the concepts of personal and general space. Tell the children: *The area within arm's reach is "personal space," the area between everyone's personal space is called "general space."*

3. Remind the children: *Be sure to stay out of other children's personal space.*

Line Formation

Keep the children in scatter formation. Define a line between two cones.

1. Point to the line between the two cones.

2. Tell the children: *On the signal, you need to move into the line formation on this line. Tomorrow class will begin in this formation.*

3. *You should be quiet enough to hear my voice. I'm going to test you on this.* On your verbal signal have the children move from line formation to scatter formation to information formation as quickly as possible. Repeat several times. End this activity in an information formation.

Concluding Activities (5 minutes)

Class Rules

The children should already be in an information formation.

1. Ask the children: *What are the class rules?* Review list.

2. *Tell us why each rule is important.* Discuss.

LESSON 2
FORMATIONS AND BOUNDARIES

Student Objectives

- Move from a circle to a line formation and the reverse.
- Move within and around boundaries.
- Move and freeze on signal.

Equipment and Materials

- 4 cones
- Signal
- Physical Education Rules poster
- Chalk or tape to mark a large circle on the floor or ground

Warm-Up Activities (5 minutes)

Movement Tasks

Use the four cones to define a large rectangle around the marked circle. Arrange the children in a line formation between two of the cones. (This is where you told them to begin today's lesson, when you practiced line formations in the previous lesson.)

1. Signal the children to *take giant steps* (or *run, hop, tiptoe, skip, run fast, walk backward*) to another boundary of the area (any space between two cones in the rectangle).
2. Repeat several times.

Skill-Development Activities (20 minutes)

Circle and Line Formations

Continue with the large rectangle defined in the warm-up activity. Have the children line up between two of the cones again. Create a circle inside the rectangle.

1. Ask the children: *Does anyone remember what this formation is called?* (Line formation.)
2. Ask the children to look at their present locations and remember them. Suggest that they look for some special landmark, like a line, clover, bare spot, or the like.
3. Describe and point out a circle.
4. Signal the children to move, in any way they want, to the circle and stand still. Adjust the children's positions in the circle as necessary so they are evenly spaced.
5. Signal the children to move back to their starting positions on the line.
6. Repeat several times until the children master the skill.

7. Signal the children to form a circle around you in a new location without a circle in chalk, tape, or the like visible.

8. Tell the children: *Return to the line.*

9. This game is more fun if you "draw out" your signal and add suspense to when changes will be made by walking around the children with deliberate steps and slow movements.

10. Repeat, ending with the children in a line between two of the cones.

Moving Within and Around Boundaries

Continue using the large rectangle, with the children in a line between two of the cones.

1. Walk the entire class around the edge of the rectangle.

2. Describe the boundaries: *This is an area "inside," and everything else is "outside" this area.*

3. Scatter the children within the area.

4. Signal the children to move carefully but randomly within the area.

5. Signal stop.

6. Tell the children: *Move around the boundaries* (outside the area, as they did earlier).

7. Signal stop. *Move randomly within the area.*

8. Signal stop. *Move around the boundaries.*

9. Repeat.

Formations Review

Continue using the large rectangle, with the children in a line between two of the cones.

Remind the children of all the formations practiced thus far (line, circle, scatter, information), of personal space and general space, and of inside and outside areas defined by boundaries. Tell the children:

> *Make a circle around me.*
>
> *Move around the outside of the area.*
>
> *Make a scatter formation inside the boundaries.*
>
> *Show me where your personal space is with your arms.*
>
> *Make a line formation between the two cones I'm pointing at.*
>
> *Show me you know where your personal space is.*
>
> *Move into an information formation.*
>
> *Move to a line formation between me and the corner cone I'm pointing at.*
>
> *Walk around inside the area in general space.*
>
> *Make a circle around me.*
>
> *Point to a boundary.*
>
> *Walk on a boundary.*
>
> *Move back into an information formation around me.*

Concluding Activities (5 minutes)

The children should have ended the last activity in an information formation.

Review the class rules. Ask the children to give a reason why each rule is important:

- *Rule 1: Follow directions.* (So everyone can learn.)
- *Rule 2: Hands off other students.* (So everyone will be safe.)
- *Rule 3: Be careful of equipment and others.* (So everyone will be safe, and there will be enough equipment for physical education.)
- *Rule 4: Stop, look, and listen on the signal.* (So everyone can learn, play, be safe, and have fun.)
- *Rule 5: Do not fight or stop practice or play.* (So everyone can learn, play, be safe, and have fun.)

ORGANIZATION

LESSON 3
SIGNALS, FORMATIONS, AND BOUNDARIES

Student Objectives

- Move and freeze on signal.
- Identify the four formations.
- State the class rules.

Equipment and Materials

- 4 cones
- Signal

Warm-Up Activities (5 minutes)

Movement Patterns

Use the four cones to define a large rectangle in the middle of the play area. Arrange the children in scatter formation inside the rectangle.

Tell the children to move in the following patterns, changing direction on signal:

> *Hop forward (backward, left, right). Repeat.*
>
> *Jog in a circle* (clockwise). *Turn around and jog in a circle in the opposite direction* (counterclockwise).
>
> *Skip forward, then jump backward.*
>
> *Walk forward, change direction, change direction, change direction* (any direction).

Skill-Development Activities (20 minutes)

Move and Freeze

Keep the children in scatter formation.

1. Describe and demonstrate the game:

   Everyone moves in the manner I tell you—for example, run, walk, hop, move high, move slowly, jump, walk backward—within the boundaries.

   When you hear the signal to freeze, stop and hold as still as possible. I will select the best frozen student and ask that student to select the next movement task.

   Then I will signal you to start moving again. Be sure you're quiet enough to hear my instructions.

2.   Have the children play Move and Freeze.

Formations Review

Arrange the children in scatter formation inside a rectangle marked by four cones.

Review all the formations practiced thus far (line, circle, scatter, information), of personal space and general space, and of inside and outside areas defined by boundaries. Tell the children:

> *Make a circle around me.*
>
> *Move around the outside of the area and freeze on signal.*
>
> *Make a scatter formation inside the boundaries.*
>
> *Show me you know where your personal space is.*
>
> *Make a line formation between the two cones I'm pointing at.*
>
> *Walk around inside the area in general space and freeze on the signal.*
>
> *Make a circle around me.*
>
> *Move into an information formation.*

Concluding Activity (5 minutes)

Review the Rules

Gather the children into an information formation.
    Ask the children to state the rules.

- Rule 1: Follow directions.
- Rule 2: Hands off other students.
- Rule 3: Be careful of equipment and others.
- Rule 4: Stop, look, and listen on the signal.
- Rule 5: Do not fight or stop practice or play.

Review the Formations and Signals

Continue in the information formation.
    Ask the children:

> *Name the formations.*
>
> *What is the signal?*
>
> *Where are the boundaries?*
>
> *What are personal and general space?*

GRADES 2-3

ORGANIZATION

LESSON 4
EQUIPMENT AND SPACING

Student Objectives

- Practice getting and returning equipment.
- Demonstrate near and far spacing.

Equipment and Materials

- 4 cones
- Enough beanbags for one-fourth of the class
- Enough hoops for one-fourth of the class
- Enough balls for one-fourth of the class
- Enough jump ropes for one-fourth of the class
- 6 carpet squares

Warm-Up Activities (5 minutes)

Formations Review

Arrange the children in scatter formation inside a large rectangle defined by the four cones.
Ask the children to complete the following tasks:

> Move into a circle formation around me.
>
> Jog clockwise.
>
> Freeze!
>
> Jog counterclockwise.
>
> Freeze!
>
> Move to a line formation between me and that cone (point).
>
> Jump up and down in personal space.
>
> Freeze!
>
> Move to a scatter formation.
>
> Run in general space inside the boundaries.
>
> Freeze!
>
> Jog around the outside of the boundaries clockwise.
>
> Freeze!
>
> Move to the line I'm pointing to (on one side of the rectangle).
>
> Hop across the rectangle to the opposite line.
>
> Make a circle around me.

Skill-Development Activities (20 minutes)

Station Rotation

Place the carpet squares one on each of the long sides of the rectangle and one in each corner. Divide the children into six groups.

1. Assign each group to a carpet square.
2. Number each carpet square, saying the numbers for each group aloud as you point to the square: *Say each number aloud with me.*
3. *On the signal, each group should move from their carpet square to the next higher number; number 6 should go to number 1.* Continue until the groups are back to their starting positions.
4. Repeat in reverse (1 goes to 6, 6 to 5, 5 to 4, and so on).

Giving Out Equipment

Divide the children into four groups, and assign one group to each corner of the play area.

1. Assign each group a type of equipment (e.g., beanbags to group 1, hoops to group 2, balls to group 3, and ropes to group 4).
2. Name a group. Have each child in the group get one piece of equipment from you, return to the group's station, and sit down with the equipment.
3. Repeat with the other three groups.

Concluding Activity (5 minutes)

Near-Far Concepts

Arrange the children in scatter formation with partners. Have the children perform and name the following concepts:

Stand back-to-back, touching backs. (Near position.)

Turn and face your partner. (Near position.)

Turn back-to-back to your partner and walk 10 steps away from your partner. (Far position.)

Partners in pairs form a line facing me, one pair behind the next so that everyone is facing me in one long line. Your partner's and your inside shoulders should be touching. (Near position.) *Move five steps sideways from your partner.* (Far position.)

Partners on this side (point to one line) *make a circle standing close together.* (Near position.)

Partners on this side (point) *make a circle standing far apart.* (Far position.)

ORGANIZATION

LESSON 5
STATIONS AND ROTATIONS, RULES AND CONSEQUENCES

Student Objectives

- Help decide the consequences for rules in-fractions.
- Move to station formation and rotate.

Equipment and Materials

- 4 cones
- Enough hoops for one-fourth of the class
- Enough balls for one-fourth of the class
- Enough carpet squares for one-fourth of the class
- Enough jump ropes for one-fourth of the class

Warm-Up Activities (5 minutes)

Near-Far Concepts

Arrange partners in scatter formation. Ask the children to respond quickly to the following statements:

Stand close to your partner.

Move as far away from your partners as possible.

Class, make a double circle, one partner standing beside the other, so one partner is on the inside and the other is on the outside circle.

Move sideways so that the inside circle is smaller, the outside circle is larger, and you and your partner are in far position.

One partner move outside the boundaries while one partner stays inside the boundary in near position.

One partner move outside the boundaries while one partner stays inside the boundary in far position.

One partner make a line on this side (point); *the rest of you make a line over there* (point).

Make the lines as short as possible, so you are in near position.

Make the lines longer, so you are in far position.

Consequences

Gather the children into an information formation.

1. Read the rules.
   - *Rule 1: Follow directions.*
   - *Rule 2: Hands off other students.*
   - *Rule 3: Be careful of equipment and others.*
   - *Rule 4: Stop, look, and listen on the signal.*
   - *Rule 5: Do not fight or stop practice or play.*

2. Ask: *Are there any questions about the rules?* (Pause.) *We have talked about why it is important to follow the rules. Having and following rules makes it easier for everyone to learn, saves equipment, and keeps us safe. What happens if someone breaks a rule?* (It interferes with learning, it may be dangerous, equipment may be broken, and there should be consequences for the rule breaker.)

3. Ask the children: *What consequences would be fair?* Discuss. Suggested consequences include the following:
   - First offense: three-minute time-out.
   - Second offense: six-minute time-out.
   - Third offense: Call parents.
   - Fourth offense: Send to principal.

4. *Note*: Remember to use behavior contracts, good behavior rewards, and good or poor behavior letters to parents. After class, make a poster of the consequences.

Stations

Use the cones to define a rectangle. Divide the children into four groups, and assign one group to each corner of the play area. Assign one type of equipment to each group.

1. Name a group and have one member of that group get the equipment for the entire group.

2. Allow the children to do creative movements with the equipment for one to three minutes.

3. Have each group rotate to the next station and repeat.

4. Continue until all four groups have been at all four stations.

5. Have one child from each station return the station's equipment.

Concluding Activities (5 minutes)

Movement Patterns

Arrange the children in scatter formation in the middle of the play area. Tell the children to move in the following patterns, changing on the signal:

Hop forward (backward, left, right). Repeat.

Jog in a circle (clockwise), *turn and jog in a circle the opposite direction* (counterclockwise).

Skip forward, then jump backward.

Walk forward, change direction, change direction, change direction (any direction).

Move in a zigzag pattern.

Move in a straight line.

Move in a curved line.

FITNESS

As you know, physical fitness and physical activity are important in reducing health risks. Children who learn to enjoy being active now are more likely to remain active as adults. So present physical activities and fitness activities that are fun for the children, combined with other activities that teach the motor skills necessary for lifelong participation. To help you in this endeavor, this fitness section has three parts: fitness testing, the Fitness Hustles, and fitness activities.

UNIT ORGANIZATION

We have designed the fitness activity lessons to be repeated as frequently as is appropriate in your program. Select the lessons you want to teach and incorporate those into your annual plan. The activities you select should reflect your personal preferences as well as the needs of your students. You can, for example, organize fitness as a five-to seven-week unit: Fitness Hustles one week, Fitness Hustles reviewed a second week, and the other activities (circuit training, challenges, and moderate to vigorous games) during the remaining weeks. Conduct fitness testing before and/or after such a fitness unit, according to your preferences and needs. As an alternative approach, you can intersperse individual lessons or weeks of fitness throughout the year. Finally, there are numerous ways to use the fitness lesson plans, so experiment to determine which suits your situation. Table F2.1 presents an overview of this fitness material.

LESSON ORGANIZATION

Each lesson begins with a warm-up, includes fitness training activities, and ends with conclud-ing activities, which are where we introduce fitness concepts. Include or delete the fitness concept (see table F2.2), depending upon your situation. For example, some teachers may prefer to use the fitness concepts as a group in the classroom rather than spread them out over several lessons.

TEACHING HINTS

Children this age are gaining competence in motor skills that will help them maintain or improve their current fitness levels. Take advantage of their natural enthusiasm and high energy levels during the fitness lessons.

Second and Third Graders

Second and third graders are typically between 7 and 10 years of age. Some girls may experience their prepubescent growth spurt at 10 to 11 years of age. So, some girls may rapidly grow taller and develop breasts. With this growth may come additional fat. Your expectations, however, for males and females should be very similar, even though some males may have greater strength than some females.

Children in this age range are usually very active and enjoy the challenges of physical fitness activities. Remember, this unit should be fun, to encourage future participation in physical activities. To this end, do not compare children to each other when you evaluate their fitness levels; instead, compare children to their own previous performances or to a standard that is challenging but attainable. Moreover, encourage participation, improvement, and enthusiasm. For example, children typically enjoy participating with their teacher. So at least some of the time it is important for the children to see you actively involved. Clearly, you are a role model. Furthermore, children will feel more comfortable trying new activities if they see you trying new activities—even if you are having trouble mastering the skill.

Obese and Overweight Students

The most challenging students to teach in a fitness unit are typically the overweight and obese students. Often these students feel frustrated, embarrassed, and incapable. But do not give up on them or allow them to avoid the fitness lessons. Instead, focus on encouraging participation and personal improvement. Allow these children to build their strength and stamina slowly so as not to discourage them altogether. In addition, discussing the value of physical activity may change the behaviors and attitudes of overweight and obese children. Finally, do not allow other children to ridicule anyone for any reason in your classes. Create an environment in which each child can feel safe, competent, and capable.

Safety Considerations

Allow children to drink water frequently, especially if the weather is hot. Children may respond to heat and cold differently than you do, so when the temperatures are extreme you must look for signs of heat stress or illness. Remember that it takes 8 to 12 weeks, exercising three or more days each week, to train the cardiovascular system. This means that children who have low endurance will need lots of time and encouragement to improve. Work toward gradual improvements in all fitness areas to avoid injuries, illness, and discouragement.

Table F2.1: Unit Plan for Grades 2-3: Fitness

Week 2: testing

Monday: introduce backsaver sit-and-reach test and fitness run
Tuesday: introduce sit-ups and push-ups
Wednesday: practice fitness run, backsaver sit-and-reach test, sit-ups, and push-ups
Thursday: testing and self-testing of fitness
Friday: testing and self-testing of fitness

Week 3: warm-up routine and Hustles

Monday: introduce warm-up routine
Tuesday: introduce Hustle 1
Wednesday: introduce Hustle 2
Thursday: introduce Hustle 3
Friday: review Fitness Hustles

Week 7: Hustles

Monday: introduce Hustles 4-6
Tuesday: review Fitness Hustles
Wednesday: review Fitness Hustles
Thursday: review Fitness Hustles
Friday: review Fitness Hustles

Week 11: circuit training

Monday: **fitness activity:** circuit 1–slow-fast and **fitness concept:** physical fitness and health
Tuesday: **fitness activity:** circuit 2–the Hustle and **fitness concept:** physical fitness, physical activity, and health
Wednesday: **fitness activity** circuit 3–progressive and **fitness concept:** components of fitness–definitions
Thursday: **fitness activity** circuit 4–stretches and **fitness concept:** components of fitness–examples
Friday: **fitness activity** circuit 5–jogging and **fitness concept:** components of fitness–measuring

Week 16: vigorous games

Monday: **fitness activity:** Parking Garage and **fitness concept:** components of fitness–training
Tuesday: **fitness activity:** Three-on-Three and **fitness concept:** cardiovascular endurance
Wednesday: **fitness activity:** Crows and Cranes and **fitness concept:** muscular endurance
Thursday: **fitness activity:** Slap Tag and Circle Tag and **fitness concept:** flexibility
Friday: **fitness activity:** Line Soccer and **fitness concept:** body composition

Week 28: fitness challenges

Monday: **fitness activity:** ropes and **fitness concept:** muscular strength and endurance
Tuesday: **fitness activity:** hoops and **fitness concept:** cardiovascular endurance and resting heart rate
Wednesday: **fitness activity:** ball and **fitness concept:** individual differences
Thursday: **fitness activity:** team and **fitness concept:** behavior and heredity
Friday: **fitness activity:** strength and **fitness concept:** risk factors

Week 30: Hustles

Monday: review Fitness Hustles
Tuesday: review Fitness Hustles
Wednesday: review Fitness Hustles
Thursday: review Fitness Hustles
Friday: review Fitness Hustles

Week 31: testing

Monday: practice fitness run, backsaver sit-and-reach test, sit-ups, and push-ups
Tuesday: testing and self-testing
Wednesday: testing and self-testing
Thursday: testing and self-testing
Friday: testing and self-testing

Table F2.2: Fitness Concepts

The following are the 15 fitness concepts presented in the Grades 2-3: Fitness lesson plans. Since the lessons can be repeated, we have suggested more than one learning activity for each concept. Thus, when you repeat the lessons, you can use a different learning activity for the fitness concept.

1. Regular exercise helps you develop physical fitness. *Physical fitness* is regular exercise or sport that contributes to health and allows us to do activities throughout the day. *Regular exercise* means that you exercise at least three times a week.
2. Physical activity, like walking, housework, or yard work, contributes to health. *Physical fitness* is exercise or sport; *physical activity* is moving.
3. Physical fitness has five parts: cardiovascular endurance, muscular strength and endurance, flexibility, and body composition.
4. A physically fit person can exercise for 20 minutes without stopping, do 30 sit-ups, some push-ups or chin-ups, stretch their body (e.g., touching toes), and has a healthy amount of body fat.
5. To measure or decide how fit you are, you could ride a bike, swim or jog for 20 minutes, do sit-ups and push-ups, and touch your toes. Someone could measure your skinfolds to see how much fat you have.
6. A physically fit person exercises regularly, jogging, cycling, or swimming, doing sit-ups, push-ups, and stretching. These exercises can help our muscles stay healthy and keep our body from storing too much fat. To be physically fit we must exercise at least three times each week for three continuous 10-minute bouts each day.
7. *Cardiovascular fitness*, or heart fitness, is also called *aerobic fitness*. A person who can jog, ride a bike, or swim for 20 minutes is demonstrating aerobic fitness.
8. *Muscular endurance* is when a muscle or group of muscles can make the same movement many times without getting too tired. Sit-ups, push-ups, and chin-ups demonstrate muscular endurance. *Muscular strength* is how much work a muscle can do one time. Muscles get stronger through exercising, for example, moving heavy objects.
9. Flexibility is important to preventing injuries. Slowly stretching our body parts helps us to be more flexible.
10. Too much or too little body fat is not healthy. Body fat can be measured with skinfolds. Our diet, physical activity, and genetics can determine how much fat we have.
11. Muscles become stronger and able to do the same amount of work more times as a result of regular exercise.
12. Resting heart rate is lowered with regular exercise. After you have been lying still for 15 to 30 minutes (or when you first wake up in the morning) the number of times your heart beats is your *resting heart rate.*
13. Each person has to do a different amount of work to become physically fit.
14. Two things decide health and fitness: the characteristics you inherit from your parents (such as height or body type) and your behaviors (what you do every day).
15. Things that may hurt our health and fitness are called *risk factors.* Some risk factors are because of the way we behave; we can change these. Other risk factors are inherited, and we cannot change these.

GRADES 2-3

FITNESS

LESSON 1
FITNESS TESTING 1

Student Objectives

- Practice the backsaver sit-and-reach.
- Practice the fitness run.
- Explain why practice and warm-up before a test are important.
- Demonstrate cooperation when practicing the backsaver sit-and-reach.

Equipment and Materials

- Envelope or bag with papers inside
- 1 carpet square or mat per child
- 4 cones
- 1 yardstick per group or 1 sit-and-reach box per group

Warm-Up Activities (5 minutes)

Pony Express

Arrange the four cones in a square or rectangular shape with 50 to 100 ft between the cones. Divide the class into four groups, and have each group stand near one cone, outside the rectangle or square.

1. Tell each group: You are a relay team on the Pony Express.
2. Explain the activity:

    On the signal, one group (point to designate) *will jog clockwise* (point) *to the next cone with one person carrying the "mail"* (an envelope or bag with papers inside). The children stay together as a group while they are jogging.

    As soon as you get the mail to the next group, hand it off to the next group, who must begin jogging to the next cone.

    Each round should increase the speed, from jogging to fast jogging and finally to running, until everyone is running as fast as possible.

    Take turns allowing different people in your group to carry the mail each round you're jogging or running.

3. Have the children run the Pony Express.
4. If desired, repeat the activity counterclockwise, gradually slowing back to the jog.

Skill-Development Activities (20 minutes)

Backsaver Sit-and-Reach

Arrange the children in scatter formation.

1. Begin with slow stretching:

    Stand with your feet shoulder-width apart and reach up overhead. Bend to each side and to the front and back. Keep your knees slightly bent. Repeat several times.

    Squat, placing your hands on the ground with your arms outside your knees, bending just enough to touch the ground.

    Slowly stand, keeping your hands on the ground—do not lock your knees straight and keep your thighs parallel to the ground. Stop if it hurts.

    Bend again and repeat several times.

Set up one backsaver sit-and-reach station for each small group you will form. Gather the children into an information formation at one station to explain and demonstrate the test.

2. Explain that before doing the backsaver sit-and-reach test everyone should warm up by stretching: *Warming up does two things: it reduces the chance of injury and improves performance on the test.*

3. Explain and demonstrate the test:

    Sit with your legs extended straight out in front of your body. Your knees shouldn't be locked.

    Place the bottoms of your feet against a flat vertical surface, like the sit-and-reach box or a curb (see figure on page 391).

    Place the foot of one leg against the knee of the other leg.

    One hand should be on top of the other with your fingers and arms extended forward.

    Reach slowly toward your toes while bending forward.

4. To measure place the yardstick or the sit-and-reach box with the 15-in mark even with the bottom of the feet and the 0-in end of the yardstick toward the child's abdomen (the yardstick on a sit-and-reach box should be affixed to the box at the 15-in mark). This way large numbers indicate more flexibility. Almost everyone should be able to reach the yardstick and therefore score. The score is determined by the number the fingers reach and hold for two to three seconds. This is to discourage "bouncing" and encourage slow stretching. For the test, record the best of three trials.

Have the children form partners or small groups, and assign each pair or group to a backsaver sit-and-reach station.

5. Allow the children to practice: *One partner does the backsaver sit-and-reach, and the other partner measures and makes sure the form is correct:*
    - *Fingers together with one hand on top of the other*
    - *Knees unlocked*
    - *End point held for two or three counts*
    - *No bouncing*

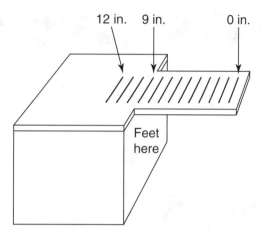

12 in.   9 in.   0 in.

Feet here

Fitness Run

Use cones or other markers to identify a running area. The total distance to be run is 880 yards; a rectangle of 100 by 10 yd fits into most playing fields and can be run four times to complete the half mile. Gather the children into an information formation to explain the test.

1. Tell your students:

   The fitness run is designed to test cardiorespiratory (aerobic) fitness.

   Practicing the test is important because each person must learn a good pace and be in shape before the test.

   Usually, it's best to begin by running slowly and increase your speed when the finish is near.

   Today we will all run together slowly, then at the end anyone who wants to run fast can sprint to the finish.

Spread the group around the outside of the rectangle.

2. Tell the children: *Jog slowly around the outside of the rectangle. Talk to each other and to me! Your pace should allow you to still be able to talk.*

3. *Help me count the laps as we complete each.* On the last lap, remind the children they may run faster if they want to. You should jog, not run, to encourage all skill levels.

Concluding Activities (5 minutes)

Discussion

Gather the children into an information formation.

1. Discuss the importance of fitness testing. Ask: *Why is practicing the test important before taking a fitness test?* (One reason is to do your best on the test. Second, to learn the "tricks" of the test, like pacing in the fitness run. Another reason is to be in shape before the test.)

2. Ask: *Why is warming up important before taking a fitness test?* (One reason is to avoid injury. A second reason is to help you do your best.)

3. *How do athletes in various sports warm up?* (Football teams often do an exercise routine, then skill drills; basketball players warm up with shooting before the game; golfers go to the practice range; and so forth.)

LESSON 2
FITNESS TESTING 2

Student Objectives

- Practice sit-ups.
- Practice push-ups.
- Cooperate by watching a partner do sit-ups and push-ups.
- List two criteria each for a correct sit-up and push-up.

Equipment and Materials

- Envelope or bag with papers inside
- 4 cones
- 1 carpet square or mat per child

Warm-Up Activities (5 minutes)

Pony Express

See Grades 2-3: Fitness, Lesson 1, page 389.

Skill-Development Activities (20 minutes)

Push-Ups

Gather the children into an information formation.

1. Describe and demonstrate a correct push-up:

    Start with your hands and the toes of your feet on the ground, hands shoulder-width apart, feet together or comfortably apart.

    Extend your legs so that they and your upper body form a nearly straight line (see figure on page 393).

    Lower your body toward the ground by bending your elbows, keeping your body straight.

    When your body is nearly to the ground, move back up to the starting position.

    Keep your body "stiff as a board."

2. Have the children practice giving you feedback on correct and incorrect push-up form. Emphasize supportive ways to offer feedback.

Arrange pairs in scatter formation.

3. Tell the children: *One partner will do push-ups while the other watches to see that the person is performing the push-up correctly.*

4. After a few minutes, have the children switch roles. Circulate, helping children give accurate feedback.

Sit-Ups

Gather the children into an information formation.

1. Describe and demonstrate a correct sit-up:

   The sit-up is really done with a rolling motion.

   Begin by lying on your back with your legs bent slightly at the knees so the bottoms of your feet are flat on the ground (see figure below).

   Choose one of the two hand-arm positions: You can cross your hands and arms on your chest so that your hands are resting on the opposite shoulders or you can place your hands on the sides of your head with a finger placed on each ear, keeping your elbows lined up (parallel) with the back of your head (keep them there, not pulling forward past the ears).

   Perform each sit-up slowly, rolling your chin to your chest to lift your head, next your shoulders, then your lower back off the ground. During the movement, you should feel the muscles under your belly button working.

   Once your lower back is off the ground, unroll to the start position.

2. Have the children practice analyzing your sit-up form.

Arrange the children in scatter formation, each with a carpet square or mat.

3. As you say "*rolllllllll*" have each child do a sit-up, emphasizing moving slowly.

4. After one sit-up ask each child to point to the muscles that did the work (the muscles under the belly button). Repeat several times.

5. Have the partners check each other's form and have them practice giving feedback as with push-ups.

Fitness Run

See Grades 2-3: Fitness, Lesson 1, page 391.

Concluding Activities (5 minutes)

Discussion

Gather the children into an information formation.

1. Discuss correct form for sit-ups and push-ups.
2. Ask: *What are the important things to remember about the sit-up?* (Rolling up, going slowly, not pulling on the head and neck.)
3. Ask: *What are the important parts of the push-up?* (Keeping body stiff as a board, bending the elbows, going close to the ground, but stopping before touching the ground.)

Alternative Learning Activities

Gather the children into an information formation for this discussion.

1. Tell the children:

   Sit-ups build up our stomach muscles. (If desired or appropriate for the particular class, introduce the word abdominal.)

   When do you use your stomach (abdominal) muscles? (Bending, climbing, and swinging.)

   Now lie down and try to stand without using your hands and arms, going directly from lying on your back to standing.

   What muscles did you use? (Stomach/abdominal.) *Do it again and think about what your stomach (abdominal) muscles are doing.*

2. Tell the children:

   Push-ups help build our arm strength.

   What does good arm strength help you with? (Lifting objects, hitting a baseball far, and so on).

3. Have the children demonstrate different ways to use their arm muscles on climbing equipment. Even when climbing a ladder, we use our arms to pull us up.

GRADES 2-3

LESSON 3
FITNESS TESTING 3

Student Objectives

- Warm up for the fitness tests.
- Practice the fitness tests.
- Help each other score the fitness tests by counting sit-ups and push-ups and measuring the backsaver sit-and-reach.

Equipment and Materials

- Envelope or bag with papers inside
- 1 carpet square or mat per child
- 4 cones
- 1 yardstick or 1 sit-and-reach box per group

Warm-Up Activities (5 minutes)

Pony Express

See Grades 2-3: Fitness, Lesson 1, page 389.

Skill-Development Activities (20 minutes)

Divide the children into six groups. Set up three stations, one for each of the following: sit-ups, push-ups, and the sit-and-reach. Set up the fitness run as described in Grades 2-3: Fitness, Lesson 1, page 391.

1. Have three groups practice the fitness run, while the other three groups rotate through the remaining three fitness activities (sit-ups, push-ups, and sit-and-reach). Allow about two to three minutes each to complete the sit-ups, push-ups, and sit-and-reach stations. You may want to time the fitness run so you have an idea of how long the children can exercise continuously. A goal for the school year of 10 to 20 minutes of moderate to vigorous, continuous exercise is appropriate. Allow less fit children to walk or jog slowly as they build up endurance so they don't get discouraged.

2. The children should walk after finishing the fitness run until you signal to switch with the other three groups.

Switch halves of the class.

3. Have the children who have completed the fitness run rotate through the other three stations, and have the children who have completed the other three stations do the fitness run.

Concluding Activities (5 minutes)

Discussion

Gather the children into an information formation.

1. Discuss the fitness testing that will occur during the next two classes.
2. Show the children the recording sheets you will use (see form F2.1) and explain that you will use the scores not to judge or grade them, but rather to show how their fitness levels improve and how much they grow during the year.

FORM F2.1 FITNESS RECORDING SHEET

Name	Height	Weight	Triceps	Calf	Subscapular	Sum skinfolds

Name	Sit-and-reach, Day 1	Sit-and-reach, Day 2	Run, Day 1	Run, Day 2	Sit-ups, Day 1	Sit-ups, Day 2	Push-ups, Day 1	Push-ups, Day 2

LESSONS 4 AND 5
FITNESS TESTING 4 AND 5

Student Objectives

- Demonstrate current level of cardiorespiratory fitness, muscular endurance, and flexibility.
- Cooperate by participating in self-testing.
- Participate in skinfolds assessment.

Equipment and Materials

- Envelope or bag with papers inside
- 1 carpet square or mat per child
- 4 cones

- Enough sit-and-reach boxes or yardsticks for one-fourth of the class (if possible)
- Skinfold calipers
- Scale to measure weight
- Tape, yardstick, or other tool to measure height
- Fitness Assessment Recording Sheet (form F2.1)
- A privacy screen if you have assistance with the testing
- Any equipment needed for game(s) played in Fitness Testing 5

Warm-Up Activities (5 minutes)

Pony Express

See Grades 2-3: Fitness, Lesson 1, page 389.

Skill-Development Activities (25 minutes)

Fitness Testing 4

Divide the children into four groups. Set up three stations, one for each of the following: sit-ups, push-ups, and the sit-and-reach. Set up a body composition testing station with the scale, measuring tape, and skinfold calipers. If an assistant is available to help you, use a privacy screen. Someone should be available to supervise the class at all times.

1. Have three groups rotate through the three fitness activities (sit-ups, push-ups, and backsaver sit-and-reach). Allow two to three minutes for each of these stations. Two groups will repeat stations 1 to 3 today.

2. For the fourth group, you or a helper (parent, assistant) measures and records height and weight of each child, taking each privately. You measure and record skinfolds at the triceps, calf, and subscapular.

3. Ask the children how many sit-ups, push-ups, and the score on the backsaver sit-and-reach test when you measure the skinfolds so these can be recorded. Measuring

height, weight, and skinfolds will take two class periods, so rotate the groups, measuring some children each day in each group. (*Note:* You also need to save 10 minutes at the end of each day for testing cardiorespiratory fitness; see "Fitness Testing 5" next.) You can record the best score from both days for the fitness tests.

Fitness Testing 5

Set up as required for the active game you select.

Assess cardiorespiratory fitness by observing the children's playing a moderate to vigorous game during the remaining 10 minutes. Remember, if the weather is hot, make sure the children have ample opportunity to drink water. Even in cool weather, children should drink water after exercising.

1. Select one or more games from Grades 2-3: Games and Sports, Warm-Ups pages 464-470.

2. As you observe children play the games (and in the fitness runs on the previous days), determine whether the child is more active than most children, similar to most children, or less active than most children. Daily living is within the context of their culture—if they cannot play with their peers this is a problem. Teachers may share this information with parents. Testing will take two days, so children will have two fitness scores for fitness runs, sit-ups, push-ups, and sit-and-reach. You can record both scores and send the best score home to parents.

Alternative Fitness Activities

1. Select activities that stress muscular strength and endurance of arms and shoulders, legs, and abdominal area (for example, climbing apparatus, overhead ladders, or chinning bars).

2. Rate the children as more active than other children, similar to other children, or less active than other children for each component (muscular strength, muscular endurance, and cardiorespiratory endurance [running]).

3. Prepare individual feedback recording sheets and the parent's letter. Send home, requiring students to have them signed and returned (see form F2.2). Encourage children and parents to talk about the fitness testing.

FORM F2.2 FITNESS LETTER AND DATA SHEET FOR PARENTS

Every School
1 Learning Lane
Home Town, USA

Dear Parent/Guardian:

We do fitness testing and assessment of growth in physical education

- to help children understand the relationship between health, fitness, and activity,
- to help the teacher assess the effectiveness of the program, and
- to track growth and fitness in the children.

How the test is scored:

- The number for push-ups and sit-ups represents the number of correct push-ups and sit-ups done without stopping (no time limit).
- The score for the sit-and-reach represents flexibility; a score of 15 represents touching the toes. Scores above 15 represent reaching beyond the toes.
- Cardiovascular fitness is scored as (1) similar to most children, (2) more active than most children, or (3) less active than most children. Children who are less active than most should be encouraged to participate in a variety of activities, especially moderate to vigorous activities.
- Height is in inches; weight is in pounds. Skinfolds represent subcutaneous fat and are the sum of three skinfolds in millimeters (mm).

During physical education we will be working on fitness. So we expect everyone to improve or maintain fitness during the year. Normally children will grow, so both height and weight will also increase. Please sign the form at the bottom, under the most recent fitness scores. Please have your child bring the form to our next physical education class. I will record the next test scores on this form. Then you and your child can see how much growth and fitness improvement occurs during the year. If you have any questions please call (teacher's name) at (teacher's phone number).

Sincerely,

I.M. Fit

— —

I have read the above letter and discussed its contents with my child.

Parent/guardian's signature_____

(continued)

Name_____ Age_____

Test	Date	Date	Date
Sit-and-reach			
Sit-ups			
Push-ups			
Fitness run			
Sum of skinfolds			
Weight			
Height			
Parent signature			

Dear parent or guardian:

GRADES 2-3

FITNESS

LESSON 6
GRADES 2-3 FITNESS WARM-UP ROUTINE

Student Objectives

- Demonstrate the steps to a fitness warm-up.
- Perform the Grades 2-3 Fitness Warm-Up Routine.
- Identify two reasons warming up is important.
- Work together as demonstrated by not bumping into each other during the activity.

Equipment and Materials

- Envelope or bag with papers inside
- Record player or tape player
- Music: "Thriller" from *A Thriller for Kids* (Side B), Georgiana Stewart, Kimbo Records (KIM 7065)
- 4 cones

Warm-Up Activities (5 minutes)

Pony Express

See Grades 2-3: Fitness, Lesson 1, page 389.

Skill-Development Activities (20 minutes)

Steps for the Grades 2-3 Fitness Warm-Up Routine

Arrange the children in scatter formation.

1. Teach each step of the Grades 2-3 Fitness Warm-Up Routine individually.
2. Have the children practice the steps in the routine as indicated.

Standing Body Stretch 1

Standing with your feet comfortably apart and your arms extended overhead, stretch up alternately with right and left arms:

Count 1, stretch left arm up,

Count 2, return to start,

Count 3, stretch right arm up, and

Count 4, return to start.

Standing Body Stretch 2

Stand with your feet comfortably apart and arms extended overhead. Stretch up with your left, then your right arm, then your left arm, and so on. Each time you lift an arm, lift one heel. You can lift your right heel with your right arm or with your left arm (in opposition). The rhythm is one count for each stretch and lift.

Side-to-Side Lunge

Stand with your feet comfortably apart, hands on your hips. Step to the right with your right foot (side lunge position). At the same time, stretch your right arm out to the side:

> *Counts 1 and 2, step and stretch to the right and*
>
> *Counts 3 and 4, return to starting position.*
>
> *Repeat to left.*

One-Half Knee Bend With Elbow Pull

Stand with your feet comfortably apart and heels flat, arms parallel to the floor at shoulder-high with elbows bent. Bend your knees while pulling your elbows back:

> *Count 1, bend knees and pull elbows, and*
>
> *Count 2, return to starting position.*

Step-Touch

Stand with your feet comfortably apart. Step to the right with your right foot, touch your left foot in place near your right foot, step to the left with your left foot, and touch your right foot in place near the left:

> Count 1, step left,
>
> Count 2, touch right,
>
> Count 3, step right, and
>
> Count 4, touch left.

Step-Touch With Arm Swing

Step-touch to right and left. With steps to right, swing your arms up to the right and overhead and clap. With steps to left, swing your arms up to the left and overhead and clap:

> Count 1, step right,
>
> Count 2, touch and clap,
>
> Count 3, step left, and
>
> Count 4, touch and clap.

Grades 2-3 Fitness Warm-Up Routine

Keep the children in scatter formation.

1. Play "Thriller."
2. After listening to the song, help the children learn, then perform the following sequence of steps:

    Standing body stretch 1 (16 counts),

    Standing body stretch 2 (16 counts),

    Step-to-side lunge (16 counts),

    One-half knee bend with elbow pull (16 counts),

    Step-touch (8 counts),

    Step-touch with arm swing (8 counts),

    Step-touch (8 counts),

    Step-touch with arm swing (8 counts),

    Standing body stretch 1 (16 counts),

    Standing body stretch 2 (16 counts),

    Step-to-side lunge (16 counts),

    One-half knee bend with elbow pull (16 counts),

    Step-touch (8 counts),

    Step-touch with arm swing (8 counts),

    Step-touch (8 counts),

    Step-touch with arm swing (8 counts), *and*

    March in place to the end of music.

Concluding Activities (5 minutes)

Discussion

Gather the children into an information formation.

1. Discuss warming up: *Why is warming up important?* (To prevent injuries and help achieve the best performance possible.)

Divide the class into two groups.

2. Have one group demonstrate the warm-up routine to music, with your leading with cues and demonstration. Have the other group watch the performers, saying the steps and counts aloud.
3. Switch group roles.

LESSON 7
FITNESS HUSTLE 1

Student Objectives

- Demonstrate the steps to Fitness Hustle 1.
- Perform Fitness Hustle 1.
- Watch classmates perform Fitness Hustle 1.

Equipment and Materials

- Record player or tape player
- Music: "Thank God I'm a Country Boy" from *Jump Aerobics*, Don Disney, Kimbo Records (KIM 2095)
- Music for Grades 2-3 Fitness Warm-Up Routine: "Thriller" from *A Thriller for Kids* (Side B), Georgiana Stewart, Kimbo Records (KIM 7065)

Warm-Up Activities (5 minutes)

Grades 2-3 Fitness Warm-Up Routine

See Grades 2-3: Fitness, Lesson 6, page 405.

Skill-Development Activities (20 minutes)

Steps for Grades 2-3 Fitness Hustle 1

Keep the children in scatter formation.

1. Introduce each step of Fitness Hustle 1 individually.
2. Have students perform steps in combinations as indicated.

Bounce in Place
Make small jumps in place with your feet together.

Skier
Jump side-to-side with your feet together.

Jog Kickbacks

Jog in place, kicking your free leg back on each step.

Knee Dips

Stand with your feet comfortably apart, heels flat, and hands on hips. Bend your knees halfway (bending further may cause injuries), *keeping your back straight and heels flat, then straighten your legs and return to the starting position.*

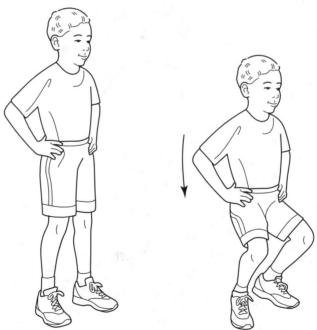

1. Introduce the routine for Fitness Hustle 1 using the preceding steps.
2. Direct the children to listen to the music for 58 to 60 counts.
3. Have the children practice the steps for the Fitness Hustle 1 in order without the music. Give the counts aloud.
4. Have the children say the steps in order.
5. Practice the steps in order with the music, giving the counts aloud.
6. Repeat the entire routine with counts.
7. Repeat the routine with the music and no counts.

Fitness Hustle 1

1. Play "Thank God I'm a Country Boy."
2. Lead the children in performing the following steps:

   Listen to music (8 counts),
   Bounce in place (16 counts),
   Skier (16 counts),
   Jog kickbacks (18 counts),
   Bounce in place (16 counts),
   Skier (16 counts),
   Jog kickbacks (18 counts),
   Bounce in place (16 counts),
   Skier (16 counts),
   Jog kickbacks (18 counts), *and*
   Knee dips (12 counts).

Concluding Activities (5 minutes)

Divide the class into two groups.

1. Have one group demonstrate Fitness Hustle 1 to music, with your leading with cues and demonstration. Have the other group watch the performers, saying the steps and counts aloud.
2. Switch group roles.

LESSON 8
FITNESS HUSTLE 2

Student Objectives

- Demonstrate the steps to Fitness Hustle 2.
- Perform Fitness Hustle 2.
- Watch classmates perform Fitness Hustle 2.

Equipment and Materials

- Record player or tape player
- Music "Devil Went Down to Georgia" from *Jump Aerobics,* Don Disney, Kimbo Records (KIM 2095)
- Music for Grades 2-3 Fitness Warm-Up Routine: "Thriller" from *A Thriller for Kids* (Side B), Georgiana Stewart, Kimbo Records (KIM 7065)

Warm-Up Activities (5 minutes)

Grades 2-3 Fitness Warm-Up Routine

See Grades 2-3: Fitness, Lesson 6, page 405.

Skill-Development Activities (20 minutes)

Review Fitness Hustle 1

See Grades 2-3: Fitness, Lesson 7, page 409.

Steps for Fitness Hustle 2

Keep the children in scatter formation.

1. Introduce each step of Fitness Hustle 2 individually.
2. Have students perform steps in combinations as indicated.

Jumping Jacks
Standing with feet together and arms at sides, jump, landing with your feet out to the sides in a straddle as your arms swing up and clap overhead. Then return to start by jumping and landing with your feet together while your arms swing back down to your sides.

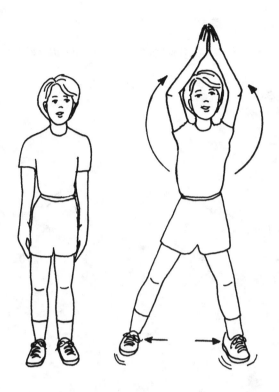

Jog and Punch Forward

Jog in place and punch forward, alternating your right and left arms.

Pendulum Rock

Bounce on your right foot with your left leg extended to the side. Then bounce on your left foot with your right leg extended to the side.

Fitness Hustle 2

1. Play "The Devil Went Down to Georgia."
2. After listening to the song, help the children learn, then perform the following sequence of steps without and then with the music:

> *Bounce in place* (16 counts),
> *Jumping jacks* (16 counts),
> *Jog and punch forward* (16 counts),
> *Jumping jacks* (16 counts),
> *Jog and punch forward* (16 counts),
> *Pendulum rock* (8 counts),
> *Knee dips* (8 counts),
> *Bounce in place* (8 counts),
> *Pendulum rock* (8 counts),
> *Knee dips* (8 counts),
> *Jumping jacks* (16 counts),
> *Jog and punch forward* (16 counts),
> *Jumping jacks* (16 counts),
> *Jog and punch forward* (16 counts),
> *Jumping jacks* (16 counts),
> *Jog and punch forward* (16 counts),
> *Pendulum rock* (8 counts),
> *Knee dips* (8 counts),
> *Bounce in place* (8 counts),
> *Pendulum rock* (8 counts),

Knee dips (8 counts),

Jumping jacks (8 counts), *and*

Jog and punch forward (8 counts).

Concluding Activities (5 minutes)

Divide the class into two groups.

1. Have one group demonstrate Fitness Hustle 2 to music, with your leading with cues and demonstration. Have the other group watch the performers, saying the steps and counts aloud.

2. Switch group roles.

LESSON 9
FITNESS HUSTLE 3

Student Objectives

- Demonstrate the steps to Fitness Hustle 3.
- Perform Fitness Hustle 3.
- Watch as classmates perform Fitness Hustle 3.

Equipment and Materials

- Record or tape player
- Music: *The Aerobic Express* (Side B), Gay Bergman, Kimbo Records (KIM 9092)
- Music: "Beat It" and "Thriller" from *A Thriller for Kids,* Georgiana Stewart, Kimbo Records (KIM 7065)

Warm-Up Activities (5 minutes)

Grades 2-3 Fitness Warm-Up Routine

See Grades 2-3: Fitness, Lesson 6, page 405.

Skill-Development Activities (20 minutes)

Review Fitness Hustle 2

See Grades 2-3: Fitness, Lesson 8, page 412.

Steps for Fitness Hustle 3

Keep the children in scatter formation.

1. Introduce the alternating stride jump (next) and review relevant steps from Fitness Hustles 1 and 2 (see new routine) to teach Fitness Hustle 3.
2. Have students perform steps in combinations as indicated.

Alternating Stride Jump

With feet together and hands on hips, jump to forward-stride position with your right foot forward and left foot back. Jump again, returning to starting position, and repeat with your left foot forward and right foot back.

Fitness Hustle 3

Keep the children in scatter formation.

1. Play "Beat It."
2. After listening to the song, help the children learn, then perform the following sequence of steps without and then with the music:

   Bounce in place (first 16 counts of the introduction),

   Skier (16 counts),

   Pendulum rock (16 counts),

   Alternating stride jump (16 counts),

   Jog kickbacks (16 counts),

   Skier (16 counts),

   Pendulum rock (16 counts),

   Knee dips (16 counts),

   Skier (16 counts),

   Pendulum rock (16 counts),

   Skier (16 counts),

   Pendulum rock (16 counts),

   Alternating stride jump (16 counts),

   Jog kickbacks (16 counts),

   Alternating stride jump (16 counts),

   Jog kickbacks (16 counts),

Skier (16 counts),

Knee dips (16 counts),

Skier (16 counts),

Knee dips (16 counts),

Bounce to the end of the music.

Concluding Activities (5 minutes)

Divide the class into two groups.

1. Have one group demonstrate Fitness Hustle 3 to music, with your leading with cues and demonstration. Have the other group watch the performers, saying the steps and counts aloud.

2. Switch group roles.

LESSON 10
FITNESS HUSTLE REVIEW

Student Objectives

- Perform warm-up routine to music.
- Perform Fitness Hustles 1-3 to music when given cues.

Equipment and Materials

- Record player or tape player
- Music: *The Aerobic Express*, Gay Bergman, Kimbo Records (KIM 9092)
- Music for Grades 2-3 Fitness Warm-Up Routine: *A Thriller for Kids*, Georgiana Stewart, Kimbo Records (KIM 7065)
- Music: *Jump Aerobics*, Don Disney, Kimbo Records (KIM 2095)
- 4 cones

Warm-Up Activities (5 minutes)

Grades 2-3 Fitness Warm-Up Routine

See Grades 2-3: Fitness, Lesson 6, page 405.

Skill-Development Activities (20 minutes)

Have the children perform Fitness Hustles 1, 2, and 3. See Grades 2-3: Fitness, Lessons 7, 8, and 9, pages 409, 412, and 415, respectively.

Concluding Activities (5 minutes)

Pony Express

Have the children begin with running and work down to walking as a cool-down. See Grades 2-3: Fitness, Lesson 1, page 389.

Note: This lesson can and should be repeated.

LESSON 11
FITNESS HUSTLES 4-6

Student Objectives

- Perform the Grades 2-3 Fitness Warm-Up Routine to music.
- Give and follow directions in Fitness Hustle 4.
- Perform Fitness Hustles 4-6 to music when given cues.

Equipment and Materials

- Record player or tape player
- Music for Grades 2-3 Fitness Warm-Up Routine: "Thriller" from *A Thriller for Kids* (Side B), Georgiana Stewart, Kimbo Records (KIM 7065)
- Music for the Hustle(s) selected:

   Fitness Hustle 4 Music: "How Will I Know," Whitney Houston, BMG/ Arista Records (B000002vcq)

   Fitness Hustle 5 Music: "Theme from 'The Dukes of Hazard,'" Waylon Jennings, RCA (ASIN B00000102T)

   Fitness Hustle 6 Music: "Let's Hear it for the Boy" from *Footloose Soundtrack*, Deniece Williams, Columbia

Warm-Up Activities (5 minutes)

Grades 2-3 Fitness Warm-Up Routine

See Grades 2-3: Fitness, Lesson 6, page 405.

Skill-Development Activities (20 minutes)

Steps for Fitness Hustle 4

Keep the children in scatter formation.

1. Introduce each step of Fitness Hustles 4-6 individually.
2. Have students perform steps in combinations as indicated.

Knee Slap

With weight on your right foot, lift your left knee and slap it with both hands. Then repeat with weight on your left foot, slapping your right knee.

Alternate Jogging in a Circle
Jog in a small circle, first counterclockwise and then clockwise.

Fitness Hustle 4

Keep the children in scatter formation.

1. Play "How Will I Know?"
2. After listening to the song, help the children learn, then perform the following sequence of steps, using the cue words provided:

   Wait (32 counts),

Bounce in place (16 counts),

Skier (16 counts),

Knee slaps (16 counts),

Alternating stride jump (16 counts),

Bounce in place (16 counts),

Skier (16 counts),

Knee slaps (16 counts),

Alternating stride jumps (16 counts),

Alternate jogging in a circle (16 counts),

Bounce in place (16 counts),

Skier to end of the music.

Steps for Fitness Hustle 5

Keep the children in scatter formation.

Knee Dip With Elbow Lift
With arms bent, elbows up, and fingers pointing down, lift your elbows with each knee dip.

Fitness Hustle 5

Keep the children in scatter formation.

1. Play "Theme from 'The Dukes of Hazard.'"
2. After listening to the song, help the children learn, then perform the following sequence of steps, using the cue words provided:

   Jog kickbacks (8 counts),

   Knee dips (8 counts),

   Pendulum rock (8 counts),

   Jog kickbacks (16 counts),

   Knee dips with elbow lift (8 counts).

Pendulum (8 counts),

Jog kickbacks with clap (16 counts).

Steps for Fitness Hustle 6

Lunge Punch

Step to the right, extending your left leg sideways. As your left foot hits the floor, make a punching motion with your right hand across your body so your arm extends over your left leg.

Front Foot Slap

Lift your left foot in front of your body and slap the inside of that foot with your right hand, then repeat with your right foot and left hand.

Extension Activities: Fitness Hustle 6

Keep the children in scatter formation.

1. Play "Let's Hear it for the Boy."
2. After listening to the song, help the children learn, then perform the following sequence of steps, using the cue words provided:

   Knee dips (8 counts),

   Jumping jacks (8 counts),

   Lunge punch (8 counts),

   Front foot slap (8 counts),

   Lunge punch (8 counts),

   Jumping jacks (8 counts),

   Jog and punch forward (8 counts),

   Front foot slap (8 counts),

   Lunge punch (8 counts),

   Jumping jacks (8 counts),

   Jogging (8 counts),

   Front foot slap (8 counts),

   Lunge punch (8 counts),

   Jumping jacks (8 counts),

   Jog to end of the music.

Concluding Activities (5 minutes)

Pony Express

Have the children begin with running and work down to walking as a cool-down. See Grades 2-3: Fitness, Lesson 1, page 389.

GRADES 2-3

LESSON 12
CIRCUIT TRAINING 1

Student Objectives

- Demonstrate Fitness Circuit 1.
- Stay on-task.
- Take turns.
- State that, "Regular exercise means exercising three times every week."
- State that, "Physical fitness means having enough energy to move all day and be healthy."

Equipment and Materials

- 6 cones
- 6 identifying signs (numbers or pictures)
- Tape (to attach signs to cones)
- Music or special signal (e.g., whistle)
- 1 blank calendar per child
- Crayons

Warm-Up Activities (5 minutes)

Pyramid

Arrange children along one side of the play area in a line, facing the other side.

1. Tell the students: *We are going to move across the activity area very slowly. When we come back we will speed up a little. We will continue until we are running as fast as we can. This is called "Pyramid" because we are building from a slow to a fast speed, just like a pyramid is built from low to high.*

2. Move across the area at least six times, each time increasing the speed.

3. Repeat, moving backward and sideways.

Skill-Development Activities (20 minutes)

Circuit Training: Circuit 1

Place six cones with either numbers or pictures for identification in a circle with 30 ft between each cone. Divide children into six small groups, and place one group at each cone.

1. Spend five to six minutes explaining the circuit. If this is a repeat lesson, quickly review the circuit by describing and demonstrating the activities for only one to two minutes.

2. At first, have the children spend about one minute at each station, with 30 seconds to travel between each station.

3. Over time as the children gain experience and strength and endurance, have them spend 2 minutes at each station and 15 seconds between each station. In addition, altering the time frames makes this fun; for example, sometimes go slowly between cones (1 minute) and short (5 seconds) at cones.

4. Tell the students: *At each cone you will do a different exercise until the signal. When the music stops (or the whistle blows) you will run to the next cone and do the exercise for that cone. Everyone will run clockwise, in this direction (point). When you hear the music, what should you be doing? (Exercising.) When the music stops what should you be doing? (Running to the next cone.) If you get to the cone and the music has not started, run in place until the music signals you to start the exercise.*

5. Have the children practice running between and stopping at the cones on the signal. Alter the amount of time between the cones by saying, *Change, move s-l-o-w-l-y, at normal speed, or fast.* You may want to accompany the verbal instruction with an arm signal. For example, move your arm in a circle so that the children can judge the amount of time to move between stations by the speed of your arm (e.g., slow arm circles for long times between).

6. Explain the exercises at each station (cone).

7. Begin the activity, continuing as time permits.

Station 1: Inchworm Stretches

Begin on hands and feet, in a stretched out push-up position. Walk your feet toward your hands, with your knees straight but not locked. Stop when your feet are as close as possible to your hands, and then walk back to the starting position.

Station 2: Three-Point Stretches

Begin on all-fours (hands and knees). *Lift your right leg, extending and straightening it to the side. Your ankle should be flexed (bent), so your toes point in the same direction as you are facing. Slowly move your leg and foot as far forward as possible, keeping the leg parallel to (level with) the ground and at torso level (point). Slowly move the leg backward so it forms a corner of a square (90-degree angle) with your body. Repeat on the right, then keep alternating legs.*

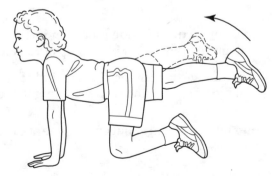

Station 3: Cat Stretches

Begin on all-fours. Slowly relax, allowing your hips to move backward, keeping your hands in place. Go back until you're sitting on your heels with your head down and arms stretched (extended) forward. Slowly reverse the movement, and still on all-fours, arch your back upward and hold for five counts, then relax your back till it's flat. Then slowly move your torso forward as your hands walk forward, keeping your knees still. Reverse to starting position and repeat.

Station 4: Leg Hug

Lie on your back with your legs extended above, forming a 90-degree angle with your torso. Turn your hands palms down, extended to the side, and press your lower back against the floor. You can hold your head slightly off the floor so you won't use your neck. Move your legs slowly over your head, as far as possible without losing balance. You can move your toes close to the ground, but do not touch the ground. Reverse to the starting position. Be sure to use your stomach (abdominal) muscles and not your arms or neck to do this exercise.

Station 5: Roller Coaster Crunches

Lie on your back with your legs extended above, forming a 90-degree angle with your torso. Turn your hands palms down and place them under your hips, and press your lower back against the floor. Place one finger from your left hand on your left ear, and do the same on your right. Twist and lift your torso, so that your left elbow points at or touches your right knee. Hold for five counts. Slowly return to the start and repeat on the opposite side.

Station 6: Jack-in-the-Box Jumps

Place your hands behind your head with your fingers laced, standing with your right leg in front of your left leg. Squat slightly, keeping your back as straight as possible. Jump up, reversing your legs so your left is now in the front. Repeat.

Concluding Activities (5 minutes)

Physical Fitness Concept

Gather the children into an information formation.

1. Explain the concept to the children: *Regular exercise helps you develop physical fitness. "Physical fitness" means that you are healthy and have enough energy to move all day without becoming too tired. "Regular exercise" means that you exercise at least three times a week for at least three 10-minute segments per exercise day.*

2. Ask the children: *What activities did you do this week? Think about last Saturday—what did you do?* (Allow children to comment.) *What about Sunday?* (Encourage children to comment.)

   Share the physical activities you enjoyed during the past week.

3. Tell the children: *We are going to keep an activity calendar* (see Form F2.3) *for one week. First, take your calendar home and decorate it using crayons. Then each day write or get help writing what you did that was physically active.*

4. When the children complete the calendars (next week), place them on display. Ask: *What physical activities do you plan to do during the next week?* (Physical education, recess activities, riding a bike or walking to school, team or individual sports outside of school, and so on.)

FORM F2.3   ACTIVITY CALENDAR

Sunday	Monday	Tuesday	Wednesday	Thursday	Friday	Saturday

LESSON 13
CIRCUIT TRAINING 2

Student Objectives

- Work independently at stations in the circuit.
- Cooperate with group members.
- Move to the beat of the music.
- Demonstrate 12 different steps.
- Give an example of physical activity and physical fitness tasks.

Equipment and Materials

- Music selection(s); for example: *The Aerobic Express,* Gay Bergman, Kimbo Reocrds (KIM 9092); *A Thriller for Kids,* Georgiana Stewart, Kimbo Records (KIM 7065); or *Jump Aerobics,* Don Disney, Kimbo Records (KIM 2095)
- 6 cones
- 6 large task cards (at least 8 1/2 in. × 11 in.)
- Tape
- Newspapers or magazines
- Scissors
- Glue
- 2 poster boards

Warm-Up Activities (5 minutes)

Pyramid

See Grades 2-3: Fitness, Lesson 12, page 423.

Skill-Development Activities (20 minutes)

Fitness Circuit 2: The Hustle

Tape the task cards to the cones, and place the cones in a large circle or rectangle. Divide the children into six groups, and place one group at each cone.

1. Describe and demonstrate the steps at each cone. Tell the children: *Each station will have two steps (exercises), which you will repeat to the music for 16 counts each.*

2. Have all children practice without and then with the music.

3. After you have gone through each exercise at least once, have the groups rotate. To rotate, have the groups jog around the outside of the six cones, going one station beyond the one they just completed (so, for example, students who did cone 1 will circle all cones and stop at cone 2).

Station 1

1. *Bounce in place* (16 counts, 8 jumps). See Grades 2-3: Fitness, Lesson 7, page 407.
2. *Skier* (16 counts, 8 to each side). See Grades 2-3: Fitness, Lesson 7, page 407.

Station 2

1. *Jog kickbacks* (16 counts and steps). See Grades 2-3: Fitness, Lesson 7, page 408.
2. *Knee dips* (16 counts, 8 repetitions). See Grades 2-3: Fitness, Lesson 7, page 408.

Station 3

1. *Jumping jacks* (16 counts, 8 repetitions). See Grades 2-3: Fitness, Lesson 8, page 410.
2. *Jog and punch forward* (16 counts, 8 steps and punches on each side). See Grades 2-3: Fitness, Lesson 8, page 411.

Station 4

1. *Pendulum rock* (16 counts, 2 counts to each side for 4 repetitions each side). See Grades 2-3: Fitness, Lesson 8, page 412.
2. *Alternating stride jump* (16 counts, 4 repetitions). See Grades 2-3: Fitness, Lesson 9, page 415.

Station 5

1. *Knee slap* (16 counts, 4 repetitions). See Grades 2-3: Fitness, Lesson 11, page 418.
2. *Alternate jogging in a circle* (16 counts, 8 counterclockwise, 8 clockwise). See Grades 2-3: Fitness, Lesson 11, page 419.

Station 6

1. *Lunge punch* (16 counts, 4 repetitions). See Grades 2-3: Fitness, Lesson 11, page 421.
2. *Front foot slap* (16 counts, 4 repetitions). See Grades 2-3: Fitness, Lesson 11, page 421.

Concluding Activities (5 minutes)

Physical Fitness Concept

Gather the children into an information formation.

1. Explain the concept to the children: *Physical activities, like walking, house- or yard work, contribute to health. Physical fitness is a result of specifc physical activities and also contributes to health.*
2. Ask children to find pictures in the magazines or newspaper that are examples of physical activity and physical fitness. Tell the children: *Let's work together to make two collages: one of physical activities and one of physical fitness. So we will have one collage showing physical activities, such as gardening and using the stairs; another collage will show physical fitness, such as jogging, weight training, and some sports. Both collages show things that contribute to health.*

LESSON 14
CIRCUIT TRAINING 3

Student Objectives

- Work independently to achieve as many repetitions as possible.
- Name the five components of health-related physical fitness.
- Demonstrate the fitness tasks in the circuit.

Student Equipment

- 1 envelope or bag filled with papers
- 4 cones for Station 3
- 6 cones or signs to mark the stations

Warm-Up Activities (5 minutes)

Pony Express

See Grades 2-3: Fitness, Lesson 1, page 389.

Skill-Development Activities (20 minutes)

Fitness Circuit 3: Progressive Circuit

Set up six cones or signs in a large circle or rectangle to mark the stations. Divide the children into six groups, and place one group at each station.

1. Describe and demonstrate each station on the circuit.
2. Have the children rotate through the circuit, allowing the children to move around the circuit at their own pace.
3. Each time around the circuit, require students to add one more repetition. For example, during the first round each exercise is repeated five times, the second round six times, and so forth.

Station 1: Sit-Ups
See Grades 2-3: Fitness, Lesson 2, page 393.

Station 2: Push-Ups
See Grades 2-3: Fitness, Lesson 2, page 392.

Station 3: Jog-Around
Define a 20-ft square with four cones. Tell the children: *Jog around five times the first round, six the second round, and so on.*

Station 4: Upper Leg Stretch 1

Stand with your legs spread frontward and backward in a lunge position. Slowly bend your front leg so your thigh is parallel to the ground as you dip the knee of your back leg. This dipping stretches your thigh. Repeat the exercise on the other leg.

Station 5: Upper Leg Stretch 2

Stand and bend your left knee by grasping your left ankle. Stretch your upper leg by pulling on your leg as your body leans forward slightly. Keep your knee bent! Relax, repeat four more times, then do with your other leg five times.

Concluding Activities (5 minutes)

Physical Fitness Concept

Gather the children into an information formation.

1. Explain the concept to the children: *Health-related physical fitness has five parts: cardiorespiratory endurance, muscular strength and endurance, flexibility, and body composition.*

2. Describe and discuss the concept: *To be physically fit, a person must train and be able to maintain all five parts of physical fitness. "Cardiorespiratory endurance" is also called aerobic fitness, or heart and lung health. "Muscular strength" refers to the amount of force a group of muscles can produce in one try. "Muscular endurance" means being able to repeat a movement several times in a row. "Flexibility" is when a joint can move through a reasonable range of motion. "Body composition" is the relationship between fat and lean tissue in your body. You need some fat but not too much.*

3. Ask the children to respond to the following statements and questions:

   • *Name some activities that maintain or develop cardiorespiratory endurance.* (Jogging, cycling, or swimming.)

   • *When do you use muscular strength?* (Lifting a weight, jumping up or forward, climbing or lifting.)

   • *Muscular endurance means being able to repeat a movement several times in a row; give some examples.* (Push-ups, sit-ups, or jogging.)

   • *Stretching helps improve which part of health-related physical fitness?* (Flexibility.)

   • *Do you remember how we measure body composition?* (Height and weight or skinfolds.)

LESSON 15
CIRCUIT TRAINING 4

Student Objectives

- Demonstrate six stretches.
- Name the five components of health-related physical fitness.
- Work independently during the circuits.

Equipment and Materials

- 1 envelope or bag filled with papers
- 4 cones to mark the area
- 6 markers and signs for the stations
- Signal

Warm-Up Activities (5 minutes)

Pony Express

See Grades 2-3: Fitness, Lesson 1, page 389.

Skill-Development Activities (20 minutes)

Circuit 4: Stretching Routine

Arrange and mark six stations in the center of a large rectangle defined by four cones. Divide the children into six groups, and assign each group to a station.

1. Describe and demonstrate the stretching exercise at each station. The first time the children do the circuit, use five to six minutes to explain the stations and rotation, and allow two minutes at each station. In subsequent lessons, allow three minutes at each station after a brief review of the six stretches and safe-stretching guidelines.

2. Remind students of the importance of stretching slowly to the point of tension, not pain. No bouncing!

3. After the first station, signal the children to leave their station, run to the outside boundary, and return to the next station in order. Continue until each group has visited each station.

Station 1: Shoulder Pull

Slowly pull your left elbow across the front of your body toward the opposite shoulder. Hold for 10 seconds. Relax and repeat with the opposite elbow.

Station 2: Arm Reach-Out

Sit on the floor. Lock your fingers together and with palms facing out, straighten your arms out in front of you. Stretch and hold for 10 seconds. Relax and repeat.

Station 3: Triceps Stretch

Lift your arms up over your head and touch your elbows. Hold your right elbow with your left hand and gently pull. Let your right hand drop behind your head as you stretch. Hold for 10 seconds and relax. Repeat, pulling your left elbow with your right hand.

Station 4: Forward Straddle Stretch

Sit on the floor with your legs straight and spread apart about three ft. Bend forward at the hip. Grasp your right knee, calf, or ankle (as far down your leg as you can go) and pull your body gently toward your leg. Hold for 10 seconds, then relax and repeat on the left side.

Station 5: Shoulder Lift Stretch

Lie on the floor with your knees bent and fingertips touching your ears. Slowly lift your head forward, stretching your upper back and neck. You should feel a gentle pull along your spine (backbone) to the shoulder blades. Hold for 5 seconds, then slowly relax to the starting position. Relax for 10 seconds and repeat.

Station 6: Frog Stretch

Lie down with your knees bent and the soles of your feet together. If you relax, gravity will pull your knees toward the ground and stretch the insides of your thighs. Relax for 10 seconds and then lift your knees up and toward each other, so they are no longer relaxed, for 10 seconds (knees do not need to touch at this point). Do not bounce!

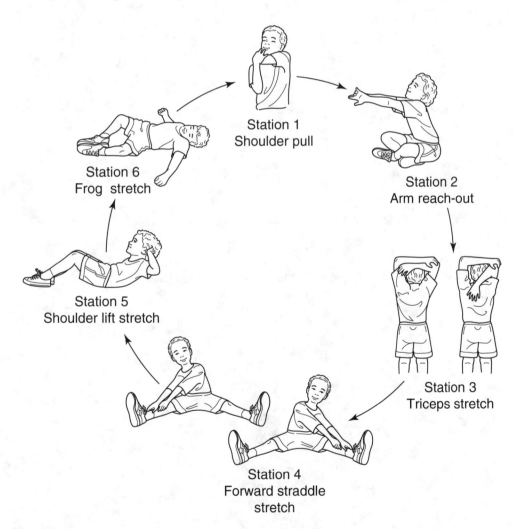

Station 1
Shoulder pull

Station 2
Arm reach-out

Station 3
Triceps stretch

Station 4
Forward straddle
stretch

Station 5
Shoulder lift stretch

Station 6
Frog stretch

Concluding Activities (5 minutes)

Physical Fitness Concept

1. Explain the concept to the children: *A physically fit person can exercise for 20 minutes without stopping, do 30 sit-ups, some push-ups or chin-ups, stretch their body (like the stretches we've learned), and have a healthy amount of body fat.*

2. Discuss the concept: *Think about the activities we did today. Which component of health-related physical fitness did station 1 help us develop?* (Flexibility.) *When we play Pony Express, what are we training?* (Cardiorespiratory fitness and muscular endurance in the legs.) *When we run and do other exercises, we are burning calories too, which means exercising for cardiorespiratory endurance also helps us keep a healthy amount of body fat.*

3. Discuss the parts of the fitness test (run, backsaver sit-and-reach, sit-ups, push-ups, and skinfolds), and each of the components of health-related physical fitness (cardiorespiratory endurance, flexibility, muscular strength and endurance, and body composition). *Physical education helps us train in each component so we can be healthy and have the energy we need to participate in daily activities.*

FITNESS

LESSON 16
CIRCUIT TRAINING 5

Student Objectives

- Match the fitness test item with the health-related physical fitness component.
- Demonstrate fitness.
- Complete the circuit.

Equipment and Materials

- 1 envelope or bag filled with paper
- 4 cones and signs to mark stations

Warm-Up Activities (5 minutes)

Fitness Circuit 4: Stretching Routine

Arrange the children in scatter formation.

Repeat each stretch 10 repetitions per minute with six seconds for each repetition: shoulder pull, arm reach-out, triceps stretch, forward straddle stretch, frog stretch (see Grades 2-3: Fitness, Lesson 15, page 432).

Skill-Development Activities (20 minutes)

Circuit 5: Jogging

Using the four cones, define a large square, 60 to 100 yd on each side. Divide the children into four groups, and place one group at each corner.

1. Describe and demonstrate each station.
2. Have the children spend most of the time moving between the cones, repeating the entire circuit as many times as possible. The groups should jog from their corner or station to the next corner or station, and they should rotate together.

Station 1: Triceps Push-Ups

Sit on the floor with your legs extended in front and your hands on the ground near your hips. Lift your hips off the floor so your body makes as straight a line as possible. Lower your body by bending your arms; raise your body by straightening your arms. Do eight times.

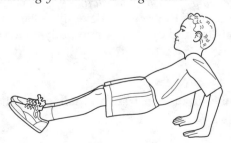

Station 2: Crunches

Lie on your back. Bend your knees and move your legs over your torso: cross your legs at the ankle with knees slightly bent, your feet over the hips or torso. Place your hands near your ears without gripping your head. One way is to carefully place one finger in each ear. Start a crunch by lifting your head and shoulders off the floor, pointing your nose toward your knees. Lower your shoulders to the starting position, but keep your head slightly off the floor. Lifting and lowering the shoulders is one repetition. Do eight times.

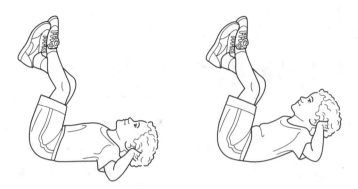

Station 3: Push-Ups

See Grades 2-3: Fitness, Lesson 2, page 392.

Station 4: Standing Body Stretch 1

See Grades 2-3: Fitness, Lesson 6, page 402.

Concluding Activities (5 minutes)

Physical Fitness Concept

Gather the children into an information formation.

1. Explain the concept to the children: *To measure or decide how fit you are, you could ride a bike, swim or jog for 20 minutes, do sit-ups, push-ups, and stretch. Someone could measure your skinfolds to see how much fat you have (what your body composition is).*

2. Make the following additional points: *The tests we do in physical education measure each component of health-related physical fitness. Do you remember why we test health-related fitness?* (To help see how healthy you are, to see how much training has helped you improve, to understand more about fitness, and to motivate you to keep improving.)

3. Tell the children: *Some jobs require a physical fitness test, for example, firefighters and the military. The parts, or components, of those fitness tests are similar to the ones used in physical education. Physical fitness tests are also used in other places, for example, health clubs and fitness centers. Do any of your parents go to a health club or fitness center?* Discuss.

4. Ask the children: *Can you name the five components of physical fitness? Name the test for each of those.* (Cardiorespiratory endurance—fitness run, flexibility—sit-and-reach, muscular strength and endurance—sit-ups and push-ups, and body composition—skinfolds.)

Extension Activities

Invite a local firefighter, police officer, or military member to demonstrate and talk about the fitness tests used in their profession.

FITNESS

LESSON 17
MODERATE TO VIGOROUS GAMES 1

Student Objectives

- Work cooperatively when on the pit crew.
- Demonstrate five different stretches.
- State that one must exercise three times per week for three 10-minute continuous bouts each day to be fit.

Equipment and Materials

- 4 cones
- 1 green flag
- Poster board or chalkboard
- Chalk or markers

Warm-Up Activities (5 minutes)

Fitness Circuit 4: Stretching Routine

See Grades 2-3: Fitness, Lesson 15, page 432.

Skill-Development Activities (20 minutes)

Parking Garage

Arrange the children on one long side of a 60- by 40-ft rectangle defined by the cones. Name three or four cars (Stealth, Camaro, and so on), and explain that each student must select one of the car types. You are the starter with the green flag to start the race. Select two or three children to be the first "pit crew." Have the pit crew stand in the middle of the racetrack (the rectangle).

1. Explain the activity:

    The object of the game is for the cars to get to the parking garage (point at the other side of the rectangle) without stopping for the pit crew—who will try to capture a car for "repairs."

    I will wave the green flag and name a car. That is the signal for those children to run to the other side. The pit crew can either circle a car or tag a car for repairs.

    Each car tagged by the pit crew replaces one member of the pit crew. The old pit crew member moves immediately to the starting line. The size of the pit crew will change because a crew member may tag two or more cars, but only one person leaves the crew. The pit crew will never be less than the number we started with.

    When cars have reached the parking garage, they must walk back to the starting line by traveling around the outside of the rectangle.

2. Have the children play Parking Garage. Start the next race (e.g., a different car) as they return. Repeat many times.

Concluding Activities (5 minutes)

Physical Fitness Concept

Gather the children into an information formation.

1. Present the concept to the children: *A physically fit person exercises by regularly jogging, cycling, or swimming, doing sit-ups and push-ups, and stretching. These exercises can help our muscles stay healthy and keep our body from storing too much fat. To be physically fit we must exercise at least three times each week.*

2. Emphasize the following points:

   The exercise should be spread out so if you exercise only three days per week, there is a day or more between exercise sessions.

   Regular exercise is healthy, but intense exercise occasionally (e.g., one time per week or one time per month) can be dangerous.

   The type of exercise can vary as long as it is done three days per week, although most people do the same activity all three days.

3. Ask the children to plan a three-day-per-week exercise program, which meets the criteria listed. Discuss how their playground and sport team activities can meet the minimum requirements if they are moderate to vigorous in intensity and if the time involved is enough—at least three 10-minute continuous bouts of exercise per day.

4. Share and discuss some good written samples.

FITNESS

LESSON 18
MODERATE TO VIGOROUS GAMES 2

Student Objectives

- Cooperate with two other children when playing Three-on-Three.
- Demonstrate correct technique in stretching.
- Define *cardiorespiratory, or aerobic, fitness.*

Equipment and Materials

- 4 cones
- 10 playground balls

Warm-Up Activities (5 minutes)

Fitness Circuit 4: Stretching Routine

See Grades 2-3: Fitness, Lesson 15, page 432.

Skill-Development Activities (20 minutes)

Three-on-Three

Define a large rectangle with the cones. Divide the children into groups of three, and give a ball to each of one-half of the groups. Have this half of the class line up along one short side of the rectangle. Have the remaining groups of three stand in the rectangle about one-third of the way from the short side where the other groups are lined up. Pair each group of three on the line with a group of three inside the rectangle (see figure on page 440).

1. Describe and demonstrate the game:

    The object of the game for the team with the ball is to move the ball from the starting line across the far endline.

    You may take five steps carrying the ball, then you must stop and pass, bounce, or roll the ball toward the endline.

    The ball must go over the endline carried by a group member or passed to a group member. Remember to use no more than five steps when carrying the ball.

    The object of the game for the other team is to take the ball away.

    When and if you take the ball away, by catching or a tie (taking ahold of the ball when an opponent is holding the ball), you immediately go to the start line and from there try to get the ball over the endline.

    Whenever the ball goes over the endline, your team will trade roles with the other team.

2. Have the children play Three-on-Three.

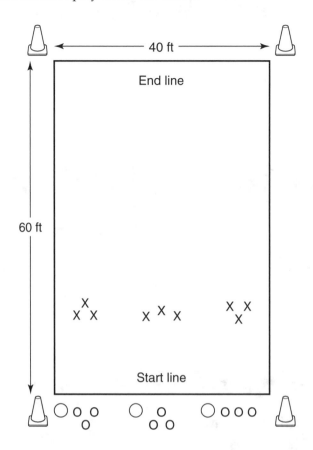

Concluding Activities (5 minutes)

Physical Fitness Concept

Gather the children into an information formation.

1. Present the concept to the children: *Cardiovascular fitness, or heart fitness, is also called "aerobic fitness." A person who can jog, ride a bike, or swim for 20 minutes is demonstrating aerobic fitness. Cardiovascular, or aerobic, fitness has three major benefits:*

   A trained heart has a lower resting heart rate, because the heart pumps more blood each beat, and so fewer beats are needed to pump the same amount of blood.

   A trained heart has more pathways for blood to travel in and around the heart.

   Training lowers blood pressure (how hard the blood pushes against the artery walls).

2. Tell the children: *All these reduce the risk of illness related to the heart.*

3. *When I say "start," count the number of beats your heart makes. You can count your heartbeats by putting your fingers on each side of your Adam's apple and pushing gently. Swallowing helps you to locate the Adam's apple. Start.*

4. Stop the count at 10 seconds.

5. Tell the children: *Now, jump up and down quickly 20 times.* Have the children count their heart rate again. The heart rate should be higher.

GRADES 2-3

FITNESS

LESSON 19
MODERATE TO VIGOROUS GAMES 3

Student Objectives

- Demonstrate fair play during Crows and Cranes.
- Name a muscular strength and a muscular endurance activity.

Equipment and Materials

- 4 cones or two long lines marked on the surface

Safety Tip

- Remind children to watch where they run so they don't hurt anyone else.

Warm-Up Activities (5 minutes)

Fitness Circuit 4: Stretching Routine

See Grades 2-3: Fitness, Lesson 15, page 432.

Skill-Development Activities (20 minutes)

Crows and Cranes

Arrange the children in two parallel lines facing each other, with half the children on each line, 30 to 50 ft apart.

1. Explain the game:

   The children in one line are "Crows;" those in the other line are "Cranes."

   As I begin saying "Crrrr . . . ," the two lines walk toward each other.

   When I complete the word "Crow" or "Crane," the line I call is "It." The children in that line run forward and try to tag the other children, who turn and try to avoid being tagged.

   You are safe when you cross the line you started from. Tagged children join the other line and play continues.

2. Have the children play Crows and Cranes.
3. Mix up which line you call to surprise the children.
4. Remind children to watch where they run so they don't hurt anyone.

Variation: Witches and Warlocks

Instead of Crows and Cranes, call the children standing on one line "Witches," and the children on the other line "Warlocks." As you call out one name or the other, draw out the "W" sound, alternating between Witches, Warlocks, and Wizards. When you say "Wizards," everyone must freeze. Anyone who moves while frozen runs a lap before the next round of play.

Concluding Activities (5 minutes)

Physical Fitness Concept

Gather the children into an information formation.

1. Present the concept to the children: *"Muscular endurance" is when a muscle or group of muscles can make the same movement many times without getting too tired. How many sit-ups, push-ups, and chin-ups a person can do helps demonstrate their muscular endurance. "Muscular strength" is how much work a muscle can do one time. Muscles get stronger by exercising, for example, by moving heavy objects.*

2. Begin the discussion: *Can you name some activities that call for you to repeat a movement many times?* (Crunches, push-ups, jogging, jumping rope, but throwing a ball is not.)

   Everyone show me an activity in which you repeat the movement many times. Correct anyone who is not doing an endurance activity. *Now switch to a different endurance activity!*

3. Tell the children: *Usually muscular endurance activities are done in sets of 10 to 12 repetitions, so you should build up to doing 10, resting briefly, doing 10 more, resting, and then doing 10 more.*

4. Continue the discussion: *Muscular strength varies from person to person and muscle to muscle. Different people have different strength levels, and different muscles on the same person have different strength levels. Muscles get stronger with training. Muscular strength and endurance work together to help us do all the tasks we need to do. Sometimes we lack the muscular strength to do an activity, but with training we improve and then can do the activity many times. Pull-ups are sometimes like that. At first, a person cannot do one pull-up, but with training, strength increases and one pull-up becomes easy. Then after more training, we can do many pull-ups because we have improved our muscular endurance.*

FITNESS

LESSON 20
MODERATE TO VIGOROUS GAMES 4

Student Objectives

- State why flexibility is important.
- Explain how flexibility is increased.
- Play fair by staying on the circle in Circle Tag.

Equipment and Materials

- Marking items for a large circle and a smaller circle
- Scissors
- Signal
- Several rubber bands of various sizes (thick, small, long)

Warm-Up Activities (5 minutes)

Fitness Circuit 4: Stretching Routine

See Grades 2-3: Fitness, Lesson 15, page 432.

Skill-Development Activities (20 minutes)

Circle Tag

Arrange children in a large circle marked on the ground with children at least 10 ft apart. A smaller circle can be marked inside the larger circle.

1. Describe and demonstrate the game:

   On the signal, run clockwise (point), *with each of you trying to tag the next person ahead in the circle.*

   If you are tagged, move to the inside, making a new circle. In the inside circle, you run counterclockwise (point), *and again try to tag the person in front of you in line. If you are tagged on the inside circle, you move back to the outside circle and continue.*

   Enter the circles where there are large spaces between children. If the circles become too crowded, we will stop and reorganize.

2. Have the children play Circle Tag.

Slap Tag

Divide the children in two equal groups, one of "Runners" and the other of "Chasers." Have each group stand on two parallel lines about 50 ft apart. Runners stand on one line facing the play area. Chasers stand on the opposite line with their backs to the play area and their hands out behind them.

1. Describe and demonstrate the game:

   The Runners sneak across and slap the palms of the Chasers.

   As soon as a Chaser's hand is slapped, both the Runner and the Chaser turn and run for the Runner's baseline at the other side of the play area.

   The Chasers try to tag the Runners before they reach their base. Every Runner who is tagged becomes a Chaser and moves to the other side.

   Each round, we will reverse Runners and Chasers.

2. Have the children play Slap Tag.

Concluding Activities (5 minutes)

Physical Fitness Concept

Gather the children into an information formation.

1. Present the concept to the children: *Flexibility is important to preventing injuries. Slowly stretching our body parts helps us to be flexible.*

2. Place a rubber band on the blades of the pair of scissors. Tell the children: *Our muscles are like the rubber band; our bones are like the scissors. In order to move further, the rubber band must stretch, just like our muscles must stretch.*

3. Demonstrate with various rubber bands. *The amount of movement in a joint is called the "range of motion." Regular stretching increases the range of motion—or flexibility—of a joint. When you have to move a joint quickly through a range of motion, like in a fall or a sport movement, a more flexible joint is less likely to be hurt.*

LESSON 21
MODERATE TO VIGOROUS GAMES 5

Student Objectives

- Cooperate when playing Line Soccer.
- State that body fat can be measured by skinfold calipers.

Equipment and Materials

- Two 8 1/2 in. playground balls
- Skinfold calipers (for demonstration)

Warm-Up Activities (5 minutes)

Fitness Circuit 4: Stretching Routine

See Grades 2-3: Fitness, Lesson 15, page 432.

Skill-Development Activities (20 minutes)

Line Soccer

Divide the class in half and arrange half the children along each of two parallel lines about 40 ft apart. Assign each child a number from one to six, arrange the children in order from one to six, repeating as many times as necessary and making sure you have an approximately equal number of each number between the teams. All players will be defenders of their line.

1. Describe and demonstrate the game:

    I will roll a ball, then another ball down the middle of the area between the two lines.

    As I roll the ball, I will call one number from one to six. All players with that number must run toward the ball.

    The object is to get the ball across the line opposite from your starting position. However, at least three players having the same number must touch the ball with their feet before attempting to kick the ball over the line.

    All of the other players defend the lines, trying to keep the ball from crossing. If these players catch the ball, it is out of play.

    When both balls are out of play (e.g., have crossed a line or are caught), I will roll them again, calling a different number.

2. Have the children play Line Soccer.

Concluding Activities (5 minutes)

Physical Fitness Concept

Gather the children into an information formation.

1. Present the concept to the children: *Too much or too little body fat is not healthy. Body fat can be measured by skinfold testing. Our diet and physical activity level are two things that help determine how much fat we have.*

2. Begin the discussion: *Extra energy (calories or food) is stored as fat. Some is under our skin; other fat is stored in our body where we cannot see it. Pinch near your belly button (umbilicus). Can you grab any fat? What about on the back of your arm between your elbow and shoulder? This is what the skinfold calipers* (show) *feel and measure. Try to pinch the fat on the inside of your calf (the lower leg). Which place has the least fat on your body?* (Calf, abdomen, or arm.)

3. Make the following points:

   It is normal and healthy to have some fat on your body.

   Different people store fat in different locations on the body; that is part of the reason we look different.

   Too much or too little fat is unhealthy.

4. To protect the feelings of the overweight or underweight child, the discussion should be nonjudgemental. Do not, for example, use words like "skinny," "ugly," or "lazy," or allow children to make comments. Keep the discussion to the facts and as scientific as possible.

LESSON 22
FITNESS CHALLENGE 1

Student Objectives

- Move in and around different shapes.
- Follow directions.
- Define atrophy and hypertrophy.

Equipment and Materials

- 4 or more cones
- 1 short jump rope per child
- 1 drum
- 1 sign that reads "Atrophy"
- 1 sign that reads "Hypertrophy"

Warm-Up Activities (5 minutes)

Slap Tag

See Grades 2-3: Fitness, Lesson 20, page 443.

Skill-Development Activities (20 minutes)

Rope Challenges

Arrange the children in scatter formation, each child with a jump rope.

1. Tell the children to try the following:

    Make a circle (a square, triangle) with the rope.

    Run (jump, hop) around the circle (square, triangle).

    Jump (hop) in and out of the circle (a square, triangle).

    Make the letter "A" (T, B S, H) with the rope.

    Jump (hop) around the letter. Repeat slowly backward.

    Jump (hop, run) over the letter.

    Think of another way to move over and around the letter.

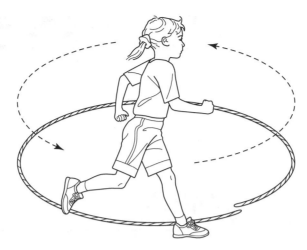

Run around circle

2. Now have the children perform the following challenges:

Put the rope in a straight line.

With your right side to the rope, jump from side-to-side over the rope. Repeat, starting with your left side toward the rope.

Face the rope, and jump back and forth over the rope.

While the drum is beating, jump continuously. You can use a side-to-side or forward-and-backward jump. (Beat the drum for 30 seconds, repeat, then beat the drum for one minute.)

Hop side-to-side over the rope, first on your right foot then on your left foot.

Try it again, hopping in a forward-and-backward pattern.

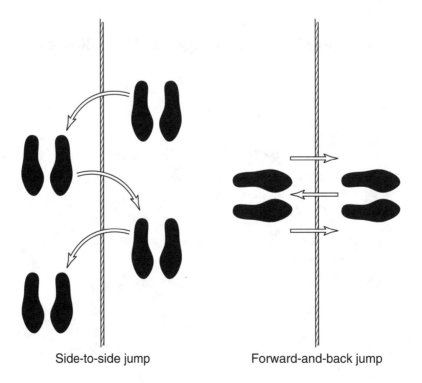

Side-to-side jump   Forward-and-back jump

Champion Joggers

Place the cones in a large oval shape.

1. Explain the activity: *On the signal, jog around the oval track marked by the cones. We will continue three to five minutes.*

2. Have the students be Champion Joggers.

3. When you repeat this activity in subsequent lessons, extend the time one to two minutes longer each time.

Concluding Activities (5 minutes)

Physical Fitness Concept

Gather the children into an information formation.

1. Introduce the concept and the terms atrophy and hypertrophy: *Muscles become stronger and able to do the same amount of work more times as a result of regular exercise. "Atrophy"* (show sign) *means a muscle becomes smaller when it is not used. "Hypertrophy"* (show sign) *means a muscle becomes larger when it is trained.*

2. Discuss muscles with the children: *Larger muscles can do more work. Training makes the muscles larger, so they can do even more work. The changes for women and children are smaller than the changes in men. When a person is sick and cannot exercise or has a broken bone so a limb is in a cast, the muscle atrophies, or shrinks.*

3. Discuss muscular strength: *Muscular strength varies from day to day, though. So some days we feel—and are—actually stronger than other days. This is normal. What do you think could cause this?* Allow the children to respond. (Stress, a previous workout [muscle fatigue], illness or infection, lack of rest, change of diet, and chemical changes in our body.) *Boys and girls have about the same muscular strength until puberty (12- to 13-years old), when body changes make it easier for boys to add muscle bulk. But no matter their age, both girls and boys gain strength and endurance when they train.*

LESSON 23
FITNESS CHALLENGE 2

Student Objectives

- Use equipment safely.
- Follow directions.
- Demonstrate locomotor skills.
- Define resting heart rate.

Equipment and Materials

- 4 cones or two long lines marked on ground
- 1 hoop per child

Warm-Up Activities (5 minutes)

Crows and Cranes

See Grades 2-3: Fitness, Lesson 19, page 441.

Skill-Development Activities (20 minutes)

Hoop Challenges

Arrange the children in scatter formation, each child with a hoop.

1. Have the children try the following challenges that develop muscular endurance and aerobic fitness:

   Spin the hoop on one arm, then on the other arm, then on one leg. Try to do 10 to 20 spins on each.

   Spin the hoop on another part of the body (waist, hips, neck).

   Spin the hoop on your body, trying to make it go slow, then fast, then slow.

   Spin the hoop on the ground like a top.

2. Have the children put their hoop on the ground:

   Jump in and out of the hoop slowly.

   Jump in and out of the hoop fast.

   Move around the hoop, jumping in and out.

   Hop in and out of the hoop.

   Run and jump over the hoop.

   Hop forward (then backward) around the hoop.

3. Now have the children pick up their hoop once again:

   Pick up the hoop and stretch with the hoop over your head.

   Holding the hoop, stretch to one side and then to the other.

   Roll the hoop from one line to the other.

   Roll the hoop and run around it as it rolls. Watch out for other hoops and children. Repeat several times.

   Roll the hoop and try to jump through it as it rolls.

   Roll the hoop so it returns to you (put backspin on the hoop).

Hoop Relay 1

Arrange the children in pairs, and give each pair a hoop. Have the pairs stand about 30 ft away from a line.

1. Describe and demonstrate the activity:

   The first child in line rolls the hoop to a line 30 ft away and back.

   The second child takes the hoop and rolls it to the line and back; this continues until time is up. The children can count the number of turns they completed if you want.

2. Have the children do Hoop Relay 1.

Concluding Activities (5 minutes)

Physical Fitness Concept

Gather the children into an information formation.

1. Introduce the concept: *After you have been lying still for 15 to 30 minutes (or when you first wake up in the morning) the number of times your heart beats is called "resting heart rate." You can lower your resting heart rate through exercising regularly.*

2. Tell the children: *Make a fist with your hand* (demonstrate, pausing for children to close their fists); *your hand is "contracted." Now open your hand* (demonstrate, pausing for the children to open their fists), *and relax. Your heart works like your hand. When the heart is relaxed—the open fist—blood enters. Then when the heart beats, or contracts (the closed fist), the blood is pushed out. The blood goes from the heart through arteries to the muscles and organs (stomach, kidneys, intestines, and so on).*

3. Tell the children: *Put your hand on your chest, be very still, and feel your heart beat.* Demonstrate and allow children to feel their heart beating. *Heart rate is the number of times your heart opens and closes in one minute. When we sleep our hearts are still beating, but more slowly. That is why it is called "resting" heart rate. When you exercise, your heart rate goes up. When you are awake but sitting still your heart rate is in between the resting and exercise heart rate.*

LESSON 24
FITNESS CHALLENGE 3

Student Objectives

- Practice ball skills.
- Use general space carefully.
- State that the amount of training for fitness is different for each person.

Equipment and Materials

- 4 cones
- 1 playground ball per child

Warm-Up Activities (5 minutes)

Parking Garage

See Grades 2-3: Fitness, Lesson 17, page 437.

Skill-Development Activities (20 minutes)

Ball Challenges

Arrange the children on a line along one side of a large rectangle defined by the cones, each child with a ball.

1. Have the children try the following activities:

    Throw the ball as far as possible.

    Now run and pick up the ball, and bring it back to this line. Be careful of your classmates.

    Kick the ball as far as possible, run after it, kick it again, go after it, and carry the ball back to this line.

    Kick the ball twice and throw it once to get it as close to the other (opposite) line as you can. Get the ball and place it on the other line.

    Throw the ball in the air and in this direction—can you catch it before it hits the ground? Repeat several times. Try to keep the ball in the air from that line to this line (point).

    Bounce the ball using both hands as you jog to the other line.

    Come back, bouncing the ball with one hand.

    Go to the other line, bouncing with alternate hands (demonstrate).

    Get on your hands and feet, with your stomach up and your back down in the "crab position." In this position, kick the ball with your feet to this line.

Roll the ball toward the other line, run, and stop the ball with your hands or feet about 15 ft away from the line (demonstrate the distance). *Run around the ball in a circle. Roll the ball 15 ft more toward the other line, stop it again, and run around it. Repeat, stopping at the opposite line. Run back here carrying the ball!*

Bounce the ball hard on the ground in front of you, catch it, move forward one or two steps, and repeat until I tell you to stop. Stop!

2. Rearrange the children in scatter formation, each child with a ball.

3. Have the children perform the following activities:

   Put the ball on the ground, and run around it three times.

   Repeat going the opposite direction.

   Jump over the ball; repeat.

   Jump sideways over your ball. Repeat, going the other direction.

   Move slowly among the balls; do not touch anyone else's ball. Stop!

   Move quickly among the balls; do not touch them! Be careful of others. Stop!

   Being careful not to bump into anyone, jump over someone else's ball, then keep going, trying to jump over every ball before I say stop! (Allow some time, and encourage children to continue jumping.) *Stop!*

Concluding Activities (5 minutes)

Physical Fitness Concept

Gather the children into an information formation.

1. Present the concept to the students: *Each person has to do a different amount of work to become physically fit, depending on how fit they are to start with.*

2. Continue: *"Training" is another word for the amount of work we have to do to be fit. We are each unique, so the amount of work we have to do to be fit is different for each of us. Part of the difference in people is inherited, or what we get from our parents. Another part is related to what we do, our behaviors. This is true for adults too. Name some jobs that require physical activity.* Allow the children to respond. *Name some jobs that require very little physical activity.* Allow the children to respond.

3. *People who are active all day long at work may need less exercise outside of work than people who sit all day long at work. Children sit in school all day long. That means that physical education and sport are very important for children. You can make more active choices at recess too. Some of you are more active than others; some of you will need to work very hard to become fit; others may already be fit, but it's still important to get plenty of exercise to maintain (keep) your fitness level.*

LESSON 25
FITNESS CHALLENGE 4

Student Objectives

- Follow verbal directions.
- Cooperate with his or her team.
- Name at least one inherited and one behavioral characteristic related to health and fitness.

Equipment and Materials

- 4 cones
- 2 hoops per group
- Chalkboard or poster board
- Chalk or marker

Warm-Up Activities (5 minutes)

Three-on-Three

See Grades 2-3: Fitness, Lesson 18, page 439.

Skill-Development Activities (20 minutes)

Team Challenges

Divide the children into teams of four or five.

1. Explain that balances take muscular strength.
2. Ask the teams to solve the following movement challenges:
   Stand on four legs.
   Balance on three arms and three legs.
   Balance with no legs on the ground.
   Move backward in a line (there are several ways to do this).
   Move sideways, with at least one side touching someone else.
   Go back the other direction.
   Move in a circle; jog in a circle.
   Run follow-the-leader-style in a zigzag pattern.
   Make a letter of the alphabet, using all team members.
   Spell a word, one letter at a time.

Hoop Relay 1

See Grades 2-3: Fitness, Lesson 23, page 451.

Hoop Relay 2

Use the cones to set up two lines, about 40 ft apart. Arrange the groups behind one line, facing the other line. Give each group two hoops.

1. Describe and demonstrate the activity:

   The first child in line drops (tosses) one hoop on the ground in front of the line. That child jumps into the hoop.

   The next child in line jumps into the hoop, and so forth.

   The last child brings the second hoop when he or she jumps into the hoop and places that hoop on the ground in front of the hoop in which the group is standing.

   Everyone in your group jumps again, one at a time, into that hoop. The last child reaches back for the hoop the group is leaving.

   Keep moving forward by going from hoop to hoop until your group reaches the endline.

   If someone falls out of the hoop, you must start over, so all group members must help everyone else.

   This is not a race. Remember the hoops can be placed close to each other, so there is no reason a child should fall out of the hoop.

2. Have the children do Hoop Relay 2.

Concluding Activities (5 minutes)

Physical Fitness Concept

Gather the children into an information formation.

1. Present the concept to the children: *Two main things help decide health and fitness: the characteristics you inherit from your parents (such as height or body type) and your behaviors (what you do every day).*

2. Continue the discussion: *Name some things you do that influence your health.* Allow children to respond. Create a list of the following five things based on the children's comments. Coax them as necessary.

   Exercise

   Diet

   Rest

   Attitude (how you feel about life, yourself)

   Lifestyle (drugs, smoking)

3. Continue the discussion: *Things you do are "behaviors," and these you can control. There are some other things that you inherit from your parents, which you cannot control. How are you like your parents?* Encourage children to respond. (Eye color, hair color or texture.) *The characteristics you inherit influence your health and fitness. Three are:*

   How easy it is to train your heart (it is easier for some people than others)

   How easy (or difficult) it is for you to get certain diseases

   What body type (shape) you have (this influences how easy it is to participate in some sports or activities)

FITNESS

LESSON 26
FITNESS CHALLENGE 5

Student Objectives

- Distinguish between risk factors that a person can and cannot influence.
- Demonstrate three muscular endurance activities.

Equipment and Materials

- 1 short rope per child
- 1 carpet square per child

Warm-Up Activities (5 minutes)

Crows and Cranes

See Grades 2-3: Fitness, Lesson 19, page 441.

Skill-Development Activities (20 minutes)

Arm and Leg Strength Challenges

Arrange the children on a long line, each child with a carpet square and a short jump rope.

1. Describe and demonstrate the stunts, explaining that they will help the children develop muscular strength.
2. Have them repeat each several times.

Seal Walk

In the push-up position, with weight on the hands and toes, walk your hands forward, dragging your legs and toes. Keep your back straight.

Jump the Rope

Stand facing a rope on the ground. Bend down, placing your hands over the rope. Supporting your weight with your arms, swing your legs over the rope.

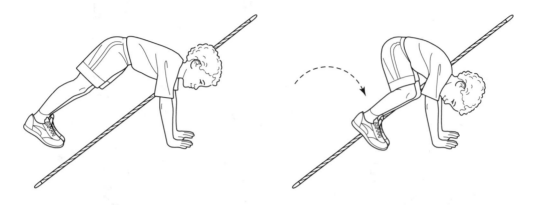

Tip-Up

Squat down and place your hands on the ground between your knees facing the carpet square. Lean forward and slowly lift your feet off the floor. Balance on your hands.

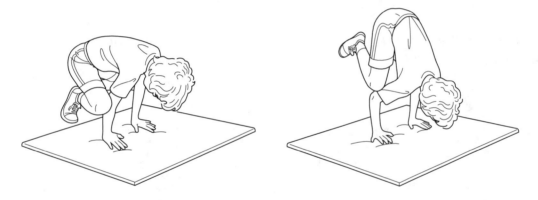

Kangaroo Hop

Bend your knees halfway and fold your arms across your chest. Keeping knees slightly bent, jump forward several times.

Cross-Legged Stand

Sit on your carpet square with your legs and arms crossed. Rise slowly to a standing position. Return to a sitting position.

Lunge

Stand on one foot with your other leg lifted straight in front of your body. Slowly bend the knee of your support leg. Repeat with your other leg.

Concluding Activities (5 minutes)

Physical Fitness Concept

Gather the children into an information formation.

1. Introduce the concept: *Things that may hurt our health and fitness are called "risk factors." Some risk factors are because of the way we behave—we can and should change these. Other risk factors are inherited, and we cannot change these.*

2. List and discuss the risk factors we can change:

    How much fat we have

    The amount of exercise we get

    The amount of cholesterol in our diet

    How much rest we get

    Substance abuse

3. List and discuss the risk factors we cannot change:

    How easily our hearts are trained

    How easily we may develop certain diseases

    The pollution we breathe

4. Continue the discussion: *There are more things we can change to be healthy than things we cannot change. If we have a risk that we cannot change, it is even more important to reduce the risk factors we can change.*

Second and third graders need to focus on skill development, refining skills, applying and combining skills, and, ultimately, using skills in games. Therefore, in this section, we introduce new skills and refine and combine skills from Grades K-1: Games and Sports. Many children in these grades will be participating in sport programs after school, which can help them become more competent movers; however, these programs often emphasize game play rather than skill development. Yet skills are too important to skim over both because sport is important in our society and because children judge each other based on motor skill performance. Certainly, as children gain skill they become more efficient and competent, which in turn enhances confidence.

UNIT ORGANIZATION

The focus of this unit is refining, combining, and applying manipulative and locomotor skills. Work to develop skill and cooperation, while deemphasizing competition.

Early lessons refine and combine tossing, throwing, rolling, bouncing, dribbling, and catching balls and beanbags. Then students work to refine kicking and foot-dribbling skills. Next, several lessons cover striking. A review of manipulative skills follows as children learn to apply them in games. The unit continues, refining locomotor and manipulative skills, and combining them in various combinations. The final lessons introduce more games in which students apply manipulative skills.

LESSON ORGANIZATION

Each lesson begins with warm-up activities, usually five-minute games of low organization. Refer to the warm-up games that open the unit often throughout the school year. Skill development activities follow; plan about 20 minutes for this segment. Usually there will be time to repeat the skill development activities until time runs out. Remember that practice is critical to skill acquisition. More turns or practice trials enhance skill acquisition and allow you more chances to give feedback to the students. Keep group sizes small for the same reasons. Finally, each lesson has five minutes of concluding activities. These are often games that use the skill(s) practiced earlier in the lesson, bringing closure to the lesson.

We encourage you to revisit many of the lessons not only to reinforce skills but also for the sheer enjoyment children get out of repeating an activity with which they are familiar. Table S2.1 summarizes the lessons in this section.

TEACHING HINTS

Children this age are enthusiastic about acquiring skills. Your encouragement and guidance can lead to a lifetime of enjoyment through games and sports. Children want to improve; one way is corrective information. Giving children feedback helps them improve and shows them you care and believe they can improve.

Individualizing Instruction

Skill levels among children will vary greatly in these grades, largely due to different experiences. Furthermore, within a child, skill levels across tasks will also vary, depending upon experience. For example, the best ball handler may be among the poorest at locomotor skills or a child with soccer experience may kick the ball well, but strike poorly. These variations are normal, and you should treat them as such. Even so, it is important that you deal with such differences. Keep in mind that skill is usually related to practice and experience. So it stands to reason that the physical educator must provide as many practice opportunities as possible. Practice—and the learning that results from practice—is hard work. Thus, encourage and reward hard work, notice improvement, and value all performance levels. In addition, make it your goal for the children to do the same. You should also make statements about skills that prepare children for practice. For example, say, "Most students have trouble with (fill in as appropriate)" or "When I was learning this skill it took lots of practice, especially with the (fill in)."

Sometimes an individual child will say a skill is too easy or even "Stupid!" Don't take offense as this can mean that the child is having trouble with the skill or has already mastered it. If the child can do the skill well, you might assign that individual a variation to make the skill more challenging or ask that child to help you or another student. If the child is in fact having trouble with the skill, encourage practice and patience, and consider giving a personal example of struggle with which the individual can relate. Finally, alter an activity to increase success rates for those who are struggling.

Class Management

Use the formations and other management tools presented in the Grades K-1: Organization and Grades 2-3: Organization lessons to help each games and sports lesson go smoothly. Remember, too, focus on having students practice and apply the skills, not on competition.

Ultimately, we encourage you to use these lessons in ways that fit your individual teaching style. Some teachers prefer control and order, while others are comfortable with more noise. Children do get excited as they learn and as they enjoy activities. Let two issues guide your decisions about management and control: safety and learning. All children should be safe, so if one or more children are "out of control" the only appropriate decision is to stop the activity and calm the situation. Likewise, if behaviors are interfering with learning, once again you must regain control of the situation. Otherwise, the level of extraneous movement and noise is largely a matter of your personal choice. Remember, however, the enthusiasm of your students is a sign you are doing a good job!

Table S2.1: Unit Plan for Grades 2-3: Games and Sports

Week 4: throwing and catching	Week 5: tossing and kicking
Monday: throwing and catching beanbags and balls Tuesday: throwing, catching, and dribbling Wednesday: throwing, catching, and bouncing a ball Thursday: dribbling and bouncing in patterns Friday: tossing and catching with a scoop and rolling at targets	Monday: tossing, throwing, and rolling at stationary targets and tossing and catching with scoops Tuesday: tossing, throwing, and rolling at moving targets Wednesday: throwing, catching, and tossing while moving and using hoops Thursday: moving the ball with the feet Friday: kicking a stationary and rolled ball

Week 6: kicking and striking	Week 12: striking and dribbling
Monday: kicking a stationary and rolled ball Tuesday: using the inside and outside of the foot, kicking for distance Wednesday: striking balloons with a large paddle from different positions Thursday: striking Friday: striking with an extension	Monday: striking Tuesday: throwing, catching, and striking stations Wednesday: kicking games Thursday: striking games Friday: dribbling, throwing, and catching games

Week 22: locomotor skills	Weeks 23 and 24: locomotor skills and parachute games
Monday: hopping Tuesday: running and jumping Wednesday: running, jumping, and hopping Thursday: run, hop, step, and jump Friday: skip, gallop, and slide	Monday: locomotor obstacle course Tuesday: create a locomotor obstacle course Wednesday: parachute games Thursday: throw and catch Friday: combining skills, throwing, catching, striking, and kicking

Week 29: manipulative and locomotor skills	Week 32: manipulative skills and review
Monday: combining manipulative skills with running and jumping Tuesday: jumping and catching or striking Wednesday: throwing and catching a Frisbee Thursday: striking with an extension Friday: new manipulative games	Monday: practicing manipulative skills in a game situation Tuesday: review games and sports Wednesday: review games and sports Thursday: review games and sports Friday: review games and sports

WARM-UPS

Balance Tag

Arrange the children in scatter formation. Designate two children as "Its."

1. Describe the game:

    The first two Its try to tag the other players. You are safe from tagging when you are standing on one foot or have no feet on the ground (as when you jump).

    Any player who is tagged becomes an It, so after the start of the game there will be several Its.

    When there are only two children left who haven't been tagged, I will stop the game, and we will start over with those children starting as the Its.

2. Have the children play Balance Tag.

Band-Aid Tag

Arrange the children in scatter formation. Designate two children as "Its."

1. Describe the game:

    Two players begin as Its. When tagged, you must hold one of your hands on the spot where you were tagged (like putting a Band-Aid over it), but you continue to play as another It. For example if you are tagged on the elbow, you must hold your hand over your elbow.

    Once you tag someone else, you are "healed" and no longer have to hold your tagged spot.

    After about two minutes, I will name two new Its, and we will start over.

2. Have the children play Band-Aid Tag.

Beanbag Tag

Arrange the children in scatter formation. Designate two players as "Its" and give each of them a beanbag.

1. Describe the game:

    The children who are It run after the other players, trying to touch them with the beanbag below the neck.

Tagged players become the new Its (or after [a set time], if an It has not tagged anyone with the beanbag, each It chooses a new It). The old Its become players.

2. Have the children play Beanbag Tag.

Circle Tag

Arrange children in a large circle marked on the ground with children at least 10 ft apart.

1. Describe and demonstrate the game:

   On the signal, run clockwise (point), *with each of you trying to tag the next person ahead in the circle.*

   If you are tagged, move to the inside, making a new circle. In the inside circle, you run counterclockwise (point), *and again try to tag the person in front of you in line. If you are tagged on the inside circle, you move back to the outside circle and continue.*

   Enter the circles where there are large spaces between children. If the circles become too crowded, we will stop and reorganize.

2. Have the children play Circle Tag.

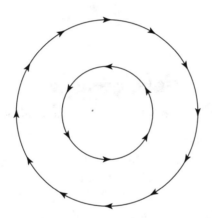

Color Tag

Arrange the children in scatter formation. Mark the boundaries of the playing area clearly.

1. Name four colors (e.g., red, green, purple, pink) and designate one "Runner." Describe and demonstrate the game:

   Each of you needs to secretly pick out one of the colors.

   The Runner will then call out one of the four colors.

   All children who have selected that color try to tag the Runner while the children who have not selected that color jog in place. The Runner tries to avoid the children by dodging and running within the marked boundaries.

   When the Runner is tagged (or after a reasonable time), we will begin the game again with the child who tagged the Runner as the new Runner. The new Runner must not choose the color that was just used. Taggers keep the same color choice.

2. Have the children play Color Tag.

Delivery Relay

Arrange the children in groups of four divided between two lines marked about 60 ft apart (see figure below). Give one child in each group a ball.

1. Describe and demonstrate the game:

   On the signal the child with the ball delivers (carries) the ball to a teammate at the other line.

   That child returns the ball to a child at the first line, and so on, until each person in your group has carried the ball over the distance.

2. Have the children play Delivery Relay.

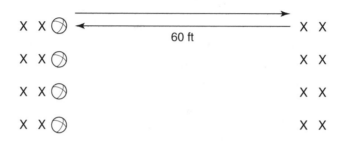

Dribble and Run

Arrange partners on a line, facing you, about 30 ft away, each pair with a ball.

1. Explain the activity:

   One partner from each pair dribbles the ball with either hand across to an imaginary line where I am standing. Concentrate on keeping the ball low (at waist level or below) and close to your body so your elbow stays bent when the ball is at its peak.

   Then return to your partner, carrying the ball and running.

   Now the second partner from each pair does the same thing.

   Then we will repeat with each partner using the opposite hand.

2. Have the children play Dribble and Run. Repeat several times.

Everyone's It

Arrange the children in scatter formation in a clearly defined large play area.

1. Describe the game:

   Everyone is It, trying to tag all the other children.

   The object is for one child to tag all the other children. You are on your honor to keep track of whom you tag.

2. Have the children play Everyone's It.

Loose Caboose

Arrange groups of three or four in scatter formation. Scatter three or four extra children about a clearly defined play area.

1. Describe and demonstrate the game:

   In each group, form a "Train," holding one another at the waist in a line (you must stay hooked together).

   The extra children are Loose Cabooses and try to hook on to the backs of the Trains.

   The Trains move around the play area, trying to avoid being hooked onto by a Loose Caboose.

   If a Caboose does connect with a Train, the Engine (the first person in that train) becomes a Loose Caboose.

2. Have the children play Loose Caboose.

Nose Tag

Arrange the children in scatter formation. Designate two players as "Its."

1. Describe and demonstrate the game:

   Two children begin as Its and try to tag the other children, who run, trying to avoid being tagged by the Its.

   You are safe from being tagged if you are standing on one leg with the other leg looped over one arm while the hand on that arm holds your nose.

   If you let go of your nose, lose your balance, or begin to run, you are no longer safe and can be tagged by an It.

   Once tagged, you become an It and switch places with the original It.

2. Have the children play Nose Tag.

Safe position: arm under knee and then holding nose

Pair Tag

Arrange the children with partners (inside hands joined) in equal numbers on two facing lines that are 50 to 60 ft apart. Have one pair stand in the center between the two lines as "It."

1. Describe the game:

   With inside hands joined, the It pair signals "Go!" and tries to tag the other pairs, who run (with inside hands joined) to the opposite side of the play area.

   As pairs are tagged they become It and join the other taggers in the middle.

   When all pairs have been tagged, the last pair to be tagged stands alone in the center for the start of a new game. Any pair that drops hands must also join the taggers in the middle.

2. Have the children play Pair Tag.

Reveille

Arrange the children in two groups along parallel lines as in the figure.

1. Describe the game:

   On the signal (a horn is best, but a whistle, bell, or other noisemaker will do), everyone runs for the opposite line.

   The first group to line up, standing at attention, gets a point.

   Take care when running past other children, so that no one is bumped or tripped.

   We will play several rounds.

2. Have the children play Reveille.

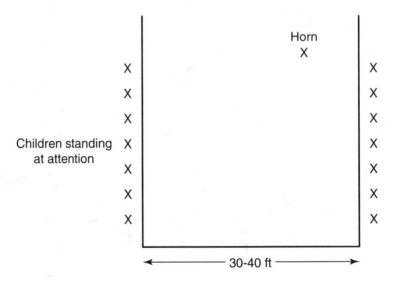

Sneaky Tag

Arrange the children into two groups, one group on a start line and the other group on X's (see figure on page 469). (You can make the lines and X's on a hard surface with tape and on grass or dirt with paint or flour.) The children on the start line are the "Sneakers," and the children on the X's are the "Taggers."

1. Describe and demonstrate the game:

   On the signal, the Sneakers move through the Taggers trying to get to the endline without being tagged. Sneakers must stay within the boundaries, and Taggers must keep at least one toe touching their X.

   If you are tagged, you run around the outside trackway and back to the start line during the next round (from finish line to start line).

   After several rounds, we will switch Taggers and Sneakers.

   Sneakers use this strategy: When a Tagger is trying to reach you on one side, run by on the other side.

2. Have the children play Sneaky Tag.

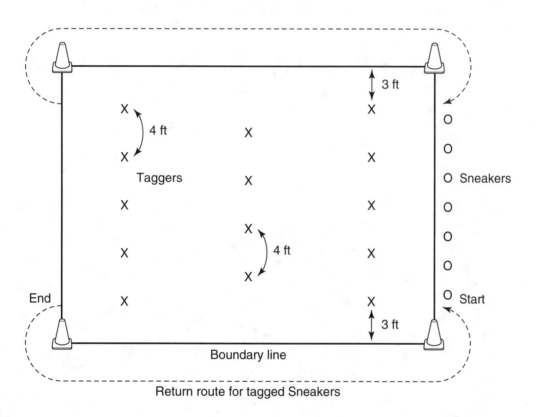

Return route for tagged Sneakers

Triplet Tag

Divide the children into groups of three ("Triplets"), with their inside hands joined. Place half the groups on each of two facing lines, 50 to 60 ft apart. Designate one Triplet group to stand in the center area between the two lines.

1. Describe and demonstrate the game:

   This game is played like Pair Tag (see Grades 2-3: Game and Sports, Warm-Ups, page 468) except that three children hold hands and play as one Triplet.

   To begin, one Triplet group stands in the center area. Only the two end children in the tagging Triplet can do the tagging, but any child in another Triplet can be tagged.

   It's important to communicate and agree on where you will run to avoid someone's getting dragged around.

2. Have the children play Triplet Tag.

Zigzag Toss

Arrange small groups of students in pairs of lines, facing each other 10 ft apart, each line with a beanbag (or an appropriate-size ball).

1. Describe and demonstrate the activity:

   The first child in line 1 tosses the beanbag to the first child in line 2.

   The first child in line 2 tosses to the second child in line 1, and so on until the beanbag gets to the end of both lines.

2. Have the children play Zigzag Toss, going up and down the lines as time allows. (This can be used as a relay race by having several sets of short lines; when the last child gets the ball, he or she runs to the front and begins again.)

GAMES AND SPORTS

LESSON 1
THROWING AND CATCHING BEANBAGS AND BALLS

Student Objectives

- Play catch with partners.
- Bounce and catch a ball with either hand or both hands.
- State that watching where the ball bounces will predict where the ball must be caught.
- Cooperate with team members during Ball Pursuit.

Equipment and Materials

- 1 beanbag per child
- 1 playground ball per child
- 1 launcher per pair, each with a small metal can attached on one end to hold
- Several balls of varying sizes and colors
- Chalk, flour, markers, or tape to mark lines

Warm-Up Activities (5 minutes)

Zigzag Toss

See Grades 2-3: Games and Sports, Warm-Ups, page 470.

Skill-Development Activities (20 minutes)

Have half the children do each of the next two activities for 10 minutes, then switch.

Launchers and Beanbags

Arrange half the children in scatter formation, each with a launcher and beanbag. Challenge the children with the following tasks:

Can you clap before catching the beanbag?

Can you turn around before catching it?

Can you catch two beanbags?

Can you catch two beanbags, one in each hand?

Bouncing a Ball

Arrange the other half of the class in scatter formation, each child with a playground ball.

1. Challenge the children with the following ball tasks:

    Can you bounce it very low and fast?

Can you bounce it with both hands?

Can you bounce it with your left hand?

Can you bounce it with your right hand?

Can you bounce it and clap before catching it?

2. Ask the children to find partners and practice bouncing to a partner.

3. Tell the children: *Watch where the ball hits, so you can guess where you will have to catch the ball.*

Concluding Activities (5 minutes)

Ball Pursuit

Arrange the children into two circles. In each circle, have the children count off by twos. Children with the same number are on the same team. In each circle, give one ball each (of different colors, if possible) to two children standing on opposite sides of the circle who are on opposing teams.

1. Describe and demonstrate the game:

   On the signal, pass the balls around the circle (in the same direction) to the next teammate until the ball of one team passes the ball of the other team.

   Your team earns a point each time one ball passes the other, and the next round begins.

2. Have the children play Ball Pursuit.

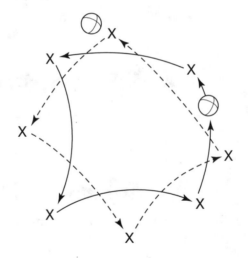

GAMES AND SPORTS

LESSON 2
THROWING, CATCHING, AND DRIBBLING

Student Objectives

- Dribble while moving.
- Refine skills of throwing and catching with a partner.
- Contrast dribbling and bouncing.
- Work cooperatively in Circle Stride Ball or in small groups in Keep Away.

Equipment and Materials

- 1 playground ball (8+ in.) per child
- Chalk, flour, or tape to mark lines
- 1 playground ball (13 in.) per group
- Signal

Warm-Up Activities (5 minutes)

Delivery Relay

See Grades 2-3: Games and Sports, Warm-Ups, page 466.

Skill-Development Activities (15 minutes)

Throwing and Catching Tasks

Arrange pairs in scatter formation, each pair 10 ft apart with one playground ball.

1. Challenge the children with the following tasks:

    Toss (throw underhand) and catch with your partner.

    Back up one step at a time until you can no longer catch and toss.

    Each of you should toss from each distance before moving.

Move the pairs back to 10 ft apart.

2. Have them throw (overhand) and catch, again backing up after each successful round, as in step 1.

After several trials, move them back to 10 ft apart.

3. Have them bounce and catch the ball, following the same procedure.

Dribbling

Arrange the children in scatter formation, each child with a ball.

1. Ask the children: *What is the difference between dribbling and bouncing a ball?* Demonstrate: *Dribbling is with one hand.*

2. Have the children practice dribbling.

3. Tell the children: *Dribble the ball rhythmically, keeping the ball below your waist and close to your body so your elbow stays bent when the ball is at its peak. Spread your fingers so your fingers and palm cover as much of the surface of the ball as possible.*

4. Have the children perform some dribbling tasks: *Dribble with your left hand. Don't move your feet. Now try with your right hand.* Repeat several times.

Line up the children across one end of the play area.

5. Ask the children: *Can you dribble and walk to there?* Point out an endline or opposite side of the play area. Have the children go back and forth several times.

Arrange partners in scatter formation.

6. Have one partner dribble around the other, then have partners switch roles. Do this several times.

Concluding Activities (10 minutes)

Circle Stride Ball

Use this activity with second graders. See Keep Away (next activity) for third graders. Divide the children into groups of six to nine each. Have the children stand in a circle with their feet spread apart so that they touch the feet of each of their neighbors. Place one child in the center of each circle with a large ball.

1. Describe and demonstrate the game:

    The child in the center tries to roll the ball out of the circle between another child's legs.

    If the child in the center is successful, the two players exchange places; if not, play continues.

    Players may not move their feet and must stop the ball with their hands.

2. Have the children play Circle Stride Ball.
3. You can also have the children play this game with the circle facing outward and the children looking back through their legs.

Keep Away

Use this game with third graders. See Circle Stride Ball (previous activity) for second graders. Arrange groups of three in scatter formation.

1. Describe and demonstrate the game:

   Two of you in each group play catch (you may bounce, roll, toss, or throw the ball) while the third person tries to gain control of the ball.

   Anyone who loses control of the ball switches roles with the child who gains control of the ball.

   At set intervals (e.g., 30 to 60 seconds), I will signal that the child trying to gain control is allowed to switch places with one of the other children if they don't get to switch by gaining control of the ball.

2. Have the children play Keep Away.

GRADES 2-3

GAMES AND SPORTS

LESSON 3

THROWING, CATCHING, AND BOUNCING A BALL

Student Objectives

- Participate in one ball game and be introduced to the rules for two ball-handling games.
- Practice the ball-handling skills of throwing, catching, and bouncing.

- Follow the rules in a game.
- Cooperate during playground ball challenges.

Equipment and Materials

- 1 playground ball per pair
- 1 tennis ball per pair
- 1 Sidewalk Tennis court per pair (see figure at left)
- 1 Four-Square court per group of 4 (see figure below)

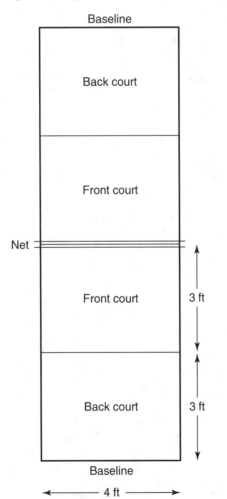

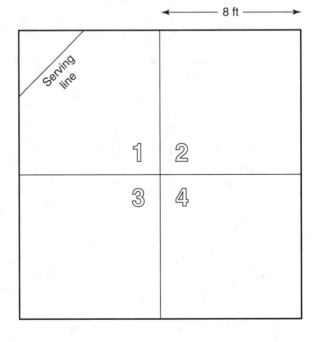

476 Physical Education for Children: Daily Lesson Plans for Elementary School

Dribble and Run

See Grades 2-3: Games and Sports, Warm-Ups, page 466.

Two-Handed Underhand Serve

Arrange pairs in scatter formation, each pair with a playground ball, standing about six ft apart, facing each other.

1. Describe and demonstrate the skill: *Drop the playground ball from waist height directly in front of your body and, as the ball rebounds, strike it with both hands into the air and away.*
2. Present and repeat each of the following sequences several times:

    Drop, bounce, and let your partner catch the ball.

    Drop, bounce, strike, and let your partner catch the ball.

Direct the children to exchange the playground balls for tennis balls.

3. Repeat step 2 with the tennis ball.

Playground Ball Challenges

Arrange the children in groups of four on the Four-Square areas.

1. Ask the children: *Can you bounce the ball around the square from* (name, to name, to name, to name)? Say this for each square in clockwise order.
2. *Now can you go the opposite direction?*
3. After they have had several tries, switch directions again.

Four-Square

Keep groups of four stationed at the Four-Square courts.

1. Describe and demonstrate the game:

    The object of this game is to be the server as long as possible.

    The first server stays the server until he or she makes an illegal hit or fails to return a ball hit into his or her square.

    Meanwhile, the other three players (nonservers) are trying to move into the server square by passing successively counterclockwise (one after the other) through the other three squares.

    You are sent to the bottom square if you make an illegal hit or fail to return a hit into your square. Illegal hits include the following: carrying the ball, hitting overhand, or allowing the ball to bounce more than once. The bottom square is the square to the server's right.

2. Have the children play Four-Square.

Sidewalk Tennis

Place one student on each end of each Sidewalk Tennis court.

1. Describe and demonstrate the game:

You must serve underhand from behind the baseline. The serve must go over the net line and into the front court.

All other hits must also be underhand, allowing one bounce or volleying the ball into either court.

The server scores a point when the opponent fails to return the ball or hits it out of bounds.

The server loses the serve if he or she fails to return the ball or hits it out of bounds.

Play each game to 15 points, but a player must win by at least 2 points.

2. Have the children play Sidewalk Tennis.

Concluding Activities (5 minutes)

Sidewalk Tennis or Four-Square

Arrange the children in pairs (Sidewalk Tennis) or fours (Four-Square). Allow the children to play whichever game they wish.

LESSON 4
DRIBBLING AND BOUNCING IN PATTERNS

Student Objectives

- Dribble in a pattern.
- Demonstrate catching, dribbling, and throwing in a series.

Equipment and Materials

- 1 playground ball
- 1 hoop (30-36 in.) per child
- 15 cones or filled 2-liter plastic bottles

Warm-Up Activities (5 minutes)

Delivery Relay

See Grades 2-3: Games and Sports, Warm-Ups, page 466.

Skill-Development Activities (20 minutes)

Dribbling in the Hoops

Arrange the children in scatter formation, each child with a hoop and ball. Have them place their hoops on the ground.

1. Tell the children: *Keep your ball close to your body, looking where you are going and not at the ball.*
2. Challenge the children with these tasks:

   Bounce your ball in your hoop while standing outside your hoop. Repeat several times.

   Dribble your ball inside your hoop and walk around the outside of your hoop.

   Now change directions! Repeat several times.

Movement Tasks

Arrange small groups of three to five, still with their hoops and balls. Have each group lay their hoops on the ground in a row.

1. Have the children dribble the balls as they walk around and through the hoops.
2. Repeat.

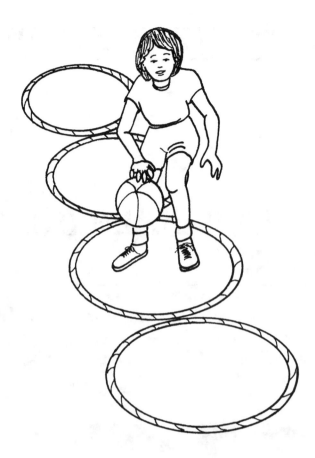

Set up three lines of five cones, with about five ft between cones (or use hoops spaced five ft apart). Divide the children into three groups, and assign each group to a line of cones.

3. Have the children dribble a zigzag pattern around the cones.

4. Repeat.

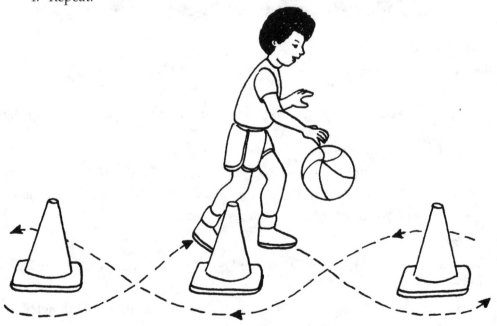

Rearrange the hoops in a row (to dribble inside), followed by the cones spread in a row (to zigzag around). Make three sets of each.

5. Have the children dribble inside the hoops, then dribble a zigzag pattern around the cones.

6. Repeat several times.

Concluding Activities (5 minutes)

Dribble-and-Throw Relay

Arrange the children into short relay lines, along one end of the play area, each group with a cone about 15 ft away.

1. Have the first child in each line dribble around the cone, then throw the ball back to the next child in line, continuing through all the children.

2. After throwing the ball, each child returns to the end of their team's line.

3. Play continuously in the available time. If you wish, determine which team has gone "through the line" the most times.

GAMES AND SPORTS

LESSON 5

TOSSING AND CATCHING WITH A SCOOP, ROLLING AT TARGETS

Student Objectives

- Toss and catch a self-tossed beanbag with a scoop.
- Hit a 2-ft-square target from 20 ft with a rolled ball.

Equipment and Materials

- Enough scoops and beanbags for half the class
- Enough targets (e.g., tires, bicycle tubes, pictures) and playground balls for half the class

Warm-Up Activities (7 minutes)

Nose Tag

See Grades 2-3: Games and Sports, Warm-Ups, page 467.

Skill-Development Activities (18 minutes)

Divide the class into two groups. Have one group begin with the Underhand Toss With a Scoop activity and the other with Playground Balls activity. Switch groups after nine minutes.

Underhand Toss With a Scoop

Arrange half the class in scatter formation with the beanbags and scoops.

1. Tell the children: *Toss and catch the beanbags with the scoops as many times in a row as possible.*
2. *Point the scoop high (low; where you want the beanbag to go.)*

Playground Balls

Arrange the other half of the class in scatter formation with the playground balls and targets.

1. Have the children practice rolling (underhand), then tossing (underhand), then throwing (overhand) the ball at the targets. Tell the children: *Reach your hand to the target.*

2. Move among and between the two groups to correct and encourage.

After nine minutes, have groups trade equipment.

3. Have students do the activity they have not yet done.

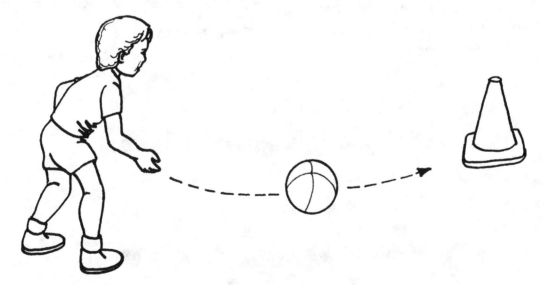

Concluding Activities (5 minutes)

Encourage the children to practice whichever skill they had the most difficulty doing (rolling, tossing, or throwing at the targets, or tossing and catching with the scoops).

LESSON 6

TOSSING, THROWING, AND ROLLING AT STATIONARY TARGETS, AND TOSSING AND CATCHING WITH SCOOPS

Student Objectives

- Toss (from 10 ft) and catch a beanbag using a scoop with a partner.
- Self-set (toss) and catch a beanbag with a scoop.
- Practice tossing, throwing, and rolling at a stationary target.
- Compare and contrast tossing, throwing, and rolling.
- Practice independently.

Equipment and Materials

- 1 scoop per child
- 1 beanbag per pair
- 1 tennis ball per pair
- 1 playground ball per pair
- 1 foam ball per pair
- 1 target (e.g., hoop, tire, traditional) per pair

Safety Tips

- Remind the children to throw or toss to their partners only when their partners are expecting the throw.

Warm-Up Activities (5 minutes)

Nose Tag

See Grades 2-3: Games and Sports, Warm-Ups (page 467).

Skill-Development Activities (20 minutes)

Movement Challenges

Arrange targets along the boundaries of the play area. Inside the play area, scatter equipment piles, each consisting of two scoops, one beanbag, and one tennis ball, one pile per pair of students. Pair off the children by having them each stand by a scoop.

1. Challenge the children with the following tasks:

   Take two giant steps away from your partner. (Partners should be about 10 ft apart.) Toss and catch the beanbag. Tossing is underhand—so your hand stays below your waist—but the ball arches high through the air.

   Now use your scoops to toss and catch the tennis ball.

   Can you toss it very high (low) to your partner?

   Can you make it go in a straight line (parallel to the ground)?

2. Repeat all challenges several times, moving the children farther apart or closer, as necessary. Continue this until most students are successful.

Have partners face the same direction, standing within arms' length of each other.

3. Challenge the children with these tasks:

   Stand next to your partner. Now toss and catch! Toss slowly.

   Toss high into the air and see if your partner can catch the beanbag.

Have the children put down the scoops, each select one type of ball, and move still in pairs to stand about 10 ft from a target.

4. Ask the children: *Can you roll your ball into the target? Rolling is also underhand—so your hand will stay below your waist—but the ball moves on the ground.*

5. Have them retrieve their balls and repeat.

6. Have each child try each type of ball and rotate to another type of target.

7. Repeat.

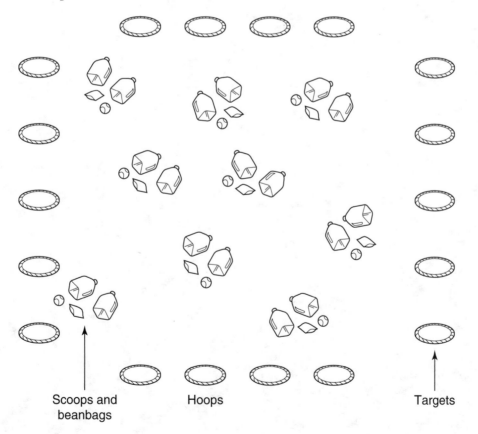

Scoops and beanbags   Hoops   Targets

Concluding Activities (5 minutes)

Move the children back to the middle of the play area. Have each child get a scoop and a beanbag. You can also have children work with partners.

1. Ask the children: *How many times can you toss and catch without missing?*

2. Have them practice.

3. Ask the children: *Who has done 5 (10, more)? Let's try again!*

LESSON 7
TOSSING, THROWING, AND ROLLING AT MOVING TARGETS

Student Objectives

- Practice throwing, tossing, and rolling at moving targets.
- Work cooperatively with a partner.
- Explain "leading" when throwing to a moving target.

Equipment and Materials

- 1 (or more) foam ball(s) per child
- 1 (or more) tennis ball(s) per child
- 1 (or more) playground ball(s) per child
- Cones to mark Individual Dodgeball areas
- Hoops
- Standard(s) and extra rope(s) from which to suspend the hoops
- Signal
- Chalk, tape, or flour to mark lines and boundaries

Warm-Up Activities (5 minutes)

Nose Tag

See Grades 2-3: Games and Sports, Warm-Ups, page 467.

Skill-Development Activities (20 minutes)

Suspended Hoops

Use standards and rope to suspend the hoops two to three ft above the ground. Arrange the children in two parallel lines on either side of the suspended hoops, about 10 ft from the hoops, each child with at least one of each type of ball.

1. Tell the children: *Throw all the balls through the hoops. Retrieve them on the signal.*

2. Repeat several times.

3. To make more difficult, you can move children farther back from the targets and/or swing the rope so the targets (the hoops) move. You can adjust the swing to the skill of the throwers.

Run and Throw

Arrange partners in two lines, facing each other, each pair with a foam ball. Identify a throwing mark 20 ft away from behind each line.

1. Tell the children: *The partner with the ball runs to the throwing mark, turns and throws the ball to her or his partner, and returns to the original position. Repeat with the other partner running and throwing from the mark.*

2. Repeat.

Throwing to a Moving Partner

Move the lines to five ft apart; give each of the partners in one line at least one foam ball.

1. Tell the children: *The partner without the ball runs directly away from the thrower, who throws the ball so the runner can catch it. "Leading" means to throw in front of a moving target so the target and the ball will meet. The thrower must anticipate—guess or figure out—how far ahead to throw.*

2. Repeat several times, allowing both partners to throw and catch.

3. Repeat, using tennis balls.

Concluding Activities (5 minutes)

Fitness Dodgeball

Define a play area with cones large enough to accommodate this activity. Arrange the children as partners in scatter formation, each pair with a foam ball.

1. Describe and demonstrate the game:

   One of the pair gets the ball; the other child is to run and dodge (try to avoid being hit by) the ball thrown by the first partner.

   All throws must be below the waist. When the dodger is hit or after a set time period, the players reverse roles.

   You must stay inside the marked play area boundaries.

2. Have the children play Fitness Dodgeball.

GAMES AND SPORTS

LESSON 8
THROWING, CATCHING, AND TOSSING WHILE MOVING AND USING HOOPS

Student Objectives

- Throw while moving, catch while moving, and move a hoop to "capture" a ball.
- Cooperate with a partner.
- Demonstrate a toss or a throw on request.

Equipment and Materials

- 1 foam ball per pair
- 1 tennis ball per pair
- 1 playground ball per pair
- 1 hoop per pair

Safety Tip

- Remind the children not to throw unless their partners are ready as well as not to throw at anyone's head.

Warm-Up Activities (5 minutes)

Nose Tag

See Grades 2-3: Games and Sports, Warm-Ups, page 467.

Skill-Development Activities (20 minutes)

Throwing to a Moving Target Through a Hoop

Arrange partners in scatter formation with partners, each pair with a hoop, foam ball, and tennis ball. Direct one partner to hold the hoop and the other to hold one ball and place the other ball on the ground.

    1. Describe and demonstrate the activity:

> *The partner with the hoop holds the hoop overhead and moves in a circle around the thrower, staying 5 to 10 ft away.*
>
> *On your signal, the thrower tries to throw the ball through the hoop.*
>
> *On your signal, the throwers retrieve all of the balls at once.*
>
> *The thrower gets to throw several times, using either ball.*

2. Have the children do the activity for about five minutes.

3. Have partners change places and repeat.

Capturing a Moving Ball

Keep partners in scatter formation with the same equipment.

1. Describe and demonstrate the activity:

   The partner with the hoop walks or jogs around the thrower.

   The thrower throws the foam ball but not directly at the target (slightly to the side or high or low).

   The other child moves the hoop to try to get the ball to go through it.

2. Have the children do the activity.

3. Repeat several times.

4. Have partners change places and repeat.

5. Repeat, using tennis balls.

Double Circle Catch

Arrange the children in two circles, one inside the other. Children in the inner circle should be about 5 ft apart. Each child in the inner circle should be facing a partner in the outer circle about 10 ft away. Give one partner in each pair a playground ball.

1. Describe and demonstrate the activity:

    Each circle begins to walk in opposite directions (point for each).

    As the circles move in opposite directions, toss or throw the ball back and forth between you and your partner as you pass each other.

    We will walk at the beginning, then jog, and then run.

2. Have the children do the activity.

10 ft

5 ft

LESSON 9
MOVING THE BALL WITH THE FEET

Student Objectives

- Move various objects in patterns with the feet.
- Control a ball with the feet.

Equipment and Materials

- 1 playground ball per child
- 1 foam ball per child
- 1 tennis ball per child
- 6 cones or plastic bottles
- 6 small colored floor markers (e.g., erasers, blocks of wood)
- Chalk, flour, or tape to mark lines

Warm-Up Activities (5 minutes)

Pair Tag

See Grades 2-3: Games and Sports, Warm-Ups, page 468.

Skill-Development Activities (18 minutes)

Movement Challenges

Define two parallel lines, 30 ft apart. Set out the six cones along line B, and arrange the children in six groups behind line A. Set the colored markers halfway between the groups of children and the cones. Give each child a foam ball.

1. Describe the activity:

    Kick the foam ball around the cone.

    Control the ball with the inside of your foot as in soccer.

    The next child in line starts when the one before is about halfway to the cone.

    Stay in your own space when you pass someone.

2. Have the children practice the skill.
3. Repeat with the tennis balls.
4. Repeat with the playground balls.
5. Ask the children: *Run to the colored marker carrying the ball, put your ball down, run to line B, turn around, run and kick your ball (just one kick if possible) back to your group, run, pick up your ball, and go to the end of the line.*

6. Have them repeat, but tell them: *Try to make the ball stop just as it gets to line A. Get as close as you can.*

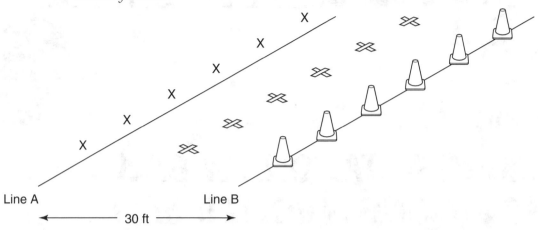

Line A

Line B

← 30 ft →

Line up partners in two groups, one partner on line A and the other on line B, each pair with one playground ball.

7. Tell the children: *Line A partners, put the ball on the marker, run, and kick it to your partner across from you (on line B). Line B partners, try to kick the ball back to your line A partner before it stops.*

Concluding Activities (7 minutes)

Kick Dodgeball

Arrange half of the children in a circle (about 15 ft in diameter). Scatter the other children inside the circle. Give several children in the circle foam balls. Place extra balls in a box away from the circle.

1. Describe and demonstrate the game:

   The object for the circle children is to kick the ball across the circle.

   The object for the center children is to stop the balls.

   Each time a circle child kicks a ball, their team will get a point, so each child counts his or her kicks.

   If a ball goes outside the circle or is captured by the center team, the ball is out of play.

   After all the balls are out of play or after two to three minutes, we will switch circle and center children.

2. Have the children play Kick Dodgeball.

LESSON 10
KICKING A STATIONARY BALL AND KICKING A ROLLED BALL

Student Objectives

- Kick a stationary ball 10 ft to a target (20 ft for third graders).

Equipment and Materials

- Station 1: several hoops, marked kicking line, 1 playground ball per pair in group
- Station 2: 1 cone and 1 playground ball per pair in group, marked kicking line
- Station 3: 1 weighted plastic bottle (with one inch of sand or water) and 1 carpet square per pair in group

Warm-Up Activities (5 minutes)

Pair Tag

See Grades 2-3: Games and Sports, Warm-Ups, page 468.

Skill-Development Activities (21 minutes)

Stations

Set up the three stations as shown in figure on page 495 and described in text. Place pairs of partners into three groups (e.g., each group with 8 to 10 children, or four or five pairs of partners). Start each group at one of the three stations.

1. Discuss and demonstrate the activities at each station. Tell the children: *One partner kicks while the other retrieves the ball. Retrieve carefully!*

2. Have the children practice the activities at the assigned station several times, then have partners switch places and repeat.

3. Rotate the groups to new stations. Repeat until the groups go through all three stations twice.

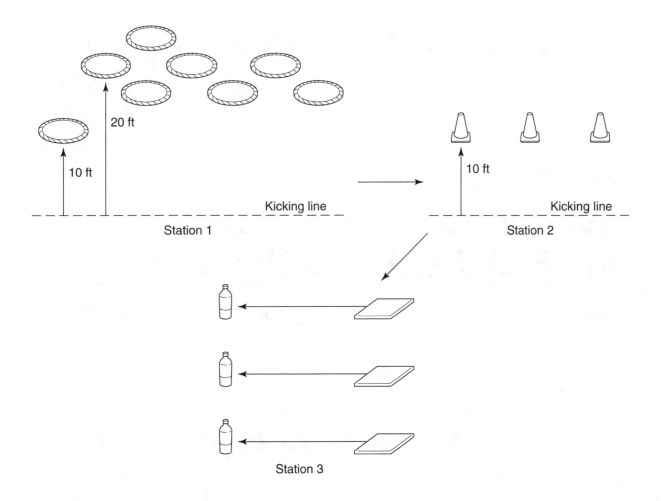

Station 1

Place the hoops 10 to 20 ft from a marked kicking line.

Kick the balls into the scattered hoops (each ball should stop in the hoops).

Station 2

Place the cones about 10 ft from a marked kicking line.

Kick the balls as far as possible toward the cones, trying to send them past the cones.

Station 3

Place the plastic bottles 10 to 15 ft away from the carpet squares.

While standing on the carpet squares, kick the balls at the plastic bottles, trying to knock them over.

Concluding Activities (4 minutes)

Kick Dodgeball

See Grades 2-3: Games and Sports, Lesson 9, page 493.

LESSON 11
KICKING A STATIONARY BALL AND KICKING A ROLLED BALL

Student Objectives

- Kick a stationary ball 10 ft to a target (20 ft for third graders).
- Kick a rolled ball 10 ft to a target (20 ft for third graders).

Equipment and Materials

- 1 playground ball per pair
- 1 hoop per group of 3

Warm-Up Activities (5 minutes)

Triplet Tag

See Grades 2-3: Games and Sports, Warm-Ups, page 469.

Skill-Development Activities (20 minutes)

Kicking a Rolled Ball

Arrange partners in two widely spaced lines, partners facing each other, about 10 ft apart, each pair with one playground ball.

1. Describe and demonstrate the activity: *The partner with the ball rolls it slowly to their partner who kicks the ball back to the first partner.*
2. Have the children repeat several times, challenging the children to kick with each foot on different turns.
3. Reverse partner roles and repeat.
4. As the partners become more skilled move them further apart, up to about 20 ft.

Foot Volley

Arrange partners in scatter formation, about 10 ft apart, each pair with one playground ball.

1. Describe and demonstrate the skill:

   The object is to kick the ball continuously between the two partners, keeping control of the ball and keeping the ball in constant motion.

> *Once you and your partner have been able to control several kicks in a row, you can count the number of volleys.*

2. Have the children practice the skill.

3. Move highly skilled pairs farther apart.

Pass to Target

Arrange children in scatter formation in groups of three, forming a 10-ft-sided triangle. Lay a hoop at the feet of one member and give another member a playground ball.

1. Describe and demonstrate the activity:

> *One child starts by kicking the ball to the other partner without a hoop, who will kick the ball into the hoop.*
>
> *The player standing near the hoop retrieves the ball and kicks it back to the first child.*
>
> *Repeat, then rotate the position of each child until all of you have had several turns in each position.*

2. Have the children do the activity.

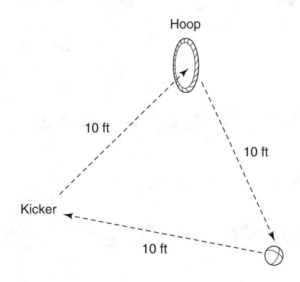

Concluding Activity (5 minutes)

Giant Kick-Around

Arrange all children in a large circle with about 10 ft between children.

1. Describe the game:

> *We will begin with one playground ball. I will choose a child who will kick the ball to the child to their right.*
>
> *That child will kick the ball to the child on their right and so forth.*
>
> *When the ball goes around the circle with no errors (no one loses control), I will start a second ball on the opposite side of the circle.*
>
> *The object is to get as many balls going as possible.*

2. Have the children play Giant Kick-Around.

LESSON 12
USING THE INSIDE AND OUTSIDE OF THE FOOT, KICKING FOR DISTANCE

Student Objectives

- Kick and control the ball with the inside and outside of the foot.

Equipment and Materials

- 1 foam ball per group
- 1 playground ball per group
- 4 cones per group

Warm-Up Activities (5 minutes)

Triplet Tag

See Grades 2-3: Games and Sports, Warm-Ups, page 469.

Skill-Development Activities (20 minutes)

Movement Tasks

Arrange the children in several short lines with cones opposite each line (see figure on page 499), beginning with one foam ball per line.

1. Describe and demonstrate the task:

   Move the ball around the cones using the outsides of both your feet.

   Move the ball around the cones using the insides of both of your feet.

   Take turns, starting with the first child in each line.

2. Have the children try the task.

3. Repeat with the playground balls.

Remove the cones and place a hoop opposite each group.

4. Explain that now the last child in line serves as a retriever. After each child kicks, she or he goes to the end of the line and becomes retriever for that line.

5. Have the groups kick for distance, one child at a time. Encourage the children: *Kick as far as possible!*

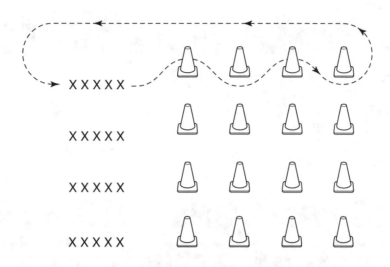

Concluding Activities (5 minutes)

Kick Dodgeball

See Grades 2-3: Games and Sports, Lesson 9, page 493.

GRADES 2-3

GAMES AND SPORTS

LESSON 13
STRIKING BALLOONS WITH A LARGE PADDLE FROM DIFFERENT POSITIONS

Student Objectives

- Strike a balloon with a paddle from two or more positions.
- Strike a balloon with a paddle two or more times in a row.
- Strike a balloon with a paddle using either hand.

Equipment and Materials

- 1 balloon per child (for indoors; plus several extra balloons, as some may break) *or* 1 crumpled paper sack or newspaper per child (for outdoors)

- 1 paddle per child
- 1 playground ball
- 3 bases
- 1 home plate
- 2 cones

Safety Tips

- Rule: Do not touch anyone with your paddle or you will serve a time-out.

Warm-Up Activities (5 minutes)

Everyone's It

See Grades 2-3: Games and Sports, Warm-Ups, page 466.

Skill-Development Activities (10 minutes)

Striking

Arrange the children in scatter formation, each child with a paddle and balloon. Challenge the children with the following tasks:

Can you hit your balloon high in the air with your paddle? Try the other hand.

Can you hit your balloon while kneeling? Try the other hand.

Can you think of any other body positions to hit from?

Using this position, hit with the other hand.

Have you tried hitting from your back (side, stomach)?

Try balancing on three body parts and hitting from this position.

Be sure to try hitting with your nondominant (or opposite) hand. How many times in a row can you hit your balloon?

Concluding Activities (15 minutes)

Lineup

Divide the children into two teams, starting one team in the field and the other at bat. The field should have two bases, home plate where the hitter stands, and another base 40 ft or more away from home. Cones can be used to mark the foul line. You can also use a softball diamond.

1. Describe and demonstrate the game:

    The hitter strikes the playground ball with a hand, then the entire team runs around the bases in single file behind the hitter.

    Each hitter has only one chance to strike (hit) the ball; it will be either an out or a run. Foul balls are outs.

    When the hitter hits the ball fair, the players on the fielding team all line up behind the player who catches the ball.

    They pass the ball quickly overhead back to the end of the line.

    They are trying to get the ball to the end of the line before the members of the hitting team all get home; if the ball reaches the end of the line before the hitting team gets home, it is an out.

    If the hitting team gets home before the ball gets to the end of the line it is a run, scoring one point for the hitting team.

    Play continues until there are three outs or all players on the hitting team have had one turn to hit.

    Then the teams will switch roles and continue playing.

2. Have the children play Lineup.

GAMES AND SPORTS

LESSON 14
STRIKING

Student Objectives

- Control a foam ball on the ground with a newspaper bat.
- Strike a suspended ball with a newspaper bat and a paddle.

Equipment and Materials

- 1 suspended ball per child
- Ropes and standards from which to suspend 1 ball per child
- 1 newspaper bat per child (rolled and taped newspaper)
- 1 foam ball per child
- 1 paddle per child

Safety Tip

- Remind children of the rules, especially those related to striking.

Warm-Up Activities (5 minutes)

Everyone's It

See Grades 2-3: Games and Sports, Warm-Ups, page 466.

Skill-Development Activities (15 minutes)

Striking Tasks

Arrange the children in scatter formation, each with a newspaper bat and foam ball.

1. Demonstrate moving the foam ball along the ground with the newspaper bat.
2. Challenge the children with the following tasks:

   Walk quickly and move the ball along the ground with the bat to the opposite side of the play area.

   Weave around other children carefully.

   Now run and move the ball back to where you started.

   Move the ball in a circle, turn, and go the other way.

Rearrange the children along several ropes that have balls suspended from them, one ball, paddle, and newspaper bat per child.

3. Demonstrate striking a suspended ball (sidearm, right, then left hand) with a newspaper bat and striking a suspended ball with a paddle.

4. Challenge the children with the following tasks:

   Strike the ball sidearm using your paddle. Try this several times.

   Change hands and try several times.

   Use the newspaper bat to hit the suspended ball. Try several times.

   Change hands again and try several more times.

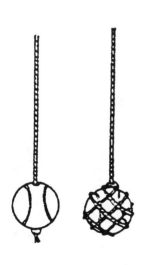

Concluding Activities (10 minutes)

Lineup

See Grades 2-3: Games and Sports, Lesson 13, page 501.

LESSON 15
STRIKING WITH AN EXTENSION

Student Objectives

- Hit a ball on a tee with a large bat.
- Run, controlling a ball with a stick.

Equipment and Materials

- 1 batting tee per group
- 1 large bat per group
- 1 paddle per group
- 1 hoop per group
- 1 foam ball per child
- 1 broomstick per child
- Flour, chalk, or tape to mark lines

Safety Tip

- Use hoops or other markers to define "on-deck" areas for all children not hitting.

Warm-Up Activities (5 minutes)

Everyone's It

See Grades 2-3: Games and Sports, Warm-Ups, page 466.

Skill-Development Activities (15 minutes)

Striking From a Batting Tee

Arrange groups of four or five around batting tees, using a hoop to mark the waiting (on-deck) area, which should be 10 ft from the tee. Give each group a bat, foam ball, and paddle.

1. Demonstrate striking from a batting tee:

    Standing facing the tee (with the intended line of flight perpendicular to the direction he or she is facing), *move your bat back slowly while turning (rotating) your body away from the foam ball.*

    Swing back toward the ball, keeping the bat level (on a plane) *with the ball.*

    Continue swinging through after contact, so that the bat points toward where you want the ball to go.

2. Have the children practice striking from a batting tee, organized as follows:

    The child next in line to bat stands in the on-deck hoop.

    The child who just batted stands 20 ft from the tee, where the striker will hit the ball, and retrieves.

The rest of the group waits behind the hoop. The striker replaces the retriever, and the retriever moves to the end of the batting line.

Repeat this rotation several times.

3. Have the children practice using a foam ball and striking with a paddle. (All other procedures remain the same.)

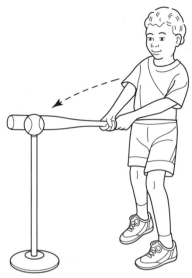

Stick and Ball Relay

Arrange the children in groups of three in relay formation along one line, facing another line 40 to 50 ft away, each child with a broomstick and foam ball.

1. Describe and demonstrate the game:

   Guide your ball with your stick to the endline and back.

   You may swing the sticks, but not more than waist-high.

   You must start over if I call a "stick foul" (swinging the stick higher than the waist) on you. You are also on your honor to call stick fouls on yourself.

2. Have the children play the Stick and Ball Relay. You can have groups play this continuously in the time available or play competitively as follows: When each child has had a turn, that team is done; the first team to finish wins.

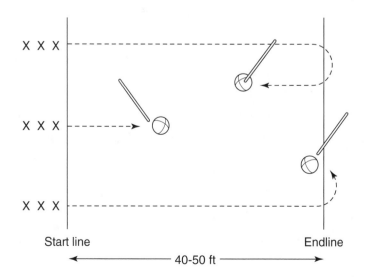

Lineup

See Grades 2-3: Games and Sports, Lesson 13, page 501.

LESSON 16
STRIKING

Student Objectives
- Strike with a hand a playground ball that has been bounced or tossed to him or her by a partner.

Equipment and Materials
- 1 batting tee per pair
- 1 paddle per pair
- 1 foam ball per pair
- 1 playground ball per pair
- 1 tennis ball per pair
- 1 large bat per pair

Safety Tip
- Spread the children apart.
- Look behind you before you swing.
- Look before you move.

Warm-Up Activities (5 minutes)

Everyone's It

See Grades 2-3: Games and Sports, Warm-Ups, page 466.

Skill-Development Activities (15 minutes)

Striking a Moving Ball With the Hand

Arrange partners in scatter formation, each pair with a playground ball.

1. Describe and demonstrate the skill:

    Stand facing the way you want the ball to go (toward the intended line of flight of the ball).

    Bounce the ball and slowly turn (rotate) your body away from the ball.

    Swing your striking arm back away from the ball and, as the ball rebounds from the ground, swing that arm forward (your body also turns [rotates] forward), making contact with the ball.

    Continue swinging through until your arm points toward where you want the ball to fly (the intended line of flight).

2. Explain further, describing and demonstrating the various lines of flight possible:

    Upward—the arm swing should be upward.

    Parallel to the ground—the arms should remain parallel to the ground (demonstrate "parallel" very clearly).

Downward—the backswing should be parallel to the ground or slightly upward, with a downward forward swing and follow-through.

3. Have half the children strike to their partners, who catch the balls and return them to the strikers.

4. Have them repeat several times, then have partners change positions.

Striking a Tossed Ball With the Hand and a Paddle

Keep partners in scatter formation, each pair with a playground ball.

1. Describe and demonstrate the skill:

    Face the direction from which the ball will be tossed.

    Step backward on the foot on the same side of your body as your striking arm and rotate (turn) your shoulders, torso, and arms back to a right angle with the line of flight, shifting your weight onto your back foot. This means the shoulder of your nonstriking arm will end up pointed at the direction from which the ball will be tossed.

    As you begin to swing forward, shift your weight to your front foot, swinging your striking arm parallel to the ground (with wrist straight) and uncoiling your body.

    Follow through toward where you want the ball to fly.

2. Challenge the children with the following tasks:

    Toss your ball to your partner, and he or she will try to hit it back to you.

    Toss your ball to your partner and allow it to bounce, then your partner will try to hit it back to you.

Collect the playground balls, and give each pair a foam ball and paddle.

3. Ask the children to perform the following actions:

    Bounce the ball and hit it to your partner.

    Toss your ball to your partner, and he or she will try to hit it back to you.

    Toss your ball to your partner and allow it to bounce, and your partner will try to hit it back to you.

    Can you hit the ball back and forth between you, both using your paddles?

Collect the foam balls, and give each pair a tennis ball.

4. Repeat steps 1 through 3.

Striking With a Bat

Keep partners in scatter formation, each pair with a bat, batting tee, foam ball, and tennis ball.

1. Describe and demonstrate the skill:

> *Decide which foot you prefer to step forward with. This is called your "dominant" foot. The other foot is your "nondominant" foot.*
>
> *Begin with your nondominant (least favorite) foot forward, feet shoulder-width apart.*
>
> *Your shoulders and feet should be in parallel lines.*
>
> *Rest more of your body weight on your back foot.*
>
> *Hold the bat with your back hand above and touching your front hand, gripping with your fingers.*
>
> *Hold the bat high, hands even with the top of your back shoulder and the bat slanted backward at a slight angle (30 to 40 degrees) over your back shoulder.*

The strike begins as your back foot pushes your body weight forward.

Meanwhile, your front foot steps forward slightly, your body rotates forward, and you swing the bat forward and downward (to parallel with the ground).

Follow through toward your target.

2. Have them hit a foam ball, then a tennis ball, off a tee. One partner retrieves the foam ball while the other hits. Repeat several times, then have partners switch.

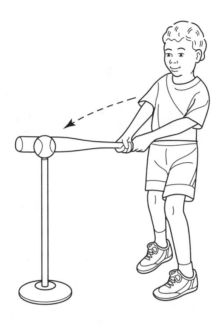

Concluding Activities (10 minutes)

Lineup

See Grades 2-3: Games and Sports, Lesson 13, page 501.

LESSON 17

THROWING, CATCHING, KICKING, AND STRIKING IN STATIONS

Student Objectives

- Work independently at the stations.
- Record own progress.
- Improve own scores after practice.

Equipment and Materials

- Station 1: 1 batting tee per child in group, 3 beanbags per tee, 1 carpet square per child, 1 large can or ice cream barrel per child
- Station 2: 30 bowling pins or plastic bottles, 3 playground balls or rubber gym balls, 3 carpet squares
- Station 3: 3 beanbags, 1 carpet square, 1 paper or plastic dot (4 in. diameter)
- Station 4: 3 launchers, 3 tennis balls, 6 beanbags, 3 scoops, 3 fluff balls
- Station 5: 18 beanbags (smooth surface) or foam balls (rough surface), 3 carpet squares, masking tape or jump ropes (for scoring area)
- Station 6: 3 batting tees, 24 hoops, 3 launchers, 3 tennis balls, 3 foam balls, 3 paddles
- Loud signal
- 1 large task card per station (at least 8 1/2 in. × 11 in.)
- 1 task sheet, optional

Safety Tip

- Have a loud signal that means all activity will stop immediately and the children will be quiet. Use the signal if things get out of hand and when it is time to rotate.

Warm-Up Activities (6 minutes)

Band-Aid Tag

See Grades 2-3: Games and Sports, Warm-Ups, page 464.

Skill-Development Activities (24 minutes)

Stations

Set up stations according to the instructions given with station explanations. Divide the children into six groups, and assign each group to a station.

1. Describe and demonstrate the activities at each station on Day 1 (12 minutes). Have the children practice at each of three stations (2 minutes each). Recording scores at stations is optional.

2. Have the children practice 8 minutes at each of three stations on Days 2 to 4.

Station 1: Beanbag Golf

Place the cans or barrels varying distances from the carpet square tees (where the children stand to throw).

The object is to use as few throws as possible to get the beanbag into the barrel. You have the option to record the number of overhand throws it takes you to get the beanbag into the can (or barrel). One child begins at each tee, and rotate everyone in your group around until you have all thrown from all the tees.

Station 2: Bowling

Set up three bowling "lanes" with 10 pins in traditional arrangement with a carpet square an appropriate distance away. Place one ball at each lane.

The bowler rolls the ball from the carpet square to the 10 pins. A partner counts the pins knocked down in two tries. If all are knocked down in the first try, the partner sets them back up and the bowler gets an additional turn (a total of three instead of two). Your score is the total number of pins knocked down. Then partners switch places. Partners repeat as many times as possible during the group's time at that station. You have the option of recording your score on the task sheet.

Station 3: Horseshoes

Arrange the carpet square and dot about 20 ft apart. Half of the children should be at the dot, and the other half of the children should be at the carpet square. Be sure to tell children to switch places halfway through the station time.

The thrower uses an underhand motion to toss the beanbag from the carpet square to the dot. If the dot is completely covered, the throw is worth three points. If the beanbag is touching the dot, the throw is worth two points. If the throw is the closest to the dot for all throwers in that round, the throw gets one point. Half the children are throwers, while the other half call out the scores and return the beanbags. After the throwers have each thrown five times, throwers and scorers switch places. Repeat as often as possible during your group's time at the station. You have the option of recording your score on the task sheet.

Station 4: Launcher Challenge and Scoop Catches

Set up three launchers with beanbags and tennis and fluff balls, and place one scoop an appropriate distance from each launcher. Be prepared to tell launchers and scoopers to trade places halfway through the station time.

Half of you start at the launchers and half at the scoops. You will trade places halfway through the station time. The children with the beanbag launchers try to do each of the following tasks. When you succeed at one task, you go on to the next (be sure these are on the station task card):

> *Catch the beanbag four out of five times.*
>
> *Catch the tennis ball four out of five times.*
>
> *Catch the tennis ball after turning around.*
>
> *Catch the beanbag in your right hand. Catch the beanbag in your left hand.*
>
> *Launch and catch two beanbags, one in each hand.*
>
> *Launch two beanbags and catch after turning around.*
>
> *Scoopers: Toss the fluff ball overhead from the scoop, and catch it five times in a row without missing.*

Station 5: Shufflebag

Mark three shufflebag courts with masking tape or ropes (a rectangle four feet by ten feet), adding six beanbags to each court (smooth surface; use foam balls on grass) and a carpet square an appropriate distance away.

Playing against a partner, kick the beanbag from the carpet square into the court, trying to get the highest points. Take turns for three kicks each, trying to push aside (displace) each other's beanbags to outscore each other. Then collect the beanbags, and begin a new round.

Station 6: Batter Up

Set up three batting areas with eight hoops arranged varying distances from each batting tee. Place a launcher, tennis ball, foam ball, and paddle at each batting area.

You have two tasks at this station:

- **Task 1:** *Strike from the batting tee to the hoop targets. Each hit scores the points assigned to the hoop in which the tennis ball lands. You have the option of recording your score on the task sheet.*

- **Task 2:** *Launch a foam ball with the launcher and strike it with the paddle (1 point for each foam ball struck with the paddle after being launched, maximum 10 points); launch a foam ball with the launcher and strike it with the bat (2 points for each ball struck with the bat after being launched, maximum 20 points).*

Concluding Activities (5 minutes)

None, but have the children make sure each station is ready for the next class or have them help put away the equipment before leaving.

LESSON 18
KICKING GAMES

Student Objectives

- Use kicking in a game.
- Cooperate with group members.
- Take turns.

Equipment and Materials

- 1 playground ball per pair
- 1 plastic bottle or bowling pin per group
- Cones to mark play area

Warm-Up Activities (5 minutes)

Nose Tag

See Grades 2-3: Games and Sports, Warm-Ups (page 467).

Skill-Development Activities (20 minutes)

Volley Kicking Review

Arrange partners in two lines, 10 ft apart, across from each other on each side of a large rectangle, each pair with a playground ball.

1. Describe the drill:

   The children in one line begin by kicking the ball to their partner in the other line.

   The partner kicks the ball back to the original partner.

   You are starting 10 ft apart, but each turn both of you succeed at, you increase the distance between you by each taking one step back.

2. Have the children practice the drill. See also Grades 2-3: Games and Sports, Lesson 11, Foot Volley, page 496.

Giant Kick-Around

See Grades 2-3: Games and Sports, Lesson 11, page 497.

Kick Dodgeball

See Grades 2-3: Games and Sports, Lesson 9, page 493.

Concluding Activities (5 minutes)

Kick Pin

Divide the children into groups of five or six, each group with a ball and a plastic bottle. The children in each group stand on a line widely spaced (10 ft between children) with the plastic bottle on the line about 20 ft from the nearest child in the line. The ball begins at the opposite end of the line from the bottle.

1. Describe and demonstrate the game:

   The first group member kicks, or passes, the ball to the next along the line, and so forth.

   The player closest to the plastic bottle kicks the ball at the bottle, trying to knock the bottle over.

   That player continues kicking the ball at the bottle until it falls over.

   The player then stands the bottle upright and runs, carrying the ball to the opposite end of the line.

   All players move one place closer to the plastic bottle, and play begins again.

2. Have the children play Kick Pin.

LESSON 19
STRIKING GAMES

Student Objectives

- Work cooperatively during a game.
- Use striking in a game.
- State at least one rule of the game.

Equipment and Materials

- 2 bases or carpet squares per Lineup field
- 1 home plate per Lineup field
- 1 playground ball per group
- 6 hoops per group
- 6 number cards (1-6) per group
- 1 carpet square or base per group

Warm-Up Activities (5 minutes)

Pair Tag

See Grades 2-3: Games and Sports, Warm-Ups, page 468.

Skill-Development Activities (20 minutes)

Lineup

See Grades 2-3: Games and Sports, Lesson 13, page 501. Stop the game and ask individual students to explain the object of the game or a rule of the game.

Concluding Activities (5 minutes)

Hoop Math

Divide the children into small teams. For each team, spread six hoops randomly around one carpet square, assigning each hoop a number card from 1 to 6.

1. Describe and demonstrate the game:

    The object of the game is for a team to score points based on striking the ball and making it land in a hoop.

    The player must stand on the carpet square or base when striking the ball.

    When the ball touches in the hoop, the team earns the number of points assigned to that hoop. A ball that does not land in a hoop earns zero points.

I will choose a number 12 or greater before each round. Each team will try to earn the number of points matching the number I choose.

Each player on a team gets one turn per round, and you can use hoops more than once each round.

2. Have the children play Hoop Math.

GRADES 2-3

GAMES AND SPORTS

LESSON 20
DRIBBLING, THROWING, AND CATCHING GAMES

Student Objectives

- Play a game using dribbling, throwing, and catching.
- Work cooperatively with teammates.
- Name two characteristics of good dribbling.

Equipment and Materials

- 1 playground ball per child
- 2 carpet squares per group of 3
- 1 hoop per group of 3

Warm-Up Activities (5 minutes)

Everyone's It

See Grades 2-3: Games and Sports, Warm-Ups, page 466.

Skill-Development Activities (20 minutes)

Hoops

Arrange groups of three with a hoop, ball, and carpet square as shown in figure below.

1. Describe and demonstrate the game:

    Player 1 dribbles the ball toward the hoop, then bounces the ball in the hoop so that it goes to player 2, who catches the ball.

    Player 2 turns and throws the ball to player 3, who catches the ball and runs to the carpet square from which player 1 began.

    Player 1 moves to the position near the hoop, and player 2 moves to the carpet square left by player 3.

    Keep repeating, so that all of you do all the tasks several times.

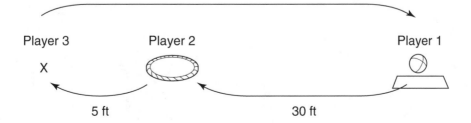

2. Have the children play Hoops.

Keep Away

See Grades 2-3: Games and Sports, Lesson 2, page 475. Allow throwing, rolling, dribbling, and catching.

Ball Challenges

Arrange the children in one long line, each with a ball.

1. Remind the children: *Dribble, pushing with your fingers, trying to dribble without looking at the ball, and keeping your arm, ball, and hand below your waist.*
2. Challenge the children with these tasks:

   Move toward me low.

   Move toward me high. Now move slow.

   Move away from me low.

   Now move toward me fast.

   Move in a circle.

   In place, move around and between your legs.

   Walking backward.

Concluding Activity (5 minutes)

Have three children at a time demonstrate their dribbling skills. Ask the children to dribble as many different ways as possible during a 30-second turn.

GAMES AND SPORTS

LESSON 21
HOPPING

Student Objectives

- Move through space using various combinations of hopping steps.
- Work cooperatively when playing Follow the Leader.
- Identify hopping (as opposed to jumping).

Equipment and Materials

- Paint, chalk, flour, or tape to mark 1 hopscotch area per group
- Signal

Warm-Up Activities (5 minutes)

Sneaky Tag

See Grades 2-3: Games and Sports, Warm-Ups, page 468-469.

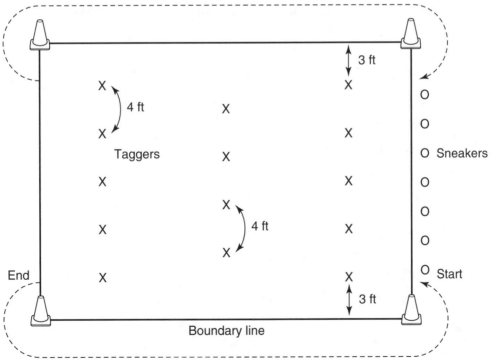

Skill-Development Activities (15 minutes)

Hopping Skills

Arrange the children in scatter formation.

1. Challenge the children with the following tasks:

   Hop forward and backward (then side-to-side).

   Hop and change direction (speed, pathway) on the signal.

   Hop a figure eight.

   Hop as far as you can.

   Hop and land facing another direction.

2. Have them repeat the challenges on the other foot.

Follow the Leader

Divide the children into groups of four to six.

1. Describe the game:

   Choose one child to lead, and the rest of you follow, imitating the leader's actions.

   The leader must use a hopping pattern (changing combinations of right- and left-footed hopping).

   Change the leader when you hear the signal.

2. Have the children play Follow the Leader, signaling groups to change leaders every 60 seconds.

Name That Skill

1. Ask a child to demonstrate hopping, then jumping.
2. Demonstrate jumping and ask a different child to name the skill.
3. Repeat with hopping.

Hopscotch

Arrange the children in groups of four to six, and place each group at a hopscotch area.

1. Describe the activity:

    Hop through the diagrams first on your right foot and then on your left.

    Repeat, going backward.

    If you step on a line or lose your balance, you must start again.

2. Have the children play Hopscotch.

LESSON 22
RUNNING AND JUMPING

Student Objectives

- Move through space, combining running and jumping.

Equipment and Materials

- 3 hoops (30-36 in.) per group (for second part of Extension Activities section)

- Tape (indoors only)
- 1 or more measuring tape(s) or yardstick(s)

Safety Tip

- If inside or on hard surface, tape the hoops down in the Extension Activities so they won't slide if students hit them.

Warm-Up Activities (5 minutes)

Color Tag

See Grades 2-3: Games and Sports, Warm-Ups, page 465.

Skill-Development Activities (20 minutes)

Running and Jumping Combinations

Keep the children in scatter formation.

1. Ask the children to perform the following combination: *Run and jump as far as you can. Use your arms on the jump.*

2. Repeat several times.

3. Challenge the children with the following combinations:

   Run 10 steps and jump as far as you can, using three jumps.

   Run 6 steps and jump four times.

   Run 8 steps and jump two times.

4. Repeat all.

Extension Activities

Keep the children in scatter formation.

1. Add your own combinations or have the children try their own combinations.

   Run and jump as high as you can.

   Run, jump high, and make your body straight (curled).

Divide the children into groups of four to six, each group with a hoop. Place the hoops 30 to 40 ft away as in figure below. Indoors, tape the hoops down for safety.

2. Tell the children: *Taking turns, run and take a long jump (by leaving the ground several feet before the hoop) and land in the hoop.*

3. Have them repeat several times.

4. For each group, add two additional hoops beyond the one in the figure, with about 2 ft between hoops. Tell the children: *Run and jump three times, from hoop to hoop to hoop.*

5. Have them repeat several times.

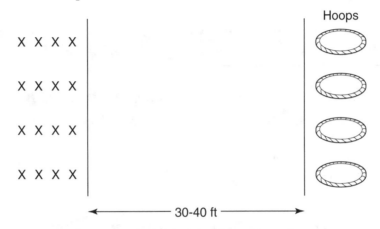

Concluding Activities (5 minutes)

Cumulative Run-and-Jump Relay

Arrange the children in four to six relay lines.

1. Describe the activity:

    The first player from each team takes three running steps and a jump (one-footed takeoff, two-footed landing).

    The next player starts from the first player's landing spot and repeats the activity, and so on until each teammate has had a turn running and jumping.

2. Have the children do the Cumulative Run-and-Jump Relay. Played competitively, the team covering the greatest distance wins. Played cooperatively, measure and add the team scores together for a class score.

3. If time allows, have the children repeat the relay, changing the required number of runs and jumps. Emphasize that speed is not a factor in winning.

GAMES AND SPORTS

LESSON 23
RUNNING, JUMPING, AND HOPPING

Student Objectives

- Move through space combining running, jumping, and hopping
- Follow instructions when playing Reveille.
- Work cooperatively when doing the relay.

Equipment and Materials

- Whistle, horn, or bell

Warm-Up Activities (5 minutes)

Reveille

See Grades 2-3: Games and Sports, Warm-Ups, page 468.

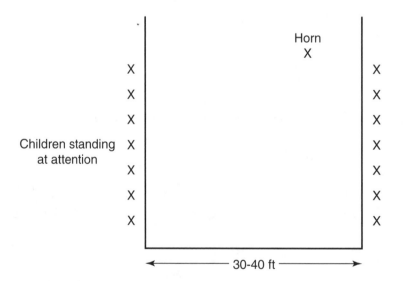

Skill-Development Activities (15 minutes)

Running and Hopping Tasks

Arrange the children in scatter formation.

    1. Ask the children to do the following tasks:

Run and hop on your right foot as far as you can.

Run and, at the signal, hop three times on your right foot and three times on your left foot.

Take 10 running steps, three hops left, and three hops right.

Take 10 running steps, three hops forward on your right foot, and three hops backward on your left foot.

Turn and, at the signal, hop as high as you can. Use your arms to lift you up.

Run and, at the signal, hop on your right (left) foot, jump, and land on both feet.

2. Encourage the children to make up and try their own combinations.

3. Have them repeat several times.

Concluding Activities (10 minutes)

Cumulative Hop-and-Jump Relay

Arrange the children in four to six relay lines.

1. This activity is the same as Cumulative Run-and-Jump Relay (Grades 2-3: Games and Sports, Lesson 22, page 525).

2. Have the children repeat the relay several times using various combinations of hops and jumps; for example:

   Three hops on right foot and two jumps (on both feet)

   One hop on left foot and four jumps

   Four hops on left foot and three jumps

LESSON 24
RUN, HOP, STEP, AND JUMP

Student Objectives

- Move through space combining running, hopping, stepping, and jumping.

Equipment and Materials

- Paint, tape, chalk, or flour to mark play area
- Whistle, horn, or bell

Warm-Up Activities (5 minutes)

Sneaky Tag

See Grades 2-3: Games and Sports, Warm-Ups, page 468-469.

Skill-Development Activities (15 minutes)

Leap

Arrange the children in a widespread scatter formation, facing you.

1. Tell them what the signal will be (whistle, horn, or bell).
2. Describe and demonstrate the skill: *A leap is a long running step from one foot to the other, where the leaper goes high and far.*
3. Challenge the children with the following leaping tasks:

   Run and, at the signal, leap three times.

   Run and, at the signal, step and jump as far as you can.

   Run and, at the signal, hop three times on your left foot.

   Run and, at the signal, hop three times on your right foot and jump as far as you can.

   Run and, at the signal, hop three times on your left foot and take a long step.

   Run and, at the signal, hop on your right foot, step, and jump.

4. Have them repeat each task several times.

Concluding Activities (10 minutes)

Cumulative Hop-and-Jump Relay

Arrange the children in four to six relay lines.

1. This activity is the same as Cumulative Run-and-Jump Relay (Grades 2-3: Games and Sports, Lesson 22, page 525).

2. Have the children repeat the relay several times using various combinations of hops and jumps. Some new examples include the following:

   One step, three hops, and two jumps

   Four running steps, one hop, one step, and four jumps

   Three running steps, one hop, one step, and one jump

LESSON 25
SKIP, GALLOP, AND SLIDE

Student Objectives

- Move through space combining skipping, galloping, and sliding.

Equipment and Materials

- Whistle, horn, or bell

Warm-Up Activities (5 minutes)

Color Tag

See Grades 2-3: Games and Sports, Warm-Ups, page 465.

Skill-Development Activities (20 minutes)

Locomotor Challenges

Keep the children in scatter formation.

1. Challenge the children with the following tasks:

   Gallop and change directions on the signal.

   Skip and stop quickly at the signal. Keep a balanced position.

   Slide right and slide left. Keep your body low.

   Slide, using big and small steps.

2. Have them repeat the tasks several times.

Follow the Leader

Arrange pairs in scatter formation.

1. See Grades 2-3: Games and Sports, Lesson 21, page 522, but have the children skip, gallop, and slide. Describe this version:

   One of you leads, and the other partner follows.

   Leaders, change directions and speeds as well as the movement to be performed at the signal.

   Followers, stay as close to your partner as you can. Watch closely for changes in speed or direction.

2. Have the children play Follow the Leader, directing partners to exchange roles frequently.

Concluding Activities (5 minutes)

Locomotor Skills

Have the children face each other in two lines, about 40 ft apart.

1. Have the children move from one line to the other, skipping, galloping, and sliding.
2. Have them repeat, using other combinations of locomotor skills.

LESSON 26
LOCOMOTOR SKILLS OBSTACLE COURSE

Student Objectives

- Travel through an obstacle course using various locomotor skills without touching the obstacles.

Equipment and Materials

- Flour, chalk, or tape for marking lines

For each obstacle course:

- 4 cones
- 10 hoops
- 8 milk crates
- 2 low balance beams

Arrange obstacle courses as shown below, 1 course per group.

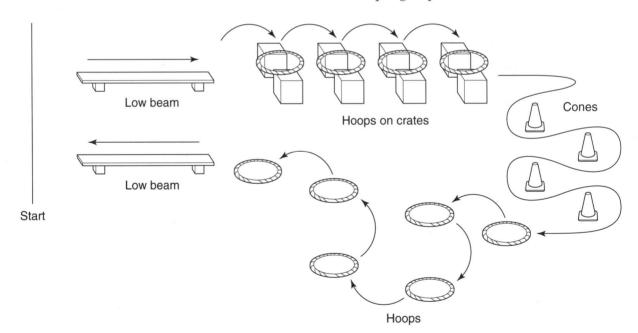

Warm-Up Activities (5 minutes)

Reveille

See Grades 2-3: Games and Sports, Warm-Ups, page 468.

Skill-Development Activities (20 minutes)

Obstacle Course

Divide the children into groups of four to six, and arrange each group at the beginning of an obstacle course.

1. Describe the activity: *Hop (on right foot) down the balance beam, jump through the elevated hoops, weave around the cones, hop (on left foot) through the hoops on the ground, and walk backward down the second balance beam.*

2. Have them repeat, using different arrangements of the equipment and other locomotor skills (e.g., gallop, slide, skip).

3. Have each group make a pattern for their course, learn it, and teach it to the other groups.

Concluding Activities (5 minutes)

Crows and Cranes

Arrange two groups facing each other on lines 20 ft apart. Two additional lines are needed 30 ft outside the first pair of lines (adjust starting lines closer together or farther apart as needed). Designate one group as "Crows" and the other as "Cranes."

1. Describe and demonstrate the game:

   I will call out "Crows" or "Cranes" (extend the first consonants of the word so the children do not know which name will be called, *C-r-r-r-rows* or *C-r-r-r-ranes*).

   The team whose name is called turns and runs to its goal line as the other team chases, attempting to tag the runners.

   All tagged players become members of the other team, and play continues. Play ends when all the runners cross the line or are tagged.

2. Have the children play Crows and Cranes.

3. Variation: Have both groups walk toward each other; as they get close together the group called runs back to the goal line.

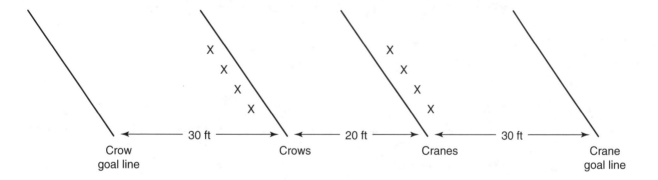

GAMES AND SPORTS

LESSON 27
LOCOMOTOR SKILLS OBSTACLE COURSE

Student Objectives

- Travel through an obstacle course, using various locomotor skills without touching the obstacles.
- Create a locomotor obstacle course.
- Work cooperatively with others.

Equipment and Materials

- Flour, chalk, or tape for marking lines
- Whistle, horn, or bell

For each obstacle course:
- 2 cones
- 2 hoops
- 2 milk crates
- 1 low balance beam

Warm-Up Activities (5 minutes)

Reveille

See Grades 2-3: Games and Sports, Warm-Ups, page 468.

Skill-Development Activities (20 minutes)

Obstacle Course

Divide the children into small groups. Give each group two cones, two hoops, two milk cartons, one balance beam.

1. Explain the activity:

   Arrange your equipment to create an obstacle course. The course must require hopping, skipping, jumping, and walking (forward and backward).

   Do your own obstacle course as soon as it is complete.

   When everyone is ready, I will select one group to demonstrate their course for the other groups.

   You will all get to try this course. Then we will learn about and try each of the other courses.

2. Have the children design and try their obstacle courses.

Concluding Activities (5 minutes)

Crows and Cranes

See Grades 2-3: Games and Sports, Lesson 26, page 533.

LESSON 28
PARACHUTE GAMES

Student Objectives

- Perform parachute activities, demonstrating cooperation.
- Follow verbal instruction to learn new activities.

Equipment and Materials

- 1 parachute
- Several fluff balls
- Several large (13 in.) playground balls
- Several smaller (6 in.) balls (2 or more colors)
- Stopwatch or clock with second hand
- Chalk, flour, or tape to mark lines

Warm-Up Activities (5 minutes)

Sneaky Tag

See Grades 2-3: Games and Sports, Warm-Ups, page 468-469.

Skill-Development Activities (20 minutes)

Parachute Activities

Arrange the children around the outside of the parachute, which is spread out on the ground.

Exchange Positions

Assign the children numbers, one through number of children.

Tell the children to hold the parachute with the left hand and circle counterclockwise. Remind them of which numbers are odd and which are even. Tell the children: *On the signal, the odd-numbered children release the parachute and move forward to take the place of the next odd-numbered player in front of them* (variations can include moving forward two places, three places, and so on). Repeat with the even-numbered players moving. Have the children use a variety of locomotor skills (walk, run, skip, gallop, slide) to move.

Run Under

Assign the children numbers from one to four.

Tell the children: *Begin in a squat position, holding the parachute with both hands. When you hear the signal, lift up the parachute to form an umbrella. I will call a number from one to four. All of you let go of the parachute, and the players with the number called must move across the circle under the parachute to the opposite side (and into the former position of another player with the same number) before the parachute floats down.* You can specify the type of movement you want the children to use (e.g., different locomotor skills, animal walks, moving backward).

Popping Popcorn

Place several fluff balls on the parachute.

Tell the children: *Shake the parachute up and down, attempting to "pop" the balls into the air but not off the parachute.*

Ball Roll

Have the children grasp the parachute, which you have laid on the ground. Place a large playground ball on the parachute.

Explain and have the children try the activity: *I will tell one child to stand and raise his or her part of the parachute. Then the next child counterclockwise* (point) *in the circle raises the parachute, and so on. The object is to keep the ball rolling around the edge of the parachute.* After the ball passes, the children may lower the parachute to keep the ball going. After some proficiency is gained, include changing the direction of the ball and/or add additional balls.

Parachute Games

Keep the children around the outside of the parachute, which is spread out on the ground.

Popcorn Game

Place several fluff balls on the parachute. Assign the children numbers, one through the number of children.

Describe and have the children play the game: *The odd numbers form one team and the even numbers another. The odd-numbered team releases the parachute and each member takes two or three steps backward. The even-numbered players have 30 seconds to pop all the balls off the parachute. Players then exchange places, and the odd-numbered team has a turn. The team with fewer balls on the parachute after the 30-second time period wins.*

Center Ball

Have two teams stand on opposite sides of the parachute (you can use the teams already created, but they don't need to remember their numbers), holding it about waist-high. Place two six-in. balls (of different colors) on the parachute.

Describe and have the children play the game: *Each team tries to shake the opponent's ball into the center pocket and at the same time keep their own ball from going into the pocket. Your team scores a point every time it puts the opponent's ball in the pocket.*

Ball Shake

Two teams stand on opposite sides of the parachute (keep teams from Center Ball or make two new teams). Place several different (e.g., 1 foam, 1 playground, etc.) balls on the parachute.

Describe and have the children play the game: *On a signal to begin, each team tries to shake the balls off the other team's side of the parachute. You may not use your hands to keep the balls on the parachute. Your team will earn one point each time a ball leaves the parachute on your opponent's side and touches the ground.*

Concluding Activities (5 minutes)

Parachute Games

Let the children choose one of the parachute games to repeat.

LESSON 29
THROWING AND CATCHING

Student Objectives

- Catch, change position, and throw to a target.
- Run and catch, then throw to a moving target.

Equipment and Materials

- 1 cone per 4 children
- 1 playground ball per 4 children (at least 7 total)
- 1 game net or a rope with standards
- Flour, chalk, or tape to mark the play area

Warm-Up Activities (5 minutes)

Circle Tag

See Grades 2-3: Games and Sports, Warm-Ups, page 465.

Skill-Development Activities (15 minutes)

Throwing and Catching Challenges

Arrange the children in four circles of six to eight children each. Have the children stand at least 10 ft apart from one another, facing counterclockwise. Give a ball to one person in each circle.

1. Describe and demonstrate the first challenge:

    The child with the ball turns and faces the child behind him or her.

    This child tosses the ball to the second person.

    The second child catches the ball, turns to face the next person in line, throws the ball to him or her, and play continues around the circle.

2. Have the children try the challenge.

3. Repeat with the children turning to face clockwise.

Next, pair up the children, and put two pairs at a cone with a playground ball.

4. Describe and demonstrate the second challenge:

    On the signal, the first pair tosses the ball back and forth over the cone.

    After each successful toss and catch, each child backs up one step.

    When the first pair misses, the second takes a turn.

    Pairs alternate on each miss.

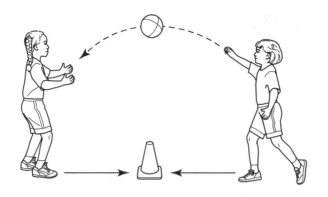

Concluding Activities (10 minutes)

Seven-Up

Arrange the children into two groups, on each side of the net (see figure below). For the playing area, a tennis court, basketball court, or any well-marked area is fine.

1. Describe and demonstrate the game:

   To begin the game, I will put seven balls into play by throwing them high into the air, throwing some to each side of the net.

   The object of the game is to catch the balls before they hit the ground and throw them high into the air, back into the opponents' court.

   If a ball hits the ground in the receivers' court, the throwing team scores a point.

   If a ball is thrown out of bounds, the receiving team scores a point.

   The team with the highest score at the end of play wins.

   We will play until one team reaches (a predetermined score [a number divisible by seven] or for seven minutes [two three and a half-minute halves]).

2. Have the children play Seven-Up.

GRADES 2-3

GAMES AND SPORTS

LESSON 30

COMBINING SKILLS: THROWING, CATCHING, STRIKING, AND KICKING

Student Objectives

- Perform the following sequences:
    - Catch, strike
    - Bounce, catch, throw
    - Catch, throw, kick

Equipment and Materials

- 1, 8 1/2 in. playground ball per group of 3
- 1 (or more) beanbag(s)
- Chalk, flour, or tape to mark lines

Warm-Up Activities (5 minutes)

Beanbag Tag

See Grades 2-3: Games and Sports, Warm-Ups, page 464. Optional variation: Use more than one It or have more than one game running simultaneously.

Skill-Development Activities (15 minutes)

Movement Tasks

Arrange groups of three in scatter formation, forming triangles with about five ft between children. Number the children, player 1, 2, and 3 in each group. Give each group a playground ball.

1. Challenge the children with the following tasks:

    Using one hand, player 1 strikes the playground ball to player 2.

    Player 2 catches and then strikes it to player 3, who strikes it to player 1, and so on.

    Player 1 bounces the ball, catches it, and throws it to player 2.

    Player 2 catches, bounces, catches, and then throws to player 3, and so on.

Spread the players in each triangle farther apart (at least 30 ft).

2. Now challenge the children with these tasks:

    Player 1 throws the ball, runs after it, and kicks the ball to player 2.

    Player 2 catches the ball, throws it, runs after it, and kicks it to player 3, and so on.

Goal Line Kick

Divide the children into two teams, and have the teams stand on two parallel lines, with one ball per team. The line you stand on is your restraining line and the other team's goal line. After the children have learned the game, run more than one game at the same time to increase opportunities for participation.

1. Describe and demonstrate the game:

   The object is to kick the ball over the opponents' line. You must kick from behind the restraining line, and only one kicker at a time from each team may be between that team's goal line and the restraining line.

   You may not use your hands, but you may use your torso or legs to block a ball from going over your team's goal line.

   Your team scores a point for each ball you send over the opponents' line.

2. Have the children play Goal Line Kick.

LESSON 31
COMBINING MANIPULATIVE SKILLS WITH RUNNING AND JUMPING

Student Objectives

- Practice running and throwing, catching, kicking, and striking.
- Practice jumping and catching.

Equipment and Materials

- 1 playground ball per group
- 7 bases per Beat Ball game setup
- Tape, chalk, flour, or ropes to mark lines

Warm-Up Activities (5 minutes)

Loose Caboose

See Grades 2-3: Games and Sports, Warm-Ups, page 467.

Skill-Development Activities (15 minutes)

Passing Drill

Make groups of four to five sets of partners each. Partners in each group face each other from about 20 ft apart (see figure on page 544). Each group has one playground ball, and the children stand about 30 ft away from an endline. To increase participation opportunities, decrease the size of the groups.

1. Describe and demonstrate the drill:

    The child with the ball dribbles the ball while running to the endline.

    At the end of the line, that child stops and gains control of the ball.

    That child's partner then runs toward the endline. As he or she approaches, the child with the ball makes a two-handed pass to the partner (leading the partner slightly, so the ball can be caught while running).

    After catching the ball, the partner throws it back to the next person in the throwing line.

    Both children go to the end of the opposite line (thrower goes to catching line; catcher goes to the throwing line).

    We will continue the drill until everyone has had several turns.

2. Have the children practice the passing drill several times.

3. Have them repeat the passing drill, but the child throwing should pass the ball high so the partner has to jump to catch it.

4. Have them repeat the passing drill, but the child passing the ball rolls it so the partner can kick it. The child passing the ball should chase it and pass to the next child in line.

5. Repeat each type of drill several times.

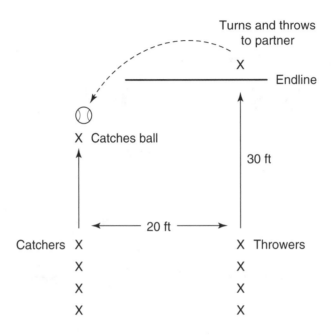

Concluding Activities (10 minutes)

Beat Ball

Divide the children into two teams, fielders and batters. Set up two sets of bases—one for the fielding team (inside bases) and one for the batting team (outside bases).

1. Describe and demonstrate the game:

   I will roll a pitch to the batter. The batter kicks the rolled ball and runs the outside set of bases.

   The fielding team catches the ball and tries to throw it around the inside bases from first to second to third to home.

   The team that finishes first (or "beats") gets a point.

   If there is a tie, both teams get one point.

   We will switch batting teams after everyone on the first team has batted.

2. Have the children play Beat Ball.

3. After the children have learned the game, create smaller teams to increase participation opportunities.

GAMES AND SPORTS

LESSON 32
JUMPING AND CATCHING OR STRIKING

Student Objectives

- Catch a ball while they are in the air.
- Practice striking while they are in the air.

Equipment and Materials

- 1 jumping box per group
- 1 playground ball per group
- 1 pin per Team Pin Ball game
- 2 bases per Team Pin Ball game
- Signal

Warm-Up Activities (5 minutes)

Balance Tag

See Grades 2-3: Games and Sports, Warm-Ups, page 464.

Skill-Development Activities (15 minutes)

Movement Challenges

Divide the children into small groups, and give each group a jumping box and playground ball.

1. Describe the activity: *One child in each group is the tosser, and the other children take turns jumping from the box. I will signal you to change the tosser each minute.*
2. Challenge the children with the following tasks:

    Jump and catch a ball tossed from straight ahead (the right, the left).

    Jump and strike (with your hand) a ball tossed from straight ahead.
3. Repeat steps 1 and 2 several times.

Concluding Activities (10 minutes)

Team Pin Ball

Arrange the children into teams as in figure below. One team is in the field and the other is at bat. Keep the teams small to increase participation opportunities. You can vary the distance to the base to increase or decrease difficulty. This game may be played on a standard ball field.

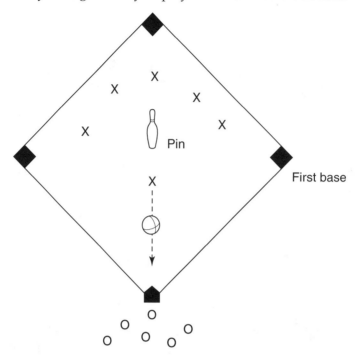

1. Describe and demonstrate the game:

    Each team tries to make runs while at bat and outs while in the field.

    The fielding team must knock down the pin by hitting it with the ball before the batter gets back to home base.

    The fielders must throw the ball from player to player when they field the ball; they may not carry it or run with it.

    Any fielding player may throw the ball at the pin, but the closer to the pin the fielding team gets the ball before throwing it at the pin, the better their chances of knocking it over.

    The batter hits a bounced ball with a hand (palm or fist) and runs to first base and back, trying to get home before the fielding team knocks the pin down.

    If the ball is foul, or if the pin is knocked down before she or he gets home, the runner is out. If the runner gets home before the pin is knocked down, she or he scores a point.

    After all the players on the batting team have had one turn, the teams switch places.

2. Have the children play Team Pin Ball.

LESSON 33
THROWING AND CATCHING A FRISBEE

Student Objectives

- Throw a Frisbee into a target from 20 ft.
- Catch a Frisbee at chest height tossed from 20 ft.

Equipment and Materials

- 1 Frisbee per child
- 6 or more hoops (30-36 in.)
- Chalk, flour, or tape to mark lines

Warm-Up Activities (5 minutes)

Circle Tag

See Grades 2-3: Games and Sports, Warm-Ups, page 465.

Skill-Development Activities (15 minutes)

Frisbee Toss

Scatter the hoops around the play area and arrange the children around them, each child about 10 ft from a hoop. Give each child a Frisbee.

1. Challenge the children with the following tasks:

   Toss the Frisbee into a hoop.

   Move farther away if you hit the target.

2. Repeat several times.

Rearrange the children as partners (10 to 15 ft apart) in scatter formation.

3. Tell the children: *Toss and catch the Frisbee. As you get better, move farther apart.*

Concluding Activities (10 minutes)

Falling Stars

Divide the children into groups of five to seven, and have the children count off starting with number one in each group. Pair off children with the same numbers directly across from each other, on facing lines about 30 ft apart.

1. Describe and demonstrate the game:

    Player 1 for team 1 throws the Frisbee toward team 2, trying to throw it over their heads.

    If player 1 is successful, team 1 gets a point.

    Team 2 tries to catch the Frisbee; if they do, they get a point.

    Then team 2's player 1 tries to throw over the heads of team 1.

    This continues until all players have had a turn.

    The team with the highest score wins.

2. Have the children play Falling Stars.

3. After each game, have winning teams play other winning teams and losing teams play losing teams.

LESSON 34
STRIKING WITH AN EXTENSION

Student Objectives

- Strike various balls with various objects.
- Strike a tossed ball with an arm.

Equipment and Materials

- 1 (or more) beanbag(s)
- 1 bat per group of 3 (make various sizes available)
- 1 paddle per group of 3 (make various sizes available)
- 1 foam ball per pair
- Several other balls of various sizes and weights
- Chalk, flour, or tape to mark lines

Safety Tips

- Have all hitters face the same direction.
- Maintain space between groups.

Warm-Up Activities (5 minutes)

Beanbag Tag

See Grades 2-3: Games and Sports, Warm-Ups, page 464.

Skill-Development Activities (15 minutes)

Movement Tasks

Scatter groups of three students around the play area, and give each group a bat, paddle, and foam ball. Within each group, have the children share equipment.

1. Describe and demonstrate the tasks:

    Take turns with the equipment and take turns as throwers and strikers.

    Each of you tries to hit each type of ball with each implement (bat and paddle).

    Repeat several times.

Rearrange pairs in scatter formation, each pair with a foam ball.

2. Tell the children: With one hand try to strike a foam ball tossed by your partner.

Punch Line Ball

Divide the class into two teams. One team stands on the fielders' line, and the other team stands on the batters' line. The two teams alternate fielding and batting. Once the children have learned the game, create smaller teams to increase participation opportunities.

1. Describe and demonstrate the game:

   I will pitch a playground ball to the first member of the batting team (or you may choose to have the children use a self-set ball from a bounce or toss).

   The batter tries to strike (punch) the ball across the fielders' line.

   The fielders try to stop the ball.

   If the ball crosses the fielders' line, the batters get a point.

   After each batter has had one turn, the fielders and batters switch.

2. Have the children play Punch Line Ball.

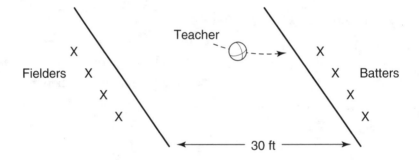

LESSON 35
NEW MANIPULATIVE GAMES

Student Objectives

- Learn two new games requiring manipulative skills.

Equipment and Materials

- 3 bases per Triangle Ball game
- 4 playground balls
- Chalk, flour, or tape for marking lines and kicking circle

Warm-Up Activities (5 minutes)

Loose Caboose

See Grades 2-3: Games and Sports, Warm-Ups, page 467.

Skill-Development Activities (20 minutes)

Triangle Ball

Divide the children into two teams—fielders and batters (see figure on page 552). Arrange the fielders in scatter formation. Form a triangle with three bases. Once the children have learned the game, create smaller teams to increase participation opportunities.

1. Describe and demonstrate the game:

   The batting team provides a pitcher who rolls the ball to the batter, who kicks the ball.

   Then all of the batting team's players line up with hands on the shoulders of the person in front of them, with the batter in the lead and the pitcher last. The entire team runs the bases linked together.

   Meanwhile, the fielding team catches the ball and throws it from player to player.

   Each player who successfully catches the ball and throws it to a teammate sits down.

   A player who does not catch the ball may not sit down but will get another try.

   Once all players are sitting, the ball is "dead."

   If the ball is dead before the pitcher crosses home, the batting team does not score a point. If the ball is still alive when the pitcher crosses home, the batting team scores a point.

   After all members of one team have batted, the teams switch places.

2. Have the children play Triangle Ball.

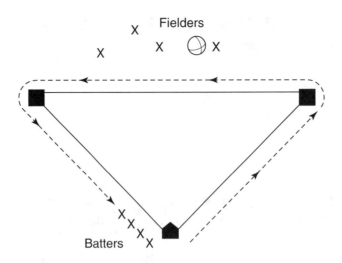

Fielders

Batters

Cross the Line

Arrange groups of four to six as in figure below. Place one child in the kicking circle, and scatter the others beyond the kicking line, which is 20-30 feet from the kicking circle.

1. Describe and demonstrate the game:

    The kicker yells "Cross the line!" while kicking the ball toward the kicking line.

    The fielders run forward in front of the kicking line and try to stop the ball without using their hands or arms.

    The child who stops the ball becomes the next kicker.

    If no one stops the ball before it crosses the kicking line, the kicker kicks again.

    If the kicker has not been "stopped" after three turns, she or he selects a new kicker.

2. Have the children play Cross the Line.

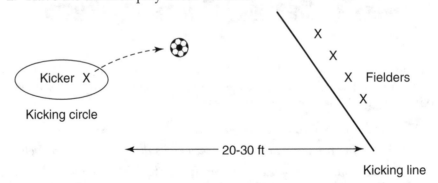

Kicker X

Kicking circle

X

X

X Fielders

X

←———— 20-30 ft ————→

Kicking line

Concluding Activities (5 minutes)

Identify one or two skills that most of the children had trouble with during the game. Have the children practice those skills in small groups.

LESSON 36
PRACTICING MANIPULATIVE SKILLS IN A GAME SITUATION

Student Objectives

- Play a game he or she knows without constant supervision by the teacher.
- Refine manipulative skills in a game situation.

Equipment and Materials

- 1 playground ball per circle in Keep It Up
- Other equipment, depending on games selected (e.g., bases and playground balls)

Safety Tip

- Keep all activity within your view.

Warm-Up Activities (5 minutes)

Balance Tag

See Grades 2-3: Games and Sports, Warm-Ups, page 464.

Skill-Development Activities (20 minutes)

Discussion

Gather the children into an information formation.

1. Ask the children which were their favorite games from the last few classes (e.g., Punch Line Ball, Triangle Ball, Cross the Line). (This can be prior to going to the play area, so you can have the appropriate equipment ready.)
2. Organize play for two or three games (keeping team sizes small), get each game started, and allow the children to keep the games going with as little supervision as possible.
3. Tell them they must settle their own arguments or else they will not be allowed to choose what they do another time.
4. Move from game to game to observe.

Concluding Activities (5 minutes)

Keep It Up

Arrange small groups into circles, scattered over the play area.

1. Describe and demonstrate the game:

   To get you started, I will toss a playground ball to one player in each circle.

   Try to keep the ball in the air as long as possible, striking the ball with one or both hands.

   The circle with the most consecutive hits wins a round (or add every circle's score for a total class score).

2. Have the children play several rounds.

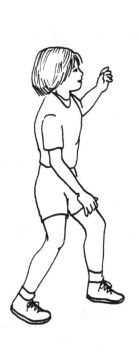

Second and third graders enjoy rhythmic activity, and for many children, physical education will be their only exposure to folk dance and the other activities in this unit. Classroom teachers often feel most comfortable with this unit, while some specialists avoid teaching these important skills. We encourage you to use these lessons regardless of previous experience with rhythmic activities. Keep in mind that children enjoy these activities and respond to an enthusiastic teacher—regardless of the teacher's skill level.

UNIT ORGANIZATION

Many physical education objectives can be met through teaching rhythmic activities. Our lessons cover locomotor skills, singing games, folk dances, rope jumping, and rhythm sticks. You may opt to teach these lessons as a six-week unit, reserving the final day to test skills or have students otherwise demonstrate what they have learned, perhaps, for example, by putting on a show for fellow students, family members, and other visitors. See the sample unit plan in table RA2.1.

There are many other ways in which you could organize these lessons as well. For example, you might enjoy teaching rhythmic activities one day each week throughout the school year or interspersing a week of rhythmic activities at various intervals throughout the year. In addition, rhythmic activities often work well during inclement weather since you can teach them indoors in relatively little space.

LESSON ORGANIZATION

Each lesson begins with warm-up activities; see the warm-up section immediately following this introduction. The skill development activities focus on moving to a beat, moving with different characteristics, and exploring creative movements. Each lesson ends with concluding activities, which typically reinforce the skill development activities and/or bring closure to the lesson. You can repeat lessons to reinforce skills and to allow children to experience the pleasure of mastery.

TEACHING HINTS

The most important factor in this unit is your attitude. When teachers present these lessons with the belief that children will enjoy and benefit from the experience, the children do! So relax and enjoy teaching these lessons. The children will not care if you are perfect, nor will they notice if you do not sing well. These activities are favorites and will "sell" themselves if given the opportunity. Keep in mind, too, that children enjoy watching adults exaggerate the movements and words. Another fun technique is for you to stop saying the words or cues and see if the children can continue without you, then pick up again after a short break.

Repetition and breaking the activities into parts also enhance learning. Teach and repeat the words or cues first. Then add the movements, preferably in parts. Break the skills into logical parts (many lessons suggest how to do this). If you or the children make a mistake, that is OK—just try again. Remember, too, that the fun doesn't have to be confined to physical education class: Many of these activities are appropriate for demonstrations, for example, at a school-wide parent's night.

Table RA2.1: Unit Plan for Grades 2-3: Rhythmic Activities

Week 13: locomotor skills	Week 14: nonlocomotor skills	Week 15: singing games and folk dances
Monday: locomotor variations Tuesday: jumping and hopping using shapes Wednesday: moving quickly and slowly Thursday: movement to feeling words Friday: body shapes and levels	Monday: swinging movements Tuesday: pushing and pulling Wednesday: galloping, sliding, and skipping Thursday: movement to a nursery rhyme Friday: singing games–Bingo	Monday: singing game–Paw Paw Patch Tuesday: singing game–Jump Jim Joe Wednesday: folk dance–Kinderpolka Thursday: folk dance–The Wheat Friday: review of singing games and folk dances
Week 25: rope jumping	**Week 26: folk dancing and singing games**	**Week 27: rhythm sticks and skill testing**
Monday: rope jumping Tuesday: rope jumping Wednesday: rope jumping Thursday: rope jumping Friday: rope jumping	Monday: folk dance–Chimes of Dunkirk Tuesday: singing game–A Hunting We Will Go Wednesday: folk dance–Dance of Greeting Thursday: singing game–Ten Little Snowmen Friday: review of dances	Monday: rhythm sticks Tuesday: rhythm sticks Wednesday: rhythm sticks Thursday: rhythm sticks Friday: skill testing

WARM-UPS

Animal Chase

Mark two goals, 30 ft apart. Arrange the children along one goal line.

1. Describe the activity:

    On the command "Animals run once," run to the opposite goal.

    On the command "Animals run two times," run across to the opposite line and then back to the original goal.

    We will continue with three, four, and so on (where the number tells you the number of trips you make from one goal line to another).

2. Have the children warm up.

3. Variations: Make the first command "*Animals run three times*," which means the children run to the opposite goal, back to the original goal, and run again to the opposite goal, without stopping. You can also increase the distance between goal lines and change the locomotor skill.

Follow My Directions

Arrange the children in scatter formation.

Give various movement directions, for example: *run in place, make a stretched shape, hop in a circle, shake three different body parts, walk on tiptoe, jump high and land softly, swing one arm and one leg, gallop forward, hop high, gallop backward.*

High, Low, Medium

Arrange the children in scatter formation.

1. Describe the activity:

    I will tell you "high," "low," or "medium."

    On "high," run high on tiptoe.

    On "low," run low with your body close to the ground.

    On "medium," run at an in-between level.

    I will change commands several times.

2. Have the children warm up.

3. Variation: Specify a different locomotor skill or allow the children to select a skill.

Locomotor Drum Movement

Arrange the children in scatter formation.

1. Describe the activity: *gallop in any direction, changing direction on a signal (drumbeat).*

2. Have the children warm up.

3. Have them repeat with skipping and sliding.

Magic Shapes

Arrange the children in a large circle.

1. Describe the activity:

   You run (skip, gallop, slide) in the circle.

   On "Freeze!" I will tell you to balance on one, two, or three body parts. For example, include balancing on one foot, seat, two knees, one foot and one hand, back, or one knee and one elbow.

2. Have the children warm up.

3. Variation: Have the children do Magic Movements rather than Magic Shapes. Commands can be to interpret feeling words (happy, frightened) or action words (run, swing).

Move and Freeze

Arrange the children in scatter formation.

1. Describe the activity:

   Walk wherever you wish around the play area to the drumbeat.

   Freeze when the beat stops.

   When the drum starts again, find another way to travel, for example, backward, sideways, in a circle, jumping, hopping, or leaping.

   Be careful to stay in your own personal space.

2. Have the children warm up.

Moving in Different Directions

Arrange the children in scatter formation. A leader, at first you, faces the class.

1. Describe the activity: *Run in general space to the drumbeat. After eight beats, the leader will signal a change in direction for the class by showing one of the signal cards, so watch for the cards.*

2. Have the children repeat the activity several times. Allow one or two children to lead.

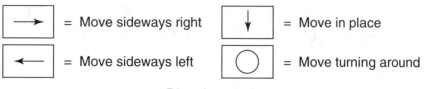

Direction cards

→	= Move sideways right	↓	= Move in place
←	= Move sideways left	○	= Move turning around

Olympic Joggers

Define a large oval track with a start line on the playground. Arrange the children at the start line. Signal the children to jog around the track until the signal to stop.

Run and Stop

Arrange the children in scatter formation.

1. Describe the activity: *When I call out "Run!" run until the whistle sounds, which means "Freeze!" Start again when I call out "Run!" again.*
2. Variation: Use other locomotor skills or specify the direction.

Stick Tricks

Arrange the children in scatter formation, each child standing by a stick laid on the floor or ground.

1. Challenge the children with the following tasks:

   With your side to the stick, jump back and forth over it to the drumbeat.

   With your side to the stick, jump back and forth over it rapidly. (Have them begin with 10 jumps and progress to 20, 30, 40, and so on.)

   Face the stick and jump over it, turn around, and jump over it again.

   With your back to the stick, jump over it.

   Jump over your stick and land facing the opposite direction (a 180-degree turn).

   Jump over your stick several times, increasing the height of your jump each time.

   Jump over your stick several times, increasing the distance of your jump each time.

2. Variation: Have the children repeat the tasks hopping.

Tortoise and Hare

Arrange the children in a large circle.

1. Describe the activity: *Run slowly in place on the signal "Tortoise" and rapidly in place on the signal "Hare."*
2. Have the children do the activity, repeating the commands several times.
3. Variation: Use the same commands, but have the children run forward rather than in place. You can also use different locomotor skills. For example, the movement for "tortoise" could be jumping slowly onto and off of a carpet square.

LESSON 1
LOCOMOTOR VARIATIONS

Student Objectives

- Walk and run at various levels and speeds.

Equipment and Materials

- 1 carpet square per child
- Red and blue shape cards
- Chalk, flour (outdoors only), or tape for marking the playing area

Colored shape cards

Warm-Up Activities (5 minutes)

Tortoise and Hare

See Grades 2-3: Rhythmic Activities, Warm-Ups, page 559.

Skill-Development Activities (20 minutes)

Locomotor Tasks

Arrange the children in scatter formation.

1. Challenge the children with each of the following tasks:

   Walk slowly (fast, with bent knees, or on tiptoes) 10 steps away from and 10 steps back to your carpet square.

   Walk to make a circle (triangle, square, or figure eight).

2. Repeat, having the students run instead of walk:

   Run with your arms overhead (bent, forward).

   Run with 8 slow steps with your knees bent (8 high steps on tiptoe).

3. Repeat 4 slow steps with knees bent (4 high steps as tiptoe).

4. Repeat 2 steps with arms overhead (2 arms bent, 2 arms forward).

5. Repeat 1 low and 2 high steps (1 low, 2 high, etc.).

Shape Card Game

Divide the children into groups of 8 to 10. Assign each group to a pathway (see figure below) marked on the hard surface.

Blue = Walk   △ = Low   □ = Fast

Red = Run   ○ = High   ◇ = Slow

1. Have the children move along the assigned pathway, using the movement suggested by the cards. For example, if a red triangle is shown the movement would be a low run.

2. Continue as time allows.

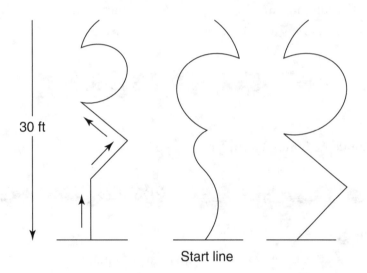

30 ft

Start line

LESSON 2
JUMPING AND HOPPING USING SHAPES

Student Objectives

- Create shapes while jumping and hopping.
- Distinguish between jumping and hopping.

Equipment and Materials

- 1 carpet square per child
- 1 drum

Warm-Up Activities (5 minutes)

Tortoise and Hare

See Grades 2-3: Rhythmic Activities, Warm-Ups, page 559.

Skill-Development Activities (20 minutes)

Movement Challenges

Arrange the children in scatter formation, each with a carpet square.

1. Provide a drumbeat.
2. Ask the children: *Jump and think of three things to do with your feet* (apart, together, forward and back, crossed).
3. Repeat, having students demonstrate another foot position.

Jumping

Keep the children in scatter formation, each with a carpet square.

1. Tell the children: *Jumping is taking off and landing on two feet. Jump and think of different shapes you can make using your arms* (in front, to the side, overhead). *Making different shapes with your arms and legs, jump 10 jumps away from your space. Be careful of your classmates.*
2. Ask the children: *Return with 10 jumps.*
3. Have them repeat: *Go backward 10 jumps.* Continue: *Jump and turn to your right and your left.*

Hopping

Keep the children in scatter formation, each with a carpet square.

1. Tell the children: *Hopping is taking off and landing on the same foot.*
2. Challenge the children with the following tasks:
   Hop on your right foot.
   Hop on your left foot.
   Hop right and turn. Hop left and turn.
   Hop and make shapes with your arms and free leg.

Concluding Activities (5 minutes)

Jumping and Hopping Shapes

Divide the children into four lines, forming a square. Describe and have the children do the activity:

On the signal, groups 1 and 3 trade places, using jumping and hopping shapes.
Now it is groups 2 and 4's turn.

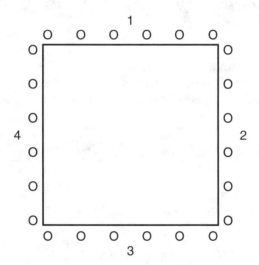

RHYTHMIC ACTIVITIES

LESSON 3
MOVING QUICKLY AND SLOWLY

Student Objectives

- Respond to commands with movements of various speeds and weights.

Equipment and Materials

- 1 carpet square per child

Warm-Up Activities (5 minutes)

Tortoise and Hare

Arrange the children in scatter formation, each with a carpet square.

See Grades 2-3: Rhythmic Activities, Warm-Ups, page 559, but have the children jump and hop onto and off of a carpet square. For example, on "tortoise" the movement could be a slow hop.

Skill-Development Activities (20 minutes)

Movement Challenges

Collect the carpet squares, but keep the children in scatter formation. Challenge the children with the following tasks:

Walk around the room as fast as you can (moving slowly).

Move many body parts (head, shoulders, hands) fast as you walk.

Move your body parts slowly as you walk (run, gallop, leap, skip).

Heavy and Light

Keep the children in scatter formation.

1. Describe and demonstrate heavy and light movements:

   "Heavy" movements are movements that are bold, slow, and deliberate and that resemble movement on the moon, carrying a weight, and so on.

   "Light" movements are movements that are fluttery, small, quick, and gentle and that may remind you of birds, flying, walking on tiptoe, a fairy, and so on.

2. Challenge the children with heavy and light movements: *Walk around the area using heavy movements (light movements).*

3. Repeat, having the children run, (gallop, leap, skip).

4. *While standing still, show me heavy movements with your arms (legs, trunk, elbows)*. Repeat with light movements.

5. *Walk around the room, using slow, heavy movements with your arms (legs, trunk, elbows)*. Repeat using fast, light movements.

Concluding Activities (5 minutes)

Pretend

Keep the children in scatter formation. Tell the children: *Pretend you are an elephant (a giant, a heavy box, thunder, a feather, a kite, a rag doll, an ant, a little person, hitting a baseball, tapping a balloon, shoveling snow, painting a picture in outer space).*

LESSON 4
MOVEMENT TO FEELING WORDS

Student Objectives

- Create movements to feeling words.

Equipment and Materials

- 1 carpet square per child

Warm-Up Activities (5 minutes)

Tortoise and Hare

See variation, Grades 2-3: Rhythmic Activities, Lesson 3, page 564.

Skill-Development Activities (20 minutes)

Feeling Challenges

Arrange the children in scatter formation.

1. Discuss the word sad: *Show me a movement that is sad (happy, curious, lonely, friendly, frightened, big, small, slow, fast, high, low, pretty, ugly, sweet, sour, warm, cold, rough, gentle, soft, hard, bouncy, smooth).*

2. Choose a sequence of two or three words to present for a movement pattern, for example, happy, sad, friendly; frightened, lonely, curious; or hot, cold, rough.

Concluding Activities (5 minutes)

Feeling Words

Keep the children in scatter formation.

1. Ask each child to select a sequence of three feeling words to create movement to.

2. Select several children to show their sequences and have the other children guess the words.

RHYTHMIC ACTIVITIES

LESSON 5
BODY SHAPES AND LEVELS

Student Objectives

- Create movements at various levels.
- Create a short dance, using body shapes and levels.

Equipment and Materials

- 1 drum

Warm-Up Activities (5 minutes)

Magic Movements

Arrange the children in a circle. This is a variation of Magic Shapes, Grades 2-3: Rhythmic Activities, Warm-Ups, page 558.

1. Explain the activity:

    You run in a circle.

    On "Freeze!" stop and create a movement to express a feeling, such as happy, sad, frightened, ugly, gentle.

2. Name some feelings and have the children try to express them, and then ask the children for additional suggestions.

Skill-Development Activities (20 minutes)

Levels and Collapse

Gather the children into an information formation.

1. Describe and demonstrate levels: *Movement can occur at different heights, for instance, high, medium, and low (e.g., on tiptoe, normal standing, and squatting).*

2. Describe and demonstrate collapse: *Drop to the floor, letting gravity pull you down in a way that looks as if you have no bones.*

Movement Challenges

Arrange the children in scatter formation.

1. Ask the children: *Stretch high and on the signal (drumbeat) collapse to the floor.*

2. Repeat rapidly.

3. Repeat slowly.

4. Tell the children: *Pretend you are a puppet and the puppet master is pulling your strings to lift you tall and high. All of a sudden the strings begin to break. Collapse your wrists, your arms, your head, your shoulders, and your legs.*

5. Challenge the children with the following tasks:

   Make a different stretched shape and on the signal collapse into a low shape.

   Pretend you are a block of ice melting.

   Combine four walking steps, a high shape, and a low shape. Cue the children: *Walk, walk, walk, walk, high shape, low shape.* Repeat, having the children jump (hop, leap, skip).

   Make a medium-level shape.

   Each time you hear a drumbeat, show me a different shape. Try wide, narrow, big, and small shapes. Beat the drum while the children practice making shapes.

   Combine four walking steps and then a high shape (a medium shape, a low shape). Repeat, having the children jump (hop, turn, leap).

Concluding Activities (5 minutes)

Have each child create a rhythmic activity, using walking, jumping, or hopping and a high, medium, and low shape.

LESSON 6
SWINGING MOVEMENTS

Student Objectives

- Create swinging movements with various body parts.
- Imitate objects and animals using swinging movements.
- Define *swing*.

Equipment and Materials

- 1 drum

Warm-Up Activities (5 minutes)

Move and Freeze

See Grades 2-3: Rhythmic Activities, Warm-Ups, page 558.

Skill-Development Activities (20 minutes)

Swinging

Keep the children in scatter formation.

1. Describe and demonstrate the skill: *A "swing" is a movement of a body part around a still (stationary) center.*
2. Demonstrate.
3. Challenge the children with the following swinging actions:

    Swing your arms forward (back, together, in opposite directions).

    Swing big. Use lots of space.

    Swing your arms from side-to-side.

    Swing one leg forward and back (from side-to-side).

    Try big swings, then small swings.

    Swing your torso.

    Make circles in space with one arm.

    Try a high circle and a low circle.

    Make circles with both arms.

    Make big and small circles.

Make circles with your leg.

Swing your head up and down (from side-to-side, around and around).

Concluding Activities (5 minutes)

Swinging Activities

Keep the children in scatter formation. Tell the children: *Pretend you are swings in the park (a tree in the wind, elephants, windmills).*

RHYTHMIC ACTIVITIES

LESSON 7
PUSHING AND PULLING

Student Objectives

- Create movements using pushing and pulling.
- Combine locomotor skills with push and pull movements.

Equipment and Materials

- None

Warm-Up Activities (5 minutes)

Magic Movements

This is a variation of Magic Shapes, Grades 2-3: Rhythmic Activities, Warm-Ups, page 558. Have the children create swinging movements with different body parts.

Skill-Development Activities (20 minutes)

Pushing and Pulling

Arrange the children in scatter formation.

1. Describe and demonstrate pushing: *To "push" you press a body part with force against an object in order to move that object from one spot to another.*

2. Describe and demonstrate pulling: *To "pull" you apply force to an object moving toward your body in order to move that object toward your body.*

3. Challenge the children with the following activities (the children should imagine objects to push and pull):

    Push (pull) with one arm (both arms, one foot, both feet, your head).

    Push a heavy object forward (downward, sideways).

    Push and pull fast (slowly).

    Push (pull), using strong movements, like pushing a heavy object.

    Push (pull), using light movements.

    Walk four steps, push, and pull.

    Push and pull in different directions.

    Walk four steps, collapse, and push and pull from a low level.

Concluding Activities (5 minutes)

Pushing and Pulling

Keep the children in scatter formation. Ask the children to perform the following activities:

> *Pretend you are pushing a lawnmower (a bicycle pump, a barbell, a swing, a giant ball, a wagon up a hill).*
>
> *Pretend you are pulling a tug-of-war rope (a kite, a church bell, a cart).*

LESSON 8
GALLOPING, SLIDING, AND SKIPPING

Student Objectives

- Distinguish between galloping, sliding, and skipping.
- Gallop, slide, and skip in different directions.
- Gallop, slide, and skip with a partner.

Equipment and Materials

- 1 drum
- 1 parachute

Warm-Up Activities (5 minutes)

Magic Movements

See variation of Magic Shapes, Grades 2-3: Rhythmic Activities, Warm-Ups, page 558. Have the children run around the circle, stopping several times to create pushing and pulling movements.

Skill-Development Activities (20 minutes)

Locomotor Tasks

Arrange the children in scatter formation.

1. Describe and demonstrate galloping: *To "gallop" you step, leap (one leg leads, the other joins).*

2. Use a drum for your start and stop signal. Challenge the children with the following tasks:

   Gallop freely in general space.

   Gallop so that your body goes high with each step. Push off hard with your back leg, and swing your arms.

   Take very large steps as you gallop.

   Gallop backward. This is very hard. Use your arms.

   Think of a movement to do with the arms (head, shoulders) as you gallop.

   Gallop with a partner.

Sliding

Make sure the children are still in scatter formation.

1. Describe and demonstrate sliding: *To slide means you step, then close (move your foot up to the other foot) going sideways.*
2. Challenge the children with the following tasks:

   Slide to the right (left).

   Look in the direction in which you're sliding.

   Try looking in the opposite direction.

   Try different pathways.

   Slide while holding both hands with a partner.

Skipping

Make sure the children are still in scatter formation.

1. Describe and demonstrate skipping: *To skip you step-hop.*
2. Challenge the children with the following tasks:

   Skip freely in general space.

   Skip and think of different positions for your arms (in front, to the side, folded in front of chest, behind back).

   Skip high (low, fast, slowly).

   Skip with a partner (two other people).

Concluding Activities (5 minutes)

Parachute Activities

Space the children around the parachute, each holding the edge with one or both hands.

Moving clockwise or counterclockwise, have the children gallop, slide, and skip, stopping on the start/ stop signal. See Grades 2-3: Games and Sports, Lesson 28, page 536.

GRADES 2-3 RHYTHMIC ACTIVITIES

LESSON 9
MOVEMENT TO A NURSERY RHYME

Student Objectives
- Clap the underlying beat of a rhyme.
- Create movements to a rhyme.

Equipment and Materials
- 1 drum

Warm-Up Activities (5 minutes)

Locomotor Drum Movement
Arrange the children in scatter formation.

1. Tell the children: *Gallop in any direction, changing direction on a signal (drumbeat).*
2. Have them repeat with skipping, then sliding.

Skill-Development Activities (20 minutes)

"Little Miss Mary"
Arrange the children in a semicircle, sitting down.

1. One line at a time, say with the children "Little Miss Mary":

    Little Miss Mary quite contrary,
    How does your garden grow?
    With silver bells and cockle shells,
    And pretty maids all in a row.

2. Say the entire verse straight through with the children.
3. Have the children repeat the verse without your joining in.
4. Clap to each syllable of the rhyme:

Lit	tle	Miss	Mar	y
Clap	clap	clap	clap	clap
1	2	3	4	5

Quite	con	trar	y
Clap	clap	clap	clap
1	2	3	4

5. Continue with other challenges:

Stand up and step in place to the beat of the rhyme.

Punch with your arms to the beat of the rhyme.

Nod your head to the beat.

(Locomotor skill) to the beat.

6. Have the children perform a sequence of movements to the beat. For example: *walk, walk, walk, jump, jump; walk, walk, jump, jump.*

Extension Activities

1. Select other nursery rhymes, and repeat the same type of activity, for example:

Rub a dub dub,

Three kids in a tub.

2. Have the children clap each syllable:

Rub	*a*	*dub*	*dub*
Clap	clap	clap	clap
1	2	3	4

3. Continue with other challenges:

Step in place to the beat.

Move a body part to the beat.

Move your whole body to the beat.

4. Repeat steps 2 and 3 with the following rhyme:

Sitting on the sidewalk,

Sipping cider,

Hey diddle-diddle,

The cat played the fiddle.

Sesame Street, Sesame Street,

I like to live on Sesame Street.

Concluding Activities (5 minutes)

Movement Sequences

Arrange the children in a semicircle.

1. Have each child create a sequence of movements to the beat of a rhyme.
2. Ask several children to show the class the movements they have devised.

LESSON 10
SINGING GAME

Student Objectives

- Sing the song "Bingo."
- Perform the movements to the song.

Equipment and Materials

- 1 drum
- Direction cards
- Music: Recording of "Bingo," optional

Warm-Up Activities (5 minutes)

Moving in Different Directions

See Grades 2-3: Rhythmic Activities, Warm-Ups, page 558. Cue the children: *Count the beats so you'll know when to look for the card.*

Skill-Development Activities (20 minutes)

Grand Right and Left

Arrange partners in a single circle. Have partners face each other. *Note:* There must be an even number of children for this to work. Have an extra child help you direct the activity, having him or her rotate into the activity as another child helps you, and so on.

Single circle,
partners facing

1. Describe and demonstrate the activity:

   Facing each other, partners join right hands, step toward each other, moving a bit to the left so that their right shoulders nearly touch.

They continue walking with their hands joined so that their right arms are extended behind them.

At this point they reach their left hands forward to the new people now facing them and join left hands (their right hands are still joined).

As they move forward, they drop right hands, pass the left shoulders of the people they were facing, and continue this pattern with each person until they reach their original partners (halfway around the circle).

2. Have the children walk through and practice Grand Right and Left. Cue the children: *Right hands to partner, right shoulders touching, left hand out, left shoulders touching.*

3. When they have learned the sequence, have them repeat Grand Right and Left without cues.

4. If the children are unsuccessful, practice with cues again. If the children are successful, continue.

5. Have them repeat, skipping.

6. Have them repeat to a fast beat. You can clap or play the music (or sing) "Bingo."

Swing

Keep the children in the Grand Right and Left setup.

1. Describe how swinging fits in with the Grand Right and Left:

   Grasping right hands, partners turn in a clockwise circle (if left hands are joined, you turn counterclockwise).

   After completing a full circle (so you are all back where you started), you stop.

2. Have the children practice swinging.

3. *Note:* This can be a half-swing or two swings in other movement sequences.

"Bingo"

Arrange the children in a circle, seated next to their partners.

1. Sing the words and give the cues to "Bingo." Have the children join in singing if they know the song:

   A big black dog sat on the porch and Bingo was his name. (Walk right eight steps.)

   (Repeat. Walk left eight steps.)

   B-I-N-G-O! (Walk four steps to center of circle.)

   B-I-N-G-O! (Walk four steps back.)

   B-I-N-G-O! (Walk four steps to center of circle.)

   B-I-N-G-O! (Walk four steps back.)

(*Note:* Spell out B-I-N-G-O slowly: Grand Right and Left to the spelling.)

2. Have the children sing the words to "Bingo" and clap to the beat.

3. Next, have the children stand in the circle, still next to their partners, with hands joined.

4. Review and demonstrate the steps to Bingo:

   Walk right eight steps.

   Walk left eight steps.

   Walk to center of circle four steps.

Walk back four steps.

Repeat four steps into circle and four steps back (out).

Turn and face your partner.

Grand Right and Left, four people.

Swing your new partner.

5. Have the children practice the steps with and without cues.

Concluding Activities (5 minutes)

"Bingo"

Perform the sequence to the music (just sing together if you don't have a recording of the song).

RHYTHMIC ACTIVITIES

LESSON 11
SINGING GAME

Student Objectives

- Skip to the song "Paw Paw Patch."
- Cooperate with a partner in a longways-set formation.

Equipment and Materials

- Chalk, flour (outdoors only), or tape to mark lines

Warm-Up Activities (5 minutes)

Animal Chase

See Grades 2-3: Rhythmic Activities, Warm-Ups, page 557.

Skill-Development Activities (20 minutes)

Paw Paw Patch

Arrange the children in two long parallel lines, with partners across from each other. Place boys in one line and girls in the other. You are in the middle between the lines so the partners can face each other and you too. This formation is called a "longways-set," facing the head of the set (in this case, this is the pair at the end near you).

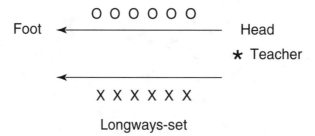

Longways-set

1. Ask the children: *Does anyone know what a pawpaw is? It is a large, elongated* (show this with your hands), *yellow, edible fruit of a tropical American tree.*
2. Sing the words to "Paw Paw Patch" (see step 5).
3. Sing the words to "Paw Paw Patch" with the children.
4. Describe and demonstrate the movements (see step 5).

5. Have the children practice the movements based on the lyrics.

Where oh where is sweet little Nellie? (Repeat two times for total of three.) *Way down yonder in the paw paw patch.* (The first person in girls' line turns to right and skips around entire set and back to place.)

Come on boys, let's go find her. (Repeat two more times.) *Way down yonder in the paw paw patch.* (First boy leads entire line of boys to the right, around the girls, and back to place.)

Picking up paw paws, put 'em in your pocket. (Repeat two more times; couples join inside hands and pantomime pick-up motion with outside hands.)

Way down yonder in the paw paw patch. (Couple 1 joins both hands and slides down set to the end, leaving a new head couple.)

Concluding Activities (5 minutes)

Paw Paw Patch

Have the children perform the entire dance, with words and movements. Have them repeat, using "Johnny" (instead of Nellie) and reversing the roles, so the girls go look.

LESSON 12
SINGING GAME

Student Objectives

- Combine jumping, running, and sliding to perform "Jump Jim Joe."

Equipment

- Music: "Jump Jim Joe" (Folkraft 1180)

Warm-Up Activities (5 minutes)

Animal Chase

See Grades 2-3: Rhythmic Activities, Warm-Ups, page 557. Use skipping or galloping instead of running.

Skill-Development Activities (20 minutes)

"Jump Jim Joe"

Arrange the children in a double circle with partners facing each other.

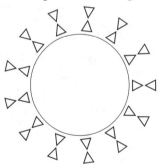

Double circle,
partners facing

1. Sing the words to "Jump Jim Joe" (see step 4).
2. Sing the words with the children.
3. Describe and demonstrate the steps (see step 4).
4. Have the children practice the steps:

   Jump, jump, jump, Jim Joe. (Jump two slow jumps and three fast jumps in place.)

Take a little turn and around we go. (Join hands with partner and circle in place with eight steps.)

Slide, slide, and stamp just so. (With hands on hips, take two slides to the right [step right, close left, step right, close left], and stamp three times.)

Take another partner, and you jump Jim Joe. (Join hands with new partner and jump three times.)

Concluding Activities (5 minutes)

"Jump Jim Joe"

Have the children perform the entire sequence several times, singing and moving.

LESSON 13
FOLK DANCE

Student Objectives

- Combine a step-close and a stamp to perform the Kinderpolka.

Equipment and Materials

- Music: "Kinderpolka (Children's Polka)" (Folkraft 1187)

Warm-Up Activities (5 minutes)

Animal Chase

See Grades 2-3: Rhythmic Activities, Warm-Ups, page 557.

1. Use the following commands:

   Animals run backward one time.

   Animals run sideways two times.

   Animals jump forward one time.

2. Repeat.

Skill-Development Activities (20 minutes)

Step-Close

Arrange the children in a single circle, with partners facing each other.

1. Describe and demonstrate the step-close: *To do the step-close, step to the side, then close with the opposite foot.*
2. Have the children practice the step-close.

Kinderpolka

Keep the children in a single circle, with partners facing each other.

1. Demonstrate and describe the movements:

   - Part 1:

   Two step-close steps to the center,

   Three stamps in place (performed slowly),

   Two step-close steps back to original position,

   Three stamps in place. (Cues: Step, close, step, close, stamp, stamp, stamp.)

- Part 2:

Repeat part 1.

- Part 3:

Clap own thighs one time,

Clap hands together one time,

And clap hands to partner's hands three times.

- Part 4:

Repeat part 3.

- Part 5:

Shake right index finger three times at partner.

Repeat with left index finger.

Turn around four steps in place,

And stamp three times.

2. Have the children practice the movements with cues.
3. Have them listen to the music.
4. Have them clap in rhythm to the music.
5. Say the cues to the music as the children perform.

Concluding Activities (5 minutes)

Kinderpolka

Have the children perform the entire sequence with the music. Repeat.

LESSON 14
FOLK DANCE

Student Objectives

- Combine walking and skipping to perform "The Wheat."

Equipment and Materials

- Music: "The Wheat" (RCA 45RP A-4146)

Warm-Up Activities (5 minutes)

High, Low, Medium

See Grades 2-3: Rhythmic Activities, Warm-Ups, page 557.

Skill-Development Activities (20 minutes)

"The Wheat"

Arrange the children in sets of three, facing counterclockwise in a large circle.

1. Have the children listen and clap to the music.
2. Describe and demonstrate part 1: *Walk 16 steps forward*.
3. Have the children practice part 1.
4. Have them practice part 1 to music.
5. Describe and demonstrate part 2: *The dancer in the center of each trio hooks right elbows with the dancer on the right and skips around with that partner in a small circle for eight steps.*

   Repeat with the dancer on the left.
6. Have the children practice part 2.
7. Have them practice part 2 to music.

Concluding Activities (5 minutes)

"The Wheat"

Have the children perform the entire sequence with music.

LESSON 15
FOLK DANCE AND SINGING GAMES REVIEW

Student Objectives

- Demonstrate one or more folk dance and one or more singing game.

Equipment and Materials

- 1 drum
- Music: "Jump Jim Joe" (Folkraft 1180)
- Music: "The Wheat" (RCA 45RP A-4146)
- Music: "Kinderpolka (Children's Polka)" (Folkraft 1187)

Warm-Up Activities (5 minutes)

Animal Chase

See Grades 2-3: Rhythmic Activities, Warm-Ups, page 557.

Skill-Development Activities (20 minutes)

Folk Dancing

Arrange the children in scatter formation.

1. Review the steps to "The Wheat."
2. Have children perform to "The Wheat."
3. Repeat with "Bingo," "Paw Paw Patch," "Jump Jim Joe," and the "Kinderpolka."

Bingo
See Grades 2-3: Rhythmic Activities, Lesson 10, page 578.

Paw Paw Patch
See Grades 2-3: Rhythmic Activities, Lesson 11, page 580.

Jump Jim Joe
See Grades 2-3: Rhythmic Activities, Lesson 12, page 582.

Kinderpolka
See Grades 2-3: Rhythmic Activities, Lesson 13, page 584.

The Wheat
See Grades 2-3: Rhythmic Activities, Lesson 14, page 586.

Concluding Activities (5 minutes)

Discussion

Gather the children into an information formation.

1. Discuss the origin of folk dances: *Folk dances are traditional activities from different countries or cultures—including our country and the cultures we represent. Often the dances represent historical events. The dances are usually done on holidays or at special events. Many folk dances are still done in costume in the country or culture. Sometimes the dances are hundreds of years old.*

2. Ask the children: *Which was your favorite dance or song?* Discuss their responses.

3. *What are folk dances?* (See step 1.)

LESSON 16
ROPE JUMPING

Student Objectives

- Perform two-footed singles and doubles (forward and backward) with a short jump rope.

Equipment and Materials

- 1 short jump rope per child
- Signal

Warm-Up Activities (5 minutes)

High, Low, Medium

See Grades 2-3: Rhythmic Activities, Warm-Ups, page 557. Allow the children to use any locomotor skill.

Skill-Development Activities (20 minutes)

Two-Footed Singles

Arrange the children in scatter formation, each with a jump rope.

1. Describe and demonstrate the activity: *To do two-footed singles, jump on both feet once for each turn of the rope.*
2. Have the children practice two-footed singles, starting slowly, then going faster.

Two-Footed Doubles

Keep the children in scatter formation, each with a jump rope.

1. Describe and demonstrate the activity: *To do two-footed doubles, jump on both feet twice for each turn of the rope. The rope turns slower for two-footed doubles.*
2. Have the children practice two-footed doubles.

Basic Jump Backward

Keep the children in scatter formation, each with a jump rope.

1. Describe and demonstrate the activity: *For this jump, throw the rope backward and jump with both feet together as the rope hits the floor. This is a variation of the two-footed single.*
2. Have the children practice the basic jump backward.

Helicopter

Keep the children in scatter formation, each with a jump rope.

1. Describe and demonstrate the activity: *With both ends of the rope in one hand, swing the rope in a circle overhead. Make sure you keep a tight grip on the rope and watch out for your classmates.*
2. Have the children practice the helicopter.

Single-Sided Taps

Keep the children in scatter formation, each with a jump rope.

1. Describe and demonstrate the activity: *With both ends of the rope in one hand, swing the rope in a circle to the side of your body.*
2. Have the children practice single-sided taps.

Double-Sided Taps

Keep the children in scatter formation, each with a jump rope.

1. Describe and demonstrate the activity: *Holding both ends of the rope in one hand, swing the rope in a circle once on one side of your body and once on the opposite side of your body.*
2. Provide a drumbeat, and have the students practice double-sided taps to a drumbeat with each hand.
3. Have the students practice jumping in place to a drumbeat while doing double-sided taps.

Extension Activities

Have the children create routines using helicopters, single- and double-sided taps, and two-footed single and double jumps.

Concluding Activities (5 minutes)

Don't Miss

Divide the class into four groups, each child with a jump rope. Each group should have jumpers of all achievement levels.

1. Describe the activity:

   Each of you will choose a type of jump and on the signal jump as many times as possible without a miss. Jumps can be two-footed singles or doubles or basic backward jumps.

   I will time you for one-minute periods, and you must each count the number of misses during each session.

   The group with the lowest number of misses wins. You are on your honor to count accurately.

2. Have the children do the activity. Repeat several times.

GRADES 2-3

RHYTHMIC ACTIVITIES

LESSON 17
ROPE JUMPING

Student Objectives

- Perform the alternate jump with a short jump rope.

Equipment and Materials

- 1 short jump rope per child
- Cones for marking jogging oval

Warm-Up Activities (5 minutes)

Olympic Joggers

See Grades 2-3: Rhythmic Activities, Warm-Ups, page 559. Continue for four or five minutes, encouraging the children to go as far as possible.

Skill-Development Activities (20 minutes)

Alternate Jump

Arrange the children in scatter formation, each with a jump rope.

1. Review two-footed singles and doubles.
2. Describe and demonstrate alternate jumps: *To do alternate jumps, jump on each foot for one turn of the rope (right, left, right, left).*
3. Have the children practice alternate jumping, jumping slowly, hot pepper (i.e., as fast as possible), in place, moving forward, and moving backward.

Extension Activities

Have the children create routines using helicopters, single- and double-sided taps, two-footed singles and doubles, and alternate jumps.

Concluding Activities (5 minutes)

Don't Miss

See Grades 2-3: Rhythmic Activities, Lesson 16, page 590.

LESSON 18
ROPE JUMPING

Student Objectives

- Perform the one-footed continuous jump with a short jump rope.

Equipment and Materials

- 1 short jump rope per child

Warm-Up Activities (5 minutes)

Olympic Joggers

See Grades 2-3: Rhythmic Activities, Warm-Ups, page 559. Encourage the children to jog a longer distance or a longer time than the last time.

Skill-Development Activities (20 minutes)

Backward Two-Footed Singles and Doubles and Basic Jump Backward

See Grades 2-3: Rhythmic Activities, Lesson 16, page 589.

Alternate Jump

See Grades 2-3: Rhythmic Activities, Lesson 17, page 591.

One-Footed Continuous Jump

Keep the children in scatter formation, each with a jump rope.

1. Describe and demonstrate the one-footed continuous jump: *For this jump, jump on the same foot for each turn of the rope. You can use either a single or double jump.*

2. Have the children practice the one-footed continuous jump, jumping right foot single (right foot double, left foot single, left foot double, slowly, hot pepper, in place, moving).

Concluding Activities (5 minutes)

Don't Miss

See Grades 2-3: Rhythmic Activities, Lesson 16, page 590. Encourage the children to select a jump skill they can perform successfully.

RHYTHMIC ACTIVITIES

LESSON 19
ROPE JUMPING

Student Objectives

- Perform leg swings with a short jump rope.

Equipment and Materials

- 1 short jump rope per child

Warm-Up Activities (5 minutes)

Jumping and Hopping

Arrange the children in scatter formation, each with a short jump rope.

1. Have each child form a circle on the floor or ground with his or her rope.
2. Challenge the children with the following tasks:

   Jump in and out of the rope circle.

   Hop in and out of the circle on your right foot. Try your left foot.

   Jump around the circle once, twice, three times.

   Jump backward around the circle.

Skill-Development Activities (20 minutes)

Leg Swings

Keep the children in scatter formation, each with a jump rope.

1. Review the alternate jump and the one-footed continuous jump (double). See Grades 2-3: Rhythmic Activities, Lesson 18, page 592.
2. Describe and demonstrate the leg swing: *For leg swings, perform a one-footed double jump and swing your free leg diagonally across the jumping leg.*
3. Have the children practice the leg swing, jumping on the right leg.
4. Have them repeat the leg swing, jumping on the left leg.
5. Have them repeat, alternating legs.

Jumping Sequence

Keep the children in scatter formation, each with a jump rope. Have the children perform the following jumping sequence:

Four jumps with left leg swing,
Four jumps with right leg swing,
Two jumps with left leg swing,
Two jumps with right leg swing,
Two jumps with right leg swing, and
Two jumps with left leg swing.

Concluding Activities (5 minutes)

Jumping Contest

Keep the children in scatter formation, each with a jump rope.

1. Have each child select a jumping step with which to move continuously.
2. Award one point every time the rope goes under the feet.
3. Find a total class score and compare to other class scores on the same level.

LESSON 20
ROPE JUMPING

Student Objectives

- Jump hot pepper and high water with a long rope.

Equipment and Materials

- 1 long jump rope per group

Warm-Up Activities (5 minutes)

High, Low, Medium

See Grades 2-3: Rhythmic Activities, Warm-Ups, page 557. Have the children skip or gallop rather than run.

Skill-Development Activities (20 minutes)

Rope Skills

Divide the children into groups of three or four, each group with a long jump rope.

Have the children practice running in the front door and running out the back door, with two-footed single and double jumps. See Grades K-1: Rhythmic Activities, Lesson 22, page 231 and Grades 2-3: Rhythmic Activities, Lesson 16, page 589.

Hot Pepper

Keep the same formation.

1. Describe and demonstrate the skill: *Jumping hot pepper is jumping with the rope turning very fast.*
2. Have the children practice hot pepper, one child at a time in each rope. Rotate turners so everyone has a chance.

High Water

Keep the same formation.

1. Describe and demonstrate the skill: *Jumping high water is jumping with the rope turning so that it gradually gets higher and higher from the ground. Turners, be careful to move up gradually, instead of quickly so the jumper will be safer.*
2. Have the children practice high water, one child at a time in each rope. Rotate turners so everyone has a chance.

"Mabel, Mabel"

Keep the same formation.

1. One by one, say and have the children practice each line of the rhyme:

    Mabel, Mabel, set the table,

    Don't forget the salt and pepper.

    (On "pepper," turn the rope faster and faster, and jumper jumps until he or she misses.)

2. Practice the entire rhyme.

"Fourth of July"

Keep the same formation.

1. One by one, say and have the children practice each line of the rhyme:

    I asked my mother for 15 cents,

    To see the elephant jump the fence.

    He jumped so high he reached the sky,

    And never came back 'til the Fourth of July.

    (Use regular jumps for the first two lines. On the third line, the rope is gradually raised and the jumper must jump higher and higher until the end of the rhyme. Again, turners, be careful to raise the rope gradually.)

2. Practice the entire rhyme.

Concluding Activities (5 minutes)

High Water and Hot Pepper

Have the children practice high water and hot pepper again, using the rhymes "Mabel, Mabel" and "Fourth of July."

LESSON 21
FOLK DANCE

Student Objectives

- Combine stamping, clapping, and running to perform "Chimes of Dunkirk."

Equipment and Materials

- Music: "Chimes of Dunkirk" (Folkraft 1188)

Warm-Up Activities (5 minutes)

Follow My Directions

See Grades 2-3: Rhythmic Activities, Warm-Ups, page 557.

Skill-Development Activities (20 minutes)

"Chimes of Dunkirk"

Arrange partners in a double circle, facing each other. See figure, page 582.

1. Have the children listen to the music.
2. Describe and demonstrate the movements for part 1.
3. Have the children practice the movements for part 1.
4. Repeat steps 2 and 3 for parts 2, 3, and 4:

   Part 1: *Stamp in place three times (left, right, left).*

   Part 2: *Clap hands three times (clap, clap, clap).*

   Part 3: *Partners join hands and circle in place eight running steps.*

   Part 4: *All join hands within each circle and slide or skip around the circle counterclockwise 16 steps. Partners, stay across from each other.*

Concluding Activities (5 minutes)

"Chimes of Dunkirk"

Keep the same formation. Have the children perform the entire sequence straight through first without, then with, the music.

LESSON 22
SINGING GAME

Student Objectives

- Combine the slide, skip, and cast off in "A-Hunting We Will Go."

Equipment and Materials

- Music: "A-Hunting We Will Go" (Folkraft F 1191 B)
- 1 drum

Warm-Up Activities (5 minutes)

Follow My Directions

See Grades 2-3: Rhythmic Activities, Warm-Ups, page 557. Use new tasks. For example, jump in a series, gallop, or move in a circle high, then low.

Skill-Development Activities (20 minutes)

Sliding to a Beat

Arrange the children in a large circle.

1. Beat the drum.
2. Have the children clap to the drumbeat (slide to the beat, slide and clap to the beat).
3. Have them repeat, sliding in the opposite direction.

Casting Off

Arrange the children in a longways-set. (See Grades 2-3: Rhythmic Activities, Lesson 11, page 580.)

1. Describe and demonstrate casting off: *The head couple separates, one going to the right and one to the left, to lead each line of dancers to the foot of the set.*
2. Have the children practice casting off.

A-Hunting We Will Go

Keep the children in a longways-set.

1. Have the children listen to the music.
2. Sing part 1.
3. Practice singing part 1 with the children.

4. Repeat steps 2 and 3 with parts 2, 3, 4, and 5.
5. Sing the entire song with the children.
6. Describe and demonstrate the movements for part 1.
7. Have the children practice the movements for part 1.
8. Repeat steps 6 and 7 for parts 2, 3, 4, and 5.

> Part 1: *Oh, a-hunting we will go. (Head couple with hands joined slides four steps down the inside of set.)*
>
> Part 2: *A-hunting we will go. (Head couple slides four steps back to place.)*
>
> Part 3: *We'll catch a fox and put him in a box. (All children stand in place and clap.)*
>
> Part 4: *And then we'll let him go. (Repeat part 3.)*
>
> Part 5: *Repeat song using words "Tra-la-la-la-la-la." (Head couple casts off using a skipping step, with each line following the leader. At the foot of the set the head couple forms an arch, and the other children skip under, making a new head couple.)*

9. Have the children practice the movements for the entire dance without the music.

Concluding Activities (5 minutes)

A-Hunting We Will Go

Continue in the same formation. Have the children perform the entire sequence several times to the music.

LESSON 23
FOLK DANCE

Student Objectives

- Combine running and stamping to perform "Dance of Greeting."

Equipment and Materials

- Music: "Dance of Greeting" (Folkraft 1187, RCA 45EP A-4146)

Warm-Up Activities (5 minutes)

Follow My Directions

See Grades 2-3: Rhythmic Activities, Warm-Ups, page 557. Vary the movement tasks. For example, sliding, making sharp movements, swinging, or skipping.

Skill-Development Activities (20 minutes)

Dance of Greeting

Place the children in a single circle, facing the center.

Single circle,
facing in

1. Listen to the music.
2. Describe and demonstrate the movements for part 1.
3. Have the children practice the movements for part 1.
4. Have them practice the movements for part 1 to the music.
5. Repeat steps 1, 2, and 3 with parts 2, 3, and 4.

Part 1: *Clap, clap, bow,*

Clap, clap, bow.

Part 2: *Stamp right, stamp left,*

Turn around in place with 4 running steps.

Part 3: Repeat parts 1 and 2.

Part 4: *Join hands and run 16 steps to the right.*

Turn and take 16 running steps back to place.

Concluding Activities (5 minutes)

Dance of Greeting

Keep the same formation. Have the children perform the entire dance to music. Cues: *Clap, clap, bow, clap, clap, bow, stamp, stamp, run around* (repeat). *Run, 2, 3, . . . 16* (repeat other direction).

LESSON 24
SINGING GAME

Student Objectives

- Perform the step-hop to a drumbeat.
- Participate in "Ten Little Snowmen."

Equipment and Materials

- Music: "Ten Little Snowmen" (RCA 45 41-6150)
- 1 whistle
- 4 or more cones (to define play area)
- 1 drum

Warm-Up Activities (5 minutes)

Run and Stop

See Grades 2-3: Rhythmic Activities, Warm-Ups, page 559.

Skill-Development Activities (20 minutes)

Step-Hop

Make sure the children are still in scatter formation.

1. Describe and demonstrate the step-hop.
2. For the step-hop, step and hop on the same foot. Repeat with the opposite foot. (Use an even rhythm.)
3. Beat the drum in an even rhythm.
4. Have the children practice the step-hop to the drumbeat.

Ten Little Snowmen

Arrange the children in a single circle, facing its center. Assign each child a number from 1 to 10.

1. Sing the words to part 1 to the tune of "Ten Little Snowmen."
2. Sing with the children as they practice the words to part 1.
3. Demonstrate the movements to part 1.
4. Have the children practice the movements to part 1.
5. Have them practice the movements while singing the words.
6. Repeat steps 1 through 5 for parts 2, 3, and 4.

Part 1: *1 little, 2 little, 3 little snowmen, (continue up to 10 little snowmen). (Squat when your number is sung in the song.)*

Part 2: *10 little, 9 little, 8 little snowmen, (continue down to 1 little snowmen). (Stand as your number is sung.)*

Part 3: *Repeat part 1. (Step-hop around the circle to the right.)*

Part 4: *Repeat part 2. (Step-hop around the circle to the left.)*

Alternate Learning Activity

Ten Little Monkeys

Arrange the children in a single circle, facing its center. Assign each child a number from 1 to 10.

1. Sing the words to "Ten Little Monkeys."
2. Sing with the children as they practice the words.
3. Demonstrate the movements to "Ten Little Monkeys."

    Hop 18 steps to the right in a circle as you chant the words.

    Point to one to three children who "fall off." Tell the children who fell off: Hold the "bump" on your head.

    Those children who have not "fallen," repeat the chant hopping in the opposite direction each time, until everyone is holding their heads on the last round.

4. Have the children practice the movements.
5. Have them practice the movements while singing the words.

    10 little monkeys jumping on the bed, one fell off and bumped his head (continue down to one little monkey).

    No little monkeys jumping on the bed, 'cause they fell off and bumped their heads.

6. The chant can be repeated in reverse order, adding children each time.

Concluding Activities (5 minutes)

Ten Little Snowmen

Keep the same formation. Have the children perform the entire sequence to music.

GRADES 2-3 RHYTHMIC ACTIVITIES

LESSON 25
REVIEW OF DANCES

Student Objectives

- Demonstrate several dances.

Equipment and Materials

- Music: "Chimes of Dunkirk" (Folkraft 1188)
- Music: "A-Hunting We Will Go" (Folkraft F 1191 B)
- Music: "Dance of Greeting" (Folkraft 1187, RCA 45EP A-4146)
- Music: "Ten Little Snowmen" (RCA 45 41-6150)
- 4 or more cones (to define play area)

Warm-Up Activities (5 minutes)

Run and Stop

See Grades 2-3: Rhythmic Activities, Warm-Ups, page 559.

Skill-Development Activities (20 minutes)

"Chimes of Dunkirk"

Cue the children: *Stamp, stamp, stamp, clap-clap-clap, circle, eight; join hands and slide three, four, five, six, seven, eight; slide, two, three, four, five, six, seven, eight.* See Grades 2-3: Rhythmic Activities, Lesson 21, page 597.

A-Hunting We Will Go

Cue the children: *Slide, slide, slide, slide, reverse slide, three, four, everyone clap, head couple cast off, bridge, and new head couple.* See Grades 2-3: Rhythmic Activities, Lesson 22, page 598.

Dance of Greeting

Cue the children: *Clap, clap, bow, clap, clap, bow, stamp, stamp, run around* (repeat). *Run, 2, 3, . . . 16* (reverse and repeat). See Grades 2-3: Rhythmic Activities, Lesson 23, page 600.

Ten Little Snowmen

See Grades 2-3: Rhythmic Activities, Lesson 24, page 602.

Concluding Activities (5 minutes)

Students' Choice

Allow the children to form their own small groups and perform their favorite dances for the class or ask the whole class to select their favorite dance to perform again. This is a good day to invite special guests to observe, such as parents, the principal, or another class.

LESSON 26
RHYTHM STICKS

Student Objectives

- Tap sticks rhythmically in a sequence.

Equipment and Materials

- 1 drum
- 2 rhythm sticks per child
- Music: "Main Street Parade" from *Modern Tunes for Rhythm and Instruments*, Hap Palmer (AR 523)

Warm-Up Activities (5 minutes)

Stick Tricks

Arrange the children in scatter formation. Have each child place one rhythm stick on the floor. Have the children perform the following two jumping activities:

Jump back and forth over the stick to a drumbeat. (Repeat several times, varying the tempo.)

Jump rapidly for 5 (10, 15, 20) jumps.

Skill-Development Activities (20 minutes)

Rhythm Challenges

Have the children sit in a circle, facing center, with two rhythm sticks each. Divide the class into two groups, one half and other half of the circle.

Pattern 1

Tap down (four counts),

Tap together (four counts),

Alternate taps down and together (eight counts),

Repeat.

Pattern 2

Tap to the side (four counts),

Tap together (four counts),

Cross arms and tap down (eight counts),

Repeat.

1. Describe and have two children help you demonstrate the activity:

   To the music, group 1 starts with pattern 1, then completes pattern 2, and group 2 starts with pattern 2, then completes pattern 1.

   Repeat, reversing so that group 1 does pattern 2, then pattern 1, and group 2 does 1, then 2.

Concluding Activities (5 minutes)

Rhythm Stick Round

Keep the children sitting in a circle, facing center, with two rhythm sticks each.

1. Have the children do the patterns as a "round," with a new student (or pair of children if you prefer) entering every four beats. For example, the first child does tap down, two, three, four and continues with tap together two, three, four as the second child does tap down two, three, four.

2. Continue until all children have done the entire routine. For variety you can have the children repeat the two patterns so that all children continue once they have started. (Every fifth child should be doing the same thing.)

LESSON 27
RHYTHM STICKS

Student Objectives

- Flip and catch a rhythm stick.
- Use the stick flip in a simple routine.

Equipment and Materials

- 1 drum
- 2 rhythm sticks per child
- Music: "Pinky" from *Modern Tunes for Rhythm and Instruments*, Hap Palmer (AR 523)

Safety Tips

- Remind the children to keep control of the sticks.

Warm-Up Activities (5 minutes)

Stick Tricks

Arrange the children in scatter formation. Have each child place one rhythm stick on the floor. Have the children perform the following tasks:

> *Hop on your right foot back and forth over the stick to a drumbeat.*
>
> *Hop on your left foot back and forth over the stick to a drumbeat.*
>
> *Hop rapidly on your right foot back and forth over the stick for 5 (10, 15, 20) jumps.*
>
> *Repeat with your left foot.*

Skill-Development Activities (20 minutes)

Front and Side Tapping

Have the children sit in a large circle, facing center, each with two rhythm sticks.

1. Demonstrate and describe the skills:

   > *For front tapping, tap the top ends of the sticks by tilting the sticks forward and touching the ends to the floor.*
   >
   > *For side tapping, touch the sticks to the floor on each side of your body (right stick to your right side and left stick to your left side).*

2. Have the children practice front and side tapping.

3. Demonstrate the following sequence while the children listen carefully: *Front, two, three, four, side two, three, four, front, two, side, two, front, side, front, two, three, four, side, two, three, four.*

4. Have the children practice the sequence (with cues if necessary).

5. Create and demonstrate your own front and side tapping sequences, and have the children repeat them.

Stick Flip

Keep the children sitting in a large circle.

1. Describe and demonstrate the skill: *Tap one end of the stick on the floor in front, then toss it, flip it over, and catch it.*

2. Have the children practice the stick flip with the right hand (the left hand; both hands simultaneously; the right, then left, then right hand).

3. Have the children perform the following routine to "Pinky."

   Side tap (four counts), *front tap* (four counts).

   Repeat (eight counts).

   Touch and flip right stick (four counts), *touch and flip left stick* (four counts).

   Touch and flip both sticks (eight counts).

4. Repeat the entire sequence.

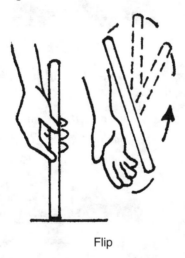

Flip

Concluding Activities (5 minutes)

Name Tap

Arrange the children in scatter formation or seat children in a large circle.

1. Demonstrate how to tap softly and loudly: *Tap out your name with the rhythm sticks. For example, "Jerry Thomas" would be loud tap, soft tap, loud tap, soft tap; "Amelia Lee" would be soft tap, loud tap, soft tap, loud tap.*

2. Have the children tap out their own and each others' names.

GRADES 2-3   RHYTHMIC ACTIVITIES

LESSON 28
RHYTHM STICKS

Student Objectives

- Flip and catch a rhythm stick to the side.
- Use the side stick flip in a simple routine.

Equipment and Materials

- 2 rhythm sticks per child
- Music: "Mai Tai" from *Modern Tunes for Rhythm and Instruments*, Hap Palmer (AR 523)

Warm-Up Activities (5 minutes)

Stick Tricks

Arrange the children in scatter formation. Have each child place one rhythm stick on the floor. Challenge the children with the following tasks:

With your back to the stick, jump over it. Repeat several times.

Jump over your stick and land facing the opposite direction.

Jump over your stick several times, increasing the height of your jump each time.

Skill-Development Activities (20 minutes)

Pass the Stick

Have the children sit in a circle, facing center, without sticks.

1. Describe and demonstrate the activity:

    As the music begins, I will lay one stick in front of one child.

    On the beat that child picks up the stick and places it on the floor in front of the child to the right (as I place another stick in front of the first child).

    As the first child picks up the second stick, the second child (seated on the first child's right) picks up the first stick and places it in front of the next child to the right. We will continue until each child has one stick.

    Then we will repeat the process, but to the left. (I will place a stick in front of the child to the left of the original first child; this will be the new "first" child.)

2. Have the children practice pass the stick to music.

Stick Flip

See Grades 2-3: Rhythmic Activities, Lesson 27, page 609.

Side Stick Flip

Keep the children in a large circle, each with a stick.

1. Describe and demonstrate the side stick flip to the right: *Tap the stick on the floor to the side, then flip it over and catch it.*
2. Have the children practice the side stick flip to the right.
3. Have them repeat to the left.
4. Have them repeat, alternating left and right.
5. Have them repeat, flipping right and left simultaneously.

Concluding Activities (5 minutes)

Stick Routine

Seat the children in a large circle, each with two sticks. Have the children perform the following routine to music:

> *Tap front* (four counts), *tap together* (four counts);
>
> *Tap to side* (four counts), *tap together* (four counts);
>
> *Touch and flip the right stick to the side* (four counts);
>
> *Touch and flip the left stick to the side* (four counts);
>
> *Touch and flip both sticks to the side* (eight counts).

LESSON 29
RHYTHM STICKS

Student Objectives

- Combine front tapping, side tapping, and flipping into a routine.

Equipment and Materials

- 2 rhythm sticks per child

Warm-Up Activities (5 minutes)

Stick Tricks

Use any of the hopping tasks. See Grades 2-3: Rhythmic Activities, Lesson 27, page 608.

Skill-Development Activities (20 minutes)

Rhythm Stick Routines

Use these activities to allow the children to enjoy and help them to refine the rhythm stick routines they have already learned. Allow the children to bring in their own music. Encourage the children to create their own routines.

Extension Activities

1. Rhythm stick routines make excellent demonstrations for school programs.
2. Paint the sticks with glow-in-the-dark paint and do the routines under black light. (This is especially effective for a Halloween night program.)

Concluding Activities (5 minutes)

Demonstration Routines

At the conclusion of each day, ask one or more groups or individuals to demonstrate their routines for the class.

GYMNASTICS

Gymnastics is a favorite activity for many children. Children who do not like gymnastics may have had a bad experience with it in the past or simply feel the skills are too difficult. Encourage all children, and work with those who are having trouble, helping them to master the basic skills. This will help them gain competence and therefore confidence.

Gymnastics enhances many aspects of physical education learning: it can develop fitness, foster cooperation, introduce a variety of skills, and allow children to express creativity. This gymnastics section builds on the lessons and activities in Grades K-1 and includes tumbling, partner stunts, and large and small equipment. The teacher may want to use Level One lessons instead if children have not had a good foundation in gymnastics. The lessons are progressive, so that lessons later in the section assume the children have mastered the content of earlier lessons.

We encourage a flexible approach to teaching gymnastics. Teach what you are comfortable with, repeat lessons as needed, and stop at any point and go to a different part of gymnastics. You know best what will work for your situation. So if you feel a part or a particular skill is inappropriate, delete that skill or lesson.

UNIT ORGANIZATION

This level includes tumbling, partner stunts, and small and large equipment. Early lessons review pretumbling skills, then progress to routines that combine skills. For second grade, consider repeating the first 10 lessons, rather than moving on to Lessons 11 through 14, as it may be better to save these tumbling lessons for experienced third graders. Several lessons incorporating partner stunts

and some fun—or silly—stunts follow. Next, students explore small equipment tasks found in Danish and modern gymnastics. The last several lessons allow the children to explore large equipment. Note that you may be able to use playground equipment for these lessons. Remember, we encourage you to do what is appropriate for your situation. Lessons 10 and 28 cover the gymnastics checklist (see the appendix), which you can use to evaluate student progress or the effectiveness of your instruction. For a summary of the content of this section, see table G2.3. Tables G2.1 and G2.2 show alternative ways to organize the lessons.

LESSON ORGANIZATION

Teach the children the warm-ups outlined immediately after this introduction so that children can quickly join in, knowing what you expect of them. Feel free, however, to vary these warm-ups, remembering that stretching is important before doing any gymnastics lesson. Keep in mind that children enjoy being the "leader" for the warm-up, so select a different child each day to lead the warm-up routine. The next part of each lesson includes the skill development activities, in which you introduce and have students practice new skills. The final section of each lesson are the concluding activities, which often combine skills or activities from previous lessons. See the equipment and material list at the beginning of each lesson.

TEACHING HINTS

As you well know, practicing skills allows students to master the skill, and repetition is an essential part of practice. Indeed, most children want many turns and do not want to stop at the end of class. You may want to vary practice by introducing a skill, practicing that skill several times for each child, then either introducing a new skill or reviewing a previous skill. Then alternate the two skills for several turns. You can continue this process, adding a new skill and practicing that with previous skills so that you do one turn of four or five skills with one child per group, then repeat the sequence with the next child in line. This type of practice is interesting. The children waiting in line can verbally state the skills they are watching others do.

Encourage, recognize, and praise good skill execution. Rather than focusing on learning new and difficult skills, help children focus on mastering and executing skills correctly. This encourages all children to participate fully as well as promotes safety.

SAFETY CONSIDERATIONS

Safety is a primary concern for any gymnastics unit, especially when using equipment. Teach, review, and enforce the safety rules and the class rules. For safety reasons, be aware that there will be times when many students are watching and few are practicing so that you can closely monitor their movements.

By second and third grades, often the most difficult children to keep safe are those who have the highest skill levels, for example, children who participate in gymnastics or dance outside of school. However, you must insist that children who have skills beyond the scope of this unit follow the rules, especially concerning performing only those activities you have assigned—just like everyone else. Although this can cause resentment, one child doing an advanced skill while other children are practicing basic skills can be dangerous. Sometimes it is helpful to simply acknowledge the fact that certain individuals can do more than you will teach. Consider also allowing such a child to demonstrate those skills at a specific time with a parent's written permission. If you address this issue immediately, you may prevent misunderstandings and injuries.

You must establish clear rules for practicing gymnastics. For example, practice only on the mats, have only one person on a mat at a time (unless specifically told otherwise by the teacher), and use equipment only as intended. We recommend dividing the children into as many groups as you have mats and space, keeping groups as small as possible to increase participation opportunities. Have each group sit in a line near the mat, waiting for turns and specific instructions. You may find it helpful to have a carpet square for each waiting child to sit on.

When starting each stunt, call the first child in each group to the mat. Do not allow children to stand on the floor at the end of the mat to begin a task. Instead, as you give instructions, children should stand (sit or lie) on the mat, beginning their turn when you say "Begin." You may want to use cues to regulate the movement, for example "bend, hands down, look at your tummy, roll." Stand so that you can see all children. If the activity requires spotting, you should spot the children. While this means more waiting for turns, it greatly increases safety. When children have learned to take turns, however, you can assign different skills to each mat, assigning one skill that you must spot, while having the children at the other mats do skills that do not require spotting. Remember to place yourself so you can see the other mats while spotting to monitor behavior. Efficient organization allows for maximum practice and safety.

Finally, it is your responsibility to see that you or another responsible adult maintains the gymnastics equipment in good order. You should check the mats and equipment to make sure everything is in good repair each day. In addition, make sure mats are cleaned regularly.

Table G2.1: Using the Gymnastics Lessons in a Six-Week Gymnastics Unit.

Week	Content	Number of different lessons	Lessons that should be repeated
1	Body parts, directions, locomotor skills	5 (1-5)	1, 5
2	Pretumbling and tumbling	5 (6-10)	9, 10
3	Tumbling	5 (11-15)	15
4	Partner stunts	4 (16-19)	16, 19
5	Small equipment	5 (20-24)	23
6	Large equipment	4 (24-27)	27

Table G2.2: Using the Gymnastics Lessons in an Eight-Week Gymnastics Unit

Week	Monday	Tuesday	Wednesday	Thursday	Friday
1	Lesson 1	Lesson 1	Lesson 2	Lesson 3	Lesson 4
2	Lesson 4	Lesson 5	Lesson 6	Lesson 7	Lesson 8
3	Lesson 9	Lesson 9	Lesson 10	Lesson 10	Lesson 11
4	Lesson 12	Lesson 13	Lesson 14	Lesson 14	Lesson 15
5	Lesson 16	Lesson 17	Lesson 18	Lesson 18	Lesson 19
6	Lesson 19	Lesson 20	Lesson 21	Lesson 22	Lesson 23
7	Lesson 23	Lesson 24	Lesson 25	Lesson 26	Lesson 26
8	Lesson 27	Lesson 27	Lesson 28	Lesson 28	Choose one lesson: 1, 4, 8, 10, 12, 15, 16, 20, or 24

Table G2.3: Unit Plan for Grades 2-3: Gymnastics

Week 8: warm-up, pretumbling, and review

Monday: warm-up practice
Tuesday: locomotor and tumbling skills
Wednesday: locomotor and tumbling skills
Thursday: locomotor and tumbling skills
Friday: gymnastics and tumbling

Week 9: stunts and tumbling

Monday: gymnastics and tumbling
Tuesday: balance and flexibility
Wednesday: handstand, backward roll, backbend, and toe-touch jump
Thursday: practice tumbling skills
Friday: gymnastics checklist

Week 10: stunts and tumbling

Monday: routine 1
Tuesday: routine 2
Wednesday: routine 3
Thursday: combined routine
Friday: partner stunts

Week 18: partner activities

Monday: partner stunts
Tuesday: partner and group stunts
Wednesday: tricky stunts
Thursday: silly-tricky stunts
Friday: small equipment

Week 19: small equipment

Monday: new skills with small equipment
Tuesday: streamers and hoops
Wednesday: streamers, balls, and hoops
Thursday: balance beam, jumping cubes, and climbing rope
Friday: small equipment

Week 20: large equipment

Monday: large equipment
Tuesday: balance beam, climbing ropes, ladder, jumping cubes, and vaulting cubes
Wednesday: balance beam, climbing ropes, ladder, jumping cubes, and vaulting cubes
Thursday: balance beam, climbing ropes, ladder, jumping cubes, and vaulting cubes
Friday: balance beam, climbing ropes, ladder, jumping cubes, and vaulting cubes

WARM-UPS

Listen and Move

1. Give the following instructions as quickly as the children can complete the tasks:

   Run 20 steps to the right.

   Make 10 big arm circles.

   Run 20 steps to the left.

   Touch your toes (bend knees slightly), reach for the sky. (Repeat 5 times.)

   Slide 10 steps to the right.

   Skip 10 skips forward.

   Jump as high as you can, 10 times.

   Hop backward 20 hops on your right foot, then your left foot.

   Twist your torso right, then left. (Repeat 5 times.)

2. Repeat the entire sequence at least once.

Steps for Grades 2-3 Warm-Up Routine

Stretches

Arrange the children in a long line on one side of the mat.

Head Stretches

Slowly move your head while providing support with your hands (chin to chest and up, then ear to shoulder and up, ear to opposite shoulder and up, chin on chest). Repeat. Place your hands palms above ears, fingers over top of skull.

Shoulder Circles

Roll your shoulders in circles forward then backward (hands on hips).

Torso Stretch

With arms extended overhead, stretch to the side, rear, opposite side, front.

Hamstring Stretch

Bend to a squat position with hands on the floor in front of your body, then slowly straighten your legs upward until your knees are only slightly bent.

Ankle Rotations

Sitting on the floor, with legs extended in a "V" position in front, move your ankles so your feet and toes make circles.

Back Arch

Rolling over onto your stomach, with legs stretched out (extended) and together behind, arms extended in front, look up to the ceiling, lift legs and feet as high as possible. Keep your stomach on the floor and your legs straight and together.

Endurance

Keep the children in a long line on one side of the mat.

Crunches

Do as many crunches as possible, up to 20. Bend your knees, place your fingers near your ears, with your hips at 90 degrees (making a corner of a square) and feet over hips or stomach (abdomen).

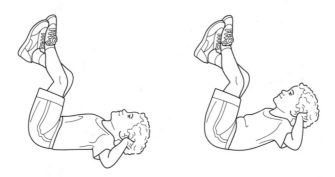

Push-Ups

Do as many push-ups as possible, up to 10. Keep your body straight, with your arms bending at the elbows to raise and lower your body.

Locomotor

Arrange the children in a large circle.

Skip Clockwise

Skip 24 steps clockwise (point), then go the other way and do 24 skips counterclockwise (point).

Vertical Jumps

Jump straight up, 5 to 10 in high (show height clearly).

Jog or Run

Try to jog or run in the circle for one minute without stopping.

Grades 2-3 Warm-Up Routine

Arrange the children in a line along one side of the mat.

1. Teach all parts of the warm-up as a routine.
2. Have the children perform the following sequence of steps:
   Head circle right, head circle left,
   Shoulder circle forward (3), shoulder circle backward (3),

Torso stretch (side, back, side, front); repeat 3 times,

Hamstring stretch (squat to straighten); repeat 5 times,

Ankle rotations inward (3), ankle rotations outward (3),

Back arches (5),

Crunches (20),

Push-ups (10),

(Move the children into a circle formation.)

Skip 24 skips clockwise, 24 counterclockwise,

10 vertical jumps, and

Run one minute continuously around the circle.

GRADES 2-3

GYMNASTICS

LESSON 1
WARM-UP PRACTICE

Student Objectives

- Learn the warm-up routine and be able to execute the routine with verbal cues.
- Walk, run, hop, skip, and jump in succession.
- Slide, gallop, and combine both skills.
- Know the safety rules.
- Give one reason for warming up before exercise.

Equipment and Materials

- 1 or more mats (4 ft × 8 ft) per group
- Background music is helpful

Safety Tips

Review the class rules and the following safety rules:

- *Rule 1: Take turns. Only one child on a mat at a time. Try once, then allow the next child to have a turn.*
- *Rule 2: Do all tumbling on a mat.*
- *Rule 3: Stay at your mat until your teacher tells you to move.*
- *Rule 4: Keep your hands to yourself.*
- *Rule 5: Perform only those activities that are assigned to the mat.*
- *Rule 6: Be a good spotter.*

Warm-Up Activities (5 minutes)

Listen and Move

See Grades 2-3: Gymnastics, Warm-Ups, page 616.

Skill-Development Activities (20 minutes)

Steps for Warm-Up Routine

Arrange the children in a long line on one side of the mats.

1. Discuss the importance of warming up: *Does anyone know why warming up is so important before exercise?* (To prevent injury and to promote conditioning by increasing flexibility, strength, and endurance.)
2. Tell the children: *"Flexibility" is range of motion in a joint.*
3. Describe and demonstrate each component of the Grades 2-3 Warm-Up Routine. See Grades 2-3: Gymnastics, Warm-Ups, page 616.
4. Have the children practice each component of the routine.
5. Go through the complete Grades 2-3 Warm-Up Routine with cues (see page 617), but with less instruction.

Safety Rules

Gather the children into an information formation. Review the safety rules as listed under Safety Tips at the beginning of this lesson (page 619).

Concluding Activities (5 minutes)

Locomotor Person

Divide the children into four groups, and place one group in each corner of the play area. Have the children move across the play area in groups using the patterns you call out, as follows, reminding them to be careful of others:

Skip.

Hop on your right foot.

Gallop with your left foot leading.

Slide with your right foot leading.

Run.

Slide with your left foot leading.

Leap.

Hop with your left foot leading.

Gallop with your right foot leading.

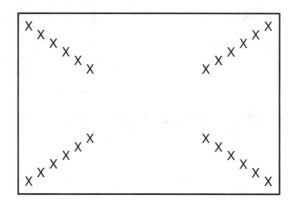

LESSON 2
LOCOMOTOR AND TUMBLING SKILLS

Student Objectives

- Demonstrate three of the following pretumbling skills: basic leap, log roll, rocker, one-legged balance, straddle scale.
- Practice independently, staying on-task.

Equipment and Materials

- 1 or more mats (4 ft × 8 ft) per group
- Background music (optional)
- Carpet squares

Safety Tips

- Have the children sit on carpet squares between turns on the mat.
- Enforce the safety rules.

Warm-Up Activities (5 to 7 minutes)

Grades 2-3 Warm-Up Routine

See Grades 2-3: Gymnastics, Warm-Ups, page 617.

Skill-Development Activities (16 to 20 minutes)

Pretumbling Skills

Arrange small groups, each at a mat. The children will take turns practicing, so line up the children to emphasize that only one child goes at a time.

Basic Leap

1. Describe and demonstrate the stunt:

   Run and take off on one foot, travel through the air, and land on the opposite foot.

   Stretch out your arms at shoulder height, slightly in front of your body.

   Practice so you can go farther and higher.

2. Have the children practice the basic leap.

Log Roll

1. Describe and demonstrate the stunt:

   Lying on one side with arms and legs together and extended crosswise on the mat, roll onto your stomach and quickly over onto your other side, continuing rolling over until you reach the other end of the mat.

You start the rolling motion by turning your head and shoulders, then your trunk and legs. Your hands and feet should not push to turn your body.

2. Have the children practice the log roll.

Rocker

1. Describe and demonstrate the stunt:

   Beginning in a tight tuck while sitting with your hands and arms tightly holding your shins, chin on chest, and forehead against knees, roll backward onto your back.

   While your body weight is on your shoulders, change the direction of the roll and rock back toward your feet until your bottom and feet are the only parts touching the ground. Continue rocking from your bottom and feet to your shoulders, and then reverse.

2. Have the children practice the rocker.

One-Legged Balance

1. Describe and demonstrate the stunt:

   Standing with hands on hips, raise one leg until your foot clears the floor and is near the knee of your support leg. Hold this position as long as possible (at least 10 seconds).

2. Have the children practice the one-legged balance.

Straddle Scale

1. Describe and demonstrate the stunt:

   Standing with feet together, slowly slide your feet out to each side with either your toes pointing in the direction of the slide or your feet parallel to each other (demonstrate "parallel" very clearly).

   As your feet move apart, lower your torso so that when your feet have stretched as far sideways as is comfortable, your torso (chest) is parallel to (flat as) the ground.

   Stretch your arms out to the side shoulder-high, so you can barely see your hands when you are looking straight forward.

   Balance in this position for five counts, then reach to the floor with your arms, put your body weight on your arms, lower your chest to the floor, and gradually move your feet and legs together. Your body will end up flat on the floor.

2. Have the children practice the straddle scale.

Concluding Activities (5 to 7 minutes)

Discussion

1. Ask the following questions about today's pretumbling skills:

   Which skill did you like best?

   Which skill was the hardest?

2. Ask small groups of children to perform their favorite skill for the class.

LESSON 3
LOCOMOTOR AND TUMBLING SKILLS

Student Objectives

- Complete a forehead touch, a forward roll, or a donkey kick.
- Maintain a balance position after executing a locomotor pattern.
- State the reason for the head position when doing the forward roll.

Equipment and Materials

- 1 or more mats (4 ft × 8 ft) per group
- Background music (optional)

Safety Tip

- Review the safety rules.

Warm-Up Activities (5 to 7 minutes)

Grades 2-3 Warm-Up Routine

See Grades 2-3: Gymnastics, Warm-Ups, page 617.

Skill-Development Activities (18 to 20 minutes)

Review the safety rules before introducing the new skills.

Forehead Touch

Arrange small groups at the mats. If there is no danger of children bumping into each other or falling off the mats, allow two or three children on a mat at once for this stunt only.

1. Describe and demonstrate the stunt:

    Kneel with your feet and knees tightly together and your hands clasped behind your back.

    Slowly lower your head until your forehead touches the mat.

    To finish, raise back to kneeling position without using your hands for balance or support.

2. Have the children practice the forehead touch.

Forward Roll

Arrange the children in small groups, each in a line at the side of the mat.

1. Describe and demonstrate the stunt:

    Begin by squatting on the mat, with your hands placed just in front of and outside your feet and your arms outside your legs.

In one motion, straighten your legs (look at your tummy with your chin on your chest if possible), shifting about half your body weight onto your hands and arms.

Bend your arms to support more weight until you are using only your feet for balance.

Then move your hips above your shoulders and forward.

At some point your hips will overbalance, and your body will roll forward.

Land on your shoulder blades.

2. Have the children practice the forward roll. Tell the children: *Remember, keep your chin tucked close to your chest. The momentum will carry your body around in a circle, but your legs must stay tucked tightly. Keep your whole body curled into a ball to help you roll!*

3. Ask the children: *What is the correct head position for the forward roll?* (Chin tucked.)

4. Ask: *Why is this position important?* (To protect the head and neck, especially to keep the head from suffering impact during the roll.)

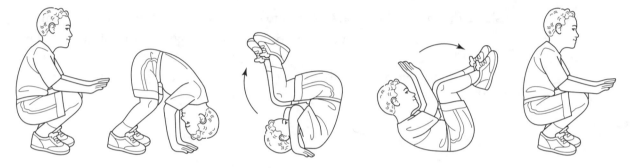

Donkey Kick

Continue with small groups, with only one child at a mat.

1. Describe and demonstrate the stunt:

The object of this task is to get both feet off the mat at the same time and to support all your body weight with your hands.

Begin by standing in the middle of the mat, facing the length of the mat. Place both hands on the mat, about shoulder-width apart.

Keep your arms straight, but bend your legs slightly. Let your hands carry some of your body weight.

As you kick your feet up and back, take all your weight on your hands. Keep your eyes focused on the mat, directly between your hands.

Be careful not to kick very hard, as this may cause overbalancing, and you may flip over onto your back. The purpose is to get both feet off the ground and support your weight with your arms, not to get into a vertical position (90 degrees is safer).

2. Have the children practice the donkey kick.

Concluding Activities (5 minutes)

Pretumbling Skills

Review with the children the skills practiced yesterday (basic leap, log roll, rocker, one-legged balance, and straddle scale).

1. Ask the first person in line at each mat to select and perform one of those stunts.
2. Then the next person has to perform a different stunt, and so on, until each child has had a turn.
3. If there is time, rotate to another first person in line and repeat. You may want to incorporate the tumbling from today's lesson as well.

GYMNASTICS

LESSON 4
LOCOMOTOR AND TUMBLING SKILLS

Student Objectives

- Practice the backward roll, the tripod, and the two-knee scale.
- Execute two different locomotor-to-balance combinations.
- State that body weight should be supported by the arms and hands during the backward roll.

Equipment and Materials

- 1 or more mats (4 ft × 8 ft) per group
- Background music (optional)

Safety Tip

- Enforce the safety rules.

Warm-Up Activities (5 minutes)

Grades 2-3 Warm-Up Routine

See Grades 2-3: Gymnastics, Warm-Ups, page 617.

Skill-Development Activities (20 minutes)

Two-Knee Scale

Place small groups, one at each mat.

1. Describe and demonstrate the stunt:

   Begin by kneeling (with your hips extended so your bottom does not touch your feet or legs), with your arms extended to the sides.

   Then lift your feet from the mat, so that only your knees are supporting your body weight.

2. Have the children practice the two-knee scale.

Backward Roll

Continue with the same setup.

1. Describe and demonstrate the stunt:

   Begin in a squat position on the mat, with your back toward the length of the mat.

   Place your hands on your shoulders with your palms up (as if to catch a penny from the sky).

   Press your chin against your chest and look at your tummy.

Rock to begin moving—lean slightly forward and then push backward with your toes.

Momentum carries your body into a roll, with your body parts touching the mat in this order: bottom, back, shoulders/hands, head/hands, hands. This allows you to recover (land) on your feet.

With a little push from your hands, you can straighten your legs and stand back up.

2. Have the children practice the backward roll.

3. Ask: *What supports your body weight during the backward roll?* (The hands and arms, not the head or neck).

Tripod

Continue with the same setup.

1. Describe and demonstrate the stunt:

    Begin in a squat, with your hands and arms placed on the mat outside your knees and legs.

    Bend forward until your forehead (at the hairline) touches the mat. Your head will serve as a balance point but will support very little weight.

    Bend your arms and make your knees touch your elbows. Support most of your body weight with your arms.

    Stop moving when your knees are resting on your elbows, your head is touching the mat, and your feet are off the mat.

    Remember, support most of your weight on your arms. Your head touches the mat but does not support much body weight.

2. Have the children practice the tripod.

Locomotor-to-Balance Combinations

Keep the children in small groups, each group at a mat. Ask the children to perform each combination as they move across the mat, one at a time:

Skipping to a one-legged balance

Hopping to a donkey kick

Walking to a forward roll

Concluding Activities (5 minutes)

Locomotor-to-Balance Combinations

Ask the children to create a similar combination to show you and the class.

GRADES 2-3

GYMNASTICS

LESSON 5
GYMNASTICS AND TUMBLING

Student Objectives
- Attempt new skills.
- Practice new and previous skills.
- Work cooperatively as a spotter.
- State one reason using a spotter is important.
- Name one skill that reverses momentum.

Equipment and Materials
- 1 or more mats (4 ft × 8 ft) per group
- Background music (optional)

Safety Tip
- Use spotters, emphasizing safety for both the spotter and the performer.

Warm-Up Activities (5 minutes)

Grades 2-3 Warm-Up Routine
See Grades 2-3: Gymnastics, Warm-Ups, page 617.

Skill-Development Activities (20 minutes)

Advanced Forward Roll
Arrange small groups, each at a mat.

1. Describe and ask a child to demonstrate the stunt:

    Begin by standing on the mat with your arms extended overhead.

    Bend and reach forward to the mat with your arms, head tucked to look at your stomach.

    As your arms begin to support your weight, straighten your legs to move your hips up and over your shoulders.

    Gradually bend your arms and allow your hips to overbalance, rolling your torso over to land on your shoulder blades. Immediately tuck your body.

    Continue rolling until your feet touch the mat. Reach forward with your arms, and stand up with your arms extended overhead.

2. Discuss the differences between the advanced forward roll and the forward roll: *How are the two stunts different?* (The beginning and ending positions and the recovery to the feet.)

3. Encourage proper technique: *Do not place your hands under your bottom to push.*

4. Have the children practice the advanced forward roll.

5. Cue the children: *Arms up high, look at your tummy, roll, stand, arms up! Stay tucked! Push with your hands. Land on your feet only!*

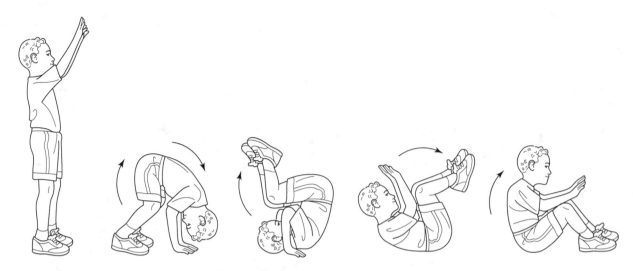

Momentum

Gather the children into an information formation. Present the idea of "momentum" to the children.

1. *"Momentum" means movement. Momentum is influenced by speed and body weight.*

2. *Two forces that influence momentum are "gravity" and "inertia." Gravity pulls things toward the earth. Gravity is why you land when you jump. Inertia means that objects try to keep going at the same speed. This means that things that are still will remain still, and things that are moving keep moving.*

3. *So, to get a still body moving, sometimes we move one or more body parts in the opposite direction first, then reverse the direction to help create momentum. Remember that once a body part is moving it wants to keep moving—because of inertia—even if we must change directions.*

4. *When we are trying to move away from earth, we must have enough momentum to overcome gravity (the pull to earth) and inertia (the body wanting to stay still).*

Shoulder Roll

Send the children back to their mats.

1. Describe and ask a child to demonstrate the stunt:

    Begin by sitting on the mat, with your back facing the length of the mat. Stretch your legs straight out directly in front of your body.

    Begin to move by reaching forward to your toes with your arms, then rolling backward, looking to one side. Stay close to the mat on this roll.

    Lift your legs and torso over the shoulder you are not looking toward.

    Extend your arms to the sides as your body passes over your head. Land on your knees.

2. Have the children practice the shoulder roll. Cue the children: *Reach for your toes, look to the side, roll, balance. Stay low!*

Handstand

Continue at the mats. At first the child's body weight is supported on the hands for only brief periods of time. As each child practices this skill, his or her balance time should increase.

1. Describe and have a child demonstrate the stunt while you spot:

   When you are first learning the handstand, your biggest goal should be to control the upward and downward movement, taking care not to overbalance and land on your back.

   Begin by standing with your arms overhead and one leg extended in front of your body.

   Step forward on your extended (front) leg (to gain momentum) and reach for the mat with your hands.

   Take your weight on your arms as you extend one leg behind your body and use the other leg for support.

   Lift your support leg off the ground with a slight kick as your arms take all your weight.

   The first leg to go up is going to be the support leg on the recovery.

   As the recovery leg takes the weight, lift your arms and step backward into the starting position with arms overhead, standing on one leg with the other leg extended forward.

2. Have the children practice the handstand. Cue the children: *Arms up high, one leg up at a time, step, lean, hands down, kick, stand. Arms straight!*

Handstand Spotting

1. Stand to the side and in front of the tumbler, near where the tumbler's hands will touch the mat.
2. Place one hand on the tumbler's thigh (to control the handstand and to keep the tumbler from overbalancing). Place your other hand under the tumbler's shoulder (to provide upward support and keep the head from hitting the mat if the arms give way).

Run and Takeoff

Continue with the same setup.

1. Describe and demonstrate the stunt:

   Many sports use this movement (e.g., springboard diving).

   Begin with several quick (running) steps leading to a hurdle.

   To hurdle raise one leg so that your thigh is parallel to (flat as) the ground and your lower leg is at a 90-degree angle to the thigh (like the corner of a square).

Reach your arms high overhead as your body lifts off the ground. Both your raised arms and lifted thigh help your body gain momentum. Momentum helps you gain height in the hurdle.

Land from the hurdle on both feet (spread about shoulder-width apart).

Follow the landing immediately with a jump to full extension.

This movement can come right before a tumbling stunt or end with a jump.

Today, I want you to practice finishing with a jump and landing on two feet.

2. Have the children practice the run and takeoff. Cue the children: *Run, run, run, step-hurdle, jump! Reach high!*

Leap

Keep the children at the mats. Mention that this is also known as the grand jeté.

1. Describe and demonstrate the stunt:

   The objects are to get as high as possible and to have your legs close to a split position while you're in the air.

   Take several running steps, push off from one leg, and land on the opposite foot as far away as possible.

2. Have the children practice leaping. Cue the children: *Run, run, run, leap! Pretend you are running and jumping over a small stream!*

Concluding Activities (5 minutes)

Gymnastics Skills

Continue with groups at the mats. Review with the children the skills practiced (advanced forward roll, shoulder roll, handstand, run and takeoff, and leap).

1. Ask the first person in line at each mat to perform one of those stunts.
2. Then the next person has to perform a different stunt, and so on until each child has had a turn.
3. If there is time, rotate to another first person in line and repeat.

GYMNASTICS

LESSON 6
GYMNASTICS AND TUMBLING

Student Objectives

- Attempt a split, a V-seat, and a 360-degree turn.
- Practice the forward roll, shoulder roll, handstand, and run and takeoff.
- Name two gymnastics skills that require balance or flexibility.

Equipment and Materials

- 1 or more mats (4 ft × 8 ft) per group
- Background music (optional)

Safety Tip

- Remind the children of the importance of warming up before practicing any gymnastics skills.

Warm-Up Activities (5 minutes)

Grades 2-3 Warm-Up Routine

See Grades 2-3: Gymnastics, Warm-Ups, page 617.

Skill-Development Activities (20 minutes)

V-Seat

Arrange small groups, each at a mat.

1. Describe and demonstrate the stunt:

   Begin sitting on the floor with your hands supporting and balancing part of your body weight.

   Place your palms flat on the floor, to the rear of your body, slightly more than shoulder-width apart.

   Keep your arms straight, and your arms and torso still (stationary). Your torso should be at a 45-degree angle to the ground (show angle clearly). Bend your legs at the knees, pulling them to your chest.

   Keeping your knees close together, extend your legs at a 45-degree angle to the ground (again, show angle clearly).

   Extend your feet and point your toes. Your legs and torso should make a "V."

   Hold this position for several seconds, and then rebend your knees and return to the starting position.

2. Have the children practice the V-seat.

3. Point out that the V-seat requires both balance and flexibility.

Regular Split

Keep the children at the mats.

1. Describe and have a child demonstrate the stunt:

   This skill also requires good flexibility, which is part of physical fitness. You can increase your flexibility quickly if you work on it, but never stretch to the point of pain.

   Begin in a position that looks like a giant step, with your legs spread apart, both feet on the ground, and both arms hanging down at your sides.

   Rotate your back leg slightly so that foot is perpendicular to the step (turned to one side). (Show very clearly.)

   Keep your torso facing forward and both legs straight at all times.

   Slide your front leg forward slowly, as far as possible, or until your legs are fully extended and touching the ground. Use your arms for support and balance.

   Never force the split! Stop whenever there is pain or pulling in your back or inside of your leg.

   With practice and increased flexibility, you should be able to straighten that leg.

2. Have the children practice the split.

360-Degree Turn

Continue at the mats.

1. Describe and demonstrate the stunt:

   Begin by standing still and straight, and pick out a target to look at directly in front of you.

   Decide whether you will turn clockwise or counterclockwise (point).

   With your knees bent and arms and torso turning away from the direction you want to turn, jump up and turn your head, torso, and arms as hard and fast as possible in the direction you want to turn.

   Land on both feet, while looking at the target. The object is to turn the full 360 degrees (full circle) without losing your balance.

2. Have the children practice the 360-degree turn.

Skill Review

Keep the children at the mats. Have the children review and practice the forward roll, the shoulder roll, and the handstand. Ask the children:

> *Which skills require balance?* (V-seat, handstand.)
>
> *Which skills require flexibility?* (V-seat, split.)

Concluding Activities (5 minutes)

Run and Takeoff and 360-Degree Turn

Continue at the mats. Remind the children to go one at a time in their groups to avoid collisions.

Have the children practice combining the run and takeoff with the 360-degree turn. Some children may do more than 360 degrees—that is great!

GYMNASTICS

LESSON 7
BALANCE AND FLEXIBILITY

Student Objectives

- Perform flexibility activities.
- Explore new positions that alter the balance point.
- Work independently to demonstrate the most difficult or favorite balance.

Equipment and Materials

- 1 or more mats (4 ft × 8 ft) per group
- Background music (optional)

Safety Tip

- Review the safety rules.
- Children with weak abdominal muscles and poor flexibility should not do the back push-up portion of the back flexibility exercise.

Warm-Up Activities (5 minutes)

Grades 2-3 Warm-Up Routine

See Grades 2-3: Gymnastics, Warm-Ups, page 617.

Skill-Development Activities (20 minutes)

Discussion

Gather the children into an information formation.

1. Introduce the concept of "center of gravity" to the children: *Your "center of gravity" is the point in your body where segments (parts) on opposite sides balance. The center of gravity moves, depending upon the positions of your body and body parts. For example, moving your arms forward changes your center of gravity, as does bending or squatting. Balancing depends upon maintaining the center of gravity.*

2. Demonstrate an example, such as those presented.

3. Use the idea of center of gravity to introduce the balance tasks in this lesson.

Knee Scale

Arrange the mats in one long line (or two medium lines), and arrange the children in a line on one long side of the mats, at least arm's-length apart.

1. Describe and demonstrate the stunt:

   Begin on all-fours, with knees together and hands about shoulder distance apart.

   Extend one leg to the rear with toes pointed, lifting the leg as high as possible.

   Look forward and hold your head high.

2. Have the children practice the knee scale.

Arabesque

Continue with the same setup, double-checking that the children are still at least arm's-length apart.

1. Describe and demonstrate the stunt:

   To begin, step onto your supporting leg, which should stay as straight as possible.

   Lower your torso toward the ground while raising your nonsupporting leg to the rear. Keep this leg straight as well. Bring your torso as close to parallel to (flat as) the ground as possible.

   Hold your arms extended to the sides shoulder-high and do not move them in relation to your torso.

   After holding the final position for 5 to 10 seconds, return to standing.

2. Have the children practice the arabesque. Cue the children: *Arms forward. Can you see your thumbs? Try the arabesque scale, but move one arm back and the other forward (with both arms back, with one leg slightly bent).*

Straight Scale

Continue with the same setup, double-checking that the children are still at least arm's-length apart.

1. Describe and demonstrate the stunt:

   Begin standing on one leg, with the other leg bent so that the foot rests on the support leg's knee.

   With your arms extended high overhead, rise up on your toes and hold for 5 to 10 counts.

2. Have the children practice the straight scale. Remind the children: *High on your toes!*

Back Push-Up

Continue with the same setup, double-checking that the children are still at least arm's-length apart.

1. Describe and demonstrate the stunt:

   Lie on your back on the mat with your knees bent, feet spread slightly (no more than shoulder-width apart).

   Point your toes forward, and place your hands palms down on the mat and fingers under your shoulders, pointing toward your feet.

Push down on the mat to raise your stomach and torso. Gradually straighten your arms and legs until your body forms an arch.

Your head should be back as far as possible (looking down toward the mat).

2. Have the children practice the back push-up. *Note*: Children tend to learn this stunt in stages: Stage 1 is to get back off the mat. Stage 2 is to get the body and head clear of the mat. Stage 3 is to get into the arched position.

3. Use the remaining time to practice the knee scale, arabesque, straight scale, and back push-up.

Back Push-Up Spotting

1. *Kneel at the child's side, with your hands placed under the midback and shoulders.*

2. *As the child pushes upward, give support. Do not lift or force the movement; rather, make the child do the work of lifting and allow him or her to arch as much as he or she can.*

3. *If the child's feet are slipping, first try moving the child's heels closer to his or her bottom; next try having someone stand at the child's feet, using his or her feet to brace the child's feet. (Do not stand on the child's feet, just keep them from slipping.)*

Concluding Activities (5 minutes)

Movement Challenges

Have the first person in each group get onto the mat.

1. Present the following movement challenges to all children, one child per group at a time:

   Show me your favorite scale or balance position.

   Can you move your arms and still balance?

   Can you think of another way to balance?

   Show me a difficult balance.

2. Continue until all children have tried each challenge.

GYMNASTICS

LESSON 8

HANDSTAND, BACKWARD ROLL, BACKBEND, AND TOE-TOUCH JUMP

Student Objectives

- Execute a backward roll.
- Perform either a back push-up or backbend, with spotting.
- Attempt a toe-touch jump.

Equipment and Materials

- 1 or more mats (4 ft × 8 ft) per group
- Background music (optional)

Safety Tips

- Require spotting during class for the backbend. Encourage children who practice at home to use a spotter as well.
- Children with weak abdominal muscles should not attempt the backbend.

Warm-Up Activities (5 minutes)

Grades 2-3 Warm-Up Routine

See Grades 2-3: Gymnastics, Warm-Ups, page 617.

Skill-Development Activities (20 minutes)

Backward Roll

Arrange small groups, each group at a mat.

1. Have the children practice the backward roll several times. See Grades 2-3: Gymnastics, Lesson 4, page 627.
2. Remind the children: *Push with your hands! Don't stop on your bottom.*

Standing Backward Roll

Keep the same setup.

1. Describe and demonstrate the stunt:

    Begin standing, with your back toward the length of the mat and your arms extended overhead.

    While bending your knees to squat, bend your arms and move your hands (palms up) to rest on your shoulders. From this point, the standing backward roll goes like the backward roll.

    Tuck your chin against your chest, overbalance backward, and roll while pushing with your hands.

    Land on your feet, ending standing tall with your arms extended above your head.

2. One child per mat at a time, have the children practice the beginning for the standing backward roll (to the point it becomes the same as the backward roll).

3. Have them practice the entire roll.

Back Push-Ups

See Grades 2-3: Gymnastics, Lesson 7, page 638.

Backbend

Assign children who are able to do a back push-up to one or two mats. Only these children should attempt backbends, with spotting. Have the remaining children continue practicing back push-ups in groups at separate mats. Keep an eye on the entire class.

1. Describe and demonstrate the stunt: *Begin with your back to the length of the mat, arms extended overhead, feet shoulder-width apart, and toes facing forward. Your torso and legs will stay still for part 1.*

    Part 1: *Drop your head back so you can look at the ceiling or sky, and continue to move your arms and head back until they are as far back as possible.*

    Part 2: *Keep your legs straight, and arch your shoulders and back as your arms and head lead the way. The object is for the bones in your back (vertebrae) to bend in succession from the top of your spine to the bottom of your spine.*

    Part 3: *Bend your legs slightly so your hands can hit the mat. Now straighten your legs, and let your hands leave the mat. Your spine straightens from the bottom up, and your arms and torso move upward. Keep your torso straight, and move your arms overhead as your head returns to start. The motion going down is slow and controlled. The motion going up is faster.*

3. Have the children practice the backbend as you spot.

Backbend Spotting

1. There are two spotting techniques that work equally well. The front-facing technique is preferred for taller tumblers; the side technique is fine for small children.

2. The front-facing technique begins with you (the teacher) facing the child with hands on the child's hips. As the child bends, the spotter provides support so the child will not fall backward uncontrolled.

3. The side technique begins with you (the teacher) kneeling at the tumbler's side, one hand on the upper arm and the other hand on the middle of the back. Again, the object is to support and control the backbend.

Backbend spotting

Toe-Touch Jump

Return to the original setup with small groups, each at a mat.

1. Describe and demonstrate the stunt:

   Begin with a run and takeoff and jump as high as possible.
   Then lift your legs into a straddle position.
   At the top of the jump, reach for your toes, trying to touch them.
   Land on both feet.

2. Have the children practice the toe-touch jump.

Skill Practice

Continue with the same setup. Have the children practice the toe-touch jump, standing backward roll, and either the back push-up or backbend.

Concluding Activities (5 minutes)

Follow the Leader

Arrange the children in a line at one end of the mats.

1. Select a "good tumbler" as the first child in line. Describe the game:

   The leader performs a forward roll on the first mat, then moves to the second mat and performs a backward roll, while the second child in line does a forward roll on the first mat.

   Then the leader moves to the third mat and does a shoulder roll, as the rest of the group follows, one at a time.

   The skill at the fourth mat is a backbend or back push-up (teacher spots).

   The fifth mat is toe-touch jump, and the sixth mat is a V-seat.

   The leader sits (in a designated spot) when she or he finishes, and the rest of you do the same.

2. Have the children play the game. Cue the children: *forward roll, backward roll, shoulder roll, backbend or back push-up, toe-touch jump,* and *V-seat.*

GRADES 2-3

GYMNASTICS

LESSON 9
PRACTICE TUMBLING SKILLS

Student Objectives

- Practice tumbling skills.
- State the safety rules on request.
- Work cooperatively with a small group.

Equipment and Materials

- 1 or more mats (4 ft × 8 ft) per group
- Background music (optional)

Warm-Up Activities (5 minutes)

Grades 2-3 Warm-Up Routine

See Grades 2-3: Gymnastics, Warm-Ups, page 617.

Skill-Development Activities (24 minutes)

Gather the children into an information formation.

Ask: *Who can state one of the safety rules for gymnastics?* Allow children to respond until all rules have been stated. See Grades 2-3: Gymnastics, Lesson 1, Safety Tips, page 619 for suggested list of safety rules.

Gymnastics Practice Stations

Create small groups, and assign each group to a mat.

1. Describe and demonstrate each station:

    Station 1: Forward roll

    Station 2: Backward roll

    Station 3: Shoulder roll

    Station 4: Toe-touch jump and 360-degree turn

    Station 5: Backbends and handstands (you spot here)

    Station 6: Splits and V-seats

2. Have the children use the space surrounding the mats to practice leaps and run and takeoffs.

3. Have the children rotate after three minutes at each station, so that each child has an opportunity to practice all the skills each day.

Concluding Activities (1 minute)

Take a minute to answer any questions the children may have and to compliment safe behavior.

GRADES 2-3

GYMNASTICS

LESSON 10
GYMNASTICS CHECKLIST

Student Objectives

- Participate in evaluation of gymnastics skills.
- The teacher will observe and evaluate the children's performance of gymnastics skills.

Equipment and Materials

- 1 or more mats (4 ft × 8 ft) per group
- Background music (optional)

Warm-Up Activities (5 minutes)

Grades 2-3 Warm-Up Routine

See Grades 2-3: Gymnastics, Warm-Ups, page 617.

Skill-Development Activities (25 minutes)

Checklist

Assign small groups to stations to practice items on the checklist.

1. As soon as you have observed all the children, or every five minutes, rotate the children.
2. For recording student results, use the Evaluation Checklist for Grades 2-3 Gymnastics in the appendix.
3. Describe each item on the checklist and what you will evaluate.
4. Have a child demonstrate each item.
5. Have the children practice the items as you observe and record.

Concluding Activities

None.

GYMNASTICS

LESSON 11
ROUTINE 1

Student Objectives

- Perform a routine with five stunts.
- Verbally state the order of the stunts in the routine.
- Compliment one of their group members.

Equipment and Materials

- 1 or more mats (4 ft × 8 ft) per group
- Background music (optional)

Warm-Up Activities (5 minutes)

Grades 2-3 Warm-Up Routine

See Grades 2-3: Gymnastics, Warm-Ups, page 617.

Skill-Development Activities (20 minutes)

Routine 1

Create small groups, and assign each to a mat. Keep groups as small as possible to increase participation opportunities.

There are two objectives today: first to foster cooperation and second to combine gymnastics skills. The children should demonstrate cooperation by spotting each other for the handstand and by encouraging and complimenting each other during practice.

1. Describe and demonstrate the routine:

   Begin standing on the mat facing the length of the mat in an arabesque. You can determine the style (arms to the side, leg bent, arms extended forward and backward along the body).

   After holding for five seconds, stand and execute a forward roll to a stand.

   Squatting, do a tripod for five seconds then stand, jump, and do a 360-degree turn, landing on both feet facing the same direction.

   End with the splits.

2. Have the children practice Routine 1, one child per group at a time. When the first child in each group has completed the routine, have the next child follow your verbal instructions.

3. Lead all the children in saying the stunts in order aloud before each turn begins.

4. Continue until all children have had several trials practicing the routine.

Concluding Activities (5 minutes)

Allow as many volunteers as possible to demonstrate the routine individually. You may also wish to have groups select their best tumbler to demonstrate.

LESSON 12
ROUTINE 2

Student Objectives

- Demonstrate a routine with three stunts and a reversal of direction.
- Take turns practicing.
- Follow instructions.

Equipment and Materials

- 1 or more mats (4 ft × 8 ft) per group
- Background music (optional)

Warm-Up Activities (5 minutes)

Grades 2-3 Warm-Up Routine

See Grades 2-3: Gymnastics, Warm-Ups, page 617.

Skill-Development Activities (20 minutes)

Routine 2

Create small groups, and assign each to a mat.

1. Describe and have one child demonstrate the routine. Have all children say the skills in order aloud:

   Begin, standing on the mat with your back to the length of the mat.

   Do a straight scale, holding for five seconds.

   From a standing position, do a backward roll back to standing.

   Run several steps toward the starting position and do a toe-touch jump on the mat.

2. Have the children practice Routine 2, one child per group at a time. When the first child in each group has completed the routine, have the next child follow your verbal instructions.

3. Lead all the children in saying the stunts in order aloud before each turn begins.

4. Continue until all children have had several trials practicing the routine.

Concluding Activities (5 minutes)

Ask each child to take a turn complimenting another child in their group (at their mat).

Balance-Off

Place two children from each group on each mat. You may want to try to distract the more-skilled children. This will make the activity sillier and less competitive.

1. Have the children on the mats do the straight scale, beginning on your signal.

   Hold the position as long as possible.

   The last child balancing will go on to perform in the next round.

   Now, let's have the rest of the children balance in the same way.

   The last child standing will move to the next round.

2. After a brief rest, have the two children who balanced longest stand on their mats doing the straight scale as long as possible.

3. Have the remaining children clap or chant to encourage them.

LESSON 13
ROUTINE 3

Student Objectives

- Demonstrate a routine with two balance stunts.
- Work cooperatively.
- Follow a peer's instructions.

Equipment and Materials

- 1 or more mats (4 ft × 8 ft) per group
- Background music (optional)

Warm-Up Activities (5 minutes)

Grades 2-3 Warm-Up Routine

See Grades 2-3: Gymnastics, Warm-Ups, page 617.

Skill-Development Activities (20 minutes)

Routine 3

Create small groups, and assign each to a mat.

1. Describe and have one child demonstrate the routine:

    Begin, sitting on the mat, with your back to the length of the mat.

    Do a V-seat, holding for five seconds.

    Then lie down immediately and do a back push-up, return to lying down, then to sitting.

    Do a shoulder roll to a knee scale; hold for five seconds.

2. Have all children say the skills in order aloud.

3. Have the children practice Routine 3, one child per group at a time. When the first child in each group has completed the routine, have the next child follow your verbal instructions.

4. Lead all the children in saying the stunts in order aloud before each turn begins.

5. Continue until all children have had several trials practicing the routine.

Concluding Activities (5 minutes)

Group Routine 3

Arrange four or five children along one side of the mat, sitting with backs facing the other side of the mat. If a group is too crowded for safety, add another mat and spread the children out.

1. Have the entire group do the routine simultaneously, as one child in the group calls out the tasks.
2. Repeat with the other groups at other mats.

LESSON 14
COMBINED ROUTINES

Student Objectives

- Perform a routine with three parts and 13 tasks.

Equipment and Materials

- 1 or more mats (4 ft × 8 ft) per group
- Background music (optional)

Warm-Up Activities (5 minutes)

Grades 2-3 Warm-Up Routine

See Grades 2-3: Gymnastics, Warm-Ups, page 617.

Skill-Development Activities (20 minutes)

Combined Routine

Create small groups, and assign each to a mat. Keep the groups as small as possible to increase participation opportunities.

1. Describe the routine:

    Today we combine the three routines we have learned, in order to make three "passes," or trips, down the mat.

    Perform Routine 1 (see Lesson 11), going forward down the mat.

    Then do Routine 2 (see Lesson 12), moving backward and then forward.

    Finally, do Routine 3 (see Lesson 13), moving backward toward the starting place.

2. Go through the details of the routine, referring to Lessons 11, 12, and 13. Have one child demonstrate as you describe the routine.

3. Have all children say the skills in order aloud.

4. Have the children practice the Combined Routine, one child per group at a time. When the first child in each group has completed the routine, have the next child follow your verbal instructions.

5. Lead all the children in saying the stunts in order aloud before each turn begins.

6. Continue until all children have had several trials practicing the routine.

Concluding Activities (5 minutes)

The Meet

Have children one at a time perform the routine, give cues, and have other children applaud at the completion of each performance. If a child does not want to perform for the class, allow him or her to wait, then encourage someone to go simultaneously. This should be fun, not a pressure-filled situation. To save time, you can have one child per group perform simultaneously or have the children perform only for their own groups at their own mat.

GYMNASTICS

LESSON 15
PARTNER STUNTS

Student Objectives

- Work cooperatively with a partner.
- Understand the terms "base," "top," and "balance."
- Demonstrate two partner stunts and attempt other partner stunts.

Equipment and Materials

- 1 or more mats (4 ft × 8 ft) per group
- Background music (optional)

Safety Tips

- Use spotting on difficult stunts.
- Children should be as equal in size as possible when working in partners.

Warm-Up Activities (5 minutes)

Grades 2-3 Warm-Up Routine

See Grades 2-3: Gymnastics, Warm-Ups, page 617.

Skill-Development Activities (20 minutes)

Wring the Dishrag

Match pairs, according to size.

1. Describe and have two children demonstrate the stunt:

   Stand facing each other with hands joined.

   Lift arms (one partner's left, the other's right), turn toward and under the lifted arms, and continue turning until you are facing each other again.

2. Have the children practice wring the dishrag.

Partner Get-Up

Have partners sit, facing each other.

1. Describe and have two children demonstrate the stunt:

   Join hands and touch toes.

   Pull until standing by balancing with each other.

   Keep your feet about shoulder-width apart.

2. Have the children practice partner get-up.

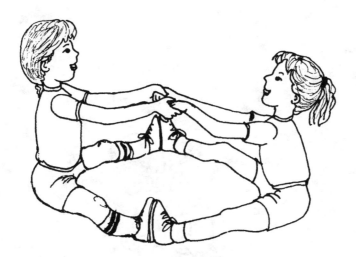

Partner Hopping

Have partners stand facing each other, about one leg-length apart.

1. Describe and have two children demonstrate the stunt: *Hold each other's right (or left) leg, then hop in the same direction using only two legs of the four legs you and your partner have.*

2. Have the children practice partner hopping.

Human Top

Have partners stand, facing each other with hands joined and toes touching.

1. Describe and have two children demonstrate the stunt:

    Lean backward until your arms and legs are straight and your two bodies form a "V."
    Then turn clockwise, keeping your toes together and your arms straight.

2. Have the children practice human top.

Back-to-Back Get-Up

Have partners sit back-to-back.

1. Describe and have two children demonstrate the stunt:

Lock your elbows and bend your legs so that your heels are close to your seat.

Push with your legs to stand with your backs still touching.

2. Have the children practice back-to-back get-up.

Quad Leg Lift

Arrange partners on the mats.

1. Describe and have two children demonstrate the stunt:

   Lie on your backs with your heads touching with your partner and extend your feet in opposite directions. Put your hands out to the side.

   Bend your knees so your feet are on the floor.

   Each of you lift one leg at the same time, until your toes touch in the air. Then lift your other leg until all four touch.

   Keep your legs up for a count of five, and then go back to the starting position.

2. Have the children practice the quad leg lift.

Wheelbarrow

Continue with pairs on the mats.

1. Describe and have two children demonstrate the stunt:

   One partner lies on his or her stomach, arms bent, supporting the body near the chest. The other partner stands near the feet of the partner on the floor and squats down (bending knees and keeping back straight).

   The standing partner lifts the feet of his or her partner off the ground. Lift with your legs, while keeping your back straight.

   At this point both partners walk forward—one using hands to walk, the other his or her feet.

2. Have the children practice the wheelbarrow.

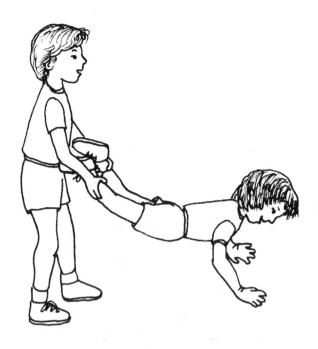

Two-Person Pyramid

Continue with pairs on the mats.

1. Describe and have two children demonstrate the stunt:

   One partner begins on all-fours (with feet and hands shoulder-width apart). We call this partner the "base." The other partner stands on the hips of the base. We call this partner the "top." Both partners face the same direction.

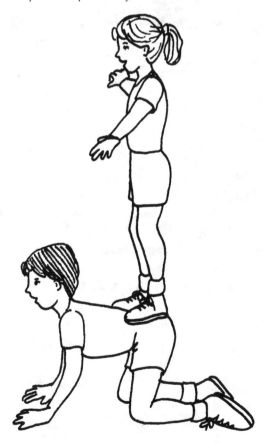

>*The top places both feet on the base's hips below the base's waist, and a few inches apart.*
>*Take turns being the base and the top.*

2. Have the children practice the two-person pyramid.

Individual Front Fall

Arrange four to six children in two to three pairs on a mat.

1. Describe and have a child demonstrate the stunt:

    >*Stand with your arms at your sides and feet together.*

    >*Lean forward and fall to the mat. At the last possible second, move your arms forward to catch your body weight and break the fall.*

    >*As your hands touch the mat, bend your arms at the elbows gradually to absorb the force as your body continues to fall to the mat.*

    >*Finish in a face-down position on the mat.*

2. Have the children practice the individual front fall. Encourage all children to try this.

Concluding Activities (5 minutes)

Wave

Have the children stand on one side of their mat, facing the width of the mat.

1. Describe and have one group demonstrate the stunt: *Line up shoulder-to-shoulder and do the front fall, one after the other. The first child begins the fall, and before she or he hits the mat the next child begins the fall, and so forth.*

2. Have the children practice the wave.

3. Repeat with all children and mats in one long line, beginning at one end of the mats and ending at the opposite end.

GYMNASTICS

LESSON 16
PARTNER STUNTS

Student Objectives

- Execute two stunts in small groups of four to six children.
- Attempt partner tumbling.

Equipment and Materials

- 1 or more mats (4 ft × 8 ft) per group
- Background music (optional)
- Chair (optional)

Safety Tip

- Match groups for physical size, pairing off into partners in each group.

Warm-Up Activities (5 minutes)

Grades 2-3 Warm-Up Routine

See Grades 2-3: Gymnastics, Warm-Ups, page 617.

Skill-Development Activities (20 minutes)

Centipede

Create small groups, and assign each to a mat. Match partners for size. For second graders you may want to do this in pairs only; third graders should be able to do this with more children.

1. Describe and have two or more children demonstrate:

   One person begins on all-fours with his or her head tucked. This child is the base.

   The second child places both hands a few inches in front of the base's hands and lies on the base's back, feet crossed loosely under the base.

   The rest of the children in the group continue, one by one, to climb onto the child at the head of the line in the same fashion, supporting most of their own body weight with their hands and arms.

   Once you are all (both) in place, the base calls out, "Right," and you all (both) move your right hands forward. Then the base calls out, "Left," and you all (both) move your left hands forward, and so on.

2. Have the children practice the centipede.

Double Wheelbarrow

Continue with the children at the mats, but create groups of three.

1. Describe and have three children demonstrate the stunt:

    Two of you start in a wheelbarrow position, one child holding the other's legs.

    The person supporting his or her weight on the hands is the "performer."

    The third child places both hands in front of the performer's hands and legs over the back of the performer.

    All three children walk forward, the performer and the third child using their hands, the base using his or her feet.

2. Have the children practice the double wheelbarrow.

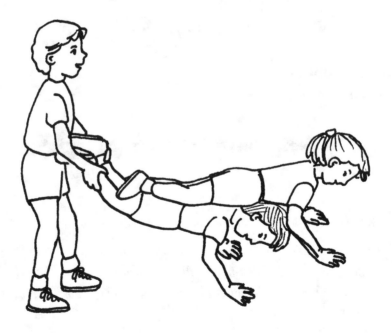

Human Chair

Continue with groups of three at the mats. Groups can be larger for children who are ready.

1. Describe and have three children demonstrate the stunt:

    One person pretends to sit in a chair (the first time you may actually want to use a chair). *This person is the base.*

    The second child sits on the base's knees. The third child sits on the second child's knees (and so on for children who are ready, until all children are sitting).

Your chair can actually move forward! The base calls out, "Right," and all children take a step with the right foot. Then the base calls out, "Left," and so forth.

2. Have the children practice the human chair.

Reverse Pyramid

Arrange partners on the mats.

1. Describe and have two children demonstrate the stunt:

   One person begins by sitting with knees bent and hands near his or her seat for support. This person is the base.

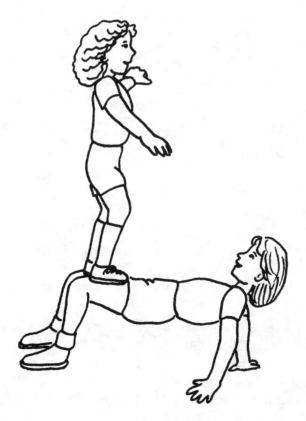

The base lifts his or her seat off the mat (similar to a crab position), so the torso is parallel to (flat as) the ground.

The second person (the top) faces the base, standing between the base's feet.

The top steps onto the base's knees and thighs (tops may need to remove their shoes).

Take turns being the base and the top.

2. Have the children practice the reverse pyramid.

Double Roll

Continue with partners at the mats.

1. Describe and have two children demonstrate the stunt:

The first child lies on the floor with knees bent and legs shoulder-width apart, feet flat on the mat. The second child stands with one foot on each side of the first child's head, facing the first child's feet.

The second child bends over and grasps the ankles of the first child. The first child grasps the ankles of the second child.

Carefully and slowly the second child lowers his or her head to the mat and does a forward roll, still grasping the ankles of the first child.

The first child, still holding the ankles of the second child, sits up and gradually moves to a stand.

You should end up back in the starting position, but reversed so the opposite child is on the mat. Repeat.

With practice this becomes a continuous (fluid) motion with no definite stopping points.

2. Have the children practice the double roll while you and/or pairs of children spot each other.

Double Roll Spotting

1. *Hold the shoulder or forearm and thigh of the child who is standing.*

2. *Help control the speed at which the standing child moves, and guide the child between the base's legs.*

3. *Spot the other partner once the top and base have reversed positions.*

Concluding Activities (5 minutes)

Partner Stunts

Continue with partners at the mats. Ask the children to demonstrate their favorite partner stunt.

LESSON 17
PARTNER AND GROUP STUNTS

Student Objectives

- Practice partner stunts.
- Identify the base and top.
- Work cooperatively with a partner or small group.

Equipment and Materials

- 1 or more mats (4 ft × 8 ft) per group, at least 6 groups total
- Background music (optional)

Safety Tip

- Match groups for physical size, pairing off into partners in each group.

Warm-Up Activities (5 minutes)

Grades 2-3 Warm-Up Routine

See Grades 2-3: Gymnastics, Warm-Ups, page 617.

Skill-Development Activities (24 minutes)

Skill Stations

Set up six stations. Match the children with partners of approximately the same size. Arrange two or three pairs of equal size on each mat.

1. Rotate the children through the mats so each group practices each stunt.
2. Assign the stunts to mats as follows:

    Station 1: Wheelbarrow and double wheelbarrow

    Station 2: Pyramid and reverse pyramid

    Station 3: Double roll

    Station 4: Partner get-up and back-to-back get-up

    Station 5: Centipede and human chair

    Station 6: Introduce the three-person pyramid (station yourself here)

3. Have groups spend about four minutes per station and then rotate.

Station 6: Three-Person Pyramid

Post yourself at this station so that you can teach and spot this new activity. Be sure, however, to keep an eye on the rest of the class.

1. Describe and have several children demonstrate the stunt:

   Two children get on all-fours to serve as the base.

   A third child stands with one foot at the center of the hips of each of the bases.

   We can put two three-person pyramids together with three bases and two tops (a total of five children).

2. Have the children practice the three-person pyramid while you spot and supervise.

3. To spot the three-person pyramid, begin standing behind the base with the top. Help the top place his or her feet over the legs of the bases. Assist the tops with balance and stepping up onto the bases.

Concluding Activities (1 minute)

Discussion

Name a stunt done today, and ask the children to identify the base and the top. In some stunts the base changes (e.g., double roll); in other stunts there are several tops (e.g., human chair) or bases (e.g., three-person pyramid). Discuss briefly.

LESSON 18
TRICKY STUNTS

Student Objectives

- Attempt individual stunts.
- Have fun!

Equipment and Materials

- 1 or more mats (4 ft × 8 ft) per group

Safety Tips

- Children who have identified or complain of lower back problems should not do the double-jointed walk.
- The double-jointed walk should only be done for short distances.

Warm-Up Activities (5 minutes)

Follow the Leader

Arrange the children in a line.

1. Ask the first leader to perform locomotor skills, such as skipping, running, and jumping, as the group follows.
2. Ask a second leader to lead additional locomotor skills that the first leader did not think of.
3. If there are no additional locomotor skills, ask the new leader to do the Grades 2-3 Warm-Up Routine.
4. When that exercise is finished, ask the next child in line to lead another warm-up exercise, and so on, until the children have done all the warm-up exercises.

Skill-Development Activities (21 minutes)

The stunts and skills today are special—each is unique. Encourage the children to learn and have fun with these activities!

Around the World

Create small groups, and assign each group to a mat.

1. Describe and have a child demonstrate the stunt:

   Begin, sitting with legs tucked tightly against your chest, knees apart and ankles together. Put your upper arms between your legs, and wrap your lower arms around your lower legs. Keep your wrists flexed so that your hands meet in front of your ankles.

Tuck your chin tightly against your chest, and roll your body to one side.

Continue the circular motion by lifting and rolling your torso.

2. Have the children practice around the world.

Walking in Place

Continue in small groups with each group to a mat.

1. Describe and demonstrate the stunt:

   The object is to appear to walk while actually staying in one place.

   Move your arms back in an exaggerated way while stepping forward, dragging the supporting leg backward.

   You must get the support leg back a step before putting the swing leg down or you will move across the floor.

2. Have the children practice walking in place.

Heel Click

Continue in small groups with each group to a mat.

1. Describe and demonstrate the stunt: *Jump as high as possible into the air, tap your heels together one or more times, and land on both feet.*

2. Have the children practice the heel click.

Double-Jointed Walk

Remember, children with lower back problems or those who complain of discomfort when attempting this stunt should not do this stunt.

1. Describe and demonstrate the stunt:

    Begin squatting with your knees apart, feet together, and arms threaded through your legs. Try to clasp your hands in front of your ankles.

    Keep your shoulders close to your knees, with both upper arms between your legs.

    Wrap your forearms around your lower legs, with your wrists bent so that you can join your hands in front of your ankles.

    While holding your head high and looking forward, walk using a side-rocking motion.

2. Have the children practice the double-jointed walk.

Knee Touch

Continue in small groups with each group to a mat.

1. Describe and demonstrate the stunt:

    Standing on one leg, hold the foot of the opposite leg behind your seat.

    Dip down until the knee of your bent leg touches the floor.

2. Have the children practice the knee touch.

Scoot-Through

Continue in small groups with each group to a mat.

1. Describe and demonstrate the stunt:

    Begin in the push-up position with your arms supporting your body weight and your legs extended to the rear with your body in a straight line.

    Without moving your hands or arms, slide your legs forward, keeping your legs as straight as possible until they pass between your arms. Continue sliding your legs through until your body is extended in front of your arms.

2. Have the children practice the scoot-through.

Concluding Activities (4 minutes)

Simon Says

Divide the students into small groups and scatter the groups around the play area, each group at a different mat. If there is room on the mats, all children can perform at once; otherwise have the children perform in order. Pick one child in each group to start as Simon.

1. Describe the game:

    Simon tries to trick the group into doing something that Simon does not "say" to do. Use the individual stunts learned in this lesson.

    Simon gives commands, some of which begin "Simon says" (and then Simon names individual stunts from this lesson). The group should perform those tasks.

    When Simon gives a command without saying "Simon says" (e.g., if Simon were to say "Do the heel click"), the group should not perform the task.

    Take turns, in order, for being Simon.

    A turn ends as soon as Simon tricks someone.

    When a different child becomes Simon, the old Simon moves to the end of the order.

    A child doing a task that Simon did not say, moves to the end of the order for performing and for being Simon, but keeps playing.

2. Have the children play Simon Says.

GYMNASTICS

LESSON 19
SILLY-TRICKY STUNTS

Student Objectives

- Learn about balance, movement, and related forces through participating in the various activities.
- Cooperate with group members to complete tasks.

Equipment and Materials

- 1 or more mats (4 ft × 8 ft) per group
- 1 yardstick per group
- Wall

Warm-Up Activities (5 minutes)

Grades 2-3 Warm-Up Routine

See Grades 2-3: Gymnastics, Warm-Ups, page 617.

Skill-Development Activities (25 minutes)

Pike Jump

Arrange the children on the mats spread arm's-length apart.

1. Describe and have two or three children demonstrate the stunt:

   Bend at the waist, holding your toes. Bend your legs slightly.

   Try to jump forward without letting go of your toes; this is impossible.

   Now try to jump backward; this is possible. The reason that you can't jump forward is that your center of gravity cannot shift forward in this position. (See Grades 2-3: Gymnastics, Lesson 7, page 637.)

2. Have the children practice the pike jump. Cue the children: *Bend over and hold your toes. Now try to jump forward. Don't let go of your toes!*

Toe Walk

1. Describe and demonstrate the stunt: *Hold the toes of each foot with the hand on the same side and walk forward, keeping your knees as straight as possible.*

2. Have the children practice the toe walk.

Earth Person, Moon Person

Create groups of three, and assign each group to a mat. Try to group children by similar height and weight.

1. Describe and have three children demonstrate the stunts: *Two of you try to lift the third person at the elbows, under two conditions.*

    In the Earth Person condition, the Earth Person (the one who is being lifted) touches hands to shoulders with the elbows pointing straight ahead (forward). There is no leverage (the elbows are in front of the center of gravity), so the lifters can't lift the Earth Person.

    In the Moon Person condition, the Moon Person (the child being lifted) holds the elbows close to the body and locked. The task of lifting is easy because the elbows are close to the center of gravity.

2. Have the children practice earth person, moon person, rotating roles.

Invisible Chair

Arrange the children in a long line against a wall, spreading them about arm's-length apart from each other.

1. Describe and demonstrate the stunt:

    Stand with your back against the wall.

    Slowly bend your knees until your thighs are parallel to the ground.

    Then cross one knee with the other as if sitting in a chair.

2. Have the children practice the invisible chair.

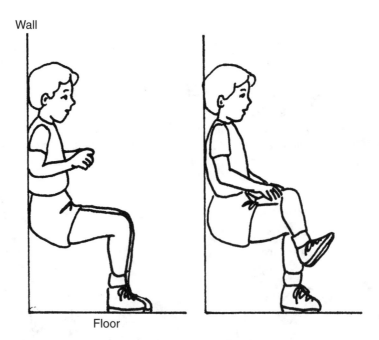

Wall

Floor

Finger Touch

Arrange the children in scatter formation or in a long line.

1. Describe and demonstrate the stunt:

   With arms extended (but the elbows and wrists slightly bent), index fingers pointing outward, and one eye closed, move your arms toward each other.

   Bend your elbows, so the meeting point of your index fingers is in front of and close to your nose.

   Repeat with your other eye closed.

2. Have the children practice the finger touch. Cue the children: *Put your arms out to the side, and close one eye. Now move your arms, trying to touch the tips of your fingers together.*

Balance Act

Create as many small groups as you have yardsticks.

1. Describe and demonstrate the stunt:

   Place an index finger under each end of the yardstick. Balance the yardstick.

   Try to move your fingers together without dropping the stick.

   Most of you will either drop the stick or your fingers will meet in the middle. The challenge is to have your fingers meet somewhere other than the middle—and still be able to balance the yardstick.

2. Have the children take turns practicing the balancing act. Cue the children: *Put the yardstick on your index fingers. Now move your fingers together. Don't stop in the middle of the stick, and don't let the yardstick fall!*

Concluding Activities

None.

LESSON 20
SMALL EQUIPMENT

Student Objectives

- Demonstrate balance using small equipment.

Equipment and Materials

- Mats (4 ft × 8 ft) as needed for safety
- Signal

- Station 1: walking cans, ropes, balance boards, beanbags
- Station 2: wands, foam balls
- Station 3: hoops, streamers

Safety Tips

- Emphasize the rule: *Do not touch others—this includes with the wand!*

Warm-Up Activities (5 minutes)

Grades 2-3 Warm-Up Routine

See Grades 2-3: Gymnastics, Warm-Ups, page 617.

Skill-Development Activities (20 minutes)

Stations

Set up the three stations as described. Divide the children into three groups. Assign each group to a station.

1. Describe and demonstrate each station.
2. Have the children practice the skills at the three stations.
3. Signal the children to rotate to the next station every five minutes (when revisiting this lesson you will have six minutes a station because explanations will be quicker).

Station 1: Balance Activities

Place the balance boards on a mat, grass, or carpet. Also have the children use the walking cans on mat, grass, or carpet. Make several ropes available.

Balance boards: *Balance on the board, with your arms out to the sides, hands on hips, beanbag on your head.*

Walking cans: *Walk in patterns (straight, zigzag, circle) on the cans. Try cans of varying sizes.*

Ropes: *Place the ropes on the ground in various patterns (straight, zigzag, circle) and walk on them.*

Station 2: Manipulative Activities

Thread the Needle: *Grasp the wand with both hands near each end, step through your arms one leg at a time, then raise the wand upward behind your back and continue until the wand is in front of your body again.*

Foam Balls: *Toss and catch the ball with your arms straight (use your legs to generate force), roll balls and chase them, and play partner toss (standing 5 to 10 ft apart, toss and catch the balls with straight arms).*

Station 3: Locomotor Activities

Hoops: *Jump rope with a hoop, roll the hoop, roll the hoop and run through it, and hula-hoop on various body parts.*

Streamers: *Move the streamer in the following patterns: figure eight, circle, letters to spell names. Try to toss and catch the streamers; jump the streamer (while circling it around your legs); toss, run, and catch the streamer.*

Concluding Activities (5 minutes)

Station Discussion and Selection

Keep children in same groups until they select a new station.

1. Ask each group to think of their favorite stations.
2. Select one group and allow each child in that group to select a station. Continue with each group until all children are at a station with the stipulation that no more than four to six children can be working on any one activity at a station.
3. Ask the children to combine two skills or create new skills at the stations they selected.

GYMNASTICS

LESSON 21
NEW SKILLS WITH SMALL EQUIPMENT

Student Objectives

- Attempt new skills using wands, foam balls, and small playground balls.
- Work cooperatively with a partner.

Equipment and Materials

- 1 or more mats (4 ft × 8 ft) per group
- 1 foam ball per child
- 1 playground ball per child
- 1 wand per child

Safety Tip

- Remind the children to treat the equipment and each other with respect, and to not touch another child.

Warm-Up Activities (5 minutes)

Circle Warm-Up

Arrange the children in a circle.

1. Describe the warm-up as the children practice it:

    Begin with your left side toward the center of the circle.

    First, hop on your left foot for 20 to 30 hops, then on your right foot for 20 to 30 hops.

    Next, skip around the circle going clockwise (point), then counterclockwise (point).

    Perform a series of jumps (10 to 20) forward, then back away from the center of the circle, and then move toward the center of the circle.

2. Select one child to perform a locomotor skill (run, walk, gallop, or the like) with the group following this leader.

Skill-Development Activities (20 minutes)

Wand Challenges

Give each child a wand, and arrange the children in scatter formation. Remind the children of the need to maintain personal space. Challenge the children with the following tasks:

Put one end of the wand on the floor, hold the other end with your pointer finger (index finger), and walk around the wand.

Can you move up and down as you do this?

Stand under (over) the wand.

Put the wand on the ground and jump over it.

Jump side-to-side over the wand.

Foam Ball Challenges

Collect the wands, and give each child a foam ball and a playground ball.

1. Have the children bounce the foam balls: *They are difficult to bounce because they are soft.*
2. Have the children toss the foam ball to themselves and catch it several times.

Roll and Intercept

1. Tell the children: *While you are walking, roll the ball as in bowling. Roll the ball slowly, continue walking, trying to walk beside the ball. Then bend and try to pick up the ball near your heel. The object is to appear to walk forward, look forward, and face forward and at the same time pick up the ball, which will trail slowly behind you as it slows down.*
2. Have the children roll and intercept the foam balls.

Playground Ball Challenges

Arrange partners facing each other, 10 to 15 ft apart.

1. Tell the children: *Roll the playground ball between you and your partner.*
2. *Now bounce the playground ball between you and your partner.*

Concluding Activities (5 minutes)

Have each pair select the foam ball or playground ball to practice tossing and catching. Have them begin at 10 ft apart and take one step backward after each successful pair of catches. Take one step forward after each unsuccessful catch.

GRADES 2-3

GYMNASTICS

LESSON 22
STREAMERS AND HOOPS

Student Objectives

- Demonstrate one streamer and one hoop skill, either locomotor or manipulative.

Equipment and Materials

- 1 streamer per child
- 1 large hoop (30-36 in.) per child
- 2-3 cones, barrels, or tall targets (to throw hoops over)

Safety Tip

- Spread the children as far apart as possible.

Warm-Up Activities (5 minutes)

Grades 2-3 Warm-Up Routine

See Grades 2-3: Gymnastics, Warm-Ups, page 617.

Skill-Development Activities (20 minutes)

Streamers and Hoop Activities

Spread the hoops around the play area, and give each child a streamer.

1. Ask the children to find an empty hoop and stand in it. Present the following challenges:

    Make big circles overhead (small circles overhead, big circles beside you, big circles in front of you, figure eights).

    Try small figure eights (any zigzagging movement).

    Walk around the outside of the hoop, with the streamer dragging on the ground.

    Skip to another hoop while moving the streamer in any motion.

2. Repeat several times.

Move the children to the outside of all the hoops (making a large formation with the hoops in the middle).

3. Select a leader to lead the group through the formation of hoops. Tell the children:
    Hold your streamer and run (skip, hop, jump) through the hoops (follow the leader).

Hoop Challenges

Collect the streamers and ask the children to each return to a hoop. Challenge the children with the following tasks:

Get inside the hoop.

Walk around the hoop (inside, outside).

Walk outside the hoop.

Jump in and out of the hoop.

Stand under the hoop.

Roll the hoop as you run with it.

Can you toss your hoop and catch it?

Concluding Activities (5 minutes)

Target Toss

Place two or three cones, cubes, barrels, or other tall targets in the play area for the children to use as targets for the hoops. Spread the targets as far apart as possible. Create groups of two or three, and assign each group to a target. Spread the children out as far as possible.

Have the children practice tossing their hoops over the targets.

GRADES 2-3

GYMNASTICS

LESSON 23
STREAMERS, BALLS, AND HOOPS

Student Objectives
- Practice skills using small equipment.
- Create a rhythmical movement sequence using small equipment.

Equipment and Materials
- 1 streamer per child
- 1 hoop (30-36 in.) per child
- 1 foam ball per child
- 1 playground ball per child
- 1 wand per child
- Music (any 4-beat music the children like)

Safety Tip
- Spread the children apart, but be sure you can still see each child.

Warm-Up Activities (5 minutes)

Grades 2-3 Warm-Up Routine
See Grades 2-3: Gymnastics, Warm-Ups, page 617.

Skill-Development Activities (20 minutes)

Streamer Routine
Scatter the hoops around the play area. Place one ball and one streamer in each hoop. Ask each child to stand in a hoop.

1. Describe and demonstrate the routine:

With the streamer in your left hand, do the following steps of the Streamer Routine:

> *Make four large circles on the left side of your body.*
>
> *Move the streamer overhead for four circles.*
>
> *Switch the streamer to your right hand.*
>
> *Make four circles on the right side of your body.*
>
> *Make four circles in front of your body.*
>
> *Perform four figure eights in front of your body.*
>
> *Walk forward eight steps.*
>
> *Switch hands.*

Lower the streamer.

Walk forward dragging the streamer eight more steps.

2. Have the children practice the Streamer Routine.

3. Have them perform the routine to music. Repeat.

4. Expansion idea: Have the children do the streamer routine in rounds, with each row starting as the preceding row gets to the end of the first set of circles.

Ball Routine

Ask the children to put the streamers down and pick up the balls.

Tell the children: *Walk around your hoop, holding the ball to your chest with both hands. Move the ball out and back in time to the music as you walk.*

Concluding Activities (5 minutes)

Hoop Creativity

With the music on, ask the children to create movement with the equipment. Stop them occasionally to point out a unique or interesting movement. Remind the children about turning the hoop (hula hoop) on body parts, tossing the hoop, and being careful.

GRADES 2-3

GYMNASTICS

LESSON 24
BALANCE BEAM, JUMPING CUBES, AND CLIMBING ROPE

Student Objectives

- Review the basic skills on equipment.
- State that only one person at a time should be on a piece of equipment.

Equipment and Materials

The more equipment you can place at each station, the more practice time your students will get.

- Mats (4 ft × 8 ft) as needed for safety (1-2 per balance beam, 1 per jumping cube)
- Signal

- Station 1: 2 or more balance beams, balls, or beanbags
- Station 2: 2 or more ropes (affixed to a wall or stake)
- Station 3: 6 or more jumping cubes and carpet squares
- Task cards (optional)

Safety Tip

- Remind the children that only one person at a time can be on any piece of equipment.

Warm-Up Activities (5 minutes)

Grades 2-3 Warm-Up Routine

See Grades 2-3: Gymnastics, Warm-Ups, page 617.

Skill-Development Activities (20 minutes)

Stations

Set up the stations as shown in figure on page 686. Use enough equipment to keep participation opportunities high. Create three groups, and assign each group to a station.

1. Describe and demonstrate each station.
2. Have the children practice the skills at the three stations.
3. Signal the children to rotate to the next station about every six minutes.

Station 1: Beam
Walk forward, walk backward, walk and carry an object (ball or beanbag), bend and touch the beam, and stand.

Station 2: Rope
Pull yourself along feetfirst, then headfirst.

Station 3: Jumping Cubes
Jump to the target, jump and clap, jump and turn, jump high, jump low, jump far, and jump short.

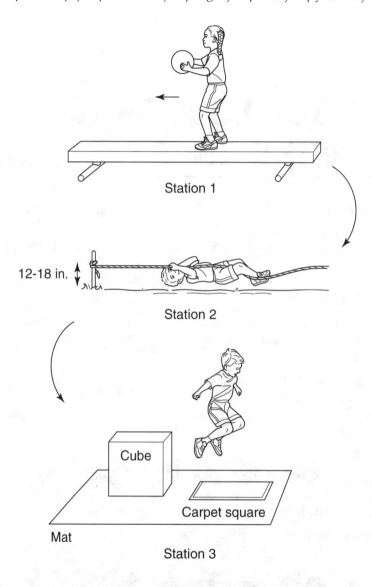

Station 1

12-18 in.

Station 2

Cube

Carpet square

Mat

Station 3

Concluding Activities (5 minutes)

Skill Review
Allow each child to show a favorite or best skill from today's lesson.

GYMNASTICS

LESSON 25

BALANCE BEAM, CLIMBING ROPES, LADDER, JUMPING CUBES, AND VAULTING CUBES

Student Objectives

- Review skills on vaulting cubes and ladder.
- Practice new skills on the balance beams, jumping cubes, and climbing rope.
- Cooperate and take turns during Beanbag Relay.

Equipment and Materials

- Mats (4 ft × 8 ft) as needed for safety (1-2 per balance beam, 1 per jumping cube)
- Signal
- Station 1: 1 or more climbing ropes suspended from above
- Station 2: 2 or more balance beams
- Station 3: 1 jumping cube (24 in.) per child

- Station 4: 1 or more wooden climbing ladders mounted to a wall or frame
- Station 5: 1 vaulting cube (wider at top than bottom, 24-30 in. high, or large paper boxes stuffed with paper) per child
- Several beanbags
- Task cards (optional)

Safety Tips

- Explain that mats should be kept under all pieces of equipment and that landings should be on the mat.
- Only one child per piece of equipment at a time.
- Emphasize safety, rather than speed, for the Beanbag Relay.

Warm-Up Activities (5 minutes)

Grades 2-3 Warm-Up Routine

See Grades 2-3: Gymnastics, Warm-Ups, page 617.

Skill-Development Activities (20 minutes)

Apparatus Stations

Set up the stations. Create five groups, and assign each to a station.

1. Describe and demonstrate each station.
2. Have the children practice the skills at the five stations.
3. Signal the children to rotate to the next station every three to four minutes.

Station 1: Vertical Rope

Reach as high on the rope as possible, grasp the rope, then lift your legs off the mat, trying to hold the rope with your ankles. Once you do this, you climb as high as possible while I hold the bottom of the rope steady.

Station 2: Balance Beams

Dip step: *Walk with your arms extended to the sides. With each step, bend the knee of your supporting leg and run the toes of your nonsupporting leg along the side of the beam.*

Minijump: *Bend your knees slightly and make a small jump, landing back on the beam with both feet.*

Station 3: Jumping Cubes

Straddle jump: *Jump off the cube, extending your legs outward in a "V" shape, then bring your legs back straight and together, landing on both feet.*

Tuck jump: *Jump off the cube and bring your knees to your chest, then extend your body and land on both feet.*

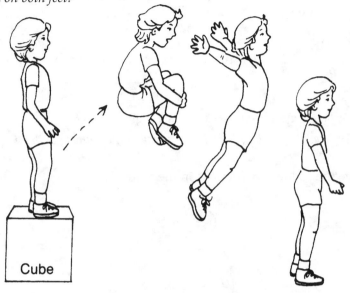

Station 4: Ladder

Practice climbing both sides of the ladder.

Station 5: Vaulting Cubes

Practice the run and takeoff first, then add the mount to practice the front running mount.

Run and takeoff: *Take several steps and lift your arms upward with the thigh of your nonsupporting leg parallel to the ground. When your body reaches the peak of this jump, your arms move to shoulder level for balance. Land on both feet. From this hurdle, you immediately jump upward in a vertical jump from both feet.*

Front running mount: *At the end of a run and takeoff, place both hands on the vaulting cube, lift your knees toward your chest, look straight ahead (never down at the cube), and balance on the cube on your knees.*

Concluding Activities (5 minutes)

Beanbag Relay

Create two or more groups, and assign each group to a beam. Further divide the children at each beam into two groups, and place one group at each end.

1. Describe the relay:

   The first child in line carries a beanbag across the beam to the first child in the opposite line.

   Continue until all of you have had a turn.

   A child who steps off the beam must begin again.

   The team to give everyone a turn carrying the beanbag without stepping off (or the fewest steps off) wins.

2. Have the children participate in the relay.

Beanbag

GYMNASTICS

LESSON 26

BALANCE BEAM, CLIMBING ROPES, LADDER, JUMPING CUBES, AND VAULTING CUBES

Student Objectives

- Practice new skills on the vaulting cubes and beams.
- Work independently.
- Define a focus point.

Equipment and Materials

- Mats (4 ft × 8 ft) as needed for safety (1-2 per balance beam, 1 per jumping cube)
- Signal
- Station 1: 2 or more balance beams
- Station 2: 1 vaulting cube per child

- Station 3: 1 jumping cube and 1 foam ball per child
- Station 4: 1 or more wooden climbing ladders, mounted to a wall or frame, and 1 foam ball per ladder
- Station 5: 1 or more climbing ropes suspended from above
- Task cards (optional)

Safety Tip

- Remind the children only one child per piece of equipment at a time.

Warm-Up Activities (5 minutes)

Grades 2-3 Warm-Up Routine

See Grades 2-3: Gymnastics, Warm-Ups, page 617.

Skill-Development Activities (20 minutes)

Beam and Vaulting Cube Stations

Create five groups, and assign each group to a station.

1. Describe and demonstrate each station.
2. Have the children practice the skills at the five stations.
3. Signal the children to rotate to the next station every five minutes.
4. You should move around the area, keeping all stations in view.

Station 1: Balance Beam Turns

Stand, facing the length of the beam with feet spread shoulder-width apart, one in front of the other. Bend your knees slightly and turn your head first (look at a still object to enhance balance; this is called a "focal point"). Then turn your body toward the open side of your body (if your left leg is in front, turn right). This is called the "squat and turn."

   Note: The focal point is the stationary object; looking at an object enhances balance. This is because peripheral vision (ambient vision) detects movement and makes rapid corrections to maintain balance. Without a focal point we rely on focal vision to make slower corrections and often lose balance as a result.

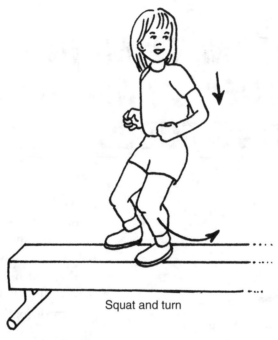

Squat and turn

Station 2: Straddle Vault on Vaulting Cube

Run and place both hands on the cube, jump, lift your hips up and spread your legs apart (one to each side of the vaulting cube). Push with your hands and jump over the cube, landing with feet together. This is similar to leapfrog.

Station 3: Jumping Cubes

Jump and clap, jump and turn, jump and land on a target, jump holding a foam ball, do a tuck jump, and do a straddle jump.

Station 4: Ladder

Climb the topside, climb the topside carrying a foam ball, climb the underside, and climb the underside with no feet.

Station 5: Vertical Climbing Rope

Climb as high as possible.

Concluding Activities (5 minutes)

Focal Point

Arrange the children in scatter formation.

1. Explain the value of a focal point: *Our peripheral vision (to the sides, around the edges of our vision) detects movement, helping us correct our balance quickly. Without a focal point, we rely on focal (main) vision and correct problems too slowly, often losing our balance as a result.*

2. To demonstrate this concept, ask the children to balance on one foot with hands on hips with eyes open (this should be easy), then repeat with the eyes closed (this should be more difficult).

3. Now have them balance on one foot using you as the focal point: *Now look at me as your focal point. Don't glance anywhere else.*

4. Begin moving around, slowly then quickly dodging up and down, side-to-side.

5. Discuss how students' balance has probably become poorer as you move around.

LESSON 27
BALANCE BEAMS, CLIMBING ROPES, LADDER, JUMPING CUBES, AND VAULTING CUBES

Student Objectives

- Follow instructions.
- Practice skills.
- Have fun!

Equipment and Materials

List is per obstacle course. If possible, set up more than one course to increase participation opportunities.

- Mats (4 ft × 8 ft) as needed for safety (1-2 per balance beam, 1 per jumping cube)
- 3 balance beams

- 3 jumping cubes
- 2 vaulting cubes
- 1 ladder and a wall
- 1 climbing rope
- Chalk, tape, or signs to number equipment
- Carpet squares (targets for jumping and vaulting cubes)

Safety Tip

- The rule for the obstacle course is: *Do not pass the person in front of you.*

Warm-Up Activities (5 minutes)

Grades 2-3 Warm-Up Routine

See Grades 2-3: Gymnastics, Warm-Ups, page 617.

Skill-Development Activities (15 minutes)

Large Equipment Obstacle Course

Set up the obstacle course as shown in the figure on page 695.

1. Describe and have one child demonstrate the course:

   Walk backward on the first beam.

   Jump to the carpet square, clapping hands at the first jumping cube.

   Hang for 10 counts on the climbing rope, with feet off the ground.

Straddle vault over the first vaulting cube.

Do the dip step on the second beam.

Jump up onto the second vaulting cube. Jump down.

Climb over the second jumping cube.

Climb up the underside of the ladder and drop off.

Jump once, then turn all the way around on the third beam.

Jump off the third jumping cube and do a 360-degree turn before landing on your feet.

2. Have one child demonstrate the obstacle course as you describe the activities.

3. Staggering their starts, have the children practice the obstacle course one or more times as time allows.

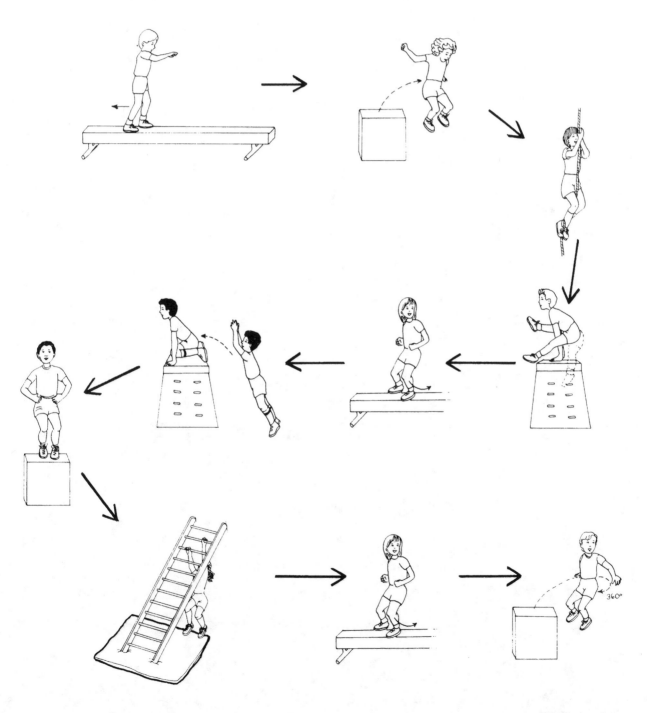

Concluding Activities (10 minutes)

Modified Obstacle Course

Allow five or six children to suggest ways to alter the course; make those changes, and let all the children try it once.

Although some schools have a dedicated health instructor, such as the school nurse, to teach basic health concepts, many physical education teachers find themselves faced with the task of teaching this part of the school curriculum. Take advantage of such an opportunity to show children the connections among fitness, lifestyle choices, and health. We designed this unit to give you an overview of appropriate content for this age level to help you get started.

UNIT ORGANIZATION

You can use the following lessons as a two-week health unit or individually as appropriate. You can also expand each lesson into a unit of its own. The topics include personal health, personal safety, body growth, living happily, substance use and abuse, nutrition, home safety, fire safety, disease and illness, and physical fitness and activity.

LESSON ORGANIZATION

We have organized each lesson in a manner similar to all other types of lessons in this book: student objectives, equipment and materials, health concept (skill development). As it enhances student learning, most lessons include a hands-on activity to reinforce the main health concept.

TEACHING HINTS

As with any lesson, being well-prepared makes for more effective teaching. Read the lesson carefully before presenting the concept to the students. Allow plenty of time for discussion and application of the concept to promote learning.

Second and Third Graders

Children this age have probably made several connections between lifestyle choices and health; for example, the amount of exercise a person gets can affect his or her body composition. These children may have many questions about health issues. Be sure to take time to explore the issues they raise. Second and third graders have become quite competent in taking care of their own basic needs, such as hygiene and fixing simple snacks or meals for themselves, and you can take advantage of the pride they feel in such accomplishments by applauding their efforts and giving them more information they can apply in their daily lives.

Continue to be sure the language you use is age-appropriate and accompanied by visual aids whenever possible, such as bright posters, models, and everyday objects. Models of parts of the human body, for example, the lungs/torso when discussing the hazards of smoking, are especially fascinating to this age group. You may be able to borrow visual aids from a secondary school in your district if your school lacks them.

Encourage discussion and participation from each child. One way to encourage discussion is to be sure to wait at least 10 seconds before calling on a child to answer your question. Encourage participation by asking for group responses, such as having the children give you "thumbs up" for "yes" and "thumbs down" for "no."

Collaboration Strategies

Inviting parents and other community members to class can greatly enhance health lessons. Parents from various health professions may serve as guest speakers. You should also include parents by asking them to help complete and/or sign health contracts, sending home information about the concepts with discussion questions, or simply inviting them to attend class. Community experts, such as pediatricians, police, health care professionals, and representatives from awareness groups (e.g., American Heart Association), are often willing to make presentations at schools free of charge. Tap into such resources whenever possible not only to supplement your curriculum but also to raise awareness among students of the many resources available to them in the community.

G R A D E S
2-3

HEALTH

LESSON 1
PERSONAL SAFETY

Student Objectives

- Identify the number-one health risk for children.
- List seven sources of risk.
- Give one strategy for reducing risk for each of five of the risks.

Equipment and Materials

- None.

Health Concept (30 minutes)

Gather the children into an information formation for the entire discussion.

Personal Safety

1. Introduce the concept to the children: *You have the right to be safe and healthy, but sometimes people or situations threaten the health and safety of children. You need to learn to protect yourselves and ask for help when your health and safety are threatened. The number-one health risk for children under 14 years of age is injury, including fires and burns, choking and suffocation, poisoning, falls, firearms, transportation (including pedestrian, car, and bicycle methods), and water safety.*

2. Discuss each of the seven risks.

Risk 1: Fires and Burns

1. Ask the children: *Can you give some examples of what might put us at risk of fires and burns?* (Being caught in a fire at home or elsewhere. The skin can be burned by many things: things that have been on the stove or in the oven [water, oil, food, or the containers for these], steam, appliances [irons, curling irons, hot rollers, ovens, stoves, radiators, space heaters], sun, and fire [matches, fireplaces, barbecue grills], and chemicals [acid].)

2. Tell the children: *Fire also uses oxygen in the air, so it can cause suffocation. How can we reduce risk from fires and burns?* (Smoke and fire alarms and detectors. Proper storage and care of chemicals and flammable materials. Having an escape plan for home, school, and other places where we spend time, observing fire exits in places we visit. Some examples of exits are emergency exits on buses, at shopping malls, and on airplanes. Use safe behavior in the kitchen [use hot pads when cooking, allow steam to escape from hot dishes by tilting the cover away, do not stand near the stove or oven]. Do not light candles, matches, or other items that burn.)

3. Encourage children to respond until all of the examples have been presented.

4. Tell the children: *If your clothes were on fire you should "Stop, drop, and roll," which means get on the ground or floor and roll to put out the fire. The idea is to smother the fire or put it out by removing the oxygen. Covering flames with natural fabrics like cotton or wool can also help put out a fire because these fabrics help reduce the supply of oxygen. Do not use synthetic fabrics that melt and burn at a low temperature. You should also get help as soon as possible, so yell for help. The best thing is to avoid open flames, so you do not need to use "Stop, drop, and roll."*

Risk 2: Suffocation

1. Tell the children: *Our body uses oxygen all the time. We get oxygen from breathing air into our lungs. Sometimes the airway is blocked on the inside; this is called "choking." Suffocation is when oxygen does not get to the lungs and brain. Suffocation can happen because something on the outside of the body stops oxygen from entering or when there is not oxygen to breathe. Fires burn oxygen, so sometimes a person suffocates when the fire uses all the oxygen. Suffocation can also occur when something covers our face or blocks the airway in our throat, stopping oxygen from entering our lungs. There are several ways to reduce the chances of choking, for example, not talking when you eat and not putting small objects into your mouth. Good ventilation is another way to reduce the risk of suffocation. This means having fresh air added to the air in a room.*

2. Discuss suffocation and choking.

Risk 3: Poison

1. Ask the children: *Can you think of a story in which poison was important?* (Snow White.) *What is poison?* (Something that makes your body sick.) Tell the children: *Too much of many medicines can be poison, but there are also chemicals that are poisons even in small amounts. Certain animals and plants can be poisonous, like some spiders, snakes, and mushrooms.* Discuss these and other sources of poison.

2. Ask the children: *How can we reduce the risk of poisoning?* (Do not taste or eat anything unless a trusted adult says it is OK. Take medicines as prescribed. Do not put your hands or feet in places you cannot see [there may be poisonous insects or animals in the space]. Keep cleaning materials, like soap and bleach, stored safely out of reach.)

Risk 4: Firearms

1. Tell the children: *Firearms are guns. Guns are never toys. Children should not touch any firearm. If you see a gun, leave the area and tell a trusted adult about the gun. Guns do not belong at school. If someone you know has a gun at school, tell your teacher. Guns should be stored safely.*

2. Continue: *Each community (state or local government) has different regulations regarding firearms; local police can provide information about the regulations in your community. Guns should be registered, and those using guns should be trained and must be responsible. When someone has a gun and acts secretive about having the gun, this is a good indication that something is wrong. It could be that the gun is not registered (legal) or that the person has the gun without permission or training or that the person's intention is to do harm with the gun.*

3. Encourage children to follow their instincts, stay away from firearms, and tell a trusted adult if they feel uncomfortable about any situation regarding firearms.

Risk 5: Falling

1. Tell the children: *Falling is normal but can be a serious health risk. If we trip, lose our balance, and catch our balance it may be embarrassing, but not dangerous. However, sometimes we do things that could be dangerous regarding falls. For example, climbing can make the fall greater. When we use the stairs we should use the handrail, no items should be left on stairs—because they can trip us—and we should take care to use facilities and equipment as it is intended. Thinking about this, should we do any of these?*

Climb up on and stand on a rocking chair to reach something in a high cupboard?

Stand on the top rung of a ladder?

Climb out the window to sit or stand on the roof?

Climb over a guardrail?

2. Discuss: *The answer is "no" to each question; let's discuss why.*

Risks 6 and 7: Transportation and Water Safety

See Grades K-1: Health, Lesson 9, page 340, for information on water safety. See Grades K-1: Health, Lesson 10, page 342, for information on transportation safety.

LESSON 2
PERSONAL HEALTH

Student Objectives

- Identify healthy behaviors.
- State that each person is responsible for his or her personal health.
- Complete the crossword on personal health.

Equipment and Materials

- Pencils
- Copies of the crossword (form H2.1)
- Chalkboard or poster board
- Chalk or marker

Health Concept (30 minutes)

Gather the children into an information formation for the entire discussion.

Personal Health

1. Introduce the concept to the children: *Each person is responsible for certain healthy behaviors, including getting enough rest, keeping clean, and eating properly.*

2. Ask the children: *Can you think of any other behaviors you do each day that help you stay healthy?* (Going to the bathroom, brushing teeth, exercising, relaxing, or playing.)

3. Tell the children: *Let's make a schedule for each day that includes many healthy behaviors.* Use the following times and help children list the things suggested on the board. Remind the children they may want or need to do the following behaviors more often than on the schedule, this is only a minimum. For example children may drink more water or wash their hands more often:

   Wake up: Go to the bathroom, wash, eat breakfast, drink water

   Morning: Exercise and/or play, drink water

   Noon: Wash hands, eat a healthy lunch, go to the bathroom, drink water

   Afternoon: Relax, exercise or play, drink water

   Early evening: Wash hands, eat a healthy dinner, drink water

   Evening: Bath or shower, go to bathroom, brush and floss teeth, relax

   Night: Sleep eight or more hours

4. Use the following crossword puzzle.

5. Review the following words listed on the handout to help the children solve the puzzle:

   bathe, bathroom, brush teeth (no space), eight, exercise, floss teeth (no space), healthy, play, relax, sleep, wash, water.

FORM H2.1: CROSSWORD PUZZLE

Use the following words to solve the puzzle (do not leave a space between two-word answers):

bathe, bathroom, brush teeth, eight, exercise, floss teeth, healthy, play, relax, sleep, wash, water

Across

1. To keep clean, we _____ every day.
2. Physical activity or _____ every day helps us stay healthy.
3. Drink _____ glasses of water each day.
4. We all need _____ for eight or more hours each day.
5. For good dental health we should _____ once each day.
6. Before meals we should _____ our hands.
7. Each day we must use the _____ several times.

Down

1. For dental health and fresh breath, we _____ three times each day.
2. Everyone needs to reduce stress and _____.
3. We should sleep _____ hours or more every day.
4. We should _____, exercise, and relax every day for our health.
5. Each of us must be responsible if we are going to be _____.
6. Every day we need to drink eight glasses of _____.

FORM H2.2: CROSSWORD PUZZLE SOLUTION

Solution

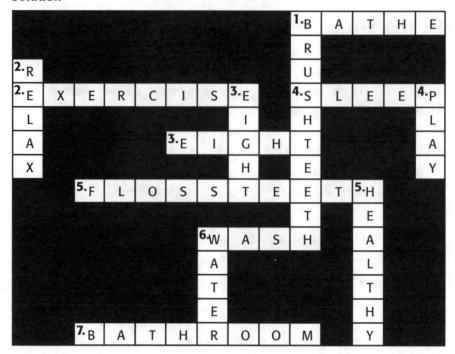

GRADES 2-3

HEALTH

LESSON 3
LIVING HAPPILY

Student Objectives

- Identify healthy ways to express emotions.
- Name one or more ways emotions can work for you.
- State that everyone needs to be loved.
- Name the steps to being a loving person.

Equipment and Materials

- 1 copy of the caring contract per child (see form H2.3)
- Chalk or marker
- Paper
- Crayons or markers

Health Concept (30 minutes)

Gather the children into an information formation for the entire discussion.

Emotions

1. Introduce the concept: *We can express all emotions in a healthy way. Emotions can work for us. Everyone has emotional needs; for example, everyone needs to be loved.*

2. Ask the children: *Can you name some emotions?* (Fear, anger, happiness, love.) *We all have the right to express our emotions in a way that won't hurt others. Let's name a good and bad way to express each of these emotions (see table H2.1).*

Table H2.1: Expressing Emotions

Emotion	Good expression	Bad expression
Hurt feelings	Saying what hurt your feelings	Just being angry at the person
Anger	Telling someone about your anger	Hurting someone or something
Love	Being kind to another person	Stalking a person
Fear	Playing with a favorite toy	Running away

3. Discuss emotions with the children: *Sometimes emotions can help us be better people. For example, when we worry, sometimes it makes us study harder, try harder, and even do our best. Other times emotions can work against us, because the emotions are out of control—that stops our best thinking. For example, worry that makes us feel sick doesn't help us do better. Anger is often an emotion out of control and usually works against us. But if we control it, anger can help us keep people from taking advantage of us. Fear can help us by making the*

blood pump faster, and it may even alert us to danger. So fear, while unpleasant, can be helpful. But unreasonable fear can keep us from enjoying things that are not dangerous. For example, fear of falling can keep you from doing something dangerous like climbing on your garage roof but it can also keep you from learning to ride a bike. So you see that emotions are complicated forces in our lives.

4. Tell the children: *Each of us has needs that cannot be met right away. For example, you may be hungry before it is time for lunch, or you want to go to a party, but it is rained out. For some of these needs time will fix the problem; however, other times it will not. For example, a friend is going to move away. You do not want your friend to leave, because you will miss the friend. However, you should try to be happy for your friend. You could write to your friend. You could spend time with someone who has moved near you—they will need a new friend too. These are ways of taking a sad emotion (loneliness) and making the best of it, rather than letting it be out of control.*

5. Ask the children: *What are some ways we show people that we love them?* (Allow children to answer and draw out the following—do something special for the person, say something special to the person, give something special to the person.) *We are kind and give something—time, compliments, friendship. When we give love, we feel better.*

6. Tell the children: *To live happily we must be in control of our emotions, use them positively, and give love so we get love.* Help each student complete a Caring Contract (see Form H2.3).

FORM H2.3: CARING CONTRACT

Date _____

Name of the special person _____

I will do the following things to show that I care:

_____

_____

_____

_____

_____

Signature of the caring person _____

GRADES 2-3 — HEALTH

LESSON 4
BODY GROWTH

Student Objectives

- Define "growth."
- State that each person has a unique growth pattern.
- Measure height and weight.

Equipment and Materials

- Yardsticks
- Scale

Health Concept (30 minutes)

Gather the children into an information formation for the entire discussion.

Body Growth

1. Introduce the concept: *From birth to maturity (when you become an adult) your body steadily grows larger. Sometime after 9 years of age for girls and 11 for boys changes are more rapid. Each person has a unique or individual rate of growth, however; each person is different.*

2. Present the following definitions:

   "Growth" means getting bigger. We grow because the body makes new cells, so we get bigger because of new cells in our body. Growth is a process, so when we think about growth we think of change.

   "Maturity" means adult or adult-like. This is when growth stops, and we do not get bigger.

   "Adolescence" starts when growth is rapid and ends with maturity. For girls adolescence usually begins between 9 and 11 years of age; for boys adolescence begins between 11 and 13 years of age.

   "Puberty" occurs during adolescence. Puberty is when the body makes many changes in addition to growing bigger. For example, hair grows on the body (e.g., armpits, facial hair in males), boys' voices change, and there are some changes inside our bodies that prepare us for becoming adults.

3. Read the following story, stopping to discuss each section. Have the children fill in the blanks as they occur. Help them as necessary.

Jennifer woke up early and put on her shorts so she could play outside. She went to the kitchen for breakfast, and her Mom said, "Jennifer, look how long your legs have grown. Your shorts still fit around your waist, but are much shorter than last summer! I think you have grown faster this year than any other year."

After breakfast, Jennifer went to the park. Mrs. Gonzales's grandson, George, was visiting. Jennifer hadn't seen him since last summer when he was visiting. George sounded funny when he said "Hi," but he looked almost the same. Jennifer and George sat on the swings to talk. George noticed that his legs dragged the ground this summer, and he was a little embarrassed about his voice, which cracked and changed while he talked to Jennifer.

4. Ask the children the following questions:

   How old do you think Jennifer and George are? (11 is a good guess.)

   Can you use a word we defined earlier to describe them? (Adolescence.) *Do you think all of our body parts grow at the same speed?* (No, the arms and legs grow more rapidly than the head and torso; also, we get taller or longer, then grow wider and "deeper.")

5. Continue the discussion: *Jennifer and George are entering* _____(adolescence), *we can tell because of rapid* _____(growth). *Jennifer and George will have* _____(unique) *growth patterns. When Jennifer and George reach* _____ (maturity), *growth will stop; then they will be* _____ (adults/adult-like).

6. Does anyone keep track of your growth? (Doctor, parent or grandparent on the wall, someone at school.)

Concluding Activity

Measure Height and Weight, Sitting Height, and Leg Length

Children can practice measuring each other for height and weight and sitting height (sitting on the floor, from the floor to the top of the head) and calculate how long their legs are by subtracting sitting height from standing height. Tell the children: *As adults our legs are around half of our body length.*

LESSON 5
SUBSTANCE USE AND ABUSE

Student Objectives

- Name the four stages of substance use and abuse.
- State that some individuals are more likely to experiment than others.
- Complete the wordfind.

Equipment and Materials

- None.

Health Concept (30 minutes)

Gather the children into an information formation for the entire discussion.

Substance Abuse

1. Introduce the concept: *Substance use and abuse has four stages: avoidance, experimentation, addiction, and rehabilitation. Some individuals are more likely to experiment and to become addicted than other individuals. Let's discuss the four stages:*

    avoidance—The individual does not use or abuse substances.

    experimentation—The individual tries one or more substances, usually with the idea it is a "one-time thing."

    addiction—The individual mentally or physically (or both) needs to use the substance.

    rehabilitation—The individual tries to stop using the substance, usually with the help of others.

2. Discuss these three points with the children:

    - *Experimentation is more dangerous and avoidance is more important for some individuals because some people are more likely to become addicted than others. Individuals with close relatives who are or have been substance abusers and addicts are also more likely to become addicted.*

    - *Avoidance is easier than rehabilitation. Even though there may be peer pressure and curiosity about substances (alcohol, tobacco, depressants, stimulants, inhalants) addiction is difficult to break.*

    - *Addiction hurts people and their families. The hurt may be physical (e.g., illness), mental (e.g., caring less for friends and family than the substance), or financial (e.g., loss of job, wasting money on the substance).*

Wordfind

Help the children do the wordfind.

FORM H2.4: WORDFIND

Abuse	Depressants	Rehabilitation
Addiction	Drug	Stimulant
Alcohol	Experimentation	Substance
Avoidance	Inhalant	Tobacco

```
A  T  S  U  B  S  T  A  N  C  E  X  O  T
D  F  A  T  L  I  T  D  P  O  L  M  S  B
P  L  E  A  V  O  I  D  A  N  C  E  D  R
M  N  O  B  P  Q  R  I  S  T  U  X  V  W
X  Y  I  U  S  E  Z  C  A  B  C  P  D  E
F  H  N  S  J  L  M  T  O  Q  T  E  V  W
G  I  H  E  K  T  N  I  P  R  D  R  U  G
T  L  A  L  C  O  H  O  L  S  U  I  Y  X
P  E  L  R  S  B  O  N  N  A  L  M  L  A
B  E  A  L  S  A  C  O  M  P  U  E  T  E
H  E  N  L  P  C  T  H  B  O  R  N  I  N
G  I  T  S  C  C  O  R  N  B  E  T  A  N
F  L  O  W  O  O  R  S  A  D  A  A  C  A
N  D  Y  S  T  I  M  U  L  A  N  T  T  O
R  E  H  A  B  I  L  I  T  A  T  I  O  N
Y  O  A  N  N  I  V  U  S  A  R  O  Y  J
E  R  R  D  E  P  R  E  S  S  A  N  T  S
```

FORM H2.5: WORD FIND SOLUTION

Solution

```
A  T  S  U  B  S  T  A  N  C  E  X  O  T
D  F  A  T  L  I  T  D  P  O  L  M  S  B
P  L  E  A  V  O  I  D  A  N  C  E  D  R
M  N  O  B  P  Q  R  I  S  T  U  X  V  W
X  Y  I  U  S  E  Z  C  A  B  C  P  D  E
F  H  N  S  J  L  M  T  O  Q  T  E  V  W
G  I  H  E  K  T  N  I  P  R  D  R  U  G
T  L  A  L  C  O  H  O  L  S  U  I  Y  X
P  E  L  R  S  B  O  N  N  A  L  M  L  A
B  E  A  L  S  A  C  O  M  P  U  E  T  E
H  E  N  L  P  C  T  H  B  O  R  N  I  N
G  I  T  S  C  C  O  R  N  B  E  T  A  N
F  L  O  W  O  O  R  S  A  D  A  A  C  A
N  D  Y  S  T  I  M  U  L  A  N  T  T  O
R  E  H  A  B  I  L  I  T  A  T  I  O  N
Y  O  A  N  N  I  V  U  S  A  R  O  Y  J
E  R  R  D  E  P  R  E  S  S  A  N  T  S
```

LESSON 6
NUTRITION

Student Objectives

- Distinguish between fruits and vegetables.
- Name some foods that are fruits and some that are vegetables.
- State the five-a-day rule.

Equipment and Materials

- Poster board or chalkboard
- Marker or chalk
- Paper and crayons for each child
- Magazines with pictures of food, scissors, and glue for each child (optional substitute for paper and crayons)

Health Concept (30 minutes)

Gather the children into an information formation for the entire discussion.

Good Nutrition

1. Introduce the concept: *Good nutrition, eating a healthy diet, is a good health habit. Nutrition also influences growth, especially body weight. The five-a-day rule means that a person should have five servings of fruits and vegetables each day.*

2. Elaborate: *Fruits contain various nutrients. Nutrients are things our bodies need that come from our diet. Fruits include such foods as melons, citrus fruit, and berries. Vegetables also contain various nutrients. Vegetables can be green leafy, yellow, beans, and starchy. Some vegetables from each of the groups include green leafy (spinach, collard greens, lettuce), yellow (carrots, sweet potatoes, squash), beans (black-eyed peas, red kidney beans, lentils) and starchy (potatoes, corn). Other vegetables include turnips, okra, eggplant, beets, mushrooms, and brussels sprouts.*

3. Ask children to name their favorite fruits while you list them. Repeat with vegetables.

4. Continue: *Vegetables can provide us with protein (from beans) and carbohydrates (from potatoes), both of which our bodies need. Protein builds cells; carbohydrates give us quick energy.* Ask children to name some foods they like that provide protein (meats, dairy, and beans) and carbohydrates (grains, fruits, and vegetables).

5. Ask each child to plan a menu for a day, drawing pictures of the foods. The menu should include the five servings of fruits and vegetables. Have the children number the servings of fruits and vegetables. Alternatively, children can cut pictures of foods for their menus from magazines.

GRADES 2-3

HEALTH

LESSON 7
PHYSICAL ACTIVITY AND FITNESS

Student Objectives

- Distinguish between physical fitness and physical activity.
- Name one benefit of physical activity.

Equipment and Materials

- 1 copy of crossword per child
- 1 pencil per child

Health Concept (30 minutes)

Gather the children into an information formation for the entire discussion.

Physical Fitness and Physical Activity

1. Introduce the concept: *Physical fitness and physical activity are part of good health and help us to grow. Physical fitness is being able to meet some standards for muscle strength and endurance, flexibility, and cardiovascular or aerobic endurance. Having a healthy amount of body fat is also part of fitness.*

2. Tell the children: *Physical activity means a person does things that require large muscles, and such a person does not spend all day sitting down. If we take a walk, use the stairs, clean house, or work in the garden, we are being physically active. Being physically fit or active reduces the risk of certain diseases (e.g., diabetes, coronary heart disease) and encourages our bones to grow stronger, helps us make bigger muscles, and keeps our bodies from storing too much fat.*

3. Do the crossword in form H2.6 individually. Down are words associated with health-related fitness; across, with physical activity.

FORM H2.6: CROSSWORD 2

Across

1. Don't ride, _____!
2. Making flowers and good health
3. _____ to work instead of driving to work

Down

1. Muscular _____
2. Over and over again
3. Heart fitness
4. Bending and stretching
5. Not too much or too little, but just right

FORM H2.7: CROSSWORD 2 SOLUTION

Solution

```
 S                         F
 T      E         W  A  L  K
 R      N                E
 E      D                X     F
 N      U      A         I     A
 G  A   R  D   E  N      B     T
 T      A      R         I
 H      N      O         L
        C      B  I  K   I  N  G
        E      I         T
               C         Y
```

LESSON 8
FIRE SAFETY

Student Objectives

- Describe the process of having a home fire plan, practicing fire drills, and designating a meeting place.
- State that the caller should hang up last when talking to a 911 operator.

Equipment and Materials

- Paper and pencils for each child (for house floor plan and escape route drawings)

Health Concept (30 minutes)

Gather the children into an information formation for the entire discussion.

Fire Safety

1. Introduce the concept: *The key to fire safety is prevention. However, we also need to know what to do when there is a fire.*

2. Discuss each of the following points.

911

If you are in a fire, get to safety, then dial 911. You should stay on the phone; do not hang up first. The emergency operator can send help for treating injuries, putting out the fire, and doing whatever else is necessary.

Fire at Home

1. Outline the planning process: *Before you have a fire, have a plan for getting out of your house safely. The plan should show and explain two escape routes for each person in your family from his or her bedroom in case one route is blocked by fire. Your home should also have smoke alarms. Check them often to be sure the alarms work. Practice crawling out under smoke where the air is better.*

2. Emphasize the need for practice: *Agree with your family on a meeting place so you can count and make sure everyone is out. Practice before there is a fire, so each person knows the alarm signal, the routes, and the meeting place. You need to know who is home, who is still in the house, and who escaped when help arrives.*

3. Help the children apply the information: *Finally, use the plan if there is a fire. Call 911 when you get to safety, and stay on the line until the emergency operator hangs up so you're sure the operator got all the information needed to help you and your family.*

Public Places

When you enter a new place, notice the exit signs. If there is a fire or fire alarm in a public place, remain calm. Move to the nearest exit. Sometimes the lights go out during a fire. Don't panic. The exit lights usually work with batteries and will stay on, so use them to guide you to the door.

Fire Extinguishers and Other Firefighting Methods

Households should have fire extinguishers, for example, in the kitchen, garage, and workshop. While firefighters use water to put out fires, some fires are made worse with water. Grease fires and many chemical fires are examples. Fire extinguishers work by removing the oxygen. There are other ways of removing the oxygen; for example, putting dirt on yard fires can stop the burning. When clothing catches on fire, rolling on the ground or in a blanket made of natural fabric can smother the flames. Public places are required to have fire extinguishers. These are usually marked clearly. All fire extinguishers have to be checked or serviced regularly. Never play with fire extinguishers; they are tools, not toys. We need them to be ready to help if a fire starts.

School children and teachers must practice how to evacuate, or leave, the school quickly. That is why we have regular fire drills. Discuss the plan and route for this class.

Applying Fire Safety Concepts

Have the children draw a map of their home's floor plan and make a fire plan to escape, including where the meeting place might be. As homework, encourage discussion with family.

LESSON 9
DISEASE AND ILLNESS

Student Objectives

- State that disease and illness can be inherited or caused by environmental factors.
- Name two or more ways to reduce the risk of disease and illness.

Equipment and Materials

- Paper and crayons or paper, magazines, glue, and scissors for each child.

Health Concept (30 minutes)

Gather the children into an information formation for the entire discussion.

Disease and Illness

1. Introduce the concept: *Two ways diseases are transmitted are through our genes (inherited) and through the environment (e.g., bacteria and viruses). Some inherited conditions are made worse or occur more frequently when certain environmental conditions are present. Our behavior influences our health by increasing or reducing our chances of getting certain illnesses. We are going to discuss three types of diseases and illnesses.*

2. Tell the children the first type of disease and illness: *First, heart disease and cancer are two diseases that have both a genetic and environmental part. We inherit risk for these diseases from our parents, but we can increase or reduce the risk through our lifestyle choices. A healthy diet, regular exercise, and low stress can reduce the risk for these diseases.*

3. *Second, some diseases can be prevented with vaccinations. Before you could go to school, you had shots with medicines to prevent the spread of the diseases that can be prevented by vaccines. Smallpox, polio, measles, and chicken pox are all diseases that can spread rapidly and be dangerous. Fortunately, they can also be prevented with vaccinations.*

4. *Third are illnesses that can be prevented or at least the risk of getting them can be reduced if we are careful. For example, many bacteria, fungi, and viruses are spread by direct contact. That means touching a person with the illness or touching something they touched. So covering our mouths when we cough or sneeze helps stop the spread of disease. Washing our hands can also prevent the spread of disease.*

5. Ask the children: *List things you can do to reduce disease risk.* (Wash their hands, cover mouth when coughing and sneezing, eat a healthy diet, exercise, reduce stress.)

6. Have the children do one of the following:

    Draw a picture of a way to reduce the risk for disease.

    Cut pictures out of magazines showing ways to reduce risk.

LESSON 10
HOME SAFETY

Student Objectives

- Identify three sources of safety risk in the home.
- Name one or more treatment for a source of home risk.

Equipment and Materials

- Poster or chalkboard
- Marker or chalk

Health Concept (30 minutes)

Gather the children into an information formation.

Home Safety

1. Introduce the concept: *Home should be a safe place, but sometimes things we do at home create unsafe situations.*

2. Discuss each of the following in table H2.2 and identify how each can be made safer:

Table H2.2: Risks

Source	Risk(s)	Treatment/Prevention
Electricity	Fire and shock	Do not play with sockets or appliances, watch for frayed cord.
Fire	Burns and suffocation	Do not play with matches or near open flames, have fire and smoke detectors.
Gas/radon	Suffocation or long-term disease	Have an alarm or test kit, check pilot lights.
Stairs	Falls	Do not play on stairs, do not store materials on stairs, keep stairs well-lighted.
Bathtubs	Falls and drowning	Do not play or stand up in the tub, have a no-slip surface or bath mat, do not go in the tub alone (have a parent or adult supervise).
Tools & knives	Cuts and shocks	Do not play with knives or tools; use only with adult supervision.
Firearms	Wounds	Store firearms, use safety locks, do not play with or touch guns, do not stay where there are guns.

3. After presenting each of the sources and discussing them, ask the children to put their heads down and cover their eyes.

4. As you say the name of the following sources ask the children: *Who has this source in their home? Raise your hand.* (Guns [firearms], knives.)

5. Now ask: *How many of you know someone who was hurt by a gun or knife?* After a chance to respond, have the children put their hands down and raise their heads. Say to the children: *Children should not play with guns or knives, even if you see them at home. You should never touch a gun or knife. It is too dangerous. I care about you, and I want you to be safe. Please do not touch these things anywhere, including your homes.*

6. *Who has the following in their home? Fire or smoke detector, carbon monoxide (gas) detector, radon test kit.* Have children raise their hands as appropriate.

GRADES 2-3 CLASSROOM ACTIVITIES

There will be times when the gymnasium or all-purpose areas are unavailable and when the weather prohibits outdoor classes. These lessons give you specific plans for making the most of these times.

UNIT ORGANIZATION

The lessons in this unit cover body challenges, body parts, fitness, rhythmic activities, manipulative activities (throwing, catching, and striking), games, and creative movement. Feel free to pick and choose among the lessons, repeating them as desired.

LESSON ORGANIZATION

These lessons are structured as the lessons intended for the gymnasium or playing field with clearly stated objectives, equipment and materials lists, and specific activity instructions. Be especially careful to adapt setup instructions to fit the particular venue you're using.

TEACHING HINTS

Teaching in a classroom setting can be a pleasure or a disaster—depending on how well-prepared you and your students are. Plan now for how you'll adapt your rules and protocols to the classroom setting, keeping student ages and abilities and safety considerations in mind. When the day comes where you must teach in the classroom, try to select a lesson that will fit in with what students have been working on in the gymnasium setting. For example, balance challenges (e.g., Lesson 1) may serve to improve gymnastics performance in the gymnasium.

Adapting Rules and Protocols

As at the beginning of the school year when you took the time to teach basic rules and protocols, it is well worth making time for training students to behave appropriately when you must hold physical education class in such a confined space. So the first lesson a particular class experiences in the classroom setting should consist primarily of showing the children how you wish to adapt the gymnasium rules and protocols to the classroom. Then each time you find yourself in the same situation, briefly but clearly review these adaptations with each class. The children will appreciate knowing what is expected of them and will respond more appropriately to the lesson.

Pay particular attention to teaching children how to make smooth transitions. At the beginning and the end of each lesson, you must find a way to set physical education apart from other curricular activities to help students focus. You might, for example, request that all other learning materials be put away, then after reviewing the rule and protocol adaptations, ask a question or two leading into the day's physical education topic, such as, "Does anyone remember what skill we worked on during our last class? What was the most important part of that skill to remember? Today we will work on a part of that skill that we can do safely in the classroom." Such an opening will draw students into the day's lesson. At the end, putting away equipment and sitting quietly doing relaxation or deep breathing exercises for two or three minutes may facilitate the transition back to academic work. You might allow the first group or row to settle down the privilege of getting a drink of water first. Children appreciate knowing what will happen and what is expected of them.

Second and Third Graders

One advantage of teaching this age group in the classroom is that they are better able to safely help you create an open space when needed by quickly and quietly moving desks aside (then back in place at the end of the lesson). Time the children with a stopwatch to challenge them to be ready quickly, taking off five seconds as a bonus to reward them for being quiet. Record this time and compare to the next classroom lesson's transition time. A classroom teacher who is willing to have the chairs stacked out of the way and the children already settled on the floor can be a real boon. Always, however, try to respect the classroom teacher's needs so that he or she will be able to move quickly into the next activity after your lesson.

Safety Considerations

You must select activities that take into account crowded conditions, low ceilings, electrical cords, and breakable objects. Then always take time to review your adaptations of your regular rules and protocols to help prevent injuries.

An important point to remember with this age group is that they are not likely to anticipate hazards when playing in the classroom setting. You must be sure to warn them of specifics, such as, "Be careful not to trip over table legs as you move toward the edges of the room" or "We usually run during this game, but today we need to walk only. Can anyone tell us why?"

Making the Most of the Situation

It is important to keep in mind that classroom days are not "throw-away" days. With a little extra effort and planning they can be wonderful extensions of your gymnasium and outdoor time with the children. You may even gain some insights into individual children as you see them in the setting in which they spend most of their school days. Such insights may help you meet their needs throughout the rest of the year. You may also be able to forge a closer relationship with their teachers, enhancing collaboration opportunities.

GRADES 2-3 CLASSROOM ACTIVITIES

LESSON 1
BALANCE CHALLENGES

Student Objectives

- Respond correctly to one half of the balance challenges.
- Attempt all the balance challenges.
- Work cooperatively with a partner.

Equipment and Materials

- 1 chair per child

Skill-Development Activities (20 minutes)

Movement Challenges

Arrange the children in lines, each child standing behind a chair, holding the back for balance. Challenge the children with the following tasks:

> *Stand on tiptoe.*
>
> *Close your eyes and hold them closed for a count of three: one, two, three.*
>
> *Open your eyes and release (let go of) one hand from the chair.*
>
> *Stand flat-footed again.*
>
> *With weight on your right foot, lift your left foot up behind you.*
>
> *Touch your left foot or toes with your free hand.*
>
> *Stand on both feet, squat down but do not let your calf and thigh touch, and stand up again. Stand on one foot, squat down as far as possible, and stand up again.*
>
> *With weight on your left foot, lift your right leg up in front of you and touch your toes with your free hand.*
>
> *Jump into the air and click your heels together two times.*
>
> *Sitting on your chair, can you balance with your feet higher than your head?*
>
> *Can you balance on your hands and knees in your chair?*

Partner Challenges

Move the children away from their chairs, and match each child with a partner.

1. Challenge the children with the following tasks:

   > *Grasp one of your partner's hands and balance on one foot.*
   >
   > *Hold one of your partner's hands and balance, one person at a high level and one person at a low level.*

2. Have partners reverse roles, then offer the following challenges:

Repeat, showing one wide balance and one narrow balance.

Balance with your partner on a total of three body parts.

Balance with your partner on a total of two body parts.

Can you balance on two parts another way?

Movement Challenges

Divide the children into groups of four (combine two existing pairs). Challenge the children with the following tasks:

Balance as a group on a total of five (three, two) body parts.

Two people balance high while two people balance low.

One person balance high while three people balance low.

Concluding Actvities (10 minutes)

Mirror Game

Have partners face each other and choose one child as the first leader.

1. Explain the activity: *The leader moves body parts or the whole body into various positions, and the other partner follows as though a mirror image of the leader. Do all movements in personal space.*

2. Have the children play the Mirror Game.

3. After the children play for two to three minutes, select a pair to show their movements to the class.

4. Have them reverse partners' roles and continue playing.

LESSON 2
IDENTIFYING BODY PARTS

Student Objectives

- Correctly identify 26 body parts on another individual.
- Correctly identify five body surfaces on another individual.
- Correctly identify right and left.
- Work cooperatively with a partner and in a group.

Equipment and Materials

- 1 beanbag per child

Skill-Development Activities (20 minutes)

Body Parts and Surfaces

Arrange the children in a large circle.

1. Ask them to stand with their right shoulders to the center of the circle. Tell the children: *Touch your head (neck, back, shoulder, hip, toe, leg, finger, wrist, elbow, ankle, knee, foot, calf, thigh, shin, stomach, chest, chin, ear, front, top side, back) on the child standing directly in front of you.*

2. Ask the children to face the center of the circle. Tell the children: *Touch your nose (eye, mouth, forehead, eyebrow, bottom).*

Movement Challenges

Distribute the beanbags, one per child.

1. Challenge the children with the following tasks:

    Put the beanbag on the floor.

    Walk around the beanbag.

    Jump over the beanbag.

    Stand beside the beanbag.

    Stand in front of the beanbag.

    Jump backward over the beanbag.

    Put the beanbag on your head and balance it there.

2. Have the children keep the beanbags on their heads for the following challenges:

    Touch your nose with your right thumb.

Clap your hands behind your back three times.

Bend and touch the floor with your left hand.

Stand on your tiptoe and turn around.

Sit down.

Stand up.

Bend and touch one knee to the floor.

Put the beanbag on your right elbow.

3. Have the children keep the beanbags on their right elbow for the following movement challenges. Some children will put the beanbag on the outside of their elbow, others will put it on the inside, others on the top—any way is fine!

    Lean to the left.

    Stand on tiptoe.

    Turn around.

    Bend and touch your toes with your left hand.

    Lean to the right.

    Toss and catch your beanbag with your elbow.

    Put the beanbag on your knee.

4. Have the children keep the beanbags on a knee for the following challenges:

    Hop forward three times.

    Touch the foot of the leg holding the beanbag to the floor.

    Stand on tiptoe.

    Lean to the right.

    Lean to the left.

    Toss your beanbag up and catch it on your knee.

    Put your beanbag on your shoulder.

5. Have them keep the beanbag on a shoulder for the next set of challenges:

    Stamp your feet.

    Clap your hands.

    Bend your knees.

    Bend your elbows.

    Touch your head to your elbow.

    Touch your head to your knee.

    Jump forward three times.

    Shrug your shoulders.

    Sit down.

    Stand up.

6. Remind the children not to touch each other. Challenge the children with the following tasks:

    Drop your beanbag, then pick it up and walk in a circle, tossing and catching the beanbag.

    Hop to the nearest wall and touch the wall with the beanbag.

    Put the beanbag on a body part (not your hand) and skip back to your place.

Challenges for Groups

Arrange the children in four small circles, one beanbag per group.

1. Challenge the children with the following tasks:

   Toss the beanbag around the circle.

   Pass the beanbag between your legs around the circle.

   Toss the beanbag under one leg and around the circle.

   Balance the beanbag on your shoulder, so the next person in line can take the beanbag off your shoulder and put it on their shoulder for the next person, and so on.

   Pass the beanbag over the first person's head, between the next person's legs, overhead, under legs, and so on around the circle.

2. Have the children think of their own challenges as time allows.

Concluding Activities (10 minutes)

Inclusive Simon Says

Divide the children into two groups. Arrange each group in a scatter formation in half of the play area. Appoint a leader for each group.

1. Describe the game:

   In each group, the leader gives a challenge. If the challenge begins with "Simon says," you should perform the challenge.

   If it does not begin with "Simon says," you should ignore the challenge.

   Children who perform a task that does not begin with "Simon says," move to the other group and play with that group.

   Leaders, use the challenges given earlier in the lesson.

   We will allow each leader to give three challenges, then have each leader choose a new person to be a leader.

2. Have the children play Inclusive Simon Says.

LESSON 3
MANIPULATIVE SKILLS

Student Objectives

- Play a game that requires listening to verbal instructions and disregarding visual information.
- Play a game in which two movement rules apply simultaneously.
- Work cooperatively with a group.

Equipment and Materials

- 1 red ball (4-10 in.) per group
- 1 ball of another color (4-10 in.) per group
- 4 beanbags

Skill-Development Activities (25 minutes)

Rabbit and Fox

Seat the class in circles of six to eight children. Give each circle two balls, one of each color.

1. Describe the game:

   The "Rabbit" is the red ball, and the "Fox" is the other ball. Cues to remember: Red, Rabbit, right.

   The Fox is allowed to travel around the circle in any direction, but the Rabbit can only go counterclockwise (point).

   The object of the game is to get both balls moving as quickly as possible without losing control of them.

   The Fox catches the Rabbit if one child holds the Rabbit in one hand and the Fox in the other.

   When the Fox catches the Rabbit, a new game begins. There is no penalty for catching the Rabbit—just start over.

2. Have the children play several games of Rabbit and Fox.

Concluding Activities (5 minutes)

Inclusive Tricky Simon

Have all the children stand at the front of the room, dividing them into two groups. Select two children to each be "Simon."

1. Describe and demonstrate the game:

   Each Simon gives commands to his or her group, but some of the time Simon demonstrates something else ("Simon says rub your stomach," while Simon actually pats his or her head).

   You are supposed to do only what Simon says, not what Simon does.

   If you do what Simon does and not what Simon says, join the other group.

   Each Simon may give three commands, then must pick a new Simon for his or her group.

   Everyone will move back to the front of the room to listen to each new Simon.

2. Have the children play Inclusive Tricky Simon.

LESSON 4
IDENTIFYING BODY PARTS

Student Objectives

- Complete a four-part movement sequence, given verbally, after a 10-second interval.
- Move one or more body parts in isolation to music.
- Play a game that requires movement and a cognitive strategy.

Equipment and Materials

- Music (break-dance, mechanical, any rhythmic music)
- Signal

Skill-Development Activities (20 minutes)

Isolations

Arrange the students in scatter formation among the desks.

1. Describe the activity:

   As the music plays, I will call out various body parts or combinations of body parts.

   Move only those parts named and hold the remaining parts still.

2. Have the children play Isolations. Cue the children: *Head (fingers, right arm, feet, left arm, left arm and leg, right arm and leg, legs and feet).*

Memory Game

Keep the students in scatter formation.

1. Present the following movement sequences. Say each sequence once, then encourage the children to remember and perform each sequence in order on a signal.

   Walk forward three steps, clap three times, and jump three times.

   Jump backward three times, turn around, and touch your toes.

   Hop in place on your left foot five times, clap behind your back three times, and jump four times.

   Touch your toes, touch your nose, lean to the left, and turn around.

   Walk in a circle, stop and clap one time, bend down, and jump up.

   Clap three times, slap your legs three times, turn around, and jump up.

2. If some of the children forget or do the wrong movements, repeat the sequence until most of the children can do it.

Concluding Activities (10 minutes)

Who's the Leader?

Select one child to be "It." The other children should be scattered around the room.

1. Describe the game:

    It leaves the room or covers both eyes while I select a leader.

    It comes back in, and the leader starts a movement and periodically changes to another movement (for example, walking in place, then touching alternate fingers to nose, then jumping up and down).

    It tries to guess who the leader is.

    When It guesses the leader, I will choose a new It and a new leader.

2. Have the children play Who's the Leader?

LESSON 5
PHYSICAL FITNESS

Student Objectives

- Perform flexibility, muscle endurance, and cardiovascular endurance exercises.
- Work cooperatively with a group.

Equipment and Materials

- 1 or 2 chairs per child
- Several tables
- Signal

Note: See instructions to determine equipment that will work in the particular classroom.

Skill-Development Activities (25 minutes)

Bicycles Everywhere

Arrange the children in scatter formation. Each student should be near two chairs or two tables or one chair and one table.

1. Describe and have two children demonstrate the game:

   I will call out "bicycles down," or "bicycles around," and you must do the action:

   "Bicycles down" means you lie on the ground and lift your hips and legs upward and support your hips with your arms, and bicycle with your legs.

   "Bicycles around" tells you to get a partner (or group of three), form a short line, place your hands on the waist of the person in front, and shuffle your feet in unison (demonstrate clearly) *as quickly as possible, moving around the space without bumping into anyone or anything.*

2. Have the children play Bicycles Everywhere.

Desk Seat Push-Ups

Arrange the children in scatter formation, each child with a chair.

1. Describe and demonstrate the activity:

   Facing the front of the chair, grasp the seat of the chair (see hand placement in figure below), *support your weight with your arms, and walk away from the chair with your feet so your legs are extended and your body forms a straight line. This is the starting position for the push-up.*

   To do a push-up, bend and then straighten your arms to lower your chest to the chair seat, then push back up to the starting position for a complete push-up.

2. Have the children do five desk seat push-ups.

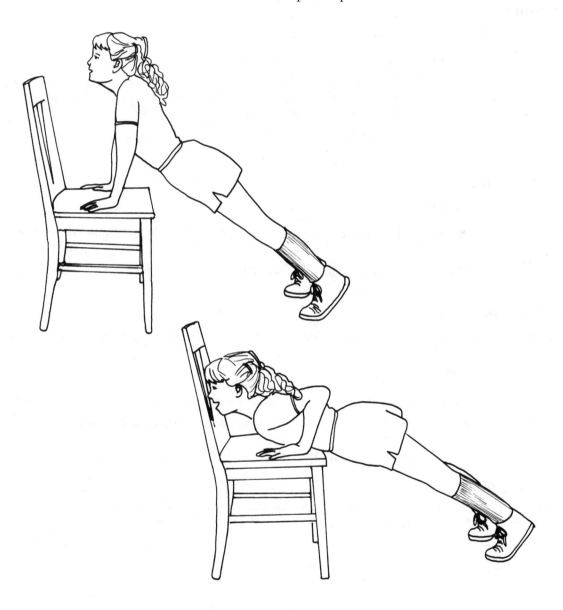

Chair Curl-Ups

Keep the children in scatter formation, each child with a chair.

1. Describe and demonstrate the activity:

    Begin by lying on the floor with your bottom against the front legs of the chair, bending your knees so your calves rest on the chair seat.

    With arms crossed on your chest, lift your head slowly from the floor and continue curling up as far as possible.

    Hold for five counts, then slowly return to starting position.

2. Have the children do 10 chair curl-ups.

Bookworm

Arrange the children in scatter formation without chairs.

1. Describe and demonstrate the activity:

    Beginning by standing, touch the floor in front of your toes with both hands, bending your knees enough for safety. Walk your hands forward until your body is straight, so they end up in starting push-up position, then reverse.

    Your feet should never move.

2. Have the children do 10 bookworms.

Book Stretching

Have the children sit at their desks.

1. Describe and demonstrate the activity: *Holding a book in both hands overhead, lean back, side, front, side.*

2. Have the children practice book stretching, five times clockwise and five times counterclockwise.

Four-Corners Fitness

Divide the children into four groups and assign each group to a corner of the room. Assign one exercise to each corner.

1. Describe and demonstrate each exercise.

2. Have the children in each corner practice the assigned exercise for one minute.

3. Signal stop and have the children rotate, allowing 30 seconds for children to get to the next corner.

4. Continue until all the children have been in each corner twice for one minute each.

Elbow-Knee Touches

Standing with feet shoulder-width apart, touch your left knee with your right elbow while jumping to a tiptoe position, return to start, and reverse so your left elbow touches your right knee.

Jumping Jacks

Standing with your feet together, arms low at your sides, jump, landing with your feet to the sides in a straddle position as your arms clap overhead, then return to start.

Skier

Standing with feet together, keep your feet together and jump side-to-side, imitating the motion of a skier.

Knee to Nose

Beginning on all-fours on hands and knees, move your chin to your chest while bringing one knee forward. After your knee and nose touch (or come as close as possible), extend the leg backward, repeat, and then use the opposite leg.

Concluding Activities (5 minutes)

Cool-Down

1. Have everyone walk slowly around the room, taking deep breaths and exhaling slowly, for one minute.

2. Have the children do the following cool-down exercises:

   Sit in a chair with your eyes closed, take a deep breath, exhale slowly, and relax your shoulders. Think about your shoulders—let them hang, don't move your fingers or arms, feel your shoulders get heavy.

   Take another breath and relax your legs.

   Your legs are so heavy you can't pick them up; they are going to sleep.

   Take another breath, and as you exhale slowly, relax your head and neck.

   Hold very still so your head doesn't bounce forward.

   Relax your arms and hands.

   Make fists with your hands; hold it! (Wait 10 seconds.)

   Now let go and relax your hands and arms. (Wait for a few seconds.)

   Now stand up and gently shake your whole body.

   Everyone sit down in your chair quietly.

LESSON 6
PHYSICAL FITNESS

Student Objectives

- Perform flexibility, muscle endurance, and cardiovascular endurance exercises.
- Work cooperatively with a partner.

Equipment and Materials

- 1 short jump rope per pair
- Signal
- 1 chair per child
- 1 book per pair

Skill-Development Activities (25 minutes)

Mountain Climber 1

Arrange partners in scatter formation. *Note*: For safety's sake, match partners by size and strength as evenly as possible.

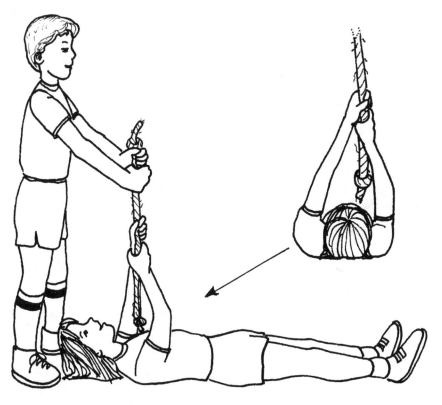

1. Describe and demonstrate the activity:

    One of you will start as the performing child and the other will help.

    The performing child lies on the floor on his or her back, and the partner stands, holding the jump rope over the performer's shoulders.

    The performer grasps the jump rope and lifts the upper body off the ground, holding this position as long as possible (keeping feet on the floor).

    I will signal "Stop!" after 30 seconds so you can rest a bit.

    After five mountain climbers, you will trade roles with your partner.

2. Have performers practice Mountain Climber 1 five times for as long as possible or up to 30 seconds each.

3. Have partners reverse roles.

Mountain Climber 2

Keep the same setup. If desired, have students change partners. *Note*: For safety's sake, match partners by size and strength as evenly as possible.

1. Describe and demonstrate the activity:

    The helping partner lies on the floor with head near the feet of the performer, who is standing.

    The performer holds the middle of the jump rope in both hands with palms up.

    The child on the floor grasps the rope with both hands.

    The performer tries to lift the rope and the child on the ground.

    Performers, be careful to gently set your partner back down.

    After 10 mountain climbers, you will trade roles with your partner.

2. Have the performers practice Mountain Climber 2 10 times.

3. Have partners reverse roles.

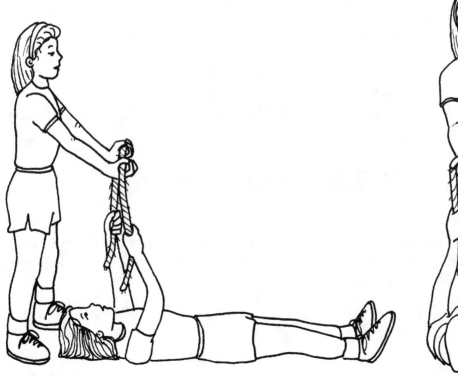
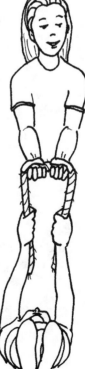

High Stepper

Arrange the children in scatter formation, each with a chair.

1. Describe and demonstrate the activity:

   Standing facing a chair, step up on your right leg, lifting your body onto the chair so both feet are on the chair.

   Step down on your right foot.

   Repeat with your left foot.

2. Have the children practice high stepper at a rate of 30 in 60 seconds.

3. Have them perform high stepper for 60 seconds and then walk around the chair for 30 seconds, repeating the sequence five times.

Partner Sit-Ups

Arrange pairs in scatter formation, each pair with a book.

1. Describe and demonstrate the exercise:

   The helping partner counts the number of sit-ups for the working partner.

   The working partner does 10 sit-ups, beginning lying with hands crossed on a book held against chest, knees bent at a 45-degree angle (demonstrate clearly).

   The working partner gives the book to his or her partner, and the helping partner now becomes the working partner.

   The new working partner now does 10 sit-ups.

2. Have the children practice partner sit-ups, three sets for each partner (a total of 30 sit-ups per child).

Echo Stretching

Keep the same setup. If desired, have students change partners.

1. Describe and demonstrate the activity:

   One partner makes up a stretching sequence; for example, touch toes (knees bent slightly), lean left, lean right, squat (no more than thighs parallel to floor), straighten legs, stand, and stretch backward.

   When the sequence is finished, the other partner does (echoes) the same sequence.

   Take turns leading, until each of you has led five times.

2. Have the children practice echo stretching, allowing enough time for each child to lead five times.

Concluding Activities (5 minutes)

Cool-Down

Have the children walk slowly around the room for three minutes, then sit or lie down quietly for two minutes as you direct them to relax. See Grades 2-3: Classroom Activities, Lesson 5, Cool-Down, page 737.

LESSON 7
RHYTHMS

Student Objectives

- Use different movements to represent different beats.
- Copy a rhythmic pattern.
- Work cooperatively as a group.

Equipment and Materials

- 1 drum, 2 wood blocks, or 2 rhythm sticks

Skill-Development Activities (30 minutes)

Changing Directions on the Accent Beat

Arrange the children in scatter formation or in rows among the desks.

1. Provide four beats, with the fourth beat louder (stronger) than the other three.
2. Have the children walk forward three steps and backward one.
3. Have them repeat several times. Cue the children: *Walk, walk, walk, back.*
4. Repeat, using any change of direction on the accent beat (e.g., sideways, or backward), *walk, walk, walk, side; or walk, side, walk, walk.*
5. Repeat, using a change of level on the accent beat. Cue the children: *Walk, walk, walk, bend.*

Patterns

Arrange the children in scatter formation.

1. Have the children walk to the following rhythm pattern, taking backward steps on the accented beats:

   Three beats, accent on the third *(walk, walk, back)*

   Six beats, accent on the second and sixth *(walk, back, walk, walk, walk, back)*

   Eight beats, accent on the eighth *(walk, 2, 3, 4, 5, 6, 7, back)*

   Four beats, accent on the first *(back, walk, walk, walk)*

2. Repeat, using any change of direction on the accent beat (e.g., left, right, or back).
3. Repeat, using any change of level on the accent beat. Cue the children: *Walk, two, three, low . . . .*

Number the children one to three and leave them randomly in scatter formation.

4. Describe the group assignments: The ones' assignment is to change levels, the twos' is to change direction, and the threes sit on the floor.

5. As the rhythmic pattern is repeated, have the children continue moving and changing as designated by group membership.

6. Stop only to let them know what pattern will come next. Here are some more examples:

   Four beats, accent on the fourth

   Three beats, accent on the third

   Eight beats, accent on the eighth

7. Rotate group assignments and repeat patterns until all groups have experienced each assignment.

Concluding Activities

None.

GRADES 2-3

CLASSROOM ACTIVITIES

LESSON 8
GAMES

Student Objectives

- Cooperate in a game.
- Participate in a simple game with little or no teacher supervision.

Equipment and Materials

- 1 beanbag per child (less one per class)
- 1 chair per child (less one per class)
- Music

Skill-Development Activities (30 minutes)

Cooperative Musical Chairs

Arrange the children in a circle around the chairs, which are arranged back-to-back in a double row. Start with one fewer chairs than children.

1. Describe and demonstrate the game:

   Walk around the double row of chairs, as the music plays.

   When the music stops, take a seat.

   The extra child sits on the lap of another child.

   As the music starts again, I will remove another chair.

   When the music stops, two children sit on the laps of other children. (No one is eliminated.)

   We will keep playing until all of you must help each other to balance on one chair!

   For safety's sake, be sure you are balancing—not sitting on each other.

2. Have the children play Cooperative Musical Chairs.

3. Repeat.

Step on It

Divide the children into circles of 8 to 10 children, each child with a beanbag, except the child who is "It."

1. Describe the game:

   As the music starts, place your beanbag on the ground and move around the circle, using a locomotor pattern selected by It (for example, walking, skipping, or hopping).

When the music stops, try to get a foot on a beanbag (including It). Be careful you don't hurt each other.

The child who does not have a foot on a beanbag is the new It and play continues.

2. Play Step on It.

Concluding Activities

None.

GRADES 2-3 CLASSROOM ACTIVITIES

LESSON 9
GAMES

Student Objectives

- Follow instructions for a simple game.
- Listen to verbal cues and respond appropriately.

Equipment and Materials

- None.

Skill-Development Activities (30 minutes)

Mousetrap

Have half the children form a circle, holding hands with arms held high. These children are the "Trap." The other half of the children are the "Mice."

1. Describe and demonstrate the game:

   The Mice move in and out of the circle by passing under the joined hands of the Trap.

   When I say "Mousetrap!" Trap children lower their joined hands. Any Mice in the circle are "trapped."

   Trapped Mice join the circle (Trap).

   We will keep playing until all the Mice have been trapped.

   Then the children who made the Trap at the start of the game will become Mice for a second game, and the Mice will become the Trap.

2. Have the children play two rounds of Mousetrap.

Run-Across

Have all the children form a circle. Assign each child a number (1 through number of children in the class; or letter—A to Z, AA, and so on), and select one child to be "It."

1. Describe and demonstrate the game:

   It calls out two or three numbers (or letters), and those children try to exchange places before It can take one of the places they've left.

   The one child left over becomes the new It.

2. Have the children play Run-Across.

LESSON 10
CREATIVE MOVEMENT

Student Objectives

- Move to music.
- Try new movement positions with stretch ropes.

Equipment and Materials

- Several long stretch ropes joined at the end to make a large circle per group (3/4 in. waistband elastic works well; the rope should provide at least a 3-ft section per child.)
- Music (1 each slow and fast instrumentals)

Skill-Development Activities (30 minutes)

Movement Challenges

Divide the children into small groups. Arrange each group evenly around a stretch rope circle (piece of elastic). Have each child in the group hold the stretch rope (elastic) with both hands.

1. Ask the children to move as they listen to the slow music and do the following challenges:

   Change levels.

   Put the elastic behind you.

   Balance on different body parts.

   Move under the elastic.

   Put part of your body on each side of the elastic.

   Change places with someone in your group without letting go. Move closer to others in your group.

   Move away from others in your group.

2. Play the fast music and challenge the children with the following tasks:

   Walk (hop) around in a group.

   Stand in one place and move your whole body to the music.

   Change levels.

   Put the elastic beside you.

3. Select children who are doing interesting movements and point them out to the class.

4. Have each child wrap the stretch rope (elastic) around one ankle and hold it in one hand. Tell the children: *Be careful not to pull on your neighbors too hard.*

5. Play the slow tune and present the following challenges:

  Change levels.

  Balance on different body parts.

  Move closer to your group.

  Move as far apart as you can.

  Walk (hop) around in a group.

Concluding Activities

None.

GRADES K-1

GRADES 2-3

GRADES 4-5

ORGANIZATION

The purpose of the five lessons in this unit is to practice the routines you want your students to follow in the instructional units. When students understand the routines, you'll have fewer discipline problems, lose less time on management, and become a team with your students, working from the same plan. Ultimately, this means you'll have more time for instruction. The skills we present in this unit are more advanced, but based upon the skills we presented in the Organization sections for Grades K-3. These lessons, however, can stand alone.

UNIT ORGANIZATION

The lessons include the following organizational tasks: rules, signals, boundaries, groupings, spacing, stations, equipment, forming groups, journal writing, cooperative teams, and discussion groups. The lessons are a fun way to introduce and/or review important skills; repeat them as needed throughout the year. For children who have experienced Grades K-1 and/or Grades 2-3, some of these lessons will be a review. Do not, however, assume the children know the content in the lessons; some will, and some won't. Even if you're sure they know these routines, it is important to review what you expect of them and to remind them that you will be using these routines. Moreover, repeating something that the children know builds confidence right from the start of the school year, creating an enjoyable and a comfortable learning environment.

Your students may have experienced developing rules several times at the beginning of pre-vious school years. You can create class rules by consensus, where you ask the students to suggest rules to make the class safe and a better learning environment. More information on consensus building is available in the Organization lessons in Grades K-1 and Grades 2-3. Alternatively, since the students may have practiced the rules in previous years, you may want to simply review the rules. In this approach, you want to be certain that each child understands the rule and why it is important.

LESSON ORGANIZATION

Like all the other lessons in this book, we have organized each lesson systematically and have included a list of clear objectives and necessary equipment to make planning easier for you. The activities start with a warm-up, progress to skill development, and end with a concluding activity. Unlike the rest of the lessons in this book, however, the content of the lessons and the instructional focus is on management and behavior. Although you may be anxious to teach movement skills and fitness concepts, remember that time spent on organization and class management now is time saved throughout the school year, as your classes will run more smoothly. Table O3.1 outlines the content of the lessons.

TEACHING HINTS

Feel free to modify certain aspects of the lessons. For example, some schools or districts have uniform consequences for rules infractions that may be different from those presented in these lessons. Further, use your individual preferences for signals and formation names. Use the lessons as presented or modify them to suit your individual situation and preferences. The key is to take a few days and cover the topics until you and your students are comfortable with the routines. This is a worthwhile investment of time, one we observe in expert teachers and know helps novice teachers be more effective.

See also Grades K-1: Organization, pages 3-18 for more information on why and how to use the organization lessons.

Table O3.1: Unit Plan for Grades 4-5: Organization

Week 1: teach and review rules

Monday: rules, signals, boundaries, and groupings

Tuesday: rules, signals, boundaries, and groupings

Wednesday: spacing, stations, equipment, and rules

Thursday: forming groups and journal writing

Friday: cooperative teams and discussion groups

LESSON 1
SIGNALS, BOUNDARIES, GROUPINGS, AND RULES

Student Objectives

- Move among line, circle, scatter, pair, and station formations.
- Form squads.
- Start, listen, and stop on an auditory signal.
- Move in, across, around, and outside boundaries.
- State rules for class behavior.
- Work cooperatively with a group to accomplish a goal.

Equipment and Materials

- Physical Education Rules poster
- 4 cones or markers
- 1 carpet square per squad
- 1 basketball or 8 1/2 in. playground ball per group

Warm-Up Activities (5 minutes)

Boundaries

Divide the children into four groups. Arrange one group on each boundary line of a large rectangle defined by the four cones. Name or number the boundaries (1 to 4, or North, South, East, and West).

1. Call out the following exchanges; students on the boundaries named exchange places with each other:

    1 and 3 (North and South)

    2 and 4 (East and West)

    1 and 4 (North and West)

    3 and 2 (South and East)

    1 and 2 (North and East)

    3 and 4 (South and West)

    3 and 1 (South and North)

    4 and 2 (West and East)

2. Tell the students: *Everyone back to starting position!*

Skill-Development Activities (20 minutes)

Advanced Information Formation

Arrange the children in concentric semicircles with the first row seated, the next row kneeling, and the last row standing. Tell the children: *This as an "advanced information formation."*

Physical Education Rules

Keep the children in the advanced information formation.

1. There are two ways to handle this section: read the rules or work with the students for a consensus on the rules. Read the rules to the students.
    - *Rule 1: Follow directions (the first time they are given).*
    - *Rule 2: Hands off (keep hands, feet, and objects to yourself).*
    - *Rule 3: Be careful of equipment and others.*
    - *Rule 4: Stop, look, and listen on the signal.*
    - *Rule 5: Do not fight or interfere with the practice or play of others (avoid hostile gestures, fighting, and game disruption).*
2. *Are there any questions about the rules?* Discuss.

Cooperative Groups

Arrange the children in groups of four to six heterogeneous learning teams every time you create cooperative groups. Place the students wisely by combining students who lack social skills with others who are more socially mature. Separate the students who tend to be disruptive by placing them in different groups. Also strive to create equal representation of students of different races, ethnic origins, social classes, and gender in each group. Finally, keep group sizes as small as possible to increase participation opportunities. Have each squad line up at a carpet square, arranged at one end of the play area.

1. Assign a role for each member of the group. Roles can include organizer or leader, timekeeper, encourager, praiser, equipment handler, facilitator, and summarizer. Explain the roles you wish the students to use:

    The "organizer" is the student who gets the group started on the group project and serves as the group leader.

    The "timekeeper" keeps time and makes sure the task is completed in the allotted time.

    The "encourager" encourages each student to work productively and reminds each student that their role is important.

    The "praiser" encourages positive interaction by making supportive remarks to each student.

    The "equipment handler" is responsible for getting and returning the equipment the group needs.

    The "facilitator" asks the teacher for help if it is needed.

    The "summarizer" keeps mental notes of the process and provides a summary at the end of the session.

2. Establish guidelines for cooperative work:

    Everyone must contribute to the work.

    Only one student can talk at a time, and the others must listen.

    Everyone must show respect for the others.

    Remember that each person has a unique role to fill.

Problem Solving

Continue with small groups.

1. Present a problem for the groups to solve; for example:

    Create a ball game that requires a circle and uses the skills of throwing, catching, and running.

    Design a play to be used in half-court basketball.

    Design an exercise plan for a week.

2. Share how you will score the work of each group on a five-point scale, ending with: *Your group can earn five points only if you collaborate and work according to the guidelines and if all students fulfill their assigned roles.*

Squad Formation

Teach the children to divide themselves into their small groups (assigned in previous section) with a designated meeting place and a set formation (short parallel lines at each carpet square arranged at one end of the play area).

1. Tell the children: *On the signal, move behind the squares, forming lines with the groups I've already assigned.*

2. Adjust children, if necessary, so that the lines are straight and nearly equal in length. Tell the children: *Remember your squad and your position in your squad.*

Concluding Activities (5 minutes)

Formations

Start this activity with the children still in their squads. Define the play area with the four cones. Ask the children to create the following formations:

Make a line facing me.

Move to scatter formation.

Make a circle around me.

Find a partner and stand back-to-back.

Move to scatter formation.

Move to squad formation.

Squad 1 go to station 1. (Point to a corner; Stations 1 to 4 are corners of a rectangle.)

Squad 2 go to station 2, (and so on; use the long sides or center of the rectangle if you have more than four squads).

Rotate (squad 1 goes to station 2, squad 2 to station 3, and so on).

Players at each station make a circle.

Make one big circle with the entire class.

Move back to squad formation.

Move to scatter formation.

Select a partner and get back in scatter formation.

Move back to squad formation.

Single File

Continue in squad formation. Designate a leader of each squad. Practice working in single file:

> *On the signal, the last person in each line runs to the front of that line and becomes the new leader.*
>
> *All leaders jog or walk around (across, inside) the area as you hear me call out the pattern.*

ORGANIZATION

LESSON 2
SIGNALS, BOUNDARIES, GROUPINGS, AND RULES

Student Objectives
- Move diagonally across an area.
- Move in an area within an area.

Equipment and Materials
- Physical Education Rules poster
- 8 cones or markers
- Large sign cards (8 1/2 in. × 11 in. or larger)
- 8 foam balls
- Chalk, flour (outdoors only), or tape for marking lines

Warm-Up Activities (5 minutes)

Single File
See Grades 4-5: Organization, Lesson 1, page 756.

Skill-Development Activities (20 minutes)

Rules
Arrange the children in an advanced information formation.

1. Ask the children to recall and state the rules.
   - Rule 1: Follow directions.
   - Rule 2: Hands off.
   - Rule 3: Be careful.
   - Rule 4: Stop, look, and listen on the signal.
   - Rule 5: Do not fight.
2. Watch for situations during the remainder of the lesson that are examples of good behavior; stop the class and point them out.

Changing Direction to a Verbal Signal
Arrange the children in scatter formation within a large rectangle marked with four cones.

Have the children move to the following commands, giving a signal when each change of direction should occur: *run (walk, hop, jump) left (right, back, forward, sideways)*.

Task Cards

Print movement tasks on cards large enough for the children to read (8 1/2 in. by 11 in. or larger).

1. Show the cards to the entire group or place the cards at the activity stations. Direct the children to read the tasks and respond with the appropriate movements.

2. Task card instruction examples (or choose other tasks that fit with your skill development plans):

   Slide right, slide left, hop in a circle.

   Jump forward, jump backward, spin, sit down.

   Run 10 steps backward, leap back to starting place.

   Gallop in a circle, hop three times, jump high.

Station Formation

Place one of the cards at each of four stations. Direct the children:

Move to the stations, forming squads with no more than six to eight (or, one fourth of the class) per squad.

Rotate (1 goes to 2, 2 to 3, and so on).

Partner Relay

Arrange the children in pairs, and assign each pair to a four-person relay team. Mark a starting line and a return line. At the return line, place a stack of cards for each relay team, one card for each pair of students. The cards should specify how the pair will return to the starting line. Task card instruction examples (or choose other tasks that fit with your skill development plans):

   Hold one hand with your partner and hop on opposite feet.

   Run backward.

   Skip with one person in front of the other.

   Join both hands and slide.

1. Explain the activity:

   On the signal, travel with your partner, using any type of movement to the return line. Then select a card from the stack of cards and read the task.

   Travel back to the starting line, using the movement specified. This is not a race.

   Continue until each pair in your group has had a turn.

   Shuffle the cards and repeat the game until time is up.

2. Run the Partner Relay.

Moving Diagonally

Have the children get back into four groups, and place one group in each corner of a large rectangle defined by four cones.

1. Have group 1 switch with group 3.

2. Have group 2 switch with group 4.

3. Repeat steps 1 and 2.

4. Have the children move to scatter formation.

5. Present the following tasks:

Can you move diagonally? Stop when you hit a boundary.

Move to a corner if you are not in a corner.

Move diagonally.

Concluding Activities (5 minutes)

Moving Within an Area

Use a second set of four cones to mark out a square in the center of the large rectangle. Divide the children into five squads. Send squads 1 and 2 to one end of the large area. Send squads 3 and 4 to the other end of the large area. Send squad 5 into the small square.

1. Explain the activity:

    Squads 1, 2, 3, and 4 will throw the foam balls over the small square, playing catch between those squads. Squad 5 players will try to catch the balls.

    If a member of squad 5 catches a ball, that child switches places with the thrower.

2. Run the activity. If squad 5 is having trouble catching the balls, enlarge the center square.

LESSON 3
SPACING, EQUIPMENT, STATIONS, AND RULES

Student Objectives

- Move quickly into squad formation.
- Use task cards.

Equipment and Materials

- Physical Education Rules poster
- Physical Education Rules Contract (optional)
- Large task cards (8 1/2 in. × 11 in. or larger)
- 4 cones or markers
- Chalk, flour, or tape for marking lines

Warm-Up Activities (5 minutes)

Forming Groups

Define a large rectangle with the four cones. Arrange the children in scatter formation inside the rectangle.

1. Explain the activity:

   On the signal, run to form groups of three.

   On the next signal, everyone must find different children with whom to form the next group.

   I will quickly signal you to form new groups.

   Remember to stay in your own space so no one gets hurt.

2. Have the children practice the activity.
3. Repeat, forming groups of five.
4. Repeat, forming groups of two.

Skill-Development Activities (20 minutes)

Task Cards

Print movement tasks on cards large enough for the children to read. See the suggestions in Grades 4-5: Organization, Lesson 2, page 758 or choose other tasks that fit with your skill development plans. Additional task card instruction examples (or choose other tasks that fit with your skill development plans):

Jump three times, turn around.

Hop in a circle and touch the ground with one knee.

Balance on three body parts.

Partner Relay

Use different tasks. See Grades 4-5: Organization, Lesson 2, page 758.

Ways to Form Two Teams

Use the following examples to form teams without embarrassing anyone or wasting class time unnecessarily.

1. Have the children form a line on one boundary line and count off (one-two-one-two, and so on). Have number 1's move across the area to the opposite boundary.

2. Have the children get in scatter formation with partners. Direct partners to split up and move to opposite ends of the play area to form the two teams.

3. Have the children sit in five squads. Divide them into columns (squads 1 and 3 and part of 5 form one team) or rows (every other person in a squad goes to one team, the remaining children go to the other team).

Concluding Activities (5 minutes)

Rules

Arrange the children in an advanced information formation.

1. Read the rules.
   - *Rule 1: Follow directions the first time they are given.*
   - *Rule 2: Keep hands, feet, and objects to yourself.*
   - *Rule 3: Be careful of equipment and others.*
   - *Rule 4: Stop, look, and listen on the signal.*
   - *Rule 5: Avoid hostile gestures, fighting, and game disruption.*

2. Describe the consequences for infractions:

   First offense: three-minute time-out.

   Second offense: six-minute time-out.

   Third offense: Call parents.

   Fourth offense: Remove from class, go to the principal or discipline office.

   Fifth offense: Send to principal.

3. Conduct a discussion about the rules and consequences.

Discussion

Continue with the children in the advanced information formation. Review the importance of having and following rules:

Why are rules important in our class?

What might happen if we didn't have any rules to follow?

What would our school be like if we didn't have any school rules?

What are some other rules that might be important?

What would happen if we didn't have a signal to stop?

What should we do if some students never or rarely follow the directions?

LESSON 4
FORMING GROUPS, JOURNAL WRITING

Student Objectives

- Form groups of different sizes quickly and quietly.
- Share their feelings about physical education in writing.

Equipment and Materials

- 1 notebook and pencil per child
- 1 color-shape-number card per child

Warm-Up Activities (10 minutes)

Forming Groups

Continue to work on forming groups with the following adaptation.

1. You can make cards before class and distribute them to the children as they enter the gym.
2. Cards should be four different colors (red, blue, yellow, green). Stamp them with different shapes (circle, triangle, rectangle, square).
3. Number the cards from 1 to the number of children in the class.
4. Present the following tasks:

    Find a partner who has the same color.

    Find a partner who has the same shape.

5. Form two groups: red and blue makes one group and yellow and green makes the second group.
6. Continue with other combinations:

    Form two groups: Group 1 = first half of numbers; Group 2 = second half of numbers.

    Form four groups: Group 1 = circles; Group 2 = squares; Group 3 = rectangles; Group 4 = triangles.

7. Continue using color and shape combinations to form groups.

Skill-Development Activities (15 minutes)

Feelings About Physical Education

Arrange children in scatter formation, each child with a notebook and pencil.

1. Ask the children: *What were your feelings when you were in physical education last year?*
2. Stimulate children's thinking by asking some of the following open-ended questions:

    I feel good in physical education when I . . .

    The activity I enjoyed most was . . .

    It was my favorite activity because . . .

    I feel uncomfortable in physical education when . . .

    I believe physical education is (or is not) important for children because . . .

3. Insist that this be a serious activity, and you should keep children's responses private, not discussing them in class.
4. Read the journals to get ideas about what children think and feel about their experiences in physical education.

Concluding Activities (5 minutes)

Discussion

Arrange children in an advanced information formation. Continue the discussion of the importance of rules:

Why is it important to stop and listen quickly on the teacher's signal?

What might happen if some children do not use the equipment in the way it is intended?

Describe what a good physical education class would look like to a stranger.

LESSON 5
COOPERATIVE TEAMS AND DISCUSSION GROUPS

Student Objectives

- Work successfully and cooperatively in a student learning group.
- Cooperate in a discussion group.

Equipment and Materials

- Physical Education Rules poster
- 2 long jump ropes per group
- List of questions in the concluding activity

Warm-Up Activities (5 minutes)

Forming Groups

See Grades 4-5: Organization, Lessons 3 and 4, pages 760 and 762.

Skill-Development Activities (15 minutes)

Cooperative Learning Groups

Arrange the children in groups of four to six heterogeneous learning teams. Place two jump ropes 40 to 60 ft apart for each group.

1. Review the guidelines for cooperative group work. See Grades 4-5: Organization, Lesson 1, page 754.

2. Discuss the concept: *In group work, cooperative effort is important.* Raise the following points:

   You are each responsible for your own work and the work of the team. The group will not be successful unless all students accomplish the goal.

   You must help each other be successful.

   You must each try hard.

3. Present a problem for the groups to solve to practice applying the concept (or choose other tasks that fit with your skill development plans):

   Discover different ways to get a ball from player 1 to player 2 and so on, using only one hand.

   Discover different ways to travel from line 1 to line 2 and back, while everyone in the group is touching each other.

Concluding Activities (10 minutes)

Cooperative Discussion Groups

Students remain in cooperative groups, sitting near you.

1. Ask open-ended questions to help each group practice working in a cooperative discussion group. Tell the children: *Discuss and arrive at a solution to these common problems:*

   What should we do with students in our class who will not follow the rules?

   How can we make sure that everybody learns in physical education?

   Should we let the best players in our class be the team captains and always get to go first in line to practice? Why? Why not?

   What are the most important things we can learn in physical education this year?

2. Question by question, have a representative from each group share the solutions with the entire class.

FITNESS

As you well know, physical fitness and physical activity are important in reducing health risks. Children who learn to enjoy being active now are more likely to remain active as adults. So present physical activities and fitness activities that are fun for the children, combined with other activities that teach the motor skills necessary for lifelong participation. To help you in this endeavor, this fitness section has three parts: fitness testing, the Fitness Hustles, and fitness activities.

UNIT ORGANIZATION

We have designed the fitness activity lessons to be repeated as frequently as is appropriate in your program. Select the lessons you want to teach and incorporate those into your annual plan. The activities you select should reflect your personal preferences as well as the needs of your students. You can, for example, organize fitness as a five- to seven-week unit: Fitness Hustles one week, Fitness Hustles reviewed a second week, and the other activities (circuit training, challenges, and moderate to vigorous games) during the remaining weeks. Conduct fitness testing before and/ or after such a fitness unit, according to your preferences and needs. As an alternative approach, you can intersperse individual lessons or weeks of fitness throughout the year. Finally, there are numerous ways to use the fitness lesson plans, so experiment to determine which suits your situation. Table F3.1 presents an overview of this fitness material.

LESSON ORGANIZATION

Each lesson begins with a warm-up, includes fitness training activities, and ends with conclud-

ing activities, which are where we introduce fitness concepts. Include or delete the fitness concept (see table F3.2), depending upon your situation. For example, some teachers may prefer to use the fitness concepts as a group in the classroom rather than spread out over several lessons.

TEACHING HINTS

This age group is rapidly moving toward puberty. Most children at this age are willing to be playful. You can utilize and maximize their strengths through physical fitness activities.

Fourth and Fifth Graders

Fourth and fifth graders are typically between 9 and 12 years of age. Some girls may experience their prepubescent growth spurt at 10 to 11 years of age. Some boys begin their prepubescent growth spurt at 12 to 13 years. This will result in a wide variety of physical sizes and shapes, maturity levels, and divergent interests. Girls may experience poorer physical performance after puberty, while for boys, puberty has a positive effect on physical fitness and performance. Your expectations for males and females, however, should be very similar prior to puberty and this growth spurt, even though some males may have greater strength than some females. Fitness is equally important for males and females, before, during, and after puberty.

Children of these ages are usually very active and enjoy the challenges of physical fitness activities. Remember, this unit should be fun, to encourage future participation in physical activities. To this end, do not compare children to each other when you evaluate their fitness levels; instead, compare children to their previous performances or to a standard that is challenging but attainable. Moreover, encourage participation, improvement, and enthusiasm. For example, children typically enjoy participating with their teacher. So at least some of the time it is important for the children to see you actively involved. Clearly, you are a role model. Furthermore, children will feel more comfortable trying new activities if they see you trying new activities—even if you are having trouble mastering the skill.

Obese and Overweight Students

The most challenging students to teach in a fitness unit are typically the overweight and obese students. Often these students feel frustrated, embarrassed, and incapable. But do not give up

on them or allow them to avoid the fitness lessons. Instead, focus on encouraging participation and personal improvement. Allow these children to build their strength and stamina slowly so as not to discourage them altogether. In addition, discussing the value of physical activity may change the behaviors and attitudes of overweight and obese children. Finally, do not allow other children to ridicule anyone for any reason in your classes. Create an environment in which each child can feel safe, competent, and capable.

Safety Considerations

Allow children to drink water frequently, especially if the weather is hot. Children may respond to heat and cold differently than you do, so when the tem-

Table F3.1: Unit Plan for Grades 4-5: Fitness

Week 2: warm-up for Fitness Hustle and Hustles	Week 3: measurements and practice testing	Week 4: testing
Monday: introduce warm-up for Fitness Hustle Tuesday: introduce Hustles 1 and 2 Wednesday: practice Hustles 1 and 2 Thursday: introduce Hustle 3 Friday: practice Hustles in cooperative groups	Monday: measure height and skinfolds and practice Hustle 1 Tuesday: measure weight and skinfolds and practice Hustle 2 Wednesday: measure flexibility and practice Hustles 1 and 2 Thursday: practice mile run and practice sit-ups Friday: practice mile run and practice sit-ups	Monday: test mile run Tuesday: test sit-ups Wednesday: fitness contract Thursday: jogging activities Friday: fitness test circuits

Week 11: circuit training	Week 16: rope jumping and individual skills	Week 27: wands and moderate to vigorous games
Monday: circuit training Tuesday: circuit training Wednesday: circuit training Thursday: circuit training Friday: circuit training	Monday: rope jumping Tuesday: rope jumping Wednesday: rope jumping Thursday: rope jumping and individual stunts Friday: rope jumping and individual stunts	Monday: wands Tuesday: wands Wednesday: moderate to vigorous games Thursday: moderate to vigorous games Friday: moderate to vigorous games

Week 28: moderate to vigorous games, Hustles, and Raging River (games and sports)

Monday: moderate to vigorous games
Tuesday: moderate to vigorous games
Wednesday: review Hustles
Thursday: review Hustles
Friday: Raging River

peratures are extreme you must look for signs of heat stress or illness. Remember that it takes 8 to 12 weeks, exercising three or more days each week, to train the cardiovascular system. This means that children who have low endurance will need lots of time and encouragement to improve. Work toward gradual improvements in all fitness areas to avoid injuries, illness, and discouragement.

Table F3.2: Fitness Concepts

The following are the 17 fitness concepts presented in the Grades 4-5: Fitness lesson plans. Since the lessons can be repeated, we have suggested more than one learning activity for each concept. Thus, when you repeat the lessons, you can use a different learning activity for the fitness concept.

1. Regular exercise maintains physical fitness. *Regular exercise* means exercising at least three times each week. *Cardiorespiratory endurance* depends on the ability of your circulatory system to provide oxygen-rich blood for energy. *Aerobic exercises* are exercises that involve the whole body and use the large muscle groups.
2. Physical fitness has five parts: cardiovascular endurance, muscular strength and endurance, flexibility, and body composition.
3. Regular exercise increases cardiorespiratory endurance and lowers resting heart rate. *Regular exercise* is moderate to vigorous activity performed at least three times a week. *Cardiorespiratory endurance* is the ability of the heart and lungs to deliver oxygen to the body tissues during exercise.
4. *Muscular strength* is the maximum amount of weight a muscle or group of muscles can lift one time. Muscles become stronger and able to do the same amount of work more times as a result of regular exercise.
5. Muscular strength and muscular endurance are related but different. *Muscular strength* is the maximum amount of weight your muscles can lift one time. *Muscular endurance* is how long a group of muscles can perform.
6. Being healthy is more than not being sick. Good health includes physical, social, and mental well-being.
7. *Heart rate* is how many times your heart contracts, or pumps, in a minute. *Resting heart rate* is your heart rate when you first wake up in the morning or after you lie still for 30 minutes. As you get older, your resting heart rate will go down.
8. *Overload training* is a way to help your muscles get stronger.
9. Different types of strength, such as arm strength and leg strength, are needed depending on the task that is to be completed.
10. *Muscular endurance* is how long a group of muscles can perform a task. Examples of muscular endurance are sit-ups, push-ups, and jogging (where the leg muscles must do the same action many times).
11. Muscular endurance can be tested many ways, for example, with a balance test or the sit-up test.
12. Individuals who exercise tend to feel better about themselves, be less prone to obesity, heart disease, and high blood pressure, and be better able to cope with stressful situations.
13. Health is influenced by many things. Fitness is one of them. Some others are diet, rest, heredity, and environment.
14. High levels of fitness have a positive influence on our lives.
15. Fitness contributes to being healthy. Fitness influences our daily lives and the length of our lives. Older people who are fit live longer and more active lives. Younger people who are fit say they are happier, have more energy, and are healthier than unfit people.
16. The abdominal muscles help hold in our stomachs and improve our posture. Good abdominal muscle endurance may help us avoid lower back pain.
17. The components of physical fitness are cardiorespiratory endurance, flexibility, body composition, and muscular strength and endurance.

LESSON 1

GRADES 4-5 FITNESS WARM-UP ROUTINE

Student Objectives

- Demonstrate the individual steps for the Grades 4-5 Fitness Warm-Up Routine.
- Demonstrate the warm-up routine.

Equipment and Materials

- Music: "Thriller" from *A Thriller for Kids* (Side B), Georgiana Stewart, Kimbo Records (KIM 7065)

Warm-Up Activities (5 minutes)

Arrange the students in scatter formation.

1. Have the children jog slowly in pace for one minute (60 steps).
2. Have the children stretch (suggest reaching up, down, and side-to-side) slowly.
3. Have the children jog faster in place one minute (120 steps).
4. Have the children walk in personal space for 30 seconds and stretch 30 seconds.
5. Have the children jog fast in place for one minute (180 steps).

Skill-Development Activities (25 minutes)

Steps for the Grades 4-5 Fitness Warm-Up Routine

Arrange the children in scatter formation.

1. Teach the individual steps to the warm-up routine.
2. Have the children practice each of the movements.

Overhead Isometric Stretch
Stand with feet comfortably apart and hands clasped behind head. Straighten your arms directly upward (stretch), lifting your shoulders toward ears. Keep your hands clasped.

> *Counts 1 and 2, stretch up, and*
>
> *Counts 3 and 4, return to starting position.*

Windmill

Stand in a straddle position with arms stretched out to sides at shoulder height. Bend knees slightly. Bend forward at the waist, touching right hand to left toe while left arm extends upward and backward, then repeat with left hand to right toe, alternating from side to side without straightening up between touches.

> Count 1, touch right hand to left toe,
> Count 2, touch left hand to right toe.

Side Bend

Standing with feet comfortably apart and arms at side, bend at the waist sideways to the left, facing forward and keeping your legs straight. Return to starting position, and repeat to the right.

Count 1, bend to the left,

Count 2, starting position,

Count 3, bend to the right, and

Count 4, starting position.

One-Half Knee Bend With Arm Movements

Standing with feet comfortably apart and heels flat, extend your arms forward, parallel to floor. Bend your knees halfway and lift your arms overhead, then return to the starting position. Bend your knees halfway again and extend your arms out to each side, then return to the starting position. For safety's sake, do not ever bend your knees more than halfway.

Count 1, stand and extend arms in front.

Count 2, bend and lift arms overhead,

Count 3, return to starting position with arms extended forward, and

Count 4, bend and extend arms out to each side.

Knee Lift

Step slightly to the right on your right foot, lift your left knee diagonally in front of your right leg and at the same time snap your fingers. Then repeat to the left.

Count 1, step, and

Count 2, lift knee and snap fingers.

Snap fingers

Step-Kick

This is a variation of the knee lift. Substitute a leg kick for the knee lift.

Count 1, step, and

Count 2, kick and snap fingers.

Grades 4-5 Fitness Warm-Up Routine

1. Play "Thriller."
2. After listening to the song, help the children learn, then perform the following sequence of steps:

   Overhead isometric stretch (16 counts),

   Side bend (16 counts),

   Windmill (16 counts),

   One-half knee bend with arm movements (16 counts),

   Knee lift (8 counts),

   Step-kick (8 counts),

   Knee lift (8 counts),

   Step-kick (8 counts),

   Overhead isometric stretch (16 counts),

   Side bend (16 counts),

   Windmill (16 counts),

   One-half knee bend with arm movements (16 counts),

   Knee lift (8 counts),

   Step-kick (8 counts),

   Knee lift (8 counts),

   Step-kick (8 counts), *and*

   March in place to the end of the music.

LESSONS 2 AND 3
FITNESS HUSTLES 1 AND 2

Student Objectives

- Practice the Grades 4-5 Fitness Warm-Up.
- Demonstrate the steps for Fitness Hustles 1 and 2.

Equipment and Materials

- Music: "Billie Jean" from *A Thriller for Kids* (Side B), Georgiana Stewart, Kimbo Records (KIM 7065)
- Music: "Flashdance" from *A Thriller for Kids* (Side B), Georgiana Stewart, Kimbo Records (KIM 7065)

Warm-Up Activities (5 minutes)

Repeat the five-step warm-up from Grades 4-5: Fitness, Lesson 1, page 770, or do the Grades 4-5 Fitness Warm-Up Routine in Grades 4-5: Fitness, Lesson 1, page 774.

Skill-Development Activities (25 minutes)

Steps for Fitness Hustles 1 and 2

Arrange children in scatter formation.

1. Teach the individual steps to Fitness Hustles 1 and 2.
2. Have the children practice each of the movements.

Twist and Bounce

With your feet together, bounce in place. At the same time twist your feet and hips to the right while twisting your arms and shoulders to the left. Repeat, alternating the twists on each bounce.

Standing Body Stretch 1

Standing with your feet comfortably apart and your arms extended overhead, stretch up, alternating right and left arms.

Counts 1 and 2, stretch left arm up, counts 3 and 4 stretch right arm up.

Step-Kick Forward

Step on your right foot and kick your left leg forward with a slight hop, then repeat, stepping and hopping on your left foot and kicking your right foot forward.

Step-Kick Sideways

This is the same as the step-kick forward, except with a kick to the side instead of a kick forward.

Jog-Punch Overhead

Jog in place and punch overhead, alternating right and left arms, coordinating the punches with the jogging steps.

Knee Dip With Shoulder Shrug

Standing with your feet comfortably apart, heels flat, and hands on hips, bend your knees halfway, keeping your back straight and lifting your shoulders. Then return to the starting position by straightening your legs.

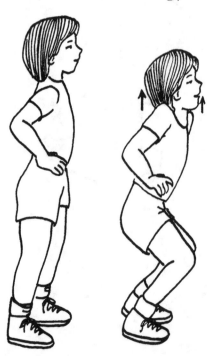

Jumping Jack Knee Lift

Step-hop in place, lifting both arms up to the sides and overhead on the hop (similar to jumping jack arm movements). Repeat step (arms down) hop (arms up) on opposite leg, and continue alternating legs.

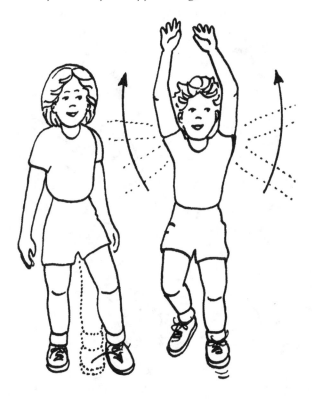

Double Rocker Forward

In stride position, double bounce on your forward leg, extending and lifting your back leg off the floor. Rock to your back leg with a double bounce, extending and lifting your forward leg off the floor. Alternate forward and backward rocking motions.

Jump and Clap

With your feet together, jump forward and bounce once in place, clapping your hands (in front of your body), once with the jump forward and once with the bounce in place. Then jump back to starting place and bounce again, hands slapping your thighs on the jump and the bounce. Continue, forward and back.

Foot Slap Back

Step on your left foot and hop, lifting your right foot behind your left leg and slapping your right foot with your left hand. Repeat the step-hop on your right foot, lifting and slapping your left foot. Continue to step-hop, alternating legs.

Heel Twist

Take your weight on your right foot, twisting to the left and touching your left heel to the floor. Repeat, taking your weight on your left foot and twisting to the right to touch your right heel to the floor. Continue, alternating right and left twist and touch.

Jog Kickback With Clap

Jog in place, kicking your free leg back and clapping with each step.

Scissors

Jump to a stride position, with one arm swinging forward and up and the other arm swinging down and back. Jump again, changing forward and back legs and arms. Continue, alternating right and left legs.

Grapevine Right and Left

Step to the side with your right foot, with your left foot crossing in back of the right, and step to the side with right again with your left leg extended out to the side, then repeat to the left. Repeat, alternating moving to the left and right until mastered. (This may also be done with a bouncy step and a kick with the extended leg.) The arms can be on the hips, extended at shoulder height, or relaxed at the sides.

Fitness Hustle 1

Keep the children in scatter formation.

1. Play "Billie Jean."
2. Use these steps or the instructions provided on Side A of the record noted in the equipment list at the beginning of the lesson.
3. After listening to the song, help the children learn, then perform the following sequence of steps:

    Listen during a short introduction (8 counts),

    Twist and bounce (16 counts),

    Repeat (16 counts),

    Step-kick forward (16 counts),

    Step-kick sideways (16 counts),

    Step-kick forward (16 counts),

    Step-kick side (16 counts),

Heel twist (16 counts),

Foot slap back (16 counts),

Heel twist (16 counts),

Foot slap back (16 counts),

Grapevine right and left (16 counts),

Scissors (16 counts),

Grapevine right and left (16 counts),

Scissors (16 counts),

Grapevine right and left (16 counts),

Scissors (16 counts), *and*

Grapevine right and left to end of music.

Fitness Hustle 2

Keep the children in scatter formation.

1. Play "Flashdance."

2. After listening to the song, help the children learn, then perform the following sequence of steps:

   Twist and bounce (16 counts),

   Repeat (16 counts),

   Double rocker forward (16 counts),

   Jump and clap (16 counts),

   Double rocker forward (16 counts),

   Jump and clap (16 counts),

   Jog-punch overhead (16 counts),

   Standing body stretch 1 (16 counts),

   Jog-punch overhead (16 counts),

   Standing body stretch 1 (16 counts),

   Twist and bounce (16 counts),

   Repeat (16 counts),

   Double rocker forward (16 counts),

   Jump and clap (16 counts),

   Double rocker forward (16 counts),

   Jump and clap (16 counts),

   Jog-punch overhead (16 counts), *and*

   Standing body stretch 1 to the end of the music.

FITNESS

LESSON 4
FITNESS HUSTLE 3

Student Objectives

- Demonstrate the Grades 4-5 Fitness Warm-Up.
- Demonstrate the steps for Fitness Hustle 3.

Equipment and Materials

- Music: "Beat Street Strut" from *A Thriller for Kids* (Side B), Georgiana Stewart, Kimbo Records (KIM 7065)

Warm-Up Activities (5 minutes)

Arrange the children in scatter formation. Do the Grades 4-5 Fitness Warm-Up Routine in Grades 4-5: Fitness, Lesson 1, page 774.

Skill-Development Activities (25 minutes)

Steps for Fitness Hustle 3

Arrange the children in scatter formation.

1. Review the steps to Fitness Hustle 3 (heel twist, jumping jack with knee lift, standing body stretch 1, jog kickback with clap, and knee dip with shoulder shrug).
2. Play "Beat Street Strut."
3. After listening to the song, help the children learn, then perform the following sequence of steps:

   Heel twist (16 counts),
   Repeat (16 counts),
   Jumping jack with knee lift (16 counts),
   Standing body stretch 1 (16 counts),
   Jumping jack with knee lift (16 counts),
   Standing body stretch 1 (16 counts),
   Jog kickback with clap (16 counts),
   Knee dip with shoulder shrug (16 counts),
   Jog kickback with clap (16 counts),
   Knee dip with shoulder shrug (16 counts),
   Heel twist (16 counts),

Repeat (16 counts),
Jumping jack with knee lift (16 counts),
Standing body stretch 1 (16 counts),
Jumping jack with knee lift (16 counts),
Standing body stretch 1 (16 counts),
Jog kickback with clap (16 counts),
Knee dip with shoulder shrug (16 counts),
Jog kickback with clap(16 counts), *and*
Knee dip with shoulder shrug (16 counts).

GRADES 4-5

FITNESS

LESSON 5
PRACTICING FITNESS HUSTLES IN COOPERATIVE GROUPS

Student Objectives

- Cooperate with a learning team to reach a goal.
- Demonstrate the steps for the Fitness Hustles.

Equipment and Materials

- Music: Hustle Warm-Up: "Thriller" from *A Thriller for Kids*, Georgiana Stewart, Kimbo Records (KIM 7065)

- Music: Fitness Hustle 1: "Billie Jean" from *A Thriller for Kids*, Georgiana Stewart, Kimbo Records (KIM 7065)
- Music: Fitness Hustle 2: "Flashdance" from *A Thriller for Kids*, Georgiana Stewart, Kimbo Records (KIM 7065)
- Music: Fitness Hustle 3: "Beat Street Strut" from *A Thriller for Kids*, Georgiana Stewart, Kimbo Records (KIM 7065)
- Large task cards (8 1/2 in. × 11 in. or larger)

Warm-Up Activities (5 minutes)

Grades 4-5 Fitness Warm-Up

Arrange the children in scatter formation. Have the children perform the Grades 4-5 Fitness Warm-Up Routine. See Grades 4-5: Fitness, Lesson 1, page 774.

Skill-Development Activities (20 minutes)

Practice Fitness Hustle Steps in Cooperative Learning Groups

Divide the children into groups of four to six. These should be heterogeneous learning teams. Print the name of each step in each Fitness Hustle on its own task card. Give each group a full set of cards for all three Fitness Hustles.

1. Review the guidelines for cooperative group work. See Grades 4-5: Organization, Lesson 1, page 754.
2. Explain: *The goal today is cooperative effort, and each person is responsible for both their learning and the team's. Every student in the group must master all the steps before the team can be successful.*
3. Distribute the task cards to each group.

4. Explain the activity:

   Take turns showing the cards to the others in the group.

   Practice the step on each card, then have the next child show a card, and so on.

   Remember to help each other, because your group will only be successful when each child in the group has mastered the skills.

   Report to me when your group is ready to take a mastery test. (Optional: *I will give a group award to the group with the best overall performance.*)

Concluding Activities (5 minutes)

Arrange the children in scatter formation.

Have a group (or the group winning the performance award) select and lead one of the Fitness Hustles for the entire class to perform.

LESSON 6
MEASURING HEIGHT AND SKINFOLDS

Student Objectives

- Have height and skinfolds measured.
- Practice Fitness Hustle 1.

Equipment and Materials

- Measuring tape
- Skinfold calipers
- Music for Fitness Hustle 1

Warm-Up Activities (5 minutes)

Arrange the children in scatter formation. Complete the warm-up routine from Grades 4-5: Fitness, Lesson 1, page 774.

Skill-Development Activities (25 minutes)

Fitness Hustle 1 and Measuring Height and Skinfolds

Divide the children into small groups.

1. Briefly review Fitness Hustle 1 with the entire group.
2. Have most groups practice Fitness Hustle 1. Keep one group with you and measure height for each child. Rotate groups until you have measured the height of all the children.
3. Begin a new rotation, measuring skinfolds on the children (you will probably need to finish this in the next lesson).

LESSON 7
MEASURING WEIGHT AND SKINFOLDS

Student Objectives

- Have weight and skinfolds measured.
- Practice Fitness Hustle 2.

Equipment and Materials

- Scale
- Skinfold calipers
- Music for Fitness Hustle 2

Warm-Up Activities

None.

Skill-Development Activities (30 minutes)

Fitness Hustle 2 and Measuring Weight and Skinfolds

Use the same groupings from Grades 4-5: Fitness, Lesson 6.

1. Briefly review Fitness Hustle 2 with the entire group.
2. Have most of the groups practice Fitness Hustle 2. Keep the other group with you and measure skinfolds, picking up where you left off in the previous lesson.
3. Rotate groups again, measuring weight.
4. Measure skinfolds at the tricpes and subscapular sites.
   - Take the sum of the triceps and subscapular sites, and using table F3.3, find the percentile reading to the left for each child.
   - You should be concerned about children who fall below the 25th percentile.

Table F3.3: NCYFS Norms by Age (in Years) for the Sum of Triceps and Subscapular Skinfolds—Boys and Girls (in Millimeters)

Percentile	10	11	12	13	14	15	16	17	18
Boys									
99	9	9	9	9	9	10	10	10	11
90	12	12	12	11	12	12	12	13	13
80	13	13	13	13	13	13	13	14	14
75	14	14	14	13	13	14	14	14	15
70	15	15	15	14	14	14	14	15	15
60	16	16	16	15	15	15	15	16	17
50	17	18	17	17	17	17	17	17	18
40	20	20	20	19	18	18	18	19	19
30	22	23	22	21	21	20	20	21	22
25	24	25	24	23	22	22	22	22	24
20	25	26	28	25	25	24	23	24	25
10	35	36	38	34	33	32	30	30	30
Girls									
99	10	11	11	12	12	13	13	16	14
90	13	14	15	15	17	19	19	20	19
80	15	16	17	18	19	21	21	22	21
75	16	17	18	19	20	23	22	23	22
70	17	18	18	20	21	24	23	24	23
60	18	19	21	22	24	26	24	26	25
50	20	21	22	24	26	28	26	28	27
40	22	24	24	26	28	30	28	31	28
30	25	28	27	29	31	33	32	34	32
25	27	30	29	31	33	34	33	36	34
20	29	33	31	34	35	37	35	37	36
10	36	40	40	43	40	43	42	42	42

Reprinted from Ross, Dotson, and Katz 1985.

FITNESS

LESSON 8

MEASURING FLEXIBILITY WITH THE BACKSAVER SIT-AND-REACH TEST

Student Objectives

- Practice the backsaver sit-and-reach test.
- Practice Fitness Hustles 1 and 2.

Equipment and Materials

- 1 sit-and-reach box per group
- Music for Fitness Hustles 1 or 2

Warm-Up Activities

None.

Skill-Development Activities (30 minutes)

Fitness Hustles 1 and 2 and Sit-and-Reach Test

Continue with the same groups as for Grades 4-5: Fitness, Lessons 6 and 7.

1. Continue the same as for Lesson 7, except measure flexibility.

2. Conduct the sit-and-reach test as follows:

   - See figure below for correct positioning (see also Grades K-1: Fitness, Lesson 1, page 24). The figure on page 792 shows a more detailed view of the box used in the test.

   - Have each child attempt to reach as far down the box as possible while keeping one knee straight, the other bent with the foot at the other leg's knee, and the palms facing down with fingers extended.

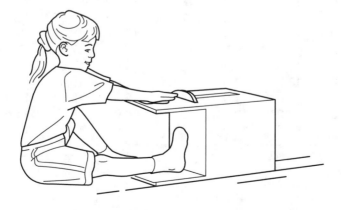

- Have each child make four trials.
- Direct the child to hold the position of maximum reach for at least one second on the fourth trial. Record this score to the nearest inch. Table F3.4 gives the norms for the backsaver sit-and-reach test.

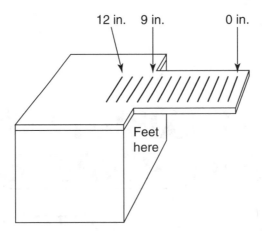

Table F3.4: NCYFS Norms by Age for the Sit-and-Reach—Boys and Girls (in Inches)

Percentile	10	11	12	13	14	15	16	17	18
Boys									
99	18.0	18.5	18.5	19.5	20.0	21.5	22.0	21.5	22.0
90	16.0	16.5	16.0	16.5	17.5	18.0	19.0	19.5	19.5
80	15.0	15.5	15.0	15.0	16.0	17.0	18.0	18.0	18.0
75	14.5	15.0	15.0	15.0	15.5	16.5	17.0	17.5	17.5
70	14.5	14.5	14.5	14.5	15.0	16.0	17.0	17.0	17.0
60	14.0	14.0	13.5	13.5	14.0	15.0	16.0	16.0	16.0
50	13.5	13.0	13.0	13.0	13.5	14.0	15.0	15.5	15.0
40	12.5	12.5	12.0	12.5	13.0	13.5	14.0	14.5	14.5
30	12.0	12.0	11.5	12.0	12.0	12.5	13.5	13.5	13.5
25	11.5	11.5	11.0	11.0	11.0	12.0	13.0	13.0	13.0
20	11.0	11.0	10.5	10.5	11.0	11.5	12.0	12.5	12.5
10	10.0	9.5	8.5	9.0	9.0	9.5	10.0	10.5	10.0
Girls									
99	20.5	20.5	21.0	22.0	22.0	23.0	23.0	23.0	22.5
90	17.5	18.0	19.0	20.0	19.5	20.0	20.5	20.5	20.5
80	16.5	17.0	18.0	19.0	19.0	19.0	19.5	19.5	19.5
75	16.5	16.5	17.0	18.0	18.5	19.0	19.0	19.0	19.0
70	16.0	16.5	17.0	17.5	18.0	18.5	19.0	19.0	18.5
60	15.0	15.5	16.0	17.0	17.5	18.0	18.0	18.0	18.0
50	14.5	15.0	15.5	16.0	17.0	17.0	17.5	18.0	17.5
40	14.0	14.0	15.0	15.5	16.0	17.0	17.0	17.0	17.0
30	13.0	13.5	14.5	14.5	15.0	16.0	16.5	16.0	16.0
25	13.0	13.0	14.0	14.0	15.0	15.5	16.0	15.5	15.5
20	12.0	13.0	13.5	13.5	14.0	15.0	15.5	15.0	15.0
10	10.5	11.5	12.0	12.0	12.5	13.5	14.0	13.5	13.0

GRADES
4-5

FITNESS

LESSONS 9 AND 10
PRACTICING THE ONE-MILE RUN AND SIT-UPS

Student Objectives

- Practice pacing in the one-mile run.
- Practice correct sit-up form.

Equipment and Materials

- Cones for marking one-mile running course (The figure below shows several layouts of fields you can use to administer the run.)
- Stopwatch
- Mats (optional)

Areas suitable for distance run test

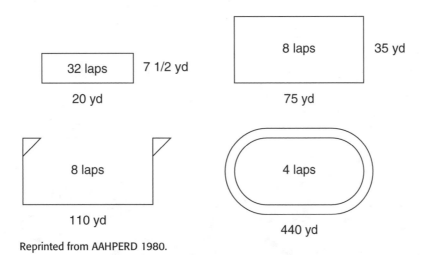

32 laps	7 1/2 yd	
20 yd		

8 laps	35 yd
75 yd	

8 laps

110 yd

4 laps

440 yd

Reprinted from AAHPERD 1980.

Warm-Up Activities

None.

Skill-Development Activities (30 minutes)

One-Mile Run and Sit-Ups

Divide the children into two groups.

1. Discuss the need for pacing in the one-mile run.

2. Describe and demonstrate a correct sit-up:

> *The sit-up is really done with a rolling motion.*

> *Begin by lying on your back with your legs bent slightly at the knees so the bottoms of your feet are flat on the ground.*

> *Choose one of the two hand-arm positions: You can cross your hands and arms on your chest so that your hands are resting on the opposite shoulders or you can place your hands on the sides of your head with a finger placed on each ear, keeping your elbows lined up (parallel) with the back of your head (keep them there, not pulling forward past the ears).*

> *Perform each sit-up slowly, rolling your chin to your chest to lift your head, next your shoulders, then your lower back off the ground. During the movement, you should feel the muscles under your belly button working.*

> *Once your lower back is off the ground, unroll to the start position.*

3. Have the children practice analyzing your sit-up form.

4. Have one group practice the pacing of the one-mile run. Encourage each child to find the fastest pace she or he can maintain while running the total distance.

5. Have the other group select partners. One partner in each pair does sit-ups for 60 seconds while the other partner holds feet; then have them switch roles.

6. After 15 minutes in each activity, allow a 2-minute rest; then have groups switch activities.

7. If the weather is hot, make sure the children have opportunity to get water when they want it.

GRADES 4-5

LESSON 11
TESTING AEROBIC FITNESS

Student Objectives

- Perform the one-mile run.
- Work cooperatively with a partner.

Equipment and Materials

- Stopwatch
- Cones to mark testing area
- Recording forms
- Music for Fitness Hustle 2

Warm-Up Activities (5 minutes)

Fitness Hustle 2

Arrange the children in scatter formation. Have the entire class practice the Fitness Hustle 2 as a warm-up. See Grades 4-5: Fitness, Lesson 1, page 783.

Skill-Development Activities (25 minutes)

One-Mile Run Test

Create partners in two groups, one partner from each pair in each group.

1. Tell the children:

    One child from each pair will run the mile first.

    The other will count the number of laps.

    I will call out each child's time as he or she crosses the finish line for each child's partner to record.

    Then we'll switch and let the other group run.

2. Give the children a short break and the opportunity to get water after running.

LESSON 12
THE SIT-UP TEST

Student Objectives

- Perform the sit-up test.
- Work cooperatively with a partner.

Equipment and Materials

- Recording forms
- Music for Fitness Hustle 2
- Mats (optional)

Warm-Up Activities (5 minutes)

Fitness Hustle 2

Arrange the children in scatter formation. Have the entire class practice the Fitness Hustle 2. See Grades 4-5: Fitness, Lesson 1, page 783.

Skill-Development Activities (25 minutes)

The Sit-Up Test

Arrange partners in scatter formation, on mats if you prefer.

1. Tell the children:

   One partner will count the number of sit-ups their partner completes in 60 seconds.
   Then partners will switch positions.

2. Have the pairs do the sit-up test, taking turns.

G R A D E S 4-5

LESSON 13
DEVELOPING A FITNESS CONTRACT

Student Objectives

- Make a fitness contract based on fitness evaluation.
- State one reason fitness is important.
- Participate in fitness activities independently.

Equipment and Materials

- Fitness Contract form (Form F3.1)
- Equipment needed for fitness stations or Fitness Hustles (see instructions)
- Large task cards (at least 8 1/2 in. × 11 in.) if using stations, one per station

Warm-Up Activities

None.

Skill-Development Activities (30 minutes)

Learning About Fitness Plans

Set up enough stations to create a circuit with task cards for groups of four to six students. To begin the lesson, however, first gather the children into an advanced information formation.

1. Discuss the importance of exercising on a regular basis and work with students so they can develop realistic goals for exercise.

2. Show the children a sample set of fitness test scores. Ask:

    In what areas does this person need to improve to enjoy a basic level of health-related fitness? (If the flexibility score was low, this would be a target area.)

    What might be a realistic, specific goal in each of those areas? (Goals can range from participate, for low-fit individuals, to a specific time or score.)

    What activities might this person do to reach each goal? (Walking and other aerobic activities are good, as well as stretching.)

    How often should this person do those activities to have a good chance of reaching his or her goals? (Three or more times per week.)

3. Help the children work to develop a similar personal fitness plan.

Divide the children into groups of four to six.

4. Have the groups rotate through a circuit, practicing the Fitness Hustles or doing other fitness activities while you meet with each child at one station to discuss his or

her personal plan and to sign a written agreement to try to improve their fitness level outside of class. Use the Fitness Contract shown (Form F3.1) or develop one that meets your needs.

5. Explain that you will give the fitness tests again later during the year so that they can see improvement.

FORM F3.1 CARDIOVASCULAR ENDURANCE PROGRAM CONTRACT

I, _____, do hereby contract to exercise for 20 minutes three times a week for 10 weeks. My exercise heart rate will be _____.

Week	Days	Type of exercise	Duration
1			
2			
3			
4			
5			
6			
7			
8			
9			
10			

Approved by _____

Date _____

LESSON 14
APPROPRIATE JOGGING ACTIVITIES

Student Objectives

- Learn specific jogging activities that can be used outside of class time.

Equipment and Materials

- None unless some area is to be marked as jogging route
- A map of your city or state

Warm-Up Activities (5 minutes)

Arrange the children in scatter formation.

1. Select four to five students.
2. Allow each student to select and lead one warm-up task, for example one stretch or other activity presented in class.

Skill-Development Activities (20 minutes)

Jogging Is Fun!

Gather the children into an advanced information formation.

1. Describe the following ways of organizing a jog to increase interest:

    Jog for a certain number of minutes (6, 8, 10, 12, 15), increasing the number as your cardiorespiratory endurance improves.

    Jog a certain number of laps around a specified area, increasing the number of laps with improved endurance.

    Jog a certain route around the school campus. (The route can be marked by you or drawn on a map with key landmarks.)

    We can keep a record of the total distance jogged by the class; for example, the total mileage of the class might equal the distance to a certain city.

    Jog single file: Groups of five to seven children run in a line; on a signal, the child in the rear weaves through the line to become the new leader.

2. Have the children practice these approaches as time allows.

Concluding Activities (5 minutes)

Arrange the children in an information formation.

1. Show the children the map.
2. Discuss how far they would travel on the map, or how many repetitions of today's jog would be needed to get to a location. Estimate the distance.
3. You can use the map to keep track of the miles the children ran and place those on the map.
4. You may want to have the children select a goal or destination.

LESSON 15
MUSCULAR STRENGTH AND ENDURANCE ACTIVITIES

Student Objectives

- Practice various circuits to increase muscular strength and endurance.

Equipment and Materials

- Equipment as needed for circuit activities
- Large task cards (at least 8 1/2 in. × 11 in.), one per station

Warm-Up Activities (5 minutes)

Fitness Hustles

Arrange the children in scatter formation. Choose a Fitness Hustle, and have the children do the Hustle. See Grades 4-5: Fitness, Lesson 1, pages 782-783.

Skill-Development Activities (25 minutes)

Muscular Strength and Endurance Circuit

Divide the students into groups of four to six students. Set up enough stations with task cards to accommodate the number of groups you have.

1. Describe and demonstrate as needed the muscular strength and endurance stations you set up. The following are sample ideas:

   Station 1: Sit-ups

   Station 2: Push-ups

   Station 3: Jumping for distance

   Station 4: Bent-knee push-ups

If playground equipment is available, use it to create a pull-ups station or have students hand-walk across horizontal ladders. Repeat stations as necessary to keep group size small (four to six).

2. Rotate groups through the circuit as long as time allows.

GRADES
4-5

LESSON 16
INDIVIDUAL STRETCHING AND CIRCUIT TRAINING

Student Objectives

- Explain what it takes to maintain health-related physical fitness.
- Define frequency, intensity, and time.
- Define and give examples of aerobic activities.
- Participate in circuit training activities.

Equipment and Materials

- 6 cones to mark stations
- 4 cones to define the Lap Cool-Down area
- 6 task cards, numbers, and tape for stations
- 1 carpet square or mat per child for Station 3
- 1 short jump rope per child for Station 4
- Chalk, tape, or cones to mark lines for Station 6

Warm-up Activities (6-8 minutes)

Individual Stretching Exercises

Arrange the children in scatter formation.

1. Briefly discuss the importance of good flexibility and how stretching can improve flexibility.
2. Describe and demonstrate the individual stretching exercises. Emphasize safety guidelines:

   Move slowly into each stretch, stopping when a slight tug is felt. It should not hurt!

   No bouncing!

3. Have the children complete the individual stretching exercises.

Sitting Toe Touch

Sitting with legs straight and feet together, reach your fingers toward your toes, bringing your face toward your knees, and hold for five seconds. Relax. Repeat several times.

Side Bend

Begin standing with feet shoulder-width apart and arms by your sides. Bend down to the right as far as possible and hold for five seconds. Return to starting position and bend to the left and hold. Repeat several times to the right and to the left.

Trunk Twister

Sitting with feet shoulder-width apart and hands clasped in front of your chest, keep your arms horizontal (demonstrate). Rotate slowly to the right and left, holding each position for five seconds. Repeat several times.

Forward Lunge

Standing with feet together and hands on your hips, lunge forward with your right leg, keeping your left leg straight. Your right knee should form a right angle (corner of a square). Hold the lunge position for five seconds and return to starting position. Then lunge with your left leg forward. Repeat several times, alternating right and left legs.

Running in Place

Run in place for 20 steps. Relax, then repeat.

Skill-Development Activities (10-12 minutes)

Circuit Training 1

Set up the six stations, taping the task cards to the cones. Divide children into six groups, and assign each group to a station.

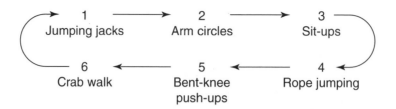

1. Describe and demonstrate each exercise in the circuit.
2. On a signal, have the children exercise at the assigned station for one minute, counting the number of repetitions, completing as many as possible.
3. Signal stop after one minute. Allow 15 seconds for students to rotate to their new stations.
4. When revisiting this lesson, gradually increase the time at each station to two minutes as students increase their strength and endurance; at the same time, gradually decrease the time allowed to rotate to the next station and prepare to exercise to 10 seconds.

Station 1: Jumping Jacks

Standing with feet together and hands by your sides, bounce up and land with your feet apart while moving your arms overhead and clapping your hands above your head. Then jump back to the starting position.

Station 2: Arm Circles

Standing with your feet comfortably apart and your arms at your sides, circle your arms forward several times, then backward several times. Repeat.

Station 3: Sit-Ups

Lie on your back with your arms folded across your chest, hands placed on your shoulders, and knees bent. Raise your body until your arms touch your thighs, then return to the starting position.

Station 4: Rope Jumping

Jump with a short rope, using a two-footed single step (one jump on two feet for each turn of the rope).

Station 5: Bent-Knee Push-Ups

Beginning in a kneeling front-support position (on hands and knees with your knees extended back as far as possible) with your back straight, lower your chin and chest to the ground, keeping your back straight, then return to starting position.

Station 6: Crab Walk

Assume a back-support position with your knees bent and your body straight. Walk on your hands and feet from line A to line B and then back to line A, continuing until the time is up.

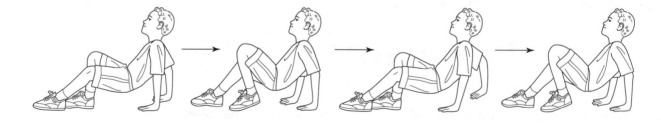

Sprint Relay

Divide the children into groups of three or four. Mark a starting line and a return line 20 yd apart. Line up the groups single file behind the starting line.

1. Explain the activity:

   On a signal, player 1 runs to the return line, runs back to the starting line, touches the hand of player 2, and goes to the end of the line.

   Player 2 runs and so on, until all the children in the group have had a turn.

2. Have children run the Sprint Relay. Repeat, using a backward run, skipping, galloping, and hopping on one foot. Repeat at least five times or for 10 minutes.

Lap Cool-Down

Use the cones to define an area about 40 by 60 ft.

Have children do seven laps of the area, using the following movements: slow jogging, jogging backward, sliding—right side leading, skipping, sliding—left side leading, walking forward, and walking backward.

Concluding Activities (10 minutes)

Physical Fitness Concept

Gather the children into an advanced information formation.

1. Introduce the following concept: *Regular exercise maintains physical fitness. Regular exercise means exercising at least three times each week. Cardiorespiratory endurance depends on the ability of your circulatory system to provide oxygen-rich blood for energy. Aerobic exercises are exercises that involve the whole body and use the large muscle groups, making the cardiorespiratory system work harder and therefore become stronger.*

2. Discuss the importance of choosing aerobic exercises when starting an exercise program for cardiorespiratory endurance. *What are some examples of aerobic exercises?* (Jogging, walking fast, swimming, bicycling, jumping rope, aerobic dancing.)

3. Discuss the three things that will determine how effective an exercise program will be:

   frequency—how often you exercise. You must exercise at least three times a week.

   intensity—how hard you exercise. You must raise your heart rate until it is 75 to 90 percent of maximum. For a 10-, 11-, or 12-year-old, the exercise heart rate needs to be at least 157 beats per minute.

   time—how long you exercise each day. You must exercise for at least three 10-minute segments per exercise day at 157 beats per minute or higher. The amount of time spent exercising is also called the **duration** of the exercise.

4. Tell the children: *To remember these, think of the word their first letters form—FIT. If a low-fit person works hard to increase cardiorespiratory fitness, that person must continue to exercise to maintain the level of fitness gained. If you miss 2 weeks of exercise, you'll lose a lot of what you worked to gain. After about 10 weeks without exercise, you'll be back to where you started.*

Discussion

Continue with the children in an advanced information formation. Discuss what the children have learned today:

What does regular exercise mean?

Can you exercise one time a week for several hours and maintain physical fitness? Why not?

How often should you exercise?

What do we mean by the intensity of the exercise?

How long should your exercise session last?

What is your favorite aerobic endurance activity?

GRADES 4-5

FITNESS

LESSON 17
INDIVIDUAL STRETCHING AND CIRCUIT TRAINING

Student Objectives

- Name and define the five components of fitness.
- Provide examples of exercises that will enhance each component.
- Participate in circuit training activities.

Equipment and Materials

- 6 cones to mark stations
- 4 cones to define the Lap Cool-Down area
- 6 task cards, numbers, and tape for stations
- 1 carpet square or mat per child for Station 3
- 1 short jump rope per child for Station 4
- Chalk, tape, or cones to mark lines for Station 6

Warm-Up Activities (6-8 minutes)

Individual Stretching Exercises

See Grades 4-5: Fitness, Lesson 16, page 802.

Skill-Development Activities (15 minutes)

Circuit Training 1

See Grades 4-5: Fitness, Lesson 16, page 803.

Have children complete the circuit with a time of one minute at each station and 15 seconds to rotate to new stations.

Sprint Relay

See Grades 4-5: Fitness, Lesson 16, page 805.

1. Have children run the Sprint Relay.
2. Repeat using an all-fours run, hopping on one foot, and jumping with two feet together. Repeat several times.

Lap Cool-Down

See Grades 4-5: Fitness, Lesson 16, page 805.

Concluding Activities (6-8 minutes)

Physical Fitness Concept

Gather the children into an advanced information formation.

1. Review the following definitions of the components of health-related physical fitness:

    Cardiorespiratory endurance is the ability of the circulatory system to provide oxygen-rich blood for energy.

    Flexibility is the range (or amount) of movement at a joint (a place where two bones meet, like the elbow).

    Muscular endurance is the ability of a muscle to repeat a movement many times without tiring.

    Muscular strength is the greatest amount of weight a muscle can lift in one try.

    Leanness means a lack of excess fat.

2. Explain that each fitness component has individual activities to train (or improve) it, but to a degree, they overlap. Say to the children: *Running is an example of an activity that enhances cardiorespiratory fitness, but also enhances muscular endurance in the legs; that is an overlap.*

3. Ask the children: *Can you name some other cardiorespiratory endurance activities?* (Cycling, swimming, aerobics.)

4. Tell the children:

    Stretching and aerobics are two activities that help with flexibility.

    Can you think of some flexibility exercises? (Toe touch, body bend, forward lunge.)

    Sit-ups and push-ups develop muscular endurance and strength in specific muscle groups. Lifting weights also helps to develop strength.

    All exercise helps to burn calories, which helps us control our body fat.

GRADES
4-5

FITNESS

LESSON 18
INDIVIDUAL STRETCHING AND CIRCUIT TRAINING

Student Objectives

- Explain how exercise affects the heart.
- Participate in circuit training activities.

Equipment and Materials

- 6 cones to mark stations
- 4 cones to define the Lap Cool-Down area
- 6 task cards, numbers, and tape for stations
- 1 carpet square or mat per child for Station 3
- 1 short jump rope per child for Station 4
- Chalk, tape, or cones to mark lines for Station 6
- Additional chalk, tape, or cones to mark lines
- Pencil and paper per child (for calculating heart rate)

Warm-Up Activities (6-8 minutes)

Individual Stretching Exercises

See Grades 4-5: Fitness, Lesson 16, page 802.

Skill-Development Activities (15 minutes)

Circuit Training 1

See Grades 4-5: Fitness, Lesson 16, page 803. Have children complete the circuit with a time of one minute at each station and 15 seconds to rotate to new stations.

Sprint Relay

See Grades 4-5: Fitness, Lesson 16, page 805.

1. Have children run the Sprint Relay.
2. Repeat several times, using different locomotor skills.

Shuttle Relay

Divide the children into groups of four and line up half of each team behind a starting line and half behind a return line. The start and return lines are 40 to 60 ft apart.

1. Explain the activity:

    On each team, player 1 runs from the starting line to the return line to touch the hand of player 2, then goes to the end of that line.

    Player 2 runs to the starting line to touch the hand of player 3, and so on.

    You will end up on the line opposite from where you started.

2. Have children run the Shuttle Relay several times.

Lap Cool-Down

See Grades 4-5: Fitness, Lesson 16, page 805.

Concluding Activities (6-8 minutes)

Physical Fitness Concept

Gather the children into an advanced information formation.

1. Review the following concepts:

    Regular exercise increases cardiorespiratory endurance and lowers the resting heart rate.

    Regular exercise is moderate to vigorous activity performed at least three times a week for 20 minutes. Cardiorespiratory endurance is the ability of the heart and lungs to deliver oxygen to the body tissues during exercise and to recover from the exercise.

2. Hold a discussion about exercise and the heart. Explain the concepts:

    The strength of the heart depends on how much it is used.

    The more regular exercise you get, the bigger and more powerful your heart becomes.

    The more powerful your heart, the more cardiorespiratory endurance you have.

    Contrary to what you might think, strenuous exercise is not bad for the heart.

3. Tell the children:

    Each time the heart contracts, or pumps, blood is pushed into the arteries, causing them to stretch. Arteries are tubes, or vessels, that carry blood from the heart throughout the body. When the heart relaxes, the artery walls contract (squeeze), pushing the blood along. The expansion and contraction of the artery walls is a pulse beat.

    Your resting heart rate is the number of times your heart beats in a minute when you first wake up or after you have been lying very still for 15 to 30 minutes. It will go down as you grow older and as you exercise more. For instance, the average 10-year-old girl has a resting heart rate of about 90, whereas the average adult woman who doesn't exercise regularly has a resting heart rate around 72. For an adult woman who exercises regularly, the resting heart rate may be even lower, about 50 or 60.

Pulse Counting

Continue with the children in an advanced information formation. Give each child a pencil and piece of paper.

1. Explain how to count the pulse at the carotid artery:

    Place three fingers on the neck, just on the left or right side of the windpipe.

    Press lightly and count the beats for 10 seconds.

    Multiply this number by six, and you will have the beats per minute.

2. Have children count their resting pulse for 10 seconds and multiply by six to determine their heart rate. (Some students will need help with the math.)

Comparing Heart Rates

Continue with the children in an advanced information formation.

1. *Take your nonexercise heart (pulse) rate. This will probably be higher than if you had rested 15 to 30 minutes or just woken up in the morning, but it will give you some idea of your resting heart rate.*

2. *Run in place for one minute.*

3. *Take your pulse rate again.*

4. *Rest for one minute, then take your pulse rate one more time. See how close the last count is to your nonexercise rate. The closer it is, the more physically fit you are.*

LESSON 19
INDIVIDUAL STRETCHING AND CIRCUIT TRAINING

Student Objectives

- Explain the *overload principle*.
- Describe ways to develop strength.
- Participate in circuit training activities.

Equipment and Materials

- 6 cones to mark stations
- 4 cones to define the Lap Cool-Down area
- 6 task cards, numbers, and tape for stations
- 1 carpet square or mat per child for Station 3
- 1 short jump rope per child for Station 4
- Chalk, tape, or cones to mark lines for Station 6
- Additional chalk, tape, or cones to mark lines
- Mats (optional)

Warm-Up Activities (6-8 minutes)

Individual Stretching Exercises

See Grades 4-5: Fitness, Lesson 16, page 802.

Skill-Development Activities (15 minutes)

Circuit Training 1

See Grades 4-5: Fitness, Lesson 1, page 803. Have children complete the circuit with a time of one minute at each station and 15 seconds to rotate to new stations.

Sprint Relay

See Grades 4-5: Fitness, Lesson 16, page 805.

1. Have children run the Sprint Relay.
2. Repeat using a different locomotor skill.

Shuttle Relay

See Grades 4-5: Fitness, Lesson 18, page 809.

1. Have children run the Shuttle Relay.
2. Repeat using a backward run, skipping, galloping, or hopping on one foot.

Crows and Cranes

Arrange children in two parallel lines facing each other, with half the children in each line, 30 to 50 ft apart.

1. Explain the game:

   The children in one line are "Crows;" those in the other line are "Cranes."

   As I begin saying "Crrrr . . . ," the two lines walk toward each other.

   When I complete the word Crow or Crane, the line I call is "It." The children in that line run forward and try to tag the other children, who turn and try to avoid being tagged.

   You are safe when you cross the line you started from. Tagged children join the other line and play continues.

2. Have the children play Crows and Cranes.
3. Mix up which line you call to surprise the children.
4. Remind children to watch where they run so they don't hurt anyone.

Lap Cool-Down

See Grades 4-5: Fitness, Lesson 16, page 805.

Concluding Activities (6-8 minutes)

Physical Fitness Concept

Gather the children into an advanced information formation.

1. Review the following definition: *"Muscular strength" is the maximum amount of weight a muscle can lift in one try.*
2. Introduce the overload principle: *To develop muscular strength, you need to understand the "overload principle." The overload principle says that you must make your muscles work harder than they are used to working if you want to increase their strength or endurance. One of the best ways to increase strength is to exercise with weights. How would you use the overload principle with weights?* (Gradually increase the amount of weight that you lift.)
3. Tell the children: *Another way to develop strength is to do body weight exercises and stunts. For example, it takes both strength and endurance of the arm and shoulder muscles to hold yourself in a push-up position.*

Holding a Push-Up Position

Arrange the children in a scatter formation. You may use mats for this activity.

1. Have each child assume a push-up position.
2. Have the children perform the following tasks:

   Keep your back straight and your head up.

   Let me see you lift your left foot.

   Now lift your right foot.

   Lift your left arm.

Now lift your right arm.

See if you can lift your left leg and your right arm at the same time.

Lift your right hand and touch your waist (touch your back, touch your left elbow, touch your right shoulder).

Lift your left hand and touch the back of your head.

Turn over and get into a crab walk position with your back straight.

Lift your right leg.

Try lifting your left leg.

Now lift your right arm.

Lift your left arm.

Discussion

Gather the children into an advanced information formation. Discuss what the children have learned today:

What components of fitness did we work on today?

What does the "overload principle" mean?

How do we use the overload principle to develop strength?

LESSON 20
INDIVIDUAL STRETCHING AND CIRCUIT TRAINING

Student Objectives

- Distinguish between muscular strength and muscular endurance.
- Participate in circuit training activities.
- Jump rope continuously for five minutes, alternating and cooperating with a partner.

Equipment and Materials

- 6 cones to mark stations
- 4 cones to define the Lap Cool-Down area
- 6 task cards, numbers, and tape for stations
- 1 carpet square or mat per child for Station 3
- 1 short jump rope per child for Station 4
- Chalk, tape, or cones to mark lines for Station 6
- Additional chalk, tape, or cones to mark lines
- 1 short jump rope per pair of children

Warm-Up Activities (6-8 minutes)

Individual Stretching Exercises

See Grades 4-5: Fitness, Lesson 16, page 802.

Skill-Development Activities (15 minutes)

Circuit Training 1

See Grades 4-5: Fitness, Lesson 16, page 803. Have children complete the circuit with a time of one minute at each station and 15 seconds to rotate to new stations.

Crows and Cranes

See Grades 4-5: Fitness, Lesson 19, page 813.

Five-Minute Jump

Arrange pairs in scatter formation.

1. Explain the activity:

The object of the game is for one team member to be jumping at all times.

One person starts jumping.

When he or she begins to tire, the second child begins jumping.

You will continue taking turns and resting as needed for five minutes.

2. Have pairs practice the activity. Over time when revisiting this lesson, encourage the children to keep jumping for longer total times.

Lap Cool-Down

See Grades 4-5: Fitness, Lesson 16, page 805.

Concluding Activities (6-8 minutes)

Physical Fitness Concept

Gather the children into an advanced information formation.

1. Review the following definitions: *Muscular strength and muscular endurance are related but different. "Muscular strength" is the greatest amount of weight your muscles can lift in one try. "Muscular endurance" is how long a group of muscles can perform.*

2. Explain the difference in more detail: *Muscular strength is usually measured by determining the heaviest weight you can lift in one try. For example, if you have weights of 10, 20, 30, 40, and 50 lb, the heaviest one you can lift with one arm is an indication of your arm strength. If you can lift the 10-lb weight easily, then you would try the 20-lb one. If you can lift the 20-lb weight but it's hard for you, then you probably cannot lift the 30-lb weight. This gives you some information about how strong your arm muscles are. Caution, though! You should not try to lift the heaviest weight possible at your age, because this can cause injury. Instead we try to carefully find a weight you can safely lift about six to eight times.*

   Muscular endurance, on the other hand, is usually measured by determining how many times you can lift a weight. To do this, you would select a weight lighter than your maximum, or heaviest, weight and see how many times you can lift it or how long you can exercise with it. In this example you might choose the 10-lb weight. Being able to lift a weight 12 to 15 times is a good guideline for developing muscular endurance.

   You don't have to use weights to increase your muscular strength and endurance. Supporting your body weight takes strength. For example, the ability to perform one push-up requires enough strength to lift your body weight. If you can't perform one push-up, then you need to practice three times a week to develop strength in your arm and shoulder muscles. If you can perform a push-up easily, then the total number of push-ups you can do is a measure of your muscular endurance. You should still exercise at least three times a week for three 10-minute continuous bouts to maintain your current level of fitness and to try to improve even more. So, push-ups may be a strength exercise for some children and an endurance exercise for others. Strength and endurance in other muscles work the same way.

3. Ask the children the following questions:

   If you can't perform one sit-up, what do you need to develop? (Strength of the stomach muscles.)

   How can you do this? (Practicing sit-ups three days a week.)

   If you can perform five sit-ups easily, then the total number of sit-ups you can do in one minute is a test of what? (Muscular endurance.)

LESSON 21
ROPE JUMPING

Student Objectives

- Explain that physical fitness is a part of good health.
- Maintain continuous activity with a long rope.
- Jog for five minutes.

Equipment and Materials

- 4 long jump ropes per group (12 to 16 ft long) (at least one rope per pair)
- Cones to mark oval field

Warm-Up Activities (5 minutes)

Jumping Through Long Ropes

Divide the children into groups of six or eight, and assign each group to a rope pattern made with four parallel long jump ropes.

1. Explain the activity:

    Starting at one end, jump over the ropes into the spaces between the ropes, first going forward, and then sideways.

    Repeat several times, hopping on the right foot, hopping on the left foot, and leaping.

    Play Follow the Leader with each child getting a turn to lead your group.

2. Have the children do the activity.

Skill-Development Activities (20 minutes)

Jumping Long Ropes

Divide the children into groups of four or five, each group with a long jump rope, in a scatter formation. Establish a rotation system for each group, with two children turning and two or three jumping.

1. Describe and demonstrate swinging: *In swinging, the turners swing the rope slightly from side to side. Jumpers stand next to the rope and jump over it as it swings.*

2. Have the children practice swinging, rotating so turners get a chance to practice jumping.

3. Describe and demonstrate swing and turn: *In swing and turn, turners swing the rope over the head of the jumper. Jumper jumps over the rope.*

4. Have the children practice swing and turn, rotating jumpers and turners. Continue

practice until most children can jump at least three jumps without missing.

5. Describe and demonstrate front door: *In front door, you turn the rope toward the jumper. The jumper runs under the turning rope (runs in the "front door") and either jumps or runs out.*

6. Have the children practice front door, rotating jumpers and turners.

7. Describe and demonstrate back door: *In back door, you turn the rope away from the jumper. The jumper begins to run as the rope leaves the ground, entering when the rope is at the top (runs in the "back door"). The jumper stays and jumps once, then jumps out while the rope is at the top.*

8. Practice back door, rotating jumpers and turners.

Continuous Jumping to Chants

Divide the children into pairs, each pair with a rope in scatter formation.

1. Say each chant, then have children practice it. Explain that jumping rope continuously is good aerobic exercise.

2. Have each pair select one of the chants and jump continuously up to 50 or until a miss occurs.

Coffee Chant

I like coffee, I like tea,

How many boys (girls) are wild about me?

1, 2, 3 . . . (up to 50 or until a miss occurs).

Chickety, Chickety

Chickety, chickety, chickety, chop.

How many times before I stop?

1, 2, 3 . . . 50.

Bobby, Bobby

Bobby, Bobby, at the gate,

Eating cherries from a plate.

How many cherries can he eat?

1, 2, 3 . . . 50.

Down in the Valley

Down in the valley,

Where the green grass grows,

Sat little Mary as sweet as a rose.

Along came Johnny,

And kissed her on the nose.

How many kisses did she get?

1, 2, 3 . . . 50.

Olympic Joggers

Mark a large oval area with cones. This can be done around the outside of a basketball court. Stagger the children around the track.

1. Explain the activity:

On the signal, jog around the oval track.

I want you to continue for three to five minutes, running as far as possible. Pace yourself but try to get your heart rate up to get the cardiorespiratory benefits.

2. Have the children jog.

Cool-Down

Walk one lap forward, one backward.

Concluding Activities (5 minutes)

Physical Fitness Concept

Gather the children into an advanced information formation.

1. Discuss the concept of being healthy (wellness): *Being healthy is more than not being sick. Good health includes physical, social, and mental well-being. Physical well-being means keeping your body fit, eating the right kinds of foods, and protecting yourself from disease. It means keeping your body in the best possible condition. Social well-being means that you can get along with others, and you can make new friends. Mental well-being means that you have a good feeling about yourself, and you know what your strengths and weaknesses are. To be healthy, you have to have good physical health, good social health, and good mental health. Health-related physical fitness is an important part of physical health. To be physically healthy, you must exercise regularly and you must exercise for all components of fitness.*

2. Read each of the following statements to the children. Ask each child to think about how the statement describes him or her. The choices for answers are "like me," "sometimes like me," and "unlike me." If "like me" is the answer then the child puts one finger in the air. If "sometimes like me" is the choice then the child puts two fingers in the air. Three fingers represent "unlike me." Discuss the results after all statements are read.

Physical Health

I like to exercise.

I do some exercise every day.

I would rather ride my bicycle (or some other moderate to vigorous physical activity) than sit and watch television.

I would rather play a game than watch others play.

I like active games better than quiet games.

Social Health

I like to meet new friends.

I get along with others when playing games.

I accept friends who are different from me.

I continue to play after I lose a game.

I make friends easily.

Mental Health

I enjoy a lot of different things.

I can name several activities I do well.

When I am unhappy, I can tell others why.

I like to compliment others.

If I need help I ask for it.

LESSON 22
ROPE JUMPING

Student Objectives

- Explain how the resting heart rate is one way to determine how healthy the heart is.
- Maintain continuous activity with a long rope.
- Jog continuously for six to eight minutes.

Equipment and Materials

- 4 long jump ropes per group (12 to 16 ft long)
- Cones to mark oval field

Warm-Up Activities (5 minutes)

Jumping Through Long Ropes

See Grades 4-5: Fitness, Lesson 21, page 817.

Skill-Development Activities (20 minutes)

Jumping Long Ropes

Practice swinging, swing and turn, front door, back door, and continuous jumping. See Grades 4-5: Fitness, Lesson 21, page 817. Remind students that these activities help develop cardiorespiratory fitness.

Continuous Jumping to Chants

See Grades 4-5: Fitness, Lesson 21, page 818.

Olympic Joggers

See Grades 4-5: Fitness, Lesson 21, page 818. Encourage the children to jog for six to eight minutes continuously.

Cool-Down

See Grades 4-5: Fitness, Lesson 21, page 819.

Concluding Activities (5 minutes)

Physical Fitness Concept

Gather the children into an advanced information formation.

1. Discuss the concept of resting heart rate: *"Heart rate" is how many times your heart contracts or pumps in a minute. "Resting heart rate" is your heart rate when you first wake up in the morning or after you have been lying very still for 15 to 30 minutes. As you get older, your resting heart rate will go down. For instance, the average 10-year-old girl has a resting heart rate of about 90, whereas the average adult woman has a resting heart rate of around 72. Everyone has a different resting heart rate. How many times the heart beats when you are resting is one way to determine how healthy your heart is. When you participate regularly in cardiovascular endurance activities, your resting heart rate will go down.*

2. Continue to discuss the heart rate with the children: *What might make your heart beat faster?* (Exercise.) *Some other things might also make your heart beat faster, for example, being angry, frightened, surprised, or excited about something.*

Pulse Counting

Divide children into groups of four.

1. Review pulse counting. See Grades 4-5: Fitness, Lesson 18, page 810.
2. Assign each group the task of recording each student's resting heart rate.
3. Discuss the differences.

LESSON 23
ROPE JUMPING

Student Objectives

- Explain how to use the overload principle to develop strength.
- Maintain continuous activity with a long rope.
- Jump a short rope cooperatively with a small group for 10 minutes.

Equipment and Materials

- 4 jump ropes per group (12 to 16 ft long)
- 1 short jump rope per trio of students

Warm-Up Activities (5 minutes)

Jumping Through Long Ropes

See Grades 4-5: Fitness, Lesson 21, page 817.

Skill-Development Activities (20 minutes)

Jumping Long Ropes

See Grades 4-5: Fitness, Lesson 21, page 817.

Continuous Jumping to Chants

See Grades 4-5: Fitness, Lesson 21, page 818.

10-Minute Jump

Divide the children into groups of three, and give each group a short jump rope. Have the groups get into scatter formation.

1. Explain the game:

    The object of the game is for one team member to be jumping at all times.

    One person should start jumping. When he or she begins to tire, the second child should begin jumping.

    When the second child begins to tire, the third child should begin jumping. Continue taking turns and resting for 10 minutes.

2. Have the children play 10-Minute Jump.

Cool-Down

See Grades 4-5: Fitness, Lesson 21, page 819.

Concluding Activities (5 minutes)

Physical Fitness Concept

Gather the children into an advanced information formation.

1. Review the definition of muscular strength: *Do you remember what "muscular strength" is?* (The greatest amount of weight your muscles can lift in one try.)

2. Review the meaning of overload: *Do you remember what the overload principle is in muscular strength and endurance terms?* (Exercising with more weight than usual.)

3. Discuss exercises for strength training: *Overload training is a way to help your muscles get stronger. You want to make your muscles work harder. If you can lift a 5-lb weight easily with one hand but a 10-lb weight is very hard to lift, then you want to use a 10-lb weight to exercise for strength. You won't be able to perform many repetitions because you have overloaded your muscles.*

4. Ask the children the following questions:

   If you can lift a 10-lb weight easily, can you develop strength by using a 5-lb weight and performing many repetitions? (No.)

   If a person can lift a 30-lb weight but can only do one or two repetitions, can he or she develop strength using the 30-lb weight? (Yes.) *What does overload training mean in muscular strength and endurance terms?* (Increasing weight to develop strength or number of repetitions to develop endurance.)

LESSON 24
ROPE JUMPING AND INDIVIDUAL STUNTS

Student Objectives

- Explain that different tasks require different amounts of strength.
- Maintain continuous activity with a long rope.
- Jump a short rope cooperatively with a small group for 10 minutes.

Equipment and Materials

- 4 long jump ropes per group (12 to 16 ft)
- 1 short jump rope per pair
- 1 mat per four to six children

Warm-Up Activities (5 minutes)

Jumping Through Long Ropes

See Grades 4-5: Fitness, Lesson 21, page 817.

Skill-Development Activities (15 minutes)

Jumping Long Ropes

See Grades 4-5: Fitness, Lesson 21, page 817. Introduce the following new chants. See also Grades 4-5: Fitness, Lesson 21, page 818.

Lady at the Gate

> *Lady, lady, at the gate,*
> *Eating cherries from a plate,*
> *How many cherries did she eat?*
> *1, 2, 3 . . . 50*

Teddy Bear

> *Teddy Bear, Teddy Bear, turn around.*
> *Teddy Bear, Teddy Bear, touch the ground.*
> *Teddy Bear, Teddy Bear, buckle your shoe.*
> *Teddy Bear, Teddy Bear, that will do.*

Teddy Bear, Teddy Bear, go up stairs,
Teddy Bear, Teddy Bear, say your prayers.
Teddy Bear, Teddy Bear, turn out the light.
Teddy Bear, Teddy Bear, say good night.

Mabel, Mabel

Mabel, Mabel,
Set the table.
Don't forget
The red-hot peppers. (Jump as fast as possible up to 50 times.)

10-Minute Jump

See Grades 4-5: Fitness, Lesson 23, page 822.

Concluding Activities (10 minutes)

Physical Fitness Concept

Gather the children into an advanced information formation.

1. Explain key muscular strength concepts: *You need different amounts of strength, depending on the task you need to do. Some activities need arm strength, and others need leg strength. Any activity that requires you to hold (support) your body weight with your arms needs arm strength. Activities in which you need to move your body around, such as running, need leg strength.*

2. Select a child to demonstrate the stunts, and let the children decide if arm strength or leg strength is needed.

Individual Strength Stunts

Divide children into groups of five or six, and arrange groups in scatter formation with mats.

1. Describe and demonstrate each of the stunts.

2. Tell the children: *Practice each of the stunts. Work together to make sure each student in your group is successful.*

Seal Walk

Get into a push-up position with the weight on your hands and toes. Keep your back straight. Walk forward with your hands, dragging your legs and toes.

Cross-Legged Stand

Sit with your legs and arms crossed. Rise slowly to a standing position. Return to a sitting position.

Jump the Rope

Stand facing a rope on the ground. Bend down, placing your hands over the rope. Supporting your weight with your arms, swing your legs over the rope.

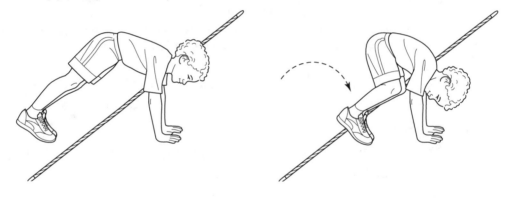

Kangaroo Hop

Bend your knees halfway and fold your arms across your chest. Keeping your knees slightly bent, jump forward several times.

Tip-Up

Squat down and place your hands on the mat between your knees. Lean forward and slowly lift your feet off the mat. Balance on your hands.

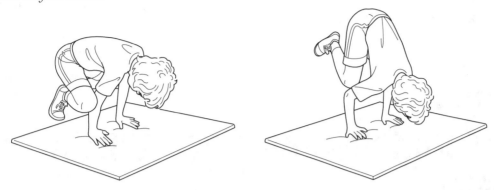

Lunge

Stand on one foot with your other leg lifted straight in front of your body. Slowly bend the knee of your support leg. Repeat on the opposite leg.

LESSON 25
ROPE JUMPING AND INDIVIDUAL STUNTS

Student Objectives

- Explain that being able to do many sit-ups requires endurance of the stomach muscles.
- Explain that being able to do many push-ups requires endurance of the arm muscles.
- Jump a short rope cooperatively with a small group for 10 minutes.
- Maintain continuous activity requiring arm and leg strength.

Equipment and Materials

- 4 long jump ropes per group (12 to 16 ft)
- 1 short rope per group
- 1 mat per four to six children

Warm-Up Activities (5 minutes)

Jumping Through Long Ropes

See Grades 4-5: Fitness, Lesson 21, page 817.

Skill-Development Activities (15 minutes)

10-Minute Jump

See Grades 4-5: Fitness, Lesson 23, page 822.

Individual Strength Stunts

See Grades 4-5: Fitness, Lesson 24, page 825.

Concluding Activities (10 minutes)

Physical Fitness Concept

Gather the children into an advanced information formation.

1. Review the definition of muscular endurance as the ability of a muscle to repeat a movement many times.

Skill-Development Activities (20 minutes)

Wand Challenges 1

Keep the children in scatter formation, and give each a wand to place on the floor. Present the following tasks:

With your side to the wand, jump back and forth over it.

With your side to the wand, jump back and forth over it rapidly 20 times.

Face the wand and jump over it. Then turn completely around, and jump over it again. Try adding a turn in the air as you jump.

Jump over the wand backward.

Jump over the wand several times, increasing the height of your jump each time.

Jump over the wand several times, increasing the distance of your jump each time.

Timed Partner Jump

Arrange partners in scatter formation.

1. Explain the activity:

   One partner holds the wand about knee-high.

   The other partner jumps back and forth over the wand as many times as possible in 30 seconds.

2. The teacher signals the start and end of this time period.

   Take turns holding and jumping.

3. Have the children do the Timed Partner Jump.

Wand Challenges 2

Gather the children into an advanced information formation.

1. Describe and demonstrate the stunts.

2. Have the children practice each stunt.

Jump Over the Wand

Arrange the children in scatter formation.

1. *Hold the wand in front of you with both hands about shoulder-width apart. The lower you hold the wand, the easier the task will be.*

2. *Jump up and over the wand.*

Wand Balance
Balance the wand on different parts of your body. See how many different ways you can do this.

Thread the Needle
Hold the wand in front of you with both hands. Bend forward, stepping over the wand with one foot and then the other. Lift the wand up behind your back and over your head to a stretched position. Release the wand and repeat.

Bridge Under

Stand very tall and hold the wand in your right hand with one end on the floor. Bend your legs and move under your right arm (the one holding the wand). Repeat with your left hand holding the wand.

Figure Eight

Hold the wand in front of you with both hands near the ends. Lift your right foot around the outside of your right arm and back over the wand. Lift the wand up over your head and down your back. The wand should not be between your legs. Release one end of the wand. Repeat, beginning with your left foot going around your left arm and back over the wand.

Cool-Down

Keep the children in scatter formation. Have the children walk for three minutes.

Concluding Activities (5 minutes)

Physical Fitness Concept

Gather the children into an advanced information formation.

1. Review the definition of muscular endurance and ways to assess muscular endurance of the stomach muscles.

2. Discuss ways to assess muscular endurance of the arm muscles.

3. Explain: *When you perform a push-up, a muscle in each arm bends (or flexes) each arm to lower your body to the floor. Then another muscle straightens (or extends) each arm to lift your body up off the floor. The flexor muscle is called the "biceps" and the extensor muscle is called the "triceps." Muscles in your body usually work in pairs, as the biceps and triceps do. The number of push-ups you can do is a test of the muscular endurance of your arms. It is testing the abilities of the biceps and triceps to repeat the push-up movement.*

4. Tell the students: *You can also determine your muscular endurance by holding a balanced position for a period of time.*

Timed Push-Up Position

Arrange the children in scatter formation.

1. Ask children: *Get into push-up position with your weight on your hands and toes and your body extended.*

2. *Hold this position for one minute.*

FITNESS

LESSON 27
WANDS 2

Student Objectives

- Explain the health benefits of physical activity.
- Maintain continuous activity with a wand.
- Perform simple wand stunts.

Equipment and Materials

- 1 wand (30-36 in.) per child
- Optional: 2 additional wands per group
- Stopwatch or clock with second hand

Warm-Up Activities (5 minutes)

Running and Dodging Games

See Grades 4-5: Fitness, Lesson 26, page 830. Choose from Follow the Leader, Partner Dodging, and Individual Running and Dodging.

Skill-Development Activities (20 minutes)

Wand Challenges 1

See Grades 4-5: Fitness, Lesson 26, page 831.

Timed Partner Jump

See Grades 4-5: Fitness, Lesson 26, page 831. Have the children try to jump for one minute.

Jump Over the Wand

See Grades 4-5: Fitness, Lesson 26, page 831.

Wand Follow the Leader

Divide children into groups of four. Give each group four to six wands. Direct each group to arrange the wands in various patterns to jump and hop into, out of, and around.

1. Tell the children: *Play Follow the Leader, changing leaders every 60 seconds.*
2. *Here are some pattern suggestions:*

    Place the wands in random order and jump forward, backward, and sideways over them.

    Place the wands in parallel lines. Jump, leap, or hop through the wands.

    Place the wands in a square or other geometric shape and jump, leap, or hop through the shape.

    Place the wands in other patterns. Jump, leap, or hop through the patterns.

Pass-the-Wand Cool-Down

Divide children in groups of four or five in a relay formation, with half of each group at opposite ends of the play area, facing the other part of the group. Ends should be about 60 ft apart.

1. Explain the activity:

    One child in each group holds the wand for that group. That child walks to the opposite end of the play area carrying the wand and hands the wand to the first child in that part of the line, relay-fashion.

    The child now holding the wand walks to the part of the group where the first child began and passes the wand to the next child.

    We will continue until everyone has had several turns.

    This is not a race; it is a cool-down.

2. Have the children do the Pass-the-Wand Cool-Down.

Concluding Activities (5 minutes)

Physical Fitness Concept

Gather the children into an advanced information formation.

1. Discuss some of the health benefits of physical activity: *Individuals who exercise tend to feel better about themselves, be less likely to experience obesity, heart disease, and high blood pressure, and be better able to cope with stressful situations.*

2. Explain that there are some things that exercise cannot do, such as increase your intelligence or change your personality.

An Exercise Quiz

Keep the children in the advanced information formation.

1. Read a list of benefits of exercise to the children.

2. Ask them to give you a "thumbs up" if the statement is true and a "thumbs down" if the statement if false.

3. *Regular exercise will:*

    Improve physical fitness. (True; training is the only way to increase fitness.)

    Make you taller. (False; growth, not exercise, does this.)

    Turn fat to muscle. (False; exercise can reduce fat and increase muscle, but these are different tissues.)

    Increase your IQ. (False; but you may be able to think better if exercise helps you feel less stressed.)

    Help maintain a lean body. (True; exercise helps to control fatness and increase muscle.)

    Improve your self-image. (True; exercise helps us be proud of ourselves.)

    Reduce the risk of heart disease. (True; exercise and diet help keep the heart healthy.)

    Allow you to read faster. (False; reading practice helps us read better.)

    Improve your cardiorespiratory endurance. (True; training is based on exercise.)

    Absolutely assure you of a long life. (False; nothing can do this, but exercise should improve the quality of your life.)

LESSON 28
MODERATE TO VIGOROUS GAMES

Student Objectives

- Explain the relationship between fitness and good health.
- Perform a stretching routine.
- Execute three sets of crunches, six repetitions per set.
- Execute three sets of regular and triceps push-ups, three repetitions per set.
- Participate in a moderate to vigorous game.

Equipment and Materials

- Chalk or tape to mark boundaries
- 1 parachute
- Signal
- Mats (optional)

Warm-Up Activities (5 minutes)

Stretching Routine

Arrange children in a large circle facing the center.

1. Describe and demonstrate each of the stretches.
2. Have children try each of the stretches.

Modified Neck Roll

Sit tall, with one hand on each side of your head covering your ears. Drop your head forward, then very slowly roll your head around in a semicircle, supporting your head with your hands, first to the left and then to the right. Do not move past the shoulders or backward. Repeat several times.

Shoulder Shrugs

Lift your shoulders to your ears, then return to normal position.

Side Stretch

Sit with feet apart and toes pointed straight ahead and knees slightly bent. Place one hand on hip and extend the other arm up over the head. Slowly bend to the side toward the hand on the hip. Hold for 10 seconds and relax. Repeat in the opposite direction.

Front and Side Lunges

Facing forward, bend to a squat with your right leg directly under your torso and your left leg extended to the side. As you bend, place your hands, palms down, on the floor on each side of your right foot to help you to balance. Keep both heels on the floor. Your left leg can be slightly bent at the knee. Your right knee should be directly over your right toes. Look forward, keeping your head up. Your back should be parallel to the floor. Hold this position for 5 to 20 seconds.

Gradually turn to your right, allowing your heels to leave the floor. Your right knee will touch or be close to touching your chest. Bend the left knee and then gradually straighten both legs to nearly extended (determine this by your comfort level—don't extend if you feel pain; knees should never be completely straight to avoid pulling the ligaments), keeping your back straight and parallel to the floor and your head up. Turn and "roll" your body over your left knee, repeating the entire sequence.

Standing Heel Stretch

Stand with one foot directly in front of the other, about one ft apart. With both feet flat on the ground and your body positioned directly above the back foot, bend your knees. Bend so your thighs are parallel to the floor without allowing your heels to leave the floor. Hold for 5 to 20 counts. Reverse feet and repeat.

3. Combine stretches into the following routine:

   Head right, two, three, four; right, two, three, four; and left, two, three, four; left, two, three, four.

   Shoulders up, down, two, three, four; again, two, three, four.

   Reach up, left, center, right, forward; left, center, right, forward.

   Heels flat on the floor—bend your right knee and hold, two, three, four, five; head up.

   Turn to the right—back straight—head up and allow your heels to come up.

   Stand, extending your legs—keep your back down!

   Turn to the front, bend your left knee—head up, hold, two, three, four.

   Turn to the left—back straight—head up and allow your heels to come up.

   Stand, extending your legs—keep your back down!

   Standing heel stretch (count 5 to 10). Reverse.

Skill-Development Activities (20 minutes)

Advanced Crunches

Gather the children into an advanced information formation.

1. Describe and demonstrate the exercise:

   Lie on your back with your hips bent at a 90-degree angle so your feet are over your hips or stomach.

   Cross your ankles and bend your knees slightly.

   With your fingers gently touching your ears on each side of your head, do the crunch by lifting your head, neck, and shoulders (to the shoulder blades) off the ground.

   End the lift when one elbow touches (or nears) the opposite knee or both elbows reach the knees.

   Do one each—right elbow to left knee, left elbow to right knee, then both elbows to both knees—then repeat the sequence. We will use the count "Right, left, both; right, left, both."

Arrange the children in scatter formation, with mats.

2. Have the children repeat this sequence six times, then rest.

3. Have the children repeat the entire sequence twice more.

Push-Ups

Gather the children into an advanced information formation.

1. Describe and demonstrate regular push-ups:

    Support your body weight on your hands and feet with your hands at the side of your body, chest-high. Your body should be straight with feet together.

    By straightening your arms, lift your body upward; then in a smooth, continuous motion, lower your body back to starting position.

    Repeat.

    Do three push-ups, then rest briefly; three more and rest; three more and stop.

Arrange the children in scatter formation.

2. Have the children do three sets of three regular push-ups.
3. Describe and demonstrate triceps push-ups:

    Support your weight on your hands and heels with your back facing the floor. Your body should be straight.

    Gradually lower your body toward the ground, then return to starting position by bending and straightening your arms. This is a difficult skill, and at first very little motion is possible.

    Repeat.

    Try to do three triceps push-ups, then rest briefly; three more and rest; three more and stop.

4. Have the children try to do three sets of three triceps push-ups.

Slap Tag

Divide children in two equal groups, one of "Runners" and the other "Chasers." Have each group stand on two parallel lines about 50 ft apart. Runners stand on one line facing the play area. Chasers stand on the opposite line with their backs to the play area and their hands out behind them.

1. Describe and demonstrate the game:

    The Runners sneak across and slap the palms of the Chasers.

    As soon as a Chaser's hand is slapped, both the Runner and the Chaser turn and run for the Runner's baseline at the other side of the play area.

    The Chasers try to tag the Runners before they reach their base. Every Runner who is tagged becomes a Chaser and moves to the other side.

    Each round, we will reverse Runners and Chasers.

2. Have the children play Slap Tag (5 to 10 minutes).

Cool-Down With Parachute Activities

Arrange children around the outside of a parachute spread out on the ground.

1. Moving clockwise or counterclockwise, have the children gallop, slide, and skip, stopping on your signal.
2. The tempo should gradually slow to walking.

Concluding Activities (5 minutes)

Physical Fitness Concept

Gather the children into an advanced information formation.

1. Discuss the relationship between being physically fit and being healthy: *Health is influenced by many things. Fitness is one of them. Can you name some others?* (Rest, diet, heredity, environment.)

2. Tell the children: *To have good health we should do what we can to help ourselves. Let's write a recipe for good health.*

3. Discuss the factors and write them down. Some suggestions: get plenty of rest; eat a balanced diet; feel good about yourself; try to avoid stress. Exercise should be included, such as running, stretching, moderate to vigorous games, sit-ups, push-ups.

4. Make them up into a pretend recipe; see sample.

Recipe for Good Health

3 days of jogging

2 days of moderate to vigorous games

3 days of sit-ups and push-ups

3 days of stretching all parts of the body

Mix with a balanced diet. Let rest at least 8 hours every day. Keep away from stress and anxiety. Serve with lots of good feelings about yourself!

LESSON 29
MODERATE TO VIGOROUS GAMES

Student Objectives

- Give examples of how physical fitness positively influences daily living.
- Perform a stretching routine.
- Execute three sets of crunches, six repetitions per set.
- Execute three sets each of regular and triceps push-ups, three repetitions per set.
- Participate in a moderate to vigorous game.

Equipment and Materials

- Chalk or tape to mark boundaries
- 1 Frisbee per pair

Warm-Up Activities (5 minutes)

Stretching Routine

See Grades 4-5: Fitness, Lesson 28, page 836.

Skill-Development Activities (20 minutes)

Arrange children in a large circle facing the center.

Crunches and Regular and Triceps Push-Ups

See Grades 4-5: Fitness, Lesson 28, page 837-838.

Crows and Cranes

See Grades 4-5: Fitness, Lesson 19, page 813.

Cool-Down With Backhand Frisbee Throw

Arrange partners in a wide scatter formation, each pair with a Frisbee.

1. Describe and demonstrate the skill:

    Grip the Frisbee with your thumb on top and fingers spread underneath. Turn the side of your throwing arm toward the target (your partner), and step forward with the foot on the throwing-arm side on the throw.

    Start the throw by moving the Frisbee across in front of your body and stepping toward the target with your front foot. Snap your wrist on the release.

You can catch the Frisbee with two hands. Once you have more practice, you may be able to catch it with one hand.

2. Have the children practice throwing in pairs. Increase the distance between partners as skill improves.

Concluding Activities (5 minutes)

Physical Fitness Concept

Gather the children into an advanced information formation.

1. Discuss how physical fitness influences nearly everything we do each day: *High levels of fitness affect our lives in the following ways:*

   We sleep better.

   We have more energy.

   We feel better about ourselves.

   We are less fat.

   We are stronger.

   We can do more physical work.

2. Continue: *Being fit improves our health and influences what we can do each day. What things do you do each day that require some level of fitness? Let's start in the morning and work through the day. What do you do when you first wake up?*

3. Allow children to list all of their daily activities: make their bed, fix breakfast and lunch, go to school, play, do chores, play sports, and so on. Relate the level of fitness to the number of things they can do.

LESSON 30
MODERATE TO VIGOROUS GAMES

Student Objectives

- Give examples of conditions that are the opposite of health-related physical fitness.
- Perform a stretching routine.
- Execute three sets of crunches, eight repetitions per set.
- Execute three sets each of regular and triceps push-ups, three repetitions per set.
- Participate in a moderate to vigorous game.

Equipment and Materials

- 4 bases
- 1 playground ball (8 1/2-in.)
- 1 parachute

Warm-Up Activities (5 minutes)

Stretching Routine

See Grades 4-5: Fitness, Lesson 28, page 836.

Skill-Development Activities (20 minutes)

Crunches and Regular and Triceps Push-Ups

See Grades 4-5: Fitness, Lesson 28, page 837-838.

Line-Up

Divide children in two teams, one on the field and the other at bat.

1. Describe and demonstrate the game:

   The hitter bounces a playground ball and strikes it with his or her hand, then the entire team runs around the bases in a single file line behind the hitter. Each hitter has only one chance to strike the ball—it is either an out or a run. Foul balls are outs.

   When the hitter hits the ball fair, the players on the fielding team all line up behind the player who catches the ball. They pass the ball quickly overhead back to the end of the line, then back to the front of the line, trying to get the ball to the end and back to the beginning of the line before the members of the hitting team all reach home.

   If the ball moves to the end of the line and back to the catcher before the hitting team is home, it's an out.

If the hitting team gets home before the ball gets to the end of the catching line and back to the catcher, it's a run.

When the hitting team has three outs, the two teams switch positions.

2. Have the children play Line-Up (15 minutes).

Cool-Down With Exchange Positions

Arrange children around the outside of a parachute that is spread out on the ground. Assign the children numbers and instruct them to hold the parachute with the left hand and circle counterclockwise.

1. On your signal, the odd-numbered children release the parachute and move forward to take the place of the next odd-numbered player in front of them (variations can include moving up two places, three places, and so on). Repeat with even-numbered players moving.

2. Have children use a variety of locomotor skills—running, galloping, skipping, and walking—to move.

Concluding Activities (5 minutes)

Physical Fitness Concept

Divide children into groups of five or six.

1. Discuss how physical fitness is the opposite of sickness or being unhealthy: *Fitness contributes to being healthy. Fitness influences our daily lives and the length of our lives. Older people who are fit have a better chance of living longer and more active lives. Younger people who are fit say they are happier, have more energy, and are healthier than low-fit people.*

2. Ask the children: *Can you give me some examples of opposites?* (Up and down, night and day, cold and hot.) *Opposites are as far apart as possible—like living in New York and in Los Angeles is about as far apart as you can be and still be living in the United States. That's like sickness and fitness!*

3. Ask each group to discuss then describe a fit and a low-fit person. Say to the children: *Remember, looks don't tell the whole story!*

LESSON 31
MODERATE TO VIGOROUS GAMES

Student Objectives

- Explain why abdominal strength is important.
- Perform a stretching routine.
- Execute three sets of crunches, 10 repetitions per set.
- Execute three sets each of regular and triceps push-ups, four repetitions per set.
- Participate in a moderate to vigorous game.

Equipment and Materials

- Chalk, tape, or cones to mark boundaries
- 1 foam ball (8 1/2- to 13-in. diameter) for every three children
- 1 parachute
- Signal

Warm-Up Activities (5 minutes)

Stretching Routine

See Grades 4-5: Fitness, Lesson 28, page 836.

Skill-Development Activities (20 minutes)

Crunches and Regular and Triceps Push-Ups

See Grades 4-5: Fitness, Lesson 28, page 837-838. Increase crunch repetitions to 10 per set. Increase regular and triceps push-ups repetitions to 6 per set.

Running the Chute

Divide the children into three equal groups. Arrange two equal groups on opposite parallel lines (60 ft long), about 40 ft apart. The remaining children should be in one group on a line at one end of the rectangle (40 ft long). Give the balls to the children on the two lines.

1. Describe and demonstrate the game:

   On the signal, the other children run between the lines as the children on the lines try to hit them below the waist with the balls. The runners try to run from one end to the other and back without being hit by a ball. Runners may move as a group or individually.

   The throwing team gets one point for each child hit below the waist. The throwing team may move into the running area to retrieve balls but must move back behind the lines before throwing the ball.

> *After the throwers get 10 points, we will switch one throwing team with the runners.*
> *After 10 more points, we'll switch again.*

2. Have the children play Running the Chute (15 minutes).

Cool-Down With Run Under

Arrange children around the outside of a parachute, spread out on the ground. Assign children numbers from one to four.

1. Explain the activity:

   > *Begin in a squatting position, holding the parachute with both hands.*

   > *On the signal, lift the parachute to form an "umbrella."*

   > *Immediately after the signal, I will call a number from one to four. The players assigned the number called must move across the circle under the parachute to the opposite side and to the former position of another player with the same number.*

   > *We will then repeat, using all numbers.*

2. Have the children play Cool-Down With Run Under.

3. Variation: All players can let go of the parachute, and then the players with the number you call out must run across as before.

Concluding Activities (5 minutes)

Physical Fitness Concept

Gather the children into an advanced information formation.

1. Explain the concept: *Abdominal (stomach) strength is important for good posture and to prevent lower back pain as you get older.*

2. Point out the abdominal muscles and the vertebrae on yourself. *When the abdomen sticks out, it stresses the back and pulls down on the backbone, forcing the vertebrae (the bones of the back) together. This pinching (demonstrate hyperextending your back so your abdomen sticks out and downward and your back is dramatically curved at the waist) is painful.*

3. Tell the children: *Doing crunches and maintaining a reasonable body weight keeps the stomach in line and doesn't stress the back.*

4. Demonstrate several forms of poor posture: slouching, leaning to one side, back swayed (abdomen protruding).

5. Ask children to demonstrate good standing posture. Tell them to make sure they do these things:

   > *Keep both feet flat on the floor.*

   > *Keep your arms relaxed and hanging near your thighs.*

   > *Hold your head high so you can't see any of your body.*

   > *Hold your hips, shoulders, and head so they make a line when viewed from the side.*

LESSON 32
MODERATE TO VIGOROUS GAMES

Student Objectives

- Name two factors that make individual training different for different people.
- Perform a stretching routine.
- Execute three sets of crunches, 10 repetitions per set.
- Execute three sets of regular and triceps push-ups, 6 repetitions per set.
- Participate in a moderate to vigorous game.

Equipment and Materials

- Chalk, tape, or cones to mark boundaries
- 1 Frisbee per pair
- 1 parachute
- Several fluff balls

Warm-Up Activities (5 minutes)

Stretching Routine

See Grades 4-5: Fitness, Lesson 28, page 836.

Skill-Development Activities (20 minutes)

Crunches and Regular and Triceps Push-Ups

Crunches: continue 10 repetitions per set; regular and triceps push-ups: continue 6 repetitions per set. See Grades 4-5: Fitness, Lesson 28, page 837-838.

Great Wall of China Tag

Arrange children on one starting line, with the ending line 40 ft away. Have two or three children stand at one of the endlines, or "behind the wall." These children are "Its."

1. Describe and demonstrate the game:

   The object is to run from one side of the playing area and leap or jump over the Great Wall (an area down the middle of the playing area, three to six ft wide) to reach the opposite side of the playing area without being tagged. Its can run through or stop in the wall.

   The rest of you must clear the wall (stepping inside or on the line is not clearing the wall) as you cross the area.

Any child who fails to clear the wall (who gets tagged) becomes an additional It. When all children are tagged or after a set time, I will select new Its.

2. Have the children play Great Wall of China Tag.

Cool-Down With Popcorn

Arrange children around the outside of a parachute, spread out on the ground. Assign children numbers. The odd numbers form team 1; the even numbers, team 2. Place several fluff balls on the parachute.

1. Explain the activity:

   Team 1 lets go of the parachute and takes two or three steps backward. Team 2 has 30 seconds to "pop" all the balls off the parachute.

   Teams will exchange places, so team 1 has a turn.

   The team with fewer balls on the parachute after the 30-second time period wins. We can play several rounds, and we will total the balls from each round to determine the winner.

2. Have the children play Cool-Down With Popcorn.

Concluding Activities (5 minutes)

Physical Fitness Concept

Arrange the children in an advanced information formation.

1. Explain that the amount of training necessary for people of different ages, genders, and needs varies, but the components of health-related physical fitness remain the same.

2. Discuss the components of physical fitness: *The components of health-related physical fitness are cardiorespiratory endurance, flexibility, leanness (body composition), muscular strength, and muscular endurance. Training is a specific routine of activity designed to develop and/or maintain health-related physical fitness.*

3. Tell the children: *People who are in very good shape—who are very fit—must work hard to improve their level of fitness. People who are in poor shape—who are not very fit—will gain fitness with an easy training program or with nearly any increase in activity. Children are usually very active. The types of activities you do tend to develop physical fitness. So you can train with moderate to vigorous exercise to increase your fitness. Remember that your age is used to select the intensity—or difficulty—of the workout. An older person trains at a lower intensity than a child, because an older person is usually not as active to start with.*

4. Ask the children: *Can you name a job in which strength is important?* (Professional football player, bricklayer's helper, furniture mover, dockworker.) *So the need for fitness may also be increased by the type of job a person has. But such a job itself helps improve or maintain a person's fitness. Hobbies may also demand and build strength—like mountain climbing or home remodeling.*

Fourth and fifth graders should still focus on refining skills and applying those skills in games. As in the earlier grades, many children in these grades will be participating in sport programs after school, which can help them become more competent movers; however, such programs often emphasize game play rather than skill development. Yet skills are too important to skim over both because sport is important in our society and because children judge each other based on motor skill performance. As children gain skill they become more efficient and competent, which in turn enhances confidence.

UNIT ORGANIZATION

Fourth and fifth graders are ready for more complex games and a greater of variety of equipment and ways of using that equipment. That is why we have them use quoits (rings), play Frisbee golf, and try juggling. This age group is also ready to be introduced to modified versions of more formal sports, such as soccer, basketball, softball, volleyball, track and field, and football. The last lesson is a cooperative game that requires problem solving in small groups.

LESSON ORGANIZATION

Each lesson begins with warm-up activities, usually five-minute games of low organization. Refer to the warm-up games that open the unit often throughout the school year. Skill development activities follow; plan about 20 minutes for this segment. Usually there will be time to repeat the skill development activities until time runs out.

Remember that practice is critical to skill acquisition. More turns or practice trials enhance skill acquisition and allow you more chances to give feedback to the students. Keep group sizes small for the same reasons. Finally, each lesson ends with five minutes of concluding activities. These are often games that use the skill(s) practiced earlier in the lesson, bringing closure to the lesson.

We encourage you to revisit many of the lessons several times not only to reinforce skills but also for the sheer enjoyment children get out of repeating an activity with which they are familiar. Table S3.1 summarizes the lessons in a unit plan.

TEACHING HINTS

Most children this age will still be enthusiastic about games and sports instruction. You may find several, however, who lack interest due to poor experiences in the past. Work hard to create success for these students so that they may become and feel more competent. These lessons include many age-appropriate games to develop, refine, and extend basic skills.

Individualizing Instruction

Skill levels among children will vary greatly in these grades, largely due to different experiences. Furthermore, within a child, skill levels will also vary, depending upon experience. For example, the best ball handler may be among the poorest at locomotor skills or a child with soccer experience may kick the ball well, but strike poorly. These variations are normal, and you should treat them as such. Even so, it is important that you deal with such differences. Keep in mind that skill is usually related to practice and experience. So it stands to reason that the physical educator must provide as many practice opportunities as possible. Practice—and the learning that results from practice—is hard work. Thus, encourage and reward hard work, notice improvement, and value all performance levels. In addition, make it your goal for the children to do the same. You should also make statements about skills that prepare children for practice. For example, say, "Most students have trouble with (fill in as appropriate)" or "When I was learning this skill it took lots of practice, especially with the (fill in)."

Sometimes an individual child will say a skill is too easy or even "Stupid!" Don't take offense as this can mean that the child is having trouble with the skill or has already mastered it. If the child can do the skill well, you might assign that individual a variation to make the skill more challenging or ask that child to help you or another student. Indeed, one effective strategy is to use highly skilled students as peer tutors. Help them to encourage and recognize improvement in the other students.

If the child is in fact having trouble with a skill, encourage practice and patience, and consider giving a personal example of struggle with which the individual can relate. Finally, alter an activity to increase success rates for those who are struggling.

Class Management

Use the formations and other management tools presented in the Grades K-1: Organization and Grades 2-3: Organization lessons to help each games and sports lesson go smoothly. Remember, focus on having students practice and apply the skills, not on competition.

Ultimately, we encourage you to use these lessons in ways that fit your individual teaching style. Some teachers prefer control and order, while others are comfortable with more noise. Children do get excited as they learn and as they enjoy activities. Let two issues guide your decisions about management and control: safety and learning. All children should be safe, so if one or more children are "out of control" the only appropriate decision is to stop the activity and calm the situation. Likewise, if behaviors are interfering with learning, once again you must regain control of the situation. Otherwise, the level of extraneous movement and noise is largely a matter of your personal choice. Remember, however, the enthusiasm of your students is a sign you are doing a good job!

Table S3.1: Unit Plan for Grades 4-5: Games and Sports

Week 5: tossing, throwing, and catching	Week 6: Frisbee tossing and games	Week 7: juggling and soccer
Monday: toss and catch quoit (ring) Tuesday: toss and catch two rings and play ring game Wednesday: toss and catch with a partner and play a game Thursday: throw and catch two rings and play a game Friday: Frisbee and backhand toss	Monday: Frisbee–to a partner Tuesday: Frisbee–curve toss Wednesday: Frisbee–distance throw Thursday: Frisbee golf Friday: Frisbee golf	Monday: juggling Tuesday: juggling Wednesday: soccer Thursday: soccer Friday: soccer
Week 12: soccer and basketball	**Week 20: basketball and softball**	**Week 22: softball and volleyball**
Monday: soccer Tuesday: soccer Wednesday: basketball Thursday: basketball Friday: basketball	Monday: basketball Tuesday: basketball Wednesday: softball Thursday: softball Friday: softball	Monday: softball Tuesday: softball Wednesday: volleyball Thursday: volleyball Friday: volleyball
Week 23: volleyball and track and field	**Week 24: track and field and football**	**Week 28: Raging River, moderate to vigorous games (fitness), and Hustles (fitness)**
Monday: volleyball Tuesday: volleyball Wednesday: track and field–running long jump Thursday: track and field–spring start and standing start Friday: track and field–baton passing	Monday: track and field–distance running Tuesday: football–forward pass and catching Wednesday: football–centering Thursday: football–carrying the ball Friday: field football–lateral pass	Monday: moderate to vigorous games Tuesday: moderate to vigorous games Wednesday: Hustles Thursday: Hustles Friday: Raging River

WARM-UPS

Circle Conditioning

Have the students stand in circle formation. With one student as the leader, have the children perform the following calisthenics. Encourage each child to try to increase the number each day.

Bent-Knee Sit-Ups

Lying on the floor with arms folded across your chest and your hands on your shoulders, bend your knees 90 degrees and raise your body until your arms touch your knees. Perform as many as possible in 60 seconds.

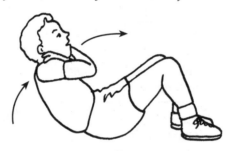

Push-Ups

On hands and toes (regular push-ups) or hands and knees (modified push-ups), bend your arms and lower your trunk to touch your chin to the ground. Then raise your body back up to the starting position, performing as many as possible in 60 seconds.

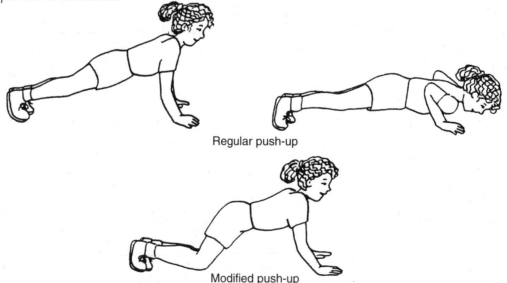

Regular push-up

Modified push-up

Straddle Sit Stretch

Sitting with legs in a straddle position, bend at your waist, extending your arms to your right foot, touch your head to your right knee, and hold for 10 to 30 seconds. Reach up as you move to repeat to the left, performing at least three times to each side.

Lateral Jump

With feet together, jump side-to-side over a line as many times as possible in 30 seconds, rest 15 seconds, and repeat.

Individual Stretching Exercises

Arrange the students in scatter formation. Have the children perform the following stretch activities.

Seated Toe Touch

Sitting with legs straight and feet together, reach toward your toes, lowering your chin to your knees. Hold for 10 to 30 seconds, relax, and repeat several times.

Body Bend

Standing with your feet shoulder-width apart and arms by your sides, bend sideways to the right as far as possible and hold for 10 to 30 seconds. Return to starting position and bend to the left and hold. Repeat several times to the right and the left.

Trunk Twister

Standing with your feet shoulder-width apart and hands clasped in front of your chin (arms horizontal), rotate slowly to the right and left, holding each position for 10 seconds. Repeat several times.

Forward Lunge

Standing with your feet together and hands on your hips, lunge forward with your right leg, keeping your left leg straight. Your right knee should form a right angle (corner of a square). Hold the lunge position for 10 seconds. Return to the starting position, then lunge with your left leg forward. Repeat several times, alternating right and left legs.

Pivot Relay

Arrange groups of five at one end of a basketball court.

1. Describe and demonstrate the activity:

   The first student in each line sprints to the near foul line and turns and runs back to the endline.

   Next he or she turns and runs to the half-court line and turns and runs back to the endline.

   Then he or she turns and runs to the opposite foul line and turns and runs back to the endline.

   Finally, he or she turns and runs to the opposite endline and returns to the starting point.

   The next student in each line repeats the action until all have had a turn.

2. Have the children run the relay.

3. Repeat the activity if time permits.

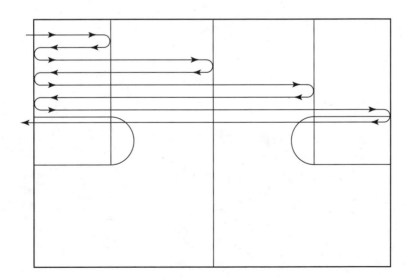

Rope Jumping

Arrange the children in scatter formation, each with a jump rope.

1. Describe and demonstrate the activity: *Turn the rope at a slow tempo and use the two-footed double step (two jumps on both feet simultaneously, for each rope turn).*
2. Have them do this 2 minutes, rest 30 seconds, jump rope for two more minutes, followed by another 30-second rest.

Running in Place

Run in place 20 steps.

Walk/Jog

Mark a jogging course and arrange the children on the starting line.

1. Start with a walk/jog for 5 minutes.
2. Increase to 10 to 12 minutes, encouraging the children to gradually increase the distance they cover.

GAMES AND SPORTS

LESSON 1
THROWING AND CATCHING

Student Objectives

- Toss up a ring and catch it with right and left hands.
- Work cooperatively with a group to achieve a goal.

Equipment and Materials

- 1 ring (quoit) per child
- 1 hoop per group
- Chalk, flour, or tape for marking Cooperative Ring Toss areas
- Cones or other markers for marking jogging course

Warm-Up Activities (5 minutes)

Walk/Jog

See Grades 4-5: Games and Sports, Warm-Ups, page 856.

Skill-Development Activities (15 minutes)

Throwing and Catching Tasks

Arrange the children in scatter formation, each child with a ring.

1. Challenge the children with the following tasks:

    Throw your ring up and catch it with the same hand.

    Practice until you can catch five times without a miss.

    Throw your ring up with one hand and catch it with the other.

    From a low level throw your ring up and catch it.

    Throw your ring up and jump high to catch it.

    Jump high and then throw your ring and catch it.

2. Repeat all several times.

3. Challenge the children: *Throw your ring up and turn around (or touch the ground, clap three times, click your heels) before you catch it.*

4. Ask the children to think of other stunts to perform.

Cooperative Ring Toss

Divide the children into groups of four to six, give each child a ring, and place each group at a game area. Mark each game area with lines 6, 12, and 24 ft from a hoop. Mark a square around the hoop about one inch larger than the hoop.

1. Describe and demonstrate the game:

   The goal of the game is for a group to achieve a combined score of 24 points.

   During each round each child must have a turn and the group must decide if the throw is from 6, 12, or 24 ft.

   Team members can throw from different lines, but the team with a total score closer to 24 points wins.

   A ring landing in the hoop scores 4 points from 6 ft, 6 points from 12 ft, and 8 points from 24 ft. All rings landing in the square around the hoop score 2 points.

2. Have the children play Cooperative Ring Toss.

3. Repeat the game several times, encouraging the children to decide the best way for their team to score close to 24 points total.

LESSON 2
THROWING AND CATCHING

Student Objectives

- Toss and catch two rings simultaneously.
- Work to improve group effectiveness in a game.

Equipment and Materials

- 2 rings (quoits) per child
- 1 hoop per group
- Chalk, flour, or tape for marking Cooperative Ring Toss areas
- Cones (if needed) for marking jogging course

Warm-Up Activities (5 minutes)

Walk/Jog

See Grades 4-5: Games and Sports, Warm-Ups, page 856.

Skill-Development Activities (15 minutes)

Throwing and Catching Tasks Using One Ring

Arrange the children in scatter formation, each child with one ring.

1. Challenge the children with the following tasks:

   Throw your ring up and step forward to catch it.

   Throw your ring up and take three (four, five, six) steps forward to catch it.

   Try going sideways and backward.

2. Allow the children to decide on the number of steps they want to take.

Throwing and Catching Tasks Using Two Rings

Keep the children in scatter formation, and give each child a second ring. Challenge the children with the following tasks:

With a ring in each hand, throw and catch one ring and then the other.

Practice until you catch 10 times without a miss.

Throw and catch with both hands simultaneously (at the same time).

Throw and catch both rings from a low level.

Throw and jump to catch both rings simultaneously.

Throw both rings and cross your arms to catch them.

Concluding Activities (10 minutes)

Cooperative Ring Toss

See Grades 4-5: Games and Sports, Lesson 1, page 858.

Discussion

Arrange the children in a semicircle. Help the children process some social and cognitive aspects of games and sports:

Why is it important to work together as a team?

What strategy did your group use to achieve 24 points?

LESSON 3
THROWING AND CATCHING

Student Objectives

- Toss and catch a ring successfully with a partner from a distance of at least eight ft.
- Encourage teammates in a cooperative game.

Equipment and Materials

- 1 ring per child
- 1 hoop per group
- Chalk, flour, or tape for marking Cooperative Ring Toss areas
- Cones (if needed) to mark jogging course

Warm-Up Activities (5 minutes)

Walk/Jog

See Grades 4-5: Games and Sports, Warm-Ups, page 856.

Skill-Development Activities (15 minutes)

Throwing and Catching Tasks for Partners

Arrange partners in scatter formation, about eight ft apart and each holding one ring.

1. Challenge the children with the following tasks:

   With the ring in your right hand, toss to your partner at the same time as your partner tosses to you. Try to catch your partner's ring!

   Repeat, using your left hand to toss and catch.

   Practice until you can catch five in a row with your right hand and five in a row with your left hand, and then move back one step farther away from your partner.

   Using either hand, throw so that your partner has to reach up to catch.

2. Have the children repeat the tasks several times.

3. Offer these additional challenges for children who are successful with the previous challenges:

   Throw so that your partner has to move different directions to catch.

   Throw different ways to your partner (under your leg, behind your back, sidearm).

4. Have the children repeat these tasks several times.

Concluding Activities (10 minutes)

Cooperative Ring Toss

See Grades 4-5: Games and Sports, Lesson 1, page 858. As the children improve, increase the total number of points needed from 24 to 32. Remind children that the goal is to work together to achieve a total number of points.

LESSON 4
THROWING AND CATCHING

Student Objectives

- Toss and catch two rings simultaneously with a partner from a distance of at least eight ft.
- Work cooperatively with a team to achieve a goal.

Equipment and Materials

- 2 rings per child
- 1 hoop per group
- Chalk, flour, or tape to mark Cooperative Ring Toss areas
- Cones (if needed) to mark jogging course

Warm-Up Activities (5 minutes)

Walk/Jog

See Grades 4-5: Games and Sports, Warm-Ups, page 856.

Skill-Development Activities (15 minutes)

Throwing and Catching Tasks for Partners

Arrange partners in scatter formation, five to seven ft apart to begin.

1. See Grades 4-5: Games and Sports, Lesson 3, page 861 for basic task ideas.
2. Have one partner hold two rings and the other place her or his rings on the ground.
3. Challenge the children with the following new tasks:

   Throw both rings simultaneously (at the same time) to your partner. Practice until you can throw and catch both rings five times in a row without missing.

   Throw both rings simultaneously to your partner so that your partner has to reach high to catch them.

   Throw both rings so that your partner has to step back (step forward) to catch them.

   Throw both rings so that your partner has to reach wide to catch them.

   Throw so that your partner has to reach high with one hand and low with the other.

Ring Tasks

Have one partner pick up the rings stored on the floor so that each partner now has two rings. Make sure partners are still in scatter formation, with five to seven ft between each pair.

Challenge the children with the following tasks:

> *Throw two rings to your partner at the same time that he or she throws two rings to you.*
>
> *Throw different ways (high, low, left) to your partner.*

Concluding Activities (10 minutes)

Cooperative Ring Toss

See Grades 4-5: Games and Sports, Lesson 1, page 858.

1. As the children improve, change the game so they need to use more cooperative planning to succeed. Describe the new rules:

   > *The first throw must be made from 24 ft, and can be made by any of the six team members.*
   >
   > *All team members must toss the ring before it goes into the hoop. The second team member throws the ring from the spot where the ring tossed by player 1 lands.*
   >
   > *Thereafter, each team member tosses the ring in any direction but the goal is for the last tosser to be close enough to hit the target.*
   >
   > *Each team can decide the best way for each team member to get a turn to throw and to get the last player close enough to the hoop to score.*
   >
   > *If each player gets a turn to toss and if the last player to toss hits the target, the team is awarded six points.*

2. Have the children play this modified version of Cooperative Ring Toss.

LESSON 5
THROWING AND CATCHING

Student Objectives

- Demonstrate the correct hand grip for the basic backhand Frisbee throw.
- Work cooperatively in a group practice activity.
- Name two things to remember about the hand grip for the basic backhand Frisbee throw.

Equipment and Materials

- 1 Frisbee per pair
- Chalk, flour, or tape for marking Cooperative Ring Toss areas
- Cones to mark jogging course and Frisbee practice areas
- 1 Frisbee target per group (e.g., hoop, box, carpet square)

Warm-Up Activities (6 to 8 minutes)

Walk/Jog

See Grades 4-5: Games and Sports, Warm-Ups, page 856. Increase the time to six to eight minutes.

Skill-Development Activities (12 minutes)

Basic Backhand Frisbee Throw

Arrange the children in two lines 30 ft apart, with partners facing each other, each pair with a Frisbee.

1. Describe and demonstrate the throwing technique:

    Grip the Frisbee with thumb on top and fingers spread underneath.

    Turn the side of your throwing arm toward the target and step forward with the foot on your throwing-arm side as you throw.

    Start to throw by moving the Frisbee across the front of your body and stepping toward the target with the forward foot.

    Snap your wrist at release.

    You can catch with both hands, but as you improve, I want you to try to catch with only one hand.

2. Have the children practice throwing and catching in pairs.

3. Increase the distance between partners as skill improves.

4. Present the following activities for partners:

    Throw with your right hand.

Throw with your left hand.

Throw at different levels.

5. Repeat all, several times.

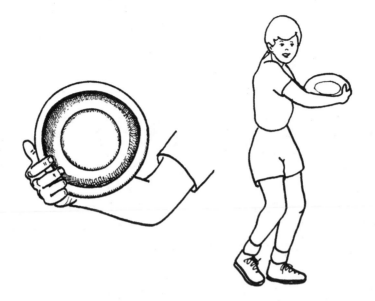

Cooperative Practice

Assign each group of four to six to a practice area.

1. Describe the activity:

   Players in each group are to help each other with the correct technique: grip; side of throwing arm toward target; foot on throwing arm side steps forward.

   The goal of the activity is for each player in the group to be able to demonstrate correct technique.

   Help each other learn!

2. Brainstorm what encouraging and helpful remarks might sound like.

3. Have the groups conduct the practice while you circulate, keeping students on-task.

Concluding Activities (10 minutes)

Toss the Frisbee

Move each group to a target area. Each target area consists of a target and lines 10 and 20 ft from the target (see figure on page 867).

1. Describe and demonstrate the game:

   The object is to toss the Frisbee using the correct backhand technique so that it lands in the target area.

   Take turns tossing the Frisbee at the target.

   Players can select the 10-ft or the 20-ft distance.

   One team point is scored for each hit from the 10-ft line, and two points are scored for hits from the 20-ft line.

   The team with the highest score wins.

You are responsible for making sure each member of your team uses correct throwing technique.

2. Have the children play Toss the Frisbee.

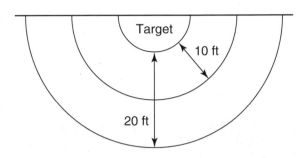

Discussion

Arrange children in a semicircle. Discuss what the children have learned today:

> *What should you remember about your hand grip for the backhand Frisbee throw?*
>
> *What are some ways that your team helped you to be successful?*

LESSON 6
THROWING AND CATCHING

Student Objectives

- Toss a Frisbee into a target three out of five times from five ft away.
- Name two things to remember about the backhand throw.

Equipment and Materials

- 1 Frisbee per child
- 1 large hoop (30-36 in.) per group
- Chalk, flour, or tape for marking lines
- Cones (if needed) to mark jogging course
- Paper and pencil per pair

Warm-Up Activities (6 to 8 minutes)

Walk/Jog

See Grades 4-5: Games and Sports, Warm-Ups, page 856. Have the children walk/jog six to eight minutes.

Skill-Development Activities (12 minutes)

Basic Backhand Frisbee Throw

Arrange the children in two lines 30 ft apart, partners facing each other, each pair with a Frisbee. Give each pair a piece of paper and a pencil on which to record their successes.

1. Have partners practice the basic backhand throw for accuracy with right and left hands from different distances. See Grades 4-5: Games and Sports, Lesson 5, page 865.
2. Have each pair keep a record of how many successful throw-catches they make: *A successful throw-catch is a backhand throw that your partner gets to and catches.*
3. *After five successful throw-catches, move back to the next lines so you are farther apart.*

Concluding Activities (10 minutes)

Frisbee Flyer

Mark play areas as shown in figure on page 869. Arrange groups of four to six on the five-ft line, each group facing a hoop and each child with a Frisbee.

1. Describe the activity:

   The object is to toss the Frisbee, using the correct backhand technique, so that it lands in the hoop.

   You each get to decide which line you will throw from, and each hit scores one point no matter which line you throw from. Keep your own scores.

2. Have the children practice throwing from self-selected distances, keeping an individual score.

3. Now have the group play as a cooperative team. Explain the rules:

   The goal is to achieve 10 points with each player tossing for his or her team from one of the four lines.

   Each hit from the 5-ft line earns 1 point, the 10-ft line earns 2 points, the 15-ft line earns 3 points, and the 20-ft line earns 4 points. The team with a score closer to 10 points after each member has had a turn wins.

4. Repeat the game several times, encouraging the groups to plan their strategies.

Hoops

5 ft ————————————————————————

10 ft ———————————————————————

15 ft ———————————————————————

20 ft ———————————————————————

GAMES AND SPORTS

LESSON 7
THROWING AND CATCHING

Student Objectives

- Successfully toss and catch a Frisbee with a partner.
- Explain what makes a Frisbee curve right or left.

Equipment and Materials

- 1 Frisbee per pair
- Chalk, flour, or tape for marking lines
- Cones (if needed) for marking jogging route

Warm-Up Activities (6 to 8 minutes)

Walk/Jog

See Grades 4-5: Games and Sports, Warm-Ups, page 856. Have the students walk/jog for six to eight minutes.

Skill-Development Activities (17 minutes)

Curving the Frisbee

Arrange partners about 24 ft apart from each other, in widespread scatter formation, each pair with a Frisbee.

1. Describe and demonstrate the skill:

   The throw is similar to the backhand throw, except that instead of holding the Frisbee flat (parallel to the ground), you hold it at a slight angle.

   For a right-handed throw, if you angle the edge of the Frisbee away from the throwing hand toward the ground at release, the Frisbee will curve to the left when you throw it. If you angle that edge upward at release, the Frisbee will curve right when you throw it.

   For a left-handed throw, a downward angle curves the Frisbee to the right and an upward angle curves it to the left.

2. Say to the children: *Using your right hand, throw a curve to the left so that your partner must run to catch it.* (Pause.) *Now make the Frisbee curve to the right.*

3. Say to the children: *Using your left hand, throw a curve to the right.* (Pause.) *Now make the Frisbee curve to the left.*

4. Tell the children: *Throw and catch with your partner while both of you are moving. Remember to throw the Frisbee in front of your partner.*

Partner Throwing and Catching Contest

Arrange pairs on two facing lines, 10 ft apart, each pair with a Frisbee.

1. In one-minute time periods, have partners see how many successful throws and catches they can make.

2. After one minute, move children who are ready to 20 ft apart.

3. Move the children who are ready another 10 ft apart each minute up to 40 ft.

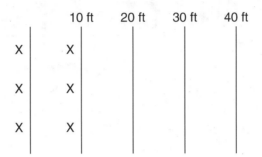

Discussion

Arrange children in a semicircle. Review the correct techniques for both right- and left-handed throws:

What technique do you use to make the Frisbee curve to the right?

What technique do you use to make the Frisbee curve to the left?

LESSON 8
THROWING AND CATCHING

Student Objectives

- Throw a Frisbee into a hoop, from a distance of eight ft, one out of three tries.
- Cooperate with a team to achieve a goal.

Equipment and Materials

- 1 Frisbee per child
- 1 hoop per pair
- 5 or 6 extra hoops for each Frisbee Golf layout
- Chalk, flour, or tape for marking lines
- 1 copy of form S3.1 per Frisbee Golf Scramble group (optional)

Warm-Up Activities (6 to 8 minutes)

Walk/Jog

See Grades 4-5: Games and Sports, Warm-Ups, page 856. Have the children walk/jog for six to eight minutes.

Skill-Development Activities (12 minutes)

Throwing for Distance

Arrange partners in widespread scatter formation, each pair with a Frisbee and a hoop. Vary the distance between partners, depending on how far the partners can throw a Frisbee (10 to 15 ft apart is a good place to start).

1. Describe and demonstrate the activity:

    One of you hold up the hoop as a target while the other child tries to throw the Frisbee through it.

    The partner with the hoop throws the Frisbee back to the other child.

    Take five tries, then switch jobs. Keep practicing until we're out of time.

2. Have the students practice. Move partners farther apart as their skill increases.

Frisbee Golf Scramble

Arrange groups of four to six at each Frisbee Golf Scramble course, each child with a Frisbee. Place five or six hoops (the exact number depending upon the space available) on the ground as shown in figure below. You can vary the distances between holes, depending on skill levels. An easier course would be one with holes about 20 to 25 yd apart; a more difficult course would have holes about 35 to 45 yd apart.

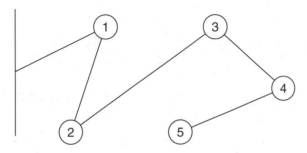

1. Describe and demonstrate the game:

    The object is for your team to throw the Frisbee into each target, using the fewest throws possible.

    Everyone starts by throwing from the starting line.

    You all take your second throw from the spot where the Frisbee closest to the target lands. So you all pick up your Frisbee and go to the spot of the closest throw. Continue until you land in the hoop.

    Take the first throw for the next hole from inside the previous target (hoop).

    The score for each hole is the number of throws it takes to get the Frisbee in the hoop. Each team keeps a separate score.

2. Have the children play Frisbee Golf Scramble.
3. Form S3.1 shows a sample score card for Frisbee Golf Scramble.

FORM S3.1 SAMPLE SCORE CARD

Name		Date
Hole	**Par**	**Score**
1	3	
2	2	
3	3	
4	2	
5	3	

GAMES AND SPORTS

LESSONS 9 AND 10
THROWING AND CATCHING

Student Objectives

- Cooperate with a partner to achieve a goal.

Equipment and Materials

- 1 Frisbee per child
- 1 hoop per pair
- Extra hoops for each Creative Golf game
- Chalk, flour, or tape for marking lines

Warm-Up Activities (6 to 8 minutes)

Walk/Jog

See Grades 4-5: Games and Sports, Warm-Ups, page 856. Have the students walk/jog for six to eight minutes.

Skill-Development Activities (22-24 minutes)

Creative Golf

Arrange groups of four to six in widespread scatter formation. Ask each group to create and play a new game using a Frisbee, a hoop, and their throwing skills.

Concluding Activities

None.

LESSONS 11 AND 12
JUGGLING

Student Objectives

- Attempt to juggle two, then three, bean-bags.

Equipment and Materials

- 3 beanbags per child

Warm-Up Activities (6 to 8 minutes)

Walk/Jog

See Grades 4-5: Games and Sports, Warm-Ups, page 856.

Skill-Development Activities (17 minutes)

Note: Repeat as Lesson 12 for children who did not learn to juggle during Lesson 11.

Juggling

Arrange the children in scatter formation, each child with three beanbags. Describe, demonstrate, and have the children practice only one or two steps of juggling at a time (see next section for descriptions of each step).

1. Describe and demonstrate steps 1 and 2.
2. Have the children practice steps 1 and 2 until they achieve some skill.
3. Encourage them to establish a good rhythm.
4. Describe and demonstrate steps 3 and 4.
5. Have the children practice steps 3 and 4 until they achieve some skill.
6. Describe and demonstrate step 5.
7. Have the children practice step 5 until they achieve some skill.
8. Describe and demonstrate step 6.
9. Have the children practice step 6 until they achieve some skill.

Steps in Juggling

Describe, demonstrate, and have the children practice only one or two steps of juggling at a time (see outline in previous section):

> Step 1—*Using your right hand, throw one beanbag up and catch it. The beanbag should go slightly above your head.*

Step 2—*Using your left hand, throw one beanbag up and catch it.*

Step 3—*With one beanbag in each hand, toss the right-hand beanbag and then the left-hand beanbag, catching each with the same hand as tossed it. This should be toss right, toss left, catch right, catch left. Now after tossing the beanbag in your right hand, toss the one in your left hand under it, catching each beanbag with the same hand that tossed it.*

Step 4—*Repeat step 3, but catch each beanbag with the opposite hand.*

Step 5—*Hold two beanbags in your right hand. Toss one in the air, then the other. Catch the first and toss it again. Catch the second and toss it again; continue.* Cue the children: *Toss the beanbag underneath (toward the left side) each time. Repeat with your left hand.*

Step 6—*Hold two beanbags in your right hand and one in your left. Toss one beanbag from your right hand, toss the beanbag from your left hand, and then toss the third beanbag. Repeat.* Cue the children: *Toss each beanbag underneath (toward the inside of the body) the one in the air.*

Concluding Activities (5 minutes)

Also use this part as Lesson 12 for children who learned to juggle in Lesson 11. Children who cannot do step 6 will not be able to do this activity; for those children, go back and help them practice the needed skills during this time.

Continuous Juggling

Arrange the children in scatter formation, each child with three beanbags.

1. Explain the following modification: *In step 6 (previous section), after tossing and catching the third beanbag, you stop and begin again. But in continuous juggling, you keep tossing until you miss or stop.*

2. Have the advanced children practice continuous juggling while you help the other children master step 6 (see previous section, Steps in Juggling).

GRADES 4-5 | GAMES AND SPORTS

LESSON 13
SOCCER

Student Objectives

- Demonstrate the technique for the inside-of-the-foot kick and the sole trap.
- Evaluate the technique of a partner and provide the partner with feedback.
- State two important things to remember about the foot when you use the inside-of-the-foot kick.

Equipment and Materials

- 1 soccer or playground ball per pair
- 1 jump rope per child
- 4 pins or milk cartons per pair of teams
- Chalk, flour, or tape for marking lines

Warm-Up Activities (5 minutes)

Rope Jumping

See Grades 4-5: Games and Sports, Warm-Ups, page 856.

Skill-Development Activities (15 minutes)

Inside-of-the-Foot Kick

Arrange pairs in scatter formation, each pair with a ball.

1. Describe and demonstrate the skill:

   You make an inside-of-the-foot kick with quick lateral (sideways) leg movements. Use it for passing and scoring attempts.

   Place your nonkicking foot alongside the ball.

   Turn out the toes of your kicking foot and kick the ball with the inside of the kicking foot. The sole of your kicking foot should be parallel to the ground (demonstrate "parallel" clearly).

2. Have the children practice the inside-of-the-foot kick.

Games and Sports   877

Sole Trap

Keep partners in scatter formation. Start with partners 8 ft apart and after some success move them to 10, 15, then 20 ft apart.

1. Describe and demonstrate the skill: *You can stop ("trap") a rolling ball with a foot by putting the sole of your foot on it.*

2. Challenge the children with the following tasks:

    Practice kicking and trapping with a partner.

    Observe your partner to see if he or she is kicking with the inside of the foot and has the toe of the kicking foot turned out.

3. Have the children do the following tasks:

    Practice kicking in different directions.

    Practice kicking so your partner has to move to the right or the left to trap the ball.

    Observe your partner to see if he or she is using the sole of the foot to trap the ball.

Concluding Activities (10 minutes)

Target Soccer

Create an even number of teams of four or five players. Place each two teams facing each other on two parallel lines about 40 ft apart, with a row of four pins or milk cartons placed midway between the two lines. Give each team one ball.

1. Describe and demonstrate the game:

    The object is to knock down the pins, using inside-of-the-foot kicks.

    The team knocking down the most pins wins.

    We will play the game for five minutes, then declare winners and play again.

2. Have the children play five-minute games.

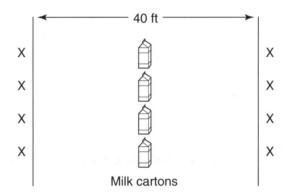

Milk cartons

Discussion

Arrange children in a semicircle. Discuss what the children have learned today:

What skills did we work on today?

What should you remember about your foot when you practice the inside-of-the-foot kick? (The sole of your kicking foot should be parallel to the ground.)

When would you use a trap?

What should you remember about the sole trap? (The ball should stop because you put the bottom of your foot on the ball.)

LESSON 14
SOCCER

Student Objectives

- Kick successfully with a partner using the inside-of-the-foot kick.
- Trap successfully using the sole trap.
- Cooperate with a partner to accomplish a goal.

Equipment and Materials

- 1 soccer or playground ball per pair
- 1 jump rope per child
- Chalk, flour, or tape for marking lines

Warm-Up Activities (5 minutes)

Rope Jumping

See Grades 4-5: Games and Sports, Warm-Ups, page 856.

Skill-Development Activities (15 minutes)

Kicking and Trapping

Arrange partners about 10 ft apart in scatter formation, each pair with a ball. Have partners practice kicking and trapping, using the following variations:

> *Kick and trap on the move.*
>
> *Travel and kick to a partner who is also moving.*
>
> *Kick with different amounts of force between you and your partner while you are both running.*
>
> *Kick and trap with your partner, using both your right and left feet.*
>
> *Kick the ball so that it rolls a specific distance (e.g., 10, 20, or 30 ft).*

Cooperative Kicking

Arrange partners on a line, each pair with a ball. Mark a second line 50 ft away and a third line 60 ft away.

1. Describe the activity: *Each child in a pair kicks the ball. The first kicker kicks as far as he or she can. The second kicker tries to kick the ball so that it stops rolling on or near the line 50 ft away.*

Change the distance to 60 ft and create groups of three or four.

2. Repeat step 1, encouraging the children to work together to accomplish the goal—to make the ball stop near the finish line after the last kick.

Concluding Activities (10 minutes)

Soccer Trap

Create fields that are 10 by 30 ft, with a 5-by-10-ft trapping and kicking area at each end (see figure below). Assign two teams of three or four to each field, one ball per field. Players stay in the trapping and kicking area for their team.

1. Describe the game:

    One team tries to kick the ball from their kicking and trapping area downfield into the opponents' kicking and trapping area. The opponents attempt to trap the ball.

    A team scores one point for each ball successfully trapped in the trapping area.

    When a ball is trapped, the team with the ball immediately tries to kick it into the other team's trapping area (a team's kicking and trapping areas are the same).

    Balls kicked above knee level or outside the field of play are "dead." When a team kicks a dead ball, the other team gets the ball.

2. Have the children play Soccer Trap.

3. If desired, the children can play the game with more than one ball by adding one or more additional balls into simultaneous play.

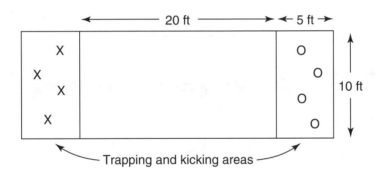

LESSON 15
SOCCER

Student Objectives

- Demonstrate the technique for the instep kick with both right and left feet.
- Adjust the force on the instep kick with both right and left feet.

Equipment and Materials

- 1 soccer or playground ball per pair
- 2 cones for Kickover
- 1 jump rope per child
- Chalk, flour, or tape to mark field lines
- Wall or solid fence to kick against

Warm-Up Activities (5 minutes)

Rope Jumping

See Grades 4-5: Games and Sports, Warm-Ups, page 856.

Skill-Development Activities (15 minutes)

Instep Kick

Arrange pairs in scatter formation, each pair with a ball.

1. Describe and demonstrate the skill:

    We use the instep kick to kick the ball long distances.

    Approach the ball from an angle, placing your nonkicking foot beside the ball six to eight in away. Flex the knee of your kicking foot to prepare for the kick.

    Contact the ball with the inside of your kicking foot at the instep (near the lower part of the shoelaces).

    Straighten the kicking leg upon contact and as you follow through.

2. Have the children practice the instep kick with partners, using the following variations:

    Kick with your right and then your left foot.

    Kick with different amounts of force.

    Kick toward a wall so that the ball rebounds to your partner.

    Kick for distance. Remember to contact the ball low.

Concluding Activities (10 minutes)

Kickover

Create fields that are 10 by 20 ft, with a 5-ft goal marked by cones at one end. Mark kicking lines at 5, 10, 15, and 20 ft (see figure below). Place two teams of three or four on each playing field, one ball per team.

1. Describe the game:

   Give each player a chance to kick the ball (using the instep kick) toward the goal.

   Your team scores one point if the ball goes over the endline and two points for a successful hit into the goal area.

   Begin at the 5-ft line. After each player gets a kick from the 5-ft line, both teams move to the 10-ft line, and so on.

   The team with the most points at the end of the playing time wins.

2. Have the children play Kickover.

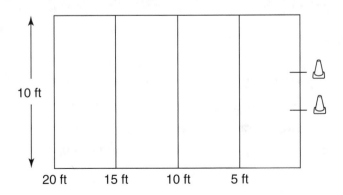

LESSON 16
SOCCER

Student Objectives

- Make progress toward refining the instep kick.
- Kick a ball in various directions.

Equipment and Materials

List is for one station circuit. If you set up more than one station circuit, you will need more equipment. See relevant text.

- 1 soccer ball per pair
- Station 1: 2 goals or targets
- Station 2: 1 cone
- Station 3: 1 large cardboard box
- 1 jump rope per child
- Chalk, flour, or tape to mark lines
- Signal

Warm-Up Activities (5 minutes)

Rope Jumping

See Grades 4-5: Games and Sports, Warm-Ups, page 856.

Skill-Development Activities (20 minutes)

Instep Kicking Stations

Set up four instep kicking stations as shown in figure on page 885. Assign a group of three or four to each station, each child with a ball. (Duplicate stations as needed to keep group size small.)

1. Describe and demonstrate each instep kicking station.
2. Have the children practice instep kicking at the stations.
3. Signal groups to rotate to a new station every five minutes.

Station 1: Passing for Goal
Mark a kicking line 25 ft from a goal line on which you have set up two targets or goals.
   Kick to the right and to the left so that the ball travels between the goal markers, practicing until you can hit the target three times in a row before moving to a longer distance. (Distance can vary according to skill.)

Station 2: Kicking to Hit an Object
Mark a field about 30 by 30 ft and place a cone in the center of the field.
Kick from any boundary of the square and attempt to hit the cone in the center. Gradually increase the distance you kick from.

Station 3: Kicking the Ball off the Ground
Mark a field 20 by 20 ft and place a large cardboard box in the center of the field.
Kick a ball so that it travels off the ground and lands in a box. Gradually increase the distance you kick from.

Station 4: Kicking for Distance
Mark two kicking lines 30 yd apart.
Take turns with a partner kicking a ball as far as possible.

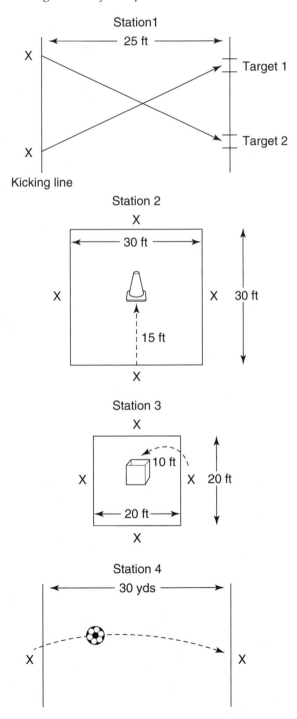

Kickover

See Grades 4-5: Games and Sports, Lesson 15, page 883.

LESSON 17
SOCCER

Student Objectives

- Kick a soccer ball with increased accuracy.

Equipment and Materials

- 1 soccer ball per pair
- 2 large hoops (30-36 in.) per kicking area
- 1 jump rope per child
- Chalk, flour, or tape for marking the field
- 1 soccer goal per field
- 4 pins or milk cartons

Warm-Up Activities (5 minutes)

Rope Jumping

See Grades 4-5: Games and Sports, Warm-Ups, page 856.

Skill-Development Activities (15 minutes)

Kicking for Accuracy

Set up four (or more) practice kicking areas as shown in figure on page 888. Arrange partners into four (or more) groups, and assign each group to one of the practice kicking areas. Give each pair a ball.

1. Describe the activity:

    One partner is the retriever, and one is the kicker.

    The kicker starts from the 10-ft line and attempts to kick the soccer ball into the air so that it lands in a hoop. The kicker must indicate which hoop he or she is aiming at, before kicking.

    After five tries, switch roles with your partner.

    If you get at least three out of five kicks into the intended hoop, move back to the 20-ft mark on the next round (and then to the 30-ft line if still successful).

2. Have the children practice, taking as many turns as possible.

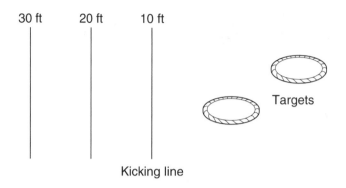

30 ft   20 ft   10 ft

Targets

Kicking line

Extension Activities

Outside-of-the-Foot Kick

Arrange partners in scatter formation, each pair with a ball.

1. Describe and demonstrate the skill:

   We use the outside foot kick for short passes.

   Place your nonkicking foot to the side of the ball and your kicking foot across in front of it.

   Contact the ball with the outside of your kicking foot.

2. Have the children practice the outside-of-the-foot kick.

Concluding Activities (10 minutes)

Select one or two of the following activities.

Goal Kickover

Place two teams of three or four on each field. The fields are identical to the Kickover fields (see Grades 4-5: Games and Sports, Lesson 15, page 883) except you should place the goalposts four ft high. Still use one ball per team.

1. Explain the rule changes:

    The rules are the same as for Kickover (see Grades 4-5: Games and Sports, Lesson 15, page 883) except for scoring.

    Your team scores one point if the ball goes over the endline and outside the goal, two points if you kick a ball through the goal, and three points if you kick a ball over the goal.

2. Have the children play Goal Kickover.

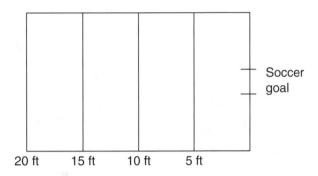

Heel Kick

Arrange partners in scatter formation, each pair with a ball.

1. Describe and demonstrate the skill:

    We also use the heel kick for short passes.

    Step slightly in front of the ball with your nonkicking foot and kick the ball backward with the heel of your other foot.

2. Have the children alternately practice the outside foot kick and heel kick.

3. Have the children vary distances, then directions.

4. Spend some time focusing on kicking for accuracy.

5. Have the children play Target Soccer (see Grades 4-5: Games and Sports, Lesson 13, page 879) or Soccer Trap (see Grades 4-5: Games and Sports, Lesson 14, page 881), using outside-of-the-foot and/or heel kicks.

Foot Traps

Arrange partners in scatter formation, each pair with a ball.
Trap the ball with the inside or outside of your foot.

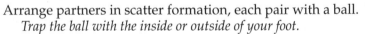

Body Traps

Arrange partners in scatter formation, each pair with a ball.

Stop the ball with your shins, thigh, abdomen, or chest. When the ball hits the ground, you should control it with your foot.

| Shin | Thigh | Abdomen | Chest |

Norwegian Ball

Assign two teams of 6 to 10 to each playing field (any large playground area will do). Have the kicking team line up behind the kicker, and the fielding team spread out in the field.

1. Describe and demonstrate the game:

   The kicker kicks the ball in any direction and runs around his or her team (a specified number of times depending upon group size and skill level; three times around is a good start.)

   The fielders must line up behind the person catching the ball. They must then pass the ball over each teammate's head down the line to the last person, who holds the ball and runs to the front of the line.

   When the runner gets to the front of the line, everyone on the fielding team sits down.

   If the fielding team does not finish all this before the runner can circle the kicking team the specified number of times, the kicker scores a point.

   After everyone on the first team has kicked, the other team becomes the kickers.

2. Have the children play Norwegian Ball.

3. Variations:

   Have the kicker run the bases of a softball field instead of running around the team.

   Have the fielding team pass the ball through everyone's legs to the last person instead of over their heads.

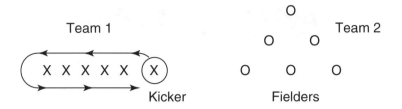

Team 1

X X X X X (X)
Kicker

O
O   O
Fielders
O   O   O

Team 2

Soccer Dodgeball

Assign two teams of 6 to 10 to each play area. Have one team form a circle about 30 ft in diameter and the other team stand inside the circle. Give the circling team one or more balls.

1. Describe the game:

    The players forming the circle try to kick the ball so that it hits a center player below the waist.

    The players inside the circle try to dodge the balls. One point is scored for each hit, but we will not eliminate anyone.

    After five minutes, we will have the teams exchange places.

    The team scoring the most hits is the winner.

2. Have the children play Soccer Dodgeball.

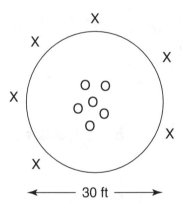

Circle Soccer

Divide the class into two teams. Have the two teams form a circle, with one team forming half the circle and the other team forming the other half, all holding hands. Hands remain joined for the game.

1. Describe the game:

    The object is to kick the ball below shoulder level between members of the other team.

    Each score is worth one point.

    I will choose one player to start the game by kicking the ball toward the opposing team.

    If the ball comes to a stop inside the circle, a player from that half of the circle may get the ball, bring it back to the circle, and restart the game.

2. Have the children play Circle Soccer.

3. Variations:

    Have two or more balls in play at once.

    Play in a line formation (two lines facing each other with teammates holding hands).

GAMES AND SPORTS

LESSON 18
BASKETBALL

Student Objectives

- Show progress in developing basketball control skills.
- Work cooperatively with a team to create a ball-handling routine.

Equipment and Materials

- 1 basketball or large (8 1/2 to 13 in.) playground ball per child
- Basketball court or similarly marked area

Warm-Up Activities (5 minutes)

Pivot Relay

See Grades 4-5: Games and Sports, Warm-Ups, page 855.

Skill-Development Activities (20 minutes)

Ball-Handling Drills

Arrange the children in scatter formation, each child with a ball.

    1. Describe and demonstrate each drill.

    2. Have the children practice each drill several times.

Circle Waist

Shift the ball around your waist using both hands (first in front and then behind your back) as quickly as possible, in both clockwise and counterclockwise directions.

Single-Leg Circles

Circle the ball around one leg as rapidly as possible, alternating legs, in both clockwise and counterclockwise directions.

Double-Leg Circles

Circle the ball around both legs, alternating directions.

Figure Eight

Circle the ball around one leg and then around the other in a figure eight pattern.

Quick Hands

Hold the ball between your legs with your right hand behind your legs and your left hand in front. Quickly change positions of your hands to catch the ball before it falls to the floor, repeating rapidly.

Concluding Activities (5 minutes)

Ball-Handling Routines

Assign groups of four to six to each practice area, each child with a ball.

1. Describe the assignment:

   Using any of the ball-handling skills from this lesson, work as a group to create a routine.

   Practice until each team member in the group can perform the routine.

   Help each other so that you can perform the routine without any errors.

   In designing the routine different children can perform different skills, depending on skill level and interest.

2. Have the groups design and practice their routines. If there is time, each group can share their routine with the class.

LESSON 19
BASKETBALL

Student Objectives

- Demonstrate the correct technique for the chest pass and the one-handed pass.
- Evaluate the technique of a partner and provide the partner with feedback.
- State two important things to remember about the chest pass and the one-handed pass.

Equipment and Materials

- 1 basketball or 8 1/2 in. playground ball per pair
- 6 cones, pins, or milk cartons per Pin Ball court
- Basketball court or similarly marked area
- Chalk or tape to mark hard surface as Pin Ball courts

Warm-Up Activities (5 minutes)

Pivot Relay

See Grades 4-5: Games and Sports, Warm-Ups, page 855.

Skill-Development Activities (15 minutes)

Chest Pass

Arrange partners in scatter formation, each pair with a ball.

1. Describe and demonstrate the skill:

    We use the chest pass for short distances.

    Hold the ball with your fingers spread, thumbs on the back of the ball, pointed toward each other. Bend your elbows and keep them close to your body.

    With your feet in a forward stride position and weight on your back foot, release the ball with a forward push of both arms. Both of your arms should apply an equal amount of force. Shift your weight forward and snap your wrists as you release the ball.

    Follow through by extending your arms toward the receiver.

    You should be able to receive the ball at chest level from your partner's passes.

2. Have the children practice the chest pass. Cue the students:

    Observe your partner to see if he or she has the elbows bent and close to the body.

    Now see if the weight is being shifted forward as the ball is released.

See if your partner's fingers are spread.

Does he or she follow through with arms extended?

One-Handed Pass

Arrange partners in scatter formation, each pair with a ball.

1. Describe and demonstrate the skill:

   We use the one-handed pass for long distances.

   Begin in a baseball-like throwing position with the ball above your shoulder and slightly behind your head.

   Place your free arm on the ball for balance.

   With the foot opposite of your throwing hand forward, shift your weight to the front foot and push the ball toward the target.

   Follow through with your throwing arm.

2. Have the children practice the one-handed pass with a partner.

3. Each child should observe their partner. For each series of 5 to 10 practice trials, ask the children to observe for specific points in technique to determine if their partner is using correct technique.

Star Drill

Arrange groups of five each in a star formation with one ball. Number the children one through five. If there is one group of six or one group of less than five, modify the pattern. Join a group if this makes equal groups of five.

1. Describe and demonstrate the drill: *The child at position 1 begins by passing to the child at position 3, then 3 to 5, 5 to 2, 2 to 4, and 4 back to 1.*

2. Have the children practice both the chest and one-handed passes in the drill several times each.

3. Challenge the students: *See how fast you can go.*

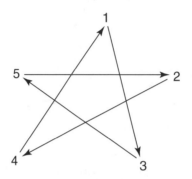

Concluding Activities (10 minutes)

Pin Ball

Set up courts on a hard surface, 40 by 60 ft, and place three cones or pins at each end. Assign two teams of six to eight to each court. Give each team two or more balls.

1. Describe and demonstrate the game:

   The object is to knock down the opponents' pins.

   Use (chest, one-handed) passes.

   Your team can run in your own half-court and throw the balls from anywhere in that area.

   Opposing players try to catch the balls before they hit their pins.

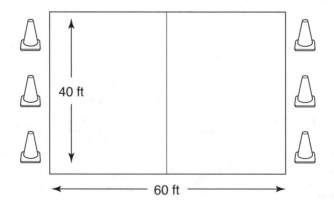

Your team scores one point for each pin you knock down.

2. Have the children play Pin Ball.

Discussion

Arrange children in a semicircle. Discuss the day's activities:

What skills did we work on today?

What should you remember about your elbows when you practice the chest pass? (The elbows should stay close to the body and move behind the ball.)

When would you use the one-handed pass?

When would you use the chest pass?

LESSON 20
BASKETBALL

Student Objectives

- Demonstrate the correct technique for stationary dribbling.
- Work cooperatively with a team to accomplish a goal.

Equipment and Materials

- 1 basketball or 8 1/2 in. playground ball per child
- Basketball court or other similarly marked area

Warm-Up Activities (5 minutes)

Pivot Relay

See Grades 4-5: Games and Sports, Warm-Ups, page 855.

Skill-Development Activities (20 minutes)

Dribbling

Arrange the children in scatter formation, each with a ball.

1. Describe and demonstrate the skill:

   Dribbling is a controlled method of bouncing the ball with one hand. We can use this skill to advance the ball in any direction on the court.

   The key is to control the ball with your fingers.

   When dribbling, bend your knees and flex your body over the ball.

   Do not look at the ball.

2. Have the children practice dribbling with the following variations:

   Dribble in place with your right (left) hand.

   Repeat until you can dribble with control at least 10 times with each hand.

   Using first your right and then your left hand, dribble low and high.

   Sit down and dribble with your right (left) hand.

   Lie down and dribble.

   Dribble with alternate hands. Remember to keep the ball low.

   Dribble under your legs and behind your back.

Dribble and move forward (backward, sideways).

Dribble with your eyes closed.

Now have the children find partners, and line them up on one side of a basketball court, each pair with a ball.

3. Present the following tasks, explaining the organization. One partner runs across the court and back and the other partner repeats the task:

    Dribble with your right hand (left hand, alternate hands).

    Dribble as fast as you can.

    Dribble in a zigzag path.

Concluding Activities (5 minutes)

Follow-the-Leader Dribble

Create cooperative groups of four or five each. Place two teams on one half of a basketball court, each child with a ball.

1. Describe and demonstrate the game:

    The first player chooses a method of dribbling and dribbles around the outside boundaries of the half-court. Team members follow the leader.

    The next player selects a method of dribbling and keeps play going.

    Continue until each child in your group has chosen a way of dribbling.

2. Have the children play Follow-the-Leader Dribble.

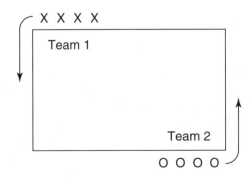

Cooperative Dribble

Keep the cooperative groups of four or five, each child with a ball.

1. Describe the game:

    The object is for each team to dribble 50 times using any five types of dribbles. For example, 5 times with right hand, 5 with left hand, 20 with alternate hands, 10 moving forward, and 10 moving backward.

    Each team chooses the types and the number of each.

2. Have the children play Cooperative Dribble.

LESSON 21
BASKETBALL

Student Objectives

- Demonstrate correct technique for the one-handed set shot.
- Cooperate with a group to accomplish a goal.

Equipment and Materials

- 1 basketball or 8 1/2 in. playground ball per pair
- Tape for marking lines
- Tape or hoops for marking shooting positions
- 1 goal per group of 4
- Basketball court or similarly marked area

Warm-Up Activities (5 minutes)

Pivot Relay

See Grades 4-5: Games and Sports, Warm-Ups, page 855.

Skill-Development Activities (20 minutes)

One-Handed Set Shot

Arrange partners in scatter formation, each pair with a ball.

1. Describe and demonstrate the skill:

    Hold the ball with your shooting hand behind and under the ball. Support the ball with the palm of your other hand.

    Bend your knees slightly to prepare to shoot.

    Now straighten your arms and legs to shoot the ball up toward the goal.

    Follow through with your shooting hand, keeping your eyes on the target.

2. Have partners shoot the ball into the air and catch each other's set shots.

Create groups of four, and place each group at a goal, each pair with a ball.

3. Have the children practice shooting from different distances, practicing first from in front of the goal and then from the sides. Encourage the students to help each other improve their technique: *Observe your partner to see if they hold the ball with their shooting hand under and behind the ball. Is the ball supported by the palm of their other hand?*

4. After several practice trials, ask the children to observe leg action during the shot: *Do your partner's knees bend slightly to prepare for the shot, then straighten to shoot?*

Concluding Activities (5 minutes)

Around the World

Place two teams of three or four at each goal with two balls. Mark the nine shooting positions with tape or hoops as shown in figure below.

1. Describe and demonstrate the game:

    The object is to see which team can have the most team members make at least one goal from any position.

    Each person can practice at any of the positions, shooting until she or he makes a basket. Work together on your team to decide where each player should shoot from.

    The first team that has all players succeed wins, and you start a new game.

    Really work to help each other!

2. Have the children play Around the World.

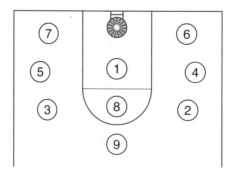

LESSON 22
BASKETBALL

Student Objectives

- Demonstrate the techniques for the pivot and the defensive stance.
- State two important things to remember about the pivot.

Equipment and Materials

- 1 basketball or 8 1/2 in. playground ball per child
- Basketball court or similarly marked area
- Tape or chalk to mark Nine-Court Basketball areas
- Signal

Warm-Up Activities (5 minutes)

Pivot Relay

See Grades 4-5: Games and Sports, Warm-Ups, page 855.

Skill-Development Activities (15 minutes)

Pivot

Arrange the children in scatter formation, each with a ball.

1. Describe and demonstrate the skill:

    We pivot to change direction and protect the ball by attempting to keep our body between the ball and the opponent.

    Hold the ball in both hands, and bend your knees slightly.

    The pivot foot (either foot) must always be in contact with the floor. The stepping foot can move in any direction around the pivot foot.

2. Have the children practice the pivot through doing the following tasks:

    Pivot using your right (left) foot as the fixed point.

    Dribble the ball in a small area, stop, and pivot.

    Dribble the ball in a small area and, on the signal, grab the ball with both hands, jump, and land on both feet. Pivot on either foot.

Defensive Stance

Keep the children in scatter formation, balls set aside.

1. Describe and demonstrate the skill:

   This skill is used to stop your opponent from passing, dribbling, or shooting. You should be ready to chase the opponent if he or she moves.

   Place your feet shoulder-width apart with one foot slightly forward.

   Bend your knees slightly and distribute your weight evenly over both feet.

   Hold the hand nearest the offensive player's dribbling side waist-high and the other hand head-high. Keep changing your hand positions in relation to the position of the ball.

2. On a signal, a leader (you or a child) points a direction (forward, backward, to the side) and gives the signal "Move!"

3. Have the students slide in the direction indicated, keeping a defensive stance, until they hear the command to stop.

4. Repeat steps 2 and 3 several times.

Nine-Court Basketball

Use tape to mark courts as shown in figure below. (If you have enough space, use a 1/2 basketball court for each court area. If not, position the nine squares at a basketball hoop with 10-in squares.) Arrange pairs (one defensive player and one offensive) in each of the nine areas (9 children on each team), one basketball per court (per nine areas). To accommodate numbers of children other than 18, use fewer areas (e.g., three squares rather than nine).

1. Describe and demonstrate the game:

   The object is for the children in the three areas closest to their team's basket to score.

   The game starts with a ball tossed in the air in area 9. You pass and defend but cannot step out of your own area. Use pivoting!

   After each goal, players rotate to the next area (rotating in counting order, with players in area 9 going to area 1), and the game begins again with a jump ball.

2. Have the children play Nine-Court Basketball.

Discussion

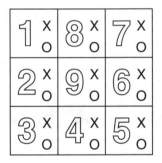

Arrange children in a semicircle. Discuss what the children have learned today:

   What skills did we work on today?

   What should you remember about your foot when you pivot?

   When would you use a pivot?

LESSON 23
SOFTBALL

Student Objectives

- Demonstrate the standard grips for pitching and throwing.
- Evaluate the technique of a partner and provide the partner with feedback.

Equipment and Materials

- 1 softball per child
- Chalk, flour, or tape for marking field lines
- Tape or chalk to mark targets

Safety Tip

- Space students so they cannot hit each other with softballs.

Warm-Up Activities (5 minutes)

Circle Conditioning

See Grades 4-5: Games and Sports, Warm-Ups, page 852.

Skill-Development Activities (20 minutes)

Softball Movement Challenges

Arrange the children in scatter formation, each child with a softball. Challenge the children with the following tasks:

> *Throw the ball up and catch it with both hands. Throw as high as possible.*
>
> *Throw the ball up and catch it with your right (left) hand.*
>
> *Throw the ball up high and run forward (backward, sideways) to catch it.*
>
> *Throw the ball up high and clap before catching it.*
>
> *Try to increase the number of claps.*
>
> *Throw the ball up high and turn around before catching it.*

Four-Finger Ball Grip

Keep the children in scatter formation, each child with a softball.

1. Describe and demonstrate the skill:

   > *Spread the fingers of your throwing hand over the bottom of the ball, and place your thumb on top (see figure on page 907).*

Never use your palm to grip the ball.

2. Have the children practice the Four-Finger Ball Grip.

Underhand Pitch

Arrange pairs in scatter formation. Holding their softballs with a four-finger ball grip, have throwers face their partners, 15 ft apart.

1. Describe and demonstrate the skill:

    Bring the ball down and back in pendular motion (demonstrate "pendular" clearly).

    As you bring your arm forward, take a step on the foot opposite your throwing or pitching arm.

    Release the ball from the fingertips as the ball passes your hip, and follow through with your arm.

2. Have the children practice the underhand pitch.

3. Encourage the children to provide feedback to their partners: *Observe your partner to see if the ball is brought down and back in pendular motion.*

4. After several practice trials, encourage the children to watch for correct leg action: *Look to see if your partner takes a step on the foot opposite their throwing arm.*

Concluding Activities (5 minutes)

Target Throw

Mark targets about the size of a strike zone (1 1/2 × 3 ft) on a wall or backstop. Mark throwing lines as shown in figure below. Place small groups at each target, each group with one softball.

1. Describe the game:

   Each of you gets five throws at the target from the closest distance, then moves back to the next line, and so on.

   Score one point for each hit from 20 ft, two points for each hit from 25 ft, three points for each hit from 30 ft, and four points for each hit from 40 ft. Keep track of your team's points, and we will find a total for the whole class.

2. Have the children practice throwing underhand at the targets. When using this activity in the future, encourage the children to beat the whole-class total.

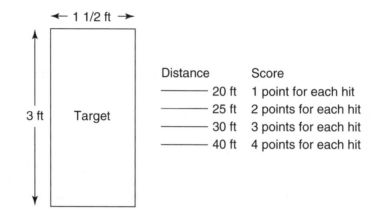

LESSON 24
SOFTBALL

Student Objectives

- Demonstrate a mature overhand throwing pattern using a softball.
- Evaluate the technique of a partner and provide the partner with feedback.

Equipment and Materials

- 1 softball per child
- 1 large cardboard box per group
- Signal

Safety Tip

- Remind students to watch out for each other when throwing and retrieving softballs.

Warm-Up Activities (5 minutes)

Circle Conditioning

See Grades 4-5: Games and Sports, Warm-Ups, page 852.

Skill-Development Activities (20 minutes)

Overhand Throw

Arrange partners in scatter formation, each pair with a softball. Have them begin by standing 15 ft apart and after five successful throws move to 20, 25, and then 30 ft.

1. Describe and demonstrate the skill:

    Using a four-finger ball grip, get into a stride position with the foot opposite your throwing hand forward and your weight on your back foot.

    With your upper arm parallel to (flat as) the ground, bring the ball back to above your shoulder, about ear-high.

    At the same time, twist your body away from the direction you are going to throw.

    Rotate (turn) your body toward the target as your throwing arm swings forward with the elbow leading.

    Snap your wrist as you release the ball.

    Take a long and strong (vigorous) step forward with the foot opposite your throwing arm as your body uncoils and your throwing arm swings forward.

2. Have partners practice throwing overhand to each other, moving farther apart as they experience success.

3. Encourage the children to observe each other for correct technique: *Observe your partner to see if he or she is using body rotation during the throw. Is there a vigorous step with the opposing foot as the throwing arm swings forward?*

Throwing Tasks

Have groups of six each make a 30-ft circle with a large box in the center, each child with a softball.

1. Describe and demonstrate the activity:

   On the signal, throw your ball, trying to get it into the box.

   On the next signal, retrieve the ball and toss again. Be safe—wait for the signal!

   Get back in position and throw again on the next signal.

   Give yourself one point for each successful throw.

2. Have the children perform the activity, signaling them to throw and retrieve. Warn the children to watch for thrown balls and not to throw when other children are in the way. Remind them to wait for the signal to retrieve.

3. After several throws increase the distance for children who are successful.

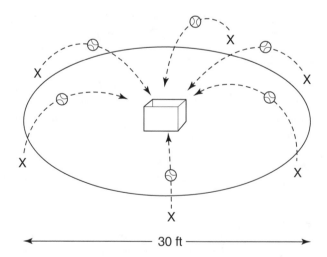

Concluding Activities (5 minutes)

Overtake Throw

Have two teams of five to seven each form a large circle (teams alternate players around the circle). Have one player from each team stand in the center as "Captain" for that team, holding a softball.

1. Describe and demonstrate the game:

    The Captain throws the ball to one player.

    That player throws the ball back to the Captain, and you continue clockwise around the circle.

    The Captains begin on opposite sides of the circle.

    The object is for one team to overtake (pass) where the other team's ball is in the circle.

    Your team earns one point for each overtake. The first person that the Captain threw to becomes the next Captain after each score.

    If a ball goes out of the circle, the team starts playing again at that point after the ball is retrieved.

2. Have the children play Overtake Throw.

3. Variation: Designate the type of throw (overhand or underhand).

GRADES 4-5 **GAMES AND SPORTS**

LESSON 25
SOFTBALL

Student Objectives

- Catch above the waist a ball thrown by a partner from a distance of at least 15 ft.
- Cooperate with a partner in a practice activity.

Equipment and Materials

- 1 softball per pair

Warm-Up Activities (5 minutes)

Circle Conditioning

See Grades 4-5: Games and Sports, Warm-Ups, page 852.

Skill-Development Activities (15 minutes)

Catching Balls Above the Waist

Arrange partners in scatter formation, each pair with a softball, about 15 ft apart.

1. Describe and demonstrate the skill:

   While waiting for the ball, stand with your feet comfortably apart and legs slightly bent. Your elbows should be away from your body with thumbs coming together in front of your chest.

   Watch the approaching ball, and move to a position under it as it arrives.

   Keep your thumbs together and your palms facing outward.

   As the ball makes contact with your hand (or glove), cover it with your other hand.

2. Have the children practice throwing and catching above the waist with the following variations:

   Throw, making your partner move back to catch.

   Throw, making your partner move to the right and the left to catch.

   Begin practice at 15 ft and increase distance to 20, 30, and 40 ft.

   Practice until you can catch at least five throws in a row before moving back.

3. Encourage the children to observe their partners and provide feedback about technique.

Concluding Activities (10 minutes)

Pop-Up

Place two teams of six to eight each in a playing area. Have one team (the throwing team) form a large circle (50 ft diameter) and scatter the other team (the fielding team) in the center. Number players from one to six (seven or eight). Give each child on the throwing team a ball. To increase participation opportunities, decrease team size.

1. Describe and demonstrate the game:

   Taking turns, the members of the throwing team throw their balls as high into the air as possible (the balls must come down inside the circle).

   When the thrower throws the ball, she or he calls out her or his assigned number.

   The player in the circle with the same number as the thrower tries to catch the ball before it touches the ground.

   Your team earns one point for each successful catch.

   Teams trade places after every person on the throwing team has thrown once.

2. Have the children play Pop-Up.

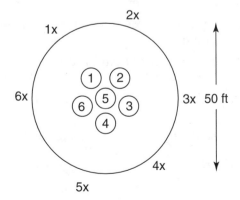

LESSON 26
SOFTBALL

Student Objectives

- Catch below the waist a ball thrown by a partner from a distance of at least 15 ft.
- Cooperate with a group to accomplish a task.

Equipment and Materials

- 1 softball per pair
- Chalk, flour, or tape to mark lines
- Signal

Warm-Up Activities (5 minutes)

Circle Conditioning

See Grades 4-5: Games and Sports, Warm-Ups, page 852.

Skill-Development Activities (20 minutes)

Catching Balls Below the Waist

Arrange pairs in scatter formation, each pair with a softball, about 15 ft apart.

1. Describe and demonstrate the skill:

   Get into a ready position and move in front of the incoming ball. Your little (pinky) fingers should be coming together and your palms facing upward.

   As the ball makes contact with your hand (or glove), cover it with your other hand.

   Stand with your weight forward on the foot opposite your throwing arm when making the catch so it will be possible for you to throw quickly.

2. Have the children practice throwing and catching above and below the waist with the following variations:

   Throw so that your partner can catch above (below) the waist. Keep your little fingers together for a ball below the waist.

   Throw so that your partner must move forward (backward, to the left, to the right) to catch.

3. Gradually increase the distance between partners.

Concluding Activities (5 minutes)

Throw and Catch Game

Arrange teams of four or five along two lines, 20 ft apart. On each team, player 1 stands on one line facing the rest of his or her team, and the remaining players line up behind the other line, across from player 1 (see figure below). Give each team a softball. Allow the catcher to vary the distance between the thrower and catcher for each throw so that students at different skill levels can be successful.

1. Describe and demonstrate the game:

   The goal of the game is for each team to work together to make sure all students are successful.

   On the signal, player 1 selects a distance and throws the ball to player 2. Player 2 throws it back and goes to the end of the line.

   Player 1 throws to each player until all are back in their original positions. Then player 1 goes to the end of the line, and player 2 becomes the new thrower.

   Rotate through all your players.

   Score one point for each successful catch.

   The team with the most successful catches wins.

2. Have the children play the Throw and Catch Game, reminding them to help everyone succeed.

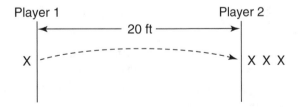

LESSON 27
SOFTBALL

Student Objectives

- Demonstrate a mature striking pattern while hitting a ball off a tee with a regulation bat.
- Evaluate the technique of a batter using a criteria sheet.
- State two important things to remember about batting.

Equipment and Materials

- 1 bat per group
- 1 home base per group
- 1 batting tee per group
- Chalk, flour, or tape for marking lines
- 1 criteria sheet per group

Warm-Up Activities (5 minutes)

Circle Conditioning

See Grades 4-5: Games and Sports, Warm-Ups, page 852.

Skill-Development Activities (15 minutes)

Batting

Set up tee ball stations with a bat, a ball, and a batting tee placed on a home plate. Arrange small groups at the stations.

1. Describe and demonstrate the skill:

    Grip the bat with hands together and your dominant (favorite) hand over your nondominant hand. (See figure on page 917.)

    Keep your feet at about right angles to the pitching mound (demonstrate angle clearly). Hold the bat up and over your shoulder, with your elbows away from your body.

    Swing the bat straight through the hitting area and contact the ball in front of the midline (point to your own midline) of your body.

    Step forward with your front foot, and shift your body weight forward when starting the forward swing with the bat.

2. Have the children practice batting, establishing a rotation system for each group, with, for example, one batter, two retrievers, and one observer.

3. Give the observer a criteria sheet that lists the major points in technique to look for:

    Bat gripped with dominant hand over nondominant

Feet at right angles to pitching mound

Bat held up and over shoulder

Elbows away from the body

Swings straight through the hitting area

Weight shifted forward

4. Have the observer observe the batter and provide feedback.

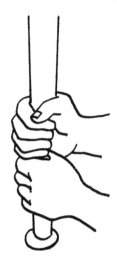

Concluding Activities (10 minutes)

Tee Ball Hit

Keep the groups at the tee ball stations. Mark lines 30, 40, and 50 ft from the tee as shown in figure below.

1. Describe the game: *Each player gets five hits and then rotates to a fielder position, with a fielder rotating in to be the new batter.*

2. *Hits are scored for their air distance (how far they travel before hitting the ground) as follows:*

   Less than 30 ft scores one point.

   Between 30 and 40 ft scores two points.

   Between 40 and 50 ft scores three points.

   Farther than 50 ft scores four points.

3. *The team with the highest score after a full round of batting wins.*

4. Have the children play Tee Ball Hit.

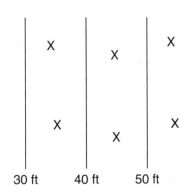

30 ft   40 ft   50 ft

5. Variations: Adjust distances according to skill level. Keep a cooperative score by adding up each team's score to find a whole-class total.

Discussion

Arrange children in a semicircle. Discuss what the children have learned today:

> *What should you remember about the technique for batting?* (The dominant hand should be over the nondominant hand, elbows should be away from the body, and toes pointed to the plate.)
>
> *Why is it important to shift your weight forward when starting the forward swing with the bat?* (To gain momentum.)
>
> *Why is it important to swing straight through the hitting area?*

LESSON 28
VOLLEYBALL

Student Objectives

- Demonstrate the correct technique for the underhand serve.
- Evaluate the technique of a partner and provide the partner with feedback.
- State two important things to remember about the underhand serve.

Equipment and Materials

- 1 volleyball per pair
- 1 jump rope per child
- Tape, chalk, or flour to mark lines
- Tape or chalk to mark targets

Warm-Up Activities (5 minutes)

Rope Jumping

See Grades 4-5: Games and Sports, Warm-Ups, page 856.

Skill-Development Activities (15 minutes)

Underhand Serve

Arrange partners facing each other from behind lines 20 ft apart, each pair with a volleyball. Mark additional lines at 30, 40, and 50 ft apart.

1. Describe and demonstrate the skill:

    Start in a stride stance (weight on back foot) with the leg opposite your hitting arm forward.

    Hold the ball waist-high in front of your front leg.

    Extend your serving arm, drawing it backward in pendular (demonstrate "pendular" clearly) *fashion.*

    To hit the ball, bring your hitting arm forward and shift your weight from your back to your front foot.

    Contact the ball with the heel of your open hand, squarely below and behind the center of the ball.

2. Have the children practice serving the ball back and forth between partners, beginning 20 ft apart and, after some success, moving back to 30, then 40, and finally 50 ft.

3. Encourage the children to observe each other for correct technique: *Observe your partner to see if he or she is drawing the serving arm backward in a pendular fashion. Is he or she shifting weight from the back to the front foot?*

Concluding Activities (10 minutes)

Target Ball

Mark targets on a wall and serving lines 30 or 40 ft from the targets (see figure below). Position each small team at a serving area, one ball per team.

1. Describe and demonstrate the game:

   Beginning with the first person in the line, each person selects a service line and serves at the target, using an underhand serve.

   Your team scores two points for hitting the center area of the target and one point for hitting the outer area.

   The team with the highest score after everyone has one turn or after a set time wins.

2. Have the children play Target Ball.

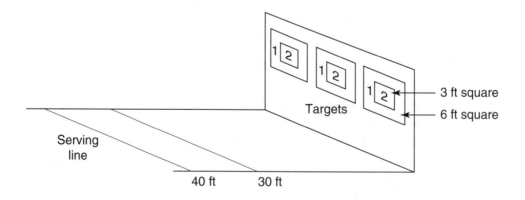

Discussion

Arrange children in a semicircle. Discuss what the children have learned today:

What should you remember about the starting position for the underhand serve? (Ball waist high and leg opposition.)

What are some things to remember when you are serving? (Stride stance, shift weight.)

Where should you contact the ball? (Heel of the open hand.)

What do you think would happen if you contacted the ball above its center? (The ball goes down.)

LESSON 29
VOLLEYBALL

Student Objectives

- Demonstrate the correct techniques for the forearm pass.
- State two important things to remember about the forearm pass.

Equipment and Materials

- 1 foam ball (8 1/2 in.) per pair
- 1 jump rope per child

Warm-Up Activities (5 minutes)

Rope Jumping

See Grades 4-5: Games and Sports, Warm-Ups, page 856.

Skill-Development Activities (15 minutes)

Forearm Pass

Arrange partners in scatter formation, each pair with a foam ball.

1. Describe and demonstrate the skill:

   In volleyball, we use the forearm pass to receive the serve.

   To prepare to make a forearm pass, get into a forward stride position with your weight on the balls of your feet.

   Contact the ball with your forearms, slightly above your wrist. Your arms should make a firm platform for the ball to contact.

   The power for the pass comes from extending your legs and hips along with raising and flexing your shoulders. So at the time of contact, extend your arms until your elbows are straight and your thumbs and fingers are extended. Meanwhile, your legs should extend until your knees and hips are straight and your toes are extended.

   This pass is also called a "bump pass," or "bumping" the ball.

2. Have the children practice bumping a ball that has been tossed: *One partner tosses a foam ball from a distance of 10 ft (tossing so the bumping partner does not have to move), and the other partner bumps the ball back. After 10 trials, change roles.*

3. Variation: Have the students take turns with a partner, bumping the ball up to each other.

Concluding Activities (10 minutes)

Keep It Up

Arrange teams of six to eight, each in a circle with one foam ball.

1. Describe the game:

    On the signal, each team starts bumping the ball.

    The team that keeps their ball up the longest wins one point.

    The team that has earned the most points at the end of the playing period is the winner.

2. Have the children play Keep It Up.

Discussion

Arrange the children in a semicircle. Discuss what the children have learned today:

What should you remember about the starting position for the forearm pass? (Forward stride, weight on balls of the feet.)

From where do you get power for the pass? (Legs/hips or shoulders.)

What should you remember about the position of your arms before and after contact? (Arms extended, elbows straight.)

LESSON 30
VOLLEYBALL

Student Objectives

- Demonstrate the correct technique for the overhead set.
- Evaluate the technique of a setter using a criteria sheet.
- State two important things to remember about the overhead set.

Equipment and Materials

- 1 foam ball (8 1/2 in.) per pair
- 1 jump rope per child
- 1 beach ball
- 1 criteria sheet per group

Warm-Up Activities (5 minutes)

Rope Jumping

See Grades 4-5: Games and Sports, Warm-Ups, page 856.

Skill-Development Activities (15 minutes)

Overhead Set

Arrange groups of three in scatter formation, each group with a foam ball.

1. Describe and demonstrate the skill:

    The overhead set is used to position the ball for a spike and as a way to pass the ball.

    To prepare to use an overhead set, move under the ball with your knees bent and hands held above your head with your elbows pointing down.

    Spread your fingers, thumbs pointed toward each other and wrists extended backward.

    Make contact with your fingers and thumbs. Extend your knees at the point of contact.

2. Have the children practice setting a ball that has been tossed. Establish a rotation system for each group, with one tosser, one setter, and one observer.

3. Tell the children: *The tosser tosses a foam ball from a distance of 10 ft (tossing so that the setter does not have to move), and the setter sets the ball back. After 10 trials, rotate roles.*

4. *The observer watches the setter and provides feedback, using a criteria sheet as a guide.* The criteria sheet lists the major points in technique to look for:

    Starting position is under the ball with knees bent and hands above the head.

Fingers are spread with thumbs pointed toward each other.

Ball is contacted with the fingers and thumbs.

Knees are extended at contact.

5. Variation: *Toss so your partner has to move to do the overhead set.*

6. Have the children practice, using this setting and bumping drill: *Partners bump a low pass to themselves and then set a pass to their partners.*

Concluding Activities (10 minutes)

Beach Ball Volleyball

Divide the children into two teams, each team scattered on one side of a volleyball or badminton court, with a beach ball. Once the students have learned the game, create small teams to increase participation opportunities.

1. Describe and demonstrate the game:

    Start the game with a serve by any player.

    You can use both the bump and the set. The object is to return the beach ball over the net as in regular volleyball. On each serve, you either make a point or lose the serve.

    A team loses the serve when it fails to return the ball within three hits, allows the ball to hit the ground, or hits the ball out of bounds. A team serves until it fails to make a point, and then the opposing team serves.

2. Have the children play Beach Ball Volleyball.

Discussion

Arrange children in a semicircle. Discuss what the children have learned today:

What should you remember about the starting position for the overhead set? (Knees bent, hands above the head, elbows down, and position under the ball.)

What part of your hand makes contact with the ball? (Fingertips.)

Is it important to extend your knees at the time of contact? (Yes.)

LESSON 31
VOLLEYBALL

Student Objectives

- Demonstrate six-player rotation in game play.

Equipment and Materials

- 1 volleyball net per court
- 1 foam ball (8 1/2 in.) per pair
- 1 volleyball per pair
- Wall or solid fence

Warm-Up Activities (5 minutes)

Individual Stretching Exercises

See Grades 4-5: Games and Sports, Warm-Ups, page 853 for descriptions of the movements. Have them do each exercise for one minute, with 20 steps of running in place between exercises.

Skill-Development Activities (15 minutes)

Bumping and Setting

Arrange partners in scatter formation, each pair with a foam ball, standing 10 ft apart.

1. Have partners practice bumping and setting a foam ball.

Arrange partners facing a wall, 5 to 10 ft from it, each pair with a volleyball.

2. Have the children practice keeping a regular volleyball in play against a wall, using both the forearm pass (bump) and the overhead set.

3. Tell the children: *Begin by taking turns for 60 seconds each.* As the children become more skilled, partners can play at the same time, alternating hitting the ball.

Rotation System

Arrange six children on a volleyball court in playing pattern, three children on the front line (near the net) and three on the back line. Have the other children sit in a semicircle to watch the demonstration.

1. Describe and demonstrate the rotation system: *You rotate when a team wins the serve. The rotation moves clockwise, and each child moves one position. The player at the net on the right moves to the back row; the other two net players move over one position. The back row left player moves to the net, the server and other back row person shift one place to the left.*

Assign two teams of six per court.

2. Have the children practice the rotation system.

Concluding Activities (10 minutes)

One-Bounce Volleyball

For each volleyball court, set the net so that the top edge is six ft from the ground, and mark a service line six to eight ft inside the court. Arrange two teams of six per volleyball court, one on each side of the net. Rotate any extra students in.

1. Describe and demonstrate the game:

   A player from the serving team serves the ball into the opponents' court. This player continues to serve until failing to make a good serve or until the serving team hits the ball into the net or out of bounds or fails to return the ball.

   Then it is a "side-out," and the opponents serve. With each side-out, players on the team winning the serve rotate positions.

   Each time the ball crosses the net it may bounce once and be hit up to three times before it is returned. Up to two players may hit the ball, but no player may hit the ball two times in a row.

2. Explain more scoring details: *Call a point or side-out if*

   a server fails to make a good serve,

   a player strikes the ball more than once,

   the ball bounces more than once,

   a player does not use the overhead set or forearm pass to hit the ball, or

   the ball fails to go over the net or goes out of bounds.

3. *Your team also scores a point for each serve that the opponents fail to return.*

4. Have the children play One-Bounce Volleyball to 15 points.

G R A D E S
4-5

GAMES AND SPORTS

LESSON 32
VOLLEYBALL

Student Objectives

- Participate successfully in a modified volleyball game.

Equipment and Materials

- 1 volleyball per pair
- 1 long rope per small volleyball court with standards
- String (12 in. pieces; optional)
- Cones, tape, or other markers to mark courts

Warm-Up Activities (5 minutes)

Volleyball Skills

Arrange partners in scatter formation. Practice any of the volleyball skills already learned.

Skill Development Activities (15 minutes)

Serving

Mark small volleyball courts (20 by 40 ft) with cones or tape. String a rope six ft high for a net on one 20-ft line. Mark serving lines 10, 20, 30, and 40 ft from the "net." Assign each team of four to a court. If desired, hang several pieces of string (12 in. long) to help players determine if the ball goes under or over the rope. Use two balls per court (one ball per two children).

1. Have the children practice serving the ball across the rope: *Begin at a line 20 ft from the net. If you only make two of your first seven serves, move up to the 10-ft line.*

2. *After 10 successful serves, move back to the 30-ft line (or 20-ft line, if you had to move up to the 10-ft line to start).*

3. Continue practice until most students can serve at least 10 good serves from 40 ft.

Concluding Activities (10 minutes)

Four-Person Volleyball

Arrange two teams of four on each side of the small volleyball courts, each court with one volleyball.

The net should be 6 ft and dividing the 20 by 40 ft court into two 20 by 20 ft halves.

1. Describe the game:

    We play this game like volleyball except for the size of the court and the number of players.

    You may move up closer to the net to serve, as close as 10 ft. You may use only legal hits (forearm pass and overhead set).

    The team with the highest score at the end of the playing time wins.

2. Have the children play Four-Person Volleyball.

LESSON 33
TRACK AND FIELD

Student Objectives

- Demonstrate the technique for the takeoff on a running long jump.
- State two important things to remember about the takeoff on a running long jump.

Equipment and Materials

- 1 tumbling mat per group
- 1 measuring strip per group
- Tape to mark takeoff lines

Warm-Up Activities (5 minutes)

Individual Stretching Exercises

See Grades 4-5: Games and Sports, Warm-Ups, page 853.

Skill-Development Activities (20 minutes)

Long Jump

Arrange the children in groups of six with each group at a mat. Assign groups based on proficiency levels to the mats, which have take-off lines at different distances.

Mark the tumbling mats with measuring strips so the jumping distance can be determined.

One child from each station will jump at once.

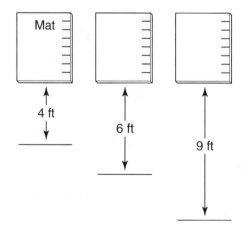

1. Describe and demonstrate the skill:

    After a short run, take off on one foot from behind the line, and jump as far as possible.

    Land on both feet.

    You must also get high in the air on the jump in order to jump far.

    Run fast to the takeoff line (or board).

    While you are in the air, lift your knees. Throw your legs and arms forward. At landing, your legs should be in front of your body. Bend your knees upon contact with the floor to absorb the shock.

2. Have the children practice running to the takeoff line and jumping onto a tumbling mat.

3. Encourage them to give feedback to their groupmates on proper technique.

Concluding Activities (5 minutes)

Long Jump Event

Keep children in groups at the jumping areas. Have each child take five jumps and record the best score.

Discussion

Arrange children in a semicircle. Discuss what the children have learned today:

> *What skill did we work on today?* (Long jump.)
>
> *What should you remember about the takeoff on a running long jump?* (Take off from one foot behind the line.)
>
> *Why do you want to get high in the air on the jump?* (To go far.)

LESSON 34
TRACK AND FIELD

Student Objectives

- Demonstrate the standing start and the sprint start for the dash.
- Demonstrate proper sprinting form.

Equipment and Materials

- 1 stopwatch per group
- Cones to mark 50-yd dash course
- Signal

Warm-Up Activities (5 minutes)

Individual Stretching Exercises

See Grades 4-5: Games and Sports, Warm-Ups, page 853.

Skill-Development Activities (15 minutes)

Standing Start

Set up a 50-yd dash course that is wide enough to keep group size small. Arrange small groups at the starting line.

1. Describe and demonstrate the skill:

    Begin with your feet in a forward stride position.

    Bend your knees slightly and lean your body forward.

    On the signal, push strongly with your front foot, bringing your back foot forward.

2. Have the children practice the standing start, running 10 yd, taking turns within their groups upon your signals.

Sprint Start

Keep the same setup as for the previous activity.

1. Describe and demonstrate the skill:

    On the call "On your mark," kneel, placing your front foot 4 to 12 in behind the starting line.

    Place your back foot 1 to 2 feet behind your front foot.

    Place your thumb and forefinger of each hand just behind the line.

    At the signal "get set," raise your back and rear end so that your back is parallel to (flat as) the ground.

On "go!" take off with a strong push off both feet, but particularly the forward leg and foot.

2. Have the children practice the sprint start, using the same drill as for the standing start.

3. Stress proper running technique with vigorous arm action, high knee action, and forward lean.

Concluding Activities (10 minutes)

Running the 50-Yard Dash

Arrange groups of four, each at a 50-yd dash area with a stopwatch.

1. Organize the activity:

   Choose two students in your group to run the dash at a time.

   Have the other two students serve as timer and starter.

   Rotate responsibilities.

2. Have the children run the dash.

GRADES 4-5   GAMES AND SPORTS

LESSON 35
TRACK AND FIELD

Student Objectives

- Demonstrate the correct technique for baton passing.

Equipment and Materials

- 1 baton per group
- Cones to mark running course
- Signal
- Stopwatch

Warm-Up Activities (5 minutes)

Individual Stretching Exercises

See Grades 4-5: Games and Sports, Warm-Ups, page 853.

Skill-Development Activities (15 minutes)

Baton Passing

Gather the children into an information formation.

1. Describe and demonstrate the skill:

   As the baton passer approaches the receiver, the receiver begins running.

   The receiver reaches back with the palm of the right hand facing upward. The extended fingers and thumb should form a "V."

   The passer places the baton across the palm of the receiver in the middle of the V.

   The receiver closes fingers and thumb around it and accelerates as quickly as possible, immediately (within two or three steps) shifting the baton to the left hand.

Line up groups of four single file with at least 10 to 15 yd between runners.

2. Have the children practice passing the baton while jogging slowly. Have them gradually increase their running speed as they become more successful passing.

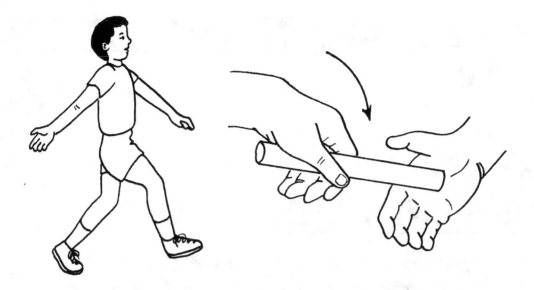

Concluding Activities (10 minutes)

Relay Running

Mark the field with cones in an oval, and place runners 25 yd apart. Have the same teams of four (from previous activity) compete, up to four teams at a time.

1. Have the children run a relay with baton passing.
2. Repeat several times, recording times.

LESSON 36
TRACK AND FIELD

Student Objectives

- Practice distance running, using a combination of running and walking.

Equipment and Materials

- Cones to mark 1/8-mi (220-yd) track and open field
- Obstacles (e.g., benches, solid boxes, and the like)

Safety Tips

- Distance runners should scan the area in front of them looking for obstacles, holes, or other things that could hurt them.
- Be careful when you go over or around obstacles.

Warm-Up Activities (5 minutes)

Individual Stretching Exercises

See Grades 4-5: Games and Sports, Warm-Ups, page 853.

Skill-Development Activities (20 minutes)

Distance Running Form

Gather the children into an information formation.

1. Describe and demonstrate the skill, emphasizing pacing:

    Carry your body in a more upright posture than when sprinting and use less arm motion.

    Take your weight on the heel rather than the ball of the foot.

    Relaxation and pacing are important. It is important to begin slowly in order not to tire quickly.

Divide the children into groups of four. Group together children of similar speeds.

2. Present distance running tasks, for example, the following progression is for practice on a 220-yd (1/8-mi) track:

    Run half lap, walk half lap.

    Run one lap, walk half lap.

Run one-half lap, walk one lap.

Run two laps, walk half lap.

3. Repeat the sequence as time allows.

Extension Activities

Distance Running

Continue running daily, gradually increasing distance.

Running on Uneven Terrain

Place obstacles, such as benches or jumping boxes, in an open field marked with starting and finishing lines.

1. Show the children how to run to an obstacle, place one foot on top, and push off to the other side.
2. Repeat several times, using different obstacles and distances, including hilly areas if possible.
3. Work up to a course that is at least one mi long.

Concluding Activities (5 minutes)

Cool-Down

Have the children walk for five minutes.

GAMES AND SPORTS

LESSON 37
FOOTBALL

Student Objectives

- Demonstrate the techniques for forward passing and catching.
- Evaluate the technique of a passer using a criteria sheet.

Equipment and Materials

- 1 junior-size football per pair
- 1 criteria sheet per child
- Cones or flour to mark fields

Warm-Up Activities (5 minutes)

Walk/Jog

See Grades 4-5: Games and Sports, Warm-Ups, page 856.

Skill-Development Activities (15 minutes)

Forward Passing

Arrange partners in scatter formation, each pair with a junior-size football.

1. Describe and demonstrate the skill:

   Grip the ball slightly behind the middle with the fingers of your throwing arm and spread them over the laces. The other hand is helping to support the ball.

   With your elbow bent and away from your body, release the support hand and take the ball back behind your ear.

   Point the foot opposite your throwing arm toward the target and take a step forward on the throw.

   With the elbow of your throwing arm leading, bring the ball forward with an overhead motion of your throwing arm. The ball should "roll" off your fingertips.

2. Have the children practice forward passing.

Catching

Keep partners in scatter formation, each pair with a junior-size football.

1. Describe and demonstrate the skill: *Catch the ball with your fingers and palms. As soon as you catch it, pull it toward your body into a carrying position.*
2. Have the children practice passing and catching.

Rearrange the children into groups of three.

3. Establish a rotation system for each group, with two passers and one observer. Provide the observer with a criteria sheet that lists the major points in technique to look for:

    Foot opposite throwing arm pointed toward target

    Foot opposite throwing arm stepping forward on the throw

    Ball taken back beyond the ear on the backswing

    Elbow leading as ball is brought forward

Begin practice with partners about 10 ft apart and observer positioned optimally.

4. Tell the children: *After five successful throws, move to 20 and then to 30 ft apart.*
5. Make sure the observer watches the passers and provides helpful feedback.
6. Practice with the following variation: *Throw, making your partner move forward and back (to the right and left) to catch.*

Concluding Activities (10 minutes)

Passing on the Fly Game

Mark 30- by 60-ft fields with an end zone 10 ft deep (vary the size of the field for children at different developmental levels). Arrange two teams of six to eight on each field.

1. Describe the game:

   Try to pass the ball while running, or on the fly, into the opponents' end zone while opponents try to catch the thrown balls.

   Your team must stay in your half of the field and cannot enter the end zone except to retrieve a dead ball.

   Your team scores one point for each ball thrown on the fly into the end zone.

2. Have the children practice.

GRADES 4-5

LESSON 38
FOOTBALL

Student Objectives

- Demonstrate the technique for centering.
- Evaluate the technique of a partner and provide the partner with feedback.

Equipment and Materials

- 1 junior-size football per pair
- Cones or flour to mark lines

Warm-Up Activities (5 minutes)

Walk/Jog

See Grades 4-5: Games and Sport, Warm-Ups, page 856.

Skill-Development Activities (15 minutes)

Centering

Arrange partners in scatter formation, each pair with a junior-size football.

1. Describe and demonstrate the skill:

    As the centering player, spread your feet wide and bend your knees slightly.

    Extend the hand of your throwing arm downward to grasp the ball as you did in passing.

    Place the hand of your nonthrowing arm lightly on the opposite side of the ball to serve as a guide.

    Toss the ball through your legs, using a wrist snap as in a forward pass.

    Player receiving the ball, stand 10 to 15 ft behind the player centering it.

2. Have the children practice centering, switching roles every five trials.
3. Encourage the children to observe each other for proper technique.

Concluding Activities (10 minutes)

Centering Relay

Have teams of four to six line up in a single file behind a line, facing a second line 10 ft away. Give the first child in each line (player 1) a football.

1. Describe and demonstrate the game:

    Player 1 from each team runs to the other line carrying the football.

    When player 1 reaches the line, he or she centers the ball back to player 2.

    Player 2 repeats the run, centers to player 3, and so on.

    After you center the ball, you go to the back of the relay line (and kneel [if playing competitively]*).*

2. Run the relay competitively or have the teams run continuously in the time available.

GAMES AND SPORTS

LESSON 39
FOOTBALL

Student Objectives

- Demonstrate the technique for carrying the ball.

Equipment and Materials

- 1 junior-size football per group of four
- 1 flag football belt with flags per child

Warm-Up Activities (5 minutes)

Walk/Jog

See Grades 4-5: Games and Sports, Warm-Ups, page 856.

Skill-Development Activities (20 minutes)

Carrying the Ball

Mark with cones several areas 30 by 20 yd. Place one child (player 1) from each team of four at the starting line (one end) with a football, and scatter the other three (players 2, 3, and 4) downfield.

1. Describe and demonstrate the skill:

    Carry the ball near your body.

    Place one hand under and around one end of the ball.

    Position the opposite end of the ball in the bend of your forearm and elbow.

2. Have the children practice carrying the ball as follows:

    Beginning at the starting line, player 1 runs down the field, carrying the ball.

    Players 2, 3, and 4 try to pull player 1's flag before he or she reaches the 30-yd marker.

    Rotate runners and taggers so everyone gets a turn carrying the ball.

    Practice several times.

Concluding Activities (5 minutes)

Football Relay

Arrange relay teams of four to six in single file on a starting line, facing a second parallel line, 30 to 40 ft away.

1. Describe the activity: *Player 1 carries the ball to the opposite line, turns, and passes the ball to Player 2, and so on.*

2. Have the children continue the relay throughout the time available (ensure everyone gets at least one turn) or, to play competitively, declare the first team to finish the winner.

3. Variations:

    Vary the distance of the throw for children at different developmental levels.

    Use only ball carrying and not passing.

LESSON 40
FOOTBALL

Student Objectives

- Pass a ball laterally with a partner.
- Run a pass pattern.

Equipment and Materials

- 1 junior-size football per pair
- Cones or flour for marking the field
- 1 hoop per group of children

Warm-Up Activities (5 minutes)

Walk/Jog

See Grades 4-5: Games and Sports, Warm-Ups, page 856.

Skill-Development Activities (15 minutes)

Lateral Pass

Arrange partners in scatter formation, one football per pair.

1. Describe and demonstrate the skill:

   Pitch the ball underhand to your partner.

   Toss the ball softly with your fingers with spiral action. To make the ball spiral, grip it on the laces, and as you toss the ball, let it roll off your fingers.

   Facing the goal, pass the ball either sideways or backward away from goal.

2. Have the children practice with partners, beginning side by side about 4 ft apart, following these instructions: *The receiver begins moving away sideways, receives the lateral pass, and runs toward the goal line. Take turns being the passer.*

Forward Passing Drill

Arrange partners in scatter formation, one football per pair. See Grades 4-5: Games and Sports, Lesson 37, page 938 for basic forward passing cues.

1. Describe and demonstrate the drill:

   In this drill, you will practice a forward pass to a receiver running a pass pattern.

   The receiver runs down the field about 15 ft, stops, turns sharply to the right or left, looks back at the passer, and catches the pass.

   The passer watches the receiver and throws as soon as the receiver turns.

   Take turns with your partner being the passer.

2. Show the children how far 15 ft is.

3. Have the children practice the drill several times.

Concluding Activities (10 minutes)

Field Football

Mark 30- by 60-yd fields. Arrange two teams of six to eight on each field.

1. Describe the game:

   The object of the game is to advance the football over the opponents' goal (endline) using forward and lateral passes.

   Begin the game with a kickoff from midfield (demonstrate, if necessary).

   Opponents try to intercept the passes or knock them down.

   If a pass is knocked down, the offensive team has to back up 10 steps (although a team cannot be backed up farther than their own goal line) and begins passing again from there.

If the defensive team intercepts, they begin advancing the ball down the field toward their endline.

Defensive players must stay at least two steps from the offensive player trying to pass the ball.

You may take only two steps after catching the ball and cannot hold the ball longer than three seconds.

Teams score two points when they pass a ball from inside the field and catch it over the endline.

2. Have the children play Field Football.

Extension Activities

Passing Accuracy

Suspend a hoop three ft above the ground for each group of children. The children should take turns passing the ball.

1. Beginning at a distance of 5 yd, have the children attempt to pass the ball through the hoop.
2. Increase the distance to 10 and then 15 yd.

Centering Accuracy

Suspend a hoop two ft above the ground for each group of children. From a distance of 10 yd, have the children, one at a time, attempt to center the ball through the hoop.

Pass Pattern Drill

Arrange the children in groups of four in scatter formation. In each group, designate a center, two receivers, and a passer.

1. Describe and demonstrate the drill:

    The center centers the ball to the passer.

    Two players run out to receive the ball.

    The passer throws to one of the receivers.

    Rotate positions after each round.

2. Have the children practice the drill, using different pass patterns for the receivers.

Touchdown Drill

Arrange groups of three to five on a field marked with cones, each group with a ball. Designate one player as a passer, one or two as receivers, and one or two as defenders.

1. Describe and demonstrate the drill:

    The receivers run 10 yd to the goal line and turn to receive the pass.

    The passer attempts to throw to the receiver(s) who has (have) run 10 yd to the goal line.

    The defender(s) tries (try) to intercept the ball.

    Rotate roles after each round.

2. Have the children practice the drill.

LESSON 41
RAGING RIVER

Student Objectives

- Work cooperatively to solve a movement problem.
- Use equipment creatively to solve a problem.

Equipment and Materials

- 1 balance beam or line on floor per group
- 1 mat per beam
- 1 hoop per group

The following equipment is per "river" you set up. Try to keep group size around six to increase participation opportunities.

- 1 mat
- 1 cone
- 1 rope
- 2 carpet squares
- 1 ball
- 1 scooter
- Chalk or tape to mark "river"

Warm-Up Activities (5 minutes)

Select one of the following cooperative games.

Balance Challenge

Have small groups of children stand in a line on a line or balance beam, which is over a mat.

1. Describe the game:

    The object is to reverse the order of the children in your group without anyone stepping off the beam (or line). For example, the last child on the right end of the line should reverse places with the last child on the left of the line and so forth.

    You will have to balance while climbing over and around each other.

2. Have the children try the Balance Challenge.

Hoop Circle

Have each small group stand in a circle with hands joined, with one hoop per group.

1. Describe the game:

    Place the hoop over your heads (hands are joined through the hoop, or the like).

    The object is to move the hoop around the entire circle without releasing hands.

2. Have the children play Hoop Circle.

Circle Untangle

Have small groups stand in a close circle with hands extended inward.

1. Describe the game:

> *Join hands and follow three rules—no one can join hands with the child on either side, no one can join both hands with the same child, and you may not let go of hands at anytime.*

> *The object is to make one large circle with hands joined. Hint: Some of you may end up facing in while others end up facing out.*

2. Have the children play Circle Untangle.

Skill-Development Activities (20 minutes)

Assign each small group a set of equipment, including a mat, scooter, cone, two carpet squares, one rope, and one ball. For each group define a "river" (two lines) about 30 ft apart.

Raging River

1. Describe the game:

> *The object is to cross the "river" (the area between the two lines) without touching the "water" (the floor). Each group must get all group members and all equipment to the other side of the river without touching any body part to the floor. If a person touches the floor, the group must start that round over.*

> *Each time your group successfully crosses, you must return, using one less piece of equipment. Remove equipment in the following order: ball first, rope second, cone third, carpet squares fourth, scooter fifth. Your final trip will be with the mat only.*

2. Have the children play Raging River. Be aware that some groups will make all seven trips, while other groups will not be able to complete one trip in the time.

3. Encourage children to work cooperatively and explore as many solutions to the problem as possible. Provide feedback as the game goes on.

Concluding Activities (5 minutes)

1. Discuss the various strategies groups used to be successful in Raging River. You may want to have groups demonstrate their strategies.

2. Expansion idea: You can use a variety of equipment to alter the game (e.g., cardboard boxes, walking cans, balance beams).

GRADES 4-5 RHYTHMIC ACTIVITIES

Fourth and fifth graders enjoy rhythmic activity, and for many children physical education will be their only exposure to folk dance and the other activities in this unit. Sometimes children this age will protest against these activities, even though they really want to do them. Be positive and remember that this will be the favorite unit for some children. Classroom teachers often feel most comfortable with this unit, while some specialists avoid teaching these important skills. We encourage you to use these lessons regardless of previous experience with rhythmic activities. Keep in mind that the children enjoy the activities and respond to an enthusiastic teacher—regardless of the teacher's skill level.

UNIT ORGANIZATION

Many physical education objectives can be met through teaching rhythmic activities. Our lessons cover locomotor skills, folk dances, rope jumping, country dance, and rhythm sticks. You may opt to teach these lessons as a six-week unit, reserving the final day to test skills or have students otherwise demonstrate what they have learned, perhaps, for example, by putting on a show for fellow students, family members, and other visitors. See the sample unit plan in table RA3.1.

There are many other ways in which you could organize these lessons as well. For example, you might enjoy teaching rhythmic activities one day each week throughout the school year or interspersing a week of rhythmic activities at various intervals throughout the year. In addition, rhythmic activities often work well during inclement weather since you can teach them indoors in relatively little space.

LESSON ORGANIZATION

Each lesson begins with warm-up activities; see the warm-up section immediately following this introduction. The skill development activities focus on moving to a beat, moving with different characteristics, and exploring creative movements. Each lesson ends with a concluding activity, which typically reinforces the skill development activity and/or brings closure to the lesson. You can repeat lessons to reinforce skills and to allow children to experience the pleasure of mastery.

TEACHING HINTS

The most important factor in this unit is your attitude. When teachers present these lessons with the belief that children will enjoy and benefit from the experience, the children do! So relax and enjoy teaching the rhythmical activities. The children will not care if you are perfect, nor notice if you do not sing well. These activities are favorites and will "sell" themselves if given the opportunity. Keep in mind, too, that children enjoy watching adults exaggerate the movements and words. Another fun technique is for you to stop saying the words or cues and see if the children can continue without you, then pick up again after a short break.

Repetition and breaking the activities into parts also enhance learning. Teach and repeat the words or cues first. Then add the movements, preferably in parts. Break the skills into logical parts (many lessons suggest how to do this). If you or the children make a mistake, that is OK—just try again. Many of these activities are appropriate for demonstrations, for example, at a school-wide parent's night.

Table RA3.1: Unit Plan for Grades 4-5: Rhythmic Activities

Week 13: locomotor and nonlocomotor sequences and streamers

Monday: locomotor and nonlocomotor sequences
Tuesday: creative movement
Wednesday: creative movement
Thursday: streamers
Friday: streamers

Week 14: folk dances and rope jumping

Monday: Virginia Reel
Tuesday: Carousel
Wednesday: La Raspa
Thursday: Crested Hen
Friday: rope jumping

Week 15: rope jumping and country dance

Monday: rope jumping
Tuesday: rope jumping
Wednesday: rope jumping
Thursday: rope jumping
Friday: country dance

Week 25: folk dancing

Monday: running waltz
Tuesday: Norwegian Mountain March
Wednesday: Schottische
Thursday: Cotton-Eyed Joe and Darling Nellie Gray
Friday: Pop Goes the Weasel

Week 26: rhythm sticks

Monday: rhythm sticks
Tuesday: rhythm sticks
Wednesday: rhythm sticks
Thursday: rhythm sticks
Friday: rhythm sticks

RHYTHMIC ACTIVITIES

WARM-UPS

Double Stick Tricks

Arrange the children in scatter formation with two rhythm sticks per child placed in parallel patterns on the ground.

1. Tell the children: *To the drumbeat, jump continuously back and forth over your own sticks.*
2. Vary the tempo of the jumping by varying the tempo of the drumbeat.
3. Have them try jumping backward. Caution the children not to step on the sticks and fall.

Follow the Leader

Arrange the children in small groups, each with a leader.

1. Explain the warm-up: *The leader of each group chooses activities to perform, and the other children follow the leader. Activities can include both locomotor and nonlocomotor skills* (give examples), *and can be performed in place or moving over, around, and under playground equipment.*
2. Variation: You can easily adapt this activity to provide variety and to challenge different age groups. For example, other children can select rhythmic steps such as the step-hop, the Schottische, and so forth.

Jumping Tricks

Arrange the children in scatter formation. Challenge the children with the following jumping tasks:

Jump up and land softly.

Jump and clap your hands overhead.

Jump and land with your feet apart and then together. Repeat several times.

Jump and land with your right foot forward and left foot back. Now trade positions of your feet.

Jump and clap hands behind your back or under one leg.

Jump up and make a quarter-turn, half-turn, or full turn.

Jump up and click your heels.

Movement to Sounds

Arrange the children in scatter formation.

1. Select several instruments (wood block, triangle, tambourine, drum, bell) and assign each a direction (e.g., forward, backward, sideways right, sideways left, turning in place).
2. Select a movement and ask the children to respond to the instrument in time with the beat.

Parachute Steps

Stretch a parachute out on the ground, and have the children stand and grasp the edges near the ribs.

1. Ask the children to stand and, to the beat of the drum, perform locomotor movements and rhythmic steps in place and around in a circle, clockwise and counterclockwise.
2. Have them try jumping and hopping patterns in place or running, leaping, skipping, and so forth around in a circle.
3. Have them perform the Schottische or step-hop in place or moving.

RHYTHMIC ACTIVITIES

LESSON 1
LOCOMOTOR AND NONLOCOMOTOR COMBINATIONS

Student Objectives

- Combine locomotor and nonlocomotor movements into a sequence.
- Create a movement sequence for a partner to copy.
- Work cooperatively with a group to achieve a goal.

Equipment and Materials

- 2 rhythm sticks
- 1 drum
- 1 tambourine
- Skill cards (listing locomotor and nonlocomotor skills)

Warm-Up Activities (5 minutes)

Movement to Sounds

Arrange the children in scatter formation. The following is an example of the warm-up described in Grades 4-5: Rhythmic Activities, Warm-Ups, page 954.

1. Explain the activity:

    The sound of the sticks hitting together is the signal to move forward.

    The sound of the drum is the signal to move backward.

    And the sound of the tambourine is the signal to move in place.

    Respond to the instrument in time with the beat and in the correct direction, running.

2. Have the children practice responding, repeating each sound several times.

Skill-Development Activities (20 minutes)

Movement Combinations

Make sure the children are still in scatter formation.

1. Have the children perform the following movement combinations:

    Leap forward (four counts), *leap backward* (four counts), *leap turning* (four counts), *jump in place* (four counts), *and collapse.*

    Hop right (four counts), *hop left* (four counts), *run forward* (four counts), *stretch* (two counts), *and curl* (two counts).

Swing right leg, forward and back (eight counts), *swing left leg, forward and back* (eight counts).

Hop in place (four counts), *hop forward* (four counts), *hop backward* (four counts), *hop in place* (four counts).

Walk forward (eight counts), *jump in place* (eight counts), *walk backward* (eight counts), *jump in place* (eight counts).

Slide right (eight counts), *slide left* (eight counts).

Run (three counts), *leap* (one count). Repeat several times.

Run (two counts), *leap* (two counts). Repeat several times.

2. Repeat challenges as time allows.

Partner Copy Activity

Arrange partners in scatter formation.

1. Select two or more locomotor or nonlocomotor skills you wish to target and a variety of counts (e.g., 4, 8, 12, 16, 24).

2. Explain the activity:

The goal of the activity is for the leader to use the skills in a sequence with the specified number of counts. For example, the task might be to use walk, hop, and jump for 16 counts. The sequence could be walk (eight counts), hop (four counts), and jump (four counts).

One of you creates the movement sequence and the partner watches.

The partner then repeats the sequence.

Then trade roles and repeat the activity using other skills and counts.

3. Present the following tasks for partners:

Walk, run, stretch, and twist for 12 counts.

Gallop forward, gallop backward, jump forward, jump backward for 24 counts.

Walk forward, walk backward, hop in a circle for 12 counts.

Skip and slide for 16 counts.

4. After several practice trials, have the children select their own movements and number of counts.

Concluding Activities (5 minutes)

Skill Cards

Divide the class into groups of four to six. Have prepared a number of cards listing different locomotor and nonlocomotor skills (see figure below for examples).

1. Describe the activity:

Each group selects four (or more) cards from the stack of cards.

The group has to prepare a sequence using the skills on the cards.

2. Allow the groups time to create and practice their sequences.

Skill cards

Walk	Curl	Swing	Leap

GRADES 4-5

RHYTHMIC ACTIVITIES

LESSON 2
CREATIVE MOVEMENT

Student Objectives

- Combine several locomotor skills while moving.
- Duplicate a partner's movement sequence.
- Work cooperatively with a group to achieve a goal.

Equipment and Materials

- 2 rhythm sticks
- 1 drum
- 1 tambourine
- Chalk, tape, or flour (outdoors) to mark lines

Warm-Up Activities (5 minutes)

Movement to Sounds

See Grades 4-5: Rhythmic Activities, Warm-Ups, page 954. Have students gallop.

Skill-Development Activities (20 minutes)

Movement Combinations

See Grades 4-5: Rhythmic Activities, Lesson 1, page 955.

Partner Copy Activity

See Grades 4-5: Rhythmic Activities, Lesson 1, page 956.

Advanced Movement Sequences

Divide the children into groups of four to six and place each group behind a line. If your space is large enough, create smaller groups so more students can move at once.

1. Describe and demonstrate the following sequence: *three jumps forward; five walking steps backward; eight galloping steps with the right foot leading; eight galloping steps with the left foot leading.*

2. Have children take turns in their groups helping each other learn and practice the sequence. Practice the sequence with the children moving across the floor until it becomes easy.

3. Repeat with the following sequences:

   Three hops forward on right foot; three hops forward on left foot; six leaps forward; four jumps forward; eight walking steps backward.

Four walking steps forward; four walking steps backward; two hops right; two hops left; four jumps forward.

Two galloping steps with right foot leading; two galloping steps with left foot leading; four walking steps forward; eight jumps side-to-side.

Concluding Activities (5 minutes)

Movement Sequences

Ask each group to create a movement sequence to perform while moving across the floor.

RHYTHMIC ACTIVITIES

LESSON 3
CREATIVE MOVEMENT

Student Objectives

- Create a floor pattern with a movement sequence.
- Identify various floor patterns.

Equipment and Materials

- Flash cards with floor patterns

Flash cards with floor patterns

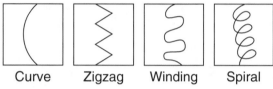

Curve   Zigzag   Winding   Spiral

Warm-Up Activities (5 minutes)

Movement to Sounds

See Grades 4-5: Rhythmic Activities, Warm-Ups, page 954. Have students jump.

Skill-Development Activities (20 minutes)

Flash Cards

Divide the children into groups of four to six, and place each group behind a line running across one end of the play area. If your space is large enough, create smaller groups so more students can move at once.

1. Show the floor patterns on the flash cards one at a time.
2. Explain the activity: *The pathway that you follow as you move across the floor is called a "floor pattern." For each floor pattern, take turns demonstrating the pattern while walking.*
3. Repeat steps 1 and 2, asking the children to move across the floor in the pattern on the cards, using the following locomotor movements: *leaping, skipping, sliding, hopping, walking backward, galloping, jumping.*
4. Repeat the activity, using combinations such as walking forward and backward and leaping and sliding.
5. Allow the groups to create their own sequences.

Concluding Activities (5 minutes)

Floor Patterns

Continue in the same formation.

1. Have each group select a floor pattern and create a sequence of three locomotor skills to use in the pattern.
2. Ask each group to show their sequence.

LESSON 4
STREAMERS

Student Objectives

- Create circles, figure eights, and letters with streamers.
- Work cooperatively with a group to create a movement sequence with streamers.

Equipment and Materials

- 2 streamers per child
- 2 rhythm sticks
- 1 drum
- 1 tambourine

Warm-Up Activities (5 minutes)

Movement to Sounds

See Grades 4-5: Rhythmic Activities, Warm-Ups, page 954. Allow the children to select their own loco-motor movements.

Skill-Development Activities (20 minutes)

Streamer Tasks

Make sure the children are still in scatter formation, and give each child two streamers. Challenge the children with the following streamer tasks:

> Move your streamers in circles (out to each side, overhead, low to the ground).
>
> Make a circle with one arm and then the other.
>
> Make large circles and then small circles.
>
> Make a figure eight with one streamer and then the other.
>
> Hold your arms out in front and move your streamers alternately up and down.
>
> Hold your arms out to your sides and move your streamers alternately up and down.
>
> Make letters in space (C, S, R, the first letter of your name).
>
> Create straight lines and curved lines.
>
> Make a square and a triangle.

Copycat

Divide children into groups of four to six and appoint a leader for each group.

1. Tell the children: *The leader leads the group in a sequence of streamer activities. Allow each child a turn to be the leader.*

Assign each child a partner.

2. Tell the children: *Partner 1 selects a streamer movement and performs the movement for eight counts. Partner 2 copies the movement for eight counts. After partner 1 has led four movements, partner 2 becomes the leader and chooses four movements.*

Concluding Activities (5 minutes)

Group Creative Project

Have the children reform their small groups. Have each group create and practice a sequence of streamer movements.

GRADES 4-5

RHYTHMIC ACTIVITIES

LESSON 5
STREAMERS

Student Objectives

- Perform a movement sequence with streamers to music.
- Work cooperatively with a group to create a movement sequence with streamers.

Equipment and Materials

- 2 streamers per child
- Music: "Frere Jacques" from *Modern Times for Rhythm and Instruments*, Hap Palmer (AR 523)

Warm-Up Activities (5 minutes)

Jumping Tricks

Arrange the children in scatter formation. Present the following jumping challenges, having the children repeat each several times (see also Grades 4-5: Rhythmic Activities, Warm-Ups, page 953):

> *Jump and land softly.*
>
> *Jump and clap your hands overhead.*
>
> *Jump and clap your hands behind your back.*
>
> *Jump and land with your feet apart and then together.*

Skill-Development Activities (20 minutes)

Streamer Routine

Keep the children in scatter formation.

1. Describe and demonstrate part 1 of the Streamer Routine:

    Part 1: *March in place with your arms out to the side* (eight counts),

    March in place with your arms extended overhead (eight counts),

    March in place with your arms out to the side (eight counts),

    March in place with your arms extended to the front (eight counts).

2. Have the children practice part 1.

3. Have them practice part 1 to music.

4. Describe and demonstrate part 2:

    Part 2: *Stand in place with your arms extended to the front, and move your arms alternately up and down* (eight counts),

Stand in place and make circles with both arms rotating forward together (eight counts).
Repeat both lines.

5. Repeat steps 2 and 3 for part 2.
6. Have the children perform the entire routine straight through to music.

Concluding Activities (5 minutes)

Divide the children into groups of four to six. Have the groups create a routine using any of the movements learned. If time allows, have each group show their routine to the class.

LESSON 6
FOLK DANCE

Student Objectives

- Name the skills in the "Virginia Reel."
- Demonstrate the do-si-do, elbow swing, and reel.
- Combine the do-si-do, elbow swing, and reel to perform the "Virginia Reel."

Equipment and Materials

- Music: "Virginia Reel" (Folkraft 1249, Melody House 74, World of Folk Dance 1623, or KIM 7037)

Warm-Up Activities (5 minutes)

Jumping Tricks

Arrange the children in scatter formation. Challenge the children with the following jumping tasks, having the children repeat each jump several times (see also Grades 4-5: Rhythmic Activities, Warm-Ups, page 953):

Jump and clap under one leg.

Jump and make a quarter-turn.

Jump and make a full turn.

Jump and click your heels.

Skill-Development Activities (20 minutes)

Step Practice

Arrange partners in scatter formation.

1. Describe and demonstrate each of the following steps.
2. Have the children practice each step before learning the next step.

Do-Si-Do
Partners walk toward each other, passing right shoulders, then passing back-to-back and walking backward in place.

Elbow Swing
Partners join elbows and run or skip around in place.

Reel

Arrange the children in a longways-set formation with six to eight couples in each set, partners facing each other (makes two lines facing).

> *The head couple turns one and a half times with the elbow swing.*
>
> *Then with the elbow swing, partners swing once around each dancer in the opposite line.*
>
> *After each elbow swing, they return to swing elbows with partner in the center.*
>
> *The couple progresses to the foot of the set.*

Repeat so each couple is "head couple" once.

"Virginia Reel"

Arrange the partners in longways-set.

1. Describe and demonstrate part 1.
2. Have the children practice part 1.
3. Repeat steps 1 and 2 for parts 2 through 6.

   Part 1: *Walk forward toward your partner four steps and walk back to your starting place four steps. Repeat.*

   Part 2: *Walk forward and join right hands with your partner, turn once, and walk back to your place. Repeat with left hands. Repeat with right hands.*

   Part 3: *Do-si-do with your partner.*

   Part 4: *Head couple takes eight sliding steps down to foot of set and returns to their starting place with eight sliding steps.*

   Part 5: *Head couple reels down the set, turns one-and-a-half times around partner, then swings with left elbow around dancer to opposite line and then back to partner with right elbow.*

   Part 6: *Head couple slides back to head of set, casts off (separates, going outside his or her line) to foot of set, and forms an arch for the other dancers to go under.*

4. Repeat entire routine with new head couple.
5. Have the children listen and clap to the music.

Concluding Activities (5 minutes)

"Virginia Reel"

Arrange children in partners in a longways-set. Have the children perform the entire sequence to music, repeating so each pair is head couple.

LESSON 7
FOLK DANCE

Student Objectives

- Combine slides, stamps, and walking steps in the dance to "Carousel."

Equipment and Materials

- Music: "Carousel" (Folkraft 1183)

Warm-Up Activities (5 minutes)

Follow the Leader

See Grades 4-5: Rhythmic Activities, Warm-Ups, page 953.

Skill-Development Activities (20 minutes)

"Carousel"

Arrange the children in a double circle, facing center. Have the inner circle children hold hands and the outer circle children place their hands on the shoulders or waists of the inner circle children. The children in the inner circle are the "Carousel Horses," the children in the outer circle are the "Riders."

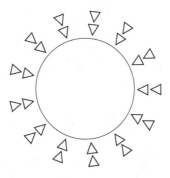

Double circle, facing in

1. Describe and demonstrate part 1.
2. Have the children practice part 1.
3. Repeat steps 1 and 2 with parts 2 through 5.
   Part 1: *14 slow slides to the left (step-close).*
   Part 2: *Stamp three times.*

Part 3: *16 fast sliding steps to the left.*

Part 4: *12 fast sliding steps to the right.*

Part 5: *Partners change places with four walking steps.*

4. Have the children practice the entire dance to music.

5. Repeat, reversing roles so the children on the inner circle move out, and vice versa.

Concluding Activities (5 minutes)

"Carousel"

Arrange the children in three double circles.

1. Have the children perform Carousel in a round, with the first circle group beginning with the music, the second circle beginning when the first circle completes the steps once, and so forth for the third group.

2. The first group can repeat again after the third group begins.

GRADES 4-5

RHYTHMIC ACTIVITIES

LESSON 8
DANCE STEPS

Student Objectives

- Combine a step and a hop in an even rhythm.
- Combine the step-hop and the bleking step in "La Raspa."

Equipment and Materials

- Music: step-hop music (any Schottische music)
- Music: "La Raspa" (Folkraft 1119, 1457)
- Music: *Folk Dance Fun* (KIM 7037)

Warm-Up Activities (5 minutes)

Follow the Leader

See Grades 4-5: Rhythmic Activities, Warm-Ups, page 953.

Skill-Development Activities (15 minutes)

Step-Hop

Arrange the children in scatter formation.

1. Describe and demonstrate the skill: *The step-hop is a walking step and a hop. You can do it in place or forward and backward. Use an even rhythmic pattern, which means give the step and the hop equal time.*

2. Have the children practice the step-hop, using the following tasks:

    Clap on count 1 and hold on count 2.

    Step in place to the music, counting one, two, one, two.

    Step only on count 1, and hold on count 2 (lifting free foot).

    Step and hop in place, alternating right foot and left foot.

    Step-hop forward, step-hop backward in a circle.

    Step-hop with a partner.

Step-Hop Sequence

Keep the children in scatter formation. Have the children create a step-hop sequence to the music, and then ask volunteers to demonstrate their sequences for the class.

Bleking Step

Keep the children in scatter formation.

1. Describe and demonstrate the step: *Spring into the air off one foot and extend the other foot in front, landing with the toe up and the heel touching the floor. Continue springing into the air, landing on alternating feet with the nonsupporting foot extended.*
2. Have the children practice the Bleking Step.

"La Raspa"

Arrange the children in one large circle, facing center.

1. Describe and demonstrate part 1.
2. Have the children practice part 1.
3. Repeat steps 1 and 2 with parts 2 and 3.

   Part 1: *Three fast bleking steps in place.*

   On count 4, pause and clap twice.

   Repeat 7 times for a total of 8.

   Part 2: *Eight step-hops to the left with hands joined.*

   Part 3: *Eight step-hops to the right with hands joined.*
4. Have the children practice the entire sequence without, then with, the music.

Concluding Activities (10 minutes)

"La Raspa"

Arrange the children in two lines, facing each other. Have the children perform "La Raspa" with lines alternating on part 1 (so one line stands still while the other line does three bleking steps, two claps, then the lines reverse). Each line does the sequence four times, for a total of eight times. The two lines do parts 2 and 3 simultaneously but in opposite directions.

LESSON 9
FOLK DANCE

Student Objectives

- Use the step-hop in the "Crested Hen."

Equipment and Materials

- Music: "Crested Hen" (Folkraft 1154)

Warm-Up Activities (5 minutes)

Follow the Leader

See Grades 4-5: Rhythmic Activities, Warm-Ups, page 953.

Skill-Development Activities (20 minutes)

Step-Hop

See Grades 4-5: Rhythmic Activities, Lesson 8, page 969.

"Crested Hen"

Arrange the children in sets of three and scatter the sets. Have each trio hold hands; one child is the center person, who will continually hold hands with the other two throughout the dance, and the other two are end persons.

1. Have the children listen to the music for "Crested Hen."
2. Describe and demonstrate the part 1 of the sequence.
3. Have the children practice part 1.
4. Repeat steps 2 and 3 with parts 2 and 3.

   Part 1: *Clap to the music.*

   Step-hop in place to the music.

   Seven step-hops to the left; on the eighth count, jump and reverse direction to the right.

Part 2: *Eight step-hops to the right.*

The end children drop hands, but the center child continues to hold their hands.

One child (on the center's left) takes six step-hops under an arch made by the arms of the other two children. The center follows under the arch. All children should step-hop the entire time.

Part 3: *The other end child (on the center's right) and the center repeat the preceding step, going through the arch (part 2).*

5. Have the children practice the entire sequence to music.

Concluding Activities (5 minutes)

"Crested Hen"

Still in trios, the children make a large circle of trios. Have the children perform the sequence one time. As the center follows the second end through the arch, direct the end to move to another set (taking 16 counts) so that each group has one new member. Continue the sequence.

LESSON 10
ROPE JUMPING

Student Objectives

- Perform the rock step, ski twist, and straddle cross jump with a jump rope.
- Jump rope to music.

Equipment and Materials

- 1 short jump rope per child
- Music: *Aerobic Rope Skipping* (AR 43); *Jump Aerobics* (KIM 2095); *Jump to the Beat* (KIM 8097)

Warm-Up Activities (5 minutes)

Follow the Leader

Divide the children into groups of four, each group with four ropes. Arrange the groups in scatter formation. This is a variation of Grades 4-5: Rhythmic Activities, Warm-Ups, page 953.

1. Explain the warm-up:

    Each group creates rope obstacles by arranging its four ropes into a formation.

    Choose a leader, who leaps, jumps, or hops through the pattern with the rest of you following.

    Give everyone a chance to lead and create a pattern.

2. Have the children warm up.

Skill-Development Activities (20 minutes)

Two-Footed Double Jump Forward

Arrange individuals in scatter formation, each with a jump rope.

1. Describe and demonstrate the skill: *Jump on both feet twice for each turn of the rope.*
2. Have the children practice the two-footed double jump forward.

Two-Footed Double Jump Backward

Keep the children in scatter formation, each with a jump rope.

1. Describe and demonstrate the skill: *Throwing the rope backward overhead, jump on both feet two times for each turn of the rope.*
2. Have the children practice the two-footed double jump backward.

Rock Step

Keep the children in scatter formation, each with a jump rope.

1. Describe and demonstrate the skill: *Using a double-jump rhythm, place one foot in front of the other, jump on the front foot, leaning slightly forward and with the same turn of the rope, and rebound on the back foot.*
2. Have the children practice the rock step with the left leg forward.
3. Have them practice the rock step with the right leg forward.

Ski Twist

Keep the children in scatter formation, each with a jump rope.
1. Describe and demonstrate the skill: *Using a double-jump rhythm, twist your knees and ankles in the same direction.*
2. Have the children practice the ski twist.

Straddle Cross Jump

Keep the children in scatter formation, each with a jump rope.

1. Describe and demonstrate the skill: *Using the double-jump rhythm, land first with your feet about shoulder-width apart, and then on the second jump, land with your feet crossed.*
2. Have the children practice the straddle cross jump.

Jump to Music

Keep the children in scatter formation, each with a jump rope. Using any of the steps learned, have the children jump rope to music.

Concluding Activities (5 minutes)

Jump Rope Routine

Keep the children in scatter formation, each with a jump rope. Direct the children to perform the following routine to music:

Eight two-footed double jumps,

Eight rock steps,

Eight ski twists, and

Eight straddle cross jumps.

LESSON 11
ROPE JUMPING

Student Objectives

- Perform toe taps and heel taps with a jump rope.
- Jump rope to music.

Equipment and Materials

- 1 short jump rope per child
- Music for jumping (See Grades 4-5: Rhythmic Activities, Lesson 10, page 973.)

Warm-Up Activities (5 minutes)

Follow the Leader

Use rope obstacles. See Grades 4-5: Rhythmic Activities, Warm-Ups, page 953 and Lesson 10, page 973.

Skill-Development Activities (20 minutes)

Rock Step, Ski Twist, and Straddle Cross Jump

Arrange the children in scatter formation, each with a jump rope. Using a double-jump rhythm, have the children practice jumping to music. See Grades 4-5: Rhythmic Activities, Lesson 10, page 974.

Two-Footed Singles

Keep the children in scatter formation, each with a jump rope.

1. Describe and demonstrate the activity: *To do two-footed singles, jump on both feet once for each turn of the rope.*
2. Have the children practice two-footed singles.

Toe Taps

Keep the children in scatter formation, each with a jump rope.

1. Describe and demonstrate the skill: *Using a single-jump rhythm, jump on your right foot while touching your left toe in front of your right foot, then repeat, jumping on your left foot. There should be one jump and one tap with each turn of the rope.*
2. Have the children practice toe taps.

Heel Taps

Keep the children in scatter formation, each with a jump rope.

1. Describe and demonstrate the skill: *Using a single-jump rhythm, jump on your right foot while touching the heel of your left foot in front of your right foot, then repeat, jumping on your left foot.*

2. Have the children practice heel taps.

Jump to Music

Keep the children in scatter formation, each with a jump rope. Using any of the steps learned, have the children jump rope to music.

Concluding Activities (5 minutes)

Rope Routine

Keep the children in scatter formation, each with a jump rope. Have the children perform the following routine to music:

> *Eight two-footed singles,*
> *Eight toe taps,*
> *Eight heel taps, and*
> *Eight two-footed singles.*

LESSON 12
ROPE JUMPING

Student Objectives

- Perform reverse toe taps and the heel-toe steps with a jump rope.
- Jump rope to music.

Equipment and Materials

- 1 short jump rope per child
- Music for jumping (See Grades 4-5: Rhythmic Activities, Lesson 10, page 973.)

Warm-Up Activities (5 minutes)

Follow the Leader

Use rope obstacles. See Grades 4-5: Rhythmic Activities, Warm-Ups, page 953 and Lesson 10, page 973.

Skill-Development Activities (20 minutes)

Toe Taps and Heel Taps

Arrange individuals in scatter formation, each with a jump rope. Using a single-jump rhythm, have the children practice toe taps and heel taps to music.

Reverse Toe Taps

Keep the children in scatter formation, each with a jump rope.

1. Describe and demonstrate the skill: *Using a single-jump rhythm, jump on your right foot while tapping your left toe behind your right foot, then repeat with your left foot.*
2. Have the children practice the reverse toe tap.

Heel-Toe Step

Keep the children in scatter formation, each with a jump rope.

1. Describe and demonstrate the skill: *Using a single-jump rhythm, jump on your right foot while touching your left heel forward. On the next turn, touch your left toe beside your right heel, and repeat with a jump on your left foot.*
2. Have the children practice the heel-toe step.

Jump to Music

Keep the children in scatter formation, each with a jump rope. Using any of the steps learned, have the children jump rope to music.

Concluding Activities (5 minutes)

Rope Routine

Keep the children in scatter formation, each with a jump rope. Have the children perform the following sequence to music:

Eight two-footed singles,
Eight reverse toe taps,
Eight heel-toe steps, and
Eight two-footed singles.

GRADES 4-5

RHYTHMIC ACTIVITIES

LESSON 13
ROPE JUMPING

Student Objectives

- Perform side taps and double-sided taps, using a single-jump rhythm.
- Jump rope to music.

Equipment and Materials

- 1 short jump rope per child
- Music for jumping (See Grades 4-5, Rhythmic Activities, Lesson 10, page 973.)
- 1 long jump rope per group of four

Warm-Up Activities (5 minutes)

Thirty-Second Jumping

Divide the children into groups of four, each group with a long jump rope.

1. Describe and demonstrate the activity:

    Two children take the ends of the rope and hold it extended about one foot above the ground.

    The other two children jump back and forth over the rope, counting the number of jumps in 30 seconds.

    Turners and jumpers trade roles.

    Repeat several times.

2. Have the children warm up.

Skill-Development Activities (20 minutes)

Reverse Toe Taps and Heel-Toe Steps

Arrange the children in scatter formation, each with a short jump rope.

1. See Grades 4-5: Rhythmic Activities, Lesson 12, page 977 to review steps.
2. Have the children practice jumping to music.

Side Taps

Keep the children in scatter formation, each with a jump rope.

1. Describe and demonstrate the skill: *Using a single-jump rhythm, jump on your right foot while tapping your left toe out to the side, then repeat with a jump on your left foot while tapping your right toe to the side. Be sure you tap for each turn of the rope (i.e., one jump and*

one tap for each turn of the rope).

2. Have the children practice side taps.

Double-Sided Taps

Keep the children in scatter formation, each with a jump rope.

1. Describe and demonstrate the skill: *This step is exactly like side taps except that there are two jumps and two taps. Jump twice on your right foot while tapping your left foot once in place and once out to the side, then repeat with a jump on your left foot.*

2. Have the children practice double-sided taps.

Jump to Music

Keep the children in scatter formation, each with a jump rope. Using any of the steps learned, have the children jump rope to music.

Concluding Activities (5 minutes)

Group Routines

Divide the children into groups of four, each child with a short jump rope. Have each group create a 32-count routine to music, using any steps.

LESSON 14
ROPE JUMPING

Student Objectives
- Jump a short rope with crossed arms.
- Jump rope to music.

Equipment and Materials
- 1 short jump rope per child
- Music for jumping (See Grades 4-5: Rhythmic Activities, Lesson 10, page 973.)

Warm-Up Activities (5 minutes)

S-Jumping

Arrange the children in scatter formation, each child with a short jump rope. Ask each child to place his or her rope on the ground in an "S" shape.

1. Describe and demonstrate the activity: *Jump over the curves of the S, then jump forward, backward, and sideways over the rope and through the S.*

2. Have the children warm up.

Skill-Development Activities (20 minutes)

Side Taps and Double-Sided Hits

Keep the children in scatter formation, each with a jump rope.

1. See Grades 4-5: Rhythmic Activities, Lesson 13, pages 979-980 to review the steps.
2. Have the children practice to music.

Arm Crosses

Keep the children in scatter formation, each with a jump rope.

1. Describe and demonstrate the skill: *Cross your arms evenly at the forearms (hands must extend outside hips) while swinging the rope and jump rope.*
2. Have the children practice arm crosses.
3. Have them practice alternating regular swings with arm crosses.

Jump to Music

Keep the children in scatter formation, each with a jump rope. Using any of the steps learned, have the children jump rope to music.

Concluding Activities (5 minutes)

Rope Routine

Keep the children in scatter formation, each with a jump rope. Have the children perform the following routine to music:

Eight two-footed singles,

Eight arm crosses,

Eight two-footed singles, and

Eight arm crosses.

RHYTHMIC ACTIVITIES

LESSON 15
COUNTRY DANCE

Student Objectives

- Perform the grapevine step to music.

Equipment and Materials

- Music: "Elvira" by the Oak Ridge Boys, *Greatest Hits* (MCA 5496)
- 1 parachute
- Signal

Warm-Up Activities (5 minutes)

Parachute Steps

Arrange the children around the parachute and ask them to hold it with one or both hands.

1. Explain the warm-up:

    Moving clockwise, slide in a circle.

    On the signal, change directions.

2. Have the children warm up, repeating the instructions several times. You can also have them try jumping, hopping, and running in place.

Skill-Development Activities (20 minutes)

"Elvira"

Arrange the children in scatter formation.

1. Have the children listen to "Elvira" and clap to the beat.
2. Have them stand in place and step to the music.

Grapevine Steps

Keep the children in scatter formation.

1. Describe and demonstrate the skill, going to the right:

   Step to the right with your right foot.

   Bring your left foot behind and step on it.

   Step to the right again with your right foot.

   Bring your left foot in front, lifting your left knee across in front of your right knee while balancing on your right foot.

   Summarize: *It takes four counts: step, back, step, cross (or lift).*

2. Have the children practice grapevine steps, going to the right. Cue the children: *Right, back, right, lift.*
3. Repeat, going left. Cue the children: *Left, back, left, lift.*
4. Have the children practice the grapevine step, going to the right and left (with a partner, in a line, in a circle).
5. Have the children practice the grapevine step to the music.
6. Have the children practice the grapevine step with a quarter-turn (pivot) on the lift, after completing the right, back, right. Cue the children: *Right, back, right, lift, and pivot.*

Concluding Activities (5 minutes)

Grapevine Line

Arrange the children in a single file line. Have the children perform the grapevine step right and left, in a line, to the music, making a quarter-turn to the left at the end of each grapevine step to the left.

LESSON 16
DANCE STEPS

Student Objectives

- Combine three running steps into a running waltz step.

Equipment and Materials

- Music: "Elvira" by the Oak Ridge Boys, *Greatest Hits* (MCA 5496)
- Music: "Norwegian Mountain March" (Folkraft 1177, RCA 45EP 6173)

Warm-Up Activities (5 minutes)

Grapevine Step

Arrange the children in scatter formation.

1. Have the children listen to "Elvira."
2. Using the grapevine step, have the children travel freely about the area to the music.
3. Ask them to change directions often, using the quarter-turn (pivot). See Grades 4-5: Rhythmic Activities, Lesson 15, page 984.

Skill-Development Activities (20 minutes)

"Norwegian Mountain March" Lead-Up

Arrange the children in a large circle.

1. Have the children listen to the "Norwegian Mountain March."
2. Offer the following challenges:
   Clap to the music, accenting the first beat.
   Run in place, counting in threes and clapping on count 1.
   Run counterclockwise in the circle, counting in threes and clapping on count 1.
   Add a slight knee bend on count 1.

Running Waltz Steps

Arrange the children in a long line facing you.

1. Describe and demonstrate the dance:
   The running waltz step is a series of running steps performed in sets of threes.

The pattern is run, run, run, with the accent on the first beat.

To accent the first beat, bend (dip) one knee slightly.

I will cue you: Dip, two, three, dip, two, three, and so on.

2. Have the children practice the running waltz step, going diagonally to the right on the first waltz step (run, run, run) and diagonally to the left on the second waltz step (run, run, run). Cue the children: *Right, two, three, left, two, three* (and so on).

Concluding Activities (5 minutes)

Running Waltz Steps

Arrange partners in scatter formation with inside hands joined. Have partners practice the running waltz step to the music, moving freely about the area.

G R A D E S 4-5 RHYTHMIC ACTIVITIES

LESSON 17
FOLK DANCE

Student Objectives

- Perform the running waltz step in the "Norwegian Mountain March."

Equipment and Materials

- Music: "Norwegian Mountain March" (Folkraft 1177, RCA 45EP 6173)

Warm-Up Activities (5 minutes)

Running Waltz Steps

Arrange partners in scatter formation.

1. See Grades 4-5: Rhythmic Activities, Lesson 16, page 985 to review the step.
2. Have partners practice the running waltz step, moving freely about the area.
3. Have the children try making curved floor patterns as they move.

Skill-Development Activities (20 minutes)

"Norwegian Mountain March"

Arrange the children in sets of three in a large circle. Have the three children in each set join hands and form a triangle. One person in each set is in front of the other two, and all three in the set are facing the same direction (see figure below). Have all sets face counterclockwise.

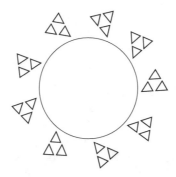

Sets of 3

1. Describe and demonstrate part 1.
2. Have the children practice part 1 by walking through the movements.
3. Repeat steps 1 and 2 with parts 2 through 4.

> Part 1: *Your trio takes eight running waltz steps* (24 counts).
>
> Part 2: *The center child backs up with six running steps. All three of you should now be standing shoulder-to-shoulder in a line.*
>
> Part 3: *With six running steps, the child on the left moves clockwise across and under the center child's right arm and the arch made by the two children. The center child follows under the arch with six running steps, and all three of you return to your original places.*
>
> Part 4: *The child on the right repeats the movement with six running steps. The center child again follows under the arch six steps and unwinds to the original position.*
>
> Part 5: Repeat parts 2, 3, and 4. Cue the children: *Left child under, center child follows, right child under, center child follows.*

4. Practice the entire sequence without the music.
5. Have the children perform the entire sequence to the music.

Concluding Activities (5 minutes)

"Norwegian Mountain March"

Continue in the same formation as shown in figure on page 987. Have the children perform parts 1 through 5, then rotate one student from each group into the adjacent group (clockwise rotation) and repeat the entire sequence. Continue.

LESSON 18
DANCE STEPS

Student Objectives

- Perform a sequence of Schottische and step-hop steps to music.

Equipment and Materials

- Music: "Military Schottische" from *Basic Dance Tempos*, Honor Your Partner (LP 501A) (or other Schottische music)

Warm-Up Activities (5 minutes)

Schottische

Arrange the children in scatter formation.

1. Have the children listen to the Schottische music.
2. Using the Schottische step, have the children travel to the music.
3. Have them repeat, using both forward and backward Schottische steps.

Skill-Development Activities (20 minutes)

The Schottische and Step-Hop Sequence

Arrange the children in a double circle, facing counterclockwise.

1. Have the children practice combining two Schottische steps and four step-hops. Cue the children: *Walk, walk, walk, hop; walk, walk, walk, hop; step-hop, step-hop, step-hop, step-hop.*
2. Have them practice in place, repeating several times.
3. Variations:

   Perform two Schottische steps moving forward (begin on the right foot), then four step-hops in place.

   Replace the four step-hops with rock steps: forward left, back right, forward left, back right.

   Perform the Schottische steps diagonally to the right and the left.

   Perform step-hops while moving forward (or turning in a circle).

Schottische Step-Hop Routines

Assign each child a partner. Ask each pair to create a routine using two Schottische steps and four step-hops.

RHYTHMIC ACTIVITIES

LESSON 19
DANCE STEPS

Student Objectives

- Combine a step-close-step in an uneven rhythm to perform the two-step.
- Combine the two-step and right and left leg swings in "Cotton-Eyed Joe."

Equipment and Materials

- Music: "Military Schottische" and "Darling Nellie Gray" from *Basic Dance Tempos*, Honor Your Partner (LP 501A)
- Music: "Cotton-Eyed Joe," (BL 257; Educational Record Center)

Warm-Up Activities (5 minutes)

Schottische Step-Hop

Arrange the children in scatter formation.

1. Have the children listen to the Schottische music.
2. Tell the children: *The Schottische step is three steps and a hop.* Describe and demonstrate the Schottische Step-Hop.

    Beginning on the left or both feet with a step right (1), step left (2), step right (3), and hop right.

    This can be repeated reversing the steps, step left (1), step right (2), step left (3), and hop left.

3. With a combination of Schottische steps and step-hops, have the children travel to the music.
4. Direct them to change directions frequently.

Skill-Development Activities (20 minutes)

Two-Step

Make sure the children are still in scatter formation.

1. Describe and demonstrate the step:

    Step on your right foot, close your left foot to the back of your right foot, and step on your right foot.

> *Repeat (step on left foot, close on right foot, step on left foot, step on right foot, close on right, and so on).*
>
> *Notice that this step has an uneven rhythm.*

2. Have the children practice the two-step. Cue the children: *Right, close left, right, left, close right, left, right. . . .*

"Darling Nellie Gray"

Make sure the children are still in scatter formation.

1. Have the children listen and clap to the music of "Darling Nellie Gray."
2. Have them perform the two-step pattern forward around the area to the music.
3. Repeat with the two-step backward (step back right, close left, and step back right).
4. Repeat with the two-step sideways (step side left, close right, step side left).
5. Repeat, varying the direction of the two-step (sideways, forward, backward).

"Cotton-Eyed Joe"

Make sure the children are still in scatter formation.

1. Describe and demonstrate part 1.

   > Part 1: *Lift your right foot out and around your left foot, keeping your weight on your left foot. (This is a brushing motion, with the ball of your right foot brushing the floor as it crosses your left foot and back.)*

2. Have the children practice part 1. Cue the children: *Brush right.*
3. Describe and demonstrate part 2.

   > Part 2: *Extend your right foot out in front of your left foot (use a kicking motion).*

4. Have the children practice part 2. Cue the children: *Kick.*
5. Have the children practice parts 1 and 2. Cue the children: *Brush right and kick.*
6. Describe and demonstrate part 3.

   > Part 3: *Take three small steps backward.*

7. Have the children practice part 3. Cue the children: *Step back, two, three.*
8. Repeat steps 6 and 7 with parts 4 and 5.

   > Part 4: *Lift left foot out and around right foot, keeping weight on right foot; return left foot.* Cue the children: *Brush left.*
   >
   > Part 5: *Extend left foot out in front of right foot.* Cue the children: *Kick left.*

9. Have the children practice parts 4 and 5: *Brush left, kick left.*
10. Describe and demonstrate part 6: *Take three small steps backward.*
11. Have the children practice parts 4, 5, and 6. Cue the children: *Brush left, kick left, back, two, three.*
12. Have the children practice parts 1 through 6. Cue the children: *Brush right, kick right, back, two, three, brush left, kick left, back, two, three.*

    > Part 7: Repeat parts 1 through 6.
    >
    > Part 8: *Take eight two-steps forward.*

13. Have them practice the two-step (part 8) to music.
14. Have them practice the entire sequence with music.

Concluding Activities (5 minutes)

"Cotton-Eyed Joe"

Arrange the children in several long lines, standing shoulder-to-shoulder, each with arms around the waist or shoulders of the next child. Have the children perform "Cotton-Eyed Joe" in these lines with the music.

LESSON 20
FOLK DANCE

Student Objectives

- Combine walking and skipping to perform "Pop Goes the Weasel."

Equipment and Materials

- Music: "Pop Goes the Weasel" (Folkraft 1329; World of Folk Dance 1623; Folk Dancer MH 1501)

Warm-Up Activities (5 minutes)

"Pop Goes the Weasel"

Arrange the children in scatter formation.

1. Have the children listen to "Pop Goes the Weasel."
2. Have the children skip to the music.
3. Have them move in various directions and try skipping backward.

Skill-Development Activities (20 minutes)

"Pop Goes the Weasel"

Arrange the children in sets of four in a large circle. Couple 1 faces clockwise and couple 2 faces counterclockwise (see figure below).

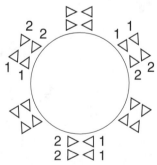

1. Describe and demonstrate part 1.
2. Have the children practice part 1.
3. Repeat steps 1 and 2 with parts 2 and 3.

Part 1: *In each set join hands and circle left with eight skipping steps.*

Part 2: *In each set walk two steps forward, raising your hands high and two steps back to your starting place, lowering your arms.*

Part 3: *Couple 1 forms an arch with inside hands joined. Couple 2 "pops" under the arch to meet a new couple. Repeat the routine with the new four-somes.*

4. Have the children perform the entire sequence to music.

Concluding Activities (5 minutes)

Folk Dances

Have the children perform a routine from a previous lesson: "Cotton-Eyed Joe" (Grades 4-5: Rhythmic Activities, Lesson 19, page 992), "Darling Nellie Gray" (Grades 4-5: Rhythmic Activities, Lesson 19, page 992), or "Military Schottische" (Grades 4-5: Rhythmic Activities, Lesson 18, page 989).

LESSON 21
RHYTHM STICKS

Student Objectives

- Combine tapping and tossing rhythm sticks with a partner.

Equipment and Materials

- 1 drum
- 2 rhythm sticks per child
- Music: "Chicken Fat" (KIM 209)

Warm-Up Activities (5 minutes)

Double Stick Tricks

Arrange the children in scatter formation with rhythm sticks placed parallel to each other on the ground at their feet.

1. To a drumbeat, have the children jump continuously back and forth over their own sticks.
2. Vary the tempo of the jump.
3. Have them try jumping backward.

Skill-Development Activities (20 minutes)

Partner Tapping

Arrange partners in scatter formation, sitting cross-legged facing each other, each child with two sticks.

1. Describe and demonstrate the activity:

   Tap sticks down,

   Tap sticks together,

   Touch right stick to your partner's right stick,

   Tap own sticks together,

   Repeat, and

   Touch left stick with your partner's.

2. Have the children practice partner tapping. Cue the children: *Down, together, right, together; down, together, left, together.*

Partner Tossing

Arrange the children with partners, sitting on the floor facing each other.

1. Describe and demonstrate the activity:

    Each of you tosses his or her right stick to your partner's right side and catches your partner's right stick.

    Repeat with left sticks.

2. Have the children practice partner tossing.

Stick Sequence

Continue with the children with partners, sitting on the floor facing each other.

1. Have partners perform the following sequence:

    Tap down, tap together, toss right, tap together (four counts). Cue the children: *Down, together, right, together.*

    Tap down, tap together, toss left, tap together (four counts). Cue the children: *Down, together, left, together.*

2. Have them repeat the pattern continuously to the music.

Concluding Activities (5 minutes)

Stick Sequence

Continue with the children with partners, sitting on the floor facing each other.

1. Have the children perform the following sequence:

    Tap down (four counts), *tap together* (four counts),

    Tap down, tap together, touch right, tap together (four counts),

    Tap down, tap together, touch left, tap together (four counts),

    Tap down, tap together, toss right, tap together (four counts),

    Tap down, tap together, toss left, tap together (four counts).

2. Have them repeat the sequence rhythmically to the music.

LESSON 22
RHYTHM STICKS

Student Objectives

- Chant the "Lummi Stick Chant" from memory.

Equipment and Materials

- 1 drum
- Large poster with the "Lummi Stick Chant" printed on it
- 2 rhythm sticks per child
- Music for stick routines (provide a variety of the current favorites)

Warm-Up Activities (5 minutes)

Double Stick Tricks

See Grades 4-5: Rhythmic Activities, Lesson 21, page 953. Have the children experiment with different types of jumps and hops.

Skill-Development Activities (20 minutes)

"Lummi Stick Chant"

Arrange the children in a semicircle so that all children can see the words on the poster, each child with two rhythm sticks.

1. Sing the chant to the children.
2. Practice the chant with the children.
3. Have the children sing the chant and tap the sticks down and together.

Lummi stick chant

Partner Routine

Arrange the children with partners, sitting and facing each other. See Grades 4-5: Rhythmic Activities, Lesson 21, page 996. Have the children perform the following sequence:

> *Tap down* (three counts),
>
> *Tap together* (three counts),
>
> *Tap down, touch right, tap together* (three counts),
>
> *Tap down, touch left, tap together* (three counts),
>
> *Tap down, toss right, tap together* (three counts),
>
> *Tap down, toss left, tap together* (three counts),
>
> *Tap down* (three counts),
>
> *Tap together* (three counts).

Concluding Activities (5 minutes)

"Lummi Stick Chant"

Arrange the students in the information formation. Ask individuals or small groups of children to perform the chant and stick routine.

G R A D E S 4-5 RHYTHMIC ACTIVITIES

LESSON 23
RHYTHM STICKS

Student Objectives

- Perform patterns 1 and 2 of the traditional "Lummi Stick Chant."

Equipment and Materials

- 2 rhythm sticks per child
- 1 short jump rope per child
- Music: "Elvira" by the Oak Ridge Boys, *Greatest Hits* (MCA 5496)
- "Lummi Stick Chant" poster

Warm-Up Activities (5 minutes)

Rope Jumping

Arrange the children in scatter formation, each with a rope. Have the children listen to "Elvira" and then jump rope rhythmically to the music, using any of the steps learned. See Grades 4-5: Rhythmic Activities, Lessons 10 through 14, pages 973-982.

Skill-Development Activities (20 minutes)

"Lummi Stick Chant"

Have partners sit cross-legged on the floor, facing each other, about two ft apart.

1. Describe and demonstrate each movement:

    Holding the sticks in a vertical position, tap them to the floor. Cue the children: *Tap down.*

    Hold the sticks parallel and tap them together. Cue the children: *Tap together.*

    Toss the right-hand stick to your partner's right hand and at the same time receive your partner's right-hand stick. Cue the children: *Toss right (left).*

2. Have the children practice each movement individually.
3. Have them practice the movements in sequence. Cue them: *Tap down, tap together, toss right.*
4. Have them repeat, tossing left-hand sticks.

Pattern 1

Arrange the children with partners, sitting and facing each other.

1. Describe and demonstrate pattern 1:

   Tap down, tap together, toss right,

   Tap down, tap together, toss left.

   Repeat four times for a total of four times.

2. Have the children practice pattern 1. Cue the children: *Down, together, toss.*

3. Continue practice until the children can toss and catch easily without missing.

Pattern 2

Continue in scatter formation with the partners seated.

1. Describe and demonstrate pattern 2:

   Tap down, tap together, toss right, toss left.

   Repeat six times for a total of six times.

2. Have the children practice pattern 2. Cue the children: *Down, together, toss, toss.*

Concluding Activities (5 minutes)

Stick Patterns

Have the children perform patterns 1 and 2 with the chant.

LESSONS 24 AND 25
RHYTHM STICKS

Student Objectives

- Perform patterns 1, 2, and 3 of the traditional "Lummi Stick Chant."

Equipment and Materials

- 2 rhythm sticks per child
- 1 short jump rope per child
- "Lummi Stick Chant" poster
- Music: "Elvira," by the Oak Ridge Boys, *Greatest Hits* (MCA 5496)

Warm-Up Activities (5 minutes)

Rope Jumping

Arrange the students in scatter formation each with a rope. See Grades 4-5: Rhythmic Activities, Lessons 10 through 14, pages 973-982. The students listen to "Elvira," then jump rope rhythmically to the music, using any of the steps learned.

Skill-Development Activities (20 minutes)

Tap Front

Arrange the children in scatter formation, sitting cross-legged on the floor, each child with two rhythm sticks.

1. Describe and demonstrate the skill: *To tap front, tilt sticks forward and tap ends to the floor.*
2. Have the children practice the tap front.

Flip

Keep the children in scatter formation, sitting cross-legged on the floor, each child with two rhythm sticks.

1. Describe and demonstrate the skill: *To flip, toss and catch a stick in the air, giving it a half-turn.*
2. Have the children practice the flip.

Patterns 1 and 2

Continue sitting in scatter formation. Have the children repeat patterns 1 and 2 with the "Lummi Stick Chant." See Grades 4-5: Rhythmic Activities, Lesson 23, page 998.

Pattern 3

Continue sitting in scatter formation.

1. Describe and demonstrate pattern 3:

   Tap front, flip,

   Tap down, tap together, toss right, toss left.

   Repeat four times.

2. Have the children practice pattern 3. Cue the children: *Front, flip, down, together, right, left.*

Concluding Activities (5 minutes)

Stick Patterns

Have the children perform patterns 1, 2, and 3 with the "Lummi Stick Chant."

GRADES 4-5

GYMNASTICS

Gymnastics is a favorite activity for many children. Girls at this age may view gymnastics as more feminine and relate gymnastics to dance or cheerleading. By the same token, some boys may dismiss gymnastics as a "female" activity. So remind boys of men's gymnastics in the Olympics and the strength required to be successful. Other children who do not like gymnastics may have had a bad experience with it in the past or feel the skills are too difficult. Encourage all children, and work with those who are having trouble, helping them to master the basic skills. This will help them gain competence and therefore confidence.

Gymnastics enhances many aspects of physical education learning: it can develop fitness, foster cooperation, introduce a variety of skills, and allow children to express creativity. This gymnastics unit builds on the lessons and activities covered in Grades 2-3. If your students have not had the opportunity to build a good base of gymnastics skills, consider using the Grades K-1 and Grades 2-3 lessons instead of these. The lessons are progressive, so that later lessons in the section assume the students have mastered the content of earlier lessons.

We encourage a flexible approach to teaching gymnastics. Teach what you are comfortable with, repeat lessons as needed, and stop at any point and go to a different part of gymnastics. You know best what will work for your situation. So if you feel a part or a particular skill is inappropriate, delete that skill or lesson.

UNIT ORGANIZATION

This level includes tumbling, partner stunts, and small and large equipment. The early lessons review tumbling, introduce new skills, then progress to routines that combine skills. For fourth graders, consider repeating the first seven lessons, instead of progressing to Lessons 8 through 13, as it may be better to save these lessons for experienced fifth graders. Several lessons teaching partner stunts follow. Next, students explore small equipment tasks found in Danish and modern gymnastics. The last several lessons allow the children to explore large equipment. Note that you may be able to use playground equipment for these lessons. Remember, we encourage you to do what is appropriate for your situation. Use the tumbling and large equipment checklists (see the appendix) to evaluate student progress and the effectiveness of your instruction. For a summary of the content of this unit, see table G3.1.

LESSON ORGANIZATION

Lesson 1 teaches a warm-up routine that you will find helpful throughout the unit. Feel free, however, to vary this warm-up, remembering that stretching is important before doing any gymnastics lesson. Note that children enjoy being the "leader" for the warm-up, so select a different child each day to lead the warm-up routine. The next part of each lesson includes the skill development activities, in which you introduce and have students practice new skills. The final section of each lesson are the concluding activities, which often combine skills or activities from previous lessons. See the equipment and materials list at the beginning of each lesson.

TEACHING HINTS

As you well know, practicing skills allows students to master the skill, and repetition is an essential part of practice. Indeed, most children want many turns and do not want to stop at the end of class. You may want to vary practice by introducing a skill, practicing that skill several times for each child, then either introducing a new skill or reviewing a previous skill. Then alternate the two skills for several turns. You can continue this process, adding a new skill and practicing that with previous skills so that you do one turn of four or five skills with one child per group then repeat the sequence with the next child in line. This type of practice is interesting. Suggest to the children waiting in line to verbally repeat the cues used to describe the skills as the other children perform them.

Encourage, recognize, and praise good skill execution. Rather than focusing on learning new and difficult skills, help children focus on mastering and executing skills correctly. This encourages all children to participate fully as well as promotes safety.

SAFETY CONSIDERATIONS

Safety is a primary concern for any gymnastics unit, especially when using equipment. Teach, review, and enforce the safety rules and the class rules. For safety reasons, be aware that there will be times when many students are watching and few are practicing so that you can closely monitor their movements.

By this age, often the most difficult children to keep safe are those who have the highest skill levels, for example, children who participate in gymnastics or dance outside of school. However, you must insist that children who have skills beyond the scope of this unit follow the rules, especially concerning performing only those activities you have assigned, just like everyone else. Although this can cause resentment, one child doing an advanced skill while other children are practicing basic skills can be dangerous. Sometimes it is helpful to simply acknowledge the fact that certain individuals can do more than you will teach. Consider also allowing such a child to demonstrate those skills at a specific time with a parent's written permission. If you address this issue immediately, you may prevent misunderstandings and injuries.

You must establish clear rules for practicing gymnastics. For example, practice only on the mats, have only one person on a mat at a time (unless specifically told otherwise by the teacher), and use equipment only as intended. We recommend dividing the children into as many groups as you have mats and space, keeping groups as small as possible to increase participation opportunities. Have each group sit in a line near the mat, waiting for turns and specific instructions. You may find it helpful to have a carpet square for each waiting child to sit on.

When starting each stunt, call the first child in each group to the mat. Do not allow children to stand on the floor at the end of the mat to begin a task. Instead, as you give instructions, children should stand (sit or lie) on the mat, beginning their turn when you say "Begin." You may want to use cues to regulate the movement, for example "bend, hands down, look at your tummy, roll." Stand so that you can see all children. If the activity requires spotting, you should spot the children. While this means more waiting for turns, it greatly increases safety. When children have learned to take turns, however, you can assign different skills to each mat, assigning one skill that you must spot, while having the children at the other mats do skills that do not require spotting. Remember to place yourself so you can see the other mats while spotting to monitor behavior. Efficient organization allows for maximum practice and safety.

Finally, it is your responsibility to see that you or another responsible adult maintains the gymnastics equipment in good order. You should check the mats and equipment to make sure everything is in good repair each day. In addition, make sure mats are cleaned regularly.

Table G3.1: Unit Plan for Grades 4-5: Gymnastics

Week 8: warm-up routine and gymnastics and tumbling skills	Week 9: tumbling skills
Monday: warm-up routine Tuesday: tumbling Wednesday: tumbling Thursday: tumbling Friday: tumbling	Monday: combining skills Tuesday: pike position, backward pike roll, forward pike roll, and handstand Wednesday: C Jump and diving roll Thursday: shoulder roll and toe-touch jump Friday: tumbling
Week 10: tumbling skills and tumbling checklist	**Week 18: gymnastics skills and movement challenges**
Monday: cartwheel and tumbling sequence Tuesday: tumbling combinations Wednesday: tumbling checklist Thursday: partner stunts Friday: partner stunts	Monday: partner stunts Tuesday: pyramids Wednesday: wands Thursday: hoops Friday: streamers and balls
Week 19: small equipment and large equipment	
Monday: small equipment Tuesday: large equipment Wednesday: large equipment Thursday: large equipment Friday: large equipment and large equipment review	

GYMNASTICS

LESSON 1
WARM-UP

Student Objectives

- Practice the warm-up routine.
- State five important safety rules.

Equipment and Materials

- 1 or more mats (4 ft × 8 ft) per group
- Rules chart

Safety Tips

- Keep close control the first days to establish the rules and a calm atmosphere.
- Children with weak abdominal muscles and poor flexibility should not do the back push-up portion of the back flexibility exercise.

Warm-Up Activities (5 minutes)

Leap and Hop

Arrange the children in a large circle.

1. Tell the children: *Run with large steps, or leap, around the area. Run in the same direction around the circle* (point).
2. *You should run or leap with your toes pointed and land on the ball of the foot.*
3. *Now reverse direction and skip with high hops and large arm swings.*

Skill-Development Activities (20 minutes)

Rules

Gather the children into an information formation.

1. Tell the children the following rules:
   - *Rule 1: Do not put your hands on anyone else, unless you are spotting.*
   - *Rule 2: Only one person on a mat or piece of equipment at a time.*
   - *Rule 3: Always warm up before doing gymnastics.*
   - *Rule 4: Be quiet when teacher is talking.*
   - *Rule 5: Spotting is an important job; when you are a spotter, do a good job.*
2. Give an example of each rule.
3. Describe consequences and other outcomes (injuries, loss of practice time, interruption of learning) of rule infractions.

4. Ask if there are questions about the rules.

Steps for Grades 4-5 Warm-Up Routine: Floor Stretches

Arrange the children in scatter formation. Describe and demonstrate each of the floor stretches. Have the children do four each of the floor stretches.

Straddle Stretches

Sitting with your legs in straddle position (spread wide apart and straight, with the inside of the ankle pointing upward—this is called "turnout"), reach toward one leg with both hands. Keep your legs straight, chin up; don't bounce. Repeat to the opposite leg. For the overhead straddle stretch, reach your opposite arm overhead and stretch down to one foot, then reverse to the other.

Pike Stretches

Sitting with your legs in pike position (legs straight and together, toes pointed), grasp the ankles and pull your chest toward your legs, then sit straight and repeat the stretch with your toes pointed upward (ankles flexed).

Steps for Grades 4-5 Warm-Up Routine: Back Flexibility Stretches

Describe and demonstrate the back flexibility stretches. Have the children do four each of the back flexibility stretches.

Back Arches

Begin by lying on your stomach. Arch your back with your legs straight and together. Lift your head up and away from the mat as far as possible, then your shoulders, chest, and so on, keeping your hips on the mat.

Leg Rollovers

Lie on your back with your arms at your sides and hands palms-down, pressing on the mat. Bend your legs at the knees, and bring your knees over your hips (in the air). Roll back, straightening your legs and pushing with your hands so that your toes touch the mat behind your head.

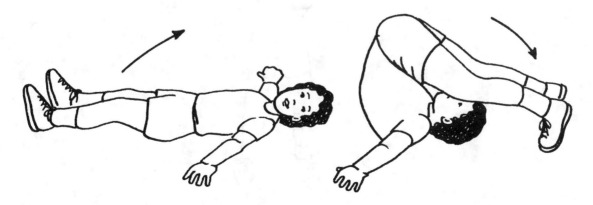

Back Push-Ups

With your feet together and legs bent so that your heels are touching your bottom, bend your arms so that your fingers are under your shoulders and pointed toward your feet. Push your body upward in an arch. Tilt your head back so you can see the mat.

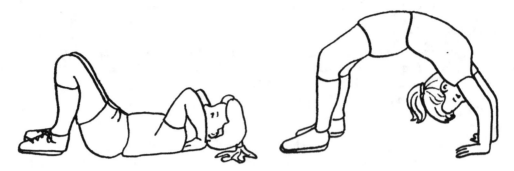

Back Push-Up Spotting

1. *Kneel at the student's side, with your hands placed under the midback and shoulders.*

2. *As the student pushes upward, give support. Do not lift or force the movement; rather, make the child do the work of lifting and allow him or her to arch as much as he or she can.*

3. *If the student's feet are slipping, first try moving the student's heels closer to his or her bottom; next try having someone stand at the student's feet, using his or her feet to brace the student's feet. (Do not stand on the student's feet, just keep them from slipping.)*

Steps for Grades 4-5 Warm-Up Routine: Standing Stretches

Describe and demonstrate the standing stretches. Have the children do eight each direction.

Torso Stretches

Standing with your feet shoulder-width apart, legs straight, and arms extended overhead, reach upward, to the side, back, other side, and front. Then repeat, going the opposite direction. This completes one repetition.

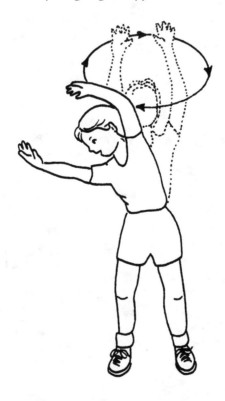

Bent-Leg Hamstring Stretches

Standing with your legs in straddle position, bend and reach toward the toes of one leg, bending that leg while keeping the other leg semistraight (in a lunge position), and reach across your body toward your straight leg. Then repeat, going in the opposite direction. This completes one repetition.

Steps for Grades 4-5 Warm-Up Routine: Endurance Exercises

Describe and demonstrate the endurance exercise parts of the routine. Have the children practice these exercises.

Running and Skipping

Arrange the children in a large circle.

Run for one minute and then skip for one minute, using big movements and lifting your body off the ground as high as possible. (Note: They will have to build up to this. Begin with running 30 seconds, resting 10 to 14 seconds, skipping 30 seconds, resting 10 to 15 seconds, running 30 seconds, resting 10 to 15 seconds, skipping 30 seconds, resting 10 to 15 seconds, gradually reducing rest periods until they are unnecessary.)

Muscle Endurance

Arrange the children in small groups on the mats.

Do up to 30 sit-ups with arms crossed on your chest and legs bent, 10 to 20 regular push-ups, and 10 dorsal back-curls, lying on your stomach with arms and legs extended. To do a dorsal back-curl, lift your arms and legs simultaneously, while arching your back upward, then return to the floor.

Push-up   Sit-up   Dorsal back-curl

Grades 4-5 Warm-Up Routine

Keep the children in small groups on the mats. Cue the children to perform the entire Grades 4-5 Warm-Up Routine straight through as follows:

Floor Stretching

Four straddle stretches right, four left,

Four overhead straddle stretches right, four left, and

Four pike stretches with toes pointed, then repeat four with ankles flexed.

Back Flexibility

Four back arches,

Four leg rollovers, and

Four back push-ups.

Standing Stretches

Four torso stretches, and

Four bent-leg hamstring stretches.

Endurance Exercises

One minute each of running and skipping,

20 sit-ups,

10 push-ups, and

10 dorsal back-curls.

Concluding Activities (5 minutes)

Rules Quiz

Gather the children into an information formation.

1. Discuss the following questions:

   How many people should be tumbling on a mat at one time? (One.) *What is the person who is helping another person do a gymnastics skill called?* (The spotter.)

   In order to understand the skills and hear directions, what must students do while the teacher is talking? (Be quiet and listen.)

   In order to prepare our bodies for gymnastics, help prevent injuries, and learn skills, we must do certain exercises every time before gymnastics. What is this group of exercises called? (Warm-up.)

   Pushing, shoving, and "horseplay" are dangerous, especially in gymnastics. What is the best way to be sure you do not hurt someone else? (Do not touch anyone else, except when spotting.)

2. The quiz should allow you to assess whether the students understand and remember the rules. If they have a problem with a rule, repeat that rule before the next lesson.

G R A D E S 4-5

LESSON 2
TUMBLING

Student Objectives

- Demonstrate the forward roll and the run and takeoff.
- Attempt a straddle roll and a heel slap.
- State two important things to remember about the forward roll.
- Practice a variation of the forward roll.

Equipment and Materials

- 1 or more mats (4 ft × 8 ft) per group

Warm-Up Activities (5 to 7 minutes)

Grades 4-5 Warm-Up Routine

See Grades 4-5: Gymnastics, Lesson 1, page 1011.

Skill-Development Activities (18 to 20 minutes)

Forward Roll

Create small groups, and assign each to a mat.

1. Describe and demonstrate the stunt:

   Bend over and place your hands on the mat shoulder-width apart and, looking at your stomach and bending your arms, shift more and more body weight onto your hands as your legs provide less and less support.

   As your center of gravity moves forward, your body will overbalance and roll forward, hitting the mat on your shoulder blades. Continue to roll in a curved position.

   Bend your legs at the knees and accept weight on your legs as your shoulders leave the mat.

   Return to standing with your arms extended overhead.

2. Have the children practice the forward roll.

Straddle Forward Roll

Arrange partners on the mats.

1. Describe and demonstrate the stunt:

   This is actually two consecutive rolls. You start by doing a forward roll then add the straddle part. Beginning in closed standing position with feet together and arms extended overhead, bend, placing your hands on the mat shoulder-width apart.

   Look at your stomach, bend your arms, and accept more and more of your body weight onto your hands as your legs decrease support.

   As your center of gravity moves forward, your body will overbalance and roll forward, hitting the mat on the shoulder blades. Continue to roll in a curved position.

   Now this stunt begins to differ from a regular forward roll. Keep your legs straight and spread apart in the straddle position, so you land on your legs for the first roll with your feet spread, body bent slightly forward, and arms extended forward.

   Begin the second roll immediately from the straddle position, with your head tucking under and your body moving forward to a shoulder-blade landing.

   Recover to standing with your feet closed, as in the regular forward roll.

   Work with your partner—one partner stands in front of the roller after the roll phase to help him or her recover. Roller, reach out to your partner and try to shake hands as you come up. This will get your arms and weight forward by moving your center of gravity forward.

2. Have the children practice the straddle forward roll.

Backward Roll

Continue with the same setup, except partners are not necessary.

    1. Describe and demonstrate the stunt:

> *Begin, standing, arms extended overhead (palms up) and your back toward the length of the mat and your chin moving to your chest. Lower your body to a tuck position by bending the knees. Overbalance your body backward to begin the roll, and remain in tuck position as your shoulders and hands contact the mat.*

> *Push with your hands to lift your body (hips, legs, and torso) over your head. Your head and neck should not support your weight and you should touch the mat as little as possible.*

> *As your feet touch the mat, straighten your arms until your feet are supporting your weight. Rise to standing with your arms extended overhead.*

    2. Have the children practice the backward roll.

Straddle Backward Roll

Continue with the same setup.

    1. Describe and demonstrate the stunt:

> *Begin, standing in a straddle balance position, with your back toward the length of the mat.*

> *Move your hands between your legs as your torso moves forward to lower your body, with your hips moving back and down, until your seat touches the mat.*

Move your hands to your shoulders as in the regular backward roll. Immediately roll your body backward, while your legs remain in the straddle position.

Recover to the straddle balance position (as shown in figure below).

2. Have the children practice the straddle backward roll.

3. Have the children extend the skill by beginning in closed standing position and rolling to a straddle balance, then rolling again from the straddle balance to a closed standing position (two rolls).

Heel Slap

Continue with the same setup.

1. Describe and demonstrate the stunt:

    The object is to touch your heels with your hands just under your seat, then land on both feet.

    Jump up from both feet, lifting both feet toward your seat while reaching back with your arms.

2. Have the children practice the heel slap.

Run and Takeoff

Continue with the same setup.

1. Describe and demonstrate the stunt:

    Many sports use this movement (e.g., springboard diving).

    Begin with several quick (running) steps leading to a hurdle.

    To hurdle raise one leg so that your thigh is parallel to (flat as) the ground and your lower leg is at a 90-degree angle to the thigh (like the corner of a square).

    Reach your arms high overhead as your body lifts off the ground. Both your raised arms and lifted thigh help your body gain momentum. Momentum helps you gain height in the hurdle.

    Land from the hurdle on both feet (spread about shoulder-width apart).

    Follow the landing immediately with a jump to full extension.

    This movement can come right before a tumbling stunt or end with a jump.

    Today, I want you to practice finishing with a jump and landing on two feet.

2. Have the children practice the run and takeoff.

Needle Scale

Continue with the same setup, except match partners; one partner practices the needle scale while the other helps balance by gently holding the knee of the nonsupporting leg.

1. Describe and demonstrate the stunt:

    The object is to stand on one foot and grasp the ankle of your supporting leg, making your legs move as close to a split position as possible.

    Begin in a scale, balancing on one leg, with your arms to the sides and your other leg extended to the rear.

    Bend your torso and grasp the ankle as you lift your nonsupporting leg as high as possible into the air, balance, then recover by reversing the movements.

2. Have the children practice the needle scale.

Splits

Continue with the same setup.

1. Tell the children: *A split is any one of several positions in which the legs are fully extended away from each other.*
2. Describe and demonstrate the straddle split and the regular split.

Straddle Split

Begin in the straddle balance position and end with your legs extended as far apart as possible. If you are very flexible, recover into a regular split. Otherwise, lean forward, taking your weight on your arms and chest, then swinging both legs together to the rear to lie on your front.

Regular Split

Begin with your feet together in a "T" position, where one foot faces front and the other foot is perpendicular to and behind the front foot, with the feet meeting the heel of the front foot to the arch of the rear foot. Slowly slide one foot forward and the other backward, until your legs are fully extended.

Note: A child may also do regular splits with only one leg moving, while the other leg remains stationary. To recover, the child leans forward with the torso over the front leg and swings the back leg around to the side until it is touching the front leg.

Discussion

Arrange the children in a semicircle. Discuss what the children have learned today:

What should you remember about the forward roll? (Head tucked, weight on hands.)
How is the straddle forward roll different from the forward roll? (Legs apart.)

LESSON 3
TUMBLING

Student Objectives

- Perform two variations of the forward and backward rolls.
- Attempt one split and one new balance activity.

Equipment and Materials

- 1 or more mats (4 ft × 8 ft) per group
- Background music (optional)

Warm-Up Activities (5 to 7 minutes)

Grades 4-5 Warm-Up Routine

See Grades 4-5: Gymnastics, Lesson 1, page 1011.

Skill-Development Activities (18 to 20 minutes)

Donkey Kick

Create small groups, and assign each to a mat.

1. Describe and demonstrate the stunt:

   The object of this task is to get both feet off of the mat at the same time and to support all of your body weight with your hands.

   Begin by standing in the middle of the mat, facing the length of the mat. Place both hands on the mat, about shoulder-width apart.

   Keep your arms straight, but bend your legs slightly. Let your hands carry some of your body weight.

   As you kick your feet up and back, take all your weight on your hands. Keep your eyes focused on the mat, directly between your hands.

   Be careful not to kick very hard, as this may cause overbalancing, and you may flip over onto your back. The purpose is to get both feet off the ground and support your weight with your arms, not to get into a vertical position (45 degrees is safer).

2. Have the children practice the donkey kick.

Tripod

Continue with the same setup.

1. Describe and have a child demonstrate the stunt:

   Begin in a squat, with your hands and arms placed on the mat outside your knees and legs.

   Bend forward until your forehead (at the hairline) touches the mat. Your head will serve as a balance point but will support very little weight.

   Bend your arms and make your knees touch your elbows. Support most of your body weight with your arms.

   Stop moving when your knees are resting on your elbows, your head is touching the mat, and your feet are off the mat.

   Remember, support most of your weight on your arms. Your head touches the mat but does not support much body weight.

2. Have the children practice the tripod.

Elbow-Knee Balance

Continue with the same setup.

1. Describe and have a child demonstrate the stunt:

   Squat and place your hands on the mat, arms inside your legs and knees touching your elbows. Hold your head up; looking straight ahead helps.

   Shift your weight from your feet to your hands, and rest your knees on your elbows.

   The critical point is to maintain balance with only your hands supporting your body weight.

2. Have the children practice the elbow-knee balance.

Knee Scale

Continue with small groups at the mats.

1. Describe and demonstrate the stunt:

   Begin on all-fours, with your knees together and hands about four in apart.

   Extend one leg to the rear with your toes pointed, lifting it as high as possible and looking forward, holding your head high.

2. Have the children practice the knee scale.

Log Roll

Continue with the same setup.

1. Describe and demonstrate the stunt:

    Lie on your stomach with your arms and legs extended.

    Begin to move by turning your head and rotating your shoulders and torso.

    Roll several turns with your body as a unit.

2. Have the children practice the log roll.

Skill Practice

Have the students practice the forward roll, straddle forward roll, backward roll, straddle backward roll, heel slap, run and takeoff, needle scale, and regular and straddle split. See Grades 4-5: Gymnastics, Lesson 2, page 1013.

Concluding Activities (5 minutes)

Skill Review

Gather the children into an information formation.

1. Ask the following questions:

    Which of the skills we practiced today was the most difficult for you?

    Which was the easiest?

    Why are some easier than others?

    Are the same skills easy for everyone?

2. Lead a discussion about body build, flexibility, and strength as factors in performance.

3. Ask each child to demonstrate a favorite skill, one from each mat at a time.

LESSON 4
TUMBLING

Student Objectives

- Demonstrate balancing in different positions and on different body parts.
- Practice and refine the basic rolls.
- Observe and evaluate the technique of a partner.
- Create a movement sequence.

Equipment and Materials

- 1 or more mats (4 ft × 8 ft) per group

Warm-Up Activities (5 to 7 minutes)

Grades 4-5 Warm-Up Routine

See Grades 4-5: Gymnastics, Lesson 1, page 1011.

Skill-Development Activities (18 to 20 minutes)

Create small groups, and assign each group to a mat for each activity.

1. Describe and demonstrate the two-knee balance, V-sit, 360-degree turn, and knee scale.
2. Have the children practice each stunt.

Two-Knee Balance

Kneeling with feet extended behind and hips straight, lift your feet off the mat and balance on your knees only.

V-Sit

Sit and lift your legs straight and together as high as possible, with your torso forming the other side of the V.

360-Degree Turn

Begin, standing still and straight. Bend your knees and rotate your arms and torso away from the direction you are planning to turn. Jump up and turn your head, torso, and arms as hard as possible in the direction of the turn. Land on both feet.

Knee Scale

See Grades 4-5: Gymnastics, Lesson 3, page 1020.

Skill Practice

Create partners within the small groups, and continue with each group at a mat.

1. Have the students practice the forward roll, straddle forward roll, backward roll, straddle backward roll, heel slap, run and takeoff, needle scale, and regular and straddle splits (See Grades 4-5: Gymnastics, Lesson 2, page 1013). Say to the students: *Observe your partner to see if he or she is using the correct technique.*

2. Ask the children: *Are there any pointers you can give your partner about technique? For example, you might say "Your head was tucked on the roll, but you crossed your ankles."*

Concluding Activities (5 minutes)

Movement Challenges That Combine Skills

1. Challenge the children with the following movement combinations:

   A forward roll, immediately followed with a backward roll

   Backward roll from straddle to straddle, then a straddle forward roll

   A regular scale into a needle scale

2. Have the children create their own combinations.

LESSON 5
TUMBLING

Student Objectives

- Change directions while skipping.
- Combine running and leaping and running and jumping.

Equipment and Materials

- 1 or more mats (4 ft × 8 ft) per group
- 1 yardstick or ruler
- Paper and pencil

Warm-Up Activities (5 to 7 minutes)

Grades 4-5 Warm-Up Routine

See Grades 4-5: Gymnastics, Lesson 1, page 1011.

Skill-Development Activities (18 to 20 minutes)

Skipping Backward

Keep the children in scatter formation.

1. Describe and demonstrate the skill: *Step back, hop, step back, hop.*
2. Have the children practice skipping backward.

Skipping Sideways

Make sure the children are still in scatter formation.

1. Describe and demonstrate the skill: *Step across the forward leg, hop, step, hop, step across the forward leg, hop.*
2. Have the children practice skipping sideways.
3. Have them practice skipping in each direction.

Change Directions

Make sure the children are still in scatter formation. Introduce changing directions while skipping.

1. Tell the children: *Without breaking rhythm, turn toward the open side of your body (the direction you can turn without moving your feet).*
2. Have the children practice skipping and changing directions.

Run and Jump

Make sure the children are still in scatter formation.

1. Describe and demonstrate the skill:

    You can jump for height or distance. Begin running, take off from one foot (a running step) and land on both feet.

    If the purpose is height, the angle of your takeoff should be steeper, and your arms should move straight up and remain overhead on the follow-through.

    If the purpose is distance, the angle of your takeoff should be lower, and your arms should reach forward toward your intended landing area.

2. Have the children practice running and jumping.

Leap

Make sure the children are still in scatter formation.

1. Describe and demonstrate the skill:

    A leap is an exaggerated running step with a very long nonsupporting phase.

    Take off from one foot and land on the other foot, lifting high into the air and spreading your legs into a split-like position. The arms can be held at shoulder height, to the side, or used to lift the body by working in oppositon.

2. Have the children practice leaping.

Run and Leap

Create small groups, and assign each to a mat.

1. Describe and demonstrate the skill: *Take several small steps then a long exaggerated one, (leap) and continue with several steps, another leap, and so on.*

2. Have the children practice running and leaping.

Jump From Knees

Continue with the same setup.

1. Describe and demonstrate the stunt: *Kneeling on the mat, with your arms extended in front of your chest, swing your arms down and backward, then quickly upward as your legs straighten and push against the mat to lift your body to a standing position.*
2. Have the children practice the jump from knees.

Donkey Kick

See Grades 4-5: Gymnastics, Lesson 3, page 1019.

Skill Practice

Assign each child a partner within the groups at the mats.

Have the students practice the forward roll, straddle forward roll, backward roll, straddle backward roll, heel slap, and regular and straddle split. Say to the students: *Observe your partner to see if he or she is using the correct technique.* See Grades 4-5: Gymnastics, Lesson 2, page 1013.

Concluding Activities (5 minutes)

Movement Challenges That Combine Skills

Have the children create their own combinations.

Split Measurement

Measure the distance from the floor to the bottom of the leg at the hip for each child in either split position. Record. You can use this later to show improvement. Reassure the children that as they work on this skill, they will get better at it.

LESSON 6
TUMBLING

Student Objectives

- Practice and refine previously introduced skills.
- Create a movement sequence.

Equipment and Materials

- 1 or more mats (4 ft × 8 ft) per group

Warm-Up Activities (5 to 7 minutes)

Grades 4-5 Warm-Up Routine

See Grades 4-5: Gymnastics, Lesson 1, page 1011.

Skill-Development Activities (18 to 20 minutes)

Skill Practice

Arrange the children in small groups at the mats.

1. Have the students practice running and leaping, and running and jumping. See Grades 4-5: Gymnastics, Lesson 5, page 1025.

2. Have them practice the donkey kick and knee scale. See Grades 4-5: Gymnastics, Lesson 3, pages 1019 and 1020.

3. Have them practice the forward roll, straddle forward roll, backward roll, straddle backward roll, heel slap, needle scale, and regular and straddle splits. See Grades 4-5: Gymnastics, Lesson 2, page 1013.

Movement Challenges That Combine Skills

Have the children create their own combinations.

Concluding Activities (5 minutes)

Skill Test

Give an informal skill test, to make sure most of the students can do the donkey kick. This is necessary for the next lesson. For those children having trouble, spend time working with them individually on the donkey kick. The other children can continue creating their own combinations.

LESSON 7
TUMBLING

Student Objectives

- Demonstrate an arm support, with or without help.
- Explain what makes the backward pike roll and the forward pike roll different from the backward and forward rolls.
- Describe the spotting technique for the handstand.

Equipment and Materials

- 1 or more mats (4 ft × 8 ft) per group

Warm-Up Activities (5 to 7 minutes)

Grades 4-5 Warm-Up Routine

See Grades 4-5: Gymnastics, Lesson 1, page 1011.

Skill-Development Activities (18 to 20 minutes)

Pike Position

Create small groups, and assign each to a mat.

1. Describe and demonstrate the skill: *In the pike position, you keep your legs almost straight and together and bend your body at the waist so that your hands reach toward your feet.*
2. Present the following challenge: *Stand (sit) in pike position.*

Backward Pike Roll

Continue with the same setup.

1. Describe and demonstrate the stunt:

   Begin, sitting with your legs straight and feet together.

   Reach forward to your toes and, using momentum gained from going forward, roll backward, keeping your legs straight. This requires strength and flexibility.

   Finish by pushing up to standing. Keep your knees as straight as possible.

2. Have the children practice the backward pike roll.

Forward Pike Roll

Continue with the same setup.

1. Describe and demonstrate the stunt: *Begin, standing with your legs straight and feet together, roll, and finish, sitting with your legs extended forward.*

2. Have the children practice the forward pike roll.

Handstand

Continue with small groups at the mats.

1. Describe and demonstrate the stunt:

    Stand with your arms overhead and one leg extended forward (this will be the support leg).

    Step forward on the support leg, reaching for the mat with your arms, lowering your torso and keeping your body in a straight line (similar to the scale) with your nonsupporting leg.

    Take your weight on your arms as you place your hands shoulder-width apart on the mat.

    Then kick your supporting leg upward until your entire body forms a straight line.

Important: Your back should not have a large arch; instead, you should lift your legs as high as possible to eliminate any arch.

2. Have the children practice the handstand with two children as spotters for each tumbler.

Spotting for the Handstand

1. Describe and demonstrate spotting for the handstand: *When spotting the handstand, it's best to stand to the performer's side, with your hand toward the performer's back, providing support under the shoulder (in case the arms "give out") to protect the head, and the other arm on the front of the thigh.*

2. When you use children as spotters, place one on each side of the performer: *Use two spotters for each performer, one on each side.*

Jump From Knees

See Grades 4-5: Gymnastics, Lesson 5, page 1026.

Straddle Forward Roll and Straddle Backward Roll

See Grades 4-5: Gymnastics, Lesson 2, pages 1014 and 1015.

Concluding Activities (5 minutes)

Skill Review

Give each child an opportunity to show a favorite task that was not practiced today. Do this in groups to save time.

LESSON 8
TUMBLING

Student Objectives

- Practice the handstand and rolls.
- Attempt a diving roll and a C-jump.

Equipment and Materials

- 1 or more mats (4 ft × 8 ft) per group
- Pillows, blankets, or additional mats for barriers
- Rope

Safety Tip

- Only students who can do the donkey kick and handstand, showing ability to support their weight on their hands, should be allowed to try the diving roll.

Warm-Up Activities (5 to 7 minutes)

Grades 4-5 Warm-Up Routine

See Grades 4-5: Gymnastics, Lesson 1, page 1011.

Skill-Development Activities (18 to 20 minutes)

C-Jump

Create small groups, and assign each to a mat.

1. Describe and demonstrate the stunt: *Jumping as high as possible, throw your arms back overhead, curve your back, bend your legs, lean your head back, and try to touch your feet to your head.*
2. Have the children practice the C-jump.

Forward Pike Roll

See Grades 4-5: Gymnastics, Lesson 7, page 1029.

Diving Roll

Arrange the children who can do a handstand on one to two mats to learn this skill. Other children should continue to practice the handstand at their mats.

   This is a variation of the forward pike roll. The roll begins with a jump (or a run and jump), going immediately into the forward pike roll (catching the weight on the arms). At first have the child put his or her hands on the mat and jump with both legs upward as in the donkey kick (rather than going into the squat) to begin the roll.

   1. Describe and demonstrate the stunt. We use a sequence of skills to lead up to the diving roll:

       First, you place your hands on the mat and kick both legs upward as in the donkey kick.

       Once you can do that, run, place both hands on the mat, and kick both legs upward as in the donkey kick.

       Once you can run and donkey kick, run and perform a forward pike roll.

   2. Have the children practice the diving roll.

Handstand

See Grades 4-5: Gymnastics, Lesson 7, page 1029.

Concluding Activities (5 minutes)

Diving Roll

Using a rope (held loosely) or other barrier on some mats, ask the children to practice the diving roll over the barrier. Make sure the barrier is soft or one that will fall if touched by the children. Folded mats make excellent barriers, as do pillows, rolled blankets, and so on. For children not wanting to try this, have one or more mats available for practicing other activities.

LESSON 9
TUMBLING

Student Objectives

- Practice and refine shoulder rolls, forward and backward rolls (in pike and straddle positions), toe-touch jumps, and handstands.

Equipment and Materials

- 1 or more mats (4 ft × 8 ft) per group

Warm-Up Activities (5 to 7 minutes)

Grades 4-5 Warm-Up Routine

See Grades 4-5: Gymnastics, Lesson 1, page 1011.

Skill-Development Activities (18 to 20 minutes)

Shoulder Roll

Create small groups, and assign each to a mat.

1. Describe and demonstrate the stunt:

   Sit with your legs extended and your back to the length of the mat.

   Reach forward to your toes, and then use this momentum to roll backward immediately, turning your head to the side.

   Bend the leg opposite the direction of the way you're turning your head at the knee, and place your knee on the mat near the back of your head, as close as possible to your shoulder.

   Support your weight with your hands and one knee, with your other leg extended in a knee scale position.

2. Have the children practice the shoulder roll.

Toe-Touch Jump

Continue with the same setup.

1. Describe and demonstrate the stunt:

   Stand and jump up, lifting your legs parallel to the ground in a straddle position. Make your feet spread as far apart as possible.

Reach for your toes with your hands, keeping your head high and looking straight ahead.

2. Have the children practice the toe-touch jump.

Skill Practice

Assign partners within groups at the mats.

1. Have the students practice the forward and backward rolls (in pike and straddle positions), the C-jump, and the handstand. See Grades 4-5: Gymnastics, Lessons 2, 7, and 8, pages 1014, 1015, 1028, 1029, 1031, and 1032.

2. Ask the children to do the following tasks:
    Observe your partner to see if he or she is using the correct technique.

    Are there any pointers you can provide your partner about technique?

Concluding Activities (5 minutes)

Movement Challenges

Continue having the children work in groups at the mats. Challenge the children with the following combinations:

C-jump, backward roll, donkey kick.

Forward pike roll, shoulder roll, knee scale.

Make your own combination.

LESSON 10
TUMBLING

Student Objectives

- Practice a 360-degree turn combined with the run and takeoff, and straddle forward roll combined with the regular or straddle splits.
- Attempt a backward roll extension, handstand forward roll, and knee turn.
- Explain how the handstand forward roll is different from the forward roll.
- Explain how the backward roll extension is different from the backward roll.

Equipment and Materials

- 1 or more mats (4 ft × 8 ft) per group

Warm-Up Activities (5 to 7 minutes)

Grades 4-5 Warm-Up Routine

See Grades 4-5: Gymnastics, Lesson 1, page 1011.

Skill-Development Activities (18 to 20 minutes)

Handstand Forward Roll

Create small groups, and assign each to a mat.

1. Describe and demonstrate the stunt:

   This is an extension of the regular handstand, with the addition of movements that begin after you have achieved balance.

   From a handstand, begin to roll by tucking your head (look at the ceiling or sky) and slightly bending your arms.

   Keep gradually bending your arms until your shoulder blades touch the mat. From here continue just like in a forward roll to standing.

2. Have the children practice the handstand forward roll, using the same spotting as for the handstand (see Grades 4-5: Gymnastics, Lesson 7, page 1030).

Knee Turn

Continue with the same setup, but two students can do this on the mat at a time.

1. Describe and demonstrate the stunt:

   Step backward onto a bent leg, which will continue to bend until the knee touches the mat.

Turn your body toward the open side, and begin to bend your front leg until both knees are together and on the mat.

Your feet should be as far apart as possible, with your front leg flat on the mat.

Your back leg is going to become your front leg as your body continues to turn and that knee lifts off the mat (the foot remains on the mat).

Stand by putting your weight on the "new" front leg. Extend the other leg backward.

2. Have the children practice the knee turn. Cue the children: *Step back, down, other knee in, turn and lift, stand.*

Backward Roll Extension

Continue with small groups, each at a mat, working with one child at a time.

1. Describe and demonstrate the stunt:

    This roll begins like any back roll. As your hips move directly over your head, push with your arms to extension so your body is in a handstand momentarily.

    Then let your feet drop to the mat and your body return to a standing position.

2. Demonstrate spotting for the backward roll extension: *Spot as for the handstand, with one hand under the shoulder protecting the head and the other hand on the ankle lifting the body upward. Timing is critical on this movement: the push must come just as the body moves over the arms.*

3. Have the children practice the backward roll extension with one tumbler and two spotters.

360-Degree Turn Combined With Run and Takeoff

Continue with small groups at the mats.

1. Describe and demonstrate the combination:

    To increase momentum, run and take off before the turn. In order for this to help, you must move continuously after the taking off.

As your takeoff ends, squat and immediately jump and turn.

2. Have the children practice the combination.

Straddle Forward Roll Combined With Splits

Continue with the same setup.

1. Describe and demonstrate the combinations:

   At the middle of the straddle forward roll, when your feet are touching the mat and spread wide, stop the roll.

   For the straddle split, lower your body closer to the mat, and for the front split, make your body face your preferred side and then lower it to the mat.

2. Have the children practice the combinations.

Concluding Activities (5 minutes)

Stunt Sequence

Put the mats in a long row.

1. Ask the children to perform the following sequence: *forward roll, straddle forward roll, forward roll, and forward pike roll.*

2. When the first person is finished with the second roll (the straddle forward roll), start the second person, and so forth.

Discussion

Arrange the children in a semicircle. Discuss what the children have learned today:

What new stunts did we learn today? (Combinations.)

How is the handstand forward roll different from the forward roll? (More momentum.)

How is the backward roll extension different from the backward roll? (More difficult, less momentum.)

LESSON 11
TUMBLING

Student Objectives

- Demonstrate two forward and two backward rolls, one additional roll, a handstand, and two different jumps.
- Practice the cartwheel.
- State two things to remember about the technique for the cartwheel.

Equipment and Materials

- 1 or more mats (4 ft × 8 ft) per group

Safety Tip

- Allow only children who can do a good handstand without help to attempt the cartwheel.

Warm-Up Activities (5 to 7 minutes)

Grades 4-5 Warm-Up Routine

See Grades 4-5: Gymnastics, Lesson 1, page 1011.

Skill-Development Activities (18 to 20 minutes)

Cartwheel

Create small groups, and assign each to a mat. Children should be grouped by those who can do the handstand and those who need to continue to practice the handstand.

1. Describe and demonstrate the stunt:

    The cartwheel is a side entry and exit to the handstand. You should not try it until you can do a good handstand without help.

    Begin with one side facing the length of the mat, your arms extended overhead, and your weight on your back foot (away from the movement), with your front foot pointed toward the length of the mat.

    Turn your head and look down the length of the mat to a spot several inches beyond the extended toe. Lean toward the extended toe and step on that foot as your other foot leaves the mat. Make your arms continue to move down until your front hand touches the mat and supports your weight.

    As your other hand touches the mat, both feet should be in the air. Focus your eyes on the mat directly between your hands.

    Keep moving your feet overhead until you are in a handstand (with legs in a straddle).

Then keep moving your legs over your body. As your first foot touches the mat, your far hand leaves the mat. Say to yourself, "Hand, hand, foot, foot."

Return to standing, with your arms extended overhead.

2. Have the children practice the cartwheel. Cue the children: *Hand, hand, foot, foot.*

Spotting for the Cartwheel

1. Stand behind the child with arms crossed (have on the top the arm in the direction of the cartwheel; e.g., for a cartwheel to the right, the right arm crosses over the top of the left arm) and hands on the waist of the child.

2. You can support and control the movement, but you must watch for bent legs (they can kick you!).

Front-to-Back Roll Sequence

Continue with small groups at the mats.

1. Describe and demonstrate the sequence: *Do not stand up at the end of the forward roll but rather, in a squat position, simply turn to face the other direction and do a back roll from the squat.*

2. Have the children practice the front-to-back roll sequence.

Concluding Activities (5 minutes)

Stunt Sequence

Line up the mats in a long line. Line up all children and stagger their starts.

Ask the children to complete the following sequence: handstand forward roll (spot if necessary), straddle forward roll to backward roll, to straddle back roll, to split.

Discussion

Arrange children in a semicircle. Discuss what the children have learned today:

What are two important things to remember about the cartwheel? (Hand, hand, foot, foot.)

What should you remember about the placement of your hands and feet on the mat? (All should be on the mat in a line.)

Is there a time when both hands and both feet are on the mat? (No.)

Is there a time when only the hands are on the mat? (Yes.)

Can someone show us the correct placement of the hands and feet?

Why is this placement sequence (hand, hand, foot, foot) important? (Provides support for balance.)

GYMNASTICS

LESSON 12
TUMBLING

Student Objectives

- Combine two or more tumbling skills.

Equipment and Materials

- 1 or more mats (4 ft × 8 ft) per group

Warm-Up Activities (5 to 7 minutes)

Grades 4-5 Warm-Up Routine

See Grades 4-5: Gymnastics, Lesson 1, page 1011.

Skill-Development Activities (18 to 20 minutes)

Tumbling Combinations

Create three or more groups, and place each group at a pair of mats lined up end to end. Remember, the smaller the group size the more participation opportunities each child will have. Call out the following combinations for the children in each group to take turns attempting:

Forward roll to backward roll

Handstand roll to forward pike roll

C-jump to knee scale to donkey kick

Run and takeoff to diving roll

Straddle forward roll to forward pike roll

Backward pike roll to straddle pike roll

Cartwheel to needle scale

Shoulder roll to knee scale

Jump from knees to forward pike roll

Concluding Activities (5 minutes)

Movement Sequences

Continue with same setup. Ask each child to create a sequence or combination and show to the group, if there is time.

LESSON 13
TUMBLING

Student Objectives

- Perform the skills listed on the evaluation checklist.

Equipment and Materials

- 1 or more mats (4 ft × 8 ft) per group
- Grades 4-5: Checklist for Tumbling (appendix)

Warm-Up Activities (5 to 7 minutes)

Grades 4-5 Warm-Up Routine

See Grades 4-5: Gymnastics, Lesson 1, page 1011.

Skill-Development Activities (23 to 25 minutes)

Tumbling Checklist

Arrange the children at the mats in the order in which they appear on your list. Use Tumbling Checklist, Grades 4-5: Gymnastics for the evaluation (appendix).

1. Ask each child to perform each skill individually, one following another as quickly as you can watch them.
2. Allow spotting when children request it.

Concluding Activities

None.

GRADES 4-5

LESSON 14
PARTNER STUNTS

Student Objectives

- Identify at least six partner stunts.
- Demonstrate three or more partner stunts.

Equipment and Materials

- 1 or more mats (4 ft × 8 ft) per group

Safety Tip

- Match children to partners of equal size.
- Remind children to be careful because they would feel bad if they hurt someone.

Warm-Up Activities (5 to 7 minutes)

Grades 4-5 Warm-Up Routine

See Grades 4-5: Gymnastics, Lesson 1, page 1011.

Skill-Development Activities (18 to 20 minutes)

Wheelbarrow

Pair up the children, and assign two or three pairs to each mat.

1. Describe and have two children demonstrate the stunt:

   One person gets into the front support position, and the partner lifts that person's legs.

   Both of you walk forward, the front person using arms and the other using legs.

2. Have the children practice the wheelbarrow.

Double Roll

Continue with the same setup.

1. Describe and demonstrate the stunt:

   The first child lies on the floor with knees bent and legs shoulder-width apart, feet flat on the mat. The second child stands with one foot on each side of the first child's head, facing the first child's feet.

   The second child bends over and grasps the ankles of the first child. The first child grasps the ankles of the second child.

Carefully and slowly the second child lowers his or her head to the mat and does a forward roll, still grasping the ankles of the first child.

The first child, still holding the ankles of the second child, sits up and gradually moves to a stand.

You should end up back in the starting position, but reversed so the opposite child is on the mat. Repeat.

With practice this becomes a continuous (fluid) motion with no definite stopping points.

2. Have the children practice the double roll.

Back-to-Back Get-Up

Continue with partners at the mats.

1. Describe and demonstrate the stunt:

   Remember this stunt from when you were younger? We are doing the same skill, but now that you are older and more skilled, we are starting from a standing position.

   Standing back-to-back, lock elbows with your partner and sit with your knees bent and your heels close to your seats.

   Push against each other and return to the start position.

2. Have the children practice the back-to-back get-up.

Flying Angel

Create pairs of partners at the mats so that one pair can spot the other pair.

1. Describe and demonstrate the stunt:

   The person providing support is called the "base." The base stands with feet more than shoulder-width apart and knees bent.

   The other partner, the "top," mounts the base by stepping onto the right thigh of the base with the right leg and onto the left thigh of the base with the left leg. The base grasps the knees of the person mounting.

   The top should stand tall with a slight arch in the back, and the base should be in a semisquat position.

2. Have the children practice the flying angel with one pair spotting another pair.

Spotting for the Flying Angel

Use four volunteers to demonstrate spotting for the flying angel: *Spotters stand on each side of the base, helping the top mount and balance by lifting at the shoulder or the elbow and holding one hand on the top's hip.*

Caterpillar

Arrange the children at the mats in groups of three (or four).

1. Describe and have three (or four) children demonstrate the stunt:

   Line up and hold hands, one hand reaching forward and one hand reaching backward between your legs to the students in front of and behind you.

   The first person in the line bends and performs a forward roll to a sitting position.

   The next person walks over the first person and then rolls to a sitting position, and so on until all in the group are sitting.

2. Have the children at each mat practice the caterpillar.

3. Have the children make one long caterpillar line. Encourage everyone in the class to get into the sitting position for the caterpillar without breaking the line!

Three-Person Pyramid

Continue with groups of three. If you have a group of four, one student can spot.

1. Describe and have three children demonstrate the stunt:

   Two children serve as the base, getting on hands and knees as close together as possible.

   The third child mounts these two by placing a foot on the hips of one base, then stepping up and placing the other foot on the small of the back of the other base.

2. Have the children practice the three-person pyramid.

Concluding Activities (5 minutes)

Centipede

Place all the mats in a row. Review how to do the centipede by having a small group of children demonstrate. (See instructions, Grades 2-3: Gymnastics, Lesson 16, page 661.)

Discussion

Arrange the children in a semicircle. Discuss what the children have learned today:

   What stunts did we learn today? (Wheelbarrow, double roll, back-to-back get-up, flying angel, caterpillar, and three-person pyramid.)

Which stunt could you use to develop arm strength and endurance? (Wheelbarrow.)

Which stunt requires leg strength? (Back-to-back get-up.)

Which stunt requires good balance? (Flying angel.)

LESSON 15
PARTNER STUNTS

Student Objectives

- Attempt three new partner stunts.
- Name at least eight partner stunts.

Equipment and Materials

- 1 or more mats (4 ft × 8 ft) per group

Warm-Up Activities (5 to 7 minutes)

Grades 4-5 Warm-Up Routine

See Grades 4-5: Gymnastics, Lesson 1, page 1011.

Skill-Development Activities (18 to 20 minutes)

Triple Roll

Create groups of three, and assign each group to a mat.

1. Describe and have three children demonstrate the stunt:

   All three of you get down on all-fours about three ft apart, facing the same side of the mat.

   The middle person begins to roll to the right, the right child hops over the middle person and rolls toward the left person, who jumps to the middle over the rolling person.

   Continue.

2. Have the children practice the triple roll.

Jump-Through

Continue with groups of three at the mats.

1. Describe and demonstrate the stunt:

   Hold hands to form a circle.

   One of you jumps over the joined arms of the other two children, who help lift the jumper's weight.

Take turns jumping.

2. Have the children practice the jump-through.

Shoulder Balance

Arrange pairs of partners on the mats.

1. Describe and have two children demonstrate the stunt:

   One person (the base) lies flat on his or her back with knees bent.

   The other partner, the top, stands between the knees of the base, leans forward, and rests his or her shoulders on the extended arms of the base.

   The top holds the base's knees and kicks his or her legs up to a handstand position.

2. Have the children practice the shoulder balance with one pair spotting another pair.

Spotting for the Shoulder Balance

Have four children demonstrate the spotting technique:

   Spotters stand on each side of the base near the waist of the base.

   They guide and balance the top by holding the top's thighs and shoulders, being careful not to interfere with the base's grasp on the top.

Concluding Activities (5 minutes)

Discussion

Arrange the children in a semicircle. Discuss what the children have learned today:

   What partner stunts did we learn yesterday? (Caterpillar and three-person pyramid.)

   What new partner stunts did we learn today? (Shoulder balance, jump-through, triple roll.)

   Which is the best stunt you and your partner can do? Which is the hardest? Show me your best!

LESSON 16
PARTNER STUNTS

Student Objectives

- Work cooperatively in partner stunt practice.
- Demonstrate one partner stunt.

Equipment and Materials

- 1 or more mats (4 ft × 8 ft) per group
- 1 playground or foam ball (8 1/2-13 in.) per group

Warm-Up Activities (5 to 7 minutes)

Grades 4-5 Warm-Up Routines

See Grades 4-5: Gymnastics, Lesson 1, page 1011.

Skill-Development Activities (18 to 20 minutes)

Back Support

Arrange pairs of partners on the mats.

1. Describe and have two children demonstrate the stunt:

   One person (the base) lies flat with legs straight and extended at a 45-degree angle. The other person stands at the feet of the base, facing away.

   The base places her or his feet on the lower back of the top person.

   The base and the top grasp hands, and the base lifts the top off the ground. You keep your balance with the top directly over the base.

2. Have the children practice the back support with one pair practicing on a mat and another pair spotting them.

Spotting for the Back Support

Describe and have four children demonstrate the spotting technique: *The spotters stand on each side of the base, each gently holding a shoulder and thigh of the top.*

Ball Lift

Continue with partners at the mats.

1. Describe and have two children demonstrate the stunt:

   Partners lie on the ground on their stomachs, facing each other, with a playground ball between and touching their heads.

The partners try to stand and not allow the ball to fall. Do not use your hands.

2. Have the children practice the ball lift.

Side Stand

Arrange pairs of partners at the mats.

    1. Describe and have two children demonstrate the stunt:

        One person gets down on all-fours to serve as the base.

        The top stands at the base's side and wraps both arms around the middle of the base, placing the hands under the near side of the base's torso and laying the arms across the base's back.

        The top then kicks into an arm support (similar to a handstand) and balances.

    2. Have the children practice the side stand.

Spotting for the Side Stand

Describe and have four children demonstrate the spotting technique:

        One spotter stands at the head of the base, the other at the base's feet.

        The spotters grasp the top's shoulders, giving support, and the top's ankles or thighs, helping her (him) balance.

Partner Flip

Continue with pairs of partners at the mats.

    1. Describe and have two students demonstrate the stunt:

        Partners stand back-to-back with elbows hooked.

        One partner leans forward while the other leans backward. Continue until the partner leaning backward is completely off the ground.

> *You can then return to the starting position or, with spotting, continue until the partner in the air flips completely over the standing partner's back.*

2. Have the children practice the partner flip with one pair spotting and one pair practicing.

Spotting the Partner Flip

Describe and have four children demonstrate the spotting technique:

> *Spotters stand on each side of the pair performing the stunt, with hands on the hips and shoulders of the top.*
>
> *Spotters guide and balance the top.*

Concluding Activities (5 minutes)

Wave

Place all the mats in a row.

1. Describe the activity:

   > *Line up shoulder-to-shoulder, facing the mat along one side.*
   >
   > *On the signal, the first child in line falls forward, catching his or her body weight with the hands.*
   >
   > *As the first child falls the next child follows, and so on, making a "human wave."*

2. Have the children perform the wave.
3. Repeat, seeing how fast they can go.

LESSON 17
PYRAMIDS

Student Objectives

- Build two types of three-person pyramids.

Equipment and Materials

- 1 or more mats (4 ft × 8 ft) per group

Warm-Up Activities (5 to 7 minutes)

Grades 4-5 Warm-Up Routine

See Grades 4-5: Gymnastics, Lesson 1, page 1011.

Skill-Development Activities (12 to 15 minutes)

Waterfall

Create groups of three, and assign each group to a mat.

1. Describe and demonstrate the stunt:

   The three of you stand side-to-side, feet touching. The middle person should take a wide stance.

   Holding inside hands with the middle person, the two of you on the outside lean to stand at an angle.

2. Have the children practice the waterfall.

Reverse Waterfall

Create groups of five, and assign each group to a mat.

1. Describe and have three children demonstrate the stunt:

   One person serves as a base and stands in the middle.

   The other two people do a handstand on each side of the base.

   The base holds the ankles of each child performing a handstand.

2. Have the children practice the reverse waterfall with three children doing the stunt and two spotting on each mat.

Spotting for the Reverse Waterfall

Describe and have five children demonstrate the spotting technique: *A spotter for each top stands beside the top and places a hand on the ankle or thigh of the top when the top goes into the handstand.*

Wide Three-Person Pyramid

Create groups of three, and assign each to a mat.

1. Describe and demonstrate the stunt:

   Two of you get down on all-fours with your heads together.

   The top person stands with a foot between the shoulder blades of each kneeling child.

2. Have the children practice the wide three-person pyramid.

Concluding Activities (10 minutes)

Giant Pyramid

Put mats in a large rectangle. Have the class form two waterfalls, two reverse waterfalls, two wide and two regular three-person pyramids, plus flying angels, shoulder balances, and so on, to include all the children in a giant pyramid.

GRADES 4-5
GYMNASTICS

LESSON 18
WANDS

Student Objectives

- Name at least three wand stunts.
- Demonstrate two skills demanding flexibility and/or balance with the wands.

Equipment and Materials

- 1 or more mats (4 ft × 8 ft) per group
- 1 wand (a dowel 30-36 in. long, 1/2 in. diameter) per child

Warm-Up Activities (5 to 7 minutes)

Grades 4-5 Warm-Up Routine

See Grades 4-5: Gymnastics, Lesson 1, page 1011.

Skill-Development Activities (18 to 20 minutes)

Thread the Needle

Arrange the children in scatter formation on the mats, each child with a wand.

1. Describe and demonstrate the stunt:

    Hold the stick near the ends, with your palms down and the stick parallel to the ground.

    Then step one leg through the stick, then the other leg, so that the stick is now behind your back.

    Then raise the stick up as high as possible.

2. Have the children practice thread the needle. Some students will be able to get the

stick overhead, others will barely be able to move it away from the body.

Stick Balance

Continue with the same setup.

1. Describe and demonstrate the stunt:

   Holding the stick upright (in a vertical position), balance it on your forefinger.

   Try this on your palm, other fingers, and even your forehead, chin, and so on.

2. Present the following challenges:

   Balance the stick on your right index finger (forehead, left shoulder, knee, foot).

   Where else can you balance the stick?

Jumping Over the Stick

Continue with the same setup.

1. Describe and demonstrate the stunt:

   Hold the stick at the ends with your palms down.

   Bend your knees, hold the stick low, and jump over the stick without letting it go.

   The stick should be behind you at the finish.

2. Have the children practice jumping over the stick.

Concluding Activities (5 minutes)

Limbo

Create small groups with children of similar skill levels, and assign each group to a mat.

1. Describe and have three children demonstrate the stunt:

   Two of you hold a stick by the ends parallel to the ground, beginning at about chest-high.

   The other children do small jumps forward as they bend backward to fit under the stick.

   After each child in your group has had a turn, lower the stick.

   Continue until no one can go under the stick.

2. Have the children practice the limbo.

Discussion

Arrange children in a semicircle. Discuss what the children have learned today:

> *What wand stunts did we learn today?* (Stick balance, thread the needle, and jumping over the stick.)
>
> *Which stunts require a lot of balance?* (Stick balance, thread the needle.)
>
> *Which stunts require a lot of flexibility?* (Jumping over the stick, thread the needle.)

GRADES 4-5

GYMNASTICS

LESSON 19
HOOPS

Student Objectives
- Move a hoop in various patterns.
- Move through a hoop.

Equipment and Materials
- 1, 30-36 in. hoop per child

Warm-Up Activities (5 to 7 minutes)

Grades 4-5 Warm-Up Routine
See Grades 4-5: Gymnastics, Lesson 1, page 1011.

Skill-Development Activities (18 to 20 minutes)

Hoop Challenges
Arrange the children in scatter formation, each child with a hoop. Ask the children to perform the following challenges:

> Roll the hoop forward with your left hand.
> Roll the hoop forward with your right hand.
> Roll the hoop backward with your right hand.
> Roll the hoop backward with your left hand.
> Hula the hoop on your waist.
> Hula the hoop on your wrist.
> What other body parts can you hula the hoop on? (Ankle, neck, elbow, and so on.)
> Toss the hoop above your head and catch it.
> Toss the hoop as high as you can and catch it. Watch out for others!
> Toss the hoop, turn around, and catch it.
> Roll the hoop forward, run, and catch it before it stops.
> Jump the hoop like a jump rope.

Boomerang
Arrange the children in a long line, facing you. Each child should have a hoop.

1. Describe and demonstrate the stunt:

   The object is to roll the hoop forward but, by placing backspin on the hoop, have it roll back. The hoop must travel just above ground level.

   Create a backspin by quickly thrusting your wrist downward just before releasing the hoop.

   Your arm "rolls" forward while your wrist and hand are putting on backspin.

2. Have the children practice the boomerang.

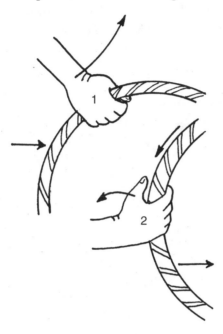

Running Through the Hoop

Continue with same setup.

1. Describe and have a child demonstrate the stunt:

   Roll the hoop and run at the same speed as and alongside the hoop.

   Then quickly turn, bend, and run through the rolling hoop.

2. Have the children practice running through the hoop.

3. Challenge the children: *Do the boomerang and run through the hoop as it returns to you.*

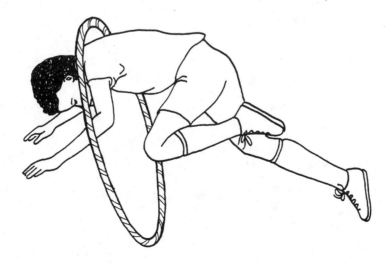

Concluding Activities (5 minutes)

Hoop Combination Challenges

Continue with same setup. You can move to two lines for the partner activity. Challenge the children to attempt the following combinations:

> *Boomerang, arm hula, toss, and catch.*
>
> *Roll to partner (both partners roll simultaneously) and run through.*
>
> *Partners stand side by side and boomerang to each other.*

GRADES 4-5

LESSON 20
STREAMERS AND BALLS

Student Objectives

- Move in various patterns and tumble while maintaining control of a ball or streamer.

Equipment and Materials

- 1 or more mats (4 ft × 8 ft) per group
- 1 streamer (or ribbon) per child
- 1 small playground or foam ball per (higher-skilled) child

Warm-Up Activities (5 to 7 minutes)

Grades 4-5 Warm-Up Routine

See Grades 4-5: Gymnastics, Lesson 1, page 1011.

Skill-Development Activities (18 to 20 minutes)

Figure Eight

Arrange the children in scatter formation, each with a streamer.

1. Describe and demonstrate the stunt: *Move the streamer in the shape of an "8."*
2. Have the children practice the figure eight.

Circles

Continue with the children in scatter formation, each with a streamer.

1. Describe and demonstrate the stunt: *Using your entire arm to make a large movement from the shoulder, move the streamer in circles overhead, in front of, and beside your body.*
2. Have the children practice circles.

Draggin'

Continue with the same setup.

1. Describe and demonstrate the stunt: *As your body turns in a circle, let the streamer follow to the side and rear, touching the ground.*
2. Have the children practice draggin'.

Throw, Turn, and Catch

Continue with the same setup.

1. Describe and demonstrate the stunt:

   Toss the streamer into the air, spin in a 360-degree turn (all the way around), and catch the streamer in the same hand.

   You can also try catching the streamer in the opposite hand.

2. Have the children practice throw, turn, and catch.

Jump the Streamer

Continue with the children in scatter formation, each with a streamer.

1. Describe and demonstrate the stunt: *Turn the streamer in a circle on the ground (begin like draggin') and, as the streamer gets spread out, jump over it as if it were a jump rope.*

2. Have the children practice jump the streamer.

Toss and Catch

Take aside a group of the higher-skilled children while the other children continue practicing streamer stunts. Collect the streamers and give each of these children a foam ball or a small playground ball.

1. Describe and demonstrate the stunt:

   Extend your arms to toss and catch.

   Squat your body slightly and then extend to your toes as you lift and release the ball.

   As the ball touches your hands, bend your knees to absorb the force of the ball.

2. Have the children practice toss and catch.

Roll and Catch

Continue working with the smaller group of higher-skilled children at a mat while the other children practice the streamer stunts.

1. Describe and demonstrate the stunt:

   Squat and roll the ball, stand, run past the ball, squat, and catch the ball as it rolls.

   Do all rolling and catching with one hand.

2. Have the children practice roll and catch.

Toss and Catch Behind

Continue working with the smaller group of higher-skilled children while the other children practice the streamer stunts.

1. Describe and demonstrate the stunt:

   Toss the ball with a straight arm, throwing it slightly behind your body and catching it with your opposite arm behind your back.

   The object is to do this without moving your feet, but this will take practice!

   At first you should move your feet to adjust your body position for the catch.

2. Have the children practice toss and catch behind.

Forward Roll With a Streamer or Ball

Allow the children to choose a ball or streamer.

1. Describe and demonstrate the stunt:

Hold the ball with your palm up and arm rotated so that your elbow is also up (do this by starting out with your arm extended and palm up, and then turning your arm 360 degrees counterclockwise until the palm is up again).

Keeping the ball on the palm of your hand, do a forward roll, using only one hand to support your body.

As you do the forward roll, "unwind" your arm holding the ball and continue to hold the ball.

Return to standing without dropping the ball.

2. The children practice the forward roll with a streamer or ball.

Concluding Activities (5 minutes)

Ball and Streamer Activities

Allow the children to select partners and either a ball or a streamer (partners should have the same equipment). Ask the children to combine, in any order, the skills learned, using the type of equipment they selected.

LESSON 21
SMALL EQUIPMENT

Student Objectives

- Demonstrate balance, flexibility, and strength, using small equipment.

Equipment and Materials

- 1 or more mats (4 ft × 8 ft) per station
- Signal
- Station 1: pogo stick(s)
- Station 2: 1 pair of stilts per pair
- Station 3: 1 rubber band (cut from inner tubes or use bicycle inner tubes) per pair
- Station 4: 1 ball and 1 streamer per child
- Station 5: 1 hoop per child
- Station 6: 1 wand per child

Warm-Up Activities (5 to 7 minutes)

Grades 4-5 Warm-Up Routine

See Grades 4-5: Gymnastics, Lesson 1, page 1011.

Skill-Development Activities (23 to 25 minutes)

Stations

Set up the six stations with mats as described. Create six small groups, and place each group at a station.

1. Describe and demonstrate each station.
2. Have the children practice the skills at the stations.
3. Signal the children to rotate to the next station every six minutes. (*Note*: You will need two days to allow each group to visit each station.)

Station 1: Pogo Sticks

Mount the stick and jump up to 20 jumps per turn, controlling direction of movement with the stick.

Station 2: Stilts

On the mat with a spotter, mount the stilts and walk.

Station 3: Rubber Stretchers

Put your feet against your partner's feet with all legs straight. Grip the rubber stretcher (rubber band) with both hands and pull. Stand facing your partner, grip the rubber stretcher, and pull, as in a tug-of-war game.

Station 4: Balls and Streamers
Practice the forward roll with a streamer or ball.

Station 5: Hoops
Practice the boomerang and running through the hoop.

Station 6: Wands
Practice jumping over the stick, thread the needle, and stick balance.

Concluding Activities

Have the children either reorganize the equipment for the next class or put it away.

LESSONS 22 TO 25
LARGE EQUIPMENT

Student Objectives

- Practice walking, leaping, running, turning, changing levels, balancing, and rolling on the balance beam.
- Practice climbing and skin the cat on one or two ropes.
- Practice hand-over-hand traveling on the horizontal ladder.
- Practice vaulting.

Equipment and Materials

- 1 or more mats (4 ft × 8 ft) per station
- Station 1: 1 balance beam (4 in. × 4 in. × 8 in. high)
- Station 2: 1 balance beam (4 in. × 4 in. × 8 in. high)
- Station 3: 1 balance beam (4 in. × 6 in. × 16 in. high)
- Station 4: 2 climbing ropes suspended from the ceiling, 8 ft apart
- Station 5: 1 horizontal ladder
- Station 6: 1 cube or vaulting box (24 in.) per child
- Task cards

Safety Tip

- Review the safety rules.

Warm-Up Activities (5 to 7 minutes)

Grades 4-5 Warm-Up Routine

See Grades 4-5: Gymnastics, Lesson 1, page 1011.

Skill-Development Activities (23 to 25 minutes)

Stations

Set up the six stations with mats as described. You can use task cards to illustrate the station activity. Create six small groups, and assign each group to a station.

1. Describe and demonstrate each station.
2. Have the children practice the skills at the stations.
3. Signal the children to rotate to the next station every six minutes. Have the children visit stations 1, 3, and 5 or 2, 4, and 6. Reverse who goes to which stations in the next lesson.

Note: To adequately teach the new tasks involved in this circuit, you may spend a short time at each station, until students have learned the skills and sequences. Use the extra time to explain the stations. Monitor new activities closely while keeping an eye on the rest of the stations.

Station 1: Balance Beam Sequence A
Walk, leap, run, turn, walk through hoop, jump through hoop, move to back-lying position, and recover to feet.

Station 2: Balance Beam Sequence B
Perform the following sequence: squat, walk backward, squat turn, knee scale, and regular split.

Station 3: Balance Beam Sequence C
Do a back-lying position, forward roll, and straddle dismount.

- Back-lying position and recover to feet—*Squatting to a sitting position with one leg off the side of beam, roll back to lie on the beam. Now both feet should be on the beam. Sit up and then stand.*

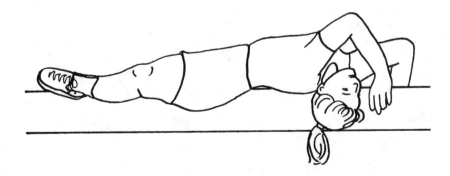

- Forward roll on the beam—*Beginning in a squat position with your hands gripping the top and sides of the beam, lift your hips and roll your torso and head forward between your arms so that your shoulder blades touch the beam. (It is important to keep the elbows as close together as possible.) Allow your legs to slowly clear your arms and finish in a back-lying position extended along the beam.*

- Straddle dismount—*Jump off beam (in the same way as in the jumping cube straddle) by splitting your legs and trying to touch your toes in straddle position. Land on your feet.*

Station 4: Climbing Ropes

Climb to the top of one rope and skin the cat on the two ropes.

Skin the cat—*Holding one rope in each hand (reach up to a comfortable height and grasp one rope in each hand), lift your legs to your chest, tilting your head back while continuing to lift your legs. Make your legs go over your head and stop when your body is in an upside-down pike. Control is important, so go slowly! At this point, you can either reverse and return to the start or continue until your the feet are on the ground.*

Station 5: Horizontal Ladder

Move hand-over-hand from one end to the other.

Station 6: Jumping Cubes

Perform the following combinations: run, take off, and straddle; jump onto cube and straddle dismount; jump onto cube and tuck dismount; jump onto cube and pike dismount.

- Straddle over cube—*Run and take off, put your hands on the box between your legs, lift your body off the floor, and spread your legs into a straddle. Then move over the cube and land on the opposite side with your feet together.*

- Jump onto cube and dismount—*Run and take off, jumping up onto the cube. To dismount, jump upward into a layout (straight body), straddle (legs split, trying to touch toes), pike (legs together, touching toes), or tuck (body in a tight ball). Look straight ahead, not at the mat below, as this may cause you to lose your balance.*

Concluding Activities

None.

LESSON 26
LARGE EQUIPMENT

Student Objectives

- Perform the tasks on the Grades 4-5: Checklist for Large Equipment (see the appendix).

Equipment and Materials

- 1 or more mats (4 ft × 8 ft) per group
- Signal
- Station 1: 1 balance beam (4 in. × 4 in. × 8 in. high)

- Station 2: 1 balance beam (4 in. × 4 in. × 8 in. high)
- Station 3: 1 balance beam (4 in. × 6 in. × 16 in. high)
- Station 4: 2 climbing ropes suspended from the ceiling, 8 ft apart
- Station 5: 1 horizontal ladder
- Station 6: 1 cube or vaulting box (24 in.) per child

Warm-Up Activities (10 minutes)

Grades 4-5 Warm-Up Routine

See Grades 4-5: Gymnastics, Lesson 1, page 1011.

Skill-Development Activities (20 minutes)

Stations

Set up six stations as described in Grades 4-5: Gymnastics, Lessons 22 to 25. Arrange small groups at each mat station. Match groups of children to the order in which children appear on the checklist.

1. Allow the children to practice at the other stations while you evaluate a group on one piece of equipment.
2. The instructions for the stations are the same as in Grades 4-5: Gymnastics, Lessons 22 to 25.
3. Use the Grades 4-5 Checklist for Large Equipment (appendix).

Concluding Activities

None.

GRADES 4-5

HEALTH

Although some schools have a dedicated health instructor, such as the school nurse, to teach basic health concepts, many physical education teachers are responsible for teaching this part of the school curriculum. Take advantage of such an opportunity to show children the connections among fitness, lifestyle choices, and health. We designed this unit to give you an overview of appropriate content for this age level to help you get started.

UNIT ORGANIZATION

You can use the following lessons as a two-week health unit or individually as appropriate. You can also expand each lesson into a unit of its own. The topics include medicines and other drugs, drug use and abuse, smoking, alcohol use and abuse, nutrition, and fitness.

LESSON ORGANIZATION

We have organized each lesson in a manner similar to all other types of lessons in this book: student objectives, equipment and materials, health concept (skill development). As it enhances student learning, most lessons include a hands-on activity to reinforce the main health concept.

TEACHING HINTS

As with any lesson, being well-prepared is essential for effective teaching. Read the lesson carefully before presenting the concept to the students. Allow plenty of time for discussion and application of the concept to promote learning.

Fourth and Fifth Graders

Children this age are usually very aware of connections between lifestyle choices and health, such as personally knowing specific people who have abused drugs or alcohol and suffered health consequences because of such choices. Depending on the child, however, his or her understanding may be incorrect, basic, or fairly sophisticated. Although their knowledge base may be quite extensive, still be sure the language you use is age-appropriate and accompanied by visual aids whenever possible. Visual aids must be age-appropriate as well, neither for older nor younger children. Children this age may also enjoy the opportunity to make visual projects to help you teach younger children, thereby reinforcing their own learning as they help others. Certainly, they still benefit from and enjoy a hands-on approach.

Encourage discussion and participation from each child. One way to encourage discussion is to be sure to wait at least 10 seconds before calling on a child to answer your question. Encourage participation from reluctant children by asking for private responses, perhaps in a journal entry.

Collaboration Strategies

Inviting parents and other community members to class can greatly enhance health lessons. Parents from various health professions may serve as guest speakers. You should also include parents by asking them to help complete and/or sign health contracts, sending home information about the concepts with discussion questions, or simply inviting them to attend class. Community

1073

experts, such as pediatricians, police, health care professionals, and representatives from awareness groups (e.g., American Heart Association), are often willing to make presentations at schools free of charge. Tap into such resources whenever possible not only to supplement your curriculum but also to raise awareness among students of the many resources available to them in the community.

LESSON 1
MEDICINES AND OTHER DRUGS

Student Objectives

- Define a drug as any substance that is taken into the body that alters its function in any way.
- Distinguish between prescribed and over-the-counter (OTC) drugs.
- Cooperate with a group to solve a problem related to drugs.

Equipment and Materials

- Paper and pencil
- Stopwatch or watch with second hand for each group

Health Concept (20 minutes)

Gather the children into an information formation until the cooperative activity.

Key Terms

Define the following terms:

drug—*Any substance that is taken into the body that alters its function in any way.*

medicine—*Any drug used for medical purposes that will facilitate cure, or prevent disease.*

prescription drug—*Medicines that can only be obtained with a physician's prescription.*

over-the-counter (OTC) drugs—*Medicines that can be bought without a physician's prescription.*

Concept Development

1. Introduce this concept: *Drugs are for sick people.*
2. Discuss general characteristics of prescription and OTC drugs.
3. Ask the children the following questions:

    Have you ever taken medicine prescribed by a physician when you were sick?

    What are some of the medicines you have taken? (Cold medication, allergy medicine, insulin shot, and so on.)

    Why did you take the medicine or shot? (Had a cold, had the flu, chest congestion, sore throat, and so on.)

4. Tell the children: *When drugs are used as medicines, they help people in many ways.*

    Help cure disease (e.g., penicillin kills bacteria [germ] that causes pneumonia).

Reduce the seriousness of the disease (e.g., steroid hormones strengthen body's defense against arthritis).

Help relieve symptoms (e.g., aspirin for aches, pain, inflammation).

Help diagnose disease (e.g., dye injected in veins to locate blockage in body vessels).

Help prevent disease (e.g., vaccinations used to boost immune system and strengthen the body defenses).

5. Tell the children: *There is risk involved when taking any drug because of the physiological and/or psychological changes that occur. Psychological changes are behaviors observed due to thoughts, beliefs, and feelings changing in a person. Physiological changes are biological responses, such as heart rate or sweating. Only physicians can legally order (prescribe) a drug. What do we call medicines (drugs) that are written up and ordered by a physician?* (Prescription or "Rx" drugs.) *Any medicine can be misused if it's not used in the ways that it was intended to be used. But prescription drugs are medicines ordered by a physician for a specific person with a specific problem or health condition. You should always take only what your doctor says is OK and only in the amount prescribed.*

6. Discuss drug abuse with the children: *Any drug that is taken for nonmedical reasons is considered drug abuse. Drug abuse can occur with OTC, prescribed, and illegal drugs. Some people misuse and abuse drugs for a variety of reasons. Why and how might individuals misuse and abuse drugs?*

7. Allow children to reply, bringing out these points:

   They are daredevils, risk-takers, gamblers.

   They are misinformed or uninformed.

   They are insecure; they have poor self-concepts.

   They are careless; they don't take their medication as prescribed.

8. Introduce this concept: *Over-the-counter drugs can be used by anyone and give temporary relief of minor pain or discomfort.*

9. Tell the children: *Over-the-counter, or OTC, drugs are the same as nonprescription drugs. They are sold in grocery stores and drugstores and do not require a written order (prescription) from a physician. Why do people use OTC drugs?* (Cold, cough, sore throat, stuffy nose, indigestion, headache, sore muscles, back pain, an abrasion or cut, poison ivy, and so on.) *People use OTCs to avoid going to a physician, the cost of an office visit, and the high cost of some prescribed medications.*

Concluding Activities (10 minutes)

Cooperative Group Activity

Divide the children into groups of five or six.

1. Assign each student a role. Roles might be organizer, recorder, timekeeper, facilitator, and summarizer. (See Grades 4-5: Organization, Lesson 1, page 754, for a complete description.)

2. Review the guidelines for cooperative work.

   Everyone must contribute to the work.

   Only one student can talk at a time and others must listen.

   Everyone must show respect for others.

   Each person must fulfill his or her role.

3. Present the problem for the groups to solve: *Propose a "Safe Drug Use Plan" for families to follow. Examples might include the following:*

   Use medicine or drugs only when you're ill.

   Use medicine or drugs only when they're given to you by a physician, your parents, or some other designated responsible person.

   Use only medicine prescribed for you or bought specifically for you. Don't take someone else's medicine.

LESSON 2
DRUG USE AND ABUSE

Student Objectives

- Define drug abuse as using drugs or medicines in ways they were not intended to be used.
- Distinguish between drug abuse and drug misuse.
- Cooperate with a group to analyze some of the reasons people give for abusing drugs.

Equipment and Materials

- Chalkboard, poster, or other way to display reasons for drug use
- Pencils
- Handout with reasons for drug use (1 per group)

Health Concept (20 minutes)

Gather the children into an information formation until the cooperative activity.

Key Terms

Define the following terms:

drug use—*Taking a drug for medical purposes, according to how it was prescribed.*

drug abuse—*The deliberate taking of a drug for nonmedical purposes and in a way that can result in damage to one's health and ability to function.*

drug misuse—*Taking a drug for medical purposes but not as it was prescribed or intended.*

addiction—*A strong psychological and physiological craving or desire for something.*

Concept Development

1. Introduce the following concept: *Drugs and medicines are often misused and abused.*
2. Ask the children: *What can happen when you use drugs or medicines for purposes that are nonmedical (abusive)? Some dangers of drug abuse are*

   overdosing (drug poisoning),

   psychological drug dependency (a strong psychological craving for a drug),

   physiological drug addiction (chemical changes in the body that require the presence of the drug in order to function), and

   becoming more likely to be accident prone (resulting from not being mentally and physically alert and having some loss of muscular coordination and agility).

3. Introduce the following concept: *Drugs and medicines are often misused.*

4. Ask the children: *What are some risks associated with the misuse of drugs and medicines?* (It may act like a poison if taken with certain other drugs, like alcohol; it may cause allergic reactions.)

5. Explain that there are several ways a person might abuse any drug or medicine:

    If you take someone else's medicine

    If you take medicine without your parents' or doctor's permission and supervision

    If you mix medications without knowing the risks

    If you take drugs that are illegal (forbidden by law)

6. Ask the children: *Why do you think people abuse drugs?* (Allow children to reply. Listen for answers listed in step 7.)

7. Tell the children: *People tend to abuse drugs for a number of reasons, whether the drugs are prescribed, over-the-counter, or illegal. These are some of the reasons people give for abuse* (show the list on a chalkboard or poster):

    Drugs make me feel good. I'm just experimenting.

    I want to escape the problems of the real world.

    Drugs make me act and feel grown up.

    Everyone else does it (peer pressure).

    I do it to be cool.

    Drugs are easily available.

    I like the risk.

Concluding Activities (10 minutes)

Cooperative Group Activity

Divide the children into groups of four or five. Give each group a handout with the reasons listed in column 1 and place to write "why" in column 2.

Ask the children: *Examine each of the previous statements about drug abuse, asking "Why?" For example, what are people really saying when their reason for abuse is "Oh, I'm just experimenting; I can stop any time I want to?" One person in each group will write the answer to "why" for statement #1. After the statement is answered, the handout is passed to another group member who will write the group response for "why" to statement #2. Continue until all of the statements are answered, and each student has written at least one answer.*

LESSON 3
DRUG USE AND ABUSE—STIMULANTS, DEPRESSANTS, AND HALLUCINOGENS

Student Objectives

- Identify stimulants that are frequently misused.
- Describe how stimulants affect the body.
- Describe the action of depressants in the body.
- Describe how hallucinogenic drugs affect the body.
- Cooperate with a group to develop a plan of action for a friend who is considering experimenting with drugs.

Equipment and Materials

- None

Health Concept (20 minutes)

Gather the children into an information formation until the cooperative activity.

Key Terms

Define the following terms:

stimulants—*Drugs that speed up the activity of the brain and nervous system.*

caffeine—*A mild stimulant found in tea, coffee, and cola beverages.*

amphetamines—*A stimulant used for medical purposes, but if abused can be very dangerous. Amphetamines can cause vision problems, restlessness, and confusion.*

cocaine—*A white powder sometimes called "snow" or "coke." Cocaine is a stimulant that used to be used in medicine to relieve pain following surgery but is now considered very dangerous.*

depressants or sedatives—*Drugs that slow down the activity of the brain and nervous system.*

hallucinogens—*Drugs that change or distort a person's sensory perceptions.*

Concept Development

1. Introduce the following concept: *Drugs cause mental and physical changes in the body.*

2. Discuss the effects of stimulants on the body: *Some drugs are useful in medicine for treating human illness and disease, but other drugs are illegal and forbidden by law. Stimulants are drugs that speed up the activity of the brain and nervous system, and some are frequently misused.*

3. Ask the children: *What can happen when you drink too much coffee or cola?*

   (Too much caffeine can cause irritability, sleeplessness, and nervousness.)

4. Discuss amphetamines with the children: *Amphetamines can be beneficial when a person uses them for medical reasons, but are very dangerous if abused. They have been used successfully in weight reduction programs, but when taken over a long time they can affect your brain so that you can't think clearly or reason for yourself. Amphetamines are sometimes called "speed," "uppers," or "pep pills."* (Your local community may have different names that you can substitute for the names given here.) *These are slang terms used for stimulant-type drugs. Cocaine, like amphetamines, can make you feel good for a little while, but the risk of abuse and addiction is too great to continue its use, even in medicine. Cocaine was once used in medicine to relieve pain following surgery, but it is not used today because of the danger. Too much cocaine can kill.*

5. Introduce the following concept: *Depressants or sedatives are valuable in the treatment of human illness but can be abused.*

6. Discuss the characteristics of depressants: *Depressants and sedatives are the same in that they slow down the activity of the brain and nervous system. When these drugs are used by physicians for medical purposes they are good and make you feel good—if you don't misuse them. Barbiturates and depressants cause sleep, but some people abuse or misuse them. How might sleeping pills be abused or misused?* (Taking too many at one time; taking them with another depressant, like alcohol; taking someone else's prescription.)

7. Discuss addiction with the children:

   "Addiction" is a term that suggests a mental and/or physical craving for a particular drug or medicine. Barbiturates are addicting. There are several slang or street terms for barbiturates: "reds," "downers," "yellow jackets," and "goofballs." (You may substitute your local community's names for these drugs) *Barbiturates usually come in pill or capsule form and appear in a variety of bright colors such as red, orange, green, blue, and yellow.*

   "Developing a tolerance" means that the body requires more (a larger amount or dose) of the same drug to achieve the feeling the drug produced the first time a person took it.

   "Withdrawal" is the physical and psychological discomfort experienced when a person gradually discontinues or abruptly stops taking a drug he or she has taken in large amounts over a long period of time.

7. Introduce the following concept: *Hallucinogens are dangerous and illegal.*

8. Discuss the dangers of using hallucinogens: *Hallucinogens are dangerous and illegal. They are drugs that change or distort a person's sensory perceptions. When a person's perception is distorted, time may be confusing or unclear. Here are some other examples of distorted sensory perception:*

   A foul odor seems to have no smell at all.

   A loud noise sounds like a whisper or a whisper sounds loud.

   A piece of ice feels like a hot coal.

   A kitten looks like a large, vicious lion.

   Colors appear super bright.

9. *Hallucinogenic drugs affect people differently. Sometimes users feel nothing until several hours, days, or even weeks later, and then they experience flashbacks. A "flashback" is an*

experience in which you think scary thoughts and believe them to be real, causing fear and panic. A flashback is sometimes called a "bad trip." Many drugs have this effect, such as "meth" and "LSD."

10. Discuss LSD with the children: *"LSD" is a very powerful, dangerous, and illegal halluci-nogen. LSD's only legal use has been in carefully monitored medical research programs. Any use by private citizens is against the law. Users of LSD often experience flashbacks. And LSD can kill. For example, people have stepped out of upstairs windows because the ground appeared to be right near them, and they've walked through windows because they simply did not see them.*

Concluding Activities (10 minutes)

Cooperative Group Activity

Divide the children into groups of four or five.

Assign the following problem-solving task: *Advise a friend who is considering using LSD because he thinks it will help him make more friends. What would you say to the friend? Should he experiment with LSD? Why? Why not?* If you have time, ask two children to role play for the class. One child will try to talk the other out of using LSD.

LESSON 4

DRUG USE AND ABUSE: MARIJUANA, NARCOTICS, AND AEROSOL SPRAYS

Student Objectives

- Describe the effects of marijuana.
- Explain why narcotic drugs are used in medicine.
- Cooperate with a group to decide a plan of action regarding the reporting of marijuana use by your best friend.
- Name aerosol sprays that are frequently abused.

Equipment and Materials

- Chart, paper, and pen for each group
- Paper and pencil for each group

Health Concept (20 minutes)

Gather the children into an information formation until the cooperative activity.

Key Terms

Define the following terms:

> *marijuana—An illegal hallucinogen.*
>
> *narcotics—Depressants that are legal only when used and administered by physicians.*
>
> *aerosol sprays—Common items found in most households that can be abused, such as spray paint and hair spray.*

Concept Development

1. Introduce the following concept: *"Marijuana" is an illegal hallucinogen.*
2. Discuss the characteristics of marijuana: *Marijuana is a mild hallucinogen compared to LSD. It causes behavioral changes in some individuals. For example, happy people become sad. Calm people become nervous and anxious. Clear-thinking people become confused. People experience a distortion of time, space, and distance. For example, they will not know what time it is; they may be late. There are some slang or street terms for marijuana: "pot," "joint," "reefer," "grass," and "weed." A person usually smokes marijuana in the form of a crudely hand-rolled cigarette. Much more medical research is needed because the long-term effects of the use of marijuana are still not absolutely known. Remember! Although we don't know everything about marijuana, the one thing we know for sure is this: Marijuana is an illegal drug.*

3. Introduce the following concept: *Narcotic drugs are legal only when used and administered by physicians.*

4. Discuss the dangers of using narcotics:

   "Narcotics" are depressants. In medicine certain narcotic drugs are used as painkillers, but even this practice must be carefully monitored by a physician. Some examples of narcotics are morphine, codeine, and heroin.

   They are all made from opium; "opium" is a substance that comes from a certain kind of poppy, a flower.

   Heroin is also illegal and dangerous.

   Morphine and codeine are drugs prescribed by doctors for patients who are experiencing lots of pain. When might a doctor prescribe morphine for a patient? (After surgery, for a broken leg, for second- or third-degree burns.) *A person might take more pills at one time or take pills more often than they were prescribed.*

   All narcotics are addicting, which is why no one should use them over a long period of time. When people become addicted to narcotics, whether through medical use or by illegal means, the person is said to be "hooked on drugs." Breaking such a bad habit is very painful; a person can become so sick that unless a doctor is supervising the process, the person can die.

5. Review the content:

   What are "narcotics?"

   What does being "hooked on drugs" mean?

   What is "morphine?"

   What does "addiction" mean?

   What are the long-term effects of narcotics use?

6. Introduce the following concept: *Household sprays can also be abused.*

7. Discuss examples of household sprays that can be abused: *Aerosol sprays are common items in most households. Can you give some examples of sprays found in the home?* (Deodorant, hair spray, window and oven cleaners, pesticides, and so on.)

8. *What are ways that toxic, or poisonous, substances can get into the body?* (Through a break in the skin, by inhaling fumes [vapors], by eating contaminated food, with needles.) *Some people deliberately abuse sprays by intentionally inhaling the vapors. When a person deeply inhales the fumes of these substances, they change the person's behavior. These fumes can also be mind-altering, causing effects like those of certain other drugs we've discussed. For example, a person may see things that are not there or imagine things that seem very real.*

9. Ask the children: *Do you know how a person might act or feel if he or she had been sniffing (breathing) an aerosol spray? Abusing aerosol sprays can produce some of the following undesirable and potentially dangerous feelings:*

   Lightheadedness

   Feeling drunk or drugged

   Silliness and giddiness

   Inability to speak clearly

   Feeling sick to the stomach

   Sleepiness and limpness

   Unconsciousness

10. Discuss inhalation with the students: *"Inhalation" is the main way that aerosol sprays are abused. Inhaling these substances causes damage to the nasal passage (nose), the throat, and the lungs (alveoli or air sacs). When a person abuses these products over a long period of time,*

brain damage can result, along with injury to other organs in the body. People who deliberately inhale aerosol vapors talk about getting a "high" or a "lift." A high or a lift is a short-lived feeling of mild intoxication or lightheadedness.

Cooperative Group Activity

Divide the children into groups of five or six. Each group needs a chart, paper, and a pen.
    Discuss the following problems and propose solutions:

> **Problem 1**—*Your best friend has let you know that she uses marijuana. Should you report your friend's use to her parents, to the police, or both? Why? Why not?*

> **Problem 2**—*Your younger brother has let you know that he wants to smoke a joint. What would you tell him? Would you report the desire to your parents? Why? Why not?*

You should move among the groups facilitating discussion.

Concluding Activities (10 minutes)

Who Knows?

Keep the children in their small groups.

1. Describe the game:

    I will ask a "Who Knows?" question, and call on a representative from a group who raises his or her hand for the answer.

    Your group should discuss the question, agree on an answer, and write it down.

    I will award your group a point for giving a correct answer and one point for a correct written answer. We will declare the group with the most points the winner for the day.

2. Ask the questions: *Who knows . . .*

    what "inhale" means? (To breathe in.)

    what a lift or high is? (A feeling of intoxication.) *what is intoxication?* (Too much of a substance leading to impaired performance.) *a type of spray?* (Pesticides, oven cleaner, and so on.)

    what long-term abuse of sprays can cause? (Brain damage and injury to other body organs.)

LESSON 5
SMOKING

Student Objectives

- Explain how smoking can be harmful to your health.
- Identify nicotine as a stimulant and the primary drug found in tobacco.

Equipment and Materials

- Paper, markers, and crayons for making "slogan posters"

Health Concept (20 minutes)

Gather the children into an information formation for the entire discussion.

Key Terms

Define the following terms:

tars—The chemical substance in cigarette smoke.

carcinogens—The things that cause cancer, a serious disease that attacks the tissues of the body.

emphysema—A breathing disorder associated with cigarette smoking.

nicotine—A stimulant and the primary drug found in tobacco.

Concept Development

1. Introduce the following concept: *Smoking is bad for your health.*

2. Discuss the harmful effects of cigarette smoke: *Tobacco smoke affects the body in harmful ways. It constricts the blood vessels (makes them narrower), it elevates blood pressure, and it increases heart rate, because nicotine acts as a stimulant to the heart and nervous system. It also reduces the ability of the blood to carry oxygen, because the carbon monoxide found in tobacco smoke is more readily picked up and carried by the blood.*

3. Discuss tars and carcinogens with the students: *Cigarette smoke also contains chemical substances called "tars." Tars are identified as carcinogenic agents. "Carcinogens" are things that cause cancer, a serious disease that attacks the tissues of the body. Smoking is a major cause of lung cancer and is highly suspect in some other forms of cancer.*

4. Discuss emphysema with the students: *In addition to increasing your risk of lung cancer, smoking can also cause emphysema, another serious health threat. "Emphysema" is a breathing disorder that destroys lung tissue and makes breathing virtually impossible. The disease puts holes in the lungs, making breathing like trying to blow up a balloon with holes in it. Cigarette smoking also increases the risk of coronary heart disease. Coronary heart disease is high blood pressure, which in turn can lead to a heart attack.*

5. Ask the children: *What are some ways to avoid the hazards caused by cigarette smoke?* (If you don't smoke now, don't start. Avoid close places where people are smoking. The smoke in the air is called "secondhand smoke," and it too is potentially harmful to your health.)

Cooperative Group Activity

Divide the children into groups of five or six with paper and crayons or markers.

1. Ask each group to create an antismoking slogan, for example, "Look out, folks, this is for real. Cigarette smoking definitely kills." Children can make a poster of their slogan.

Gather the children into an information formation to continue the discussion.

2. Introduce this concept: *Tobacco in any form is dangerous to your health.*

3. Discuss other forms of tobacco use that are harmful to your health: *The most common forms of tobacco use are as follows:*

   Smoking—cigarettes, pipes, cigars

   Chewing—plug tobacco

   Dipping—snuff

4. Tell the children: *Nicotine is a stimulant and the primary drug found in tobacco. Cigarette smoking is the most common form of tobacco use, although chewing and dipping are on the increase. Because we have evidence that smoking, chewing, and dipping can kill you, why do you think people today ever start smoking?* (See list in step 5.)

5. Discuss smoking as a habit with the children: *Smoking, like drinking alcohol, can become a habit. We know that adult role models and peer pressure have a lot of influence on whether a person ever starts smoking. People give other common reasons why they smoke:*

   It's just a habit (something to do).

   It stimulates them (stimulates the appetite, wakes them up, increases their energy level).

   It helps them relax (settles them down).

   It's a crutch (helps reduce stress).

   They're "hooked" (they have a psychological and possibly physical dependence).

6. Discuss various reactions to smoking with the children: *Different people respond to smoking in different ways. For example, some people think it is "cool," some people think it helps them to relax, and others are addicted. The same person may experience different responses to smoking. For example, some people think it helps them to wake up or think faster. Sometimes people don't want to stop smoking because they believe smoking decreases their appetite or when they stop smoking, it makes them feel bad. They are addicted to nicotine and to the habit of holding or handling cigarettes.*

Concluding Activities (10 minutes)

Cooperative Group Activity

Have the children meet again in their small groups.

1. Ask each group: *Brainstorm about why people smoke.*

2. Then ask each child to complete the following written statements.

3. Place the statements on the chalkboard or give them to the children on a handout.

   I will not smoke because . . .

   I will avoid places filled with smoke because . . .

LESSON 6
ALCOHOL USE AND ABUSE

Student Objectives

- Name two characteristics of alcohol.
- Name two things alcohol does to you as a depressant.
- Explain how alcohol abuse can destroy the quality of life.
- List some of the mental and physical effects of alcohol abuse.
- State reasons why people drink alcohol.
- State reasons why people do not drink alcohol.

Equipment and Materials

- Handout or chart for last Cooperative Group Activity (see text, page 1087)

Health Concept (20 minutes)

Gather the children into an information formation for the entire discussion.

Key Terms

Define the following terms:

> *ethyl alcohol*—*The primary ingredient found in distilled beverages (like whiskey), beer, and wine.*
>
> *alcoholism*—*A disease where the person drinks large amounts of alcohol over a relatively long period of time.*
>
> *cirrhosis*—*A fatal condition of the liver that results from damage to the organ caused by alcohol consumption.*

Concept Development

1. Introduce the following concept: *You should know about alcohol before you use it. Alcohol is the number-one drug problem in our nation today. "Alcohol" is a depressant that dulls your senses, affects your speech and vision, and interferes with your general ability to perform any task (like walking, running, and dancing).*

2. Discuss the characteristics of alcohol:

   "Ethyl alcohol" is toxic, but not as toxic as other forms of the chemical are. Do you remember what "toxic" means? (Poisonous.) *Can you name another form of alcohol that's highly toxic but beneficial in medicine?* (Methyl alcohol is the active ingredient in rubbing alcohol.)

   Ethyl alcohol is made from fermented fruits, juices, or cereal grains.

   Alcohol is colorless. It is a "flammable" liquid, meaning that it burns quickly and easily.

The amount of alcohol in a beverage varies from one kind to another. Distilled beverages, such as whiskey and rum have the highest alcohol content. Beer has the lowest alcohol content (five to seven percent). All alcoholic beverages carry a label revealing the proof of the alcohol. Alcohol proof is a number on an alcoholic beverage label that is twice as much as the amount of alcohol contained in the drink. For example, 86 proof whiskey is 43 percent alcohol. Whiskey that is 50 percent alcohol has a label that reads 100 proof.

3. Discuss alcohol abuse: *Not everyone who uses alcohol is a problem drinker. Many adults drink alcohol in moderation and are sensible. These are responsible users. However, excessive use of alcohol is abuse. Abuse of alcohol can lead to alcoholism. "Alcoholism" is a disease where the person drinks large amounts of alcohol over a relatively long period of time, leading to dependency and addiction. You can never become an alcoholic if you never start drinking.*

People who abuse alcohol seldom get the most out of life. They tend to

> *argue and fight with other people,*

> *get angry and do embarrassing things,*

> *act silly and immature,*

> *act irresponsibly, failing to meet their obligations, and*

> *lose good friends and family members who try to help them.*

4. Tell the children: *Alcohol abuse takes the quality out of living, and the abuser is often ashamed when he or she sobers up. "Sobers up" means the effects of the alcohol have gone away, or the alcohol is out of the bloodstream.*

Cooperative Group Activity

Divide the children into groups of five or six.

1. Discuss the following questions:

   Would you drink a glass of whiskey if it were offered to you? Why or why not?

   Would you purposely choose friends who drink? Why or why not?

   Do you plan to drink when you're 21? Why or why not?

   Do you want your friends to drink? Why or why not?

Gather the children back into an information formation.

2. Introduce the following concept: *Drinking alcohol can be dangerous to your health.*

3. Discuss how alcohol can be dangerous to your health: *Alcohol acts as a depressant on the nervous system. Depressants slow down the activity of the brain and nervous system. In small amounts, alcohol acts like a tranquilizing drug, making the user feel relaxed, less tense, and less inhibited (self-conscious). Responsible drinkers do not use alcohol in large amounts or when it might be unsafe even in moderation. For example, small amounts are not safe when taken with certain medications or when you're going to drive a car.*

4. Discuss the effects of alcohol consumption: *Too much alcohol is bad because it messes up your thought processes, muscle control, coordination, and reaction time. You cannot remember things, and your judgment is poor. With heavy drinking, all your senses are dulled. Alcohol consumption can kill, depending on the amount of alcohol in the bloodstream at one time. Years of drinking alcohol can damage the brain and liver. "Cirrhosis" is a fatal condition of the liver that results from damage to the organ caused by alcohol consumption. The liver is a large gland that secretes bile for digestion and helps produce blood. When a person's brain is damaged severely by alcohol, he or she is no longer able to make judgments, learn anything new, or remember important things.*

Concluding Activities (10 minutes)

Cooperative Group Activity

Return the children to their small groups. Place the statements on the chalkboard or give them to the children on a handout.

      1. Ask the children to write their reactions to the following written statements.

          My reasons for choosing not to drink now are . . .

          My reasons for choosing not to drink as an adult are . . .

      2. Allow groups to share their reactions.

HEALTH

LESSON 7
NUTRITION

Student Objectives

- Explain why it is important to eat a balanced diet.
- Propose a diet that follows healthy dietary guidelines.

Equipment and Materials

- Food Guide Pyramid poster

Health Concept (20 minutes)

Gather the children into an information formation for the entire discussion.

Key Terms

Define the following terms:

> ***nutrients***—*Substances obtained from food and used by the body for good health.*
>
> ***carbohydrates***—*Nutrients that provide energy for the body.*
>
> ***protein***—*A nutrient that provides energy and can serve as working parts of cells.*
>
> ***vitamins and minerals***—*Nutrients that can be in food or supplements (e.g., pills); these are building blocks (calcium in bones for strength) or fuel (calcium in muscles for movement).*
>
> ***fiber***—*A part of food that helps us digest. It is sometimes called "bulk" because it is not a nutrient; however, it is necessary for healthy digestion.*

Concept Development

1. Introduce this concept: *A balanced diet is important for good health.*
2. Discuss important dietary guidelines: *A balanced, healthy diet provides nutrients that are necessary for good health. Nutrients are found in foods, and the body uses them for energy. There are over 40 different nutrients, and most foods provide more than one nutrient. There are six main types of nutrients: carbohydrates, fats, proteins, vitamins, minerals, and water. Each nutrient provides something that's important for good health. It's important that you eat a balanced and varied diet that provides some of each one of the nutrients.*

Think About Your Diet Activity

1. Read the following statements and ask the children to complete each phrase with the first thought that comes to mind. Select several children to share their thoughts.

> *My favorite food is . . .*
>
> *I eat breakfast because . . .*

Eating a balanced diet means . . .

One food I do not like is . . .

The most important meal for me is . . .

2. Tell the children: *A balanced diet includes foods from each food group. Different foods contain different nutrients your body needs. To make sure that you get all the nutrients you need, you should eat a variety of different kinds of foods. To make sure you have a balanced diet, you need to select some foods from each one of the food groups. The food groups can be seen on the Food Pyramid Guide poster* (show the poster to the students). *You should eat 6 to 11 servings of bread, cereal, rice, and pasta, 3 to 5 servings of vegetables, 2 to 4 servings of fruits, 2 to 3 servings of milk, yogurt, or cheese, and 2 to 3 servings of meats (and other proteins, such as beans and nuts).*

3. Discuss other things to remember for a healthy diet: *Other things to remember for a healthy diet are:*

   A desirable weight is important for good health, and a balanced diet can help maintain a desirable weight.

   A low fat diet can help prevent atherosclerosis and some forms of cancer. Atherosclerosis is when arteries become blocked by fat from the blood; this blocks blood flow.

   Choosing a diet with lots of fruits, vegetables, and grains can help prevent heart disease.

   Use sugar in moderation.

   Limit salt (sodium).

   Avoid alcohol.

4. Introduce the following concept: *Foods made from grains (with flour), rice, and cornmeal are important sources of carbohydrates.*

5. Discuss the importance of carbohydrates for a healthy diet: *Carbohydrates are important nutrients. Foods from the bread group are a major source of carbohydrates. Fruits and vegetables are also sources of carbohydrates. The bread group includes all foods made from grain products. What are some examples of foods made from grains?* (Rolls, cereal, bagels, pasta, tortillas, pancakes, waffles, crackers, noodles, macaroni, hamburger buns, muffins, biscuits.) *Some foods in the bread group are better for you than others. Breads and rolls made from whole grains are more nutritious. Examples are whole wheat rolls and rye bread. Whole grains are better for you because they contain fiber and more nutrients. Fiber is a low-calorie material that helps your digestive system work more efficiently. Fiber is found in many foods, but you find more fiber in whole-grain foods like whole wheat bread. We should eat six or more servings from the bread group each day. A serving can be as small as a half cup of something or one slice of bread.*

6. Introduce the following concept: *Fruits and vegetables are important sources of nutrients in a diet.*

7. Discuss the importance of including fruits and vegetables in a diet: *There are many different kinds of fruits and vegetables, and they all contain some nutrients. There are many different types of fruits* (have the children help list them):

   Citrus fruits—oranges, tangerines, grapefruits, and lemons

   Melon fruits—watermelon, honeydew melon, and cantaloupe

   Berry fruits—strawberries, blackberries, raspberries, cranberries, and blueberries

   Other fruits—apples, apricots, prunes, plums, pineapples, pears, mangoes, grapes, raisins, dates, cherries, bananas, pomegranates, and papayas

8. *There are also many different types of vegetables* (have the children help list them):

   Green leafy—mustard greens, turnip greens, collard greens, lettuce, kale, and spinach

Yellow vegetables—carrots, squash, sweet potatoes, and pumpkin

Beans—kidney beans, lima beans, navy beans, pinto beans, black-eyed peas, and lentils

Starchy vegetables—potatoes and corn

Other vegetables—turnips, okra, eggplant, celery, asparagus, beets, cabbage, zucchini, artichokes, cauliflower, cucumbers, mushrooms, onions, radishes, and brussels sprouts

9. Introduce the following concept: *Meats are important sources of many nutrients, especially protein.*

10. Discuss the importance of protein in a diet: *The meat group includes various kinds of meats, fish, and poultry. Can you name foods from the meat group?* (Beef stew, pork chops, ham, beef liver, hamburgers, steaks, sausage, bacon, luncheon meats, and beef and pork roasts.)

    Can you think of fish that we might eat? (Fish can include flounder, bass, tuna, trout, redfish, red snapper, mackerel, salmon, cod, sardines, crab, shrimp, oysters, and lobster.)

    Poultry includes chicken and turkey.

    Some other foods can serve as alternatives to meat, such as eggs, dried beans, nuts, and dried peas. If you don't like meat, these other foods are also good sources of protein.

11. Introduce the following concept: *Foods from the dairy group provide important nutrients in a diet.*

12. Discuss foods from the dairy group: *Can you name foods from the dairy group?* (Things made from milk as well as milk itself. Products made from milk include cheese, cottage cheese, pudding made with milk, yogurt, and ice cream. Milk can be whole, skim, low-fat, evaporated, or buttermilk.)

Concluding Activities (10 minutes)

Cooperative Group Activity

Divide the children into groups of five or six.

1. Ask each group to plan a day's menu that follows healthy dietary guidelines.

2. Direct the groups to discuss different ways to follow the guidelines. If there is time, have the students share their plan with the class.

3. Hint: School food service personnel may have materials about nutrition, meal planning, and the food guide pyramid.

LESSON 8
NUTRITION

Student Objectives

- Identify dietary sources of carbohydrates.
- Identify sources of fat in the diet.
- Propose guidelines for avoiding fat in the diet.
- Define cholesterol.

Equipment and Materials

- 1 sample of each of a variety of packaged foods (crackers, cookies, canned soup, canned vegetables, canned fruit, or milk)
- Food Guide Pyramid poster

Health Concept (20 minutes)

Gather the children into an information formation.

Key Terms

Define the following term: *cholesterol—A white, powdery, fatty material found in the body that can clog arteries.*

Concept Development

1. Introduce the following concept: *Carbohydrates provide the body with energy from sugars and starches.*

2. Discuss sugars and starches in the diet: *Both sugars and starches have four calories per gram. Most of us probably eat too much sugar—much more than we need. What are some foods with a lot of sugar?* (Candy, cake, soda pop, sugar-frosted cereal, fruit drinks, honey, jam, Popsicles, doughnuts, pies, pastries, ice cream.) *Starches can be converted to energy—sugar—or stored for later use. Many starches contain fiber, which is very important in our diets. Fiber helps our digestive system move food through the stomach and intestine. Fiber helps keep the digestive system clean, by helping it to empty regularly.*

Cooperative Group Activity

Divide the children into groups of five or six.

1. Explain: *As you know, many children like to eat candy, cake, or pie for snacks.*

2. *In your group, make a list of five healthful snacks that could replace snacks full of sugar.* (Some suggestions are fruits, raw vegetables, popcorn, cheese and crackers, peanut butter and crackers, and nuts.)

3. Groups can share their ideas.

4. Introduce the following concept: *Fats do several important jobs, but most of us eat too much fat.*

5. Discuss fats in the diet: *Fats provide us with energy and can be stored for use when we need them. Fats also do several other things: They carry some important vitamins into the body and help us use vitamins. And most people believe fats make food taste better. We get fats from animals and plants. Meat (pork, beef, chicken) has a lot of fat in it. Fat from animals is also found in butter, milk, cream, and eggs—products that come from animals. Oils like vegetable or corn oil provide us with plant fat. Plant fat is better for you than animal fat, because it doesn't have "cholesterol," a fatty substance that can clog the arteries. Unfortunately, most people eat too much fat. One tablespoon of vegetable oil each day gives us the fat we need, and most of us eat a lot more than that, hidden in our food. What are some foods that provide fat in our diet?* (Meat, butter, cream, mayonnaise, salad dressing.)

Concluding Activities (10 minutes)

Test for Food Fat

Give each group a different food product with a food label.

1. Tell the children: *Read each label. How many calories from fat, how many grams of fat and what percentage of fat is in the product? What about saturated fat and unsaturated fat? Are these listed?*

2. Have the groups determine if their food product is "healthy," or less than 30 percent fat, providing some of the minimum daily requirements for a healthy diet (e.g., protein and vitamins).

3. Have the groups give thumbs up (healthy product) and thumbs downs (unhealthy product).

G R A D E S
4-5

HEALTH

LESSON 9
FITNESS AND HEALTH

Student Objectives

- Define "obesity."
- Explain that eating extra calories results in a person's gaining weight.
- Explain that the number of calories your body needs depends on your age, weight, height, gender, and the amount of exercise you get.

Equipment and Materials

- 1 copy of table H3.1 per group (see page 1098)
- 1 pencil per child
- 1 piece of paper per child

Health Concept (20 minutes)

Gather the children into an information formation until the cooperative activity.

Key Terms

Define the following terms:

> *obesity*—*When you have too much body fat.*
>
> *calorie*—*A unit of measurement used to describe the amount of energy in food.*

Concept Development

1. Introduce the following concept: *Obesity is bad for your health.*

2. Discuss obesity and health: *"Obesity" is when you have way too much body fat. Fat is also called "adipose tissue." We all have a certain number of fat cells in our bodies. We also have muscle, bone, blood, and nerve cells. As you probably know, our bodies are made up of billions of tiny cells that we can't see. You become fat or obese when your fat cells grow larger and/or when the number of fat cells increases. The main reason fat cells get larger, and sometimes increase in number, is eating more food than your body needs. Sometimes the body also stores excessive fat because its chemistry is upset, but this is rare. Such a condition requires a doctor's care. Most people who have too much fat simply eat more food than their body needs.*

3. Discuss energy from food with the children: *The food you eat provides your body with energy. The amount of energy in the food is usually measured in "calories." One pound of fat is equal to 3,500 calories. So when you take in more calories than you use, your body stores the extra calories as fat. If your activity level stays the same (if you use the same amount of energy) and you eat 3,500 extra calories, you'll gain one pound of body fat. This can be done a little at a time—if you ate one extra piece of cake that has 100 calories each day for 35 days, you could gain one pound (100 × 35 = 3,500 calories).*

4. Introduce the following concept: *The number of calories your body needs depends on your age, weight, and height, whether you are a boy or a girl, and the amount of exercise you get.*

5. Discuss the calorie needs of children 8 to 10 years old: *Your body uses energy at all times. All of your body systems continue to work even when you're sleeping, so you use some calories during the night. Many more calories are needed if you're active. And some activities use more calories than others. The more vigorous the activity, the more calories used. Do you remember what the total number of calories you need depends on?* (Your age, height, weight, gender, and activity level.) *It matters whether you are a boy or a girl because as boys and girls mature, girls typically add fat, while boys add muscle. Boys also grow taller and heavier. All of these factors help boys burn more calories per pound of body weight than girls. Do you remember what will happen if you take in more calories than you need and you don't exercise enough to work them off?* (You'll gain weight.) *Children 8 to 10 years old need about 2,400 calories each day to provide you with the fuel your body needs to move and grow.*

Concluding Activities (10 minutes)

Cooperative Group Activity

Divide the children into the same groups used to make healthy menus.

1. Provide each group the Caloric Values of Some Foods chart (see table H3.1).

2. Ask each child: *Recall the menu plan we did a few days ago, and figure the number of calories in the plan.*

3. Ask children to decide if their plan was healthy. Also state one thing each person in the group could do to eat a healthier diet.

Table H3.1: Caloric Values of Some Foods

Meat group	Calories
Beans, kidney, 1/2 cup	115
Beef, ground, lean, broiled, 3 oz.	222
Beef, sirloin steak, lean, broiled, 3 oz.	176
Chicken, meat and skin, baked, 4 oz.	275
Egg, boiled, 1 large	82
Fish, fried 4 oz.	250
Flounder, baked or broiled, 4 oz.	159
Ham, slice, 3 oz.	195
Liver, calf, broiled, 4 oz.	221
Peanut butter, 2 tbsp.	174
Pork chops, fried, 8 oz.	475
Tuna, in oil, chunk style, 3 oz.	168
Turkey, light meat, without skin, roasted, 3 oz.	150
Veal cutlet, broiled, 3 oz.	184

Fruit and vegetable group	
Apple, with peel, 1 med.	80
Banana, 1 med.	101
Beets, sliced, cooked, 1/2 cup	32
Broccoli, cooked, 1/2 cup	25
Cantaloupe, 1/4 med.	40
Cherries, sweet, raw, 10	30
Corn, sweet, whole kernel, 1/2 cup	70
Cucumber, pared, 1/2 small	10
Grapefruit, 1/2 med.	40
Green beans, cooked, 1/2 cup	17
Lima beans, cooked, 1/2 cup	84
Orange, 1 med.	64
Orange juice, fresh, 1/2 cup	54
Peach, 1 med.	38
Pear, 1 med.	100
Peas, green, cooked, 1/2 cup	57
Pineapple, canned in water, chunks, 1/2 cup	71
Potato	
Baked in skin, 1 small	144
Chips, 1 oz.	150
French fried, 15 (3 oz.)	200
Spinach, cooked, 1/2 cup	20
Tomato, 1 med.	27

Milk group	
Cheese, cheddar, 1 oz.	113
Cheese, cottage, 2% fat, 1/2 cup	102

Milk group *(continued)*	Calories
Ice milk, vanilla, 1/2 cup	112
Milk, skim, 1 cup	86
Milk, whole, 3.3% fat, 1 cup	150
Milk shake, 8 oz.	300
Yogurt, fruit varieties, 1 cup	225
Yogurt, plain, low-fat, 1 cup	138

Bread and cereal group	
Cornflakes cereal, 1 1/4 cups	110
Corn grits, plain, cooked, 1/2 cup	63
Hard roll, 1	156
Popover, 1	150
Rice, brown, cooked, 1/2 cup	104
Rice, white, cooked, 1/2 cup	87
Rye bread, 1 slice	57
Spaghetti, cooked, plain, 1/2 cup	78
Tortilla, 1	43
White bread, 1 slice	63
Whole-wheat bread, 1 slice	56

Others	
Butter, 1 tbsp.	100
Chocolate, 1 oz.	150
Doughnut, glazed, 1	250
Jelly beans, 15	150

Combinations	
Bacon, lettuce tomato sandwich	400
Burrito, bean	350
Burrito, beef	450
Cheese and bacon burger	500
Cheese burger	350
Cheese pizza, 1 slice (1/4 of a 14" pizza)	354
Enchilada, beef	350
Fried chicken with french fries (15)	650
Grilled cheese sandwich	400
Hamburger	300
Hamburger with french fries and catsup (1 tbsp.)	525
Ice cream cone, 1 scoop	200
Nachos, 4	125
Spaghetti with meatballs, 1 cup	350

Reprinted from Merki 1983.

LESSON 10
FITNESS AND HEALTH

Student Objectives

- State that a person is born with a tendency to be fat or lean.
- Explain that a skinfold measurement tells you how much body fat a person has.

Equipment and Materials

- 1 copy of form H3.1 per child (see page 1100)
- Skinfold calipers (optional)
- 1 tape measure per group

Health Concept (20 minutes)

Gather the children into an information formation until the cooperative activity.

Concept Development

1. Introduce the following concept: *Obesity tends to run in families.*

2. Discuss the relationship between obesity and genetic makeup: *Children who are obese usually have obese parents. You are born with a tendency to be fat or lean, tall or short, depending on your parents. This is called "genetic makeup." You inherit from your parents many characteristics or traits. Your weight is simply one of these. Children also learn their eating and exercise habits from their parents. If the parents overeat and don't exercise, the children are likely to do the same.*

   But you can be lean even if you inherit a tendency to be fat or have learned bad eating or exercise habits. For example, if you exercise a lot and decrease the amount of food you eat, you can become lean even if your parents are overweight.

3. Discuss the concept of weight loss: *To lose weight, we need to look at calories used through exercise and calories eaten. Consider the relationship between the two. If you burn more than you eat, you will lose weight. If you eat more than you burn, you will gain weight. If you burn and eat the same amount, your weight will stay the same. If you want to be lean and your parents are overweight, you might have to work a little harder.*

4. Introduce the Body Image Questionnaire (see form H3.1). Encourage children to take a realistic look at their bodies and answer the questions on the questionnaire. They can complete this assignment at home.

5. Introduce the following concept: *A trained person can measure body fat with skinfold calipers or other means of estimation.* If available, show the children the calipers.

6. Discuss the measurement of body fat: *The purpose of a skinfold test is to measure a person's amount of fat. Pinch the skin near your waist and wiggle it between your fingers.* (Pause.) *Now pinch the skin on the back of your arm (triceps) and wiggle it between your fingers.* (Pause.) *The material under your skin is fat. Everyone has a layer of fat under the skin. Everyone must have some fat. Fat helps us stay warm. It stores energy from food for use later*

and even makes each of us look different. But too much fat is unhealthy. Walking around with too much fat stresses your body, because you're carrying weight that serves no purpose. People tend to have more fat in different locations on their bodies—some people have more fat on their stomachs, and others have more fat on their arms and legs. Pinch the skin on the inside of your calf (pause) and then on your back just under a shoulder blade (scapula). (Pause.) Most of you will notice the thickness of the skin is different in all those places.

FORM H3.1 BODY IMAGE QUESTIONNAIRE

Think about the way you look. Would you like to change things about your body if you could? Describe your feelings in the blanks provided.

1. **I would like to change the following things about my body if I could:**

_____

_____

_____

_____

_____

_____

2. **Reasons why I would make the changes:**

_____

_____

_____

_____

_____

3. **Ways I can go about making changes:**

_____

_____

_____

_____

_____

_____

Reprinted from Thomas, Lee, and Thomas 1990.

Concluding Activities (10 minutes)

Cooperative Group Activity

Divide the children into groups of five or six, and give each group a tape measure.

1. Using the tape measure, ask children to measure a different body part on each group member (you may want to have students of the same sex measure each other). Ask if there is anyone who wants you to measure them or help them measure.

2. You can take measurements at waists, hips, chests, knees, calves, and necks.

3. Explain: *When you measure around—called the circumference—the measurement includes skin, muscle, bone, fat, and other tissues. So when you lose fat those circumferences get smaller. Because children are growing, however, their circumferences usually don't get smaller; their bones, muscles, and organs are all getting larger to make the circumferences larger, even when the child may be losing fat.*

4. *Note*: The American Medical Association recommends a balanced and normal diet combined with exercise for children who are overweight or overfat. Severe restriction of calories through dieting is not recommended for children. If children or parents discuss obesity with you, recommend that they see a physician and begin a balanced diet and exercise plan to reduce fat.

GRADES 4-5 CLASSROOM ACTIVITIES

There will be times when the gymnasium or all-purpose areas are unavailable and when the weather prohibits outdoor classes. These lessons give you specific plans for making the most of these times.

UNIT ORGANIZATION

The lessons in this unit cover recreational games, fitness, rhythmic activities with poi poi balls, Lemon Twister, and Balloon Volleyball. Feel free to pick and choose among the lessons, repeating them as desired.

LESSON ORGANIZATION

These lessons are structured as the lessons intended for the gymnasium or playing field with clearly stated objectives, equipment and materials lists, and specific activity instructions. Be especially careful to adapt setup instructions to fit the particular venue you're using.

TEACHING HINTS

Teaching in a classroom setting can be a pleasure or a disaster—depending on how well-prepared you and your students are. Plan now for how you'll adapt your rules and protocols to the classroom setting, keeping student ages and abilities and safety considerations in mind. When the day comes where you must teach in the classroom, try to select a lesson that will fit in with what students have been working on in the gymnasium setting. For example, Fitness With a Partner (Lesson 6) may not only serve to improve fitness but

also to enhance teamwork and cooperation in the gymnasium.

Adapting Rules and Protocols

As at the beginning of the school year when you took the time to teach basic rules and protocols, it is well worth making time for training students to behave appropriately when you must hold physical education class in such a confined space. So the first lesson a particular class experiences in the classroom setting should consist primarily of showing the children how you wish to adapt the gymnasium rules and protocols to the classroom. Then each time you find yourself in the same situation, briefly but clearly review these adaptations with each class. The children will appreciate knowing what is expected of them and will respond more appropriately to the lesson.

Pay particular attention to teaching children how to make smooth transitions. At the beginning and the end of each lesson, you must find a way to set physical education apart from other curricular activities to help students focus. You might, for example, request that all other learning materials be put away, then after reviewing the rule and protocol adaptations, ask a question or two leading into the day's physical education topic, such as, "Does anyone remember what skill we worked on during our last class? What was the most important part of that skill to remember? Today we will work on a part of that skill that we can do safely in the classroom." Such an opening will draw students into the day's lesson. At the end, putting away equipment and sitting quietly doing relaxation or deep breathing exercises for two or three minutes may facilitate the transition back to academic work. You might allow the first group or row to sit in their seats quietly the privilege of getting a drink of water first. Children appreciate knowing what will happen and what is expected of them.

Fourth and Fifth Graders

One advantage of teaching this age group in the classroom is that they are better able to safely help you create an open space when needed by quickly and quietly moving desks aside (then back in place at the end of the lesson). Time the children with a stopwatch to challenge them to be ready quickly, taking off five seconds as a bonus to reward them for being quiet. Record this time and compare to the next classroom lesson's transition time. A classroom teacher who is willing to have the chairs stacked out of the way and the children already settled on the floor can be a real boon. Always, however, try to respect the classroom teacher's needs so that he or she will be able to move quickly into the next activity after your lesson.

Safety Considerations

You must select activities that take into account crowded conditions, low ceilings, electrical cords, and breakable objects. Then always take time to review your adaptations of your regular rules and protocols to help prevent injuries.

An important point to remember with this age group is that although they may anticipate hazards when playing in the classroom setting, they may still get "carried away" with an activity. You must be sure to warn them to remember they're in the classroom setting and that they must make adjustments accordingly. Say, for example, "Nobody really wins a game if someone gets hurt."

Making the Most of the Situation

It is important to keep in mind that classroom days are not "throw-away" days. With a little extra effort and planning they can be wonderful extensions of your gymnasium and outdoor time with the children. You may even gain some insights into individual children as you see them in the setting in which they spend most of their school days. Such insights may help you meet their needs throughout the rest of the year. You may also be able to forge a closer relationship with their teachers, enhancing collaboration opportunities.

LESSON 1
RECREATIONAL GAMES

Student Objectives

- Roll a softball after a four- or five-step approach, with the last step in opposition to the ball arm.
- Hit spots (targets) on the floor with a rolled softball.

Equipment and Materials

- 1 or more softballs per small group
- Tape

Skill-Development Activities (30 minutes)

Bowling History

Have the children listen from their desks.

Bowling has been around for many years, in many different cultures. The Dutch brought bowling to New York before George Washington, our first President, was born. Regular bowling balls are made of hard rubber and weigh from 10 to 16 pounds. But we can practice the skills of bowling with a ball that is much smaller and lighter than a regular bowling ball.

Four-Step Approach

Arrange the children in scatter formation or standing in rows with children three to four ft apart. The children should be in small groups taking turns rolling a ball toward a wall.

1. Describe and demonstrate the skill:

    Starting position: Begin standing with feet together and hands together holding the ball, palms up, waist-high in front of your body. Lean your torso slightly forward.

    Move both hands forward, with the hand holding the ball moving a little beyond the free hand. At the same time, the foot on the side of the body holding the ball moves forward a step.

    As your foot touches the ground, the downswing should be in progress. The ball goes back, passing the line of your body as the next step occurs, and begins to move upward behind your body.

    As the ball reaches the top of the backswing, the third step begins, which is a quick step with the ball almost hesitating.

    The forward swing is a downward and forward motion with the last step, which turns into a slide to the release and follow-through.

2. Ask the children: *Show me the starting position.*

3. Walk the children through the four-step approach: *Right, left, right, slide.* (Help left-handed bowlers reverse the motions.)

4. Repeat.

Four-Step Delivery

Arrange the children in six or more lines with at least one softball per line. Mark target X's on the floor with tape.

1. Describe and demonstrate the skill:

    Use the four-step approach with a ball. The object is to have the ball touch the ground, as the foot slides after the last step, and roll forward.

    The ball should remain in contact with the ground at all times after it leaves your hand.

    The ball should move toward the target and eventually roll over the target.

    You don't have to throw the ball forcefully (hard), and remember, the ball should remain on the ground at all times after it leaves your hand.

2. Have the children practice the delivery and retrieval of their own balls. Say to the children: *Right, left, right, slide.*

3. Point out the targets, and have the children practice the delivery, trying to hit the targets.

Concluding Activities

None.

Extension Activities

Many commercial bowling alleys have portable lanes, which they will bring to your school for demonstrations. The staff will provide instruction, allow the children to practice, show equipment, and so forth.

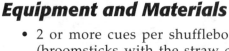

LESSON 2
SHUFFLEBOARD

Student Objectives

- Cooperate as members of a group.
- Hit a target with the disk.
- Demonstrate the use of varying forces by stopping the disk at specified places.
- Learn to bump a disk out of play.

Equipment and Materials

- 2 or more cues per shuffleboard court (broomsticks with the straw cut off, or shuffleboard cues)
- 4 or more disks per shuffleboard court (6 1/2 in. shuffleboard disks or large sand-filled margarine tubs)
- 1 shuffleboard court per group of 4 students

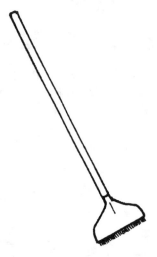

Skill-Development Activities (30 minutes)

Shuffleboard History

Have the children listen from their desks.

Shuffleboard is a game that was played long ago with a penny pushed on a table. The object of the game was to land the penny on the scoring areas and to knock other pennies off the scoring area. Over time people shifted to larger disks played on special shuffleboard courts, a popular feature on the decks of ships crossing the ocean. Passengers liked the game so well they began playing it on land.

Shuffleboard Skills

To set up "courts," either push tables and desks back or use the aisles as "courts." Divide the children into as many groups as you have space and equipment.

1. Select four students to help you demonstrate the game while the other students watch and listen:

   The object of the game is to push disks into the scoring area. Using the cue, a player pushes the disk toward the other end, trying to make it stop in the scoring triangle.

   To start, line up four disks in each 10-off area.

   Using the cue, one partner pushes a disk toward the other end, trying to make it stop in the triangle.

   The other person on that end plays a disk, also trying to stop it in the triangle at the other end.

   Remove those disks.

   Then the players at the opposite end repeat the process.

2. Divide the children into groups of four and assign each group to a shuffleboard court. If necessary, have one group of three or five students.

3. Have the students practice pushing the disks, until they are successful at stopping the disks in the triangle.

Bumping

Keep the same or change the groups of four children.

1. Tell the children: *"Bumping" means attempting to knock the opponents' disks out of the triangle and leave your own disks in the scoring area.*

2. Have the children practice pushing and bumping the disks, until they are successful at stopping the disks in the triangle and bumping.

Concluding Activities

None.

LESSON 3
DECK TENNIS

Student Objectives

- Throw the ring in an arc.
- Throw the ring within the boundaries.
- Catch the ring with one hand.

Equipment and Materials

- 1 ring per group of 4 children
- Tape to mark the courts
- String (or nets) (*Note*: You can adjust the size of the courts to the space available. Hallways make a good playing area; consider using halls that do not have classrooms off them.)

Skill-Development Activities (30 minutes)

Deck Tennis

Have the children listen from their desks. Have enough playing areas set up to accommodate teams of four (and one group of three or five if necessary).

1. Describe the game and rules:

    This is a game of throwing and catching.

    You are "on your honor," in that players are expected to call their own fouls. No one calls a foul on another person. (Stress the importance of playing fair and calling your own fouls.)

    In doubles a player stands in each of the court areas.

    The server begins in the right court, behind the endline, tossing the ring in an arc so that it arrives in the court opposite.

    The receiver must catch the ring in one hand. The ring must never touch any body part other than that hand.

    The receiver can take one step and then must throw the ring into fair territory across the net. This continues until someone fouls. Fouls are the following:

    - *A wobbling throw (on the serve or returns)*
    - *A throw that does not arc*
    - *A ring that goes out of bounds*
    - *Failing to catch a ring*
    - *A ring that lands in the neutral area*

2. Continue describing the game:

> *If the receiving team fouls, the serving team gets a point.*
>
> *If the serving team fouls, they give up the serve.*
>
> *If a serve is fair but touches the net, the serve may be replayed one time.*
>
> *The serve alternates from the right to the left court, and each time the serve changes, it alternates between the team members.*
>
> *The winning team is the one that reaches 15 points first, but the team must have at least a 2-point lead to end the game.*

3. Begin a game, demonstrate, and explain the rules.

Divide the children into groups of four, and assign each group to a playing area.

4. Have the children play Deck Tennis.
5. Observe and offer help as the groups play.

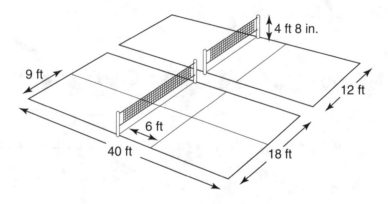

Concluding Activities

None.

LESSON 4
GAMES

Student Objectives

- Play a game requiring locomotor skills and balance.

Equipment and Materials

- 2 erasers

Skill-Development Activities (30 minutes)

Eraser Tag

Select two children; one will be the tagger ("It") and the other will be the dodger. Each child balances an eraser on the head.

1. Describe the game:

    It attempts to tag the Dodger. The rest of you sit in your seats as the Tagger and the Dodger walk quickly around the furniture.

    If the Tagger drops the eraser, he or she must pick it up and put it back on the head.

    If the Dodger drops the eraser, it is considered a foul.

    If It tags the Dodger, or if the Dodger fouls, the game is over.

    The Tagger becomes the Dodger, and I will choose a new It.

2. Have the children play Eraser Tag, continuing until all children have played.

Concluding Activities

None.

LESSSON 5
FITNESS

Student Objectives

- Perform flexibility, muscle endurance, and cardiovascular endurance exercises.

Equipment and Materials

- 1 chair per child
- 1 book per child

Skill-Development Activities (25 minutes)

Four-Corners Fitness

Assign each of the following exercises to a corner of the room. Divide the students into four groups and assign each group to a corner.

1. Describe and demonstrate each exercise.
2. Rotate children every minute, allowing them 30 seconds to walk slowly to the next corner.
3. Repeat until all the children have been in each corner.

Elbow-Knee Touches

Standing with feet shoulder-width apart, touch your left knee with your right elbow while jumping to a tiptoe position, return to start, and reverse so your left elbow touches your right knee.

Jumping Jacks

Standing with feet together, arms low at sides, jump, landing with your feet to the sides in a straddle position as your arms clap overhead, then return to start.

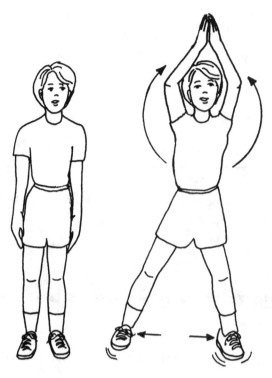

Treadmill

Beginning with hands and feet on floor supporting your weight and hands shoulder-width apart, bend one leg so the knee touches your stomach or chest (knee does not support weight but the foot does). Give a little jump, so legs reverse positions, and repeat rhythmically.

Knee to Nose

Beginning on all-fours, move your chin to your chest while bringing one knee forward. After your knee and nose touch (or come as close as possible), extend the leg backward and lift your head up and looking at the floor, repeat, and then use the opposite leg.

Chair Stretching

Arrange the children in scatter formation or in rows among the desks, each child with a chair.

    1. Describe and demonstrate the activity:

Sitting in a chair with both feet flat on the floor, reach forward, extending both arms as far as possible.

Stretch your arms to the right side and touch the floor on the right.

Return to sitting and touch the floor on the left.

Move both arms overhead, and look backward, reaching arms backward as far as possible.

Your feet should not lift from the floor nor your bottom from the chair.

2. Have the children practice chair stretching. Cue the children: *Reach forward, sit up, arms out, reach right, sit up, reach left, sit up, arms up and together.*

3. Repeat 10 times.

Chair Leg Stretching

Continue with the same setup.

1. Describe and demonstrate the activity:

   Sitting in normal position, grasp one knee with both hands, bend that knee, pulling your thigh to your chest (do not lean forward).

   Now lift the leg, relax, lower the leg slightly, grasp the leg on the backside of the knee, straighten the leg (keeping your back against the back of the chair).

   With your toes pointed, flex your toes and hold, bend knee, and return to normal sitting position.

2. Have the children practice chair leg stretching. Cue the children: *Grasp, pull, relax, regrasp, stretch toes pointed, bend ankle and hold, bend knee, and stop.*

3. Have each child perform 10 repetitions of chair leg stretching.

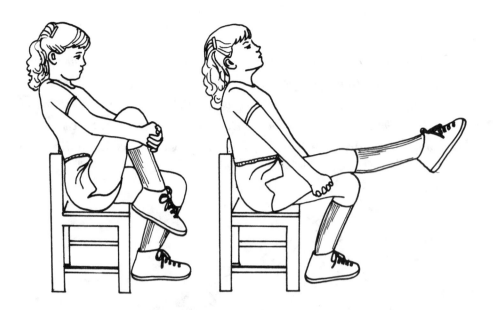

Chair Busters

Continue with the same setup.

1. Describe and demonstrate chair busters, part 1: *Standing behind the chair with your arms extended (stretched) and hands on the back of the chair and keeping your body straight, lower your weight onto your arms until your chest touches the back of the chair; hold, then return to the starting position.*

2. Have the children do 15 chair busters, part 1. Cue the children: *Lower slowly, bending arms, and hold, two, three, four, five; push up, arms straight.*

3. Describe and demonstrate chair busters, part 2: *Sitting on the chair, holding on to the chair seat with both hands, bring your knees to your chest; keeping your legs bent, hold, and then return to start.* Cue the children: *Lower slowly, bending arms, and hold, two, three, four, five; push up, arms straight.*

4. Have the children do 15 chair busters, part 2. Cue the children: *Legs up, hold two, three, four, five; legs down.*

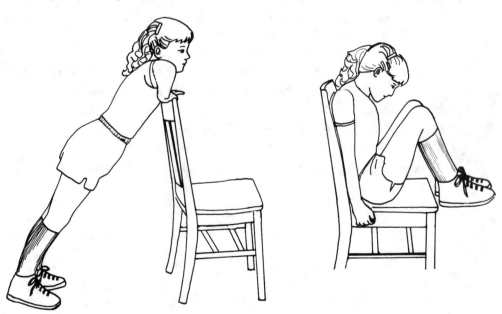

High Steppers

Continue with the same setup.

1. Describe and demonstrate the activity:

   Stand facing the chair, and place your right leg on the chair seat.

   Step up on your right leg, lifting your body into standing position on the chair.

   Stand on the chair with weight on both feet, then step down on the right foot.

   Repeat, starting with the left foot.

   Keep repeating, alternating feet for one minute.

2. Ask the children to walk slowly around the room, taking deep breaths and slowly exhaling for 30 seconds, repeating the sequence five times.

Chair Curl-Ups

Continue with the same setup.

1. Describe and demonstrate the activity:

   Begin by lying on the floor with your bottom against the front legs of the chair, bending your knees so your calves rest on the chair seat.

   With arms crossed on your chest, lift your head slowly from the floor and continue curling up as far as possible.

   Hold for five counts, then slowly return to starting position.

2. Have the children do 15 chair curl-ups.

Bookworm

Arrange the children in scatter formation without their chairs.

1. Describe and demonstrate the activity:

   Beginning by standing, touch the floor in front of your toes with both hands, bending your knees enough for safety. Walk your hands forward until your body is straight (you end up in starting push-up position), then reverse.

   Your feet should never move.

2. Have the children do 15 bookworms.

Book Stretching

Have the children sit at their desks.

1. Describe and demonstrate the activity: *Holding a book in both hands overhead, lean back, side, front, side.*

2. Have the children practice book stretching 15 times, clockwise and counterclockwise.

Concluding Activities (5 minutes)

Cool-Down

Arrange the children in scatter formation, each with a chair. Have the children perform the following sequence of cool-down activities:

Sit in a chair with eyes closed, take a deep breath, exhale slowly, and relax your shoulders. Think about your shoulders—let them hang, don't move your fingers or arms, feel your shoulders get heavy.

Take another breath and relax your legs.

Your legs are so heavy you can't pick them up; they are going to sleep.

Take another breath, and as you exhale slowly, relax your head and neck.

Hold very still so your head doesn't bounce forward.

Relax your hands and arms.

Make fists with your hands; hold it! (Wait 10 seconds.)

Now let go and relax your arms and hands. (Remain quiet for a few seconds.)

Now stand up and gently shake your whole body.

Everyone sit in your own chair quietly, two, three, four, five.

LESSON 6
FITNESS WITH A PARTNER

Student Objectives

- Perform flexibility, muscle endurance, and cardiovascular endurance exercises.

Equipment and Materials

- 1 short jump rope per pair
- 1 textbook per pair

Skill-Development Activities (25 minutes)

Partner Pushing

Arrange partners in scatter formation.

1. Describe and have two children demonstrate the activity:

   Stand back-to-back with arms hooked at elbows and legs extended slightly to the front.
   Push against each other for five counts, and then relax (remaining in the same position).
   Repeat this 10 times.

2. Have the children practice partner pushing.

Partner Pulling

Keep partners in scatter formation.

1. Describe and have two children demonstrate the activity:

   Sit on the floor, facing each other with feet touching and holding hands. One partner has legs bent at the knees, and the other partner has legs straight at the knees.

   By gently pulling the arms and pushing with the legs, change roles so the opposite child has legs bent and straight.

   Repeat this 10 times.

2. Have the children practice partner pulling.

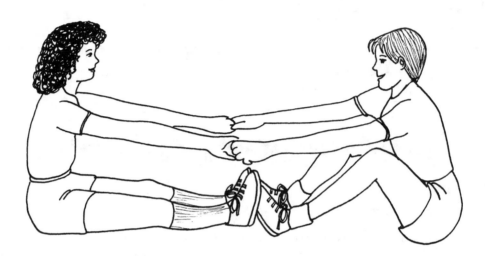

Partner Stretching

Keep partners in scatter formation, still facing each other. Have each pair choose a leader

1. Describe and demonstrate the activity: *The leader stretches left, front, right, or back, and the other partner performs the same movements going the opposite direction (for example, if the leader goes forward, the other person goes backward). Each of you should lead 10 times for a total of 20 stretches.*

2. Have the children practice partner stretching.

Partner Treadmill

Keep partners in scatter formation, on all-fours, facing each other.

1. Describe and have two children demonstrate the activity:

   The first partner brings one leg up between the arms, then quickly extends that leg and brings the other leg forward (this is like running in place but with hands on the floor).

   The first partner repeats this 10 times, then the second partner does this 10 times, then the first repeats 10, and so on, until each of you has had 10 turns.

2. Have the children practice partner treadmill.

Wiggle Worms

Keep partners in scatter formation, lying on their stomachs beside each other, facing opposite directions.

1. Describe and have two children demonstrate the activity:

   Stretch (extend) your arms and legs.

   One partner lifts arms and legs off the floor and holds for five counts, while the other partner lies very still.

   Change roles and keep repeating until each partner has had 10 turns.

2. Have the children practice wiggle worms. Cue the children: *Up, two, three, four, five, switch two, three, four, five, switch, two, three, four, five.*

Mountain Climber 1

Divide the children into pairs in scatter formation. One child lies on the floor, and the other child stands holding the jump rope. *Note*: For safety's sake, match partners by size and strength as evenly as possible.

1. Describe and demonstrate the activity: *The bottom child grasps the jump rope and lifts the upper body of the other child off the ground, holding this position for as long as possible (keeping feet on the floor). Listen for the signal to stop. Do this 10 times, then switch roles.*

2. Have the children perform the mountain climber 1.

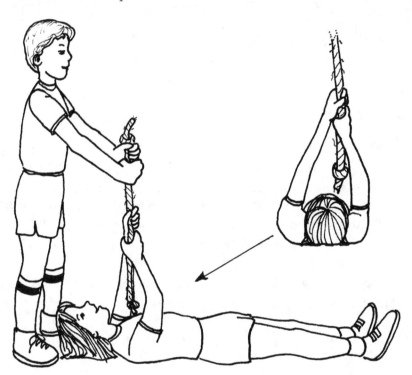

Mountain Climber 2

Keep the same setup. If desired, have students change partners. One child lies on the floor with head near the feet of the other child, who is standing holding the middle of the jump rope in both hands. *Note*: For safety's sake, match partners by size and strength as evenly as possible.

1. Describe and demonstrate the activity: *The child on the floor grasps the rope with both hands. The standing child tries to lift the rope and the child on the ground. Lower your partner gently back down to the floor. Do this 10 times, then switch roles.*

2. Have the children perform mountain climber 2.

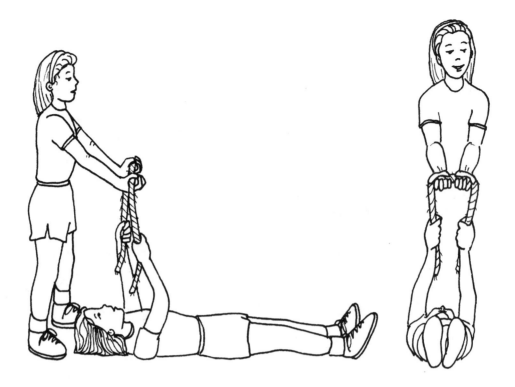

Partner Sit-Ups

Arrange pairs in scatter formation.

1. Describe and demonstrate the exercise:

   The helping partner counts the number of sit-ups for the working partner.

   The working partner does 10 sit-ups, beginning lying with hands crossed on a book held against his or her chest, knees bent at a 45-degree angle (demonstrate clearly).

   The working partner gives the book to his or her partner, and the helping partner now becomes the working partner.

   The new working partner now does 10 sit-ups.

   Keep switching until you have each done four sets (40 sit-ups per child).

2. Have the students perform partner sit-ups.

Echo Stretching

Keep the same setup. If desired, have students change partners.

1. Describe and demonstrate the activity:

   One partner makes up a stretching sequence, for example, touch toes (knees bent slightly), lean left, lean right, squat (no more than thighs parallel to floor), straighten legs, stand, and stretch backward.

   When the sequence is finished, the other partner does (echoes) the same sequence.

   Take turns leading, until each of you has led 10 times.

2. Have the children practice echo stretching, allowing enough time for each child to lead 10 times.

Partner Treadmill

See Grades 4-5: Classroom Activities, Lesson 6, page 1120.

Concluding Activities (5 minutes)

Cool-Down

Have the children walk slowly from corner to corner or around the room to cool down.

G R A D E S 4-5 CLASSROOM ACTIVITIES

LESSON 7
FITNESS

Student Objectives

- Perform flexibility, muscle endurance, and cardiovascular endurance exercises.

Equipment and Materials

- None

Skill-Development Activities (25 minutes)

Fitness Stations

Divide the children into six groups, and assign each group to a fitness station.

1. Describe and demonstrate the exercise at each station (3 to 5 minutes).
2. Ask the children to perform as many repetitions as possible for 1 minute, then have them rotate to the next station (allow 15 seconds transition time per rotation).
3. Have the children rotate through the six stations three times (taking approximately 22 minutes).

Jumping Jacks
Beginning standing with feet together and arms low at sides, jump, landing with your feet out to the sides in a straddle as your arms clap overhead, then jump back to starting position.

Sit-Ups
Keep your knees bent and arms crossed on your chest. Have a partner hold your ankles.

Elbow-Knee Touches
Standing with feet shoulder-width apart, touch your left knee with your right elbow while jumping to a tiptoe position, return to start, and reverse so your left elbow touches your right knee.

Push-Ups
Keeping the body straight, lower your body until your chest touches the floor, and then return to starting position.

Leg Stretching
Sitting, stretch left, right, and center, first in straddle position and then in pike position with your toes flexed and extended.

Knee to Nose
Beginning on all-fours on hands and knees, move your chin to your chest while bringing one knee forward. After your knee and nose touch (or come as close as possible), extend the leg backward and lift your head up and looking at the floor, repeat, and then use the opposite leg.

Concluding Activities (5 minutes)

Cool-Down

Have the children walk around the room, taking deep breaths and exhaling slowly for one minute.

GRADES 4-5   CLASSROOM ACTIVITIES

LESSON 8
RHYTHMIC SKILL

Student Objectives

- Move a poi poi ball to a beat.
- Execute three or more skills with poi poi balls.

Equipment and Materials

- 2 poi poi balls per child (1- to 2-in. Styrofoam balls on 18- to 24-in. strings)
- Background music

Skill-Development Activities (30 minutes)

Poi Poi Ball Skills

Arrange the children in a circle or in rows, each child with one poi poi ball. Make sure there is enough room between children to prevent interference with each other.

1. Present the following tasks:

    With your arm extended in front of your body, make the poi poi ball go in a circle by rotating your wrist.

    Slowly bend your elbow, moving the ball closer to your body.

    Extend your arm.

2. Repeat several times.

3. Have the children move the poi poi ball to the other hand and repeat step 1 challenges and add: *Turn the poi poi ball in a clockwise circle (counterclockwise circle).*

4. Have the children switch to the opposite hand:

    Make circles overhead (on the right side of your body, under your lifted leg, on the left side of your body).

    Make a circle on the left side of your body, then immediately repeat on the right side of your body.

5. Have the children switch the poi poi ball to the opposite hand:

    Make figure eights (overhead, on the right side of your body, under your lifted leg, on the left side of your body).

    Make a circle on the left side of your body, then immediately repeat on the right side of your body.

6. Have the children repeat with the poi poi ball in the opposite hand.

Give each child another poi poi ball.

7. Present the following tasks:

Make circles with both balls going clockwise (counterclockwise).

Make circles with the ball in your left hand going clockwise and the ball in your right hand going counterclockwise. (The circles will be moving toward each other on the upswing.)

Make one circle overhead with one ball and one in front with the other ball. Make one circle to the side with one ball and half-circles around the opposite thigh with the other ball. Alternately make half-circles on each side of your body with one ball on your right side and the other ball on your left side. Make one figure eight overhead with one ball and one to the front with the other ball. Make one figure eight in front with one ball and one to the side with the other ball.

Clackers

Keep the same setup.

1. Describe and demonstrate the activity:

Start with the ball in the left hand going clockwise and the ball in the right hand going counterclockwise (the circles will be moving toward each other on the upswing).

Slowly move your hands together so that your right hand is on top of your left hand and the wrist motion is up and down.

2. Have the children practice Clackers.

Concluding Activities

None.

LESSON 9
LEMON TWIST

Student Objectives

- Jump the Lemon Twist in place five times consecutively.
- Jump the Lemon Twist while moving across the floor.

Equipment and Materials

- 1 Lemon Twist per pair

Skill-Development Activities (30 minutes)

Lemon Twist

Arrange partners in scatter formation. Have one child per pair attach the rope to an ankle.

1. Describe and demonstrate the activity:

    The object is to spin the end piece in a circle with your roped ankle as the center of the circle.

    Each time the end piece moves toward your free leg, jump over the twister.

    You can do this by rocking back and forth from foot to foot.

    Take turns practicing with your partner. When one of you gets tired, let the other take a turn.

2. Have the children practice the Lemon Twist.

Concluding Activities

None.

LESSON 10
GAMES

Student Objectives

- Play a game that requires striking.

Equipment and Materials

- 1 or more balloons
- 1 string (enough to tie across the room)
- Tape (optional)

Skill-Development Activities (30 minutes)

Balloon Volleyball

Move the desks and chairs to clear a space for the game play. Suspend a string through the middle of the play area, five to six ft high. If the chairs and desks are not movable, run the string between two rows so that approximately half the children are on each side of the room, forming two teams. Two teams are on opposite sides of a string that is tied five to six ft off the ground. Spread the children three to four ft apart. (Taped X's on the floor help keep children in position.) This game can be played from chairs (or desks) if the space is limited or if the chairs cannot be moved. Children must remain in their seats at all times. You can mark the boundaries of the play area with tape or simply designate boundaries to determine when a balloon has left the playing area.

1. Describe and demonstrate the game:

    Each team begins with 15 points.

    To begin, I will toss the balloon to one team. The children on that team try to hit the balloon (staying in their positions as much as possible) until it goes over the string.

    The other team then hits the balloon until they return it over the string.

    If the balloon touches the ground, goes out of bounds (hits a desk or goes out of the playing area), or is caught by a child, play stops. The team that made the error loses a point.

    While play is stopped you will change positions, so that the children in the back row move to the front row, the front moves to the middle, the middle moves to the back.

    To restart play, I will toss the balloon to the team that did not start play on the last round.

    The game ends when one team has zero points.

2. Have the children practice Balloon Volleyball (as you explain the rules again).
3. Have the children play Balloon Volleyball.

4. Variations:

   Play with more than one balloon.

   Place a weight in the balloon (a penny, marble, sand).

   Play with the children holding one hand behind their backs.

Concluding Activities

None.

TYPES OF EVALUATION FORMS

The following evaluation forms are arranged by activity category: Games and Sports, Rhythmic Activities, and Gymnastics. There are three types of evaluation forms: checklists, rating scales, and skill test scoring forms.

CHECKLISTS

There are two types of checklists. The first type of checklist is used to evaluate an entire group of students. Place one student's name in each column as indicated on the checklist. Observe each student, checking the appropriate box when a skill is performed correctly. The second type of checklist is for separate evaluation of individuals. Fill in the student's name, his or her class, and the observation date at the top of the form. Then check "yes" if the skill is completed correctly, or "no" if the skill is not completed correctly. Both types of checklists can tell you which skills you need to stress in class, and can help you give feedback to the children about which skills they need to practice.

RATING SCALES

Rating scales are used to follow the development of skills in an individual child over a period of time. Write the child's name on the scale and the date of the first observation in the space above the first column. In each column, place a 3, 2, or 1 corresponding to the student's ability level when performing each skill. You can add other items to the list of skills as needed.

The next time you observe the child, place the date of this second observation over the second column and follow the same procedure. You may want to space your observations; for example, record the ratings in September, December, and May. This records the development of a child's skills across time.

For children without mature or developmentally appropriate motor patterns, you should provide extra instruction by including additional instruction on those patterns. Then fill in the numbers that are appropriate for the demonstrated characteristic, taking into account the developmental levels of the children.

SKILL TESTS

The third type of evaluation form is the skill tests scoring form. To use skill tests scoring forms, fill in the student's name, his or her class, and the observation date. Then have the child complete the test. Record his or her score(s) using the standards listed. These standards can be used to motivate the children to attain higher scores.

GRADES K-3: GAMES AND SPORTS CHECKLISTS/SKILL TESTS SCORING FORMS

CHECKLIST FOR FUNDAMENTAL PATTERNS

Running

Name

Foot contact is a rolling motion (heel-to-toe) or all toe contact (speed dependent).

Arms move in opposition to legs in a pumping motion.

Steps are on a line directly under midline of the body.

Thigh reaches parallel to ground on front swing.

Heel touches (or nearly touches) buttocks on backswing.

Support leg is extended fully to push body off the ground.

At some point during each stride, neither foot is on ground.

Comments:

Comments:

Comments:

(continued)

Jumping (For distance)

Name

Crouch is evident prior to jump.

Arms swing down and backward prior to jump.

Arms swing vigorously forward and upward before and during take-off.

Legs are extended at take-off.

Legs and arms are extended during flight.

Landing is balanced.

Landing is on both feet at same time.

Comments:

Comments:

Comments:

(continued)

CHECKLIST FOR FUNDAMENTAL PATTERNS *(continued)*

Hopping

Name

Body is airborne taking off from one foot and landing on same foot.

Balance is maintained.

Arms assist body in upward motion.

Hopping is rhythmic on both dominant and nondominant feet.

Arms are not used for balance.

Knee of nonsupport leg is pointed to ground.

Comments:

Comments:

Comments:

(continued)

Overhand throwing (For distance)

Name

As throw begins, trunk is rotated away from intended line of throw.

Foot in opposition to throwing arm takes a vigorous stride forward.

Hips rotate to a forward-facing position in advance of trunk.

Forearm lags well behind elbow as trunk begins its forward rotation.

Total action appears fast and vigorous.

Comments:

Commènts:

Comments:

(continued)

CHECKLIST FOR FUNDAMENTAL PATTERNS *(continued)*

Catching

Name

Arms begin at side of body, awaiting projection of ball.

Eyes follow ball into hands.

Ball is caught with hands only (no trapping against body).

Arms move toward body by elbows bending.

Body position and/or location is adjusted to match flight of ball.

Comments:

Comments:

Comments:

(continued)

Kicking

Name

Several steps are taken prior to kick.

Last step prior to kick is a leap onto support foot.

Knee of kicking foot is completely extended at ball contact.

Ankle of kicking foot is completely extended at ball contact.

Follow-through lifts child off ground.

Body leans forward on backswing.

Body leans backward on follow-through.

Total movement is smooth and coordinated.

Comments:

Comments:

Comments:

(continued)

CHECKLIST FOR FUNDAMENTAL PATTERNS *(continued)*

*One-arm striking with an extension
(Racket)*

Name

Holds racket with Eastern forehand grip
(handshake).

Positions feet shoulder-width apart.

Faces thrower in ready position to start.

Steps backward onto foot on racket side.

Rotates trunk backward, and shifts weight
onto back foot as ball approaches.

Holds racket up and out from body.

Follows flight of ball with eyes until
just before contact is made.

Shifts body weight forward in direction of
intended hit.

Rotates hips and trunk in direction of intended
hit.

Moves arm forward using a level horizontal
swing.

Comments:

Comments:

GRADES K-1: RATING SCALE FOR RHYTHMIC ACTIVITIES

RATING SCALE FOR RHYTHMIC ACTIVITIES

Name _____   Class _____

	Date_____ First			Date_____ Second			Date_____ Third		
Skill	3	2	1*	3	2	1	3	2	1
Is able to create original shapes.									
Is able to									
clap to drumbeats,									
step to drumbeats.									
Is able to vary the direction of locomotor skills:									
Walk,									
Run,									
Jump.									
Is able to produce the actions for simple singing games:									
Baa, Baa, Black Sheep,									
Looby Loo.									
Remembers a simple rhythmic stick routine.									
Is able to perform rhythmic jump rope activities:									
Basic jump forward,									
Basic jump backward.									

*3 = nearly always, 2 = sometimes, 1 = seldom

GRADES K-1: CHECKLISTS FOR GYMNASTICS

LOCOMOTOR SKILLS

Name

Walking variations

Straight line

Zigzag pattern

Circle

Curved pattern

On heels

On toes (tiptoe)

Backward

Sideways (right)

Sideways (left)

Running variations

Fast

Slow

Arm opposition

Nonsupport phase

No bouncing

Jumping variations

3 consecutive jumps

Jump backward

Jump upward

Jump forward

Jump in circle pattern

(continued)

Name

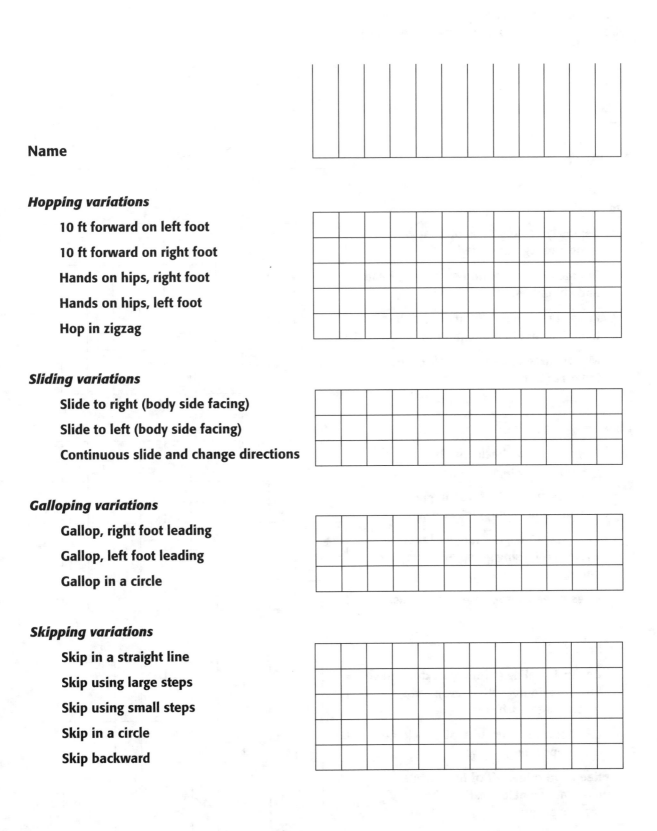

Hopping variations
- 10 ft forward on left foot
- 10 ft forward on right foot
- Hands on hips, right foot
- Hands on hips, left foot
- Hop in zigzag

Sliding variations
- Slide to right (body side facing)
- Slide to left (body side facing)
- Continuous slide and change directions

Galloping variations
- Gallop, right foot leading
- Gallop, left foot leading
- Gallop in a circle

Skipping variations
- Skip in a straight line
- Skip using large steps
- Skip using small steps
- Skip in a circle
- Skip backward

CHECKLIST FOR TUMBLING

(Kindergarten competencies are noted with #.)
(First grade should do all skills competently.)

Name

Log roll#

Begins lying crosswise on mat with arms and legs extended.

Initiates rolling motion by turning head and shoulders.

Keeps body straight and doesn't use hands or feet to make motion.

Makes three complete turns, or moves length of mat.

Rocker#

Begins lying on back with hands grasping knees.

Initiates motion by thrusting head forward and "pumping" body.

Achieves 90-degree range of motion without releasing grasp of hands and knees.

Does three consecutive repetitions.

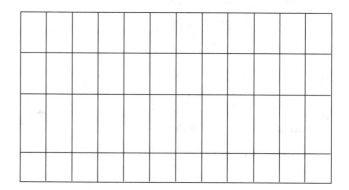

Two-knee balance#

Begins kneeling (with hips extended so buttocks do not touch legs), arms extended to each side.

Lifts feet from mat so that only knees are supporting body weight.

Keeps both feet off of floor while maintaining balance. Balances for five seconds.

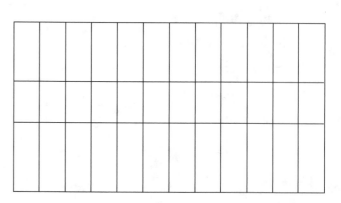

(continued)

Name

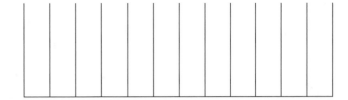

Forward roll#

Begins squatting on mat, hands placed on mat in front of and outside feet.

Has arms outside of legs.

In one motion, straightens legs while looking at tummy.

Begins to support body weight with arms; keeps hips above shoulders and moving forward.

Lands on shoulder blades.

Keeps legs tucked.

Lands on feet (first).

Does not use hands to push under hips.

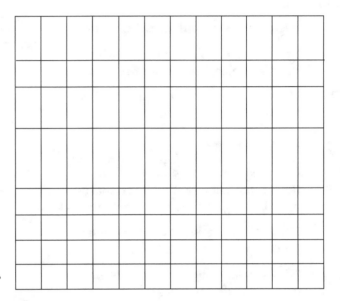

Backward roll#

Begins in squat position with back to length of mat.

Places hands on shoulders, palms up.

Presses chin close to chest.

Begins motion with rocking movement.

Touches mat with bottom, back, shoulders-hands, head-hands, in sequence.

When hands touch, child pushes by extending arms.

Recovers (lands) on feet (first).

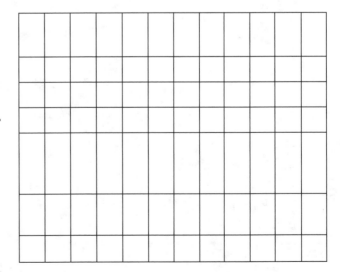

(continued)

CHECKLIST FOR TUMBLING *(continued)*

Name

One-leg balance

    Begins standing with hands on hips.

    Keeps one leg raised until foot clears
floor, stopping near knee of support leg.

    Maintains balance for 10 seconds.

Forehead touch

    Begins in kneeling-squat position
(knees, legs, and feet on floor; buttocks
on calf of leg), hands joined behind back.

    Bends slowly forward until forehead
touches mat.

    Raises to kneeling position without
using hands for balance.

(continued)

Name

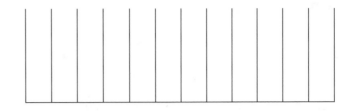

Donkey kick

Begins standing.

Bends at waist, hands placed
shoulder-distance apart on mat.

Kicks feet and legs out and up behind
while supporting body weight with arms.

Moves feet up and down together.

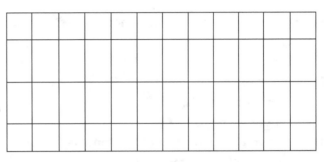

Tripod

Begins in squat with hands and arms
on mat outside knees and legs.

Bends forward until forehead
touches mat.

Bends arms and touches knees
to elbows.

Supports body weight with arms.

Maintains balance for five seconds.

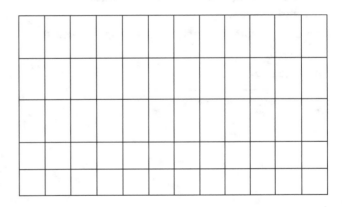

Elbow-knee balance

Begins in squat with hands on mat
outside legs.

Touches elbows to knees.

Holds up head.

Shifts weight from feet to hands.

Maintains balance for five seconds.

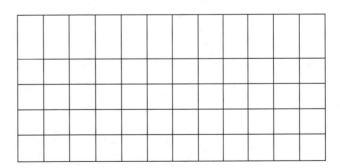

GRADES 2-3: RATING SCALES FOR RHYTHMIC ACTIVITIES

GRADES 2–3: RATING SCALE FOR CREATIVE RHYTHMIC ACTIVITIES

Name_____ Class_____

	Date_____			Date_____			Date_____		
	First			Second			Third		
Skill	3	2	1*	3	2	1	3	2	1
Is able to vary the *rhythm* of locomotor skills: Walk,									
Run.									
Is able to vary the *speed* of locomotor skills: Walk,									
Run.									
Is able to demonstrate heavy movements,									
light movements.									
Is able to create a movement to a stimulus (word, feeling, rhyme).									
Can create a simple dance using locomotor skills and shapes.									
Is able to produce the actions for singing games: Bingo,									
Paw Paw Patch.									

*3 = nearly always, 2 = sometimes, 1 = seldom

RATING SCALE FOR RHYTHMIC ROUTINES

Name_____ Class_____

Skill	Date_____ First 3 2 1*	Date_____ Second 3 2 1	Date_____ Third 3 2 1
Jumps rhythmically using the following skills:			
Two-foot singles (forward)			
Two-foot double (forward)			
Basic jump (backward)			
Rhythm Sticks			
Taps rhythm sticks in time to music.			
Remembers rhythm stick tapping routine.			
Can flip and catch rhythm stick.			

*3 = nearly always, 2 = sometimes, 1 = seldom

RATING SCALE FOR FOLK DANCE

Name_____ Class_____

Skill	Date_____ First 3 2 1*			Date_____ Second 3 2 1			Date_____ Third 3 2 1		
Performs folk dance steps in time to music or drumbeat:									
Step-close,									
Slide.									
Remembers step sequence for singing games and folk dances:									
Chimes of Dunkirk,									
Dance of Greeting,									
Ten Little Snowmen.									
Displays rhythmic movement in performance of singing games and folk dances:									
Chimes of Dunkirk,									
Dance of Greeting,									
Ten Little Snowmen.									

*3 = nearly always, 2 = sometimes, 1 = seldom

GRADES 2–3: CHECKLIST FOR GYMNASTICS

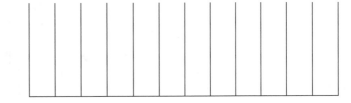

Name

Advanced forward roll

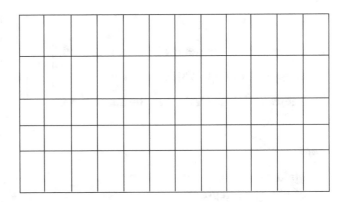

Begins standing with arms extended overhead.

Tucks head and supports body weight with arms.

Lands on shoulder blades.

Rolls to feet without hand assist.

Finishes standing with arms extended overhead.

Shoulder roll

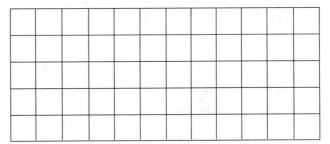

Begins sitting with back to length of mat.

Turns head to side.

Keeps one leg straight during roll.

Lands on bent knee.

Finishes in knee scale.

Handstand

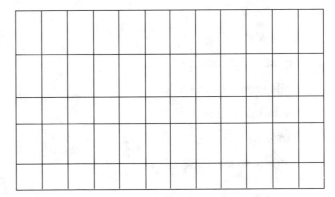

Begins standing with arms extended overhead and one leg extended forward.

Steps forward onto extended leg while reaching for mat with arms.

Supports weight with arms.

Brings legs together overhead and maintains balance.

Requires no spotting.

(continued)

GRADES 2–3: CHECKLIST FOR GYMNASTICS *(continued)*

Name

Leap

    Takes a running start.

    Leaps with more height than normal run.

    Leaps with longer stride than run.

    Keeps both legs straight at the same time.

V seat

    Makes legs and body form angle
of about 45 degrees.

    Keeps legs straight.

    Maintains balance.

360 turn

    Begins standing straight.

    Jumps up and rotates 360 degrees.

    Has a balanced landing.

Backward roll

    Begins standing.

    Squats with palms upward.

    Rolls with curved back.

    Pushes with hands.

    Lands on feet.

    Returns to standing position.

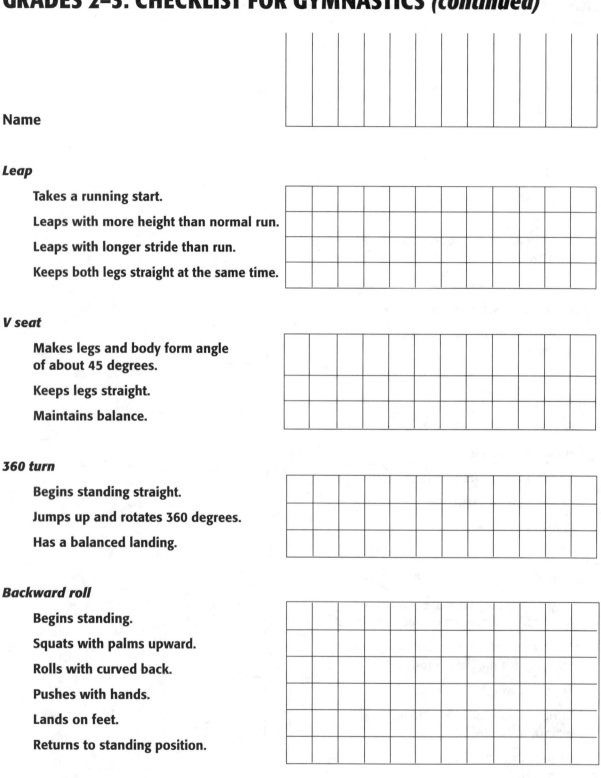

GRADES 4–5: GAMES AND SPORTS CHECKLISTS, RATING SCALES, AND SKILL TESTS SCORING FORMS

RATING SCALE FOR THROWING AND CATCHING ACTIVITIES

Name_____   Class_____

| | Date_____ | Date_____ | Date_____ |
| | First | Second | Third |
Skill	3 2 1*	3 2 1	3 2 1
Is able to juggle two beanbags.			
Is able to juggle three beanbags.			
Demonstrates correct backhand technique for Frisbee throwing.			
Throws Frisbee with accuracy.			
Catches Frisbee successfully with right hand,			
left hand.			

*3 = nearly always, 2 = sometimes, 1 = seldom

CHECKLIST FOR SOCCER SKILLS

Name_____ **Class**_____

Observation Date_____

Inside-of-foot kick

	Yes	No
Places nonkicking foot alongside ball.		
Kicks ball with inside of foot.		
Turns out toe of kicking foot.		
Keeps sole of kicking foot parallel to ground.		
Kicks accurately.		

Instep Kick

	Yes	No
Approaches ball from an angle.		
Places nonkicking foot alongside ball.		
Keeps knee of kicking foot fixed in preparation.		
Straightens kicking leg upon contact.		
Kicks with force.		

SKILL TESTS FOR BASKETBALL

Name _____ **Class** _____

Observation Date _____ **Passing Score** _____

Dribbling Score _____

Passing test

Description: Mark a restraining line 8 ft from a wall. On the "go" signal, the student passes the ball against the wall, catches it, and continues passing and catching as many times as possible in 15 seconds. Any type of pass is allowed. The student must retrieve a ball out of control and return to the line to continue passing.

Standards

15 or more = excellent

6 to 14 = average

Below 6 = poor

Dribble test

Description: Arrange five cones at 10-ft intervals, with the first cone 5 ft from the starting line. The student starts behind the line and on the "go" signal dribbles zigzag around the cones and to the starting line. The score is the number of seconds it takes to dribble the course.

Standards

15 seconds or less = excellent

16 to 20 seconds = average

21 seconds or more = poor

CHECKLIST FOR BASKETBALL SKILLS

Name _____ **Class** _____

Observation Date _____

Chest pass
	Yes	No
Ball is held with fingers.		
Elbows are bent and close to body.		
Feet are in stride position at release.		
Wrists are snapped at release.		
Arms follow through toward receiver.		

Dribbling
	Yes	No
Ball is controlled with fingers.		
Knees are slightly bent.		
Body is flexed over ball.		
Head is up with eyes looking forward.		

One-hand push shot
	Yes	No
Ball is held with shooting hand behind and under ball.		
Ball is supported by nonshooting hand.		
Knees are flexed in preparation.		
Legs and arms are straightened as ball is released.		
Shooting hand follows through toward target.		

CHECKLIST FOR SOFTBALL SKILLS

Name _____ **Class** _____

Observation Date _____

Underhand pitch

	Yes	No
Uses four-finger grip.		
Uses pendular motion in backswing.		
Takes step on foot opposite throwing arm while bringing ball forward.		
Pitches with accuracy.		

Overhand throw

Uses four-finger grip.		
Brings ball back with upper arm parallel to ground.		
On backswing, rotates body away from direction of throw.		
As throwing arm swings forward, leads with elbow.		
Releases ball with snap of wrist.		
As arm swings forward, steps forward with opposing foot.		
Throws with force.		

SKILL TEST FOR SOFTBALL

Name _____   **Class** _____

Observation Date _____   **Catching Score** _____

Catching balls above the waist

Description: The student being tested stands inside a 30-ft circle. A thrower throws 20 fly balls from a line 60 ft from the center of the circle so that the ball will come down within the circle. The student being tested catches each ball, rolls it to the side, and assumes a ready position for the next catch. One point is scored for each ball caught.

Standards

15 to 20 = excellent

10 to 14 = average

9 or fewer = poor

CHECKLIST FOR VOLLEYBALL

Name _____   **Class** _____

Observation Date _____

Underhand serve

	Yes	No
Begins in stride stance with leg opposite hitting arm forward.		
Uses pendular motion in backswing.		
While bringing arm forward, shifts weight to forward foot.		
Contacts ball with heel of open hand.		

Forearm pass

Prepares for pass by assuming forward stride position with knees flexed.		
Contacts ball with forearms.		
Extends elbows at contact.		
Extends legs at contact.		

Overhead pass

Moves under ball and bends knees.		
Prepares for hit by placing hands above head, elbows pointing down.		
Contacts ball with fingers and thumbs.		
Spreads fingers with thumbs pointed toward each other.		

CHECKLIST FOR TRACK AND FIELD

Name _____   **Class** _____

Observation Date _____

Long jump

	Yes	No
Takes short run prior to jump.		
Takes off from one foot.		
Lands on two feet.		
Lifts knees during flight.		

Baton receiving

Reaches back with palm of right hand facing upward.		
Extends fingers with thumb forming a V.		
After receiving baton, shifts it to left hand.		

CHECKLIST FOR FOOTBALL

Name _____ **Class** _____

Observation Date _____

Forward pass

	Yes	No
Grips ball slightly behind middle with fingers spread over laces.		
Points foot opposite throwing arm toward target.		
During backswing, keeps elbow bent and away from body.		
Takes ball back beyond ear on backswing.		
Leads with elbow during forward swing.		
Throws ball with overhead motion of arm.		
Rolls ball off fingertips.		
Throws accurately.		
Throws with force.		

Centering

	Yes	No
Spreads feet wide with body forward over ball.		
Grasps ball with passing grip.		
Balances weight while passing ball through legs.		

GRADES 4-5: RATING SCALES FOR RHYTHMIC ACTIVITIES

RATING SCALE FOR CREATIVE RHYTHMIC ACTIVITIES

Name_____ Class_____

	Date_____			Date_____			Date_____		
	First			Second			Third		
Skill	3	2	1*	3	2	1	3	2	1
Creates rhythmic sequence using									
locomotor skills,									
streamers.									
Jumps rope rhythmically using the following skills:									
rock step,									
ski twist,									
straddle and cross step.									
Remembers words to Lummi Stick Chant, Koo-ee.									
Performs Patterns I, II, and III of traditional rhythm stick routine with partner.									

*3 = nearly always, 2 = sometimes, 1 = seldom

RATING SCALE FOR FOLK AND COUNTRY DANCE

Name_____ Class_____

	Date_____			Date_____			Date_____		
	First			Second			Third		
Skill	3	2	1*	3	2	1	3	2	1
Remembers step patterns for dance steps:									
step-hop,									
bleking,									
grapevine,									
schottische.									
Perform dance movements and steps to music:									
do-si-do,									
elbow swing,									
step-hop,									
bleking,									
schottische.									

*3 = nearly always, 2 = sometimes, 1 = seldom

GRADES 4–5: CHECKLIST FOR LARGE EQUIPMENT

LOCOMOTOR SKILLS

Name

Beam

    Leap

    Turn

    Knee scale

    Back lying

    Walk forward

    Walk backward

Rope

    Climb < 10 ft

    Climb 10-20 ft

    Climb > 20 ft

    Skin the cat

Horizontal Ladder

    Full length

    Half

Jumping Cubes

    Jump up

    Straddle dismount

    Tuck dismount

    Straddle over

GRADES 4-5: CHECKLIST FOR TUMBLING

Fill in children's names across the top. Use "+" to indicate a skill performed correctly and "-" to indicate a skill performed incorrectly. Skills followed by * should be observed in 4th grade, mastered in 5th grade.

Name

Skills

Straddle backward roll

Heel slap

Needle scale

Splits

360 turn

Skipping backward

Skipping sideways

Changing directions

Run and leap*

Jump from knees*

Backward pike roll*

Forward pike roll

Handstand

C jump

Knee turn

Combine 360 turn with run and take-off

Combine forward roll straddle and splits

Front to back roll sequence

Diving roll*

Handstand forward roll*

Backward roll extension*

Cartwheel*

ABOUT THE AUTHORS

Katherine T. Thomas, PhD, is an associate professor of health and human performance at Iowa State University, where she teaches a variety of teacher education and motor development courses. Dr. Thomas also has taught at Arizona State University, Southeastern Louisiana University, and Southern University, Baton Rouge. Her research and numerous publications focus on skill acquisition in sport and exercise and the relation of physical activity to health. She has external grant funding in excess of $800,000 to study physical activity and is the physical activity consultant for the USDA's Team Nutrition. However, Dr. Thomas calls her early professional experiences as a graduate assistant and as an instructor in elementary schools and a college teaching laboratory the most relevant to the writing of this book. These experiences enabled her to find out firsthand what does and doesn't work in a physical education class.

Dr. Thomas is a member of AAHPERD and the North American Society for the Psychology of Sport and Physical Activity (NASPSPA). She received her doctorate in physical education from Louisiana State University in 1981.

Amelia Lee, PhD, is a professor and chair of the department of kinesiology at Louisiana State University. In addition to her 25 years of experience as a teacher educator, Dr. Lee taught physical education at elementary schools in Louisiana and Texas for 10 years. She has published many articles on children's learning and motivation in physical education and has served as a physical education consultant to more than 20 school districts. Dr. Lee is a member of the American Educational Research Association (AERA), and she has received the Scholar Lecture Award from the AERA's Special Interest Group on Learning and Instruction in Physical Education. She is a member of the American Alliance for Health, Physical Education, Recreation and Dance (AAHPERD) and has received an Honor Award from AAHPERD's Curriculum and Instruction Academy. Dr. Lee earned her doctorate in physical education from Texas Woman's University in 1972.

Jerry R. Thomas, EdD, has taught elementary physical education methods and children's motor development for more than 30 years. Currently, he is a professor and chair of the department of health and human performance at Iowa State University. Dr. Thomas also has taught as a professor at Florida State, Louisiana State, and Arizona State Universities. He has written more than 125 published papers, including many on children's motor skills. Dr. Thomas is former president of the American Academy of Kinesiology and Physical Education and NASPSPA. In addition, his scholarly work in physical activity has earned him the titles of C.H. McCloy Lecturer for children's control, learning, and performance of motor skills; Alliance Scholar for AAHPERD; and Southern District AHPERD Scholar.